Central Asia and Tibet

Towards the Holy City of Lhasa

Vol. 1

SVEN HEDIN

Central Asia and Tibet

Towards the Holy City of Lhasa

(In Two Volumes)

by

SVEN HEDIN

With 420 Illustrations from Drawings and Photographs, Eight Coloured Illustrations from Paintings and Five Maps

Vol. 1

Low Price Publications

2012

Sven Hedin (1865-1952)

First Published 1903
Reprinted in **LPP** 1997, 2012

ISBN 10: 81-7536-101-8 *(Set)*
ISBN 13: 978-81-7536-101-0 *(Set)*

ISBN 10: 81-7536-102-6 *(Vol. 1)*
ISBN 13: 978-81-7536-102-7 *(Vol. 1)*

Published by
Low Price Publications
A-6, Second Floor, Nimri Commercial Centre,
Ashok Vihar Phase-IV, Delhi 110052 (INDIA)
tel.: +91.11.27302453 fax.: +91.11.47061936
url: www.Lppindia.com e-mail: info@Lppindia.com

Printed at
Salasar Imaging Systems
Delhi

PRINTED IN INDIA

Dedication.

THE ENGLISH AND AMERICAN EDITIONS

OF THIS WORK ARE DEDICATED BY SPECIAL PERMISSION

TO

HIS EXCELLENCY

LORD CURZON OF KEDLESTON,

VICEROY OF INDIA,

WITH GRATITUDE AND ADMIRATION

BY THE AUTHOR.

PREFACE.

In offering, as I do in the following pages, the results of my latest travels in Central Asia to the English-speaking world, my first duty must be to thank all those who have in various ways contributed to the success of the journey. In the first place, my sincere and earnest thanks must be tendered to His Majesty King Oscar of Sweden and Norway. With his accustomed generosity and enlightenment he made possible the inception of an undertaking, the success of which was in no slight degree due to his valuable assistance and his distinguished patronage. During the many years which I have devoted to the exploration of the little-known interior of Asia His Majesty has always followed my movements with the warmest interest and sympathy, graciously encouraging me to fresh efforts, and honouring me in the most flattering way after each new success. To him, therefore, I desire to express my deepest and most heartfelt gratitude.

To His Imperial Majesty the Czar of Russia I also owe a heavy debt of gratitude for the invaluable support he was pleased to afford me. The services which his Cossacks rendered me were such as money alone could not repay. In my caravan there was not the faintest echo of those bloody and hostile passages which in the past have more than once clouded the relations between Swedes and Russians. Seldom have I been served with such signal devotion and zeal as I was during the three years I had the good fortune to have associated with me these four Cossacks of the Czar's great army. At the same time may I also express my heartfelt thanks to His Excellency, General Kuropatkin, Russian Minister of War, for the valuable assistance he so kindly rendered me? After the very substantial help which King Oscar so generously gave me by way of a start, I experienced no difficulty in raising the funds necessary for my journey, long and important though it was. I had no need to appeal to any except my own countrymen; and amongst them I had on this, as on former occasions, no more liberal friend than M. Emanuel Nobel, of St. Petersburg.

The Swedish edition of this book I have dedicated to my deeply revered parents, as a slight token of the love and affection I owe them for all they have done for me in the past. By a happy inspiration, I have asked, and obtained, the kind permission of His Excellency, Lord Curzon, Viceroy of India, to dedicate to him the English-American edition. It affords me the sincerest pleasure thus publicly to thank him for the truly magnificent hospitality which he and Lady Curzon showed me when I was in Calcutta and Barrackpur. It was owing to Lord Curzon's influential favour that my visit in India turned out so exceedingly pleasurable, in fact, I shall never forget it. But whilst thus tendering the evidence of my gratitude to the able and successful administrator, I desire also, by my dedication of the book to Lord Curzon, to express my admiration for the learned geographer, and, at the same time, render my homage to one who is counted amongst the profoundest of living students of the geography and politics of Asia. I congratulate the powerful empire which has such posts as the Viceroyalty of India to bestow upon the noblest and best of her sons; I congratulate her still more in having sons like Lord Curzon to whom she can entrust the rule of a dependency compared with which most of even the Great Powers of Europe are but as pigmies beside a giant.

It also affords me great pleasure to offer my respectful thanks to the *Royal Geographical Society* for the distinguished and flattering reception it has always accorded to me, for the unique and highly valued honours it has bestowed upon me, and for the proofs of hospitality, sympathy, and kindness with which I have been overwhelmed by those of its members with whom I have had the good fortune to be brought into contact, but more especially to Sir Clements R. Markham, its esteemed president, and Dr. J. Scott Keltie, its valued secretary. By both the officers and members of the Royal Scottish Geographical Society I have been no less honoured and encouraged; and herewith I tender to them also my heartfelt thanks.

This book cannot claim to be anything more than a digested and ordered diary of my latest travels in Asia, together with a description of the regions which I have crossed and recrossed to an added total of some six thousand English miles. If the narrative should be found somewhat heavy and lacking in variety—it will be an exact counterpart of the regions I have travelled through. Travel in Asia is not a dance upon the dropping petals of the rose. Life, with the slow-moving caravans of its boundless deserts and untrodden mountain solitudes, cannot help being monotonous. I have, however, tried to convey an impression of the manner of life, and of how the days pass, amid the lonely desolation of those illimitable wastes. And in any case my labours bring their own reward, in the consciousness that they have contributed, in some degree at least, to the advancement of human knowledge.

In this book I have contented myself with merely an occasional glance at the scientific results of the journey. The fuller and detailed account of them is reserved for a separate work, to which I would like to be allowed to refer the reader who is interested in the geography of Central Asia. The work in question will appear in the course of the next three years, and will be accompanied by an atlas in a couple of folio vols. I shall be happy to answer any inquiries about the *Scientific Results*, as well as to enrol the names of subscribers; for the production of the work must necessarily be costly, and its success will, of course, depend upon the number of subscribers who come forward.

As I can make no pretensions to being either a historical or an archæological scholar, I have seen fit to quote the opinions of two gentlemen, who are well conversant with such subjects, with regard to the ruins of the ancient towns that I had the good fortune to discover beside the ancient lake of Lop-nor. I allude to Professor Himly, of Wiesbaden, and Mr. Macartney, Agent of the Government of India at Kashgar. Dr. M. A. Stein's *Sand-buried Ruins of Khotan* did not, unfortunately, appear in time for me to refer to it in the text. Nevertheless it cannot be overlooked. It is a work which is as admirable in execution as it is important for the valuable matter it contains. Indeed, it would not be easy to conceive an abler survey, at once clear and full of the keenest insight, of the historic and archæological problems connected with Central Asia. It is certain to mark an era in the investigation of that part of the world. This classic production —for such it is bound to become—cannot be too warmly recommended. The great admiration I have for it must be my excuse for dwelling for a moment upon one or two of the numerous fascinating topics it suggests.

In the first place I desire to acknowledge the loyal spirit in which Dr. Stein has recognised my claim to be the first discoverer of Dandan Uiliq (though I confess I never heard this name applied to the site), and of Kara-dung. With regard to the shifting of the Keriya-daria towards the east, I would refer to my paper in *Petermann's Mitteilungen*, Ergänzungsheft, No. 131, p. 37 (1900). The following pages will afford abundant proofs of the tendency of the rivers of East Turkestan to shift their beds. Had Dr. Stein enjoyed the same opportunities that I have had for studying their courses, and the rapid alterations they undergo, he would have found nothing surprising in the fact that the Keriya-daria has shifted its course 23½ miles further to the east. That is a movement which would require for its accomplishment neither centuries nor thousands of years. Once the bed of an East Turkestan river gets choked with mud, it is only a question of a comparatively few years for it to alter its course.

The detailed results of my investigations on the Mus-tagh-ata, and the Eastern Pamirs generally, are not yet published, but they will, I trust, be published ere long. The materials which I collected for a map of the region are at this moment in the hands of the geographical firm of Justus Perthes in Gotha; in fact, I have made an arrangement with them to publish the whole in another separate monograph of the well-known *Petermann's Mitteilungen.*

Dr. Stein is to be congratulated upon having exposed the scandalous fabrication of "ancient MSS." which for a time went on wholesale in Khotan. Fortunately he discovered it before more serious or more mischievous results were able to ensue.

I ought perhaps to state that the reasons why I so seldom advert to the travels of my predecessors and contemporaries in the same parts of the world have not been either forgetfulness or want of due recognition of them; but simply because my own materials have been so voluminous that the requisite space has been wanting.

Finally, I must thank my publishers, Messrs. Hurst and Blackett, for the generous and obliging spirit in which they have met me throughout. They are issuing the book in what I can only describe as a first-class manner, and I trust the result will amply compensate them for the trouble and sacrifices they have made.

The present book has been translated by Mr. J. T. Bealby, the same gentleman who so ably translated *Through Asia.* To him also I desire to offer my sincere thanks for the painstaking and diligent care he has bestowed upon the English rendering. Unless I am mistaken, it is an excellent piece of work.

SVEN HEDIN.

Stockholm,

21st August, 1903.

CONTENTS.

INTRODUCTION.

STOCKHOLM TO KASHGAR.

II.

FLOATING DOWN THE LONELY TARIM.

A JOURNEY BY BOAT THROUGH THE DESERT.

III.

ACROSS THE TAKLA-MAKAN DESERT.

THE LAND OF PERPETUAL TWILIGHT.

IV.

LOP-NOR AND ITS SISTER LAKES.

A REEDY WILDERNESS IN THE DESERT.

V.

IN NORTHERN TIBET.

MOUNTAINS, LAKES, AND QUAGMIRES AT HIGH ALTITUDES.

LIST OF ILLUSTRATIONS.

LIST OF MAPS.

KEY TO THE TRANSLITERATION OF THE MAP-NAMES.

å	on the map	is	rendered by	o	in the text.	
ch	„	„	„	kh	„	
dj	„	„	„	j	„	
e (final)		„	„	eh	„	
g (final)		„	(sometimes)	gh	„	(e.g. tagh)
gi	„	„	rendered	ghi	„	
j	„	„	„	y or i	„	
s	„	„	(generally)	z	„	
sch	„	„	rendered	sh	„	
tj	„	„	„	ch (as in "church")		
tsch	„	„	„	tch or ch		

Introduction.

Stockholm to Kashgar.

CHAPTER I.

FROM STOCKHOLM TO OSH.

It was midsummer day in 1899, and our Northern summer was looking its very best—the lilacs in bloom and the trees full of leaf—when I left Stockholm for the fourth time, bound for the heart of Asia. In honour of the day the shipping in the harbour was decorated with flags and bunting, and merrily it fluttered in the breeze that came in crisply off the Baltic. Nobody was down on the pier to see me off except my father and mother, brothers and sisters, and a few intimate friends, when the *Uleåborg* slipped quietly away, carrying me the first stage on my long and adventurous journey. Whatever vicissitudes I may have encountered, whatever privations I may have undergone, during the three following years, nothing was harder to bear than the wrench of that first day. To tear myself away from the place where all my affections have been rooted since infancy demanded far greater resolution than any effort I was called upon to put forth by the contingencies of subsequent travel. But, the bitterness of leave-taking over, a pleasant surprise awaited me. I found amongst the passengers on board my old friend and teacher, Professor Brögger. His company greatly cheered me, and helped me to shake off the depression of spirits which had naturally come over me.

For this journey my equipment was incomparably greater and more complete than on any previous occasion. All told, my baggage weighed no less than 22 cwt., and was stowed away in two dozen cases, most of them specially made for convenience of transport on the backs of horses. A list of the instruments I took with me, as well as some brief mention of the more important items in my equipment, will be found in the subjoined footnote.*

* The astronomical instruments consisted of a Universal Traveller's Theodolite by Hildebrand and three chronometers, two of which came from V. Kullberg in London.

The cost of carrying such a quantity of baggage by passenger train right across Russia, Caucasia, Transcaspia, and West Turkestan, a distance of 3,200 miles, would of course have amounted to a considerable sum. But it did not cost me a single penny. His Majesty the Czar was so interested in my journey that not only did he grant me a free pass for myself and my baggage over the whole of the Russian railway system, but he directed that my belongings should enter and leave the

These instruments, although requiring, under all circumstances, the greatest care and the most delicate handling, suffered no harm whatever throughout the journey, and were just as good at the end of it as they were at the beginning. My topographical instruments embraced a levelling tube, with staff-scales and other accessories, a levelling mirror, tape, compasses, a prismatic compass, with dioptric fittings, and a plane-table with stand and diopter. I had two first-rate velocity instruments made in Stockholm, which could also be used when rowing. The meteorological equipment was almost entirely supplied by Fuess, of Berlin, and consisted of a hypsometer, five boiling-point thermometers, an Assmann's ventilated psychrometer, a couple of actinometers, an anemometer, a rain-gauge, and a large number of ordinary thermometers, wet-bulb thermometers, maximum and minimum thermometers, thermometers for investigating the temperature of the soil, etc. The Royal Nautical Meteorological Office in Stockholm kindly lent me a deep-sea thermometer with capsule and reversing propeller. The self-registering barometer and self-registering thermometer, each to run fourteen days, were specially made for me by J. Richard, of Paris ; and both worked splendidly. One great advantage they possessed was that their glass cases fitted so closely that neither sand storm nor atmospheric dust was able to penetrate into them and impair their working efficiency. On the other hand I had, on this score, a good deal of trouble with the ventilated psychrometer. I used three areometers of Stockholm make, which answered well, except that their graduation might have been better adapted to the altogether exceptional salinity of the Tibetan lakes. Although I took with me no less than 58 pairs of spectacles, very few came back whole. The clouded spectacles for use amongst snow, and tinted various shades of grey and blue, some also with unground glass, were in great demand amongst the men of my various caravans and with the natives generally. I carried the same weapons, a gift of the head of the famous Husqvarna small-arms factory, which I used in 1893-97. The same gentleman further presented to me for this journey four Swedish army officers' revolvers, a large number of smaller weapons of the same kind—these were chiefly intended as presents for native chiefs and others—and a plentiful supply of ammunition. The four Cossacks used their own new Russian army magazine rifles, so that altogether we possessed the somewhat imposing force of ten rifles and a score of revolvers.

Amongst my remaining equipment I have space to mention only a few articles, such as a folding bed from a Malmö firm, which I used in summer ; in winter, and whilst journeying through Tibet, I generally slept on the ground. I have very special satisfaction in mentioning the James Patent Folding Boat, which I obtained from the Military Equipment Stores and Tortoise Tents Company of London. It consisted of two sections, which, when in use, were joined together, the whole making a very light load for one horse ; indeed, the boat was so light a man could carry it. Its appurtenances embraced two oars with rowlocks, mast, sail, and two life-buoys. On various occasions this little boat not only proved of inestimable service, it also afforded me many an hour's genuine pleasure, as the following pages will abundantly show.

My photographic equipment was by the same maker as before, and answered in every respect admirably. I also had with me a Watson's camera, the identically same instru-

empire without payment of customs. This meant an appreciable lightening of the expenses of my journey; and it meant also a great gain in both comfort and prestige.

From the 26th to the 30th June I stayed in St. Petersburg, enjoying the hospitality and unwearied, kind offices of the Swedish representative at the Russian court, M. Reuterskiöld. My sincere sorrow may therefore be conceived when, only one week later, I learned of his sudden and unexpected death. And here I would desire to express how great a debt of gratitude I owe to the new Swedish minister who succeeded him, Count August Gyldenstolpe, for the obliging assistance he rendered

ment which lay buried for nearly a year under the sand of the Takla-makan Desert. But besides these I was also provided with a Richard's Verascope camera, in every respect a superior type of instrument; a Kodak junior, and a Daylight Kodak, both from Eastman. The lenses I used were the very best that could be obtained; and the plates, which made the heaviest item in my baggage, were Edwards's *anti-halo*. As I also provided myself with a complete stock of chemicals and appliances for developing, fixing and printing negatives, I developed myself the greater portion of those I took (some 2,500 in all) at various times during the course of the journey. Upon reaching home I still had 700 plates left to develop.

Finally I may mention a number of small things, such as knives, daggers, chains, watches, compasses, musical boxes, etc., etc., which were intended as presents to the natives. A first-class Eskilstuna knife is valued in Central Asia at a great deal more than its monetary value. In many cases gifts of this character are more esteemed than hard cash, and they also have this advantage, that they are cheaper.

My stock of stationery, paper for mapping, diaries and note-books, writing materials, dry ink, and so forth, also made up a pretty heavy packet, as will be more easily understood when I state that my maps filled 1,149 sheets and my diaries extended to 4,500 pages.

For the conveyance of the more fragile and perishable of my effects I got a Stockholm firm to make me six trunks, with water-tight casings and cork framework. These were light and strong and suffered no injury, whereas wood or iron would not have stood the racketting. Another firm in the same city provided me with a strong case fitted with 300 test-tubes for holding various natural history preparations.

In the way of edible stores I carried eight cases of preserved foods, which proved of immense service, especially such delicacies as turtle, "Emperor," and ox-tail soups, which only required to be heated over the fire just as they were in their tins. Then, for giving flavour and body to a soup made of mutton or antelope flesh, there was nothing to beat Liebig's *Extract of Meat*.

I also took with me a few books, *e.g.*, a Bible, Psalm Book, and a small book of devotion called *Dagens Lösen (Good Thoughts for Every Day)*, which formed a link between me and dear ones at home. Besides these, I had Supan's *Grundzüge der physischen Erdkunde*, Geikie's *Great Ice Age*, Hann's *Klimatologie*, Kern's *Buddhismus*, Rhys-Davids's *Buddhism*, and two or three scientific works of reference, as well as Odhner's *Svenska Historia* (*History of Sweden*) and a few books of light literature. A separate portfolio contained copies of every map of Central Asia that had been published by previous travellers in that region. By the help of these I was enabled not only to avoid going over their routes again, but also to confine my own energies almost entirely to breaking fresh ground.

me, and the great patience with which he watched over and furthered my interests in St. Petersburg, both at this initial stage of my journey and all through the three years of its continuance. My friend M. Emanuel Nobel gave me his generous assistance, and further crowned his kindness by arranging that I should be able to draw what money I needed at the branch of the Volga-Kama Bank in Tashkend.

The pleasure of my stay in St. Petersburg was greatly enhanced by daily intercourse with my old benefactor and friend, Baron Adolf Nordenskiöld, who also was at that time visiting in the Russian capital. Little did I anticipate that that was the last time I should see him! He also was carried off during my absence from home, to the deep sorrow of all who loved and admired him, a loss to our country and an irreparable loss to science.

I will not dwell upon my journey through Russia. The country has been already sufficiently described by myself and others. But I will hasten to reach the scene of my new experiences and my new geographical discoveries.

My last months in Stockholm had been a time of strenuous, hard work. It was therefore delicious to rest, stretched at full length in my comfortable berth in the train, free from the correcting of proofs, the answering of telephone calls, the sending of wires, the reading of newspapers, and the thousand and one demands which civilized life makes upon a man's time and thought. Delicious to let my mind dream on unchecked and weave plans for the future, as one straw-thatched village after another swept pass me, and one copper-green bulb-shaped church tower after another peeped up on the horizon, flew past, and disappeared again. Meanwhile every beat of the engine piston was bringing me nearer and nearer to my goal.

Before us, behind us, and around us, as far as the eye could reach, stretched the monotonous steppes of Russia, forming a gently undulating or rather almost perfectly level expanse of green—green in all its shades. The hay was already cut, and the face of the country was dotted with endless rows of haycocks. Flourishing corn-fields alternated with the shorn meadows. No trace or sign here of the famine which prevailed in the eastern governments of the empire. My route was *viâ* Moscow, Voronezh, and Rostoff, over the majestic Don, and so on to Vladikavkaz—the same route I followed on my first journey south in 1885. But this time I turned east at Beslan, one station north of Vladikavkaz, and proceeded towards the Caspian Sea, and thus skirted the northern foot of the gigantic mountain-wall which shot up its peaks and crests into the thin air to the south, its sides streaked with snowfields, its summits wreathed in fantastically-shaped clouds. The surface sank slowly towards the sea, and the railway gradually deviated from the mountains. It was a little after seven (3rd July) when we left Beslan; but, owing to the more southerly latitude, the sun had already set. The sky rapidly flushed into a deep purple, and shortly afterwards it became intensely dark. My thoughts flew back to our bright and joyous summer nights at home, which I was destined not to enjoy again for many and many a month. As we ran down towards the largest inland sea in the world, the blackness of the night was from time to time illumined by the flashes of summer lightning which played about the brows of Caucasus, as though the mountains held hidden volcanoes in their arms. The distance between the lonely little stations grew greater and greater; in some cases it was as much as 18 miles. The only sound which broke the stillness of the steppes was the occasional chirping of a cricket. The temperature rose to over 80° Fahr. during the day, a sure indication that we were approaching more southerly climes; but as yet the nights were still balmy and beautiful.

Petrovsk, on the Caspian, a humdrum little place, offering nothing of interest, has scarcely grown at all since the railway was built from Beslan, although the new route is the shortest way to Transcaspia and West Turkestan, and obviates the necessity of crossing over the Caucasus, in this having the advantage over the route *viâ* Baku and the Georgian military railway. There is not one building of importance in the little town; the only features it possesses are the church, the barracks, the railway station, one hotel, a Tatar mosque, and a watch-tower for fires. The country around is sadly lacking in vegetation. Greyness and barrenness are its predominant traits, and the hills which encircle it are equally bare and sterile. True, there is a public park inside the town, besides a few scattered groups of trees; but the place is very exposed, utterly without shade against the sun as without shelter against the storms which beat in off the Caspian. Some few years ago Petrovsk was a sort of holiday resort and bathing-place, to which the people of Baku were accustomed to run over in the summer. But during the last eighteen or twenty years the town has been haunted by a malignant fever, and as a consequence of this many of its former inhabitants have left and gone elsewhere to live. The harbour is but a poor affair, consisting of little better than an artificial pier, or rather of two pier arms which, like a crab's claws, embrace a small basin, where vessels are loaded and unloaded by a crowd of sunburnt, bare-footed Tatars, dingy with dirt.

It was five o'clock on the afternoon of 5th July when the *Tzezarevitch Alexander* started for Krasnovodsk, a journey which takes on the average about 32 hours. We were not long in steaming out of sight of the coast and its low hills. Under the impulse of a fresh south-east wind the sea ran high, and the paddles laboured hard, especially during the night when the wind blew strongest. There were only a very few first-class passengers on board, mostly Russian officers serving in Asiatic Russia, some with, others without, their families. But the fore-deck was crowded with Asiatics—Sarts, Tatars and Armenians. Right out in the open the water was a transparent bluish-green, and the crests of the waves were tipped with foam. But throughout the whole of the passage we did not catch a single glimpse of either sail or steamboat. As we approached the Asiatic coast the wind gradually dropped and the sea grew smoother, and early on the morning of the 7th July we sighted the hills and promontory of Krasnovodsk. But before we could make the port, we had to luff to the south to get round a long and narrow peninsula which protects the bay on the west. The sea shallows a long way out from land; the lead had been going all the afternoon.

Krasnovodsk is one of the wretchedest places under the sun. It possesses not a single tree, is totally destitute of other vegetation, and has no drinking water, for the water in the wells is as salt as the water of the sea itself. Every drop of water has to be fetched from further inland in big wooden casks fastened on waggons specially made for the purpose. The white, one-storied houses, with their flat roofs, are fully exposed to the noontide sun. I could not help pitying the poor Russians who are condemned to serve in such a parched and dreary hole.

In the middle of the day the thermometer rose to 98°.5 Fahr. in the shade, nor was the burning dryness of the atmosphere in any degree tempered by the proximity to the sea. When I visited West Turkestan in 1891 the Transcaspian Railway started from Uzun-ada. But in consequence of a destructive earthquake, which visited that town in the year following, when the earth rose and fell like the waves of the sea, and the rails were so twisted and bent that every bolt and nut in them started, Krasnovodsk was again made the terminus in 1893.

General Kuropatkin had done me the great kindness of telegraphing to Krasnovodsk, ordering the railway authorities to give me a whole carriage to myself all the way through to Andijan. After stowing away all my baggage, I still had room to arrange myself as comfortably as if I had been in an hotel. I had a writing-table, chairs, and lounges ; and as mine was the last carriage on the train, I had a free and uninterrupted view of the country from the back of it. The keys of the carriage were in my possession, and I was completely isolated from all the other passengers in the train. This was a great advantage during the hot days of that desert journey. I could dress as scantily as I pleased, and every now and then go into my sleeping compartment and refresh myself with a *douche*.

We left the Caspian at five o'clock in the afternoon, and after skirting for three hours the shore of the Balkan Gulf, we turned eastwards and plunged into the desert. At midnight the thermometer dropped to 82°.5, and my energies, which had become torpid in the torrid heat of the day, once more revived. Early on the morning of the 8th we reached Kizil-Arvat, and at two in the afternoon Askabad. The station master of the latter place was Colonel Svinhufvud, a bright and congenial Finn, whose acquaintance I made on my first journey in these parts.

My meeting with him was marked by the following characteristic incident. I asked him to give orders to uncouple my carriage at Merv and hang it on to the first train that ran down to Kushk. For, whilst studying the Russian railway time-table, it had occurred to me, why should I not run down and have a peep at the much-talked-of fortress of Kushk and the region towards Herat ? My ticket said in plain and unmistakable language, that " Dr. Sven Hedin was to be granted free passage for himself and his belongings over all the Imperial Russian railways, both in Europe and Asia."

But Colonel Svinhufvud smiled significantly, and taking out his pocket-book, drew forth a telegram from the Minister of War, which he read to me. " In case Dr. Sven Hedin should contemplate going to Kushk, please inform him that that line is closed to all travellers."

That was explicit. However, I thought to myself that the Russian military authorities did quite right to keep jealous watch upon a place of such great strategic importance as Kushk. I was told that the line was even closed to ordinary Russians, and that nobody was allowed to travel by it except those who formed the garrison of Kushk.

That same afternoon we passed Kahka, the place where I struck the line in 1890, when I rode over from Meshhed *viâ* Kelat-i-Nadiri. All these places are typical oases strung along the southern edge of the Kara-kum Desert, and are watered by intermittent streams that flow down from the barren, greyish-brown, weathered slopes of Kopet Dagh on the frontier of Persia. To the north of the line the country was a good deal more uniform. Strips of steppe alternated with patches of sandy desert, what little vegetation there was was burnt up by the sun, the heated atmosphere pulsed in liquid waves along the tops of the sand-hills, and every now and again the eye was cheated by a mirage, which generally took the form of a pleasant grove of trees standing on the shore of a tranquil summer sea. Shortly after noon the thermometer rose to 106°.2 Fahr. in the shade. When I put my head out of the carriage window I could, it is true, feel a distinct breeze, but it was burning hot, like the heat-waves which radiate from a baker's oven.

We reached Merv at 2.30 a.m. on the morning of the 9th July. Then, after crossing another division of the Kara-kum, we came at midday to the large and flourishing oasis of Chardjui, where the arrival of our train in the bustling station was evidently the chief event of the day.

Just beyond the station of Amu-daria we slowed down whilst crossing the strong wooden bridge * which there spans the Amu-daria. It took us 26 minutes to get across. As the river was just then at its highest, it was like riding across a vast lake. Although a tremendous volume of water, brown as *café au lait*, rolled on underneath the bridge in one solid mass, it was easy to see that it was compounded of different currents; and the main stream was accompanied on each side by minor currents. Both above and below the bridge the river seemed to have no termination. Its bosom was strewn with drift-wood and snags,

* When I returned home in the summer of 1902 this was replaced by a new iron bridge.

and the water flowed absolutely without noise, except for a little gurgling against the piles which supported the bridge.

After crossing another dreary belt of desert, in which the sand-hills were over 30 feet high, we arrived at New Bokhara, a place which did not exist when I visited this region before, but now it bids fair to become a thoroughly Russian town. The Emir, the descendant of the Great Tamerlane, has built a palace there, in the Russian style of architecture. Between Bokhara and Samarkand I had the rare pleasure of travelling with my old friend and countryman Dr. Fegræus, who holds the appointment of geologist at the Nobel Works in Balakhani and Baku. I was quite sorry to part from him at Samarcand, whither he was journeying. We sat and talked in my saloon carriage the whole night long; and after the thermometer dropped to 77°, we felt it quite a refreshing change after the 105°.8 of the day. We chatted in Swedish, toasted our absent friends in wine from Tashkend, puffed away at our pipes, and discussed old times in Stockholm and Upsala.

I left Samarkand and its luxuriant vicinity on the morning of 10th July. The river Serafshan (Zarafshan) is now crossed by a new bridge flung over beside the picturesque ruins of the old one, and beyond it the train runs through deep cuttings in the loess; it was as if we were travelling through a dry ravine or earthen avenue. On the other side of Jizak the railway traverses a monotonous, level steppe. The new stations along this part of the line are named after Russian generals who have distinguished themselves in that part of Asia, *e.g.*, Chernyayeva, Vrevskaia, and so on. Finally, after rolling across the Syr-daria on a good iron bridge, the train steamed into the large and bustling station of Tashkend, the capital of West Turkestan. The importance of this place will undoubtedly increase when the new line is opened, about the end of 1903, from Orenburg.

In Tashkend I stopped to visit His Excellency the Governor-General of Turkestan, S. M. Dukhavskoi (who shortly afterwards was carried off by death), as well as my old friends of the Pamir Boundary Commission, Colonel Salessky and M. Bendersky, the topographer. I also took the opportunity to have my chronometers regulated at the observatory. On the evening of the 12th I continued my journey, returning first to Chernyayeva, where I had to wait the greater part of a day for the train from Samarkand. Fortunately there was a large tent close to the station, with a bath inside, which affords passengers some measure of relief from the noonday heat. We started again at five p.m.; but it was not until three hours later that we began to feel any sensible abatement of the heat of the day. And I need hardly say that our heartiest blessings accompanied the sun when he disappeared in the west.

After that the train traversed the fertile valley of Ferghana, threading its way amongst gardens and orchards, villages, cultivated fields, and grassy steppes, with first the Turkestan moun-

Islam Bai.

tains, and after them the snow-capped peaks of the Alai Mountains framing in the valley on the south. Every now and again we ran alongside the Syr-daria. At various places, beside the villages and at the points where the roads crossed the railway, we saw groups of Sarts. They have not yet grown accustomed to the wonderful "machine" which flies past at such a marvellous rate on the *temir-yoll* (iron road). At nine in the evening we reached Andishan (or Andijan), the terminus of the Russian Central Asiatic Railway.

As the train slowed down to the platform, I saw standing

waiting for me, as calm and steadfast as when I last parted from him, my faithful old servant Islam Bai. He was dressed in a blue *khalat* (Kirghiz coat) and wore on his breast the gold medal which King Oscar gave him. He was just the same, looked vigorous and hardy, but had aged a little, and his beard was greyer. He said himself, he was now an old man. I greeted him warmly, had him up into my carriage, and there we sat and talked for three hours on end, partly about his long, four months' journey home from Urga in Mongolia in 1897, and partly about the journey I was just beginning. Islam grasped my plans at once, and entered into them with the greatest interest. And as I stood and watched him setting out for Osh, with all my baggage loaded upon *arabas* (Turkestan carts), I felt glad I had such a faithful fellow to entrust it to. From that moment onwards he again officiated as my *karavan-bashi* (chief or captain of the caravan), and attended to all my wants, anticipated my wishes and procured everything that was required for the equipment and furnishing of my successive caravans. Poor Islam Bai! Alas! that the journey which thus began for him in the rosiest colours should close in such an unhappy, such a pitiable fashion!

CHAPTER II.

OVER THE PASSES TO KASHGAR.

At Osh I spent two very pleasant weeks in the company of my excellent friend, Colonel Saitseff, of the Pamir Boundary Commission, and his amiable family. He held the appointment of *uyäsdny natyalnik* (district commissioner) of the district of Osh, ruling over a population of some 175,000, of whom 35,000, all Sarts, together with 150 Russians and a garrison of 800, were concentrated in the chief town. The commissioner's residence stands in the midst of a park, buried in luxuriant vegetation, on the right bank of the Akbura, and commands a magnificent view down the valley. My stay in Osh was, however, somewhat marred by a violent inflammation of the eyes. This trouble tried my patience severely; though after all I did not really lose much through the involuntary detention, for Islam Bai was all the time busy organising the caravan and getting it ready to start, engaging servants, seeing after two tents being made, and laying in the requisite stores, such as sugar, tea, stearine candles, petroleum, leather trunks, saddles, and so forth. I and Colonel Saitseff went one day to see Islam in his own home in the Sart quarter. He lived in a poor and simple hut of clay, standing in a little plot of ground which he owned, and had a wife and five children. I left with them presents in money and other things, by way of comforting them for the approaching absence of their prop and stay. During my previous journey I paid Islam 25 roubles (about £2 13s.) per month; now I increased this to 40 roubles (£4 4s. 7d.), a large salary for an Asiatic, especially as Islam had rations and everything else free. I deposited his first year's salary with Colonel Saitseff, who agreed to pay over to his family 10 roubles every month.

As soon as my eyes were better, and everything was ready, I resolved to make a start. Accordingly the caravan set off early on the morning of the 31st July, and went as far as Madi.

Kader Ahun, Islam Bai, and Musa at Nagara-challdi.

Meanwhile, after a festive dinner, with giving of toasts and drinking of champagne, at Colonel Saitseff's house, I quitted Osh in the afternoon, escorted on the way by my host and his wife, and by a small cavalcade of young ladies and Russian officers. At Madi we found one of my tents set up in a grove of trees, while the *min-bashi* (chief) of the district had furnished a large *yurt* (Kirghiz tent) with chairs and tables. These last groaned under a plenteous *dastarkhan* (repast), consisting of such luxuries as *ash* (rice pudding), chickens, sweetmeats, tea, etc. At dusk my friends rode back to Osh, and I was finally cut off from civilisation; and when at nine o'clock that same evening I took my first series of meteorological observations, I felt I was once more "on the travel," and my thoughts flew back to the "thousand and one" nights I had spent, only a few years before, under similar conditions, in the heart of the great and desolate continent of Asia. It was delightful to be once more "tented" in the open air, with the boundless expanses of the vast continent before me, and a multitude of new hopes and new projects began to swarm through my brain.

Islam had procured for me two fine pups. One of them, a setter, was called Dovlet; the other, a creature of mixed Asiatic blood, was named Yolldash. I had them tethered to my tent, so as to train them to be its watchful guardians, and they were not many days before they learned what was expected of them. I grew so fond of these two beasts, that when I subsequently lost them, I missed them terribly.

The *personnel* of my caravan consisted of Islam Bai, its leader, of Kader Ahun and Musa, two *jighits* (couriers) of Osh, each engaged permanently for 15 roubles a month, and of four *karakesh* (horse-owners), who accompanied the 26 horses which I hired, at the rate of eight roubles a head, for the whole of the journey to Kashgar, a distance of 270 miles. These men had two tents for their own use, and around them the baggage was stacked up like bastions, making quite an interesting scene on the outskirts of the town. At first, and for as far as the new-made driving road extended, I preferred to travel on wheels.

Our real start was made on the morning of 1st August, but the day was already wearing on when we at length got on the move. The weighing and dividing of the baggage, so that the two cases which were slung one on each side of a packhorse should balance evenly and be of the same weight, naturally took up a good deal of time.

My stately caravan of 26 horses, with its mounted captain at its head, presented a truly stirring sight as it filed out into the uncultivated country beyond the little village. The landscape was at first open and bare, but soon grew more diversified and in part covered with yellow grass. Then the hills gradually closed in on both sides, until they finally formed a typical valley. The "going" was first-rate, but the heat was scorching—a remarkable contrast to Osh, with its orchards and plentiful supplies of water. We came upon the *auls* of the Kirghiz immediately outside of Madi. These tented villages, with the big flocks and herds of sheep, goats, cattle, camels, and horses grazing around them, quite brightened up the landscape. The Kirghiz of Ferghana spend the summer up amongst the mountains and in the valley of the Alai. The most conspicuous feature of their nomad life is the women, with their red garments, their ornaments, and high white head-gear.

The next day we crossed over the little pass of Chigherchigh, climbing up to it by a gently sloping valley of red and yellow clay, moderately clothed with fine grass, on which the Kirghiz were grazing their flocks. Two Kirghiz horsemen, catching up the long ropes which hung from the carriage-pole in front of my horses, set off up the pass at full gallop. But over on the other side the slope was much steeper, and the road zigzagged every few yards, so that I had to keep the brake jammed hard against the back wheel to prevent the phaeton from going faster than might have been agreeable, or even safe. The Ileh-su, the little brook which trickled down the eastern face of the pass into the Gulcha river, rippled merrily amongst the stones and bushes with which it was fringed, and often broke into creamy cascades. After a little the steep descent came to an end, the valley opened out, and before us lay, embosomed amid slender poplars, the little town of Gulcha, with its half-dozen Russian houses, its barracks, telegraph station (the last that the Russians have in this direction), bazaar, and fort garrisoned by a *sotnia* (company) of Cossacks. Gulcha stands on the right bank of the Kurshab or Gulcha-daria, which carried a considerable volume of water, notwithstanding that it was only 2¾ ft. deep—deep enough, however, to enter the bottom of my carriage when I crossed it.

The road from Gulcha kept to the right bank of the river, which flowed along a broad and stony bed, though in several arms. But the previous winter's fall of snow having been inconsiderable, the volume was less than usual. The road, notwithstanding that it ran up and down over the hills and ridges, was first-rate. It is maintained with great care, and is repaired every spring, for it is generally destroyed by avalanches and melting snow, especially on the passes. The bridges which spanned the river were made of wood, cleverly strengthened with upper beams, and were thrown across at places where one span would easily reach from bank to bank. What a contrast to the wretched, swaying contrivances of the Kirghiz

A Bridge above Gulcha.

which I saw on the occasion of my first visit nine years before! But since then the road itself has acquired strategic importance, in that it is now continued up the Alai valley to Bordoba (Borteppeh), and then on further *viâ* Kizil-art and Ak-baital to Fort Pamir. You can now drive the whole of the way from Osh, and the Russian outpost on the Murghab is supplied with provisions and building materials by cart. Artillery also can now cross the desolate plateaus of the Pamir. At several points along the route, *e.g.*, at Bordoba and at Kara-kul, the Russians have built station-houses of stone, well masked with earth, so that they merely look like hills or mounds, and might easily be passed without observation by anybody unacquainted with their position. Each of these rest-houses contains a room with fire-places, store of provisions, samovars, and so forth, and is intended to afford shelter to travellers and couriers (*jighits*) during the winter, when the snowstorms rage.

The higher we ascended the more distinctly the river became concentrated into one well-defined channel, as well as shut in on both sides by steep crags. We had already passed a few isolated poplars (*terek*); now junipers (*archa*) began to make their appearance, scattered along the mountain sides. Partridges were very plentiful, and not at all shy. At the little clay fort of Kizil-kurgan (red fort) some Kirghiz were awaiting me with tea. A little further on I pulled up under the shade of a grove of fine poplars to wait for the caravan, and fell asleep, and slept as I had not slept for many a long day. And I was really in need of it, for I had rested very badly during the first nights of the journey, through not being yet accustomed to the restless life of the caravan, especially the noises of the camp, such as the neighing of the horses and the barking of the dogs. But I had barely slept an hour when I was awakened by shouts and whistlings, and my caravan defiled past me. At its head rode one of the men on an ass, leading the three horses which carried my cases of valuable instruments. The rest of the caravan was divided into three sections, each in charge of one man, whilst others of the men walked beside the horses to adjust the loads when they slipped or no longer rode well and evenly. Last of all came Kader Ahun, leading in a string a new dog I had bought. The shrill echoes of the horses' bells made very pleasant music in the pass. Slowly the long string of animals filed on past me, disappeared in a dip of the road, emerged into view again, once more vanished, and yet once again appeared in sight, slowly climbing a steep acclivity. But I was not long in catching them up, in a part of the valley where the road ran as it were along a shelf, protected by a parapet, high up above the river, which was there spanned by several bridges.

After traversing a glen dotted with poplars, and called Kirgaul, the road grew more stony, and for long distances ran along the shoulders of perpendicular screes and gravelly slopes, the bases of which were washed by the stream. An affluent, which emerged from a *yilga* (glen) called Billauli, contributed pretty nearly one-half of the volume of water in the main river. At the entrance to every side-glen we obtained picturesque glimpses into the heart of the mountains. Poplars became more and more common and the bushes more plentiful; the path ascended

My First Caravan.

somewhat, cascades increased in frequency, and the ripple of the stream waxed louder and louder. In a particularly inviting poplar grove on the right bank of the river, in an expansion of the valley known as Kulenkeh-tokai, we granted ourselves our first day's rest. It was indeed an ideal place to rest in, being so still and quiet, for the horses were sent off to graze on certain *yeylaus* (summer pastures) in the neighbourhood. The sky was overcast, the air pleasant, and at intervals there was a drizzling rain, through which the sun peeped out occasionally. It blew alternately up the valley and down the valley, and the sound of the wind among the leafy trees was like a consecration hymn. I lay and listened to that old familiar murmur, and dreamed myself back among the crowds of incidents which made up my former journeys, and my imagination reached out towards the coming years and the vicissitudes—disappointments and losses, successes and discoveries—which they had in store for me. Although I was not yet fully habituated to the loneliness of caravan life, I was sufficiently impressed by the difference between my present occupation and those of the past two years. The melancholy crooning of the poplars and the increasing murmur of the river alike seemed to bid me exercise that patience which is the surest guarantee of future success. The camp seemed silent and deserted, no curling smoke betrayed the presence of a fire, and there was not a human being within sight, for my men were all fast asleep inside their tents. Nothing broke the solemn stillness save the ripple of the water and the stirring of the wind in the tree-tops.

Shortly after midnight we were treated to a copious downpour of rain, which pattered briskly on the tent-canvas. It was quite cheering and refreshing to hear it after the oppressive heat of Turkestan; indeed, on towards morning the air felt decidedly cool. This unexpected shower woke up the camp, and my men rushed out to drag the packing cases and baggage under cover.

Shortly after striking camp on the following morning we crossed the river two or three times, but after that kept for the most part to the right bank. At Sufi-kurgan we passed on the left hand the glen of the Terek, which leads up over the pass of Terek-davan by a shorter, but more difficult, route to Kashgar. Above that point the main stream diminished in volume, but the valley itself widened out again, and its grey, regularly-sloping bottom contrasted strikingly against the terraces of red sand, gravel-and-shingle, and common clay which walled in the river steeply on both sides. We pitched our camp in the open valley of Bosuga, where pasture was plentiful and Kirghiz *auls* were numerous, while the mountain slopes all around were clothed with junipers, in some places standing so thickly together as to form forests. On this, as on the preceding day, we marched 26 miles; the *verst* posts still lined the side of the road.

My pups Dovlet and Yolldash were perfectly killing. They were only a couple of months old, and unable to run very far;

A Short Rest by the Way.

so I packed them into a basket, fastened at the back of the carriage. At first they were so amazed at this strange manner of travelling that they were unable to utter a sound. However they soon grew accustomed to it, and Dovlet, who was luxuriously inclined, used to keep a sharp eye upon Yolldash, and if he refused to let him have the softest place to lie in, used to give him such a lesson that the poor beggar whined most pitifully. But upon being let out of their prison when we pitched camp, their joy was unbounded, and they became the very best of friends, and frisked and raced, and tumbled over one another, as though there had never been any differences at all between them. By this time they were quite at home in the camp, and at night always slept beside my bed.

And first-rate watch dogs they proved, for at the least suspicious sound they barked furiously. They always had their meals with me, but oh! what appetites they had!

The night of the 6th August was decidedly cold; the thermometer fell nearly two degrees below zero (Fahr.), and I had to unpack my furs, felts, and winter cap. The rarefaction of the air did not, however, occasion me the least inconvenience, although the loss of breath which followed upon any strenuous exertion proved that we were subject to what the natives call *tutek*, or the feeling that is experienced when crossing a lofty pass.

The road continued upwards beside the Talldik rivulet, and sometimes even ran down into the bed of the torrent, but eventually it quitted it and wound up the mountain slope. After passing more side-glens, two or three of which led up to the pass over the Alai Mountains, we came to the foot of the real ascent. This was neither excessively steep nor dangerous, for the road has been made to climb up by innumerable short zig-zags, each protected by a parapet. The rock through which it has been cut is a black, much-folded slate. On the summit of the pass of Talldik, within an inclosed area, there stands a post, to which are attached two cast iron plates, proclaiming that the pass is 11,500 feet high, and 58 miles from Gulcha, and that the road was made when A. B. Vrevsky was Governor-General of Turkestan and N. J. Korolkoff was Governor. The work was begun on 24th April and finished on 1st July, 1893, under the superintendence of Major Grombtshevsky. On the other side of the pass, that is, going down into the Alai valley, the descent was not so steep, and it needed but a very few turns to bring us down to the stream which led to Sarik-tash. But on that side of the pass there was not a single juniper; the slopes above the Alai valley were entirely destitute of timber.

At Upper Sarik-tash I dismissed my *arabachi* (coachman), giving him a good tip and a dagger, for he had driven me capitally, and without a single mishap to horse or vehicle, all the way from Osh. Henceforward I travelled on horseback, and to begin with tried a new Hungarian saddle from Budapest. We were not long in coming to Sarik-tash, properly so called, where the glen from the pass of Talldik led down into the Alai valley. After that we turned to the east, leaving the last verst-posts of the Russian road behind us. To the south we now had the magnificent mountain system of the Trans-Alai, each mountain giant clad in a pure vesture of snow, softly tinted with light blue, while most of the loftiest summits were wreathed in clouds. These were particularly numerous towards the west, and consequently we were unable to see Peak Kaufmann. Directly opposite to us when we came out into the Alai valley was the glen of Kizil-art, up which ran the road from Bordoba to the pass that I crossed on my former journey (1894). Looking westwards we had an unlimited view down between the two huge mountain-ranges of the Alai and the Trans-Alai, the valley between them being broad and open, and abounding in

A Camel Caravan Fording an Arm of the Kizil-su.

pasture, as might readily be inferred from the great number of large *aghils* (sheep folds) and the immense flocks of sheep which dotted the mountain-sides in many places. The Kirghiz horsemen who met our cavalcade invariably dismounted and greeted us on foot.

At its eastern end the Alai valley is shut in by a ring of mountains, nicked however by the flat pass of Tong-burun, which forms at one and the same time the eastern threshold of the valley and the main watershed in that part of the world. At intervals we crossed over low spurs of the Alai, *e.g.*, Katta-sarik-tash, all stretching towards the south, that is towards the middle of the valley. Gradually all the rivulets and tor-

Nagara-challdi.

rents which coursed down these stony side-glens became united into one stream, the Kizil-su, the main artery of the Alai valley.

During the greater part of the day it hailed, and sometimes rained, although the fall was slight; but as we drew near to our camping-ground at Äylämä, the weather grew much worse and the rain came on faster. Hardly was the tent up, when down upon us burst the storm, but fortunately we all got safely under shelter without being drenched. August though it was, the weather was quite autumnal, and the air raw and cold, and heavy clouds hung about the mountains. As this place was said to offer the best grazing all the way to Kashgar, we resolved to give the horses a day's rest. All along we were escorted by Kirghiz horsemen, who kept us supplied with fuel; and besides having a yurt always ready for us, they fetched us mutton and milk from the nearest auls. This second day's rest was no better than the first; it literally poured with rain. Autumn had, it was evident, already begun amongst these mountains of Ferghana. But we comforted ourselves with the reflection that in such weather it was more comfortable to be snug and dry inside a good roof than to be getting wet through in the saddle.

The next day, the 9th of August, was a splendid day, with a bright blue sky; and we climbed slowly up towards the pass of Tong-burun, or rather it is a broad *bel* (saddle), which the Kirghiz hardly deem entitled to the name of a pass. All the same, the little cairn, which stood on its softly rounded, convex summit, marked a very important geographical fact, namely, that here we had the watershed between the drainage basins of the Sea of Aral and Lop-nor. Hence it was a more important dividing line than Talldik itself, which merely separated the basin of the Syr-daria from that of the Amu-daria. From this watershed the contour sloped all the way to Lop-nor.

After riding a short distance up the glen of Shura on our right, we climbed the steep slope which overhung it. It was a tough pull for the horses; some of the loads slipped, and occasioned delay. We were now quite close to the mountains that formed the eastward continuation of the Trans-Alai; but they were muffled in snow, and had their summits shrouded in clouds.

After that we travelled along a sort of flattened ridge, leaving the Kizil-su (of Kashgar) on our right, and eventually dipped down into the depression of Kho-yilga. This last possessed no definitive drainage channel, but had a large number of peculiar pits or cavities of great size, into which the rain water gathered;

at least it would appear so from the horizontal deposits of mud which covered them at the bottom. In some of the crevices small junipers had taken root, and the region abounded in bobacs or steppe marmots (*Arctomys Bobac*).

Next we descended a steep gravelly slope or terrace until we came to the confluence of the Kizil-su and the Kok-su ; and then continued over crests and along terraces zigzagging over broken ground and across more or less deep ravines. As we advanced the vegetation grew scantier and scantier, and the junipers stood further and further apart.

The next important feature we encountered was the broad valley of the Nura, furrowed at the bottom by its deep and strongly scarped river-bed. The Nura was a more considerable stream than the Kizil-su, and its water just as red as that of the Red River (Kizil-su) itself. It was anything but an agreeable stream to ford, for the treacherous stones which littered it were invisible owing to the muddiness of the water, and sometimes came within an ace of bringing our horses to their knees. Had we been a month later the river would have been in full flood, and we should have been unable to cross it at all ; as it was, our travelling cases were in considerable danger. Fortunately the river was lower than usual owing to the dull, cold weather of the past few days. It is astonishing what a difference two or three days of bright, warm sunshine make in the volume of a stream like this. After their confluence, the united Nura and Kizil-su formed quite a respectable stream.

Our route lay along the slopes which overhung the right bank of the river, the path climbing and dipping incessantly, until at the top of the last pass we beheld, far down below us, the white walls and towers of the Russian frontier post of Irkeshtam, which is held by a Cossack garrison. Irkeshtam is a customs station as well as a frontier blockhouse, and in the chief customs' officer there, M. Sagen, I found again an old acquaintance, whom I had met on a former visit to Kashgar. This gentleman was a great lover of animals, and had a private menagerie, consisting of a wolf, some foxes, and a bear, the last tethered beside his den in the middle of the courtyard. Some time after my visit Bruin, who was completely untamed, contrived to wriggle himself loose from his chain, and went and paid his respects in the couriers' room, to their no little consternation. But Master Bruin's adventure had for him a tragic termination, for the men took refuge on the roof, and from

Crossing the Kizil-su on the Way to Kashgar.

that point of vantage bombarded the poor beast till they killed him.

Half an hour's ride beyond Irkeshtam we struck the Red River again; by this it had swollen into a turbulent torrent of muddy water, 2 ft. 7½ in. deep and with a temperature of 9°.9 C. or 49°.8 Fahr. We were now within the confines of the Celestial Kingdom, which stretched hence eastwards all the way to the Pacific. The road led along the left side of the Kizil-su, and then through a narrow gorge up to the pass of Torpag-bel. After that we crossed the barren, sandy, gravelly steppe of Däsht, diversified by sparse tufts of grass and numerous water-channels, all now dry; indeed the entire landscape, which was shut in on every side by mountains, wore an altogether arid appearance. The outliers of the Pamirs, amongst which we were now travelling, were everywhere diminishing in elevation, until finally they ended in low hills and ridges of gravel-and-shingle, seamed by trenches, gulleys, and erosive furrows. Nevertheless the hard rock, a black slate, cropped out almost everywhere.

Thence crossing over the little pass of Kara-davan, we reached, at first by a steep descent, but afterwards by easier slopes, the broad, open valley of Yeghin, at the bottom of which, on the left bank of the biggish stream which threaded it, stood a Chinese fort. There we found encamped a caravan of 150 camels bound for Kashgar. When they started again, about three o'clock in the afternoon, it was quite a sight to see the big, clumsy animals ploughing their way across the Kizil-su, churning up the water as if they were so many paddle-boats.

Our route led on down the valley, which gradually narrowed, while the river hugged closely the foot of the cliffs on the right. A thin belt of vegetation—poplars, willows, scrub and grass—accompanied each bank of the stream. Below the confluence of the Yeghin with the Kizil-su, the valley widened out again, so as to embrace within its precipitous rocky arms a beautiful little wood, traversed by a cheery rivulet. This region was known as Nagara-challdi, and was the queen of all the oases on the road to Kashgar.

We pitched our camp a couple of hundred yards below the confluence of the Nagara-challdi with the Kizil-su. Here on 11th August, which again was set aside for a day of rest, I measured the volume of the latter stream: it amounted to 1,492 cubic feet in the second. Had a stream of that magnitude been confined to one channel with a swift current, it would have been anything but easy to cross it; but fortunately for us it was divided amongst four shallow arms, so that we got the caravan over on the following morning without mishap. I was very pleased to find there was relatively so great a volume of water in the Kizil-su, for this stream was one of the main feeders of the Yarkand-daria, down which I hoped to float right away to the region of Lop-nor.

At first we rode along the right bank, passing on our left a blockhouse of clay, built by Yakub Beg of Kashgar. During the next few hours we forded the river no less than four times. At the first fording in the morning we found that the volume had increased over 700 feet cubic during the night, and it continued to increase at each successive crossing. In a large triangular expansion of the valley, at a spot where a little rivulet came down from the north through the glen of Ala-yukka, stood the square clay blockhouse of Ullug-tshat, the nearest stronghold to the Russian frontier which the Chinese maintain in this direction.

We crossed the Kizil-su for the last time in another similar triangular expansion of its valley called Semiz-khatun, where, amid poplars and bushy scrub, stood another little *kurgan* (fort). But this time the passage was nothing like so easy, for the current was there confined to one channel, and its volume had swollen so rapidly that it now measured 3,000 to 3,500 cubic feet in the second. The muddy reddish current rolled on with a sullen, scowling face, underneath which lurked many deep and treacherous pits.

Islam Bai rode into the river to see what the ford was like, but all at once he plumped into deep water and got a thorough ducking. Kader Ahun, who tried it in another place, fared even worse; for he stumbled into a regular trap-hole, his horse lost its footing, and the two together were whirled away by the current, each only just managing to keep his head above water. Kader usually carried my kodak, but luckily he had handed it over to me immediately before going into the river. After that one of the karakeshes stripped to the skin and mounted bareback, and by dint of letting his horse go where he liked, managed at last to find a firm ledge, which ran diagonally across the stream as far as a little tongue of gravel, and thence turned back again up-stream. The other men followed their comrade's example, and having stripped led the caravan animals across

Camel Caravan on the Way from Osh to Kashgar.

in small detachments, first the three horses which carried our supply of food, then the tent, the tinned goods and other baggage, and last of all the horses which bore my instruments and photographic outfit, each animal being convoyed across singly by the three men, who were ready to come instantly to the rescue should the animal stumble or fall. It was impossible to sit and watch without a feeling of great anxiety the heavily-laden horses struggling against the fierce energy of the current, for the ledge I have mentioned ran for the greater part of the way

Fording the Kizil-su.

up-stream, so that the water broke like a cataract against the horses' chests.

Luckily we all got over without mishap, for the packages that were likely to suffer from wetting were tied up higher before the horses entered the river. Then, after readjusting the loads, and drying ourselves a little, we continued our way, and pitched camp for the day at Yaz-kitchik, beside a Kirghiz aul or tent-village. Here we said good-bye to the Kizil-su, which flowed away to the south.

It was a cool and beautiful evening, with a bright moon and glittering stars, and through the stillness of the night there echoed from afar the dull jingling of the camels' bells from the big caravan travelling to Kashgar. The sound roused our dogs to frenzy ; nevertheless the low but solemn rhythm had for me a great charm ; it was eminently symbolical of the calm, majestic gait of the lordly camel. Gradually the echoes came nearer and nearer, we heard the shouts and singing of the camel-drivers more and more distinctly. Then they went on past us in the darkness of the night, filling the air with a tumult of noise and confusion. And finally the riot died away amongst the mountains.

The last few days' march ran through a perfectly mono-

M. Nicolai Fedorovitch Petrovsky, Privy Councillor and Russian Consul-General in Kashgar.

tonous region—barren and destitute of vegetation—while the hills drooped and drooped until finally they ended in level plains.

On the 13th August we crossed over the Mäshrab-davan, the summit of the pass being marked by a little fort and three *masars* or burial-cairns, hung about with rags. The following day's march took us through a deep, narrow glen, almost absolutely sterile, and shut in on both sides by the familiar folded red sandstone, the layers of which varied greatly in hardness and consistency, the hardest frequently jutting out in overhanging friezes and laminated cornices. The ground under our feet consisted of the same sort of materials. Before we got to the *serai* or shelter-house of Kan-jugan we were caught by a rain storm of unexampled violence, and had to run up the tents in a great hurry. But it was of no avail; we all got wet to the skin. The water stood on the ground and splashed up at every footstep we took; and inside the tent, amongst the dripping cases, the air was cold and damp, and I was not sorry to put on my furs. A temperature of 12°.6 C. or 54°.7 Fahr. at 5.30 p.m. was quite an unusual thing at that season of the year in those localities.

On the 15th August we travelled to Min-yoll, and on the 16th made our last day's march into Kashgar, after being met at Kalta by Consul-General Petrovsky, Mr. George Macartney, and some Russian gentlemen then living in the capital of East Turkestan, followed by an escort of Cossacks.

CHAPTER III.

FROM KASHGAR TO THE YARKAND-DARIA.

I REMAINED in Kashgar from the 17th August to the 5th September, organising and equipping the caravan I was to lead into the deserts of innermost Asia. I need not say how hospitably I was entertained by my good old friend Consul-General Petrovsky, and how he helped me, as he had so often done before, in every possible way. He placed his ripe and valuable experience absolutely at my disposal, as also the well-nigh omnipotent influence which he enjoys in East Turkestan. Indeed but for his invaluable assistance many of my plans would have been altogether impracticable; but with it they turned out eminently successful. The first business we took in hand was to exchange my capital, amounting to some £1,200, into Chinese silver. At that time, in the bazaars of Kashgar, a yamba* was worth 71 roubles, (£7 10s.), but the market was so small that the purchase of 160 yambas all at once, sent the rate of exchange up to 72 roubles in the course of two or three days.

The business was arranged by a crafty old broker, Isa Hadji, and when the transaction was completed it appeared he had not fleeced us out of more than 36 roubles (£3 16s.). As it turned out, it proved an exceptionally good thing for me, because not long afterwards the yamba appreciated very suddenly and greatly in value; and yet the Volga-Kama

* One yamba=50 sär. One sär=16 tengeh=1·48 roubles=37 grams of silver=10 miskal=3 shillings. One tengeh=50 pul. One miskal=10 pung; 1 pung=10 li. The rate of exchange of Chinese silver is subject to great fluctuations. The yamba seldom weighs exactly 50 sär, but varies as a rule between 49 and 51; and as the monetary standard of Central Asia is the Chinese coinage, it is always necessary to have a Chinese balance at hand when exchanging money in any quantity. New silver coins, not exceeding a maximum value of 8 tengeh, have recently been introduced into East Turkestan. These are current along with the usual Chinese silver "shoes," an exceedingly inconvenient form of coined money.

I also took with me a Kashgar boy named Kader because of his knowledge of Arabic writing.

My first object was to get the whole of the caravan to Lailik on the Yarkand-daria. There I intended to divide my forces. While I, along with two or three of the men, and a very small portion of the baggage, floated down the Yarkand-daria or Tarim, the main body of the caravan would travel by the great caravan-road leading through Maral-bashi, Aksu, and Korla to some rendezvous in the Lop region; where, according to arrangement, I also expected to be joined by two Buriat Cossacks in the end of December.

The Two Cossacks—Sirkin and Chernoff.

Now Consul Petrovsky thought it would be very unwise to send such a big caravan, with such a large store of money, all through East Turkestan without protection, and offered to let me have two of the West Turkestan Cossacks of the consulate guard as escort, until I should be joined by the Buriats. It was a splendid idea, and I at once accepted the offer, with gratitude. The Governor-General of West Turkestan readily accorded his permission, and the two Cossacks were at once attached to my service. These men, Sirkin and Chernoff, proved first-rate servants, and rendered me invaluable help during the ensuing year; in fact, I never had better. The arrangement was that they were to continue to

A Rope-dancer in Kashgar.

receive their regular pay all the time they were in my service, but were to ride their own horses, and provide their own saddles, weapons, and ammunition.

I also arranged with M. Petrovsky, that any letters which arrived for me at Kashgar during the course of the autumn and winter were to be sent to the Lop country by four successive *jighits* or couriers. The days on which they were successively to start was definitely fixed before I left, so that I knew pretty well when each man ought to arrive. And as these couriers were not to be paid until they delivered my mail-bag, I felt

Market at Kashgar.

pretty easy with regard to that matter. The arrangement worked splendidly, for M. Petrovsky took it in hand himself. Thus I had the pleasure, of priceless worth to the solitary traveller, of getting news from home occasionally, and keeping in some fashion in touch with the great world.

The days passed swiftly amid the bustle of preparation, visiting and dining. Of the numerous friends whom I made during my former visits to Kashgar I saw a good deal; amongst others, of Mr. Macartney, the English political agent, whose home was now brightened by the presence of a charming wife. I also had the pleasure of meeting again my excellent old friend, Father Hendriks, as well as the Swedish missionary Mr. Högberg, and his wife, and the two new missionaries whom they had added to the station.

The Chinese officials, Khan Dao Tai and Tsen Daloi, were old acquaintances; but Tso Daloi, who had something to do with the police, was a new revelation. He appointed two *durgaz* (policemen), with instructions to see that the inhabitants of the city supplied the caravan with everything it needed—of course, in return for a handsome equivalent.

I was not, however, the only traveller who at this time happened to be present in the westernmost city of China; for on the 21st August, Colonel McSwiney arrived, the same member of the English Boundary Commission in whose company I spent so many happy days on the Pamirs in 1895. He was on his way back to India *viâ* Turkestan, Kashgar, and Pamir, after making a short visit to England. The next day after there came two French travellers, M. St. Yves and a young lieutenant, who after a few days' rest continued their homeward journey by way of Pamir.

When all our stores and other equipments were ready, the loads were made up and weighed, and finally fastened to a wooden framework. Two of these were then bound together in such a way as to make a short double pair of steps. In this way they were easier to lift and lash on the back of a kneeling camel. Then, having said good-bye to my friends in Kashgar, and thanked M. Petrovsky for his invaluable kind offices, and having duly celebrated my departure by a last merry feast, I started, at two o'clock on the afternoon of 5th September, to make the first stage in my journey proper.

When the camels were arranged in file, the men mounted on horse-back, and all ready for starting, M. Petrovsky took a couple of negatives; then a last greeting, a last farewell, and off we went to the dull, but significant, tingle-tingle of the camels' bells. Our road lay along the western wall of the city, past Chinneh-bagh, Mr. Macartney's house, and Kum-därvaseh, where I said adieu to my countrymen, the Swedish missionaries. We had just reached the bridge over the Kizil-su, whose water both in colour and consistency bore a striking resemblance to tomato soup, when the sky darkened in the north-west, and heavy densely packed clouds came trailing out of the mountains. But the day had been hot and sultry, and foreboded a storm. Nor was it long before we encountered the first violent gusts of wind. Up they whistled the fine yellow dust which covered the road, and drove it on before them in dense whirling clouds. Then it began to rain, and soon came down in torrents; in fact

From a photograph by] [CONSUL-GENERAL PETROVSKY.

The Start from Kashgar—In the foreground, from left to right, the two Cossacks, Kader, the Author, and Islam Bai.

I have seldom seen such rain. In a very few minutes the road was converted into a muddy puddle, and the entire caravan —men, animals, and baggage—looked as if they had been steeped in a river. Yet we had no alternative but to keep pushing on; for every house and *serai* (rest-house) in the vicinity was crowded with people. The road was, as it generally is, full of animated traffic, and when the storm burst, everybody rushed into the nearest available shelter. Besides, none of these places was spacious enough to contain our big caravan; consequently, we had to remain where we were and face the rain as best we could. The storm raged for an hour and a half with undiminished violence; the sky was repeatedly lit up with dazzling flashes of vivid, bluish-white lightning, and the thunder crashed again and again as if all the artillery of heaven were being discharged at once. Never have I heard it more awe-inspiring; it literally deafened us. But both camels and horses took it quite composedly, and tramped stolidly on southwards between the rows of willows; whilst we men derived what consolation we could from the thought that we could not very well be wetter than we were.

But, uncomfortable though the rain was, its effects were still more unpleasant. For now the road was for long stretches under water, and the soft clayey soil became so slippery, that the camels with their flat, yielding, padded feet, had the utmost difficulty in keeping on their legs. They slipped and slided incessantly, until at last their legs went from under them, and they fell. This occasioned repeated halts, for we had to stop until we got them up again. Very often they went down so suddenly and with such *aplomb*, I could well have believed they had been tripped up by some invisible giant, and when their heavy loads dumped on the ground the mud flew for yards. Shouts, cries arose from every side! The caravan halted to a man. The men rushed up and tried to get the foundered beast straight and on his legs again, or if he lay awkwardly, set about unloading him, and then had to reload him again. In consequence of this we crawled like snails through the treacherous mire. The worst places were those in which the road was uneven, and dipped down into the hollows and then mounted up again. Here we had to cut notches or steps with spades, or dig up dry soil and strew it over the soft and treacherous surface. Even then it required two men to guide each camel, and help him to maintain his balance.

Thus although our first day's march out of Kashgar was only a short one, it proved to be anything but easy. I have never left that city under more unpropitious circumstances. I could not help thinking that Heaven itself took this emphatic way of putting us in mind of the dangers and difficulties which beset the path of the traveller amongst the poplars of East Turkestan. But this was the last downpour I was destined to see or feel for many a long day; the next happened two years later, when I was in the vicinity of Lassa.

Meanwhile night was come, and in the labyrinth of bazaars and alleys which abut upon the northern town-wall of Yanghi-shahr or "New Town" of Kashgar, the paper lanterns were already lighted. It was there the road turned off to the east. Immediately outside this, the Chinese town, the road lay for nearly an hour's march completely under water, so that as we went splashing between the orchards and gardens, fields and clay-walls, we seemed to be fording the bed of a shallow river. All that could be seen in the darkness were the dark silhouettes of the poplar avenues; but the rain had stopped, and the sky was clear. The road too was better, and the camels were now able to keep their feet. It was late when we halted for the night and pitched a makeshift sort of camp at Musulman-nachuk. As a matter of precaution I deemed it advisable to post guards about the baggage.

The road thence to Lailik was for the most part known to me. I travelled over it in 1895. Hence there is no need for me to linger over it.

On 6th September we travelled through a remarkably well cultivated, though rather sparsely inhabited, region, the road being good and dry, and bordered by canals. We met two or three caravans bringing in white cotton stuffs from the Khan-arik district. Although our baggage was still wet and heavy, it gradually dried in the sun. Beyond Khan-arik we went along a magnificent avenue of mulberry trees, willows, and poplars, which afforded us ample shade. The poplars were topped to prevent them from growing too high, though the branches at the pollarded end were like a thick sheaf of vertical rods. For long stretches not one ray of sunshine was able to pierce the dense foliage, and it was a great pleasure to ride underneath its cool green arches. Indeed, in these places the road was more like a tunnel; while the camels, stalking through it with their long, even, swinging gait, put me in mind of a string

Fording a Canal near Kashgar.

of freight waggons, tunnelling their way through greenery, a remarkably striking picture. The heaviest burdens were carried by the camels which bore the Chinese silver money, especially one gigantic fellow, who stalked along with no less than forty yambas on his back. As the loads were now well balanced and nicely adjusted, we were no longer delayed through having to stop and regulate them. All that was now required was an occasional hitch or pull at the load on one side or the other. Camels have a voracious appetite, and as ours marched along they levied tribute from both willows and poplars, often snapping their nose-rope to do so. For, if the rope is drawn too tight,

My First Caravan in the Desert East of Kashgar.

it readily breaks in the middle, where the two ends are fastened together by a thinner piece of string, without doing injury to the animal's nose. The canals which bordered both sides of the road not only brought moisture to the roots of the trees, but also, by means of smaller irrigation rills, supplied water for flooding the rice fields.

Each of my men had his appointed duty and fixed place in the line of march. First rode the two *durgaz* from Kashgar; then followed Faisullah, mounted on the leading camel, and by his side Niaz Hadji on horseback. On the sixth camel sat little Kader, gathered in a heap, and on the seventh Islam Bai. The second detachment was led by Turdu Bai, and in its wake rode Musa. The two Cossacks guarded the flanks;

while I generally brought up the rear. In this way we threaded our way through orchards and gardens and villages, between fields of maize and wheat, over *ariks* (irrigation channels), some with bridges, others without, across barren steppes and small patches of sand, where a few forlorn and isolated sand-hills, some ten feet or so in height, turned their steeper sides towards the east. That night we encamped in the town of Yupoga, and it was only by dint of searching several dug-out pools in the large canal of Khan-arik that we discovered sufficient water for our needs, for the supply was that year shorter than usual.

As the animals of a caravan are always more susceptible to fatigue during the first few days than when they have been travelling some time, I decided to make the 8th September a day of rest. The pack-saddles had not been off since we quitted Kashgar, and it was desirable to see whether the camels' backs or humps were being chafed.

The temperature was now steadily falling at night, but the day gradually grew warmer as we got away from the irrigated region and from the mountains. At two or three bendings of the road, the villagers had prepared refreshments for us in the shape of water-melons and sugar, in the hope of getting a little *douceur* in return—a form of polite attention which in the long run is apt to become irksome. We were soon through the town; and out on the "tussocky" steppe that lay beyond it we met a number of peasants, some on horse-back, others on asses, and yet others riding on the backs of oxen, but all carrying the produce of their fields and gardens to market in Yupoga. Every now and again a chain of barren sand-hills ran across the steppe; but between them were flocks of sheep, fields of maize and cotton, and dreary ariks, all perfectly dry except for a little moisture left in one or two places from the last flooding by the Khan-arik.

In the middle of a sand-pit we came upon the lonely masar of Habdan Buzrugvar, decorated with streamers and yaks' tails fastened to poles. In this part of Turkestan it is no uncommon thing to find these saints' burial-places hidden away in sand-pits. On the right-hand side of the road was a belt of tamarisks, covered with graceful blossoms, which awakened melancholy reminiscences of the heather in our Swedish woods at home. The high road narrowed gradually to a mere path, evidence that the traffic decreased as the desert was approached. Upon reaching the environs of Terem, we once more encountered

Poplars and Pool of Water near a Roadside Rest-house in the West of East Turkestan.

the long irrigation canal of Khan-arik. Its sandy bottom, twelve and a half feet wide, was perfectly dry; but a number of little bridges thrown across showed that it did contain water sometimes. The avenue which flanked it consisted of young trees, but they stood wide apart, and there were sad gaps in the rows; many of them were broken down, while in other places they were entirely wanting on one side. With a view of shortening the long desert march which lay before us on the morrow, as I remembered well of old, we continued on through the town and its bazaar, and pitched our camp beside

A Short Rest in the Desert.

the last house immediately before the desert. The bazaar of Terem was quite empty and deserted; all its traders had gone to Yupoga.

On the 10th September I made for many a month to come my last journey by land. During the night the temperature dropped to 8°.3 C. or 46°.9 Fahr., a grim change from 30°.0 C. or 86°.0 Fahr. during the heat of the day. When I rose in the morning the greater part of the caravan was already on foot ready to start, and the rising sun poured a flood of golden light across the steppe, which alone separated us from the river. The day was hot, and the march long and tiring, and there were more than customers enough for the water-melons we carried with us. Belts of steppe alternated with strips of desert. Thus.

sand-dunes were sometimes sparsely dotted with tamarisks, sometimes quite bare. The people call the former *kara-kum* or "black sand"; the latter *ak-kum* or "white sand." At length we perceived evidences that we were approaching the river, in little groves of *tograk* (poplars), and I observed that they wore an increasingly fresher appearance and were fuller of leaf as we drew nearer to the great stream. When we at length reached the broad bosom of the Yarkand-daria it was dusk. At the point where we struck it the river was divided into several arms, and as the left arm, alongside which we were marching, was too shallow to make a fitting starting-point for my contemplated river trip, we pushed on for some distance north, in the dark, the bushes and branches of the scrubby timber crackling and crunching under the camels' hoofs. But as the way did not improve, and the moon dipped her silver crescent behind the woods, we halted where we were, and pitched our camp at random, all thoroughly tired after a thirteen hours' tramp. However, here we were at the river, and I was now about to try a method of travel which was entirely novel to me.

In the Desert near Terem and Lailik.

II.

Floating Down the Lonely Tarim.

A Journey by Boat Through the Desert.

CHAPTER IV.

BOAT-BUILDING AT LAILIK.

I COULD afford barely a week in which to complete the preparations for my long journey down the Tarim, so that there was not a moment to lose. The first thing next morning, the 11th September, I opened negotiations with the begs, or beks, and *kemichis* (ferrymen), by sending Islam to Merket to see if he could buy a ferry-boat. This proved an easier task than I had anticipated. In the first place, I was afraid the Chinese would be suspicious of my purpose. I also feared that, after the experiences of my disastrous journey across the desert in 1895, the inhabitants of the district would be deterred from rendering me any assistance; for it was from Merket I started on that occasion, and the beg of the place had got into trouble through it, having been summoned before the Dao Tai, or Chinese Procurator, of the province, and censured for not providing me with a trustworthy guide. However, there was now a new beg at Merket, and he had been commanded by the Dao Tai, not only to give me a helping hand, but to treat me as a person of distinction. After a few hours' absence Islam came back and reported he had found a man who was willing to sell his boat for 1½ yambas (£10 15s.).

During Islam's absence I took the Cossack Sirkin, and tried the canvas boat I had bought in England, launching her on the side-arm of the river beside which we were encamped, and which, itself augmented by numerous small feeders entering from the main stream, rejoined this last some distance lower down. As there was a gentle breeze from the south-east, I set up the mast and hoisted sail, and away we went, the little boat behaving splendidly and sailing as steady as a rock. Then, having tried her so far, we took her through one of the small connecting channels out upon the broad river itself, and there she went every bit as satisfactorily, though we drifted down stream at a pretty smart pace. Except for a few tiny eddies, which moved as the current moved, the surface of the river was perfectly placid, and there was neither sound nor sign of rapids. The little craft seemed, in relation to the current on which it was floating, to be standing perfectly still. Nevertheless, the banks flew past us with remarkable swiftness. And what a delight it was to be borne along in this easy fashion! It was a foretaste of the exquisite pleasure I was to derive from my several hundred miles' journey down that important river. At length I began to think it a very long way to the point where our side-arm rejoined the main stream, and also awoke to the fact that we ourselves were drifting a considerable distance

The Canvas Skiff when Rigged.

from camp. It was high time to turn back. Accordingly we got out and dragged our little craft across the tongue of soft, tenacious clay, yellow or bluish-black in colour, which separated the river from its lateral branch.

There was a current also in the latter, and although it was not at all strong, it was powerful enough to make the task of rowing against it rather fatiguing work. Sirkin therefore landed, ran through the underwoods, and presently came back bringing with him a man and two horses. Mounting one of these, my Cossack rode up the middle of the stream, towing the little boat behind him by means of a rope. In some places the bottom was dangerous, and the horse very nearly got stuck fast in the tenacious clay; sometimes also the water was decidedly deep.

Once Sirkin went in up to his waist, while the horse, unable to touch the bottom, was carried down by the current at the imminent risk of being upset altogether. The Cossack flung himself off into the water and swam towards the boat, which I steered in his direction. But it was hard work for him to swim in his clothes, and just as he was reaching up to my outstretched oar he suddenly went down. But he soon came up again, and at last contrived to get hold of the boat-side, and very nearly upset her clambering in. All this took place so quickly that

Tent of my Men at Lailik.

I had no time to feel anxious; and yet how easily a disaster might have happened had the man taken cramp, or even been unable to swim! General Pievtsoff lost one of his Cossacks in a whirlpool in the same river only a short distance lower down. The horse meanwhile swam ashore, but had the utmost difficulty in forcing his way through the tenacious mud, though by dint of desperate effort he did so eventually. Sirkin was faint and exhausted by his exertions; but the water looked so inviting that, flinging off my clothes, I jumped in and had a most refreshing bath.

All this, however, brought us no nearer to the camp, and we should have been completely stranded had not some of my men of their own accord come along the bank in search of us. Then, harnessing themselves to a long rope, they towed me from the bank, I meanwhile keeping the boat out in deep water by means of an oar used as a rudder.

When we got back the encampment presented a most animated picture. My tent was surrounded by a crowd of visitors, amongst them certain of my old friends of 1895, notably the beg of Anghetlik, the worthy Tokta or Togda Khoja; the former beg of Merket—Mohammed Niaz—and his sons; the *on-bashi* (chief of ten men) and *örtängchi* ("hosteler") of Lailik; besides several of the inhabitants of Merket, and women dressed in long garments of a thin red material, with their children on their arms.

At first the conversation turned on my unfortunate desert journey of 1895, the talk being frequently interrupted by such ejaculations as "Ai Khoda!" "Taubeh!" and "Ya Allah!" After that we discussed my projected journey down the Tarim, and the possibility of using a ferry-boat for the purpose. In order to settle the matter, I went to the ferry between Lailik and Merket, followed by the greater part of the crowd. The boat which Islam had picked out was a first-rate affair, newly built of sound, rough-hewn planks, held together by stout iron clamps, and as near as possible watertight. The only objection I had to it was that it was very big and very heavy. For although that would be an advantage so long as we were in the upper reaches of the river, who could guarantee that the current was equally deep and powerful everywhere lower down? If this heavy monster were to run aground on the sandbanks that lay hidden underneath the surface, the chances were it would be an awkward business to get her afloat again. I discussed this matter from every point of view with the ferrymen of Lailik. Most of them recommended me to take the craft as she was; others advised cutting her lengthwise, so as to make out of her two lighter and more easily managed boats. Others again suggested that I ought to build two new boats, of medium size and specially constructed for the purpose I had in view. This last would have been the most sensible thing to do, but it could not be carried out without fetching wood and other materials all the way from Yarkand, and that would have meant the loss of much valuable time.

I decided, in the first place, to move the craft down the river to a point on the right bank immediately opposite to our camp ; and this was done on the following morning. Before, however, I could use her, the ferry-boat would have to be altered and reconstructed, and for that purpose it was necessary to build a kind of slip or dry dock. The left bank where we were encamped was not suitable for that purpose, for between us and the main river, and separated from it by a low tongue of wet mud, was the shallow lateral branch I have already mentioned. The right bank in its turn laboured under a disadvantage of another kind, for the river had eaten it away, leaving a steep descent of six feet sheer. But Häkim, the beg of Merket,

Our Building-slip.

requisitioned close upon a hundred men, who came with their spades, and in a very short space of time converted the bank into a gentle slope. Then, laying down wooden rollers, they hauled the big, clumsy boat up out of the water by main force, to the accompaniment of a good deal of shouting and singing. Häkim Beg, who had a larger strain of Chinese than of "Mohammedan" blood in his veins, stood on the "captain's bridge," and directed the proceedings. It was not that he made the boat any lighter to move, but his authority kept the men in order, especially as he held a long rod in his hand, which he flourished about as the ring-master does his whip in a circus. The sons of the desert worked like Trojans, and bit by bit hauled the heavy boat out of the water on to dry land, and thence hoisted her up on to two or three pairs of cross-timbers, placed amongst the hawthorn bushes.

This successfully accomplished, we paused to consider what was the next thing to be done. Various circumstances had to be taken into account. One man told me that the greater part of the water which flowed past Lailik was deviated into a broad, shallow arm that led to the small lakes of Maral-bashi, and from them was distributed by means of ariks or small irrigation channels to the fields of the oasis just named. At the same time the Yarkand-daria itself took a more easterly course towards Chahr-bagh, and was said to be just then shrunk to a narrow, but swift current, so that it was extremely doubtful whether our big craft would be able to make her way along it. On the strength of this information, I thought it best to begin by removing the uppermost plank all round the vessel's sides, bow and stern. With this and some other pieces of wood which I bought we constructed a smaller ferry-boat, for use in case deficiency of water should force us to abandon the bigger craft. For I had made up my mind to descend the Tarim all the way to Lop-nor, and I was determined to do it somehow or other.

For convenience in crossing the river from our camp to the boat-building yard on the other side, we hired, for as long as we wanted it, one of the ordinary ferry-boats which ply between Lailik and Merket. Most of my own time was spent on the other side of the river, where the boat-building was going on, partly that I might superintend the work, partly that I might see everything was done precisely as I wished it; for in all probability the new vessel was destined to be my home for several weeks, and I wanted it to be as comfortable as possible.

And the men worked away with a will. I could easily imagine I was spending a summer afternoon in a saw-mill beside the Ångerman river at home. Cunning sawyers came from Yarkand, and clever carpenters and joiners from Merket, each man with his tools, and earned wages such as they had never earned in their lives before. We also made a smithy amongst the bushes, with a brick fire-place and bellows, and merrily the hammers rang and the sparks flew, whilst the iron clamps were beaten out for holding the woodwork together. Our friend the beg was everywhere, directing and controlling, with the greatest energy and zeal, the "host" of men who were at work building our ark.

From Kashgar I had brought with me two camel loads of

Traffic between the Building-slip and the Camp.

thin planks of strong, well-seasoned poplar wood, for the purpose of constructing a foredeck or platform, on which to put up my tent. These we nailed fast to the edge of the bulwark on the right-hand side (looking down stream), and on the left-hand side to a strong beam which was supported by two or three vertical pieces of short, stout timber. Along this side of the boat, between the beam just mentioned and the outer bulwark, we left a narrow gangway from one end of the vessel to the other.

Behind the platform, nearer amidships, we erected a small square room or cabin of vertical posts and matchwood planking. This I originally intended to use as a sleeping apartment; it would be more easy to keep it warm than the tent during the cold nights of autumn. But eventually it was converted into a photographic dark-room, where I developed and enlarged the negatives I took during the journey. The floor of the cabin was the bottom of the boat; but the structure also took in a breadth of about two feet of the floor of the tent, that is to say of the foredeck. This, extending along the whole of one side of the cabin, served as a table. Another similar table was made against the right-hand bulwark for jars, bottles, and other receptacles containing chemicals. Between the ribs of the cabin we fitted in three long, narrow window-frames, which I also brought with me ready made from Kashgar. One of these was fixed into the front wall next the tent, its lower end resting on the foredeck or table, and this we glazed with dark red glass. When I developed negatives at night or on dark afternoons, I used to put a candle outside this window in the tent, where it was protected against draught and wind, partly by the tent itself, partly by means of a wooden screen which almost entirely surrounded it.

The other two window-frames were glazed with white glass, and put one in the outside wall, the other in the back wall. When I stood up, I could see through them, namely, the river behind us and its right bank at the side; but when I wanted to develop negatives, I had contrivances for shuttering them up so effectually that not a single ray of light came through. I kept my clean water for photographic purposes in four large, iron-hooped barrels, which stood on a low shelf along the back wall. For washing the plates I devised the following contrivance. On the outside of the cabin roof, at the left-hand top corner, on a specially strengthened platform, I fixed a large tub, or barrel, with an india-rubber tube leading out of it at the bottom; this was carried through the cabin roof, and into a samovar provided with a tap. When the samovar was full, I shut off the supply by a clamp round the tube; and when the tub was empty I had only to call to one of the men, and he at once filled it again. The river water was always a turbid grey owing to the mud and dust, and of course quite unsuited for photographic purposes; but there was everywhere plenty of clear crystal water in the small side lagoons, which lay all along the river. On the other hand, it was not practicable to drain away the dirty water which accumulated in the bottom of the boat when I was developing; but, as the boat, in consequence of the unequal distribution of our top-hamper, had a good list to the right, the waste water generally ran over to that side out of my way, and was laded out in the morning. In fact it was scarcely any inconvenience, for I lived for the most part in the tent, a good three feet above the bottom of the boat.

When the framework of the cabin was finished, we threw over it a double set of black felt carpets, and nailed them tight down at the corners and along the edges. The doorway, which opened out on to the narrow gangway on the left-hand side, could be closed by means of felt curtains fastened at the top.

The heat inside the black cabin was unbearable in the daytime, even as late as September; but as the autumn advanced, I suffered less and less from that discomfort. Indeed, I seldom had much to do there during the day, except to go and look at any plates that might be drying, or fetch a scientific instrument or something of that kind out of the laboratory.

Behind the cabin in the middle of the boat we piled up some of our supplies, and two or three saddles, in case we should be compelled to abandon our floating palace and take to horses, as well as the boatmen's belongings; whilst the men themselves found plenty of accommodation in the stern. There they built a small round fireplace of bricks—that was our kitchen. There, also, when the autumn nights began to grow cool, and still more when the nights turned decidedly cold, as they did at the beginning of winter, the men built up big, roaring fires of wood to keep themselves warm.

While all this was being done, we were equally busy with other preparations for our long journey. Sirkin the Cossack spent his time at the smithy, making a couple of strong anchors, or rather six-clawed grapnels, which proved of great service on

Building the Black Cabin.

several occasions. The smaller of the two was meant for the English canvas boat, and was dropped every time we went out in her into the middle of the river to measure its velocity. The smaller ferry-boat was soon finished, and its seams caulked with old cotton steeped in oil.

Nevertheless, I began to grow anxious, as I watched the river dropping an inch or so every twenty-four hours. But we pushed on with the work as fast as we could, still hoping that, if only we could clear the shallows of Maral-bashi, we should be able to carry out our voyage right through to Lop-nor.

The whole of the last two days at Lailik were taken up with the final preparations. The baggage was divided into two sections, one for the boat trip on the Tarim, the rest for the camel caravan. For the former I retained only such things as were absolutely indispensable; yet even then they filled three large boxes. Two of the boxes contained my scientific instruments, writing and sketching materials, clothes, books, etc., and the third was completely filled with the photographic outfit. When everything was at length ready, I paid the carpenters, joiners and smiths who had helped us; the beg meanwhile standing by to see that none of the men got more than they were justly entitled to.

Our little flotilla was launched on the 15th September. I took a short experimental turn in the bigger boat, and it answered capitally in every respect. The day was celebrated as a general holiday by all the inhabitants of the neighbourhood, who came down in large numbers to witness the launching. Every one of them brought "gifts" *in natura*, such as sheep, poultry, eggs, bread, melons, grapes, and apricots, so that we were well supplied for several days to come. In the evening I made a feast for the notables of the place and for the workmen who had laboured at the boats. The banquet consisted of rice pudding and mutton, tea and fruits, and whilst we ate and drank, music was discoursed by a big musical box I had brought with me for such occasions as these. When it grew dark we hung up Chinese lanterns amongst the tents, and through the bright stillness of the night echoed the melancholy strains of *nagaras*, *dutaras*, and other stringed instruments, stirring awake in my memory reminiscences of my former stay in the place. Then as now I was on the eve of setting out upon a momentous journey, with Lailik and Merket for my starting-point. Yet how different were the circumstances! On the first occasion my object was the weird and murderous desert; now, however, on the route we were about to follow, we should not at any rate suffer from want of water. The very same musicians who played the overture to my desert journey were now inaugurating the new one; while dancing-girls, clad in long robes of white, with heavy plaits of black hair hanging down their backs, and their heads crowned with small bag-caps, danced barefooted to the strains of the music, the measure being a slow one, with jerky, whirling movements. I photographed the sirens on the following morning, but a goodly proportion of their charms were then seen to be due to the beautifying effects of the Chinese lanterns.

Musicians and Dancing-girls at Lailik.

Although everything was now ready for a start, I sacrificed yet one day more, partly that I might make some measurements, and partly that we might get on board certain stores which would come in very useful later on. Along the right bank of the river, which lay 8 ft. 2 in. above the level of the water, I measured a base-line of 1,250 mètres (1,367 yards). This distance was covered by the ferry-boat, of course on the river, in 26 minutes, and by the skiff (canvas boat) in 22 minutes 17 seconds; the difference being due to the difficulty we experienced in keeping the bigger vessel in the middle of the current, while the smaller boat was quite easy to manage. The ferry-boat consequently travelled, at any rate over this particular stretch of the river, at the rate of nearly 50 mètres, or 52½ yards, in the minute, or a little more than 1¾ miles an hour. Walking at my usual rate when on the march, I found it took me 13 minutes 45 seconds to travel over the same measured base-line, and I required an average of 1,613 paces to do it in; consequently 52½ yards were the equivalent of 64½ of my paces. As my standard therefore for mapping the river, I assumed that we drifted downstream at the rate of 50 mètres, or 52½ yards, in the minute, and to correspond to that distance I measured 1 mm. (=.0394 inch) on the map. Of course I need hardly say that the rate at which we drifted varied very considerably at different times and in different parts of the river; but this I corrected by measuring the velocity of the current several times a day. At the point of departure the volume of the current was 3,468 cubic feet in the second, its maximum depth (quite close to the right bank) was 9 feet, its bed 442 feet wide, and its greatest velocity almost exactly 2 miles an hour.

My big ferry-boat was 37 ft. 9 in. long, 7 ft. 9 in. broad amidships, 2 ft. 9 in. high, of which 9 in. were below the water-line when the vessel was fully loaded and manned. Consequently, when there was less than 9 in. depth of water we ran aground, and this we did every day. The black cabin was 7 ft. wide, 7 ft. 1½ in. long, and 6 ft. 3½ in. high. The fore deck, or platform, on which my tent stood, was 12 ft. 1½ in. long, 7 ft. broad, and lay 2 ft. 5½ in. above the bottom of the boat. The smaller ferry-boat measured 19 ft. 8 in. in length by 3 ft. 4 in. in breadth

Finally, on 17th September, we made a definitive start, the caravan animals being loaded up very early in the morning. My plan was to send them on by land, under charge of the Cossacks and Niaz Hadji, *viâ* Aksu and Korla to Arghan, a place on the Tarim near its termination in the desert. They were to be at the rendezvous in 2½ months' time, when we would endeavour to get into touch with one another by means of couriers or special messengers. My men took with them letters of recommendation from Consul-General Petrovsky to the Andijan *aksakals* (consular agents) of the two towns named, besides a pass of portentous size from the Dao Tai, which was escorted from one town to another by a couple of Chinese subjects, generally Mohammedan begs or gendarmes. The servants I brought with me from West Turkestan were provided with Russian passes, each having a Chinese and a Turkish translation. To the two

Cossacks, Sirkin and Chernoff, I gave presents in money, besides which they were to have free rations so long as they were escorting the caravan, so that when they returned to Kashgar they would be able to lift their ordinary pay without any deduction.

The camels were in the very pink of condition, having fattened on the young foliage of the forest during the time we

A Girl of Lailik.

were delayed at Lailik. I directed the men to take the greatest care of them on the way to Lop-nor, and not overtax them, so that when the winter began they might be in at least as good condition as they were when they left Lailik, and able without difficulty to face the hardships of a journey through the desert. I gave Niaz Hadji 4½ yambas (£33 15s.) for the maintenance of the entire caravan, and for the purchase of large supplies of rice, flour, and several other stores which we should want later on; while it was Sirkin's duty to keep a short diary as well as the caravan accounts. Having bade their adieux, the men climbed into their saddles, and the caravan disappeared

An Ordinary Ferry-boat on the Yarkand-daria.

amongst the bushes, and soon the echo of their bells died away in the distance.

I only took with me on board Islam Bai, who officiated as cook, body-servant, and general factotum, and Kader, whose proper calling was that of Mussulman secretary, though he generally filled in his time by acting as Islam's assistant. The crew of my flotilla consisted of four men, known as *suchis*, or watermen, also as *kemichis*, or boatmen, each armed with a long, stout punting pole. One man was in the prow, and two in the stern of the big ferry-boat. Their duty was to keep her off the steep banks, especially where the river made sharp turns; and owing to the strength of the current their task was by no means an easy one, and called for unceasing vigilance. The fourth boatman took charge of the smaller ferry-boat, which generally piloted the way, partly to indicate the depth and partly to warn us of shallows and sand-banks. This craft was laden to the gunwale with provisions, such as flour, rice, and fruits. The wages of these men were ten *sär* (=£1 10s.) a month and free rations. But I had some difficulty in persuading them to accompany me all the way to Lop; they had a childish terror of such distant regions, never having heard of them before.

Whilst the last touches were being given to the equipment and the provisioning of the ferry-boat, the baggage was carried on board, and Islam busied himself with arranging his cooking paraphernalia—his saucepans, cans, plates, porcelain cups and so forth—in their proper places near the fireplace on the after-deck. The tent was set up on the platform, and its loose ends nailed down fast to the boards on which it stood, and inside it I laid down a bright-coloured Khotan carpet. My camp bedstead stood at its left-hand side (looking downstream), with a big packing case at the end of it. The other two big cases stood on the right-hand side, where they made a table on which I kept my various instruments, maps, and such like things, generally in a state of picturesque confusion. My working table, which consisted of another large packing-case resting upon a trunk that contained my winter clothing, stood at the forward edge of the platform, right in the doorway of the tent, and I made a bench to sit upon out of the big box in which I packed my photographic apparatus. By unfastening the back of the tent I could get access to the roof of the cabin, where we kept a number of articles, such as sails, oars, the velocity-instrument, and so on, that were too heavy to blow away. There also I kept my meteorological instruments, namely, the self-registering barometer, self-registering thermometer, maximum and minimum thermometers, Assmann's ventilated psychrometer, and three aneroids, besides Robinson's anemometer. The records of the last-named were, however, of very little value, for throughout the whole of the distance the valley of the Tarim was protected by the woods and high banks which bordered it. But the records of my self-registering instruments were of the very greatest interest. The readings of the barometer showed distinctly the slow and gradual descent of the stream towards the east; while the zigzag curves of the thermometer drooped lower and lower as the autumn advanced and finally passed over into winter.

The ferry-boat had been brought over as close to the left bank of the river as the spit of sand I have mentioned would allow; but for all that the men still had to wade out a considerable distance in the muddy water. Tucking up their gowns, a crowd of natives and their children came out to bid us a last good-bye, and forced upon us a number of "gifts," which we hurriedly paid for, and dismissed the bringers.

The scene on board was altogether so charming that I almost pitied those we left behind in the water, watching us as we noiselessly glided out into the current of the big river. These people had viewed all our preparations with a sceptical mien, and were now amazed to see how well everything had succeeded. It was exactly two in the afternoon when I gave the signal for the start. The boatmen thrust in their punting-poles, and we were off. The banks marched swiftly past us, and once round the first turn, we disappeared for ever from the memorable locality of Lailik and Merket.

Almost the very instant we started I sat down at my writing-table, and there I remained for months as though glued to the spot; it was at one and the same time my commander's bridge and my tower of observation. Before me lay ready to hand a piece of clean paper—the first sheet of my big map of the Tarim—mariner's compass, watch, field-glass, measuring scale, pens, knives, compasses, ink eraser, telescope, and so forth, and I set to work immediately. My table stood so far forward in the tent opening that I commanded an uninterrupted view of the landscape, not only before me, but also on both sides. Dovlet and Yolldash were at home almost from the first minute.

The Author at Work on the Ferry-boat.

During the day, so long as it was warm, they lay and panted underneath the fore deck; but as soon as it grew cool in the evening, they came out and kept me company in the tent.

Were I asked *why* I took this river journey, and *what results* I expected from it, from a geographical point of view, I should reply—in the first place, it was the only remaining route through East Turkestan which I had not already travelled over; and, in the second place, the course of the Tarim had never been mapped. Pievtsoff, myself, and one or two other travellers had journeyed from Maral-bashi to Yarkand by the caravan route which runs alongside the river; between Shah-yar and Karaul Carey and Dalgleish, and at a later date I myself, had threaded the forests which border the river bank; whilst the lower course of the stream had been traversed first by Przhevalsky and later by Prince Henri of Orléans and Bonvalot, Pievtsoff, Littledale, and the present writer. But the roads and tracks which accompany the river only touch it at occasional intervals, at the extremities of its windings; that is to say, they form, as it were, the bases of the curves described by its course. From them, however, it is obvious that no idea could be formed of the actual course of the river itself, of its general features, peculiarities, or other characteristics. What little knowledge we possessed about the Tarim was thus derived from transitory glimpses of it, and was consequently possessed of little or no scientific value. The map of the river which this journey enabled me to make proved how widely different the actual Tarim is from the course assigned to it on the previously existing maps. My voyage was, in short, a voyage of geographical discovery, and in every way eminently worth the months of labour which it cost me.

No river outside of Europe has been mapped with the same degree of minuteness or accuracy. And not only did I by continuous and daily labour gather materials for a detailed monograph on the largest river in the heart of Asia, and traverse a route which had never been traversed by anybody before, but I also discovered a mode of travel fraught with the most idyllic charm. To one hitherto accustomed to journey on horseback or to measure the endless distances of the desert from the back of a swaying camel, it was a pleasure altogether unlike anything before experienced, to have the current carry one along without jolt or jar, tranquilly, peacefully, noiselessly—to me a pleasure without parallel to sit at my work-table in the welcome shade and have the landscape come to meet me, unrolling itself like an ever-changing panorama, while I watched it as from a cosy box in a theatre. And it was equally delightful to feel that I was, so to speak, always at home, and in my own study, with my own sleeping-chamber close by, and my various instruments about me ready for use both day and night.

Indeed, I considered myself better off than if I had been on a European or American river-steamer. In the first place, I was quite alone, and there was nobody whom I need heed except myself. When the weather grew hot, I simply flung off my clothes and jumped straight into the river from my working-table—a thing I could not of course do on a river-steamer in Europe. And if we came to a spot which for any reason offered an inducement to stop, I was free to stay there as long as I chose. I had my meals served on the table where I worked as often as I wished it, and seldom have I enjoyed my food better than during my life on board that Tarim ferry-boat. My bed and couch were as comfortable as any in a big city; and there was always an abundance of pure water and fresh air, the latter frequently laden with the aromatic scent of the poplars. Close beside me hung portraits of those who were near and dear to me. I could look at them every day, and rejoiced in the thought that their love and affection accompanied me throughout the whole of my long and solitary journey. I generally had several books lying on my improvised table, but it was very seldom I found time to look into them; every minute was taken up with work which would brook no delay. And so deeply was I interested in this work, that I should not have been sorry had the journey lasted twice as long. If I am tempted to dwell rather too minutely on this trip down the Tarim, I can only urge in extenuation that I look back upon it with the most unfeigned pleasure; and who does not like to linger over times and scenes in which he has been perfectly happy?

CHAPTER V.

LIFE ON THE UPPER TARIM.

ON then we drifted with the silent but steadily moving Tarim; travelling at the same rate as the current, for we frequently had the same pieces of drift-wood keep us company for hours together. And how still and peaceful it was! Not a sound, except an occasional dimple or the ripple of the current as it broke against a branch jutting out from the bank, or the sudden "plump" of the punting-poles into the water, as the boatmen, warned by a shout from Kasim in the little ferry-boat, strove to steer clear of some shallow or sand-bank.

We had not gone very far when we perceived the banks dotted with groups of natives, both men and women; but their melons, their sheep, and other "good things" no longer tempted us, we were amply provisioned for the present. The Tarim bent and serpentined in almost every conceivable direction; for instance, we directed our course successively to the north-west, south-east, north, north-west, and north-east. The trend of the woods indicated for a long distance ahead in which direction the river wound; but at first the atmosphere was not clear, and the poplar groves grew fainter and fainter in the distance. At Kalmak-yilgazi there was quite a crowd of people collected on the right bank at a point where we drifted nearest in. But finding we did not stop, they ran after us, and at last waded out in a shallow place in the river, and climbed on board, and came and laid their wares on the foredeck in front of my study table. It turned out that the people who hit upon this stratagem for getting the better of us were the wives, children and other relatives of my boatmen. We had therefore no alternative but to accept with thanks what they brought, and—pay for them.

We got aground for the first time half an hour after we started; but the jar was so slight that I hardly knew the boat had stopped, and was only convinced of it by seeing the water flowing away from us on both sides. Without more ado the boatmen jumped into the river and pushed off, and away we went again. Every time we grounded, I seized the opportunity to measure the velocity of the current. At the inner angles of the curves, the river banks were often 9 to 10 feet high. The boatmen, especially Palta, who was my nearest neighbour in the forepart of the big boat, knew the name of every stretch of bank and patch of wood for several days below our starting point, so that at first there was no need of a guide. The nomen-

Women and Children Wading out to the Ferry-boat with Supplies.

clature almost always conveyed some meaning and instruction. For instance, a particular belt of wood was called Tonkuzlik, because it was frequented by wild boar; and a ford was known as Kalmak-yilgazi (the Mongol ford), because Mongols are said to have lived near that part of the river in former times. A hostelry or guest-house (*lengher*) on the great caravan road, which we almost touched at a sudden turn in the river, was called Mohammed-Ili-lengher after the man who built it. It stood so close to the river that its tall and slender poplars towered like cypresses above the scrub and tangled thickets which bordered the bank.

At this place the stream two years ago altered its course for a short distance; the old bed, which was plainly discernible at the junction, was called Eski-daria (the Old River). Subsequently, we observed a great many instances of the same

An Encampment on the River Bank.

thing, and each was faithfully entered on my map. In each of these abandoned side-arms there were almost always a number of little pools (*köll*=lagoon) of perfectly fresh water. In the district of Avvat the river grew so narrow and the current so strong that our big boat swung completely round in a whirlpool.

In the afternoons, we were frequently incommoded by the flashing of the sunlight upon the water when we turned up the west-going reaches. But when we travelled north or east the colouring was magnificent; the sun, shining from behind us, completely transformed the landscape.

Our provision boat presented quite a picture of rustic wealth, with its stacks of green-stuffs and its melons, especially when the hens cackled or the cock crowed; for it also carried a small colony of poultry, whose function it was to supply my breakfast table with fresh eggs. Our live-stock included also a few sheep, penned on the after-deck of the big boat.

As soon as our day's journey was finished, the first business was to make the flotilla fast to the bank, lest the boats should get loose and drift down stream during the night. The men encamped on shore round a fire, over which they boiled their tea-kettles and cooked their supper. Their beds consisted of felt mats (*kighiz*) for mattresses and sheepskins (*pustun*) for coverings. I usually sat far on into the night, occupied with writing up my diary and similar work. As I sat and wrote the only sounds which broke the silence were the land-slips at the inner angles of the river's windings, where the banks were most undermined by the erosive power of the current. Sometimes, the loosened masses of silt or sand fell with a sudden plunge into the stream, as if they had been crocodiles, but fortunately those creatures did not exist in the Tarim. When the moon came out she shot a belt of silver across the broad river. In the far distance a dog began to bark. At first the gnats were very troublesome, but soon the nights grew too cold for them.

The first morning on board was fresh and cool, for I always slept in the tent. For one thing, I had then no need to keep a look-out for scorpions, which were too abundant on the banks to be pleasant. One consequence of our pulling into the bank for the night was that by the morning the ferry-boat became so deeply embedded in silt and sand, that it cost the men a good hour's work with spades and poles to get her out. Whilst they were doing this I usually took my breakfast, and by the time I had finished, it was generally about 9 o'clock. The character of the river and its surroundings remained constantly the same, everywhere uniform. The only relief to the sameness was afforded by the young poplars, and bushes and thickets of hawthorn, which clothed the steep banks, and shot their roots out over the river, through the accumulations of silt or sand or clay which bordered it. The native names for these sheer-cut earthern banks were *kash* and *yar*, prefixes which mean "bank terrace," and occur in, for example, the words Kashgar and Yarkand.

The *kemichis* or boatmen whom I had engaged turned out first-rate fellows, who did their work splendidly. Their names were, Kasim Ahun, Naser Ahun, Alim Ahun and Palta; a fifth man, Kasim the On-bashi, gave us some help during the first few days and then returned home. All alike thoroughly understood the management of the ferry-boat, and were perfectly familiar with the peculiarities of the river. They were able to tell almost invariably from the formation of the banks, and the rippling and dimpling of the surface, whether we were in deep water or shallow. The presence of sand-banks in the middle of the river was frequently indicated by an accumulation of drift wood—trunks of poplars, twigs and branches of various kinds, and bundles of reeds—sometimes all densely matted together. The occurrence of a treacherous sand-bank immediately under the surface was generally revealed by an exceptional smoothness of the water directly above it, as well as by the quickening of the current immediately beyond it.

Here I may conveniently point out the principal differences between the convex and the concave banks which we encountered everywhere throughout the river's windings. The latter, being directly exposed to the full force of the current and its centrifugal power of erosion, were in general cut sheer down to the water's edge, and so presented a perpendicular face some 6 to 10 feet in height; and the main body of the current swept in upon its face with undiminished violence. Consequently it was in these places that we found the greatest depths and the maximum velocities. The projecting angles made by the convex banks were called by the natives *aral* or *aralchi*, which, properly speaking, means "island," and this indifferently whether the river turns to the right or to the left. They consisted in general of a flat, crescent-shaped, but sometimes blunted, accumulation of silt, always however clearly and sharply defined, deposited by the gentle current that flows over these shallow places when the river is in flood. Had we started some six weeks earlier, the silt peninsulas would have been under water, and our course would consequently have been a little shorter, while the stream would have flowed faster. But at the time we navigated it, the current had already fallen so considerably as to barely fill the actual bed of the river. And as this wound in and out to the uttermost extremity of every concave curve on both sides, the line we actually travelled over was all the longer, and it was impossible to shorten it by cutting off corners.

On the other hand, these circumstances were all in favour of an accurate topographical mapping of the Tarim, for the shallow parts were now exposed, and it was easier to study the laws and tendencies of the river's erosive energy. Except for one short stretch, there was always sufficient depth to float the ferry boats; and the slowness of the current—on the second day of the journey the velocity was less than 1½ miles an hour—was in no sense a drawback. On the contrary, it enabled me to make my map more detailed and more complete. As it was, the rate at which we moved barely gave me time to jot down all the notes and observations I desired to make. Throughout the whole of the journey my time was fully occupied, and I was seldom able to leave my table except to sleep.

In this region, the river presented several tolerably straight reaches. For instance, we often got stretches which it took us 25 minutes to drift down, equivalent to lengths of about three-quarters of a mile. But very soon the river became more sinuous, and the straight reaches seldom exceeded three to four minutes (150 to 200 yards) in length. This hardly gave me time to note down the observations relative to one stretch before I was called upon to deal with the next. The level did not fall gradually and uniformly, but, so to speak, from step to step; and as it cut its way through the sand-banks and silt peninsulas, it left sharply eroded edges, which from time to time crumbled and crashed down, as I have already said, into the water. But as we proceeded, we found that the accumulations of silt grew bigger, while the stream itself shrank more and more into its principal bed.

To return again to the topographical features and the native nomenclature. A projecting point was called *tumshuk*; and on the lower side of this there was generally a concealed sandbank, which would become exposed when the river dropped sufficiently. These were the worst places we had to contend with; the men were obliged to use every effort to keep the boat off them. If, in spite of all their exertions, we still ran aground, they at once jumped in and pushed the boat off, wading round her to find out how deep the water was in her immediate vicinity. But the bottom was so soft, and the contact so gentle, that I seldom knew we were aground until I heard the men shouting *laiga tegdi* (contact with clay), *toktadi* (stopped), or *turdi* (stuck fast). Their cries when we got off again were *tyshdi* (glided off, literally fallen), *mangdi* or *mangadi* (she goes). If it was the prow that ran aground, the boat whirled completely round (*tollanup ghetti*), making me feel quite giddy. Then in a moment the features of the scene were totally changed. The sun seemed to have turned crazy, for whereas a minute ago it was at our backs, now it shone directly in our faces.

The natives also have special names for the several phenomena which regularly occur in connection with the river. The slight crumplings of the surface above a shallow they called *kainagan-su* (boiling water) or *kainagan-lai* (boiling mud). When the stream bifurcated, they employed the simple terms "right arm" and "left arm." When one of these was smaller than the other, it was called *kitchik-daria* (little river) or *parcha-daria* (part of the river). To a cul-de-sac they gave the name of *bikar-daria*; to an abandoned arm the name of *eski-daria* or *kona-daria*, or, if it contained a separate pool, *köll* (lake). Whenever the river divided, we were generally in great perplexity as to which arm we ought to follow, and it very often happened that we anchored where we were, whilst some of us went forward in the skiff and explored the more likely arm. A deep trench in the river bottom was known as *akin* or *chukkur-su*, and a shallow as *tais*. *Ittik akkadi* and *asta akkadi* indicated that the current was flowing fast and flowing slowly respectively.

The boatman Palta sat on the fore-part of the big ferry-boat, his legs bare and his punting pole in his hands, attentively watching the river and keeping as nearly as he could in the wake of Kasim, who steered the smaller pioneer ferry-boat. He constantly had a melodious song on his lips about some king's adventures; but, like the other men, he was deeply interested in the voyage, and in all that went on on board the boats.

We several times saw shepherds with their flocks on the banks of the river. The former dwelt in huts made of branches and foliage, woven about the trees that stood on the brink of the stream. In a westward bend we again touched the caravan route to Maral-bashi, and found a man waiting for us with greetings from the caravan.

I measured the river again at Besh-köll (the five lakes), the place on the right bank where we halted for the next night. It was $283\frac{1}{2}$ feet wide, had a maximum depth of $7\frac{1}{4}$ feet, a mean velocity of $1\frac{5}{8}$ miles an hour and a maximum velocity of two

Natives of the Tarim Region.

miles, and its volume was 2,992 cubic feet in the second. These figures showed a remarkable diminution in the current as compared with the last measurements.

On 19th September we had a fresh set of experiences in river navigation. Very early in the morning it began to blow a strong breeze from the north-west, and we soon discovered that not only did it check the rate at which the boat drifted, but in the broader parts of the river, what with the slower flow and the opposition which the tent and the black hut offered to the wind, actually brought her to a standstill. On the other hand, the smaller ferry-boat now went the faster of the two. At first we steered east, with the sun in our faces, but at 8 o'clock we turned due north, and so obtained shelter against the wind; the rest of the day was bright and pleasant.

The river kept for a considerable time to the north, and the north-west wind, which was blowing at the rate of over eight miles an hour, caused us to lose 16¼ yards every minute, and drove the boat close up against the right bank, so that the men had to work desperately hard to avoid a collision. One sudden violent gust whisked away the map sheet upon which I happened to be working, and we had to pursue it a long distance in the skiff before we recovered it.

Later on, we turned to the east and south-east, and had the wind at our backs; after which the boat travelled three-quarters of a mile an hour faster than the current, which itself was moving at the rate of one and a half miles an hour. But at the next bend we turned to the north-west, and the wind became so strong against us that we were forced to stop. It was clear, therefore, that unless I made allowance for the wind, by measuring the difference between the velocity of the current and the velocity of the ferry boat, my map would present a highly distorted and incorrect chart of the river's true course.

At Shäshkak, where we next encamped, the bank was seven and a half feet high, and we had to cut steps up it. The place was inhabited by four shepherds and their families, who owned some two hundred sheep, in addition to goats and cattle. Besides that, they cultivated the ground, and grew maize and wheat, their fields being watered by an artificial canal led out of the river below Besh-köll. Here the river was not more than 139¾ feet wide, and its volume only 2,372 cubic feet in the second, showing an alarming drop within the last twenty-four hours. This made me anxious. The shepherds told me it was nearly two months since the river was at its highest at Shäshkak, and in another ten or eleven weeks it would have shrunk to its winter volume, and about a week later would be frozen over. In spring, they said, it was, in several places, possible to wade across the river.

When we awoke at sunrise next morning, the sky looked rather ominous. The night had been the coldest we had hitherto had, the thermometer dropping to 2°.9 C. or 37°.2 Fahr. The country was enveloped in a kind of twilight, due neither to fog nor cloud, but to fine drift-sand, which was being swept along by a *sarik-buran* or "yellow storm," although we saw no other signs of its presence, owing to the fact that the ferry-boat lay under the shelter of the high bank. The landscape wore a gloomy aspect, and the tamarisks and thickets of reeds which grew along the banks became lost to sight at about a hundred yards' distance. The boatmen thought, and rightly, that under these circumstances it would be difficult to advance, and so we decided to wait until the weather improved.

On this and similar occasions I whiled away the tedium of waiting by taking a sail in my little canvas boat, although. having neither keel nor rudder, it was not exactly suited for that form of sport. Of course, I only sailed it with the wind, using an oar over the stern instead of a rudder. But on this occasion the wind was so strong, the boat skimmed along like a duck, the foam spouting high off her bow. I thoroughly enjoyed it as, avoiding the principal current of the river, I sped on upstream. The banks raced past me, the forest vanished in the haze, I fancied I was careering across an open fjord at home, and that the mud islands were so many holms. After a couple of hours of this glorious sport, I thought it was probably time to go back. So, dropping mast and sail, I steered into the main current, intending that it should carry me home. But I was reckoning without my host. The wind was so violent, it almost stopped the surface current entirely. However, I hit upon a way to counteract its influence. A foot below the surface the river flowed with its usual force, so I set an oar vertically downwards into the water, and then lashed it to the boat, and after that I dropped down stream quite easily.

At one point where I tried to land, the ground was extremely treacherous. It gave way under me, and I sank in up to my waist; indeed I should have gone in further only I caught hold of the edge of the boat in time to save myself. After that I had to take a bath with my clothes on, to get rid of the mud which clasped my nether extremities like a suit of mail.

At last I caught, through the haze, a glimpse of my white tent on the ferry-boat, and in a few minutes I was alongside her. As a rule we kept the skiff fastened to the stern of the big ferry-boat; it was useful for landing in without laying-to the larger craft. Islam Bai often got one of the other men to put him ashore in her, and then roamed the woods for hours together, and when he came back, he generally carried pheasants, or ducks, or both in his hand. By cutting off the windings of the river he travelled faster than we did, and in that way generally managed to get ahead of us. Hence it was no unusual thing for us to come suddenly upon him, sitting on a projecting spit of sand waiting for us. And as we drifted past, one of the boatmen would go off in the skiff and fetch him on board. Islam found the journey extremely monotonous, and was glad of these little hunting expeditions as a most welcome break to its uniformity.

The weather continued on the 21st September to be cold and autumnal; in fact, it was so raw and disagreeable we were glad to don our winter clothing. The sky was overcast and gloomy, as if it were full of threatening rain-clouds. However, it was nothing but dust, brought, as was usually the case, by the east wind, for the sky was always bright and clear when it blew from the west. The wind kept in the east all day, and blew strongly and steadily, obscuring the landscape and making it difficult for us to make headway. During the night, the river had risen six inches, a circumstance not at all surprising when you bear in mind that its height was dependent upon the state of the weather in the mountains. A bright, pure atmosphere in the latter often causes the river to rise, even in the autumn, though of course only for short periods and at long and irregular intervals.

In one sharp bend, where the river turned completely back upon itself, through an angle of 180°, we sounded a depth of close upon 20 feet, while the current was terribly slow. If I had not had my map constantly before me, I should have been hopelessly befogged as to the direction we were going in, the river wound about so. Although its general course was towards the north-east, yet not infrequently we were steering for short distances towards the south-west.

The company of my dogs, and, above all, their pranks and frolics, helped to brighten many an otherwise solitary hour. They were by this thoroughly at home on board and perfectly reconciled to our method of travel. When anything on shore struck them as being suspicious, especially men or animals, they went and stationed themselves right forward and kicked up a fearful din, and the moment we stopped for the night, they, without waiting for the plank to be pushed out, leapt instantly ashore, and began to chase one another through the woods. But when supper-time came they were never absent from my side, and they always slept in my tent.

The water in the river was now so chilly that the men never jumped in if they could avoid it. The gnats were extremely troublesome, especially in the still, quiet corners (*bulung*) of the river, while in the forest they were perfectly unbearable. They were a small grey insect, scarcely visible until just about to settle and sting; but the moment a breeze cropped up, away they went. Thus the stillness had its disadvantages as well as the wind.

At another point we saw a large troop of men and horses, the former dismounted, waiting for us on the bank. They turned out to be the beg of Aksak-maral and his attendants, and were on their way to Merket. As they had prepared a copious repast (*dastarkhan*) against our arrival, there was nothing for it but to land and partake of the good things they had provided.

We again measured the river. In fact, we usually stopped a little before sunset, so as to get our measuring over before dusk, and we always chose for our night-camp a place where the whole volume of the river was confined in one narrow channel, and there was sufficient firewood to be had on shore. I generally made my measurements from the little skiff, which was held in position by Sirkin's grapnel, and Islam Bai and one of the boatmen usually helped me. The breadth I measured directly with a tape some fifty yards long; if it failed to reach across, we stuck a stake in the bottom of the river at the fiftieth yard, and then measured off the remaining distance. After that we took the depth at a series of points along an imaginary straight line, and the velocity at two or three different depths at the same points. At the camp of Att-pangats the volume was 2,087½ cubic feet in the second. Thus the stream was gradually dwindling, though this was not perceptible to the eye; for although there was about the same quantity of water in the river-bed, it moved at a slower rate.

On the morning of the 22nd September a flock of wild geese passed overhead, steering in a well-ordered phalanx toward the south-west, their goal being no doubt India. The atmosphere was now buoyant and still, though not perfectly clear; there was still a sort of haze or shimmer in the air. As early as eight o'clock it grew so warm that we were glad to go back to our summer suits. A narrow irrigation canal, which led off to the right and turned a mill a little distance away from the river, showed that the latter, even in its present low condition, lay above the level of the adjacent country.

About an hour after starting, we caught sight of some people amongst the trees on the left bank, apparently waiting for us, and we soon recognised them. It was Sirkin, Niaz Hadji, and the on-bashi or chief of Ala-ayghir, where the caravan had arrived two days before. We took the three men on board, and great was their delight in our new method of travel. The poplar woods were now considerably larger than they had been hitherto, so that we resembled a monastic procession moving with majestic and solemn silence through their leafy cloisters. The trees grew most luxuriantly at the inner angles of the windings, where the water gets at their roots all the year round. When we came abreast of Ala-ayghir our men returned to the caravan; and from this time onwards we were entirely cut off from them until we met them in the Lop country. But before they left me I bade them find out my former faithful servant Parpi Bai, who accompanied me on my last journey through Asia, and who was living at Kuchar, and ask him to meet us at Karaul on the lower Tarim.

At Togluk, the place where we spent the night, the river was only 116 feet broad, and had a maximum depth of 16⅓ feet, a mean velocity of one and a quarter miles an hour, and a volume of 2,105 cubic feet in the second, or a trifle more than at the last measurement. This meant, there had been a more copious influx of water from the mountains during the last twenty-four hours.

Early the next day we left on our right a side-arm of the river, which, although it was not more than 30 to 35 feet wide, and shallow, nevertheless raced along like a torrent, the reason being that the water was taking a more direct way than the main stream. Possibly it was the beginning of a new channel, into which the principal river would ere long pour itself. In one of the inner angles just here we were caught, despite our watchfulness, in the eddy of the back stream, and it was no easy matter to get out again. The punting-poles, although 15 or 16 feet long, failed to reach the bottom. The only thing we could do was for one of the men to paddle ashore with a rope, and then for them all to haul the boat back into the current.

Shortly after this we approached the point at which the river itself bifurcated. The left arm, known as the Kona-daria (Old River), was the smaller, and flowed past Maral-bashi; the right arm, the Yanghi-daria (New River), carried the larger portion of the current, and was said to have been formed only four years previously. The two arms reunited over against Aksak-maral. Hence the Yarkand-daria had, thus high up, made a deflection to the right; and as we proceeded, we found the same thing repeated several times. This tendency was, however, most pronounced in the region of Lop, as will be shown later on.

Immediately after entering the main stream, the Yanghi-daria, or Kotteklik (Dry Timber Place), as it was also called, because of the large quantity of driftwood and logs of dead poplars which had become stranded upon its sandbanks, we stopped for an hour's rest. My men asserted we were now close upon some dangerous rapids, of which I had lately been hearing a good deal. At Lailik I was told that when we got to Kötteklik we should have to descend a fall with a drop of eight fathoms. This had now shrunk to one fathom; but all the same, we should, I was told, want 30 or 40 men to help us down. The only way to pass the place comfortably was to carry all the baggage on shore and haul the ferry-boat down the fall.

Accordingly, I commissioned the on-bashi of Ala-ayghir to have a score of labourers ready at the falls by the following morning. Meanwhile, I measured the volume of water in the two arms of the river, as they flowed on each side of a long narrow island, which was never entirely covered even in seasons of high flood. However, as the day was yet young, and as it was, moreover, still and bright, I resolved to go on with the ferry-boat, and have a look at the "dangerous place." Accordingly, on we went, threading our way through veritable islands of driftwood, the passages being so narrow, there was scant room for the boat to get between them, and the suction of the current was very considerable. For the greater part of the way the men were obliged to wade and haul the boat along with ropes, otherwise she would inevitably have stuck fast. Even as it was, she several times struck against the snags and submerged poplars, and every time she did so, she swung right round, till she came stern on. Every now and again the men who were wading first suddenly plumped into deep water, to the great amusement of the rest.

After a while we began to hear the river foaming and churning some little distance ahead. This, the men said, was the first cataract (*sha-kurun*). It did not look at all formidable, the fall not being more than three or four inches. Our boat took it quite leisurely, without the slightest list or lurch. This was followed by two other cataracts, each equally insignificant. One of them was, it is true, of considerable volume, but a little distance below it the river shallowed again.

After we were well past this so-called "dangerous place" the river resumed its former appearance, though it was now narrow and deep, and our ferry-boat travelled at a right good pace. In fact, we shot into one sharp bend so swiftly, and the boat swung round upon us so suddenly, that we collided with the bank, and stuck fast; and the upper box which formed my table would infallibly have gone overboard, only luckily Palta seized hold of it in time. We were overtaken by the on-bashi and his score of labourers at our camping-station, beside a solitary poplar in the district of Kötteklik-ayaghi. They were tremendously taken aback to find we had cleared the cataracts without their help, and soon returned home again.

At this place we were visited by the beg of Aksak-maral; and, as he was well acquainted with this part of the country, I invited him to go with us and guide us for two or three days. He was immensely interested in the way we travelled, but was of opinion we should have encountered great difficulties had we started when the river was in full flood. We could not have found punting-poles long enough to reach the bottom; the boat would have been altogether unmanageable owing to the swiftness of the current, and we should have been in collision with the banks at every turn and winding of the river. Another drawback would have been the heat, owing to the earlier season of the year; and yet a worse evil than this would have been the midges. Which I can well believe, for even in the autumn they were a perfect plague, especially in the thickets and scrub at sunset. In point of fact, we had, he said, chosen precisely the most favourable season for our undertaking.

The volume of the Yanghi-daria or Kötteklik was only 1,303 cubic feet in the second; consequently we had lost 802 cubic feet, which was, of course, drained off by the Kona-daria that ran through Maral-bashi. If the river divided again, should we be able to proceed?

CHAPTER VI.

THE ENCHANTED FOREST.

On the 24th September, after an early start, we made a long and interesting stage down a newly-formed arm of the Yarkand-daria. Here we said good-bye to Kasim the On-bashi, who was returning to Lailik, taking with him part of the other boatmen's earnings, which he undertook to hand over to their families or parents. Almost from the first the river was very deep and narrow, and barely 70 feet wide, and the breadth continued to decrease. There could be no question as to the recent formation of the arm we were navigating, for several times we came across green tamarisks and poplars standing on little mounds of earth in the middle of the stream. Others of these tiny islets, however, consisted simply of a mass of lumber, branches, twigs and similar flotsam, which had caught on a snag or piece of timber sticking up from the bottom of the river. In one place we observed two poplars with their roots actually in the water; they had no doubt been surprised by the current. The banks now presented a very different character from what they had hitherto done. They were no longer the high, deeply-scarped terraces we had been accustomed to travel between, but were far less distinctly marked, as indeed would naturally be expected in a newly-formed river-bed. For the same reason the tongues of silt at the projecting headlands were either very rudimentary or wanting entirely.

In the course of the day we came to an awkward and uncomfortably narrow passage, blocked with driftwood, partly massed together, partly forming slight barricades, through which we had somehow to make our way. The waterway was in some places so narrow that the ferry-boat grazed both sides, and we were compelled to proceed with the utmost caution. And seeing that the current was here very swift, and sometimes broke into white-crested waves, a collision would almost certainly have been serious. One man stood at each corner, pole in hand, and did his best to keep us clear of all impediments; while Kasim piloted the way in the commissariat boat. However, the worst mishap we experienced was getting wedged in between two accumulations of driftwood. At once every man leapt into the water, and began to push and heave and pull, all singing together in unison. Having got our craft free, one or two of the men waded on a little way ahead to see what depth of water there was in front of us.

By this the river had dwindled to a paltry rivulet, and I began to fear we should not reach the Aksu-daria and the Tarim proper. Except for two or three very short stretches, the current zigzagged backwards and forwards between scrubby forests, thick reed beds, and single tograks (poplars). But ere long it contracted into a kind of canal, flowing with an exceptionally swift current some six feet below the level of the adjacent country. The wind retarded our rate of travelling, though not very seriously, for its force was broken by the forest and the high banks. In some places the river divided and passed on each side of genuine islands, covered with vegetation. Every time it did so we wondered if there would be water enough to float us, or whether we should be compelled to haul our vessel all the way back to the bifurcation. Some of these side-arms were relatively very short, and soon rejoined the main stream; others again were a few miles long; and yet others were entirely cut off at both ends, as was proved by the transparency of the water they contained.

At length, however, the river widened out, and we obtained an extensive prospect towards the north-east, backed in the far distance by a solitary mound of drift-sand called Karaul-dung (Watch-house Mound). But this open, lake-like expanse soon contracted again. We chose a passage on the right of Karaul-dung, but had only gone a short distance when we stuck fast, just above a sort of threshold across the river—with only two or three inches of water over it. The bottom consisted of fine, tenacious blue clay, spiked with the stems of decayed *kamish* (reeds).

We tried to push our craft over, we tried to haul her back; all in vain. She was held fast by the bottom suction. There was nothing for it but to lighten her by shifting on shore all the heavy baggage, boxes and stores. This done, we again essayed to move her by united main force, but we only drove her deeper into the mud. I therefore asked the beg of Aksak-maral to go to his village, and fetch men to help us. He at once landed and mounted, for two of his attendants had accompanied us all day on horseback. At the end of a couple of hours he came back, bringing with him about thirty men, who, as soon as they saw what was wanted, set to work with a will; and as I, too, encouraged them by my example, their efforts were speedily crowned with success. Foot by foot we hauled the colossus over the rapids; but a very little lower down she stuck fast again, and this time worse than before.

What was to be done now? The mud was so slippery and so tenacious, we had great difficulty in keeping our feet. We were in a queer fix. We no longer knew where the caravan was. We could not move the big, clumsy ferry-boat, and the smaller one was nothing like big enough to carry all our baggage. It looked as if we should have to construct a new building-slip, call in carpenters and smiths from Aksak-maral, and build another vessel, smaller and lighter than the one which had run aground. Yet what a loss of time that would involve! And the river was falling every day! I could not, I literally could not, bring myself to abandon my projected journey here, as it were, on the very threshold. No; we must somehow go on as we were, let the cost be what it might. Eventually we turned the boat round two or three times on its own axis, and by that means softened and loosened the mud so that we were able to push her through it, and in that way got her into deep water. After a little we came to the last and biggest of the cataracts, which was over 18 inches deep everywhere, while the fall amounted to seven or eight inches. The current was so violent the men were afraid it would capsize our leviathan. Hence, as a matter of precaution, I had the whole of the baggage once more transferred to dry land; but I stayed behind myself, being resolved to stick to the vessel as she shot the rapids—to the great concern of my men, who feared we should both be overturned in the boiling waters at the foot of the cataract. However, they guided the boat to the edge of the fall, and then, pointing her nose in the right direction, let her go. On she glided as tranquilly as possible, and when the fore part was far enough advanced, down it went like a see-saw, striking the water with a loud smack, while the after end rose high into the air. A little ploughing with the prow, a few yards more of uneasy, agitated motion, and we were safely over. As soon as might be, we halted for the night, for it was already dusk. Then I dismissed my auxiliary corps, who one way or another had had a lively afternoon of it, and sent them home well rewarded for their exertions.

That afternoon the gnats were a perfect plague. They came in vast clouds, and it was utterly impossible to keep them off. When you have both hands engaged, and are half naked so as to be ready for an impromptu bath at any moment, the gnats of Turkestan can make themselves veritable fiends of torment. It was as if they had been patiently waiting for our arrival to hold a carnival of malice on the exposed parts of our persons. I wonder what they lived on before we went there?

At this place the river had a volume of only 802 cubic feet in the second; consequently its various side-arms had deprived it of very nearly one-third of its total flood. The successful issue of my project began to look extremely doubtful.

The sand-dune of Karaul-dung, which was about 35 feet high and covered with tamarisks and tussocks of grass, rose steeply on the very brink of the river, and its top commanded an extensive view of the whole district. The tiresome cataracts we had recently passed presented themselves from its summit as a broad expansion of the river, now split into several arms, which in seasons of flood become reunited into one stream. On the left the Yarkand-daria was bordered by steppe, on the right by scrubby forest; while farther to the east it appeared to be swallowed up by a dense forest of tall poplars. Half a mile to the south and south-east, beyond a narrow belt of vegetation, were the yellow crests of the billowy dunes of the desert.

When we started again next morning, the river once more resembled a canal, some 16 to 20 feet wide, and with a current of considerable depth and velocity, so that incessant vigilance was required to prevent our craft from running aground; in which, indeed, we were not always entirely successful. The channel we were in was also a recent creation. In some places the river had cut its way clean through the sand-dunes which lay in its path, the sand in the middle of the dunes being held in position by the roots of the tamarisks that grew on it. Some of these cuttings were 12 to 20 feet deep, and their sandy walls looked as if they were just waiting for us, ready to plunge down and bury us, ferry-boat and all, the moment we got underneath them. The surface of the ground hereabouts consisted entirely of sand, more or less continuous, except that immediately

An Idyllic Journey down the Tarim.

[VOL. I.—*To face p.* 106.

adjacent to the river there was a strip of mud or silt, too soft to bear a man's weight.

This day we were no longer tormented by the gnats; but on the other hand we were delayed by the east wind. One or the other of these vexations we were almost always bound to have; for no sooner did the wind drop than the gnats came. The atmosphere was thick, and the air cool and autumnal. Our chief desire now was to reach the point where the new channel which we were navigating became reunited with the Kona-daria or Old River. After that we should not only get more water, we should also return to civilized regions. For the new arm had carved its course through an entirely uninhabited country.

At last the wind became so disagreeable that we resolved to submit to its vagaries no longer; and, upon reaching an inviting nook on the right bank, near a few old poplars, known as Kum-atchal, we encamped, although the place was absolutely barren and uninhabited.

Amongst our live stock was a goose, which we brought all the way from Lailik. It travelled with Kasim in the commissariat boat, and was originally intended to be killed and eaten; but its staid and irreproachable respectability led to its being gradually promoted to be the "pet of the regiment." It was a comical bird, and often paid visits to the big ferry-boat, and waddled about wherever it liked. Every now and again it would come and have a peep at me in my tent, and was so tame, it used to come when it was called. Although it was a captive wild goose, it never made any attempt to fly away; but then we kept its wings clipped. When we encamped, the bird used to drop down into the river and swim about all round the ferry-boat; but it always returned of its own accord to its accustomed place on board. Eventually we lost the creature somewhere, though I do not now remember how or when.

After a sail in the skiff, in which I was accompanied by the beg of Aksak-maral, whose amazement at such a means of progression knew no bounds, I spent the evening in developing photographic negatives, and found the work so fascinating that I kept on at it until three o'clock in the morning, and then went to bed with the resolution to continue the work next day if the wind still remained contrary. No wonder then I was drowsy when Islam came and woke me at seven o'clock next morning. But when he told me that the wind had dropped and the sky was clear, I was up like a shot, and having given orders to lift anchor, hurriedly swallowed down my breakfast.

Before starting I dismissed our friend the beg of Aksakmaral, and sent back with him all his men except one, Mohammed Ahun by name, whom, being a *pavan*, or hunter, and well acquainted with the country thereabouts, I retained to act as guide.

Shortly after we started, our particular arm of the river was rejoined by another, which had separated from it two days before, and which brought with it a most welcome addition to the volume of the current. After this the Yarkand-daria again showed its former characteristics—a broad current, numerous alluvial deposits, and deeply eroded vertical banks. Its course now lay through a luxuriant poplar forest, interrupted here and there by small beds of reeds and belts of sand. The tops of the trees were beginning to grow torpid through the chilly autumn nights, and the foliage was deepening its tints to yellows and russets. The spell of cold wind we had just experienced was the herald of autumn's approach, and when, towards noon, the east wind again began to shake itself, the dry leaves which littered the ground set up a melancholy, joyless dance. Occasionally the wind freshened a bit, though not enough to retard our progress. The current was here pretty strong, flowing at the rate of nearly 1¾ miles an hour.

The banks were now 6 feet to 10 feet high, and perfectly vertical, and showed plain indications of the river having flowed at more than one different level in the past. On the right bank high sand-dunes appeared at intervals, shooting straight down into the river which gnawed away at their feet. These were the extreme outliers of the great "ocean" of sand-hills which covered the desert to the south and south-east. Once, when sweeping round into a sudden elbow, with a swift current under our keel, we came into collision with a decaying poplar, which stood in the stream about two yards or so from the right bank. The men did not perceive it soon enough to clear it entirely, and we scraped and bumped all along its stem, while its big branches very nearly swept my tent clean away. The box which contained the meteorological instruments was also for one moment in great jeopardy; but I just managed to get hold of it in time, and saved it.

At last we reached the long-wished-for confluence of the Kona-daria. But, except for a pool of bright blue water close to its mouth, its broad bed was dry. Two or three times we ran aground upon the submerged sandbanks, it being difficult to detect their presence owing to the crumpling of the surface by the wind.

In this part of its course the Yarkand-daria flowed on the whole towards the north-east, though at times it turned towards the north, the east-north-east, and occasionally towards the east-south-east, describing in each of these directions the most fantastic curves and sinuosities imaginable.

But the region was still uninhabited. We did not see a single human being, nor a single hoof or horn during the whole of this day, the 27th September. The only creatures which disturbed the solemn silence of the woods and waters were a solitary eagle and a few ravens, though in the sands beside the river we often observed the fresh tracks of wild boar and deer which had been down to the river to drink.

The measurements I took that afternoon were of great interest. The river was 261 ft. wide; its mean depth 2½ ft.; its maximum depth 3½ ft.; its mean velocity 1¼ miles an hour; and its volume 1,225½ cubic feet in the second, or close upon half as much again as when I measured it last. This increase was due to the fact that by this the stream had again caught up all the side-arms which it had previously shed off. During the day we sounded depths of as much as 26¼ feet.

Thus we glided on day after day down the still, but persistent river, and day by day my map of it grew bigger and bigger in volume. During the night of the 27th September the surface dropped over three inches. I always measured the level of the stream at every camping station, and for precaution's sake measured it by two distinct methods. Choosing a quiet and sheltered spot, where there was practically no current, I put down a graduated pole till it rested on the bottom. The other device was to thrust the pole horizontally into the vertical bank, and from its outer end drop a plummet swinging in a graduated arm.

The banks were still uninhabited, but we did see two or three shepherds' huts (*söreh*), each consisting as a rule of a roof of branches and leaves resting on four uprights. It was clear that the district had been visited at some time or other, and been deserted when the grazing gave out. The river itself, gathered into a single bed, with a depth which in some places was as much as 23 feet, still rolled on in its usual fashion, through the majestic silence of the woods. The trees, poplars of a venerable, though dwarf and gnarled appearance, whose green crowns were beginning to change into gold and red, as if adorning themselves for a merry autumnal carnival, stood in close array, and made a magnificent framework for the glinting river. The Lailik boatmen had never seen any forest like it; its autumnal splendours drew from them repeated exclamations of astonishment and delight. They called it Östäng-bagh, which properly means "the orchard beside the canal," the general name for the irrigated parks and gardens of the East Turkestan oases. And there was really no hyperbole in this expression of their feelings. The magnificence of colouring which the foliage of these poplar woods presented was a source of genuine delight. Often and often again I could not help fancying I was being drawn in a car of triumph through a magic wood, by invisible elves and gnomes, along a pathway paved with sapphires and crystals. And there was a mystic charm also in the unbroken silence which brooded over both river and forest alike. You hardly dared to speak, lest you should break the magician's spell. Solemnly and in a deep and serried phalanx stood the poplars, as they had stood for hundreds of years, guarding the borders of the river, and mirroring their crowns of autumnal gold in the life-giving stream, the sustainer of the woods, the milk-mother of the wild deer and the royal tiger, the bourn of life to the lonely shepherd of the desert. There they stood like a dark wall, at once the antithesis and the rival of the hungry desert behind them—stood in silence, in an attitude of reverence, as if listening to some hymn of a thousand years that was breathed up through their branches in adoration of the Supreme, a hymn which the wanderer and the traveller *may* indeed hear, if only his ear is attuned to the moving and matchless notes of Nature's greatness. Their one and only object in existence seemed to be to pay homage to the wonderful river, which not only brought the life-sustaining moisture to their roots, but saves the whole of East Turkestan from becoming one of the most desolate and barren regions on the face of the earth. In their reverent worship of the Tarim they were like the Brahmins and other Hindu pilgrims, who strain onwards to Benares, if only they may die in the sacred waters of the Ganges, which they also reverence with a holy love.

The forest stretched right down to the very brink of the river; but the steep faces of the banks were screened by a thick belt of yellow reeds, and immediately behind them the bushes formed an absolutely impenetrable thicket, through which nothing penetrated save the wild boar, by tunnels and dark gangways into which no ray of sunshine ever strays. High up on the sky-line ran the green coping of the poplars' crowns, making a dense curtain of foliage which seldom allowed a glimpse of the tree-trunks to gleam between—green, but green shot with various shades of rich brown, so rich that they would have been harsh had their effect not been softened by the hazy sky behind them. And all this glory of colour, all these silent har-

A View down the River from my Tent. On the right is my Work-table, on the left my Bed and Palta the Boatman.

monies of nature, were mirrored mile after mile on the sensitive surface of the placid river. I never grew tired of admiring it.

Thus we glided on through the heart of Central Asia, beside one of the greatest deserts of the earth, as though we were floating down the avenue of a park, a canopy of green leaves above our heads and a mantle of refreshing shade wrapped about our shoulders. Truly a wonderful journey! No need now for the boatmen to be incessantly on the watch. The river carried us safely and well. Our craft might have been a gondola drifting through the water-streets of Venice, save that our palaces were the groves of the poplar forest. Even the rude boatmen of Lailik felt the magic spell of those ever-silent woods, and almost slumbered at their posts. As for me, I kept expecting every moment to see the nymphs of the forest rocking on the branches that overhung the river, and laughing as they watched the reflection of their own dainty figures dimpling on its surface; nor should I have been the least surprised had I heard the plaintive notes of a pan's pipe, the music of the shepherd's god, come stealing through the forest trees. Yet no revelation from the world of faërydom came to break the solitude of our journey. All the forest had to give us, apart from its wealth of poetic suggestions, were the wilting leaves it showered down upon the bosom of the Tarim, like the yellow flowers which the devout Hindus scatter upon the waters of the Ganges.

Our fluvial highway was on the whole very sinuous. At one place, although we drifted 200 yards in a straight line towards the north-east, our actual route of travel measured a distance of 1,600 yards; in other words, we described eight-ninths of a circle in order to advance the remaining ninth. It was very seldom indeed that the river flowed in a straight line, and then only for a short distance. Its course through the woods was in fact like that made by a snake wriggling through the long grass. This added very greatly to the work I had to put into my map; for, if it was to be accurate, I could not, of course, afford to disregard all these little windings and sinuosities.

Towards evening the gnats began as usual to dance for their supper—and got it. I protected myself as well as I could with olive oil; but the boatmen, who always went barefoot, had a pretty rough time of it. Smack! smack! was heard unceasingly from each end of the boat, accompanied by exclamations such as "Annangnisskeh!" "Kissingnisskeh!" "Kaper!" words which are much more expressive if left untranslated.

At Yallguz-yiggdeh, where we encamped for the night, the forest thinned out a little, and was intermingled with sparse young forest trees and tamarisks, and broken by belts of reeds and sand-dunes. That night around the fire on shore we held a council of war. Mohammed Ahun, the hunter, the only man who knew anything about that part of the country, declared the river would freeze in two months' time. Hence, with the view of saving time, I ordered that for the future we should start every day as soon as we could see, that all meals were to be taken on board, with the exception of supper, and that our daily quantum of bread was to be baked in the oven on the after-part of the big ferry-boat. The men were anxious to get to

Masar-alldi or Avvat, for they were ill-supplied with *chapans* (cloaks), pelts, and boots.

Mohammed Ahun, the hunter, told me that two or three miles from the right bank of the Yarkand-daria I should find the dry bed of the Khorem, in which I discovered pools of fresh water in 1895; and that beyond it to the south-east stretched the boundless desert.

That evening the volume of the river was only 1,010 cubic feet. Owing to our stoppages during the night the river dropped at a relatively faster rate than it would have done if we had drifted continuously day and night without stopping; though the relation was of course affected also by the losses due to evaporation and absorption into the ground.

Copious dews now began to fall during the night. They came on shortly after the sunset, and in the morning the deck was as wet as though a shower of rain had fallen. On the 29th September we travelled for the most part between alternating steppes and young, virgin forests; the venerable poplars of the past day or two only survived in small groups and in single trees standing at wide intervals apart. In the morning appearances looked more favourable. The river was less sinuous than usual, and the air was perfectly still, so still that the chief thing which affected the anemometer was the steady pace at which we travelled. But about noon these favourable conditions came to an end. A crisp breeze sprang up, and the river once more began to meander in the old way. In the elbows or inner angles of the curves the current was sometimes as much as 29½ feet deep; and the back-stream, which was generally set up on the surface in these *köll* or *bulung*, as they were called, once or twice brought us to a standstill. As a rule we managed to punt ourselves out of them; but when the wind was against us, it was necessary to send a man on shore with a line to haul us out, and sometimes we had to yoke the skiff in front of the colossus, and tow her out.

Here the river was not only deep, it was also broad, and carried a comparatively large volume of water; but its rate of flow was relatively slower.

At Tuzluk-kash we passed a shepherd's encampment, standing on a peninsula which was surrounded on eleven-twelfths of its circumference by the river, and bought a sheep for 48 tengeh (nine shillings). The many windings of the stream in this part of its course made our actual route twice as long as it would have been could we have gone in a straight line as the crow flies. For example, on the 29th September we only advanced 5 miles towards the north-east, whereas we actually traversed 12 miles, at the rate of close upon 1½ miles an hour. As a result of the slower rate of flow and the greater depth the water became more transparent. It occurred to me that I might measure its transparency, and with that end in view I constructed a very simple instrument, consisting of a bright metal disk fixed to the bottom of a graduated rod. By its means I determined the transparency by ascertaining the depth to which the disk was visible when plunged vertically into the river.

Great though my enjoyment of the journey was, I was never able to quit my post for an instant to stretch my legs. We hardly ever travelled more than ten minutes in a straight line; as a rule, we seldom went longer than two or three minutes at a time without altering our direction. Hence, I had to keep my eye upon the compass. In fact, in this part of the Yarkand-daria I was tied down so closely to my map, that at one o'clock, the time for taking the readings of the meteorological instruments, we were often obliged to pull into the bank and stop whilst I did it. My first observations were made with pencil in a common note-book, which always lay open before me; these, when we stopped for the night, I transcribed in ink into a diary. In the part of its course in which the river wound most frequently, I was so incessantly occupied that I had hard work to keep my cigarette alight, and if it chanced to go out hardly found time to relight it; and many a time the tea which Islam made for me stood on the box by my side until it was cold before I got an opportunity to drink it.

The map, however, grew under my hands as the days went by, and I worked away at it with real enjoyment. It was planned on such a large scale that every turn of the ferry-boat's course is shown, every deviation it made to right or left, every halt by the river's bank, every crossing from one side to the other; in fact, it presents an exact reproduction of all the vessel's movements to and fro upon the surface of the river. The sharply-outlined banks or steep terraces, at the foot of which erosion works with the greatest effect—the bottom of the river suffers but little from this cause, and what there is is counterbalanced by the deposition of sedimentary matter—are indicated by sharp, black lines; the alluvial peninsulas as white crescents; and every island, sandbank and subsidiary side-channel is duly laid down in its proper place. The poplar woods are marked by tiny circles, the reed-beds by small arrow-heads, bushes and thickets by dots, tamarisks by barbs, and sand-dunes by the conventional stippling generally used to indicate mountains. When the forest thinned out, as it did on the 29th September, I marked every individual poplar tree. I believe, if I were to visit that region again, I should recognise every one of them as an old acquaintance.

The place we encamped at that day was called Kiyik-teleh-chöll ("the desert of the antelope willow"), an open steppe, where the gnats were not quite so troublesome as usual. The volume of the river was 982 cubic feet in the second.

During the following night the Yarkand-daria again fell 8¼ inches. We must consequently keep pushing on as fast as we can. On the 30th September the air cleared a little, and we caught sight of my old friend the Masar-tagh, towering skywards to the north-north-east. At first we could only perceive the faint outline of the mountains; but as the day wore on they became more and more distinct, until we were eventually able to distinguish the spurs and indentations of the range, as well as make out its brown colouring. This brought some relief to the monotony of our outlook, and formed a new topic of conversation. For a considerable distance the mountains lay directly ahead of us; then they appeared on our right, and after that on our left; and finally they stood right astern of us, and we seemed to be sailing away from them. It was only after we got this conspicuously fixed landmark that we saw clearly how greatly the river wound to and fro.

By this time the woods had disappeared, and the country become more barren. Grass and reed steppes stretched away from both banks, and it was the rarest sight to see a solitary young poplar lifting its head above the grass which nobody apparently cared to appropriate. Our hunters detected signs of deer and other wild animals. Islam seldom shot anything but ducks and geese: age was beginning to tell upon him. As for myself, I have not the destruction of so much as even a crow upon my conscience. During the whole of the journey I never fired a single shot. I did, it is true, carry a revolver for self-protection in case I should be attacked; but it was always packed away in one of my trunks, though in which of them I hardly ever knew.

At a desolate place on one of the banks, Kasim, the man

who steered the commissariat boat, found a solitary stray lamb. We took it on board and carried it with us, intending to hand it over to the first shepherd we met. Had we left it where it was, it would very soon have fallen a prey to some prowling wolf.

The sinuosities of the river were not quite so capricious as on the preceding day; but the east wind checked us a good deal. One peculiarity of this particular part of the river was that its banks were much higher than they had hitherto been, namely, 12 to 16 feet above the surface of the current. One punting pole, although nearly 20 feet long, was seldom long

A Shepherd's Hut near the Masar-tagh.

enough to reach the bottom, and when measuring the depth it became necessary to lash two of them together. Sometimes both banks were equally high, and without a trace of alluvium; this was, of course, in the straight stretches. Here, although we were sheltered from the wind, we could see but little of the surrounding country. In one locality, however, we perceived a few shepherds, who possessed a clumsily-made boat, sadly different from the slender, graceful canoes used by the Lopmen.

The mean velocity of the current at Camp no. XII., situated in an unnamed district, was over $1\frac{1}{4}$ miles an hour, and the volume 883 cubic feet in the second, consequently 99 feet less than on the day preceding. In the direct line we had advanced 7 miles, though our actual course measured $11\frac{1}{4}$ miles, a far better record than that of the day before.

Day by day it became an increasingly anxious question, whether we should succeed in getting through before the river became ice-bound.

CHAPTER VII.

A REEDY LAKE AND A MOUNTAIN CLIMB.

DURING the ensuing night the current dropped another half inch, and it was transparent to a depth of 5½ inches. Away to the north, a faint contour, which might well have passed for rising mist, had it not been for its serrated edge, showed the mountain range of the Tian-shan. The Masar-tagh too came out much more distinctly. Every hour its structural features, and the play of light and shade across them, became more and more intelligible; and I was able to map them in the perfection of comfort, as we slowly drifted on towards them. On my map I indicated the individual peaks of the range, easily recognisable by Roman numerals.

The river-bed was sharply eroded, but narrow, and the banks 10 feet high. The depth of the current was however less, and the velocity 1½ miles an hour. We frequently ran aground, and did not always succeed in getting off easily owing to the pressure of the water. Steppe country predominated on both banks. Amongst the steppe fauna which we observed, a species of hawk was very common. Two or three times we caught sight of shepherds and their flocks.

Before long we came to the outlying spurs of the Masar-tagh, their feet actually washed by the river, so close did they advance to it. I should not have been surprised had there been falls or rapids here, where the Yarkand-daria and the mountains came into contact; but there was nothing of the kind. The river, instead of forcing a path through them, swung off to the south-east, so as to skirt the southern extremity of the range, and in that way turn their flank. Immediately above the point where it deviated, the river was joined by two turbulent rivulets, both entering through deep trenches cut through its steep bank; they brought bright, clear water from a string of lakes, which were fed by the overflow of the Kona-daria of Maral-bashi.

Soon after we turned and began to skirt the base of the Masar-tagh, we perceived huts and people on the banks, then four *gumbez*, or mausoleums, on a declivity of the mountains, and shortly afterwards an old *guristan*, or burial-place. A little past this last we halted beside the huts of Kurruk-assteh.

The burial-place just mentioned was known as Hazrett Ali Masar, from the *masar*, or tomb, which it enclosed. The same name is also applied to the range as a whole. At the foot of the masar the Yarkand-daria gave off a large arm, the Kodai-daria, which I visited in 1895. It had, however, dried up ten days before our arrival, and therefore deprived us of none of our current; although from the middle of July to the 30th September it had drained off water to irrigate several villages on the Aksu road. Here again, as so often throughout its entire course, the great river manifested a tendency to shift its course to the right. But the Chinese *amban*, or governor, of Maral-bashi, wishing to check this tendency, and save the crops of the vicinity, had issued orders for a dam to be built before another year, so as to deflect the stream back into the Kodai-daria. Accordingly, at Kurruk-assteh, we found five men watching a pile of some thousand beams and other pieces of timber, which had been brought thither on *arbas* (carts) from the nearest forest. As soon as the river dropped sufficiently, the amban intended to raise a *corvée* of the people of the neighbourhood and have the dam built. Fortunately for us, it would be a month yet before the work could begin, and by that time I hoped we should be so far away that this stoppage of the river would in no way affect us.

We decided to stay at least one day at Kurruk-assteh. Summoning the on-bashi of the place, I commissioned him to go to the bazaar of Tumshuk, and buy pelts and boots for my boatmen, and I also bade him procure a supply of rice, flour, and vegetables. He promised to return by the following evening. Unfortunately I was not able to send any of my own men with him, for there was only one horse in the whole of the district. But I trusted to the man, and gave him the money to pay for what he bought.

After developing photographic plates until 3 o'clock in the morning, and having a good sleep after it, I devoted the rest of the day to a well-earned and much-needed holiday. As a rule, I worked sixteen hours every day, and often grew quite stiff from sitting still so long at a time. By way of a thorough change, therefore, I took a good walk, and climbed to the top of the hill of Hazrett Ali Masar, to have a look round the neighbourhood—the boundless steppes; the yellow desert, with its weird and lofty sand-dunes, here also called Takla-makan; and the winding river, which from the point of view where I stood looked like a mere trench, a glittering narrow blue ribbon flung across the face of the open country.

At dusk I measured the volume of the river, and was agreeably surprised to find it 1,897 cubic feet in the second; that is to say, more than double the quantity of water at the last measurement. This satisfactory state of things was due to the two affluents which joined the river above Kurruk-assteh; and as the water they contributed was perfectly clear, the transparency of the Yarkand-daria was now increased to 8⅓ inches.

But we heard nothing of the on-bashi. It grew late, and yet he did not return. I began to think he had run away with my money. If he had, we were in no position to follow him, for we had no horses. Nor did he come on the following day either. We were, therefore, obliged perforce to wait. This enforced delay I turned to account, by making another excursion to the left bank of the river, that is, towards the north-west.

I walked as far as the two affluents I have mentioned, to see how Kasim caught fish. The place he had chosen for his operations was the spot where three rivulets met, all coming from the lake of Shor-köll, one of the basins fed by the overflow of the river of Maral-bashi. In other words Shor-köll was a steppe-lake, or, if you like, a swamp, for it was impossible to get to it by reason of the broad expanse of soft ground, covered with luxuriant grass and reeds, which hemmed it in. This irregular, polyp-shaped lake, with its multitude of creeks and little bays, its thousands of islands and peninsulas, was the filtering basin of the two affluents already mentioned, so that the water which they contributed to the Yarkand-daria was, as I have already said, as bright and clear as crystal.

At the place where Kasim was fishing, the eastern affluent tumbled down a waterfall about five feet high, divided in the middle by a small islet. Down the incline it raced in boisterous tumult, and boiled and churned itself into foam at

Our Camp at Kurruk-assteh.

the foot of the cascade. The banks were here six to eight feet high, and rose straight out of the water.

The fish (*balik* or *asman*) frequented the boiling pool at the bottom of the fall; though they frequently showed themselves above the water, when with a clever, elastic bound, they tried to leap up the fall, exactly as salmon do. The instrument Kasim used for catching them was a kind of eel-spear, a sixteen-foot rod or javelin called a *sapp*, consisting of two parts, the lower made of tough tamarisk wood, the upper of pliant willow. At the end were two hooks (*satchkak*), with the points pointing

Kasim Fishing.

downwards and the barbs pointing upwards. They were loosely fixed, so as to become detached the moment they struck; but were secured to the rod 18 or 20 inches higher up by means of a strong cord.

In the space of about a minute, Kasim captured two big fellows, and after that several others. He stood on the edge of the water, holding his spear ready poised like a harpoon, and when he caught a glimpse of a fish, down went the instrument like an arrow. You heard the shaft whizz, you saw it vibrate, you saw the foam fly, and the water splash, and the next moment there was a big *asman* flopping and floundering on the bank, spiked on the end of the *sapp* as though it had come there by witchcraft. It was both a novel and an interesting spectacle, and we were supplied with fish for several days to come.

Late that evening the on-bashi turned up at last, bringing with him everything he had been commissioned to buy. He had also procured me a new guide, a hunter.

During the night of the 3rd October, it blew such a gale that the tent-poles creaked and the ropes whipped incessantly against the canvas. Next morning also there was a strong breeze; and as it came from the east-north-east, it was of course adverse to us. In fact, it blew so hard that the surface of the river was an expanse of combing crests, which fell over short and abrupt, owing to their being forced against the current. This rendered the task of piloting us more difficult, as it was impossible to see which side of the river the current ran. It was, however, very pleasant to hear the waves rippling against the ferry-boat; but they were no friends to us, they kept us back and hindered us. The tent too proved an obstacle to progress, because, catching the wind like a sail, it caused the boat to tilt over to the lee-side. I therefore had it taken down, after first removing all my loose effects to the inside of the black cabin. All this made our rate of advance painfully slow. The only time we were able to progress at a normal rate was when we obtained shelter from the wind under the high river-banks. If only it would blow from the west, were it only for one day! But no, the wind was always against us.

The bed of the Yarkand-daria now ran to the east-north-east, and during the whole of this day (4th October) it resembled an artificially made canal. Its breadth was everywhere the same, 150 to 200 feet; the banks, which were lined with luxuriant reeds, scrubby bush, young forest, and thickets, were exceptionally high; and the curves well rounded and easy, without any very sharp or awkward turns. There was no trace of alluvial deposits.

During the course of the day the river did, however, describe one curve which came very near to being a complete circle. We heard a shepherd singing in a clear and melodious voice in the woods close beside us. Then the river swung off to the north, and the song died away in the distance. A fresh bend, and we again heard the song. It grew nearer and nearer, and at last there it was again, quite close to us. The singer had never moved, but sat all the time in the same spot in the forest, watching his sheep as they grazed amongst the trees; it was the river which had looped round upon itself, so as to bring us once more within sound of the man's glad and light-hearted song.

To the east we saw two other isolated hills peeping above the horizon. They were the Chokka-tagh and Tuzluk-tagh, from which I started on my disastrous journey across the desert in 1895. The lake beside which we rested on that occasion was called Yugan-balik-köll (Big Fish Lake), and was fed by rivulets from

Kasim with his Catch.

the Yarkand-daria, to the right of which it lay. As the name indicates, the lake was well stocked with fish; and in the spring the inhabitants of Charvak and Masar-alldi visit it for the fishing, which they carry on by means of canoes hewn out of poplar-stems. Another source of livelihood to the inhabitants of these two places is mining rock-salt in the Tuzluk-tagh (Salt Mountain), the produce of their labour being transported on arbas (carts) in winter when the river is frozen over.

At Yugan-balik, three shepherds' families lived all the year round in charge of a thousand sheep belonging to merchants of the two towns just mentioned. The animals are shorn twice a year, in the autumn as well as in the spring ; and then the owners come and fetch the wool away—the same custom which I observed in the regions beside the Khotan-daria and the Keriya-daria. In this same locality—Yugan-balik—tigers were very common, having increased greatly in numbers of recent years. The year of our visit (1899) they had already carried off five horses and several sheep ; but they were shy of human beings, and took very good care not to go anywhere near the sheep-folds.

It was a beautiful afternoon, still and peaceful, and we continued our journey until it grew so dark it was impossible to distinguish the outline of the banks. The air was unusually warm, owing to the veil of fine dust which the gale had brought, and which now hung over the country like a low canopy, preventing excessive evaporation, and even hiding the stars above our heads.

On the 5th October, we drew near to the Chokka-tagh, though only very slowly, for the river had begun to wind about again in the most extraordinary fashion. Sometimes the Chokka-tagh was directly in front of us, and sometimes we had in the same position the Masar-tagh, which we left the day before ; but before night, the latter range became shrouded in the dust-haze and disappeared altogether from sight. Both banks were bordered by narrow belts of tender young forest, but behind them, as far as the eye could reach, stretched one unbroken expanse of golden reeds. Owing to the adverse wind we only covered about two-thirds of our usual distance. The wind, as it came sweeping across the ocean of reeds, struck upon me, on my elevated captain's "bridge," with almost the freshness of a sea-breeze.

At Sorun, where we halted till we should get the spell of still weather that usually set in in the afternoon, I received from some shepherds the comforting information that, with the next new moon the wind would drop, and that we should then get still, calm weather, for it always happened so at that season of the year. As, however, the wind continued to blow till a late hour of the night, I decided to encamp where we were, and make an excursion to the Chokka-tagh and the lake of Sorun. The latter, like the Yugan-balik-köll, was fed by the Yarkand-daria. Whenever the river lies at the higher level, the water flows down naturally into the lake; then, when the surface of the lake rises above the level of the river, the reverse process takes place; but in both cases the connecting stream flows along the same channel. At the time of our visit the Yarkand-daria was the higher of the two, and so much of its flood was drained away by the lake, that, of the 1,897 cubic feet which it had measured at Kurruk-assteh, it now retained only 989 cubic feet. On the other hand, the water was transparent to a depth of 13⅓ inches.

It was a good thing we halted as we did, for on the 6th October it blew a veritable *sarik-buran* (yellow storm) or fierce sand-storm, and the atmosphere became so heavily charged with dust that the Chokka-tagh, although quite close to us, looked like a grey wall all in one and the same vertical plane, without depression or protuberance of any kind. I walked as far as the Tuzluk-tagh and climbed two of its summits to get an idea of our surroundings. In 1895 we travelled along the northern foot of this mountain without seeing the Sorun-köll, though now it lay spread out at our feet like a map, half overgrown with reeds and its shores dotted with solitary poplars.

The view I obtained was indeed so attractive that I resolved to explore the region further, invested as it was with so many memories of my former visit; in all human probability I should never set eyes on it again. But to do this, it would be necessary to stop where we were over the 7th October. And although we had every reason for hastening on, lest we should get frozen fast in the ice before our journey was finished—really I could not resist the temptation.

And sure enough, the next morning it blew just sufficiently to make it difficult to continue our river-journey, yet not too much to spoil a splendid sail across the lakes in the little skiff. As, however, it would be too far to row all the way back, I sent a man off early along the eastern side of Sorun-köll with a bullock arba to bring the boat back.

I used the same vehicle to get her down to the lake; yet, as the shore was shallow, and it consisted of soft mud, we had, all the same, to carry her a good way out. After she was got afloat, it became my turn. Whilst Naser Ahun carried me down on his back, Islam, who was anxious to go with me, splashed along barefooted behind through the ooze.

There was a crisp and steady breeze, and away we went due south, right across the lake, out of one open reach into another.

The kamish (reed) fences were nowhere thick, and as we slipped past each successive promontory, the boat gently brushed against the outermost reeds, without being stopped. All round the shores, however, the reeds formed a pretty continuous ring, especially on the west side, though they also hid several creeks and projecting points and narrow passages, which gave access to the little lakes immediately to the west. The eastern shore was more evenly rounded off by the scree which came down the mountain-side.

The water of the lake was perfectly fresh, and so transparent that we could everywhere see the bottom, with its *Algæ* and decayed reed-stalks. At 11 o'clock in the morning its temperature was 13°.7 C. or 56°.7 Fahr. The greatest depth we sounded was 6½ feet, and in all probability this was also the maximum depth, for we kept mostly in the middle of the lake.

At one place we saw a beautiful sight—a flock of fourteen snow-white swans, sitting the water in their usual proud and stately way; but when we approached them, they rose with a great flapping of wings, and went and settled farther off.

At intervals we caught glimpses of the clayey shore through gaps in the reeds; and small islets, with tamarisks growing on them, and low sand-dunes covered with grass, were not at all uncommon. In the south the lake expanded into a large open sheet of water, shut in by thick beds of reeds. I naturally thought that was the end of the lake; but two of the natives, who had followed us on horseback along the eastern shore, pointed out a natural channel through the reeds connecting with another lake, Chöll-köll (Desert Lake).

Except for a narrow lane of open water some six or ten feet wide, the passage was entirely overgrown with reeds, and so tall and luxuriant were they that they made a sort of fence or wall on both sides. The wind, however, was behind us, and our little skiff cleft her way through with the greatest ease, her yard bending down the rustling reeds as she brushed against them. The channel was on the whole pretty straight; still, it inclined a little first to one side and then to the other, just sufficient to prevent us from seeing very far ahead, so that several times we fancied we had dived into a watery *cul-de-sac*. But no; each time the prospect opened out again, and so on our brave little skiff glided like a swan. All this while the nodding plumes of the reeds which walled in this lacustrine gallery were so far above our heads that they completely hid from us the crests of the adjacent mountains; and yet we were so close to dry land that we talked the whole way to the horsemen who were guiding us, although we never saw a glimpse of them.

This channel was considerably deeper than the lake itself—namely, as much as 12 feet, and the water a dark blue colour. The breadth also increased gradually; for although (including the reed belts) it was nowhere less than 30 feet, it often widened out to 100, and sometimes to over 150 feet. Several circumstances seemed to point to its having been made by human hands, others that it coincided with an ancient river-bed; yet it was clearly nothing but a natural water-course, kept open by the alternate ebb and flow between the Yarkand-daria and the lake of Chöll-köll.

The whole place swarmed with wild duck. They kept diving and swimming along in front of us, and sometimes, when we got close to them, they swept up in such numbers that the water was churned into foam. Then down they would plunge like a hail-shower, bob under, and come up again, quacking incessantly. Unfortunately, Islam had forgotten to bring his gun with him. We never dreamt there would be such a splendid opportunity as this. At length we approached the Chöll-köll, which was free of reeds. Simultaneously, the wind began to die away. But as I had already mapped its western shore in 1895, there was no object to be gained by sailing across it.

When Islam saw the enormous flocks of wild duck—actual clouds of them—rise, terrified by the appearance of our white sail, and scurry backwards and forwards across the lake, he was unable to contain himself any longer. So I gave him permission to ride back to camp and fetch his gun, as well as to row the boat back through the channel which we had just threaded.

Whilst he was doing that, it suddenly entered my head to walk across the Chokka-tagh, that is eastwards, and then find my way back to camp round its northern extremity. A shepherd of the locality told me the distance was deceptive, the range was further off than it looked, and even after we got over it, we should have as far again to go as the distance we had sailed during the last four and a half hours. But I had made up my mind, and was not to be deterred by his representations. It was a fine opportunity to complete my map of the region—an opportunity I could not afford to neglect. It was half-past three o'clock, the sun was nearing the top of the Tuzluk-tagh, and it was evident to the simplest understanding, that we could not get back to camp before midnight. And yet get there we must at all costs, else the chronometers would run down.

Hence after dinner, I chose Palta and the shepherd just mentioned to accompany me, and we set off to the east-south-east, making for a notch in the long crest which topped the range. Although we walked at a smart pace, and steered a straight line for the pass, at the end of an hour we did not seem to be any nearer to our goal. At the end of the second hour, however, we approached the foot-hills of the range. Seen from the lake whence we started, these appeared to merge immediately into the main chain itself; but we now perceived that they were parted from it by a long stretch of rising ground.

As we advanced, the features of the country changed. We crossed a series of concentric zones, which girdled the mountains, each different in character from the others. Nearest to the lake lay a strip of low, sterile soil, inundated when the Yarkand-daria was in flood, but at this time covered with a slight sprinkling of salt, a proof that the water of this land-locked lake was not perfectly fresh. Next came a belt of reed-steppe; and after that a zone of older salt deposits (*shor*), now dry and crystallised, and the whole brittle and crunching when trodden upon. Lastly, we came to the slope which mantled the western foot of the chain. Its fall towards the lake was extremely gentle, only 3°, and it was covered with débris, and furrowed by vast numbers of tiny runnels, at this time dry, but interlacing, dividing, and sub-dividing like the arms of a veritable delta. The nearer we approached to the mountains, the more rugged did they grow, until at last the fractured edges were several feet in height, so that we could only make progress by going round them.

At last the ascent grew steeper, and we were forced to stop to catch our breath. From the top of the scree we obtained a splendid view of the lake behind us. It was broader than I thought it was when I saw it, foreshortened, in 1895. Its southern end had in no respect altered, but was broken in the same irregular manner by little bays and marshes as when I last beheld it on 22nd April, 1895. My mind became filled with sad and solemn thoughts as my eyes fell again upon the steppe where our tent stood that unhallowed day, while away to the south stretched the murderous desert "ocean" in which my caravan perished. There before me lay, peaceful and tranquil, the copious lake, which would have preserved the lives of both men and camels, had we only possessed sufficient foresight to carry with us a larger supply of the water which it wasted by evaporation upon the desert air to no man's profit.

The towering crests of the sand-dunes were now bathed in purple and red, and glowed like burning volcanoes in the setting sun. They were giant graves covering the dead. And as my thoughts penetrated the dread wilderness of sand, where I knew that my servants and camels lay sleeping their last long sleep, my heart was oppressed with uneasiness. Could they forgive me—me, one out of the only three creatures which escaped alive out of that fiery Gehenna—could they forgive me as I stood thus, surrounded by every comfort, and gazed out towards the spot where their tortured spirits were dissociated from their suffering bodies? Did brave old Mohammed Shah, as he now cooled his parched throat under the palm-trees of the heavenly Bihesht—did he perchance urge his accusation against me? For it was indeed I, I who was responsible for that terrible journey through the most deadly and most accursed region on the face of all the earth. I fancied I could hear the murmur of a death-song stealing upon my ear from the heart of the desert, and expected every moment to see the spectres of the poor camels which perished in such unspeakable agony stealing forth from behind the sand-dunes, in search of him who misled them and deceived them, forcing upon them that mad and desperate, that agonising, that utterly hopeless, struggle with death. I remembered as well as if it were only yesterday, how the big tears dropped from their wistful eyes, and were mockingly gulped up by the burning sand. *

The scree, or curtain of débris, was now very uneven, and sparsely dotted over with steppe tamarisks, whose long, stiff needles reminded me of the pine needles of my Northern home. We put up a couple of deer, which in long, elastic leaps fled, light as a dream, up the slopes of the Chokka-tagh, their feet scarce seeming to touch the ground.

After crossing several minor crests, we finally struck into a *yilga* (eroded glen), which led us to the summit of the range.

* See *Through Asia*, vol. I, pp. 519-574.

There we halted a short while, to survey our position and decide in which direction we should continue our journey. The pass on which we stood was about 650 feet above the level of the lake. A precipitous ravine shot down to a plain at its foot, which stretched away as far as the eye could reach to the east-north-east. Immediately to the east were high sand-dunes. The sun set behind Tuzluk-tagh, and it grew rapidly dusk, the dark shades seeming to grow up out of the ground like mist, and once more the pall of night was spread over the desert, the mountains and the lake.

Our next business was to get down on the other side without mishap. The descent was so steep, the men wondered how we were going to manage it. But manage it we did, mostly by slipping, sliding and glissading. In this rapid scramble I found my geological hammer very helpful, for on such excursions as this I always carried it with me. After a while the descent became easier, and we were soon down in the valley; then hastening along it, we reached the spur which shut it in on the left. Beyond that we could just dimly discern a fresh spur to the north. This also we should have to get past, before we could obtain a glimpse of Sai-tagh, a little isolated hill close to the camp, on which our men were to kindle a fire when evening set in.

After walking diagonally across the gravelly scree, for it extended also to this side of the mountain, we came to level ground, covered with sand, where the going was much easier in the dark. Being unaccustomed to such long tramps, I began to feel very tired, and so at the end of every 2,000 paces or so we granted ourselves a five minutes' rest, flinging ourselves down full-length on the cool sand. For I was counting the steps we took, so as to be sure of the distance, as well as to complete the circle, which began and ended at our encampment.

On the left we had the dark silhouette of the mountain; on the right the sandy desert, which even here rose into barren dunes, so high as to be easily mistaken for a spur of the mountains themselves. At length we caught sight of the reflection of a fire, though we could not see the fire itself, owing to an intervening height. Do you know what it means to travel towards a fire on a dark night? When you are tired it encourages you as a beacon of hope; but you can march on and on for hours without getting any nearer to it. At length, however, after going a few thousand more paces we passed the end of the intervening ridge, and then saw distinctly the fire and its leaping tongues of flame. When the fire drooped, as it sometimes did, the distance seemed to grow as long as ever it was; but when a fresh armful of dry fuel was flung upon it, we fancied we should soon reach the bright flames which we now saw so distinctly. At intervals we stopped and shouted, but as yet got no reply. Finally, however, there came back a faint answering shout, and we knew we were drawing near to our goal.

As soon as my men were sure it was we, they set fire to a row of dead and dried poplars, and an hour later we made our entrance in fine style through the magnificently illuminated forest. There we found two horses waiting for us, and I do not think I ever put leg across a saddle with a more grateful sense of relief. Islam and the other men, who had grown uneasy at our prolonged absence, met us with torches, and so lighted us home across the marshes and rivulets which ran down to the river.

A twenty-four miles' tramp when you are not accustomed to walking is not a bad piece of work. It was midnight when at length I sat down again in my tent and ate my supper; then I wrote up my note-books and diary, and finally crept into bed. Such was the first hard day I spent in the heart of Asia; but it was by no means the last.

CHAPTER VIII.

RIVER-WINDINGS, WOODS, AND MASARS.

THE 8th of October was a glorious morning, as still as the Sabbath, with a beautifully bright atmosphere, so that the mountains stood out sharply and distinctly down to the smallest feature. Not a dimple on the river, which stretched out before us, sparkling like a mirror, as it lazily dawdled round its long sweeping curves, shut in between its high, sharp-cut banks, with their fringes of cheerful young forests, yellowed by the breath of autumn, and their belts of luxuriant reeds.

Our heavy colossus glided on her way so sedately and so tranquilly that there was very little for the men to do, except give an occasional push when we entered the angles or rounded the curves. Most of them were indeed tired after the exertions of the previous day, and silence and peace reigned on board. Palta lay stretched at full length on the fore-deck exposed to the full blaze of the sun, leaving his punting-pole to young Ibrahim, the son of our new guide, who was simply called the Mollah.

The isolated little hill of Sai-tagh stood close beside the river; in fact, the water washed its foot, swinging in so close to it as to leave room for nothing more than a shepherd's path and two or three young poplars. Its western declivity, which fell at an angle of 34°, was naked rock, though further away from the stream its flanks were carpeted with sand. Towards the north it was continued by a chain of low eminences running parallel to the river. On one of these ridges we perceived a small burial-place, consecrated by its quietude and soothing restfulness. Here our Mollah, who knew his Koran, recited certain prayers, whilst the rest of the men kneeled about him. Its principal monument was a mausoleum of sun-dried brick, cubical in form and surmounted by a cupola (*gumbez*), erected to the memory of some eminent man, probably a highly-honoured shepherd or hunter, and around it were several other tombs. On the very summit of the ridge were two other graves, without any covering beyond a few pieces of timber and some stones, and with the north end—for they lay north and south—quite open, so that we were able to see the heads of the skeletons which lay within. One of the graves was divided, so as to accommodate two corpses. Neither of the graves appeared to be very old.

At noon a slight breeze sprang up in the south-west, and as we were travelling towards the north-east, we went along at a spanking pace. We encamped for the night on the left

The Yarkand-daria at Sai-tagh.

bank, at a place called Moreh. Here the volume of the river was 886½ cubic feet in the second. At this place I suffered a great loss—my favourite dog Dovlet died. Poor Dovlet! he was excellent company, friendly, cheerful, and full of comical impulses, and I always played with him for a little while every evening. When we left Osh, he was a miserably thin little pup; but under my care he had grown into quite a handsome dog. After he was buried I felt quite lonely and melancholy, and it was several days before I got over his loss, I missed him so.

The morning of the 10th October was bitterly cold. At six o'clock the thermometer registered only 3°.0 C. or 37°.4 Fahr.;

and when we started, the river was as silent as the grave, except for the melancholy croaking of a small colony of ravens. The banks were desolate ; although in one spot the sight of tree-trunks and branches blackened by smoke showed that shepherds must once have encamped there. The woods were now almost entirely yellow ; their green tints were few and far between.

I discovered I had quite a treasure in my guide, the Mollah ; he was a perfect geographical lexicon, and knew inside and out the topography of that almost unknown region. Spectacles on nose and with a big sheet of paper in front of him, he made me a map of it, with every place and route delineated and named ; and he showed me at what points the desert approached nearest to the river. I had afterwards several opportunities of testing his map, and found it singularly correct. He had ranged these woods several times when hunting, and had three times been all the way to Shah-yar. With the boatmen he was exceedingly popular, for he entertained them many a long hour with reading, having brought with him two books which described the travels of the earliest Mohammedan missionaries in East Turkestan.

In another little cove we surprised a troop of wild swine, the old ones perfectly black, the young ones, four in number, brown. For a moment they stood gazing in amazement at the huge monster which came floating down the river towards them, then they all turned tail and disappeared into the reeds, going off at a smart trot and all together in a clump.

Towards evening we approached the district of Ak-sattma, where a certain *bai* (rich man), Kurban by name, the owner of 2,000 sheep and a large number of cattle, had built two huts at the foot of a sand-dune, near a few solitary poplars. As he also cultivated wheat and melons, we were able to replenish our stores in a satisfactory way.

Although the day wore late, we decided to round yet one more *chugulup* (loop). The twilight spread itself over the glittering stream, its placid surface as smooth as glass except for a few slight dimples. The evening was so silent, you could hear your own heart beat. I drew forth the musical-box and set Islam to attend to it ; and the men, whom I thought it would cheer up, listened silently and reverently. Kasim in the pilot-boat dropped back, so as to keep as near to us as he dared. Sad and melancholy were the strains as the chords of *Cavalleria Rusticana* echoed along the slumbering reaches of the river; festal and melodious as the lively measures of *Carmen* vibrated through the forests. Then followed a folk-song, of serious import, to which the wondering woods and waters listened in silent sympathy. But when the echoes of the neighbourhood were awakened by a stirring march, fancy converted our homely ferry-boat into a triumphal barge, making her state entry into some desert capital, to the accompaniment of trumpeters' fanfares and the crash of regimental music. It was a delightful evening, and as peaceful as it was charming. The air was loaded with the scents of the forest, and the fragrance of the meadows and the reed-beds, and a profound silence, as of some holy temple, reigned over all—river, forest, steppe and field. Amid that deep, oceanic silence the smallest sound struck with an exaggerated effect upon the ear. The least movement of bird or beast seemed to fill the air with ringing echoes; a duck swimming in a sheltered nook of the river, a fish splashing in the pitch-black shadow under some high, steep bank, a fox rustling amongst the reeds, even a handful of sand-grains dropping upon the water from some overhanging shelf above the river—all smote upon the solemn stillness of that lovely autumn night in the heart of Turkestan. The shades of night came down upon us fast, whilst we, like spectres and ghosts from another world, drifted on deeper and deeper into the heart of that weird, lone land, the denizens of whose sleeping woods no doubt listened with creeping awe to the changing melodies of our instrument. The strains of a musical-box are not the most noble sounds with which to delight the ear of man; but the surroundings—the time, the scene, the accompanying associations—invested them with a magic charm and effect there was no resisting; while the profound silence around begat in the mind dreams of great and daring deeds that might yet be achieved.

But while we rested for the night amongst the yellowing poplars on the shore, the unslumbering river carried further the great flood of water which had borne us along during the day, and so gave it one day's start of us. It was so late in the evening when I measured the river, that I had to do it by torch-light. The volume was 943 cubic feet in the second.

A slight, moist dew lay over the Yarkand-daria when we started at seven o'clock the next morning, the 11th October. Our course ran at first towards the south, so that the rays of the rising sun, filtering through the mist, caused the figures of the men, standing in the pioneer ferry-boat and skiff, to throw dark silhouettes against the veiled background of the river. The river still preserved the same characteristics, being every bit as sinuous as heretofore. This, and the strong wind which lay in our teeth, prevented us from travelling very far that day. These eternal windings were enough to make a man dizzy. Sunshine and shadow, wind and shelter alternated incessantly. One while we were freezing; then a little while after the sun was hot enough to scorch us. Now we crawled along slower than the snail, anon we rivalled a race-horse. In the transverse loops the current lost a good deal of its innate force through friction and pressure against the perpendicular banks, but by way of counterbalance it expended its force in other work, namely, in eroding the banks. And experience confirmed this inference, for we always moved slower after passing such spots.

At Moreh, where I lost Dovlet, the men, having run out of *naz* (snuff), sent young Ibraham to the bazaar of Chiggan-chöll to buy a fresh supply. The lad had a fifteen-mile tramp to reach the place, and joined us again two days later at a spot called Duga-jayi-masar. In addition to an armful of melons, carrots, beetroot, onions, and bread, he also brought his mother and younger brothers, so that during the next few days we had fresh passengers on board. At the camp we had just left the banks rose seven feet above the surface of the river, and the ground inside the forest had not yet dried from the summer overflow. That is to say, the river had fallen more than six feet since that happened. The farther we advanced the narrower and deeper grew its bed, and the slower flowed its current. The breadth indeed seldom exceeded 50 feet. As I was getting impatient to reach the Aksu-daria, where the Mollah assured me we should have three times the quantity of water we now had, we generally drifted eleven hours every day. No wonder then I grew stiff and numbed with sitting so many hours bent over my work-table. With the view of getting a little change in this respect, I contrived a sort of lounge of felt rugs and cushions in the skiff, and arranging my writing and drawing materials, and the necessary instruments, conveniently about me, lay there and worked in the lap of comfort. By keeping a good distance ahead of the big ferry-boat, I got away from all disturbing sounds, and, pipe in mouth, pen in hand, and map on knees, I revelled in the solitude and idyllic stillness of the

Burial-place at Sai-tagh.

scene. I cannot conceive an easier or a more comfortable way of travelling through an unknown region.

During the night of the 12th October we had our first touch of frost; the thermometer fell to $-1^\circ.1$ C. or $30.^\circ0$ Fahr. In the evening of that day the river measured 867 cubic feet in the second. The next day the Yarkand-daria wound about worse than it had ever done since the journey began. At the end of three and a half hours we found ourselves abreast of the identically same poplars we had started from first thing in the morning. The day was bleak and raw, and we were glad to get into our furs. While Islam and the Mollah preferred to tramp through the woods, cutting off the winding loops by traversing their bases, the rest of the men crouched on board wrapped in their *chapans* (cloaks), keeping a watchful eye that we did not run aground: they would not relish jumping into the water on such a day. After seven hours we picked up Islam and his companion; they were lying fast asleep beside a dying fire. Out of the seven hours which had elapsed since they left us, they had been waiting no less than five; and had it not been for their fire, we should never have seen them, but have gone past, leaving them fast asleep where they were.

The first nights of frost left their mark upon the forests; the foliage everywhere was now fast turning yellow. The wind scattered the leaves so thickly over the surface of the river, that it became spotted all over with yellow, and our ferry-boat drifted on through a veritable avenue of hanging gold. The movements of the floating leaves showed clearly how the least breath of air influenced the rate at which our craft drifted. Sometimes the leaves travelled faster than we did; sometimes it was we that went the faster; but in a dead calm, we kept equal pace one with the other.

On the evening of the 14th October we encamped in the district of Yiggdelik. The river immediately above that place was unusually straight, and as we had a light breeze behind us, we made good progress. On the right bank, where we stopped, we found in the forest, on the top of a sand-dune planted with tamarisks, a pole erected, to signify that there was a masar or holy man's tomb in the vicinity. Our Mollah had been there several times before, in quest of rubies, which he declared were to be found amongst the sand-polished flints that covered a wide, open stretch of country between the desert and the forest. He said he had spent the night close to the gumbez (dome) of the grave, and had seen a pale, flickering flame hovering above it. But he was said never to have found any rubies. Towards the south-south-east we perceived the extreme outliers of the "sea of sand," namely, a double-humped dune of gigantic dimensions. I should readily have taken it for a small detached mountain group, had the Mollah not assured me that it was actually built up of sand.

The first part of our journey on the 15th October resembled a tangled cord, but the latter part was quite normal. As a rule, when the river wound greatly, it was also narrow and deep, with a slow current; but when it straightened out it became shallow and broad, with a swift current, in other words the fall was here greater. Sometimes it seemed as though the river did not know which way to turn, but paused to consider, wondering whether it had not better stop for good and all. Already the thermometer reached a minimum of –4°.1 C. or 24°.6 Fahr.

My boatmen now began to lose heart a little, as we thus went on day after day, getting further and further away from their homes and hearths in Lailik, and penetrating ever deeper into unknown deserts and unknown woods. But their courage revived again after we reached Kuilushning-bashi; for there a fine fellow named Yussup Do Beg, who was grazing his sheep in the vicinity, comforted them with the assurance that when their task was finished it would be the easiest thing in the world for them to return home again by the great caravan-road through Aksu. By this the first of the jighits, or couriers, who was to bring my letters from Kashgar, was, or ought to be, on his way to Dural. I arranged, therefore, with Yussup to have him stopped at Aksu, and sent on from there down the river to meet us, or rather to wait for us; which he did.

On the 17th October we struck one of the deltaic arms of the Kodai-daria, but it contributed only an insignificant increment to our current, a thing not indeed to be wondered at, seeing we had already found it dry at the point where it broke away from the main stream. Of course that might be, and yet there might be water still remaining in the river lower down. For some distance after this the Yarkand-daria flowed due north, and we did not lose anything like so much time in winding in and out of its sinuosities. Yet for all that we traversed one which described as nearly as possible a complete circle, the chord of its arc being only forty yards long. The next time the river was in full flood it would infallibly break through that narrow neck of land, and so cut off the loop. The banks were here 11 to 13 feet high, and were being undermined at each end, so that the neck was already rapidly growing narrower. In this part of the river, similar abandoned loops or back-waters (*boljemal*) were pretty common. In almost every case there remained in them a little crescentic pool (*köll*) of clear water.

A Shepherd Bringing us a Sheep.

At a point on the right bank where there was an abundance of thickets and dead forest we perceived a column of smoke curling upwards amongst the trees, followed soon afterwards by leaping tongues of flame. The Mollah said they were fires made by the shepherds to scare tigers and wolves away from their flocks. During the past few days we had several times seen traces of tigers on the banks. And true enough, when we came abreast of the place, behold there were two or three shepherds; but the moment they caught sight of our ferry-boat, with its white spectral tent and pitch-black hut, they took to their heels and fled as if the Foul Fiend were after them, abandoning sheep and dogs and fires to their fate. We shouted, we sent messengers after them; but no, they were gone, and we never set eyes on them again. For this I was sorry; I wanted to get some information about the district.

The tendency which the river here showed to straighten its course by cutting off its loops was due to the conformation of the surface. This consisted of loose sand, which crumbled down at the least touch, so that the river was able to carry on its work of erosion without any particular difficulty. And it was a necessary consequence of the variability of the river's course that the forests thereabouts were thin, and had seldom grown to any great age. It was no uncommon sight to see the poplars standing on the very verge of the river, ready to topple in the moment the current should have undermined them sufficiently; indeed, many of them lay already prone on the water, merely held precariously by their roots. The volume of the stream had by this diminished to 716 cubic feet in the second. But the transparency had decreased from 15½ inches, which it registered only a little way back, to 8 inches. This again was a consequence of the loose and porous character of the containing soil.

On the 18th October the wind was again contrary. When our course lay due north, it blew from that quarter; and when we turned towards the north-east, the wind also changed and met us again; but eventually it fixed itself in the east. The river-bed was tolerably open and flat, so that we got little protection from the banks and the belts of vegetation which accompanied them. On the windward side the tent-canvas was as taut as a drum, and by putting our hands upon it we obtained some idea of the force with which the wind was driving our craft to leeward. The men had to work hard all day long to keep us clear of the banks; indeed, so hard were they put to it that they had great difficulty in finding time to eat their frugal breakfast of bread and melons. The bosom of the river was more encumbered than usual with drift-wood, branches, snags, and flotsam of all kinds, loosened from the shallows and banks in which it had been fastened. The sky was heavy with clouds, and the wind whistled shrilly through the thin and stunted poplars. The volume increased again to 788 cubic feet in the second. As soon as I had finished my measurements, I took a stroll through the forest, followed by Yolldash; but before I got very far the forest proper came to an end, or rather it passed over into bushes, steppes, and finally the outermost fringe of the desert.

The next day the wind was again a serious hindrance to us, especially after it quickened into a tempest on a small scale. The atmosphere was thick with drift-sand, so that all we could see of the sun above our heads was a faint yellowish-red blurr. It was impossible to see where we were going to, the banks became swallowed up in the haze even when quite close to us, and the wind howled and shrieked through the young forest trees, tossing the hard, dry, rattling leaves about their ears, like a bull in a hay-field. At the inner angle of the sharper loops, where the counter current set up a sort of eddy, there were immense accumulations of fallen leaves, putting me in mind of miniature sargasso seas. Round and round they swirled in a densely-caked mass, swinging off at their extreme outer edge in a long, trailing tail, which gradually found its way back into the main current, where the leaves once more danced along until they were caught in the next eddy.

For some hours we struggled on against the gale, and were just on the point of stopping, when the Mollah declared that, if we would only have patience for one hour longer, the river would bend round to the south. And he was right; it did. And then, oh, what a change! On we flew before the wind, the banks swept past us like railway-trains, the water hissed off our bow. But it was too good to last; the river soon turned again, and once more pursued its favourite direction towards the north-east. But upon reaching a sheltered nook we pulled up and rested some hours.

After the wind slackened a bit we continued our journey. Then about twilight it dropped altogether, and as the moon came out, and converted the smooth river into a silvery highway, pointing straight towards the east, we resolved to push on still further by moonlight. I had my photographic developing-lamp lighted, so that I might be able to see the compass, chronometer, and map, without having my eyes blinded to the features of the moon-lit landscape before me. The boatmen, hovering between the faint reflection of the red light behind them and the pale blue light immediately in front of them, assumed quite a fantastic appearance, their dark silhouettes being etched with almost unearthly sharpness upon the mirk and glittering river where the moonbeams played. The banks loomed up dim and solemn against the sky on each side of us, as though they were sketched upon the landscape with the blackest of graphite ; and it was only very occasionally that a quivering rod of moonlight struggled through the intense blackness of the poplar-woods. The beauty of this scene at night, in the heart of the Asiatic solitudes, was to some extent lost upon those of the men who had to jump overboard into the river and push us off whenever we came rather too sharply into collision with the banks, as we did once or twice.

It was quite late at night when we at last stopped beside the Yekkenlik-köll, where there was an abundance of excellent fire-wood. As soon as we got a good fire started, we flung across it four whole poplar-trunks ; and as they crackled and spluttered, their vivid flames lit up the silent woods for a wide distance round, and penetrated into their deepest recesses, unveiling their mysterious secrets, and laying them bare to the cold eye of night. When, early the next morning, we pushed off from the camp, there was nothing left of the massive logs except a heap of grey smouldering ashes.

On the 20th October the bed of the Yarkand-daria continued to exhibit the same characteristic features with a truly wonderful uniformity—the same formations, the same types of curve and winding, the same sharp angles, eddies, and sandbanks as heretofore, each successively cast in precisely the same mould as its predecessors. A lace pattern could not have shown a more persistent uniformity. The banks or river terraces were 16 to 20 feet high, and very often our 20-foot punting poles were not long enough to reach to the bottom. The surface of the river was now literally patterned with leaves, which lay as thick upon it as ever they did around the forest-monastery of Vallombrosa ; and in the whirling pools where the river turned, the reed-stems writhed like snakes amongst their swirling masses.

When we came to the Masar Khojam, which stood a little way back from the river, we left Kader behind to keep watch upon the boats, and all went to visit it. The tomb commemorated the memory of a saint named Hazrett-i-Akhtam Rezi Allahu Anhu, who lived in these regions in the time of the Prophet. It consisted of a few dry clay mounds of a greyish yellow colour, surmounted by stakes bearing bunting and antelope skulls, the whole enclosed by a fence of brushwood, to prevent the sheep and cattle from profaning the sanctity of the place. On the south side it was flanked by a very primitive *khanekah*, or prayer-house, consisting of a few vertical posts covered with a simple roof, and on the east by an *ayvan*, or verandah, supported by two pillars. The building was 10 feet high and over 35 feet long, and was surrounded by a fenced-in court-yard, to which access was gained by an entrance-gate. A few gnarled and aged poplars grew in the vicinity.

The Mussulmans paid their devotions at the shrine by holding a long service, in the course of which the Mollah's deep, strong voice, reciting *Allahu ekbar!* resounded through the brooding stillness of the forest. And it cannot be denied that there was something touchingly solemn in their worship. We were engulfed by an earnest silence as of the open sea. Nothing stirred, nothing moved, except the drowsy leaves, which, touched by the faintest breath of the breeze that came through the lips of the forest, shivered as they still hung precariously by their now brittle stalks. It would be impossible to find a more peaceful place for a shrine—far away from the noisy haunts of traffickers and beside a lonely river, which was now for the first time being navigated by man. Not a sound fretted the noontide hush of the forest, except that a shy hare slipped away as we drew nigh. "La illaha el-Allah!" echoed the deep voice of the Mollah, full of earnestness and conviction, and the sound travelled a long way through the motionless poplars. The saint's memory is celebrated on a day towards the end of November by the inhabitants of Avvat, who betake themselves to his shrine in great numbers, and stay there three days, carrying provisions with them and encamping in the forest. Masar Khojam would be just the place for a hermit.

The name of our next camping place, Kalmak-kum (Sand of the Kalmucks or Mongols), proved that some time or other in the far distant past Mongols had dwelt beside this river. There we found three shepherds, with their families and some 300 sheep. My curiosity was excited by a peculiar contrivance (*tor*) they had for trapping birds of prey. It consisted of four flexible rods, stuck into the ground at the corners of a square, and bent inwards so as to hold open a sack-like net, with a hole in the middle. Immediately below the hole the hen or pigeon was tied which served as bait. As soon as the hawk tried to fly off with his booty, the elastic rods sprang apart, drawing together the opening of the sack, and in that way he was caught.

The volume of the river again dropped very considerably, only measuring 593 cubic feet in the second. The prospects of success once more began to darken.

CHAPTER IX.

THE LONELY TARIM.

THE 22nd October was quite a red-letter day in our journey, for we had the straightest piece of the river we had hitherto met with. There was only one place which occasioned us any difficulty whatever, and that was caused by the bifurcation of the stream. We chose the shorter arm, although it was considerably the smaller, and choked with drift-wood and lumber; but it turned out in places so shallow that we were forced to haul our ferry-boat after us. The temperature of the water had fallen to 10° C. or 50° Fahr., so that I had no longer any inclination for a swim. Kasim, however, held different views as to the utility of a bath; for whilst standing on the stern of the pioneer-boat, pushing it along in the usual way, he over-reached himself, and fell backwards into the river, to the unspeakable amusement of his fellow-boatmen.

Our broad highway now stretched on a long way ahead, until it disappeared in the far distance. To the eye it wore the appearance of a succession of black and white horizontal reaches, the former being the sand-banks and alluvial deposits, the latter (the white patches) the stretches of open water foreshortened.

The following day's journey, although short, brought a good deal of diversity, and compelled the men to keep their eyes well open all the time. As we drew nearer to Avvat, the shepherds increased in number, and their huts stood at pretty close intervals on both banks of the river. During the course of the day we passed the point where the Kashgar-daria (our old friend the Kizil-su) entered the Yarkand-daria by two narrow mouths, both of them for the most part choked with sand and mud and vegetation. The two together brought but a slight increase in the volume of water.

Not long after we started in the morning we perceived a horseman on the bank. No sooner did he catch sight of our flotilla than off he went and disappeared behind the bushes. He was evidently a scout sent to keep a look-out for our coming; and very soon afterwards we saw a troop of horsemen riding towards the river. They dismounted, spread carpets on the ground, and offered us *dastarkhan* of grapes, melons and bread. It turned out to be the *yoll-beghi* or road commis-

A Hunting Eagle.

sioner of Yanghi-Avvat, who had been sent to welcome us. After a short rest, we continued our journey, taking the commissioner on board with us, whilst his retinue accompanied us on the left bank.

About an hour later, behold! another band of horsemen, dressed in gay-coloured khalats, two or three of them evidently men of some distinction, and again we had to stop and partake of *dastarkhan*. This was the principal *bai* (rich man) of the Andijanliks (West Turkestan merchants) of Avvat. Him also we received on board, whilst the rest of his company rode beside us on the right. Thus we were escorted by a cavalcade on each bank; while Islam Bai on board did the honours with tea round the fire-place on the after-deck.

A little bit further on, a third body of horsemen were awaiting us on a projecting headland, which they had almost covered with various fruits, eggs, bread, and a whole slaughtered sheep. This was no other than the beg or governor of Avvat, who desired to offer us welcome in his own august person. He also came and joined the company on the after-deck, which was thus getting quite populous. What with this and the successive clusters of mounted men riding along the banks, I warrant the turbid waters of the Yarkand-daria had never in all their history witnessed a more magnificent or more imposing spectacle. Amongst the horsemen were eight falconers, two of whom carried eagles, the others falcons, all duly hooded. In this part of the world falconers form an indispensable adjunct in any formal parade or procession. Later in the day they gave us an exhibition (*tamashah*) of their birds' powers, by letting them kill four hares and a deer, all of which were presented to me.

When we came to the village of Mattan we found all its inhabitants assembled on the bank, and a little beyond there we halted for the night. The bank was so steep we had to cut steps in it to get up on *terra firma*. There we rested a whole day. Yet the time was not wasted; for I spent it in developing photographic plates, in determining the astronomical position of the place, in measuring the volume of the river, which I found to be 657 cubic feet, and in gathering information about that region generally, and about the river in particular, below the confluence of the Aksu-daria. I was told there were no hindrances down to that point, and beyond it we should find a flood, which would carry us along at a glorious pace.

After duly rewarding everybody for their services, and the beg had found for us a fresh hunter well acquainted with the country, besides a new dog called Hamrah, we plunged once more, on the 25th October, into the wilderness. The river-bed was broad and flat, but sharply defined, being inclosed between banks nine feet in height, with steeply-scarped sides, showing that they marked the extreme compass of the river when in full flood. But the actual stream, now shrunk to a mere ribbon, meandered to and fro from the one bank to the other, threading the sand-banks and alluvial deposits with which it was so thickly beset. Being shallow, it moved slowly, and was frequently divided by islands of silt. Once we took the wrong arm, and were forced to turn back, which cost us a couple of hours of valuable time. The current had now shrunk to a miserable 505 cubic feet in the second. But from the indications on the banks it was plain the river had, during that same summer, been 4½ or 5 feet higher; in other words, the flood must have attained unprecedented dimensions.

One thing, however, was in our favour—namely, in October the river usually rises again for a short time. This we were told in Mattan, and the event proved the information to be correct. The reason of this apparent anomaly is, that as water is then no longer required for irrigation higher up the river's course, the innumerable ariks and irrigation canals begin, often through the medium of springs, to restore their contents to the river from which they originally derived them, and the consequence is the stream slowly rises. On the 26th October, the volume had increased nearly 100 cubic feet—that is to say, it measured 601 cubic feet.

The 27th October was a notable day; we knew that before its close we should reach the long-hoped-for confluence of the Aksu-daria. It was a glorious autumn morning, still and peaceful, and the river glittered like a mirror, and every bush and tree was reflected on its surface with such distinctness that we had to keep lifting our eyes to the banks to distinguish the image from the reality.

The forests hereabouts were not old; all the poplars were young trees. On the other hand, there was an abundance of tamarisks and other bushes.

We were now all agog to catch the first glimpse of the big tributary, which the men of Lailik had never seen, but only heard speak of, so that they approached it with a certain amount of curiosity. "Look! when you get past those poplars—then you'll see it!" declared the Mollah; and when he proved to be wrong, he repeated his assertion, that it would be behind the next bend. Evidently he was not so well acquainted with this part of the river as he was higher up.

Meanwhile, the velocity of the current was decreasing, and at last it moved so slowly we were forced to use our punting-poles. And as the men pushed and punted they sang together in unison. Once Alim's pole stuck fast in the bottom, while the boat went on without it. But he was not to be put out by such a small matter; flinging off his clothes, he jumped in, swam to the pole, tugged it out, and then swam back to the boat with it. Yet the temperature of the water was only 9°.0 C. or 48°.2 Fahr.

In the afternoon there was a dead calm, and it grew as hot as on a summer's day, so that I took off my coat, and sat and worked in my shirt-sleeves, sniffing the fragrance of the dishes of apricots, grapes and pears which lay on a carpet at my feet. Two more hours, and the river opened out before us, and there was the noble Aksu-daria in all its majesty. "Voi! Voi!" cried the men of Lailik, as they gazed with rivetted eyes upon the mighty stream. "And are we to venture out upon that heaving flood?" they asked.

Curiously enough, immediately above the confluence the Yarkand-daria suddenly changed its direction towards the north-west. Then it was joined by the Aksu-daria, which came from the north-north-west, and the united stream assumed an easterly direction. From this point the river assumed the name of the Tarim; although it was likewise known as the Yarkand-daria as far as the Lop country. So far as the direction of the conjoint river was concerned, it was the Aksu which exercised the preponderating influence; and from what the natives told me, it must, at all seasons of the year, be the more powerful stream of the two.

Leaving the last projecting point of the Yarkand-daria on our right, we now crossed over to the left bank. During the last hundred yards or so the current of the Yarkand-daria had not only ceased to move, it was in some places even turned back, owing to the more powerful pressure of the Aksu-daria. We came within an ace of being caught in one of these back-flows; but just in the nick of time the men managed to get on shore and moor the boat, otherwise we should infallibly have been swept into the vortex. It was my purpose to halt here at the confluence of these two rivers—Yarkand-darianing-kuilyshi—to investigate the channel more minutely before proceeding further.

I utilized the holiday for various purposes. Amongst other things, I determined the astronomical position of the confluence; developed and copied negatives, and took others; and made an excursion in the skiff to sound the most convenient channel for our elephantine craft, a task which occupied me until long after midnight. The water in the big river was very turbid

Our Landing at the Confluence of the Aksu-daria.

as compared with that of the Yarkand-daria, which had gradually cleared as a consequence of its long, slow fall. Vast flocks of wild geese, all ordered in wedge-like battalions, perfectly marvellous in their regularity and "dressing," flew overhead, with a few skirmishers thrown out between the compacter masses. The long journeys which these sagacious creatures make, all the way from Lop-nor *viâ* the Yarkand-daria to India, have always excited in me the utmost admiration and wonder. They flew at an altitude of 600 or 700 feet above the earth, and kept up an incessant screaming as they flew. There seemed that day to be no end to them. No sooner had one battalion dwindled to a mere speck on the verge of the horizon, than up there hurtled another, all from the east, and all screaming vociferously. Perhaps they are like the rain-water that falls in the mountains, impelled by some imperious power which Nature has implanted in them and which they are constrained to obey like automata. But I prefer to think that the meaning of their incessant "snattering" is that they are discussing the route they should pursue, and where the next resting-place is to be, and what the dangers are which threaten them. Anyway, I always followed them with yearning eyes, as on unwearied wing they soared on and on, high up above the trials of earthly life.

When, on the morning of the 29th, we pushed off from land, the boatmen's "Bismillah!" rang out with greater emphasis than usual, and each man stood at his post with muscles strained and knuckles whitening under the resolute grip with which he held his punting-pole. However, it was not so dangerous as they imagined. It is true our craft was seized in a sort of eddy, and given a good spin; but after that, she proceeded on her way as sedately as heretofore. At first the velocity was as much as 2¾ miles an hour, but later on it decreased. The river-bed, however, made such a wide gap in the earth, and its steep banks were so far apart, that the woods which lined them looked like mere black lines on the horizon.

Not long after we started we came to the ferry where the great highway between Khotan and Aksu crossed the Tarim by means of a boat, which was capable of carrying over six camels at once.

In the evening a flock of wild geese dropped into the river a short distance from our camp. They chattered and ducked and splashed, till the air rang again with their hubbub. But when we arose next morning they were already gone, except one solitary bird, which, exhausted by the fatigues of the journey, had lingered behind ; but it, too, rose, and flying low and screaming anxiously, struggled on westwards in the track of its companions.

At several places along the steeply-scarped banks we observed traps for catching fish. They consisted of a sack-like net or big basket, into which the fish were drawn by means of a long enclosure or passage made of rods stuck vertically into the river-bottom.

The next day the river was wonderfully straight ; not one of its angles was as sharp as 90°, but all were obtuse and elongated. Hence the fair-way was very little longer than the track which ran along its left bank to Shah-yar. The latter crossed on its way a narrow belt of sand, called Kizil-kum, the dunes of which were visible from the river.

Shortly before twilight came on, I began to keep a sharp look-out to my right—that is to say, to the south—so as not to go past the mouth of the Khotan-daria without observing it. At length a wide gap showed itself in the young forest, and through it ran a broad river-bed, five or six feet above the level of the Aksu-daria, and now perfectly dry and deserted. During the short season in which the Khotan-daria does carry water, it is said to swell to a really large river ; and this seemed to be borne out by facts, for the Tarim, just below its confluence, was considerably broader, and there was also a much larger deposit of alluvium. The direction of the main river was however in no sense influenced by its affluent. The latter again called to my mind my ill-omened journey across the desert in 1895 ; but I looked upon the Khotan-daria as a friend that had once saved my life.

The country thereabouts was flat and open, and very uniform. All its features were moulded on the grand scale. The water surfaces were wide-spread, the alluvial formations exceptionally extensive, the river-banks more than half-a-mile apart, and the forests so far distant from the middle of the Tarim that we had much ado to hear the noontide breeze as it swept through their poplars. In the immediate vicinity of the banks the region consisted of kamish (reed) steppes, intermingled with tamarisks, tussock grass, and scrub, with only a very occasional group of aged poplars.

The boatmen were in good heart, and observed with the

greatest interest the new world which was unrolling itself before their eyes. The yoll-beghi accompanied us, and as he sat in front of my tent he plied me with valuable information about the locality, the names of the topographical features, the shepherds, the villages, the variations in the volume of the river at the different seasons of the year. Our new dog, Hamrah, was gradually reconciling himself to his fate, and making himself at home. He condescended to honour Yolldash with his company at meal times, but would not yet condescend to play with him. One of the cocks had learned to come and sit on the ridge-pole of my tent to crow, and the hens often paid a visit to the big ferry-boat, where they wandered about as they pleased, picking up what they could.

The boat glided so swiftly down the broad highway of the mighty river, that it was a good way on into the night when we stopped, though it was not without difficulty we did so, beside a precipitous bank. Whilst the boatmen were sitting round the fire their loud and animated conversation became blended with peculiar sounds from the forest. In answer to my inquiry, they told me it was a vixen's whelps which had lost their mother and were now seeking for her.

The instruments showed that we had here a volume of 2,797 cubic feet, but that the depth was less than in the lower course of the Yarkand-daria—namely, barely over 6½ feet.

On the morning of the 31st October, the surface of the river was slightly crumpled; but we put off and once more drifted away down the great and lonely Tarim. But before we got very far from the silted reed-beds, where we had stopped for the night, the wind freshened, and within a short time it was blowing an uncommonly stiff gale. I was wearing proper winter attire—furs, felts, and felt-boots—but was soon chilled to the bone by that treacherous wind, which drove straight into the tent, threatening to tear the canvas loose and waft it away like a balloon. My fingers became stiff and numb, and I could not use my pen with the precision I desired; I had to get up every now and then and rub them, as well as stamp to keep myself warm generally. Owing to the broad and open character of the river, the wind swept along it with unmitigated force. Yesterday the water was as smooth as glass; to-day it was churned into foam-crested waves, which struck against the prow of our big craft with such violence that they made the old hulk shiver from end to end. Both banks were enveloped in a yellowish-grey mist, a smoke of fine dust, which the wind scooped up from the earth. As the tent threatened to go altogether, and as the stream, powerful though it was, made no headway against the wind, I commanded a halt, although we had only been travelling a couple of hours.

As soon as we had effected a landing, and made a fire and warmed ourselves, I hoisted sail on my little English skiff, and, to the amazement of the Lailik boatmen, went spinning back along the way we had come. And brave little thing that she was, she literally flew like a bird; the worst gusts seemed to lift her so that her keel just skimmed along the surface. I went over a sandy shallow as though it were nothing at all. The mast creaked, the steering-oar was strained; but it was perfectly glorious to be driving through the sublime solitudes of Asia before the fierceness of that uncurbed tempest. The ferry-boat was soon lost to sight behind a projecting headland. There were none to bear me company except the hissing waves and the yellowing woods and the unloosed fury of the wind. A feeling of supreme content came over me. I felt as though the unbounded spaces of the desert belonged to me, and as though, despite Chinese mandarins and Turkestan begs, I could order everything as I pleased. The wind whispered into my ears that that mighty river had flowed on and on, century after century, for thousands of years, waiting for me to come and wrest from it its dearest secrets; that it was a Higher Will which bade the Tarim wind its smooth highway through the desert, and so offer me an easy passage to the hidden heart of that vast continent. Who was there to dispute with me the ownership of that entrancing stream? The shepherds, may be, who pastured their flocks along its banks, and fled like frightened antelopes when we shot noiselessly upon their sight from behind a jutting headland. Who was there to stop us and demand from us toll and pass? The tigers, maybe, whose emerald green eyes gleamed out upon us at night from among the leaves of the dark tamarisk thickets. No man knew the river better than I did. The native hunters, the half-civilized children of the wild woods, whom we picked up one day and dropped the next as soon as their topographical knowledge came to an end—perhaps they knew better? Nay, not so. Their knowledge only extended as far as they were wont to range in their hunting excursions in pursuit of the flying deer; but beyond the well-known land-marks all was guesswork. They knew neither where the great river came from, nor whither it was carrying its never-ending flood. I, on the contrary, gathered into my diary everything that the natives knew about it. I lived with the restlessly changing river, mile by mile, and yard by yard; every evening I felt its pulse and took the measure of its life-blood in feet and inches; and though I knew that the river which had flowed on there for thousands of years was always the self-same river, yet I also knew that from time to time it changed its bed, as well as that, after it had hurried on to its dissolution in the far-distant Lop-nor, it was nevertheless destined to rise again transformed, and so repeat again and again its periodic circulation between heaven and earth and earth and heaven. I was as it were the archives in which the life-history of the Tarim was deposited in word, picture, and map, and not one day passed without that material being augmented, growing slowly into a monograph on one of the greatest of Asiatic rivers, of which these chapters give but a small portion.

When you are flying along before such a wind as that you are apt to be forgetful of the rapidly increasing distance behind you. At length, however, I did awaken from my dreams. Steering in towards the nearest bank, I drew my boat ashore and made her fast, and then, penetrating a little way into the forest, I made a fire and ate the *déjeuner* I had brought with me.

As I drifted slowly back with the current, my thoughts ran upon the immediate future, which presented itself before me in the brightest colours. What experiences destiny had in store for me, I knew not; but one thing I did know, that if an enterprise is to succeed it must be planned with prudence and foresight. And as I thus thought, a host of questions pressed in upon me. Should I get through with my purpose before the winter set in? Where should I establish my standing camp, which was to serve as a base for the various expeditions I had in view? Would the jighits succeed in finding me? Would it be good news they would bring me from home?

I got back on board, and set to work to copy negatives. As a matter of precaution I wanted to have two prints of every photograph I took, as well as two copies of the notes and other observations I made. For example, during the day I jotted down my observations with pencil, in small pocket-books, and then copied them out again in the evening into my diary in ink. As for the sheets of my map, I copied them over again as I went along, in the intervals between recording the successive compass-bearings. All this, of course, caused me a great deal of extra labour, but at the same time it inspired me with a feeling of confidence; one set of my work would surely get home safely.

The only thing which sorely tried my patience was the wind, or rather the fact that the wind was so often against us. On the 1st of November the river turned to the north, and—the wind, too, blew from the north. All day long the tent sheltered me, although the sun would now have been very welcome, for even with a temperature of 10° C. or 50° Fahr. in the afternoon, the air was decidedly raw and cold. During the night, however, the thermometer dropped to −8°.8 C. or 16°.2 Fahr., and the water which stood beside my bed, as well as the ink in my inkstand, was frozen, and oh! it made me shiver to creep in between the icy sheets. It would, of course, have been a simple thing to have put a stove in the tent, but I held off from it as long as I possibly could, I did not want to disturb the self-registering instruments.

At a place called Dolan-kemizi we found an unwieldy little ferry-boat, built of poplar-trunks and steered by a broad-bladed oar over the stern. But no sooner did the ferry-man, who lived in a hut on the bank, catch sight of us than he took to his heels and ran off as fast as he could put foot to ground. Three bais who lived in that part of the country owned between them no less than 10,000 sheep, and the ferry-boat was for the purpose of conveying the animals and their wool across the Tarim.

When we came to the district of Kara-tograk, the river shallowed, and was churned into foam as it plunged down the successive ledges, that were formed in its bed. Here we raced along at a dizzy rate, and were making straight for a projecting headland, where a violent collision seemed inevitable, when we were saved by the current itself swerving to one side, so that we merely grazed the branches of some tamarisks which hung out over the stream. It was a near thing, and I was not sorry to see the bank receding behind us, as we swung off towards the middle of the Tarim.

Immediately adjacent to the river the banks were overgrown with reeds, and a little way back from them, and parallel to them, ran a belt of poplars. Below Kara-tograk the Tarim straightened its course in a way it had never hitherto done;

for it stretched away towards the north-north-east in an almost imperceptible curve, framed in on both sides by yellow lines of reed-beds; while in the far-off distance it seemed to blend with the sky and spread out its waters through all the immeasurable spaces of the world.

During the past few days we had observed that the river rose a little; this was due, as I have already explained, to the re-opening of the ariks and irrigation canals. In two or three places the sand-dunes advanced quite close to the bank, and then broke off abruptly almost as it were hanging over the water. Here it was possible to see with what fierce energy the powerful current undermined them, as one huge avalanche of sand after another was precipitated into the flood below. In those places where the banks consisted of clay, they were not only often perfectly vertical, but sometimes even hung over the water. Once, just as we were skirting one of these impending eaves of clay, the mass broke off and soused plump into the river, drenching the whole of that side of our boat, and setting up such a succession of waves that the heavy colossus fairly rocked on her keel. Again and again we heard what sounded like the booming of heavy guns from some distant fortress; it was these clay avalanches taking their final plunge into the torrent below.

At Leshlik, where we encamped that evening, the boatmen amused themselves with a comical spectacle or game. Two of them took each a companion on his back. The hands and feet of the rider were tied, while the man who carried him took a stick and began to dust away as hard as he could on the back of the opposing cavalier. The riders, bound and helpless, grew angry, and began to abuse one another, each egging on his bearer to give his opponent what for. This exhortation they, nothing loth, zealously strove to fulfil; and when one of them managed to get a good opportunity, his stick went like lightning. Whereupon the victim eagerly called upon *his* walloper to go in and give him (the rider) his revenge. And so they went at it, first one and then the other, until the two riders both got their jackets thoroughly well dusted. Now Palta and Naser were the "steeds," while Kasim and Alim acted the part of riders, and consequently it was their garments upon which these delicate attentions were bestowed. The former laughed until the tears came into their eyes; while Kasim and Alim howled with rage. As for the onlookers, of whom I was one, we literally split our sides with laughter. Kasim and Alim, wishing to have their revenge, proposed to exchange places with their "steeds," and try the game again. But the other two men objected; they had laid on in pretty good earnest, and they no doubt thought that, in this case at any rate, it was better to give than to receive. The game brought, however, one advantage with it; it thoroughly warmed all who participated in it; and in the light of our big red-blazing fire the figures of the men and their ludicrous motions were highly comical to look at.

CHAPTER X

FIRST SIGNS OF WINTER.

THE temperature of both air and water was slowly but steadily falling; clearly the day was not very far distant when we should find ice drifting on the surface of the river. On the banks, the moist places which had been recently flooded were already frozen hard in the morning, though they thawed again during the course of the day. The cold, however, in no way affected the crew in the after-part of the ferry-boat. They used to make up a big fire and sit round it in their new sheepskin coats, and gossip, tell tales, listen to Kader as he read to them, and bake their bread. The boatmen also took turns in going there to warm themselves; but it was only when we came to a long, straight stretch of river that I was able to leave my writing-table and follow their example.

In the still, cold morning air, when sounds rang out sharply and travelled a long way over the water, we heard what seemed like whole rows of houses being pulled down; but it was only the avalanches of sand and silt, which, after freezing during the night, now became loosened as they thawed, and tumbled headlong into the river. We went along at a glorious pace, leaving the banks rapidly behind us, while small cataracts became more and more frequent.

Kasim as usual led the way in the smaller ferry-boat, and kept constantly calling back to warn us of shallows, snags, tottering avalanches of sand or silt or clay—everything, in fact, which seemed likely to cause us trouble. Palta was the navigating lieutenant of the other ferry-boat. He was always cool and collected, and never lost his good humour, except when some manœuvre had to be hurriedly carried out to avoid a collision, and then he bellowed like a bull of Bashan at his mates on the after-deck. The other men placed the most implicit reliance upon his skill, because for several years past he had had charge of the ferry between Lailik and Merket.

But this day none of them got any rest; the Tarim swept along so fast that every man had to be constantly at his post, his eyes intent upon the river and his punting-pole in his hand, ready for any emergency. Only once, however, did they fail; that was in a sharp elbow, where the current took the bit between its teeth and drove in straight upon the steep, high bank. In such cases the crew were wont to hold off the prow with their poles, bring the boat to a sharp angle with the strand, and then swing her stern round till she came parallel with the current. But on this occasion they failed; the current was too swift for them; we were travelling at the rate of nearly three miles an hour. Bang against the bank went the boat, butting at it with all her might. Apart, however, from one or two somersaults, and a few shovelsful of earth dropping on board, no harm was done.

After we passed the forest-dune of Balik-ölldi (the Dead Fish) the velocity of the stream was still further increased. Three years ago the river, leaving the Kona-daria (the old bed), together with its forest-belts, on the left, carved for itself a new channel of close upon two days' journey in length.

Upon entering its new channel the river completely altered its character. It became narrow and straight, and had every appearance of not having yet completed its work of erosion. The country through which it ploughed its way was utterly barren, the soil being sand; the only relief to the prevailing desolation was an occasional poplar and a few tamarisk groves. The margins of the new channel were defined with the greatest distinctness, making a straight, deep, narrow trough, completely filled from side to side with water. All along the sand was continually tumbling down the precipitous slopes, so that a cloud of smoke, as it were, hung over each bank. We were several times in danger of being swamped by these sand avalanches, and once at least the men on the after-deck got a thorough good splashing as a huge mass toppled into the water close beside them. And as the current was swifter than ever it had been before, the greatest vigilance and care were called for on our part to prevent a catastrophe. In fact, we felt rather helpless.

All at once we heard a desperate shout from Kasim, "Stop! stop!" The river was not more than a chain wide, and in the

Our Camp at Ala Kunglei Buzrugvar.

very middle of the fair-way a poplar stem was stuck fast in the bottom, and around it a large quantity of driftwood, reeds, and other flotsam had accumulated, making a small island. In fact, driftwood and so forth was generally more abundant in these new-made arms than in the older parts of the river, owing to the fact that every scrap of brushwood which was carried into the water along with the crumbling banks was swept down by the current; though this was not always the case elsewhere. The flood chafed against the impediment in its path till it was white with foam and tossing spray. Had the ferry-boat come into contact with that snag, it would infallibly have been swung round, wedged fast, and capsized. We were only 50 or 60 yards from the dangerous point, and an upset seemed unavoidable. I sat with my heart in my mouth, wondering if the expedition was to be shipwrecked in this boiling cauldron. The men shouted backwards and forwards, and there was a fearful uproar on board. But at the last moment Alim managed to jump ashore with a line, although, owing to the steepness of the bank, he as near as nothing fell back headlong into the river. But he recovered himself, and scrambling on to firmer ground began to haul away with all his might, while the other men helped him all they were able by pushing vigorously against the stream, shouting frantically, "Ya Allah! Ya Allah!" The lumbering craft came to a stop a few feet above the poplar, and as she hung amidstream the river boiled and heaved along her sides.

While the men were getting the big craft into form to pass this dangerous obstacle, I stepped into the skiff, and anchoring it in the middle of the river, proceeded to take the velocity. But the suction of the current was so strong, it was not easy to keep my balance. Indeed I came within an ace of going overboard; while the boat half filled with water, and my map-sheet got saturated. For the moment the anchor bit in the bottom, the skiff heeled over so much that she came broadside on to the current, but as soon as the rope which was attached to the anchor was pulled round to the bow, she straightened herself into line with the stream, and there hung, swinging to and fro like a pendulum, while a seething eddy gurgled away on each side of her bow. The velocity was over $3\frac{3}{4}$ miles an hour; and this rate was maintained all the next day.

After this no further incident occurred whilst we were travelling through this desolate region, which, to judge from the character of its banks, was a close neighbour of the great desert of sand which lay to the south. Hunters going in that direction were said occasionally to come across the tracks of wild camels not far from this Yanghi-daria (new river); but those shy denizens of the desert never showed themselves at the river itself.

Upon reaching the masar of Ala Kunglei Buzrugvar, where some shepherds were dwelling, we deemed it advisable to stop for the night, especially as the men wanted to go up to the shrine to thank the saint for having brought them safely through the perils of the day. It was, however, anything but easy to stop our leviathan in full career. I put to shore in the skiff; then Alim flung me a line, at which I hauled away until I got the big boat so close in to the bank that he was able to jump out and take the line from me. And even when our clumsy craft was moored fast to the bank, her old timbers creaked and groaned, and the water splashed and gurgled against the skiff which lay fastened under her stern. The avalanches thundered down the banks, the sand whistling as it trickled after them, and the fire on shore crackled and hissed; but except for these things the entire neighbourhood was wrapped in peace, especially as the dogs were still, there being literally nothing for them to bark at.

The banks here rose 15 feet above the actual level of the stream, while the high-water line was five feet higher still. During the night the river rose half an inch; its transparency extended down to only $2\frac{1}{8}$ inches.

The next day the Tarim was not quite so straight, but the velocity still remained the same. The chief danger we had to guard against was the back-current in the sharp elbows. In one of these the skiff was on the point of being crushed between the two bigger boats, but I managed to save her just in the nick of time. Very early that morning we had our first glimpse of ice, on a small sheltered pool on the bank.

Before the day was over we came, on the left, to the reunion of the Yanghi-daria and the Kona-daria, and after that the stream reverted to its normal character. A short distance below the confluence the river embraced a small reed-grown islet, which, with its perpendicular edges, looked like a river-fortress. We encamped for the night at Tellpel, where dwelt nine shepherds, with their families, in charge of 8,000 sheep.

The shepherds in this part of the country used a different

Fishing Apparatus on the Tarim, as used at Tellpel.

sort of fishing apparatus from that which I have described above. It consisted of a net stretched fanwise on a light, triangular framework of rods, and was fastened so as to hang outspread just above the surface of the water, while by means of a line going back to land, it could be raised or lowered at will. When the net was let down and spread out the fish were frightened into it, and it was then closed by means of the side-rods, then whirled round like a paper-poke for sweets, and hauled up to land.

The yoll-beghi had now left us; but at Tellpel we picked up a fine old fellow named Mollah Faisullah, who was 54 years of age, had a big white beard, wore horn spectacles, of Brobdingnagian dimensions, and was always cheerful and talkative, and read aloud to the men on the after-deck. He was invaluable.

On the 4th and 5th November the river once more altered its character, becoming narrow and violent, with a sharply defined channel. On both sides it was bordered by a vast steppe of yellow reeds, amid which a few solitary sand-dunes bearing tamarisks stood out like islands. It was, in fact, something intermediate between an old and a new-formed bed; indeed, I was told it was some eight years old. The name of the old course, which the stream abandoned eight years before, was Kök-chöll-dariasi. All this showed that the Tarim does change its course, though in these longitudes for short distances only. At the same time it was interesting to notice that whenever it did so, it always left the old channel to the north, or, in other words, shifted to the right.

One thing which contributed to relieve the monotony on board was the doings of our dogs. Sometimes they would jump overboard, swim to land, and accompany the flotilla the whole day long on the bank. But they never succeeded in learning the laws which determined the river's course. When the ferry-boat drifted along the inner side of an elbow or curve they kept close beside it; but when it was carried by the current right across to the inner side of the next elbow near the opposite bank, they always took to the water, and swam across, so as to remain in our immediate vicinity. This manœuvre they repeated time after time; it was impossible to make them understand that if only they waited we were bound to come back to them again. Some days they crossed the river a score of times, and became so done up that they howled from sheer weariness. Yolldash was killing as he splashed about, gasping for breath, and spluttering to get the water out of his throat.

At Initshkeh the river had a volume of 2,847 cubic feet in the second, and it was easy to see it was slowly rising; in one night, indeed, it rose two inches. This measurement took me a good three hours to accomplish, and had to be made by the light of a lantern. The river was too wide to allow of a rope being stretched from bank to bank in the usual way, to which to fasten the skiff. In fact, the current was too violent —3¼ miles an hour—we could not get the rope across at all. I tried to row across, but had to give it up. Instead of a rope we flung across a thin piece of sail-twine, divided by white knots, and at every knot anchored the skiff and took our measurement.

During the night of the 4th and 5th November the river rose another inch; and the banks were here 16¾ feet high. The Tarim turned again towards the north-east. On a sandy tongue of alluvium at Hässemet-tokai a dozen big vultures, clumsy birds of a dark-brownish grey, almost black, in fact, sat and watched our approach, merely turning their heads like sun-flowers as we slowly circled round the projecting headland on which they were assembled. What brought them there was the carcase of a horse, which lay half out of the water in an angle of the river. Most of the flesh was already devoured, and the foul birds appeared to be sated; for they had flown a little way off, and were digesting what they had gorged upon, in company with two or three unabashed ravens. A little lower down we passed a couple of score more vultures, sitting immovably on the leafless branches of some dead poplars. There they perched, in the stunted forest, like spirits of the infernal regions or the harpies of death, their weird aspect being quite in keeping with the Stygian scrub and air of desolation which marked their surroundings. It was a much pleasanter sight to watch the wild-geese sailing through the air in their irreproachable phalanxes, a single bird in the van and the others trailing out behind it like an arrow-head, except that one of the barbs was generally longer than the other.

Another characteristic of this part of the Tarim was the large quantity of driftwood which floated on its surface, and of poplar-stems which stuck up snag-like from the mud at its bottom. Several of the latter would eventually sink; others were just on the point of breaking off and floating away. As only one end was fast in the mud, the other lay along the surface, where it wriggled and nodded like a water-snake swimming towards us. But what deceived us was the eddy, caused by the current striking against the impediment. It was not the poplar, but we who were moving, and as we drifted over it we could hear it snapping like a water-ogre down below.

On the 6th November we picked up a fresh guide at the sheep-fold of Bostan. All the same, we still kept old Mollah Faisullah on board, for he was cheerful and amusing, and read to the other men stories about the deeds and sufferings of imams and heroes, and about fabulous cities, each with a thousand gates, and a thousand watchmen beside each gate. The people of Bostan wanted to give us some melons; but we declined them, melons were too tender to stand the frosty nights.

This day the river made only one bend, but that was a double one, like the letter S, with an island in the one loop and deposits of mud in the other. At Dung-kotan the banks presented a very curious formation, owing to the river having washed away or cut in half the poplar-studded sand-dunes which there touched it. They looked like so many gigantic prompters' boxes. The tree-roots stretched obliquely down the steep banks and were rooted in the bottom of the river, so that they resembled taut violin strings or nets set to catch fish

We camped that night at Kara-dashi, not very far from the place where, in 1896, we first found water after our dangerous journey across the desert north of the Keriya-daria.

Next day we observed several reed-huts, and even houses of clay, and occasionally a canoe moored to the bank, clear indications that we were once more drawing near to inhabited regions. The canoes now began to resemble somewhat those which I remembered in the Lop country, being long and narrow. hewn out of a single poplar; but in contrast to the Lop canoes their fore-part was prolonged into a sort of perforated handle, and the stern formed a little platform on which a man could sit. The paddle, by which they were propelled, was shovel-shaped.

My boatmen appropriated a tiny specimen of these craft, in which Alim gave us quite an exhibition. No matter how he paddled the thing, it would not go straight forward, and, in spite of his frantic efforts to balance and control it, gave him many a lurch now to one side, now to the other. When we reached

Chong-aral, the men exchanged it for a larger one. For it was by no means our intention to steal the canoe, and so levy a contribution upon the peaceful inhabitants of the river-side; we desired to pay for it, and did pay for it later on in the afternoon. After that Islam and the Mollah travelled in the canoe, which thus added another vessel to our flotilla.

The country hereabouts was extraordinarily open. The woods receded so far apart as to appear mere black lines on the horizon. It was only very occasionally that a solitary poplar broke the dead level of the interminable reed-beds which fringed the banks.

A branch of the Shah-yar-daria (Mus-art), which came from Khan-tengri, entered the Yarkand-daria from the left in the district of Gädyiz. It was 95 feet wide at the actual confluence, and apparently preserved the same breadth as high up as we were able to see. Its bed was filled with stagnant water, beautifully clear and of a blue colour, and transparent to a depth of 30¾ inches, whereas the Tarim was transparent to a depth of 1½ inches only. The dividing-line between the two was very sharply drawn, the muddy water merely flushing and clouding the clear. The fact is, the arm of the Shah-yar-daria, with its standing water, formed virtually a continuation of the containing bank of the Tarim, which accordingly merely brushed against it in passing.

Whilst I was engaged examining this affluent from the skiff, an old man arrived, wearing a violet chapan, and attended by several other persons, and offered me his services; he was the yoll-beghi, or road-commissioner of Chimen. And he brought with him letters from Niaz Hadji and the Cossacks, reporting all well with the caravan.

When we reached the village of Terez, we found a great quantity of gifts in kind awaiting our arrival, such as sheep, fruits, two boxes of pears from Kuchar, a box of pomegranates, besides hares, pheasants, hens, eggs, and milk—a very welcome replenishment of our commissariat. Our vehicle of travel had this advantage over camels, that, no matter how heavily we loaded it, it never murmured, and went just as well, and just as far in the day, equally whether heavily or lightly laden.

That night we encamped at the point where the river was crossed by the high road from Kara-dash and Kungarchak-bel to Chimen, Shah-yar, and Kuchar, the very place, in fact, where I forded the river on the ice in 1896. Khalil Bai, the same honest old man who gave me the hospitality of his house on that occasion, now came to meet me, in spite of his seventy-three years, supporting himself on a long staff. I was always pleased to see the old friends of my previous journey; accordingly I sat and talked with the old man beside the fire for a long time.

At Chimen we rested two days, which I partly employed in determining the position of the place astronomically, in measuring the volume of the river (2,454¾ cubic feet), and in getting through various arrears of work. Here also we were found by Abdurrahman, the first of the jighits or couriers from Kashgar, who brought me nothing but the best of news in his

Canoes on the Middle Tarim.

sealed post-bag. I sent him back to Kashgar with my own letters, and at the same time gave him a hermetically soldered tin-box containing negatives. Further, I engaged a fresh hunter as guide, and bought a supply of oil in case it became necessary to continue our journey at night by lamplight.

The 10th November was the first real winter's day we had. The morning was bitterly cold, a moist fog clung to the earth, and only disappeared after a determined wind got up in the south-west. The ground was white with rime-frost, as also were the ferry-boat and its black cabin. The air was grey and misty, the sky obscured with clouds, the entire landscape clothed in the cold blue-white tones of winter. Fortunately, I had left the last negatives I developed the night before lying in the bath-trays, which were only just frozen on the surface. Had I set them up in the frames to dry they would have been frozen, and so ruined. It was not until after 11 o'clock that the thermometer rose above freezing-point, so that I judged it wise to warm the dark room a little, to prevent the negatives from freezing whilst they were drying. At 10 o'clock in the morning the thermometer stood at −2°.0 C., or 28°.4 Fahr., and at five o'clock at −1°.0 C., or 30°.2 Fahr.; it was above the freezing-point not more than five hours altogether. The outlook for a successful termination of my project began to look dark; for if the river began to freeze now, we were hardly likely to reach the end of the journey before we got fast in the ice. Meanwhile we were all longing to get away from Chimen, which not only stood in an open and exposed situation, swept by every wind and every storm, but was in a bare country, where firewood was a scarce commodity. Abdurrahman the courier was taken across the river in a canoe, with his horse swimming beside him; poor beast, I pitied it on such a cold morning! But I confess I was quite relieved when I saw the man safe on the other side, with my precious packets in his hands.

The beg of Shah-yar, who had come with a mounted retinue to pay his respects to me, gave me a present of a new dog, a most comical little pup called Dovlet, who looked like a fox and was a veritable four-legged clown. From the very first he proved himself an excellent watch-dog, and was at once established as the prime favourite of all the two-legged passengers on board, except the cock.

My old friend Khalil Bai, in return for a present I had given him, was anxious to show his sense of politeness by accompanying us on horseback to our next encampment. But we induced him to take his place in the circle which sat around the blazing fire on the after-deck; but even there he shivered with cold, and longed for the great camp-fire of the evening.

Lifting anchor, then, we glided softly away from the shore and the people gathered on it, and were soon carried by the strong wind out of sight of their wondering eyes. The flotilla numbered four vessels. As we generally had two guides with us now, I directed one of them to lead the way in the canoe. He was followed by Kasim in the heavily-laden commissariat boat. Favoured by the south-west wind, we made a long day's journey. The open river-bed wound away towards the east,

The Beg of Shah-yar and his Attendants Waiting to Receive us at Chimen. The Ferry-boat on the Left.

and except for the patches of forest which it occasionally brushed against on either side, it ran through a region of unbroken kamish steppe, intermingled with extensive high-water alluvial deposits.

On the 11th November we passed several shepherds' camps, the sheep belonging to the bais of Shah-yar; and on the 12th the woods along the banks began to be more plentiful and more beautiful. Every morning now every sheltered nook and side channel was frozen over, and sometimes we saw thin cakes of ice, which had been formed close to the bank, swimming down the stream.

Our Pilot-canoes from Chimen.

In this part of its course the river was called Ughen or Öghen, also Terem or Tarim. The canoes which now dotted its banks were made on precisely the same pattern as those of the Lop country. Every day thousands of wild-geese passed westwards over our heads. In all probability these were the last of the pilgrims, warned to make a hasty departure by the rapid approach of the wintry cold. There was now scarcely a leaf left on the poplars; they had put off their autumn attire, and stood bare and naked, awaiting winter's approach. The fallen leaves lay on the banks in heaps and rustled quite crisply under the wayfarer's footsteps.

On the following day, in a sharp north-going loop, we passed the confluence of the Inchikkeh-daria, coming in from the left. In the tent it turned so bitterly cold that, in order to obtain some advantage from the sun's warmth, I transferred myself to the skiff. The temperature of the water at midday was only $3\frac{1}{2}°$ above freezing-point; and the long punting-poles were cased with ice. Every angle which the midday sun was unable to penetrate into was fringed with a margin of ice a foot broad and half an inch thick. As a rule it hung out a little above the surface of the water, the river having dropped since it was formed. The main mass of the forest stood however somewhat back from the margin of the river, and only sent a few outposts close up to it. That evening we had to hunt for some time in the darkness before we hit upon a suitable camping-ground. Islam and Naser were put ashore, and went off on foot, and it was getting quite late before we saw their signal-fire blazing up in the distance. They had pitched upon a place where an old *sattma* (shepherd's hut) stood, and, banishing all respect for the crazy affair and its owner, had used up the materials of which it was built to feed their fire with.

Our days now passed quietly, peacefully, and monotonously. The advent of winter made scarce any difference in our manner of life. The chief thing was, that we now wanted a larger supply of firewood; but our caterer in this respect was not at all stingy, if only we took care to choose a proper place for camping in. Young forest was no use; it must be dry wood. I was not wakened now until half-past six, and it was no joke to tumble out and struggle into your icy clothes in about 20° of frost. Under these circumstances dressing was performed with the utmost dispatch, the niceties of the toilet being accurately proportioned to the number of degrees registered by the thermometer. But this proceeding over, and the first series of meteorological observations taken by seven o'clock, it was quite a pleasure to hurry up to the fire, which crackled right cheerfully in the grey of the morning. As I stepped on shore I was received from every side with friendly and polite greetings of "Salaam aleikum!" At that hour the men were generally busy over their breakfast, which consisted of boiled mutton, with bouillon, into which bread was crumbled, and tea. As I sat by the fire, I usually had my breakfast too. After that I measured the banks, and when all was ready, and the men were thoroughly awake, I cried "Mangeleh!" (Let us go!), and in a minute the mooring-ropes were loosened, the poles were in the water, and off went the big boat again on her long and lonely journey down the Tarim.

Fortunately, the river was now so deep that we very seldom ran aground, and when we did so we were mostly able to get off again by using the punting-poles. The after-deck of the big ferry-boat presented quite a picturesque scene—boatmen, sheep, poultry, sacks, and packing-cases, all mixed together in any sort of order, while the column of smoke from their fire trailing down the river behind us invested our imposing craft with the fictitious dignity of a steamboat. It was on the after-deck the men baked their bread, there they dried my wet clothes on an outstretched rope, there they washed their dishes, and there they made such implements and household utensils as they needed. Naser was employed in shaping with his axe a specially long-bladed punting-pole, with which to prize out the ferry-boat when she got into a back-current. Kasim and Kader had somehow somewhere got possession of a couple of canoes, with which they manœuvred the commissariat boat, when their punting-poles failed to reach the bottom. When the time hung heavy on their hands, one of them would start a song, in which all joined, and very tuneful their voices sounded amid the great silence of the woods. But towards evening their songs would die away; they began to long for the rousing, roaring camp-fire. But we usually continued a good while after sunset, steering our course by the light of the moon. There was neither fire nor light on these deserted banks, except the feeble gleam which the fire on our own after-deck shed upon the reeds at their margins, while on the river the moon's rays broke on the curling eddies which dimpled its surface.

When at length I called "Indi toktamiss!" (Now we will stop), everybody on board at once woke up. The ferry-boat was made fast. A few brands were carried on shore to light the camp fire, followed by such cooking-pots as were required. Then the *ash*, or rice-pudding, was mixed with pieces of meat and vegetables in a huge pan. After that another of the men took ashore the box containing my dinner ware. The tea, seasonings, and jams were set out near the fire. As all the ingredients for the ash had been already prepared on board, it was not long before Islam came to announce that "Ash tayyar!" (Dinner is ready). Nor did the men tarry long before they donned their sheepskins, and arranged themselves in a circle round the fire. So long as the flames were strong and high, their only concern was to protect their backs; but when they grew sleepy, they pulled the sheepskins closer round them, crept in nearer to the dying fire, which they left to take its chance through the night, and were always industriously snoring away a good long time before I had finished jotting down my notes and writing up my diary, and was able to follow their example.

CHAPTER XI.

WITH THE YUMALAK-DARIA THROUGH THE DESERT.

ON the 14th November we travelled at a mean rate of 1¾ miles an hour. During the night it froze, and when we awoke in the morning all the boats of our flotilla were frozen in, though the ice was thin. The only one which could possibly suffer from this was the little skiff, whose canvas hull ran a risk of being cut by the sharp edges of the ice. The alluvial deposits along the shore were as hard as stone, and when struck by the ice-coated punting-poles, gave back a hard, grating, almost ringing noise. During the day, however, we observed only one piece of floating ice, about 5 or 6 square feet in area; indeed, it was quite a chance we saw it at all in the muddy water. So far the frost had never penetrated deeper than three-quarters of an inch; but even that was sufficient to give rise to very peculiar mouldings, flakes and bell-shaped mounds along the line of the water's edge, caused by the soft mud underneath having been washed away, whilst the frozen layers were held fast by the frost. But as soon as the sun began to beat down upon them with any degree of power, they of course thawed, and then toppled headlong into the river. We did not see any more wild-geese; even the very last of the stragglers seemed to have gone now.

A little way ahead we perceived four men standing on the bank as motionless as statues, watching us; but when we drew nearer, off they went in headlong flight, and left all their belongings behind them. These included four fierce dogs, which pursued us for some time, barking frantically. After that we saw the shepherds' horses, and they, too, accompanied us a little way.

As soon as it grew dark I bade our only guide, Rehim Bai, go on first in the canoe, and pilot the way, or rather illumine the way, for he carried, fastened to a sloping pole, an enormous Chinese lantern, with a strong oil lamp inside it. I instructed him to keep about two hundred yards in advance, and from him I took my compass-bearings quite as well as I took them by daylight. The reflection from the lantern, playing upon the rippling surface, made Rehim's canoe look like a Venetian gondola.

The volume of the river at our next camping-ground, Teppeh-teshdi, was 2,691 cubic feet in the second, that is to say, 236 cubic feet more than at the last measurement.

Immediately after starting on the following morning, we passed the boundary-line between the two *tabesi* or administrative districts of Shah-yar and Kuchar, the boundary being marked by a conical stack of poles, to the east of which the shepherds of Kuchar alone had the right to graze their sheep.

A great number of ducks were wintering in the Tarim, and Islam was often fortunate enough to surprise them.

In the neighbourhood of Källälik, where we stopped for a short noontide rest, we discovered an unusually well-built hut of clay, surrounded by several sheep-folds. The only creatures we saw, however, were a dog, some poultry, and some lambs; but we readily understood that the inhabitants had fled as soon as they caught sight of our ferry-boat. A fire was burning in the hut, and over the fire hung a kettle, while clothes and other objects lay scattered over the floor. We explored the thickets in the vicinity, but found nobody. At length, however, a solitary boy showed himself in the distance, but we had regularly to hunt him down before we could catch him. The poor fellow was, however, so terrified that we could not get him to open his mouth, let alone give us any information. He simply stood all a-tremble, without daring to lift up his eyes.

I wonder what strange stories are now current in the forests of the Tarim with regard to our remarkable colossus and its prolonged voyage! How many and many a time did we not find empty huts, which their owners had only just deserted! What must these simple shepherds have thought when they saw such an odd-looking monster approaching them silently, like a crouching tiger? Did they imagine it was some monstrous amphibian, with terrible antennæ, which it moved backwards and forwards? Many took to their heels straightaway, as though the Author of all Evil were after them. Others probably stood at a safe distance, on the edge of the forest, to see what was going to become of this unspeakable thing. And I dare say yet others are running still, as terrified out of their wits as if they had seen a hobgoblin of the forest. Who that knows the genius of the Asiatic mind for exaggeration and superstition can doubt that a plentiful crop of legends and tales has already grown up around the track of our uncouth leviathan, and that these in process of time will crystallize into a marvellous relation of the triumphal progress of some river deity, desert king, or forest magician along the great watery highway of his dominions?

At Khadeh-dung, where a sand-hill, 26 feet high, overhung the river, I dismissed, on the 16th November, the guides whom we had brought with us from Chimen; their knowledge of the local topography was exhausted. Hence, as we found nobody to take their place when we started again, we had no guide except the sinuous windings of the river itself. Our chief concern now was to get hold of a man who could go with us and give us local information. At length we saw a shepherd boy tenting his sheep, and we managed to get quite close to him without being observed; but when he did perceive us, off he went at full speed. But have him we must; so once more we organised a regular chase, which, though it cost us a good deal of valuable time, ended in the capture of our quarry. The boy told us that the name of the district was Sarik-buya, and that before evening we should find an inhabited place on the left bank. This information turned out to be correct, and we obtained there a capable pilot.

The sun was no longer strong enough to thaw the sheets of ice which formed on the lagoons beside the river; but the ice continued to increase in thickness until it would bear the dogs, which, when swimming to dry land, had often experienced great difficulty in scrambling through the thin ice which fringed the bank. These marginal braidings of ice were now visibly increasing in size; and it was evident it was their intention to stretch a bridge right across the river from bank to bank, and incorruptibly block our way. The small patches of drift ice, which now became quite common floating on the surface, came from the entrances to these lagoons, and from the river-ice immediately adjacent to the banks, not out of the lagoons themselves.

It had now become the established rule for our day's

journey to be extended to twelve full hours, the moon being assisted every evening by the rays of the Chinese lantern. This evening we saw in the distance a solitary fire on the bank. It turned out to be at Dung-kotan, a place which I visited in 1896, and consequently made a fixed-point for my map. Kader, the bai who dwelt there, gave me a good deal of very valuable information about the changing characteristics of the river at different seasons. He also told us that tigers were very common in that locality. I bought from him the skin of a big fellow which had been shot there about a fortnight before. The year before that, too, tigers had been shot at Dung-kotan.

It is an astonishing thing that these simple forest-men, with their primitive muzzle-loading muskets, should really tackle and destroy such a beast as the tiger. Of course, they have to resort to craft, or else they would never do it. Suppose a tiger has carried off a horse, or a cow, or a sheep, and gone into the reeds with it. There, having satisfied the first cravings of hunger, he leaves what he does not eat, and when he goes away from it, always follows a well-trodden shepherd's track. It is this peculiarity which has procured him his Turki name of *yollbars* (the panther of the path). His footprints reveal where he has gone into the reeds and whence he may be expected to emerge; while the remains of his feast betray that it is his purpose to return to the same spot when he gets hungry again. Then it is that the natives place a spring-trap (*kappgan* or *tosak*) in the path, concealing it well with branches, brushwood, and leaves, while underneath it they dig a hole about two feet deep. If luck is against the tiger, he steps into the trap and is held fast. Now, the trap is made of iron, and is so heavy that the tiger is only able to drag it after him when he moves backwards. Consequently, it is impossible for him to run off with it, especially as the jaws have a terrible grip and are set with sharp teeth. Although the animal's spoor is very distinct and easy to follow, his enemies generally let at least a week pass before they venture to approach him. Meanwhile, the tiger, being deprived of the power to move where he desires, is unable to procure food, and consequently gets famished with hunger, and begins to pine away. At length, however, the shepherds approach him on horseback, and generally shoot him from the saddle, so as to be safe against attack if the tiger, making a last desperate effort, should try to throw himself upon them. The animal whose skin I had just bought was already done for when his enemies approached within about forty-five yards of him, and lodged the fatal shot in his left eye. Yet so great was the respect his destroyers had for him that, although the first ball made him roll over on his side, they nevertheless gave him five more before they ventured to draw close up to him and dismount. Their triumphant satisfaction at slaying the worst enemy of their flocks may well be conceived.

The tosak is a cunningly-devised instrument, like the English rabbit-trap or rat-trap, a semi-circular scissors or shear-like arrangement, the two sides of which are made to clap together by means of two steel springs of enormous power. The inner edge of each side is set with sharp teeth, which, when the trap is closed, interlock with perfect exactitude. The springs are so powerful that it requires a strong man, exerting his full strength, to force the toothed edges back into the position they are to remain in when the trap is set. The ring is then pushed close up to the two claws, and kept in place by a simple combination of a cord and two pins. It is the tiger's weight as he steps upon the cord which causes the trap to spring and hold him fast by the paw. On one occasion a tiger was caught by the toes only; but he tore himself away from them and, though maimed, escaped.

Lower down the river, towards the Lop country, tigers are quite common, especially on the left bank. They seldom show themselves during the day, but at night haunt the shepherds' tracks.

The slayer of the tiger accompanied us on the 17th November. The river, which pursued a general east-north-east course, was narrow and winding, and was accompanied by a labyrinth of ancient beds containing stagnant water, side-channels which only filled when the river was in full flood, and marginal lagoons surrounded by reeds and forest. On the left lay a very extensive lagoon, and on the right was the Hassanak-daria, a peculiar *cul-de-sac*, into which the river only penetrated at high flood, and there stood without going any farther. Speaking broadly, my map of the Tarim is only an instantaneous photograph, for every year some fresh branch or other is carved out, old loops are abandoned, new marginal lagoons are formed, while others dry up. It is, in short, a restless and unstable stream, and as the country is flat, it incessantly changes its course in a very capricious manner.

After the sun had set, the moon rose—a ruddy-yellow globe climbing up a light blue sky; but as she brightened and grew whiter, the sky took on a deeper shade of colour. Viewed against this background, the contours of the inclosing river-banks stood out as sharp-edged as silhouettes clipped out of black paper. The wan, wintry tones which nature had assumed made everything look hard and frigid. The Tarim glistened like a sheet of cold blue steel, and the only places where it showed signs of movement were just round the snags,

The Yumalak-daria (Tarim), seen from Koral-dung.

which stuck fast in the bottom. The moon hung so low down in the sky that its orb seemed to roll across from the one bank to the other, according as the river wound to the right or to the left.

We met the first Lop-men at Lämpa-akin on the 18th November. They were a party of three, an old man and his two sons, proceeding up the river in three canoes, with their nets and other accoutrements for fishing. They were taken so utterly aback when we suddenly came upon them in the middle of a loop that they never dreamt of trying to escape, although it would have been easy enough for them to do so, in their light, swift nutshells. After a good many objections, the old man consented to go with us, while his two sons pursued their journey; and, as it turned out, he was intimately acquainted with the district.

At Koral-dung (the Watch-Hill), on the right bank, through which ran the boundary between Kuchar and the Lop country, we rested for a long time. The river there had a volume of 2,571 cubic feet in the second. Immediately south of the hill lay, glittering in the sunshine, the greenish-blue lake of Koral-dungning-köll; its water was as clear as crystal, half-frozen over, and surrounded by tamarisk thickets and kamish fields of extraordinary density, through which ran numerous tiger tracks, showing that these black-striped beasts were in the

Koral-dungning-köll:

habit of haunting the place at night. During the summer these reed marshes were flooded; indeed, the ground was still moist at the time of our visit, although there was no water except in the shallow marginal lagoons. From that point the lower Tarim was called the Yumalak-daria, or the Round River; it stretched at first towards the north-east, but soon afterwards turned to the south-east—a narrow ribbon winding through a vast wilderness of reeds.

On the other side of Atchal the river underwent another metamorphosis; it shrunk to a breadth of only 66 feet, was as much as 23 feet deep, and without a single trace of alluvial formation. The high terraces which confined it were frozen as hard as stone; if by any chance our craft came into contact with them, it was like touching a quay of marble. On the right of the river at this part lay the lake of Ak-kumning-yugan-köll (" the Big Lake in the White Sand "), embosomed among sterile sand-dunes, and so great that the voice of a man shouting on one side of it could not be heard across on the other side.

On the 19th November we again passed a long string of marginal lagoons. Indeed, this tendency to shed off side lagoons was characteristic of the Lower Tarim, and became more pronounced in proportion as Lop-nor was approached. Tograk (poplar) forests now became very common again. Except for these, the river-bed was bordered by tall strong yellow reeds, which leaned picturesquely out over the river like hanging hedges. As our heavy colossus brushed against them, their brittle stalks crackled, snapped, and broke.

That evening the sunset gave rise to remarkable colour effects, the entire expanse of the reeds being lit up with an intense ruddy yellow glow, as if somebody had set them on fire. Dark and silent, the inky-black water of the Yumalak-daria wound through the thickets where the royal tiger had his lair. The ice-sheets which covered the lagoons whistled and whined. Occasionally a flash as of lightning would gleam across the dark river in front of us, as some sheet of floating-ice, hitherto invisible, was caught edgewise in an eddy and tilted up a glassy corner, upon which the rays of the sinking sun caught, broke, and dispersed as if scattered by a prism. The dead poplars, swart and naked, stretched their gnarled and rotten arms out over the river as though even in death blessing its life-giving waters.

Again the river began to serpentine and wind to such an extent that I frequently found it necessary to take two or three hundred compass-bearings in the course of a single day. We had secured yet another Lop-man to act as guide, and in one of the marginal lagoons we went past, he caught us a few fish. The lagoon in which he caught them was long and narrow, and lozenge-shaped; it lay behind a tongue of alluvium, and was covered with ice strong enough to bear a man. It is in such pools, where the water is still and clear, that the fish are wont to be found at that season of the year. Having placed his net across the mouth of the lagoon, the man drew back a little in his canoe; then, standing in its stern, he drove it with all his might, with a broad-bladed paddle, against the edge of the ice, immediately above the outspread net. The ice, being brittle, broke under the weight of the canoe and the force of the impact. Then the Lop-man smashed it right through to the far end of the pool, and pushed the ice adrift upon the river; after which he drove the fish into the net with his paddle, and then went and picked up the net and drew it into his canoe. When, however, the ice proves too thick to be broken in this way, the Lop-men frighten the fish into the net by beating its surface with their paddles. In the larger marginal lagoons fishing is carried on all winter, even after connection with the river is cut off.

The concluding portion of our day's journey on the 20th November led due east-north-east. With my telescope I discovered, a long way ahead, half-a-score men waiting for us on the bank. They were the begs of Tograk-mähälläh and Kara-chumak, two villages situated in the vicinity. They told me they had been ordered by Fu Tai, governor-general of Urumchi, to go and meet a *chong mähman*, or "distinguished guest," who was coming down the Yarkand-daria. The Chinese had thus got their eyes upon us, although from a distance, and rumours of our journey had travelled far and wide. But for all that, they neither knew where we started from nor yet where we were going to; all they knew was that we were extraordinarily strange beings. More than two years after this, when I was in Ladak, I was asked by some Indian merchants whether I knew anything about a white man who had spent several months sailing in a boat down a big river a long way off to the north. Such a thing would be impossible, they declared, on the Indus.

Yunuz Beg, the most distinguished man amongst our new friends, had been expecting us for several days, and had ridden some distance up the river to meet us, but failing to find any trace of either boat or sail, had returned to the place where we encountered him. Now, however, he was eager to bring forward his stores of sheep and melons and fresh fish.

Ketchik, the place where we encamped, was a very interesting spot. The name signifies "ford," and was acquired because the road from Kakteh to Karaul crossed the river there. These crossing-places generally occur in the perfectly straight reaches, where there are no deep trenches, pits, or excavations in the bottom. On the left our river was joined by a large dry bed full of mud. This I learned was formerly used by the Tarim, which had come down that way for a period of at least fifty years, for the old man who was my informant remembered it from his childhood; but four years before our visit, the river had completely deserted its old course, to which it did not now bequeath one single drop of water, even when at its highest. The new branch, which did not reunite with the old river until several days' journey lower down, ran towards the south-east, through an entirely desolate tract of country, in which before its advent there had existed nothing except a series of shallow lagoons. Here again we had an illustration of the changeableness which characterises the hydrographical relations of those regions, and which became more pronounced the nearer we approached to the Lop country and the more insignificant the fall of the Tarim became.

The region we travelled through during the next few days was therefore a *terra incognita* to most of the natives. The velocity of the new stream, the first day we spent on its bosom, was approximately 3¾ miles an hour. The begs and all their gifts having been stowed on board, away we went, preceded by two Lop canoes, one of them navigated by four men. The latter went splendidly; being but a narrow trough, all four men paddled standing, and only the last one of the four was visible, although the four paddles struck the water separately without any regard to simultaneity. The reed-beds were still tolerably dense, though tangled, and no longer grew in one continuous mass, but were broken into belts and disconnected patches. The river was undecided about which direction to pursue. It described no big or definite loops, although it was full of small sinuosities, as though seeking and trying to find the way which would suit it best. Time after time the current was divided by small islands lying athwart its course. Here we might easily have gone astray, had the canoe-men not darted on ahead and tested the depth of the passages with their paddles. Even with their help we were kept in a state of perpetual suspense by the contracted water-gaps, poplar snags, accumulations of reeds and floating jetsam of all kinds, as well as by sharp turns and foaming rapids. Besides, every now and again, we encountered a living poplar, standing on its own roots in the middle of the river—a clear proof of the recent formation of the channel. These spreading trees were so dangerous and so threatening, that we sometimes deemed

Stopping for Breakfast on the Yumalak-daria.

it advisable to lower the tent and take down the meteorological observatory just before we came to them. On the right the river was bordered by a chain of lakes, the last of which, Buya-köll, communicated directly with the main stream through a channel beset with a great number of tiny islets—in fact, a Swedish *skärgård* in miniature.

On the other side of that place we struck the Chong-ak-kum (Great White Desert), as the great desert was there called. At the same time the sand-dunes closed rapidly in upon both banks, and in proportion as they did so the belts of vegetation which accompanied the river grew thinner and thinner. The transition was very sharp. We left the last of the poplars behind us, while on our right the reed-belt swung back so as to admit the absolutely barren sand-dunes right up to the river, where they came to an abrupt termination at the water's edge or at the margin of the flat alluvial deposits in the river-bed.

As soon as it grew dusk, I transferred myself to the skiff and followed immediately behind the Lop-men's canoes; but it was so cold, I ordered one of the men to bring me a fire-basket and place it on a piece of planking in the bottom of the little boat. Owing to the alarming pace at which we went, the boatmen were kept incessantly on the *qui vive*. But as soon as we entered the sandy desert, with the high dunes on both sides of us, it darkened rapidly, and so we halted. The Lop-men had with great foresight filled their canoes with drift-wood, which they fished out of the river, so that we soon had a couple of big fires roaring away. In this region the river was called Tärim, Yanghi-daria, or Chong-daria, in addition to the names I have already mentioned.

On the 22nd November the Yumalak-daria flowed towards the south-east. Its new channel was carved through the outer margin of the sandy desert, and any dunes which chanced to stand in its path had been swept aside by the irresistible energy of its hungry flood. Against this great power of nature, animated as it was by the inflexible law of gravitation, the sand was absolutely powerless.

On both sides we were now shut in by sand-dunes rising to a height of 50 feet; those on the right bank, where the sand was the more developed, were often entirely sterile. And yet it was not a hopelessly barren region; for every now and again we came across a solitary poplar, while tamarisks, true children of the desert, were relatively numerous, and a narrow ribbon of reeds still clung to each bank. It is a surprising circumstance that the sand-dunes should possess sufficient consistency at their base thus to present perpendicular faces to the water; the reason is, their lower strata were wet. Higher up the sand was loose, as it generally is, and there the sides of the dunes were seamed with tiny channels, down which the sand trickled until it came to the edge of the precipice. This it descended in a series of little falls and cascades, and these sand rivulets continue to flow as long as they are fed from above. But when the time-glass is exhausted, the dune becomes "dead," eaten away, as it has been, by wind and current. Yet even then the orbit of the sand is not completed; for it is caught up again and driven further on in its restless wanderings by another force. The "desert ocean" has its pilgrims also, and its inorganic life is as much subject to laws of periodic movement as the organic life which pulses under the shade of the palm-trees in more genial climes.

On these fabulously desolate shores there was an utter absence of organic life—not a human being, not a four-footed animal, not even a raven or a vulture, the privileged visitors of the desert. The only indication of any creature ever having been there was a *saldam* in a poplar-tree, a species of look-out made of branches and twigs plaited together, in which some hunter hid himself whilst lying in wait for antelopes that might chance to come down to the river to drink at sunrise. Again we were engulfed in that awful Asiatic silence, a silence as of the dead. No greeting came to meet us from the heart of the desert. The river, the river alone, sang its rippling song to the unresponsive sand, a song which would very shortly congeal on the lips that sang it.

And every hour which passed that same singing Tarim carried us deeper in amongst the dunes, into a land that was utterly unknown, for even our Lop-men had never been there before. If ever we stood in need of pilots to point out the way, this surely was the time, and they were our men. Dipping in their paddles, in a moment or two they were out of sight behind yonder projecting elbow. But anon they came back, to warn us of some critical passage or other they had discovered. They were the light, swift cruisers which scouted around our heavy battleship, and darting on in front showed us the fairway. Strange! Very strange to be crossing one of the earth's greatest deserts—by water! Not so very long ago I had nearly died there for want of it!

On one occasion our canoe-men came and reported that the river divided into five arms, and guided us to that which they considered to be the principal one. The pass ran between two islets of flotsam—reeds, branches, and rubbish—and was so narrow that the water was lashed into foam on both sides. Guiding our clumsy craft as straight as we could, we glided into the watery alley. Both her sides were scraped; nevertheless we struggled through and came out into open water; but then we ran aground. The river was equally shallow every-

A Canoe Making a Reconnaissance.

where from bank to bank; yet advance we must, let the cost be what it might. And we *did* get over, thanks to the slight rise which had taken place in the current during the past twenty-four hours. Had the current fallen to the same extent, it would have been far worse. How often did we, I wonder, just scrape over sand-banks and shallows without suspecting it! I dare say that many a time it was such a near thing it would have been impossible to put a sword-blade between. So far the river had been gracious to us; might it still continue so!

In a poplar-grove, where we landed, and where I took some photographs, we observed large numbers of tiger-tracks; but though I went on that occasion, as well as on others, a little way inland, and looked about me from the top of a hill, I never had the good fortune to see that fierce, yet fascinating, beast in his native haunts.

This Yanghi-daria, or New River, furnished yet another illustration of the great river's tendency to deviate to the right. If any deviation took place on the left bank, the water invariably found its way back into the main stream; but not so on the right. There the new branch strove to get away from its parent, and sought to carve a new path for itself still further in the same direction. Once, long ago, the Tarim used to empty its waters into the ancient lake of Lop-nor; now it pours them into a new lake, far to the south, having thereby taken a gigantic step towards the right.

During the last few days we had not seen very much ice; the current was too swift to permit of its formation. Still by eight o'clock at night the thermometer was down to $-6°.0$ C. or $21°.2$ Fahr. Day by day the race between ourselves and the frost—the moment when the river should become totally frozen over—grew more and more interesting. There could not be many days left to us now, for each succeeding night it grew colder. Yet I dreaded the hour when we should be compelled to say good-bye to our floating home, and abandon her to her fate. Clumsy though she was, ungainly though she was, I had learnt to have an affection for her—something akin to the feeling one cherishes for the farm where one has lived long and prospered. She had made us a comfortable home; she had carried us safely through the whole of East Turkestan. She had spared us the daily recurring worries of pitching tents, of packing and unpacking, of unloading and loading up, and the care of a troop of caravan animals. Besides that, I had a dark-room always ready, my instruments were always working and in good order, I had everything I needed conveniently within reach, and when I wanted a glass of cool fresh water, I had only to stretch out my hand to get it.

On the 29th November we had a volume of 2,497 cubic feet all day long. That was of course sufficient; but the ice! When would it stop us for good and all?

CHAPTER XII.

FIGHTING THE DRIFT-ICE.

For the first part of our journey on the 24th November the Tarim was once more inclosed between belts of forest; for it swept round two long curves, shaping itself like the letter W, the points of which touched the desert on both sides, though the stretches between were lined with woods. At intervals we met Lop fishermen, and saw long rows of fish hung up to dry outside their temporary quarters. At intervals, too, we observed a dried fish-skin hanging on a pole; this was to indicate that fishing was forbidden there, owing to somebody having claimed the fishing rights. The fish-skin was the owner's notice board.

This day we came within an ace of suffering shipwreck. The current swept with undiminished force and violence, close in against the bank in an exceptionally sharp angle, and there a gigantic poplar, undermined by the stream, had fallen prone across the river, hanging just over the current at about one yard above the surface. The remaining portion of the river's breadth was occupied by a broad eddy, which swung round very slowly, and set up a back current. It was an easy matter for a Lop canoe to pass under the overhanging poplar, but had the ferry-boat come into collision with it, everything would infallibly have been swept overboard—tent, boxes, packing-cases, black cabin, everything—or if we had drifted sideways against it, and our top-hamper had offered sufficient resistance, we should in all probability have been capsized. It would have been a trial of strength between the upper framework and the tree, and the latter was so massive it looked as if nothing could move it.

As it happened, the big ferry-boat was just then leading the flotilla, and was slipping unconcernedly down-stream without the least suspicion of anything being amiss. But just as we were on the point of entering the quickened current immediately under the bank, there came a desperate cry of warning from Palta. The poplar was only about a score of yards in front of us. The river was deep; the punting-poles were not long enough to reach the bottom. In, then, with the new-made sweeps, two men to each, for they were heavy and long. The men shouted. The river broke into a kind of cataract, it was moving so swiftly. One moment more and we should be shipwrecked. Down we drifted, straight upon the poplar. Could nothing be done? Was there no means of averting a catastrophe? The men worked like demons. I seized hold of my map-sheets and note-books, determined to save them if I possibly could, for if once they had gone down in that muddy water, it would have been good-bye to them for ever. Islam and the beg ran to the fore part of the boat, ready to grasp hold of the poplar and as far as they could break the force of the collision. But just at the last moment the boatmen succeeded in swinging our leviathan off into the eddy, where she slowly spun round and finally glided off on the back current. Yet even then we were not safe. The stream would have brought us back to the ill-omened poplar again had not Alim jumped into the water—it was only (!) 1°.4 C. or 34°.5 Fahr.—and though it reached up to his arm-holes, hurried to the left bank with a rope. Fortunately the bank was low, and he had no difficulty in landing. After that he towed us safely past the danger.

Whilst we were being slowly turned by the eddy, Kasim and Kader went spinning past us with the commissariat boat and the skiff, both driving straight down upon the poplar. But they saved themselves by a clever manœuvre. Warned of what lay ahead of them, they unfastened the skiff, and giving her a vigorous push as they flew past, managed to send her close up to the big ferry-boat, where we caught hold of her, and held her fast. Meanwhile they steered their own craft close in under the right bank, so that Kader was able to jump ashore with a line. Nevertheless, their craft got in amongst the branches of the poplar, and Kasim had to hang on to it to prevent himself from being swept overboard. It was only by the skin of their teeth that they escaped coming to grief.

Now if this adventure had happened at night, it would not have been the ice that would have brought my river journey to an abrupt termination. But good luck was once more a passenger

Our Way Stopped by a Fallen Poplar.

[VOL. I.—*To face page* 200.

with us, and we were allowed to drift on further down our watery highway. But my Lailik boatmen began to be filled with amazement, not to say consternation. They thought the river never would come to an end, but went winding, winding on for ever towards the east. When they thought of the enormous distance they had travelled since they left their homes, their brains turned dizzy; they were utterly unable to form any numerical idea of what it amounted to. All they knew was that between themselves and their homes at Lailik there stretched an interminable maze of storms and mists, of sand-deserts and impenetrable woods.

Canoes on the Lower Tarim.

By the time we had recovered from our fright, the sun was beginning to set, and I turned on the musical box to cheer the men up a bit. Islam had just come to bring me a dish of fresh-cooked fish, which had a most delicious smell, and I was comforting myself with the thought of getting something nice and hot to warm me, when we heard frantic cries for help from up-stream, where Kasim and Kader were following in our wake. The shouts were so piercing and so full of anxiety that we were all alarmed. I at once gave the order sharply to pull in to land; but we were right in the middle of the stream, and it took some little time to pilot our stupid monster to the bank. I was afraid one of the men was on the point of being drowned, or was actually already drowned.

The moment we touched land, all the men rushed away back up-stream, plunging through the thickets, scrambling through the reeds. I shouted to them to send me word instantly what had happened. After a while one of the Lop-men came back, and said that the commissariat boat had been capsized by an unseen snag. As soon as I was satisfied that both the men were safe, I felt easy, and fell to on my fish, which however had, in the meantime, grown cold.

The end of the adventure was of a tragi-comical character. Down the river came, merrily dancing on the water, the various effects which had been spilled from the commissariat boat, and hard after them the Lop-men in their canoes, fishing up whatever was worth saving—buckets, tubs, boxes filled with flour, baskets full of fruit, flat disks of bread like the leaves of a new kind of water-lily, punting-poles, and a multitude of odds and ends scattered widely over the river from bank to bank. A certain number of things had been rescued at the spot where the misfortune happened, amongst others our two sheep, which swam ashore; but several others, such as an axe, a spade, a lantern, and so forth, were irrecoverably lost.

We encamped where we were, Islam and Alim making up two huge fires. It was very late when the other men came in with their boats and such of their wet cargoes as they had been able to collect. Kasim was greatly cast down, but he was really no way to blame for the accident. Whilst he and Kader were endeavouring to avoid a snag that stuck up from the bottom of the river, they got caught in an eddy, and from that were flung into a strong current, which carried them straight down upon another snag that they did not see, and consequently could not guard against. The skiff received the first impact, a long rent being torn in her side, though fortunately above the water-line. When the commissariat boat went over, Kader, who was unable to swim, scrambled into the skiff; but Kasim clung to the poplar stem which caused their shipwreck, and there sat and shouted for help until a canoe fetched him off.

On the 25th November we were joined by the *shang-yas*, or begs, of Chong-tograk and Arelish, each bringing a canoe with him, so that our flotilla now numbered ten vessels, and we made quite a stately procession as we slowly moved along the face of the Tarim. The two begs stationed themselves beside Palta in the prow, and took a turn at the oars, that is to say, the new sweeps or flat-bladed punting-poles; so that we

Gigantic Sand-dunes on the Right Bank of the Tarim near Tokkuz-kum.

[VOL. I.—*To face page* 202.

now moved a little faster than the stream. Whilst Islam was sewing a patch over the rent in the one half of my little skiff, one of the natives manœuvred the other half, to the intense amusement of his compatriots. We encamped at Tokkuz-kum (the Nine Dunes). My Mohammedan friends were of opinion that, provided the weather kept calm, we might continue for another three weeks; but if a *buran* (black tempest) were to come on, the river might be stopped in the course of a single night. The lower part of its course froze first, and after that the upper part; in other words, the frost travelled up-stream against the current. They told me, as the result of observation, that the colder the water the faster it flowed. This might be true theoretically; but it was hardly likely to be perceptible to the naked eye.

On the following day we were carried directly towards the highest part of the Tokkuz-kum dunes—gigantic, and in the highest degree imposing, accumulations of yellow drift-sand. They too, like the other dunes I have mentioned, were stragglers from the great desert; but they advanced so close to the river that their bases were washed, and even undermined, by the water. These dunes were the biggest accumulation of sand I have ever seen, and I could not resist the temptation of stopping and climbing to the highest point to take a look round such an interesting country.

Leaving the ferry-boat moored to the left bank, we paddled over in the canoes, and started to climb the steep slopes. But it was hard work; the sand was so loose, we sank deep into it at every step, and often slipped backwards. Eventually however we reached the top, and found ourselves on the summit of a steep wall that went straight down into the river. The scene which met our eyes was one of singular majesty. I was amazed at the astonishing forms into which the active powers of nature had sculptured and modelled the relief features of the earth's surface. I knew what it was to travel over an oceanic expanse of sand, crumpled into ridges, hundreds of feet high. Many and many a time my eyes had rested upon the all-dominating "waves" of sand, sand, sand, and once more sand, which follow one another for endless miles across that stupendous "desert ocean," and it was a precisely similar landscape which now lay unrolled at my feet. But here I stood at the northern fringe of the great desert ocean, and its edge was as sharp cut as the sea-coast or the shores of a lake. The outermost verge of the desert consisted of a wall or terrace, a bent bow of absolutely unadulterated sand, which plunged straight down into the river at an angle of 32°. The sand in the vicinity of the river possessed a greater degree of consistency or firmness than the sand in the interior of the desert. This was owing to the more abundant degree of humidity which visited it, partly in the shape of dew, partly in the form of actual moisture which it sucked up mechanically. And it was in consequence of its greater firmness that the sand assumed the peculiar contours—depressions, terraces, and cones—shown in the accompanying photograph (compare also illustration facing p. 202). Seen

Tokkuz-kum.

from the left bank of the river opposite, this great wall of sand looked perfectly vertical, and suggested that, if a man were to attempt to come down the face of it, he would start a fresh avalanche, and be infallibly swept to destruction. These dunes were about 200 feet high, and persons standing on the top of them appeared to be exceedingly small.

The view down the river was in its way equally impressive. Deep down below our feet the stream wound like a canal, and disappeared in the east in a labyrinth of eccentric sinuosities. A tiny lagoon was ensconced between two of the dunes, but was sadly cramped for room. The margin of the desert was just as sharply marked on the eastern side of this colossal aggregation of sand as it was on the western. The poplar woods began again quite abruptly without any transition, the trees standing in thick clumps on the very skirts of the dunes.

A short distance lower down we came to Al-kattik-chekkeh, where dwelt Istam Beg and ten families in huts built of reeds and laths, and placed all together in a clump for the sake of protection against cold, and wind, and the heat of summer. The entire population of the place, some forty souls in all, men, women and children, in all their picturesque rags and dirt, were immortalised on the accompanying photograph (p. 207). Amongst them was an old man of ninety, who sixty years before had come thither from Kara-köll. He was blind, and sat crouched over the fire, and wept because he had lost his sons, and had nobody to look after him and care for him. He also spoke of the capricious changes in the course of the great river; but his memory was defective, and I could place but little reliance on the information he gave me.

After we had measured the river, which had 2,663 cubic feet in the second, Istam Beg invited us to go and fish in a creek on the inner side of a silt bank. The pool was covered with ice 1½ inches thick, and the method of procedure was that already described, except that on this occasion two nets were used. The first was dropped across the mouth of the creek. After that the ice was broken for a distance of ten or eleven yards, and at the edge of the ice, as it was then left, the second net was dropped. Then the two nets were drawn together. This manœuvre was repeated two or three times, until the end of the creek was reached, and the last haul of course gathered in all the fish that remained. The water was only three or four feet deep, and the nets were kept vertical by means of stones fastened to the bottom and bunches of dry rushes tied at the top. These latter served also as "floats," for they bobbed up and down when a fish got fast in the meshes immediately underneath. Then that part of the net was swiftly lifted with a paddle, and the fish killed by a blow on the head. The total catch amounted to twenty-six fish.

Our days were now reckoned. There was no blinking the fact any longer, for although the temperature of the water kept a little above freezing-point during the day, it always sank below it during the night, and in the morning our flotilla was frozen in and had to be hewn out. The Lop-men had warned us, that after the first drift-ice appeared, it would only be ten days more before the river ceased to flow, and this moment we were now anxiously expecting every day. It came on the 28th November. When I stepped out of my tent in the morning, I found the entire surface of the river spangled with patches of soft, porous ice, consisting of crystals and needles which had been formed on the bottom, or at any rate below the surface of the water, and which on coming to the top became agglomerated together into flat cakes or disks, often as white as snow on the top. These formations, an unfailing harbinger of the speedy freezing of the river, were called *kömul*, or *kadeh*. As soon as they appear, the fish desert the river, and take refuge in the creeks and marginal lagoons; whereupon the Lop-men become high busy gathering in their stock of fish for the winter months.

It was a cold, dull morning, and the sky was cloudy. We chopped out our boats with axes and iron-bars; but a fringe of ice which remained clinging to them along the water-line never thawed all day long. Everything was frozen; ropes and lines were as hard as wood, and the velocity-instrument was sheathed with ice, and had to be thawed at the fire before we could use it. The natives had protected their canoes by drawing them up on land. Although we had a fire fore as well as aft, we all shook with cold; the men, however, kept up their spirits by singing all day. I suspect the Lailik boatmen would not be overpoweringly sorry if we did get frozen fast: it would mean that the journey was then over for them, and they were free to return home.

From now onwards for the rest of the journey we had to steer our course amongst these drifting sheets of ice. They formed a fresh source of interest for the men, who never grew tired of watching their erratic progress down the capricious river. Being always most numerous in the centre of the stream, they were constantly being drawn into the eddies. They jostled one against another, until some of them were pushed back into the current. They ran aground on the sandbanks, which jutted above the water's level. They went dancing down the stream like little islands afloat. They collided with one another. They ground their edges together. They ran atilt against our boats. They were smashed to pieces; they were fused together. They stuck fast in the bank, and spun round and round. In short, they played the most fantastic tricks imaginable, until they disappeared—which the greater part of them did by one

The Village of Al-kattik-chekkeh.

o'clock, and by four o'clock every one of them was gone. But we had had our warning: in a few days the river would be impassable.

That day the Tarim's course was unusually changeable. It began in a very promising fashion by stretching out towards the north-east. But when it reached Köttektu-körruk, a little fishing lagoon wedged in between two sand-dunes, it unexpectedly wheeled quite round to the west; then, encountering firm sand on the left bank, it flung itself back through a series of erratic windings to the north-north-east.

Drift-ice on the Lower Tarim.

We encountered several fishing-parties. One canoe was so heavily laden, its gunwhale was just level with the water.

We stopped to take our measurements at Siva on the left bank, where there were some fine poplar woods. This was in all probability the last time I should be able to perform this duty in the old way, for my little skiff, which the men called *kagaz-kemi*, or "the paper boat," would not stand much contact with the drift-ice. The volume was 2,559 cubic feet in the second. From observation of the high-water marks and other indications, I should judge that, when in full flood, the river here carried something like 6,110 cubic feet in the second, or even more.

On the 29th November winter took another big stride onwards. The thermometer dropped during the night to

$-16^{\circ}.0$ C. or $3^{\circ}.2$ Fahr., and the temperature of the water was just at the freezing-point. The river wore a strange and unfamiliar aspect; its surface being so thickly strewn with white drift-ice, that it would have been easy to imagine it had frozen and then been covered by a thick fall of snow. It was not, however, quite so bad as that yet. The white-sprinkled surface kept up an incessant movement, like a gyrating side-walk; and each succeeding day the *kömull*, or *kadeh*, became more abundant. To stand on the bank and fix our gaze steadfastly upon the glittering white belt as it hastened on and on made our eyes swim, until we fancied it was the river that was motionless and we ourselves that were drifting up stream.

The night before this we made a very unfortunate choice of a camp—namely, in a small sheltered creek. When we awoke in the morning, we were frozen in so fast that we could without risk walk all round the boats, and it took a pretty good while to cut a canal through the ice to let us back into the river. The outer edge of the ice-sheet was washed by the current, which piled up upon it a rampart of drift-ice as white as snow. The patches of floating ice were bigger and more compact than we had hitherto seen them, and when they crashed together it was as if somebody were smashing porcelain. All day long we were accompanied by sounds which resembled the playing of chimes in a distant church, and the millions of ice crystals sparkled like diamonds in the sunshine. The incessant "sissing" and whizzing of the melting ice-needles, and the painfully bright light which they gave off in the process, had a stupefying, almost a hypnotic, effect upon the senses.

Upon examining it closer, I found that the kadeh consisted solely and entirely of tiny laminæ and spicules of ice, all exceedingly thin, but fused together in large numbers. So long as they remained under the water, they possessed the same colour that it did; but when they emerged above the surface, they at once became as white as snow. The disks of drift-ice, which were composed of this loosely-aggregated, supersaturated material, were seldom more than a yard in diameter, and generally round, owing to their never-ending friction with one another and with the banks. Owing to the same cause each disk was edged with a raised flange, about four inches high, which also gleamed white by reason of the upper face of the disk being a smooth, bluish-grey surface, at the same level as the surface of the river.

Journey of Night amongst the Drift-ice of the Tarim

Vol. 1—to face page 210

Thus we were surrounded by a countless number of snow-white rings, the burial-wreaths, as it were, of the great river. For months we had been living its life, now we were to be partakers in its burial.

The sun of course failed not to exercise considerable influence upon these floating disks ; but at noon the river was still covered with them, and, though they thinned out somewhat, they did not all disappear entirely.

All day long we had the lofty and sterile sand-dunes on our right ; but between us and them there was always a belt of yellow kamish intermingled with poplars, brownish-grey, leafless and melancholy. The ground was everywhere frozen hard, so that the men were no longer afraid of venturing into marshy or recently inundated places. The river here exhibited the same characteristics as the Yarkand-daria below Lailik. We had again the same big broad alluvial islands and headlands, and the river-bed was wide and fenced in by high escarpments, crowned by ancient woods.

A lofty piece of sterile sand, near the right bank, was called Ansash-kum, after an old *pavan*, or hunter, long since dead, who used to climb it to see if he could detect any antelopes or wild camels in the vicinity. The latter, which used occasionally to come through from the desert, never show themselves near the river now ; although Kamber Shang-ya of Kara-chumak declared that he had shot seven farther south, beside the dry course of the Opgan-daria. But the shepherds of the Tarim forests know nothing of the wild camel visiting them, and when asked about it invariably answered, they had heard there existed such a creature, but a long, long way off in the desert.

We went on for about an hour in the dark, guided by the rays of our Chinese lantern, but it was ticklish work shouting and halloing at every sandbank and shallow. We only ran aground once, however, but then such a quantity of drift-ice accumulated behind the ferry-boat, it was more difficult than usual to get her off. When we pulled up for the night, we took precious good care not to enter any of your sheltered creeks ; we did not want to be caught in an icy rat-trap. On the contrary we anchored in the very middle of the current ; but the little skiff we drew up on land, safe out of harm's way. The big ferry-boat was moored with her stern towards the bank and her fore-part sticking out into the river, for I thought I should like to have my Venetian balcony hanging over the running water. But as I sat at my table and entered my observations for the day, every disk of ice that drifted past knocked against the old craft, making her creak and shiver from head to foot at each blow.

By this the ice had begun to form in earnest along both banks, and every day the fringe grew broader and broader. For the present, however, the frost confined its attention to the quiet waters close in under the banks, where there was no current, and to the accumulations of driftwood and flotsam which were held fast nearer the middle of the stream.

All night the drift-ice went on bumping, scraping and jarring against the ferry-boat; but it did not in any way disturb my sleep, and in the morning it was not quite so plentiful as on the previous day, for the thermometer only fell two or three degrees below freezing-point. In fact the river was barely half covered with ice; yet strange to say, although the sky was clouded, so that the sun's rays were unable to get through, the greater part of the ice eventually disappeared. By evening the few *kadeh* which remained were extremely soft, as well as few and far between. The river's course was unusually straight. We made a long day's journey (the 30th November), and all day we had on our right the high sand, resembling a mountain-chain with its weathered, denuded, and rounded forms, putting me in mind of the ranges of northern Tibet. We did not see a single human being, nor even a column of smoke. The only signs of the existence of man were certain skeleton platforms made of posts, which were said to be used by some pavan or other as a safe place in which to leave the antelopes he shot, out of the reach of wild beasts. Of birds we saw one pheasant, one hawk, a couple of ravens; these were the only living creatures.

I generally worked 14 hours a day, beginning at 6.30 a.m. when the fire-basket was brought into the tent. I did not take my breakfast of boiled fish until after we were well started. I also ate my dinner on board; the dinner-service was there quite ready to hand, and it was not always so convenient to land in the dark. Time was now so precious, that I did not lose one single minute. My barber, Islam Bai, even cut my hair as I sat at my work-table.

The next day, the 1st December, the Tarim still preserved the same character, flowing in wide curves towards the north-east, accompanied by plenteous forests, and backed by the yellow sand of the desert, which, however, was increasing perceptibly in volume. The river maintained the same level, neither rising nor falling. The transparency went down to 2¾ inches, and the erosion terraces were five feet high. At the only elbow which penetrated the sand we landed, and from the top of the dune took a few views, one of which is here reproduced. There was now a greater difference than formerly between the different parts of the river. The actually flowing current was grey, and thickly beset with white disks of drift-ice; whereas the lagoons at the margins of the river and behind the alluvial deposits were a clear greenish blue, and covered with glassy ice some four

View up the Tarim from the Right Bank (1st December).

inches thick, which crackled and "hummed" when you walked across it. Towards the south-east the eye travelled across a veritable wilderness of sand-dunes, until it became utterly lost in the unaccountable distance; and even to the north-west there was a belt of desert sand, though it could not well be very extensive. If we except a few stray tamarisks, the total breadth of the zone of vegetation between these two pieces of desert did not exceed a mile and a half. As a rule the margin of the actual river-bed was everywhere bordered with reeds.

I was awakened early by a noisy bumping against the bottom of the ferry-boat; it was the kadeh rising to the surface. During the night these ice-disks were not visible; but directly the sun rose, up they came. If, in the morning, you felt the bottom of the river with a pole, it was hard and slippery like ice ; but later on in the day, after the kadeh had loosened its hold, it became soft and spongy like ordinary sand. The noise which the drift-ice made grating against the side of the ferry-boat was pretty much as if sugar were being sawn by machinery. At first it made the dogs perfectly frantic, and they barked furiously at the innocent ice-disks. But they soon grew accustomed to them, and after they became still more numerous, and consequently drifted closer together, they even used them as stepping-stones for getting to land.

It was a splendid day, quite warm, and with the help of the fire-basket the temperature in the tent rose to 5°.0 C. or 41°.0 Fahr. We only got aground once ; and it was quite a novel experience to see the ice-disks, which had for hours been floating beside us, and in front of us, now all at once go streaming on past us, whilst we stood still. As a rule the ice gave us warning of the shallows and sandbanks. It was itself often as deep as the draught of the ferry-boat, and consequently used sometimes to ground in its turn, and then we would hear it crunching and crashing as it began to pile itself up above the impediment. The Lop-men asserted that the kadeh increased the velocity. But I doubt that ; these repeated collisions were calculated to have the opposite effect. When the river flowed quite straight, we drifted along quietly in the midst of the riotous scrimmage ; but when we got caught in an eddy, where the ice-disks were present in greater numbers, it became more difficult than usual to get past them.

On the 2nd December we travelled altogether 14½ miles, moving at the rate of 1½ miles an hour, and that almost in a straight line, for the curves were insignificant. The river rose a little during the night ; but the water remained just as muddy, no doubt in consequence of the formation of the ice at the bottom. The great sand-dunes of the desert drew back a little from the banks, and eventually disappeared altogether. The marginal lagoons preserved the same character as heretofore ; each was connected with the river by a narrow throat or canal, now, however, closed, so that the fish which had fled into them to escape the kadeh were caught in a veritable trap. These tiny lakelets were almost always named after the man who owned the right of fishing in them.

We were now approaching, on the left, the Ughen-daria,

an arm of the Tarim which I visited on my former journey. The patch of desert on the north had come to an end as well as the greater desert on the south, and as the Ughen-daria was bordered by extensive forests, the tract of country in the angle between the two rivers formed an almost continuous forest.

The least breeze made me feel the cold very much more, for it expelled the warm air from the tent, and then the ink soon froze in my pen. The sky was covered with heavy clouds, which hung close down over the earth like a piece of cloth outspread, but did not discharge one single flake of snow. Towards evening, however, the sun peeped out underneath this gloomy canopy like a ball of glowing fire, producing light effects of gorgeous splendour. The entire volume of the atmosphere appeared to be on fire with some inflammable gas, the reeds were a flood of purple, the poplars stood with outstretched arms as if still intoxicated by the glowing kisses of the departing sun, and the lower fringes of the sky burned in every shade of vivid violet. This glorious spectacle lasted, however, merely a few minutes, and was immediately followed by the twilight, which painted everything without distinction its own iron-grey shades. The giant reeds, which had so recently resembled a guard's regiment drawn up on parade, with their full plumes nodding in a bath of gold, were now as uninteresting and monotonous as any ordinary fence of commonplace palings.

We were dying to reach inhabited districts again, the banks of the river were so terribly lonely. Were there actually no shepherds at all in this God-forsaken region? Our guides' local knowledge was giving out; we wanted fresh men, who knew the country better. Yet not a vestige of life or habitation was to be seen between the poplars, except occasionally the tracks of antelopes, wild boar, foxes, and hares.

When it got too dark to see, I commanded "Halt!" The canoes danced along the water like will-o'-the-wisps, their lanterns swinging to and fro at the ends of the poles, and flinging their unsteady light upon the circling disks of ice with which the river was embossed. The eyes were irresistibly drawn to those swinging censers of light; they so completely dominated the scene. That evening we again chose an unsuitable place for our camp, but this time it was owing to the absence of firewood. With the object of getting light by which to search for this indispensable necessary, as well as to illumine the neighbourhood, the men set fire to the dense thickets of reeds which clothed the banks. They crackled, they hissed, they roared as the devouring flames rapidly got the mastery over their dry flags and stems. It was a stupendous firework-display; and the sight of the cataract of reddish yellow glare, which it poured forth unceasingly over the murky water, with its thousands of swirling ice-disks circling down it, was one I shall not easily forget. Those ice-disks! I could not help fancying they were water-spectres, the cobold children of old Father "Nick," who were let loose for a nightly frolic or carnival before the long Lent of their winter sleep. They put me in mind of a procession of outlawed Mussulmans, with white turbans wound round their heads—wooers of the wilderness, bedecked with garlands of everlasting flowers of perishable ice.

CHAPTER XIII.

ICE-BOUND.

On the morning of the 3rd December the river was three-parts canopied with ice; but the relative amount of area covered varied of course at different times during the day. When the river contracted, the ice was driven closer together, until not a single inch of water was visible, and our flotilla had the appearance of being frozen fast in a moving ice-field. But no sooner did the channel widen out again than the ice-disks separated, and the water once more gleamed out between them. Oh, those erratic patches of floating ice! How they dashed themselves against the frozen bank, till the air rang again with their metallic laughter! I never grew tired of studying the veined marbled patterns they drew upon the face of the river, nor of observing their glittering shapes—running nooses, arabesques, trailing garlands, slow merry-go-rounds, chaotic forms incessantly metamorphosing themselves into creatures strange and yet stranger—the embodiments of the river's capricious and ever-shifting fancy.

All day the current moved at a satisfactory pace, and we drifted on without let or hindrance past the luxuriant forests and imposing stragglers of the great sandy desert, which continually sprang into view one after the other in a succession of remarkable pictures. But we were no longer journeying on the still and placid waters of the Yarkand-daria. The air was full of murmurs from the grinding ice, murmurs which never ceased, but grew louder and louder in proportion as the river contracted. The icy fringe along each bank was now growing rapidly wider. Three or four days more, and the gap would be completely closed up. Even now those reaches, in which the current slowed down, were in several places coated with a film of ice as bright as glass.

Then the forest thinned out again, the river once more widened, and the country became more open, allowing us to see unrestricted in every direction. Very often the stream stretched straight away in front of us without stop or termination, white as snow, a veritable winter highway. To the right we beheld in the far-off distance, between the scattered poplars, the desolate and menacing front of the desert dunes, and to the left, equally at a great distance away, the thick black line of the forests of the Ughen-daria.

Upon reaching the embouchure of the canal of Dashi-köll, we were surprised by two horsemen, who had been sent in quest of us by Hassan Beg of Teiz-köll. The beg's son was waiting for us, they said, with ten other men at Momuni-ottogo, a good way down the river. The two scouts had arranged that, when they found us, they would notify the fact to their companions by lighting signal-fires. Accordingly we soon saw their smoky pillars ascending skywards ; and when we reached Momuni-ottogo our visitors were waiting for us, with dastarkhan ready and big fires blazing merrily away.

Hassan Beg's son brought us important news. My caravan had halted at Teiz-köll three days before ; the day previous to our arrival it was to be at Yanghi-köll ; and from thence was to proceed onwards to Arghan, the rendezvous fixed upon before we started from Lailik. As we might now expect to be frozen in at any moment, and it would be important to have the camels close by when that occurred, I sent a mounted messenger to Niaz Hadji and the Cossacks, bidding them halt wherever they might be. I learnt further that my old friend Khalmet Aksakal of Korla was with the caravan, and that Parpi Bai, my old servant of 1896, was awaiting me at Karaul.

With regard to the river, I was told, it remained frozen in that region from the beginning of December to the beginning of March, although for another fortnight after that it was covered with melting ice. It did not begin to attain full flood until the beginning of August, and did not reach its highest level before the end of September or beginning of October. After that the stream dropped continually day by day, but for a short period before the ice began to form it remained stationary. Then, shortly after the river became completely frozen across, the water rose again, and lifted up its blanket of ice. This was said to be due to the damming of the river through the packing together of the drift-ice. But as soon as the dam burst,

The Ferry-boat at the Confluence of the Ughen-daria with the Tarim.

the water dropped again. The river was at its lowest ebb in June, when it is possible to ford it on horseback in several places.

It is of course self-evident that the difference between high-water and low-water in the Lower Tarim, owing to its immense distance from its sources in the mountains, must be far less than it is, for example, in the Yarkand-daria at Yarkand or the Aksu-daria at Aksu. The further you descend the river the more does this difference tend to disappear. The volume of the current is also regulated to no slight degree by the innumerable lagoons and marginal lakes which cling like parasites to the Tarim, and suck up its life-blood all the way down its lower course. The spring freshets, which sweep down the Yarkand-daria, the Aksu-daria, the Khotan-daria, and the Kizil-su, with such torrential violence, gradually lose their uncontrollable energy as they travel along. For every one of these countless lagoons, which has dried up during the course of the summer, has to be filled again, and this drains away an immense amount of water. And it is only after they are all full that the river begins to rise in its lower course. Then, when the supply from the upper regions begins to decrease, and finally ceases altogether, these innumerable reservoirs act as regulators of the lower parts of the stream. At the time we left Lailik, it was high-water here in Momuni-ottogo and Karaul; but now in the beginning of December the river had, for some two months or more, been emptying its muddy waters into the terminal lakes of the Tarim system.

Here, then, at Momuni-ottogo we were once more in contact with friendly and helpful natives. The night was dark and biting cold, and the monotonous murmurs of the drift-ice were every now and again drowned by the peculiar sound which attended the formation of the glassy ice on the quiet, tranquil river. The day had been in every way a memorable and happy one. We had made a long and instructive stage, and we had heard good news. But it was also the first Sunday in Advent, and we stood now on the threshold of the Tarim's sepulchre, for the river was being buried more and more under the wreaths of its own white immortelles.

During the last three days the velocity had increased. On the 4th December we travelled at an average rate of 2¼ miles an hour; but sometimes even this was uncomfortably fast, for as our ferry-boat scraped and crunched against the edges of the fixed ice she made them hiss and snarl angrily. When an eddy got hold of her, she drove slap-dash in amongst the ice-disks, scattering them without ceremony. The poplar woods gradually died away, and at Karaul, where we struck the confluence of the Ughen-daria, the country was entirely naked, except for reed-beds, low sand-dunes, and tamarisks.

We stopped at Karaul, for there Parpi Bai and a number of other natives were waiting for us. My faithful old servant hastened on board, and seizing my hands carried them to his forehead; but he was so affected at seeing me again that for a long time he was quite unable to speak. He, too, like Islam Bai, had aged, and got grey hairs in his beard; but in all other respects he was the same fine fellow he always had been. In fact he looked particularly well, owing to the very appropriate dress he wore, a dark blue chapan and a blue cap edged with fur.

We stayed over the whole of the next day at Karaul. I wanted to take an astronomical observation, as well as measure the volumes of the Ughen-daria and the Tarim. The former had no drift-ice at all; but the latter was choke full of it, so that it was more difficult than usual to measure it. The main river carried a volume of 1,967 cubic feet, the Ughen-daria a very much smaller amount. On the other hand, whereas the Ughen was transparent down to 27 inches, the Tarim was transparent to only 3 inches; and the different waters could be clearly distinguished a quarter of a mile below the confluence.

The aksakal of Korla, who also met me here, brought with him two or three boxes of pears and grapes—but the fruit was sadly spoiled by the frost—and a few hundred cigarettes which the Russian Consul at Urumchi had sent me four years before, but which only now reached their destination.

Karaul stands at the point where the river makes the great bend to the south-east which takes it direct to Lop-nor without any further tedious windings. The current was strong; and once, when we struck against a tograk stem that jutted up from the bottom, our boat was helped over by the pressure of the drift-ice. All the same it was anything but a comfortable feeling, for one side was lifted clean out of the water, and after scraping the whole of her length over the obstruction, she banged down again with a loud splash. During the course of the day the sand again approached the right bank. In this, the last section of its course, the river contracted and assumed the form of a narrow canal, hemmed in by deeply-scarped banks, and with only a few small deposits of alluvium.

The Meeting of Parpi Bai and Islam Bai at Karaul.

The 7th of December was our last day on the Tarim. We knew it first thing in the morning, for the caravan was waiting for us at Yanghi-köll, only one day's journey further on, and just below that point the river had frozen over two days before. We started the day therefore with mixed feelings. The Lailik boatmen were glad that the hour of their deliverance had at last struck. Islam and Kader were anxious to get back to their own companions and the life ashore. As for myself, although I was very pleased the journey had been so successful, and had ended at such a convenient place, I nevertheless began the last day of it with feelings of melancholy, for I should be truly sorry to leave the dear old ferry-boat, which for the past two months and a half had made me such a peaceful home.

We were escorted on the bank by three other begs and a large cavalcade of horsemen from the surrounding villages; but I would not allow anybody to come on board, except the beg of Yanghi-köll, a man with whom we were destined to have a good deal to do in the future.

That last day proved to be one of the most interesting of the entire journey; for it brought us into a region wholly unlike any we had passed through before. The river flowed, as I have already said, due south-east. To the east, steppes of grass and kamish stretching to infinity, dotted at wide intervals with solitary poplars; to the west, an unbroken expanse of high and sterile sand-dunes, their bases advancing to the very brink of the river. In spite of this, however, they made room for a chain of peculiar lakes, peculiar in that they were entirely embosomed in sand, and did not support one blade of vegetation on their borders. General Pievtsoff had noted some of them; but neither he nor I were at all aware that their number was so great. I determined therefore to explore them more thoroughly, to map them, and sound them; but I shall return to this again later on.

The river was now in general narrow, and only expanded when it cut into the sand-dunes in getting round a corner. Its bed was choke full of drift-ice, that is to say, two-thirds of it; it was only the centre, the actual current, that was free. In several places we only just managed to get through at the cost of breaking the edges of the fixed ice, which, upon being broken, rang like glass. The ice-disks were getting too crowded, they had not room to swim, but ground against one another, mounted on top of one another, and piled themselves into little ridges on the margins of the fixed ice. Notwithstanding this they continued to sweep on down the river with irresistible force. The centre of the disks, which only a few days before was so soft, had by this become considerably firmer; a single frost, very little sharper than usual, would cause them to freeze together in one continuous and immovable mass.

The first of the long series of desert lagoons, which hang like grapes on a stalk along the right bank of the Lower Tarim, was called Tuz-algutsh-köll, or the "Lake where Salt is taken." Although I knew I should have a good opportunity later to examine these highly interesting formations, I could not resist landing even now to have a general look at this one. It was squeezed tight in amongst the sand-dunes, and the ice which covered it glittered like a mirror set in a gold frame. The little channel which connected the lake with the river was stopped up with a dam of branches and clay. In this way the lake would be cut off from the Tarim for a space of two or three years, because the natives believe that the fish grow fatter and acquire a better flavour after the water has become faintly saline.

The second lake of the series was the Seit-köll, which penetrated close upon one day's journey into the sand. It was connected with the river by three outlets, all of them stopped, to prevent the flood entering from the river at the next season of high water. One of the three must at some time or other have been traversed by a strong current, for there was a little mill standing on it.

Near the outlets of these lakes were several abandoned villages. At one, Seit-köll, twenty-three families had dwelt; at Tuz-algutsh, nine; and, a little higher up, at Teiz-köll, twenty-five. Their dwellings, huts made of poplar wood and kamish, were still standing, and looked quite new and habitable; yet there was not a living creature about them, nor a single footprint visible in the sand that was heaped up against them like drifted snow. I was told that these villages, as well as several others lower down the river, had been abandoned seven years before owing to a visitation of small-pox (*chichek*), which literally decimated them. The Chinese authorities had transferred the survivors to the left bank, where they had assigned them parcels of land. Previous to the outbreak these people had lived almost entirely upon fish; but since then they had completely changed their mode of life, and now cultivated the ground, and sowed wheat, and eked out their livelihood by breeding live stock. The soil, however, was only of moderate quality, and although

Ördek in his Canoe, and Palta and two other Men in a Double Canoe, on the Ughen-daria.

they might easily have irrigated their fields by digging rivulets from the river, they did not do so, and the produce was not sufficient to support them, so that they were often forced to sell their sheep to buy themselves flour from Korla. The wealthiest of these people owned as many as a thousand sheep; but the greater part of them were poor, and every summer went back to their old fishing-grounds, the lakes, to fish. Yet they were very careful not to enter their former huts, which awakened such sad memories in the minds of most of them, but lay in the open air. Now, however, the Chinese have introduced

Low Continuous Sand-dunes at Karaul.

compulsory vaccination, although the natives are sceptical as to its efficacy.

We landed again at Seit-köll, and climbed a high dune, which commanded a magnificent view of the lake. This last, which was said to be over 24 feet deep, stretched away about 25° west of south, and resembled a fjord ensconced between vertical cliffs. It was entirely frozen over, though the ice was reported to bear at the outside only.

The elbow at which Seit-köll was situated penetrated deeply into the sand, forming as it were an advanced creek. Originally the great sandy desert extended a long way towards the north-east; but it had been gradually forced back by the river. Thus here again the Tarim was apparently deviating towards the right.

The explanation which the natives of the country offered me as to the origin of these desert lakes was extremely fantastic. They asserted that the canals or outlet channels were dug first, and that, when the river was seeking new passages for itself at the time of high flood, it found its way into them, forced back the sand-dunes, and formed these large lakes. It hardly requires to be pointed out that no amount of digging of canals would have given rise to these lakes had not certain indispensable conditions of nature been already present. From the hydrographical standpoint, the lake of Dashi-köll also was very peculiar. Although it lay quite close to the river bank, it was

Abandoned Huts at Seit-köll.

nevertheless separated from it by a considerable ridge of sand. But quite recently the stream had swept the ridge completely away, leaving lake and river connected and at precisely the same level, so that when the one rises the other rises also, and *vice versâ*. Close beside the breach were some poplars, sticking up without rhyme or reason through the ice. Here again we obtained a fjord-like view, penetrating into the desert.

Nor were these the only lakes of the series; but the others are dealt with lower down.

At a place called Arelish we were met by Chernoff and Faisullah, and yet lower down by Niaz Hadji and several other men of the caravan, all of whom escorted us along the bank, in company with a troop of dogs which they had recently acquired.

The Outermost Sand-dunes at Yanghi-köll.
Parpi Bai, Palta, and Islam Bai.

Their delight at seeing us all safe and sound after our long and trying voyage was indescribable. They had scarcely believed it possible I should be able to navigate our uncouth monster of a boat all those hundreds of miles, whilst they were taking so many wearisome steps along the dusty highways of Turkestan. Having joined hands with our caravan, we were now free to stop wherever we pleased. But when Chernoff told me that only two hours lower down the drift-ice had piled itself up into a barrier, and then frozen into one solid mass, I resolved to push on that far with the help of our lanterns.

The night was however a long way advanced before we came in sight of the big fire which the men of the caravan had made on the left bank, immediately above the barrier of ice. Here then we pulled in for the last time, and went up to the fire to warm our stiff and frozen limbs.

Thus ended our peaceful and fairy-like journey. Those long and happy days, with their ripe harvest of experiences, our adventures and excursions, our monotonous life on board, our Venetian evenings, and the never-ending woods which had strewn our path with their yellowing leaves—all this, as I looked back upon it, seemed like a dream. Never was a journey of that magnitude carried through so comfortably and so successfully. Nothing could well have made a more seasonable transition from the sedentary life I had been leading in Stockholm to the years of toil which now lay before me. I had been carried, as it were, on a triumphal car to the very heart of Asia, and whichever way I turned, there was the unknown beckoning me with its magnetic finger. It was a remarkable coincidence, that we should have been stopped just at the point at which the caravan had arrived. The original rendezvous was Arghan; but the ice prevented us from getting there. This, however, turned out eventually to be no loss, but on the contrary an advantage. For Yanghi-köll was the best possible starting-place for the long and perilous excursions which I had planned to make across the desert both east and west. It was, further, another great advantage not to be too far away from Korla, the nearest town where we could procure what we required for the further equipment of our caravans. It was only a three days' journey thither for a man on horseback.

CHAPTER XIV.

IN WINTER QUARTERS.

THERE was no longer any need for haste, and oh! how delightful it was the next morning, the 8th December, to be able to sleep on in peace, undisturbed! I spent the day copying photographic plates, while the Cossacks went to look at a place that seemed to be exceptionally well suitable for winter quarters, situated on the left bank a few hundred yards above the spot where we had stopped. Thither they removed all the baggage and put up their tents. One of the advantages of the site selected was a tiny harbour, with low, but vertical banks. It was, of course, frozen over, but we broke the ice with axes and iron bars. Our ferry-boat had also frozen fast with a vengeance during the night, and had to be liberated from her icy fetters in the same way. Then she was hauled along to the new harbour, and moored to the bank. This last precaution was a work of supererogation, for it was not long before the boat was embedded in solid ice a foot thick. During the course of the winter the water underneath her became partly frozen also, and our far-travelled dwelling became founded as it were upon a bed of granite.

At first I lived on board, for I had everything handy about me; and I made abundant use of the dark room.

The first evening in our new winter camp gave rise to one of those deplorable and tiresome discoveries which are common when you are so childish or so good-natured as to place too great confidence in the honesty of a Mohammedan. Before leaving Lailik I gave Niaz Hadji 4½ yambas (£36) for the expenses of the journey, partly to provide sustenance for the caravan, partly to make certain other purchases. The amount ought to have been more than sufficient, and there should have been a surplus over; but instead of that my karavan-bashi not only spent it all, but had actually borrowed another four yambas on the way, which I was now called upon to pay. Accordingly, placing myself on the high seat of justice, to wit a flour sack, beside the fire, I held a searching inquiry, while round about me stood the accused, his accusers, the witnesses, and the spectators. The affair was both solemn and tragic, and I would willingly have paid another two or three yambas to have been spared the painful necessity of sitting in judgment upon my own employé. But it had to be done, both for the sake of the example and warning it would be to the rest of the men, and because it was an occasion on which it was incumbent upon me to exert my authority as leader of the expedition. Calling Niaz Hadji forward into the firelight, I bade him give an account of how he had dealt with the talent I entrusted to him. What sort of an answer he made will be readily imagined by those who have had anything to do with Mohammedans. He tried to show that not a tengeh had been diverted from its legitimate purpose, and that he had honourably and faithfully discharged his office; but he lied. For Sirkin had, at my request, kept an account of the disbursements, so that it was easy to control the caravan-leader's statements. Besides this, the man was also accused of unseemly behaviour towards the other men, whom he looked down upon and treated with contempt. At Aksu he had paid his own debts, at Korla his son's debts, and had wound up by bringing the latter gentleman along with him at my expense.

I did not want to be too severe upon him, especially on a day which had ended so agreeably for me; besides, I was not free from reproach myself for putting the temptation of such a large sum of money in his way. I condemned him to be dismissed from my service, and the sentence was to take effect on the following day.

Strange beings, those Mussulmans! You never can be quite sure of them. The very men who had accused Niaz Hadji now came to me to intercede for him, begging me to keep him, even if it were only to cook the other men's food. But no; I had pronounced judgment, and would not alter it, although I felt truly sorry for the poor old man, Mecca pilgrim though he was, especially as he had formerly served Przhevalsky. I promised to forget the affair, and when he left us gave him half a yamba to stop his tears and help him tide over the winter. This was the end of his "story," and no doubt he thanked his stars that he had got off so well.

The next thing was to get the camp settled down, and to

organise a fresh caravan for the next expedition I contemplated. This took up three days, the 9th, 10th, and 11th of December. I sent Khalmet Aksakal to Korla to buy candles and sugar, and sailcloth for various purposes, and then bade him go on to Kara-shahr, and buy two Mongolian *kibitkas* (tents) and five mules, as well as change some silver ingots into small coin, that is to say into tengehs* of Yakub Beg's period, which are still current between Korla and Charkhlik, at the rate of 21 to a sär (3s.). I also sent along with him Musa Ahun to bring back the things Khalmet bought at Korla, and gave the latter my budget of letters, with instructions to send them on to Kashgar. The writing of these also kept me very busy.

It was now time to send back the four boatmen to their distant home in Lailik, and as they had behaved so well, and always been such pleasant fellows to deal with, I doubled their wages and gave them in addition enough to pay their expenses all the way home. They were deeply touched, and with tears in their eyes recited their *Dua!* and *Allahu akbar*; and really I too was quite sorry to part from them, they had proved themselves such capital fellows. It was arranged that they should accompany the Aksakal on foot to Korla, where he was to buy them good horses so that they might ride the rest of the journey. I never heard anything more of them, but trust they reached home in safety.

Notwithstanding this serious diminution in the number of my employés, the camp was still the scene of considerable life and bustle. Islam Bai now became karavan-bashi; and he and the two Cossacks were my principal assistants. Parpi Bai I appointed to look after the horses; when they did not require his attention, he amused himself with hawking, and fed his hawks upon live poultry, anything but an edifying spectacle. Turdu Bai and Faisullah took charge of the camels, one of them being always on watch whilst the animals were out grazing. A fine old fellow from Aksu, sixty years of age, but frank and happy as a boy, Kurban by name, acted as errand-boy, taking the horses down to water, and carrying out his meals to the man who watched the camels. Ördek, a Lop-man, and a first-rate fellow, who had an exceptional knowledge of all that region, was engaged, amongst other things, to do labourer's work about the camp, such as carrying water for cooking purposes, gathering

* See the table of monetary values, p. 40.

dry wood in the nearest forest, which the camels afterwards fetched in, and getting in provender for the horses. Although we chopped a hole through the ice in the little harbour, and always kept it open, we made a practice of taking our drinking water and water for cooking from the middle of the river, where there was always a fresh, pure current. The begs of the neighbourhood arranged that their Lop-men should sell us fodder for our animals, and the first day or two they brought in no less than a thousand bundles of clover and a thousand bundles of straw, which they let us have at the current rates. Finally I engaged a smith, and the first thing I set him to do was to help Sirkin make me a pair of skates. My idea was to use them for travelling across the lakes I have spoken of; but they were not sufficiently well made to allow of my doing anything more than pottering about close at home.

The camp was continually visited by troops of Lopliks, or Lop-men; for no sooner did our neighbours learn that we had settled in their country, and founded a little village in the wilderness, than they began to make pilgrimages to visit us, and they never came empty-handed; besides which I gleaned a good deal of useful information from them. Thus people were coming and going unceasingly, and from my tent on the ferry-boat, where I sat at work, I heard an unbroken murmur of voices as from a busy market-place.

My men's tent was erected underneath the only poplar there was in the camp, and behind it all the camel-loads were packed up on the framework just as they had been lifted from the animals' backs. The cook carried on his operations over a fire in the open air, surrounded by a big barricade of fire-wood, which was continually being added to as the winter advanced. The camp was guarded by five watch-dogs which the men had brought with them from Kuchar and Korla. Two of these were greyhounds, capital dogs, and very affectionate. I christened them Mashka and Taigun, and they soon became prime favourites. They were exceptionally handsome beasts, big-boned, tall, and white coloured, with very short hair. For this reason they were very fond of being near the fire; while at night they slept in my tent in coats, or rather bags, of white felt, which I had specially made for them. It was very comical to see how cleverly they learnt to creep under these coverings without help from anybody, and how grateful they were, and what sighs of comfort they breathed, when I tucked them snugly in. But on the field of canine battle they were unsurpassed, and kept all the dogs of the neighbourhood in a state of terror. Nor have I ever seen animals that waged battle in a cunninger way than Mashka and Taigun. They would snuffle about their antagonist until they got an opportunity to seize a hind-leg, whereupon they would swing him round, and drag him away at such a pace that he very soon went head over heels, and when he got up, he invariably fled, howling and limping on three legs. At feeding time not one of the other dogs durst look at a piece of meat until after these two were fully satisfied. They were excellent company, and made a good substitute for the first Dovlet that died; but alas! their days too were numbered.

After they came into the camp I cannot say that Yolldash exactly fell into disgrace; it was rather that he withdrew into private life, and never ventured inside my tent when the new-comers were there. But he always slept faithfully outside it, and when I stepped out and patted him, he jumped and barked with delight. Yollbars ("the tiger") was a gigantic dog of a dark brown colour, a son of the Lop jungle with wolf's blood in his veins. He was kept bound by an iron chain close to the camel-loads, and was so fierce that nobody ever ventured to go within the radius of his tether. He was a perfect model of a watchdog, a sort of Knight of the Deadly Fangs; but even with him I soon became good friends. Yollbars was an important member of our caravan, and afterwards accompanied us on the road to Lassa; and when, two years afterwards he disappeared without leaving a trace behind him, he was greatly missed by everybody. I love dogs; they take the keenest interest in everything that happens in and to a caravan, and never shirk their duty.

When I stepped out of my tent on the morning of the 10th December, I was surprised to see the wooden framework of a house standing ready fixed on the bank. This excellent idea was due to the beg of Yanghi-köll, who had "commandeered" his people, procured the beams, and begun the work at daybreak. The framework consisted of upright posts, narrow spars, and laths, strongly bound together with withies and ropes. Later in the day it was provided with walls, consisting of bundles of reeds set up on end all round it, and the roof also was made of layers of reeds. The method of construction was that common throughout the Lop country, and when finished it was quite an idyllic dwelling, and was even large enough to be divided into two

Our Winter-quarters at Yanghi-köll. The men, going from left to right, are Kader, Turdu Bai, Kasim, Chernoff, Parpi Bai, Sirkin, Niaz Hadji, Khalmet Aksakal, Islam—the last five kneeling—and behind them Faisullah, Palta, Musa, and others.

fair-sized apartments. The idea was that one of these should be used as my living room, while all the baggage was stowed away in the other. However, I remembered what once happened to Schweinfurth, who lost the collections and notes which it had taken him years to gather, because he stored them in a hut of an inflammable character. I preferred therefore to leave my stores outside in the open air, though I took the precaution of covering them down with felting and sailcloth. Had it been my intention to spend the whole winter at Yanghi-köll, I should of course have had a complete and comfortable house built entirely of wood, and put into it the windows of the dark room

Tura-sallgan-uy.

which I had on board the ferry-boat; but I had other plans in view. This camp was a first-rate place, but I only spent a few days there on three separate occasions; and it even acquired a certain degree of fame throughout the Lop country. The Lopliks bestowed upon it the name of Tura-sallgan-uy, that is the "House built by the Great Man," and they assured me that the name would persist to all time as a constituent of the geographical nomenclature of the neighbourhood, just as a certain spot on the Kunchekkish-tarim is called to this day Uruz-sallgan-sal, or the "Russian built a Ferry-boat," because Kozloff once crossed the river there on a raft of dry tograk-stems.

The hut was eventually overtaken by the fate that comes to all the perishable things of earth. Next summer when the floods came, they swept it away, and along with it destroyed both our little harbour and pier and the poplar tree which stood close beside it; but by that time we were gone, and our Penates transferred to higher and safer ground.

How peacefully these few days passed at Tura-sallgan-uy; I was no prouder when, as the guest of His Majesty Shah Nasr-ed-Din, of Persia, I trod the mirrored halls and marble salons of Emaret-Sepa-Salar than I was within the kamish walls of this airy domicile in the land of Lop, where the wind whistled its melancholy, never-ending funeral marches through the stalks of the reeds.

We also built for our eight horses a roomy stable of similar materials, leaving one long side of it open to the camp. Along the other ran the manger, that is to say, two canoes, out of which the horses ate their maize and hay. Further, we bought more poultry, as well as some sheep and cows, which gave us a supply of milk. Thus I speedily gathered about me a farmyard, which, although not exactly a model of its kind, was at any rate the most comfortable and the most delightful of any I have ever had to do with. The space between the huts, the tent, the stack of camel-loads, the "kitchen," and the little harbour formed an open courtyard, the market-place of our village, and in the centre of it a fire was kept burning night and day. This was the place of honour, the place where carpets were spread and guests received; it was our "club." But although our fire was not allowed to go out until May of the following year, it was not tended by vestal virgins, but by bearded barbarians. It was the duty of our night-watchmen, who were relieved every second hour, and looked after by the Cossacks, to replenish the fire; in fact during the cold winter nights they generally sat beside it when not making their periodical rounds.

Ever since my arrival I had been trying to gather information about the desert to the south-west; but the knowledge which the natives possessed of its secrets really amounted to very little. That gigantic wall of sterile sand-hills which stretched alongside the right bank of the river had for me an attraction, a fascination there was no resisting. Yet one thing I felt perfectly sure of, and that was, I was going to venture a perilous assault upon their fortifications by crossing the Takla-makan Desert at its widest part. But as I have said, I could glean very little information of value about it. What astonished me most was the horror with which the people spoke of the desert. Their usual names for it were simply Kum (Sand) or Chong-kum (Great Sand), though also Shahr-i-Kettek-kum (Town in the Dead Forest Sand), this last name being derived from a legendary town which was said to be buried in its interior. For a man to lose himself there, they regarded as the worst evil that could by any possibility happen to him. Nobody had ever been far into the desert, neither the camel-hunters of former times nor the gold-hunters of the present day. The farthest they ever ventured was two days' journey from the river; then, overwhelmed by the terror of that awful sand, they always hastened back. If we were so foolish as to try to cross it—well, we were committing sheer suicide, for we should never come back again. But I quieted their fears, telling them it was not the first time I had dared to beard the lion in his den.

To the south-west of Tura-sallgan-uy there was a break in the line of the sand-dunes, and through it, they told me, ran a track to the basin of Bash-köll, in front of which was a village called Yanghi-köll-uy, where several of our purveyors and new friends lived. The little information I did obtain about the desert only whetted my desire to investigate it. Beyond the lakes, they told me, and in the line of their longer axes, stretched several bare, open depressions, resembling the beds of dried-up lakes; these, according to the natives, were formed by the north-east wind sweeping the sand away. They called them *bayir*; but nobody was able to tell me how far they extended into the desert. All they could say was, they had always heard that many hundreds of years ago there lived, a long way towards the south-west, a heathen race, ruled over by one Atti Kush Padishah. Holy imams had gone there to preach the faith of Islam, but the people refused to listen to the new faith; so the imams cursed them, and invoked God's vengeance upon their country, and it rained sand for several days, until the country, and all its inhabitants, and all their cities, were buried under it.

Before making a definitive start, I decided to undertake a short trip for purposes of reconnaissance, and accordingly I called my people together round the fire in the evening, and issued my orders for the following day, the 11th December. They were to lead across the river the camels I proposed to take with me, to prepare the requisite supplies of provisions and fodder, and to keep open the communication between both banks as best they could. During my absence the hut was to be made as comfortable as possible, so that it might serve as a dwelling-place. They were to divide one of the big apartments, namely that which stood next the river, into two smaller ones, and the inner of the two was to be provided with a double wall of reeds, as well as lined on the inside with felts, to shut out the draught. The floor was to be strewn with reeds and carpets, but in the middle of the floor they were to make a fire-pit, and in the roof immediately above it a hole for the smoke to escape by. All this was to be done by the time I returned; the truth was I found my tent too cold, with the temperature at 18°.0 to 20°.0 below zero.

It was, however, by no means an easy matter to get the camels across the river. For the first thing, we were mistaken in supposing the ice bore. A violent wind had rent apart the seams last frozen; then they froze to again during the night of the 10th December, but not sufficiently to bear the weight of a camel. To have made the animals swim across would have been to kill them. The only way out of the difficulty was to transport them across on the big ferry-boat, yet she was held fast as in a vice. However the Cossacks were not to be beaten. They gathered people and chopped a passage-way for her through the ice, thick as it was. Then, at a point in the river immediately above the camp, where it was only 102 feet wide, and where there was open water right across except for a narrow fringe along the right bank, they stretched a rope four times backwards and forwards across. The depth exceeded 28 feet, and the current flowed at the rate of 2¼ miles an hour. This happened to be the very last place which became permanently frozen. Then by means of the rope the men hauled the ferry over, carrying one camel at a time on the after-part. As soon as they were all safely across, they were led away to the nearest pasture.

In the afternoon we were honoured by the visit of a Chinese *siah* or secretary. He was sent by the amban or governor of Kara-shahr to ask after the state of my health; but in reality he was a harmless spy, sent to find out what sort of a traveller I was. Late in the evening we had another visitor, namely, my old friend and former host, Naser Beg, of Tikkenlik, who stayed all night, and gave me some useful information. For one thing he told me "a Russian" had come to Charkhlik from

Dung-khan (*i.e.*, Sa-chow), and would be with me within a week. I suspected this was not a Russian, but the French traveller, M. Bonin. He also reported that the lakes of Avullu-köll, Kara-köll, Arka-köll, and so forth, which I discovered during my former journey, still remained about the same size. He told me too that in the days of his forefathers begs had come from Turfan to exact, on behalf of the Chinese, tribute of otter skins from the inhabitants of the Lop country. The route these envoys used to take ran to the east of the Bagrash-köll, over the Kurruk-tagh and the Kum-daria, then across the Ilek (or Koncheh-daria) at Turfan-köbruk, and so on to Kara-köll. This we know from Chinese sources actually was the case. Otters (*kama*) do frequent the lake of Chivillik-köll and several of the other lakes in that locality; but so far as I could ascertain they are not present in the Kara-koshun. This difference is important and significant; it suggests that the northern lakes are not in connection with the southern lakes, but are an entirely new formation. The otters are caught on the ice after a snow-fall; for although the fall of snow in these parts is very slight, it is nevertheless sufficient to show which way an animal has gone. When the hunter has tracked his otter to a hole, he waits until the creature comes up again from his fishing, and stabs him with a kind of fish-spear (*senjkak*), or catches him in a net the moment he pops his head above water. If there happen to be several fishing holes, each hole is trapped and watched; but the sport is never indulged in unless there has been snow.

About two years previously Naser Beg had been at Tuzun-chappgan, and from a hill close by had observed a cloud or mist (*bulut*) about a day's journey to the north-east; he thought it arose from some unknown lake to the north of Kara-koshun. It was his opinion that it was the lake into which the Kum-daria, the present dry river-course which extends along the foot of the Kurruk-tagh, formerly discharged its waters, a conclusion which showed sound judgment, and which, so far as I was able to ascertain subsequently, was perfectly correct.

All this and a good deal more I was told by the fat and jolly beg, and I let his words sink into my memory; nor were they without influence upon my subsequent plans.

CHAPTER XV.

RECONNOITRING IN THE DESERT—M. BONIN.

THE weather on the 12th December, the day fixed for the beginning of the excursion, was not at all inviting; it was blowing hard from the south-west, and we became chilled to the bone the moment we stepped outside of either tent or hut. The wind swept through the gap of the Bash-köll as if it were being pumped through a funnel, and the dense banks of clouds which obscured the sky tended to make the day still colder. The Cossacks were dressed in furs like Arctic explorers, and each carried a hunting-piece. Besides them, Faisullah, Ördek, and Pavan Aksakal (the White-bearded Hunter) also took part in the trip. The last-named, a big, good-natured old fellow from the village of Yanghi-köll, was one of our best friends in this locality, and did everything in his power to serve us. The caravan consisted of only four camels, which we took turns about in riding. After loading them up on the right bank, we set off for the village of Yanghi-köll and the canal of Bash-köll. As this last was cut off from the river ten years ago, its water was now salt; we therefore took with us a supply of ice for drinking and cooking.

The village, which consisted of 20 families, used formerly to stand on the canal of Yanghi-köll, but eight years ago eleven of the inhabitants died of small-pox, after which the survivors flitted to the mouth of the Bash-köll, carrying the old name with them. When a man fell ill of the small-pox, everybody near him fled, leaving the sick man to his fate. Pavan Aksakal was the oldest man in the little community, and cleverly controlled the fishing in the lake.

After leaving the village we continued along the south-east side of the Bash-köll, which was frozen all round close in shore, hard enough to bear the weight of a man. Further from the shore the ice was very thin and precarious, while in the middle of the lake were several large open sheets of pure blue water, a striking contrast to the desolate yellow sand piled up all round the shores. The cause of the lake not being entirely frozen over was the slight admixture of salt it contained. There were a few ducks and swans floating on the open reaches. This lake was barely 12 miles long, and seldom more than $1\frac{1}{4}$ miles wide, in two or three places even only half that width. It stretched due south-south-west, and resembled a fjord penetrating the sand-dunes, which at its extreme end were barely lifted above the horizon. The lake did not, however, at that end quite reach the base of the sand-dunes, but was separated from them by a strip of gently sloping ground, consisting of sand and silt, very soft in summer, but at the time of our visit frozen as hard as a stone. If the channel, which formerly connected the lake with the river, were to be opened again, this low-lying strip of soft soil would be inundated to the depth of 5 or 6 feet. The immediate extremity of the lake was girdled by a belt of luxuriant reeds, some 25 to 50 yards broad, while close at the foot of the dunes were patches of tamarisks. On the east side of the lake, along which we were travelling, the dunes descended at the steep angle of 33°, but on the opposite side they resembled a giant staircase, coming down by terraces. This difference was accounted for by the east wind, the wind which predominates throughout the whole of the Lop country. Except for an occasional poplar, more rarely a small grove, the landscape wore a strangely uniform aspect.

As there was plenty of firewood at the southern end of the lake, we halted there. Just before dark we collected a big pile of dry tamarisk branches, and, gathering round the fire in the happiest frame of mind, ate the excellent dinner of partridges, rice-pudding, and tea which the Cossacks had prepared, and then, after I had written out my notes for the day, we rolled ourselves in our furs and were soon asleep, the sky above being our only covering.

The next morning the earth was white with rime-frost, which indeed lay so thick that the dunes looked as if they were covered with snow. The thermometer showed −8°.0 C. or 17°.5 Fahr., and as the lofty dunes on the east side of the lake shut out the rising sun, we felt it pretty cold.

Beyond the lake the sand went up by steps, which were not at all steep, and then quite suddenly all vegetation ceased. From the top of the ascent we observed to the south-west a *bayir* or depression, which was probably half a mile long and a quarter of a mile broad, moist and barren in the middle, where it showed indications of salt, and with thinly-scattered clumps of grass along the sides. Its general shape was that of a cauldron, for it was shut in all round by a ring of steep, gigantic dunes, and resembled the bottom of a former lake, which the drift-sand had carefully shunned. Seeing how these bayirs are so freely exposed to every wind that blows, it is amazing they were not long ago filled up with sand.

To the south and south-west was nothing except a sea of sand, with sharply-defined protuberances, the culminating crests or ridges of the accumulations of individual sand-dunes. It was like looking out over the waves of the wild Atlantic, except that they were waves of stationary sand, not of moving water. One naturally inferred that there were numerous bayirs hidden in the valleys between. The protuberances or crests of the dunes lay closer together in this neighbourhood than they did in the western parts of the Takla-makan Desert, and very often the dunes were steep on both sides, showing how changeable the winds are. The prevalent wave-formation proved, however, that the east wind is the stronger, and blows more frequently than any other wind.

Having obtained this general survey of the region and its contours, and ascertained that this point was not altogether favourable for making a start from, seeing that the bayir of Bash-köll, with its easy and level floor, only extended a short distance, I decided to choose some other point of departure, and to return now to Tura-sallgan-uy by way of the lake of Yanghi-köll. Accordingly we turned due east, and so had the steep slopes of the dunes against us. Before, however, we could face all these giant stairs, we were obliged to make a long detour in order to get the camels over the stupendous "wave," or ridge, which parted the two lakes. The animals did not feel at all sure of themselves on the uneven surface, and grew terrified. Upon reaching the summit of the pass two of them went over it on their knees, so as to be nearer to the ground in case they should fall.

Whilst the caravan continued on further, Pavan Aksakal guided me to the top of a lofty dune, some 350 feet in height, which commanded a splendid view of the whole country, and from which our camels down below looked no bigger than beetles. South-west of Yanghi-köll I noted three big bayirs, separated by considerable masses of sand, which were like pits in the billowy surface—islands amid the ocean of sand. North-east lay the lake, covered with glittering greyish-blue ice, and beyond it the immense wall of sand which rose between Yanghi-köll and the right bank of the Tarim.

After having with some difficulty piloted the camels over a formidable ridge, we went down into the big oblong bayir which lay next the innermost part of the Yanghi-köll. The bottom was entirely free from sand, and consisted of concentric belts of different formation. The outermost ring, next the foot of the dunes, consisted of powdery dust, into which the camels dropped a foot or more; then came a girdle of marshy soil, and inside that a ring of salt. The north-eastern part of the bayir contained one large pool and several small ones, all with intensely salt water. Beyond this bayir, and still towards the north-east, followed a patch of reeds six to seven feet high; there we found a suitable spot to camp in, with plenty of dry wood.

Our bayir was separated from the lake by a sandy neck of land, about 100 feet high. At its foot were some springs, the water of which was fresh when it first bubbled out, but grew salt after it accumulated at the bottom of the depression. Viewed from this sandy ness, the landscape formed a particularly attractive picture. The Yanghi-köll was so long and so straight that its northern end, next the river, where there was no sand, was invisible. For all we could tell, we might have been standing at the head of a fjord, with the open sea behind the projecting headland, equally as on the shore of a desert lake embosomed amid gigantic sand-dunes. But while the north-west corner of the lake was lit up by the rising sun, the steep sand-walls of the south-eastern angle were plunged in deep shade, and flung their shadows far out across the bright grey-blue surface of the lake. Here the vegetation was scanty, whereas on the diametrically opposite shore it was more fully developed. About a dozen scattered poplars in all might have been counted on both shores together. The water was fresh, and was reputed to be 5 fathoms deep or more. The lake had been cut off about two years, and was to continue in that condition seven or eight more, all for the sake of the fishing. But a few open places near its north-eastern shore indicated the presence of subterranean springs. These, however, did not yield sufficient water to compensate for the loss by evaporation and other causes, and that the lake was shrinking was evident from the ice, for it was higher at the margins than in the middle.

Our route lay to the north-north-east along the lake side.

As we advanced we found the lake diversified by lagoons, peninsulas, and islands, but these existed nowhere else. In respect of size, shape, and general appearance, the Yanghi-köll was exactly like the Bash-köll, in that it resembled a fjord. Sometimes the track took us down upon the ice, which was as pure and transparent as glass, and the water underneath it as bright as crystal. At a depth of two or three fathoms the minutest object was plainly visible at the bottom. At first we had a sort of feeling that we were actually travelling on the water itself. The picture at the bottom was like a scene in an aquarium—algæ as motionless as coral, and big black-backed fishes which hung without movement, half asleep amongst the clusters of algæ. When the Cossacks awakened them out of their semi-dormant condition by stamping on the ice, they gently moved their fins, and calmly and slowly glided into the depths below. The smaller fish dashed along in shoals underneath the ice close to the shore. There the ice was no less than four inches thick, but a hundred paces from shore it was not more than one inch thick. I have never seen a more magnificent sheet of ice. I was almost tempted to stay beside it all winter, simply for the sake of skimming along its smooth surface in a home-made ice-yacht; it would have been better than risking my life amongst those awful sand-dunes. Continuing alongside the channel which connected the Yanghi-köll with the Tarim, we came to the latter, and, advancing along its right (western) bank, eventually reached the point from which we started. There we found our ferryman awaiting us with his big boat, and were received by Islam Bai and Parpi Bai.

On the 15th December I sent Chernoff, Islam, and Ördek on horseback to examine the Seit-köll and the country to the south-west of it, to see if it would afford a suitable starting-point for our contemplated desert journey. They executed their task both quickly and well. Chernoff and Ördek, who took part in both reconnaissances, were consequently in a position to institute comparisons as to which was the better route. After an absence of 36 hours they returned, bringing with them a rough route-sketch of the country they had traversed. My scouts assured me that they nowhere saw sand-dunes like those we had encountered beside the Yanghi-köll; also that the accumulations of sand which divided the depressions from one another were passable even for horses. From the furthest point they reached towards the south they saw a string of bayirs stretching onwards in the same direction, that is towards the south-west. This would make at all events, the first few days' journey very much easier. Early though the season was, the sand-dunes were already white with rime-frost, and Ördek observed that if we ran short of water, we should be able to quench our thirst with the rime. I suspected, however, it was only in the vicinity of the river that the rime-frost was so copious, and that it would decrease as we penetrated into the desert.

Once more I enjoyed a couple of delightful days' rest at Tura-sallgan-uy. Meanwhile the tent was fitted up and converted into a comfortable dwelling. It will be remembered that the inner half of it was to be divided again; this was

Native Huts at Aktarma, a Village near Yanghi-köll.

now effected by letting drop a thick red felt carpet from one of the beams which supported the roof. Although I transferred my boxes, instruments, writing-table, etc., to the innermost room, I found it impossible to keep it warm, and I durst not introduce a stove amongst all that dry straw; one spark would have been enough to set it ablaze. To overcome this difficulty I opened up a doorway through the back wall of the hut, setting up the tent immediately outside it, and there installed the stove. The outer side of the tent was stitched up, and earth was then banked up against it all round to keep out the draught. After that I slept in the tent again. In the outer division of the hut we kept a variety of bulkier stores, such as saddles. my skiff and its belongings, and various other things. Thus I dwelt in a three-roomed house, and felt so comfortable that it demanded a good deal of resolution to quit it for a cold, perilous, and wearisome march through the desert.

But who could this Oruz Tura (Russian lord) be who was said to be approaching the region where we were? I knew that M. Charles Eudes Bonin had left China, intending to cross the continent *viâ* Sa-chow, Lop, and Urumchi. Surmising that the mysterious traveller might be he, I sent a special messenger to meet him, with an invitation to come and dwell with me. I entrusted the message to Parpi Bai, thinking M. Bonin would be interested to meet a man who had accompanied the Prince of Orleans and M. Bonvalot in their journey across Tibet, and who had witnessed the murder of Dutreuil de Rhins.

Parpi Bai returned on the evening of the 16th, bringing an answer couched in the politest terms of French amiability. M. Bonin, for it was indeed he, had reached the *örtäng* or rest-house of Jan-kuli, some six miles north of our village, and so, taking horse, I rode thither by the light of a brilliant moon, and found the distinguished traveller in a room filled with smoke from a fire in the middle of the floor, surrounded by his Annamite, French-speaking attendants.

Nothing is more delightful, when you have been travelling a long time in a desolate region, than to encounter a European. In this case the pleasure was doubly enhanced because M. Bonin was a quiet, yet bright and charming, man and a scholar, and it was quite a treat for me to sit and listen to his remarkable experiences and hypotheses. He had discovered an old pilgrim-route across the Astyn-tagh into Tibet, and an ancient highway which led from Sa-chow towards the quarter where the old lake of Lop-nor was situated. With regard to the variability of this lake-basin, he entertained the same ideas that I did.

M. Bonin gave me a capital supper, and after breakfast the next morning we rode together to Tura-sallgan-uy, where we spent an unspeakably pleasant and agreeable day together. My French guest examined with the greatest interest our little village and all its "lions"—the huts, the fire-place, the harbour, with its frozen-in boats. We went over together all the sheets of my map of the Tarim and its innumerable windings, and after the moon got up we had a little sail amongst the drift-ice.

But as the evening was cold, I invited my guest into the tent, and got up a roaring fire in the stove. Then my men served up

M. Bonin and the Author at Yanghi-köll.

a Lucullan banquet, embracing everything our larder and store-room were able to offer. The chief dishes were Swedish "Emperor" soup, Tatar *shisslick* (mutton grilled on a skewer), and Turkestan *ash* or rice pudding, followed by a number of canned fruits and so forth, washed down by the only bottle of wine my cellar afforded — a bottle which in an unguarded moment Colonel Saitseff had smuggled into one of my trunks. The banquet, which was also honoured with music, lasted on into the small hours of the morning; and then, while I took a shakedown in the airy "salon," M. Bonin turned in in the tent. It was one of the happiest days I ever spent in the heart of Asia.

Next morning, the 18th December, M. Bonin's far-travelled Chinese cart was driven into our courtyard. The moment was come to part, he to return to his own country, I to disappear into the trackless wilderness of the "desert ocean." He had his task behind him—he had done his work; whereas mine lay before me —a host of enigmas shrouded in an impenetrable mist. When everything was ready, M. Bonin and his attendants were photographed standing under the big Chinese lantern which hung at the end of a post fixed in the middle of the courtyard. The French traveller wore a long red cloak, with a *bashlik* (hood) of the same colour, and looked like a Lamaist pilgrim. A warm shake of the hand, and "Au revoir!" He mounted into his cart, and disappeared behind the bushes, and I was once more alone; but I look back upon our meeting as one of the pleasantest episodes in the whole of the journey.

The river was now frozen so hard immediately above our camp that it bore a man on horseback, and in consequence of the vast quantities of water which in this way became fixed at the bottom of the river, the level steadily dropped, and the current in the open 16-foot channel in the middle was scarcely perceptible. The melting of this solid mass of winter ice occasions in spring a pioneer flood, which the natives call *mus-suyi*, or "ice-water"; it was this we seized advantage of in the following year to get our big ferry-boat farther to the south-east.

The 19th December was the last day for a long time to come that we were to spend at Tura-sallgan-uy, and it was wholly occupied with preparations for the trip across the desert. The depression which began with lake Tana-bagladi-köll was pitched upon as the starting-point.

For the new expedition I appointed as caravan-bashi Islam Bai, the faithful and experienced companion of my former journey across the Takla-makan Desert. The other participators in the march were Turdu Bai, Ördek, and Kurban. We had with us seven camels and one horse, and of the dogs I chose Yolldash and Dovlet II., for I did not wish to compel the sensitive greyhounds to sleep in the open air in the bitter winter cold. A supplementary caravan, with Parpi Bai, Faisullah, and a Loplik Khodai Verdi and three camels were to go with us the first four days, and then return.

With the view of safeguarding my travelling-cases against fire, I had them taken out of the hut and carried back on board the big ferry-boat. My meteorological observatory still remained on the roof of the dark-room, and there the instruments continued to work all through the winter. I had already instructed the Cossack Sirkin how to use them, and now left him in charge of this important branch of my work; besides which, he was appointed chief and captain of the whole camp. It was with an aching heart that I left my two Cossacks behind; but they were necessary for the protection of the camp. They lodged in their own tent, transferring to it the stove, and I gave them two yambas (£15) to meet all expenses, besides a superfluity of provisions. They were made responsible for the safety of the camp and the protection of all the animals I left behind me, amongst them being three young mules, which I had recently bought at Korla for the extraordinary cheap price of only 70 sär (£10 10s.) for the three, and the animals held out for two-and-a-half years. Altogether seven men were left behind at Tura-sallgan-uy, and there they spent a peaceful winter.

Considering the heavy sand we were to march across, I had the loads made as light as possible, and to that end cut down our stores, etc., to the lowest possible margin. We took rice and flour for ten days, ready-baked bread sufficient to last a fortnight, and *talkan*, or roasted flour, which is eaten just as it is, also for a fortnight. For my own use I had in addition a few cases of tinned foods, tea, sugar, and coffee, while the men carried Chinese cube tea. That is to say, we were provisioned only as far as Cherchen, for there we should be able to renew our supplies.

Besides these things, I packed into the only box we carried with us the alt-azimuth and its stand, meteorological instruments, levelling glass, kodak, itineraries, measuring-tape, test-tubes, maps of East Turkestan, and a host of small articles and my clothes. The chronometers I always carried in my pocket.

I was awakened at 7 o'clock on the morning of the 20th

M. Bonin.

December by Islam, who came to tell me there was a violent storm blowing from the south-west; did I intend to start? I at once saw that he was right, for the tent bulged like a sail, and the smoke came "pouthering" out of the bottom of the stove chimney. But I had fixed upon that day for starting, and it is not wise to put off a thing when you have once made up your mind to do it. Hence, whilst I ate my breakfast, the baggage was conveyed over to the other side of the river, where the begs of the neighbourhood and their people came to see us set out on an expedition from which they fully believed we were destined never to return.

The camels were led over the ice on a sanded track and loaded up. My box of instruments, bedding, and cooking utensils made one camel's load; the men's clothing and the larger packages of food a second; the third camel was laden with wood cut into huge blocks; the fourth carried maize for the animals themselves; and the three last were laden with blocks of ice, packed into *tulums* or goat-skins. The three reserve camels carried heavy loads of wood and ice. All the travellers were well provided with winter clothing and heavy furs.

III.

Across the Takla-makan Desert.

The Land of Perpetual Twilight.

CHAPTER XVI.

TRAVERSING THE BAYIRS.

OUR route lay at first between the river on the right and the sand-hills on the left, and led due west amongst open brushwood and thin kamish-beds. However, we soon left the Tarim, turning in towards the sand and striking along the south-east shore of the lake of Tana-bagladi. This, both in form and general appearance, resembled the lakes I have already described, except that it was considerably shorter. Upon reaching its southern extremity, we halted, cut four small holes in the ice, and let the camels drink all they possibly could hold ; this was the last water they would get for a long time to come. And the sagacious animals seemed to understand what lay before them, for they drank and drank, as though they never meant to stop. The little white horse also—he came from Kashgar—as well as the dogs, and the men, all had a good drink ; for, although we carried a supply of ice with us, it might easily happen that later on we should be pinched for the precious fluid. We made our first camp beside a frozen saline pool on the other side of the dunes which shut in the lake on the south.

With the idea of getting as much shelter as we possibly could, we made a big clearing in the heart of the reeds, then lighted a fire of dried grass, and fed it sparingly with chips from one of the wood blocks ; but our only covering was the sky. Parpi Bai, who officiated as cook, washed the rice, and put a piece of lard into the pan, then, when it began to splutter, he added small pieces of meat, onions, and vegetables, and finally poured the rice in, and on the top of all a can of water. That done, he covered the pan with a lid. The whole was left to boil until the water had entirely disappeared, partly as steam, partly through absorption by the rice. Such is the orthodox way of preparing the regulation *ash* or Turkestan rice-pudding.

The next day, thanks to the favourable nature of the ground, our march proved in all respects satisfactory. Our route was determined entirely by those remarkable bayirs, which extended in one long line 35° west of south. Shortly after starting we crossed over a low and easy transverse ridge or threshold, and went down into bayir no. 6. At its lower end—that is the end which came nearest to the river—were a few saline pools surrounded by incrustations of salt. The second and third bayirs were both smaller; but the fourth reassured us, for it was as big as the first three put together.

All these bayirs appeared to lie at one and the same level, and were perfectly flat, as well as separated from one another by short belts or necks of sand. Fortunately for us the sand of which they were built up was not steep. The bottom of the bayirs was seldom hard. In these early ones it consisted of fine moist dust, into which the camels sank fifteen or sixteen inches at every step, so that our progress was slow and tiring. In fact, it took us two minutes to travel 110 yards, so that we moved at the rate of less than two miles an hour. The leading camel had the worst of it, for it fell to him to trample a path for those that followed; while the last of the string had almost a well-beaten path to walk on. I rode behind the camels on my little white horse, but all the men went on foot, except Parpi Bai, who rode on the top of a load of wood.

In shape all the bayirs resembled one another, and it was soon apparent that they owed their formation to the same physical agencies. Except for the absence of water, they were all exactly like the marginal lagoons of the Tarim. Like the Tarim lakes, too, they were inclosed on both sides by sand; but the dunes which shut them in on the south-east formed a continuous barrier, shooting down into them at an angle of about 33°, whereas the slopes on the north-west side ascended very gently, making it pretty certain that at their farther or western base there was another bayir.

It was of course abundantly evident that the route we had chosen was the only possible direction for us to travel in, since it would take us straight to our goal, the village of Tatran on the Cherchen-daria, a day's journey below the town of Cherchen. It is almost absolutely impossible for even a foot-passenger to travel in that desert either to the east or to the west. Every now and again a tongue of sand jutted out across the level floor of the bayir; but these were low, and it was quite easy to make a detour round them.

We halted and formed Camp no. II. near the far end of bayir no. 4; though, as there were no reeds to afford us shelter, we were exposed to the full force of the whirling drift-sand. The one all-engrossing topic of conversation, as we crouched round our two modest fires, was, how far did these helpful bayirs extend? For, so long as we were able to travel along them, there was no danger. Upon climbing to the top of the highest dune to obtain a survey of the country around, my eyes fell upon what was little short of an appalling spectacle. Imagine

The Caravan Threading its Way between Mountains of Dritt-sand.

an ocean of sand, crumpled into gigantic waves, and suppose these waves to come rolling straight in upon you, and to be suddenly arrested just when on the point of breaking and overwhelming you. You will then be able to conceive the scene which I looked upon—an ocean of stupendous waves—waves not of water, but of loose sand, poised and threatening, and ready to burst and roll onwards again the moment the magic *sesame!* was uttered. According to the topographical results of my former journey, the distance we had to travel to reach Tatran was 177 miles, or almost twice the distance I journeyed when I crossed the same desert from the lakes of the Masar-tagh to the Khotan-daria, and yet the latter had been long enough to kill an entire caravan. Both Islam and I—we shall neither of us ever forget that journey—realised only too well how perilous an enterprise our present project was.

With the wind blowing keenly from the west, and the air so heavily charged with dust as to convert the broad daylight into twilight, and with the thermometer down at 11°.0 C. or 12°.2 Fahr., I was naturally reluctant to take off my furs. Accordingly during the whole of the two months this expedition lasted, I slept every night, except when in Cherchen, in the open air, and that without feeling the least ill-effect from it. Even thus early we husbanded our chips of wood and lumps of ice.

Parpi Bai was unwell, and I should have sent him back from Camp no. II., only he was unable to walk in his heavy furs, nor could he travel all the way to Tura-sallgan-uy in a single day. We made room for him therefore on the back of one of the camels, and carried him with us. But this was the last of my expeditions in which the poor fellow was to take part; his days were numbered.

The next day we marched 14 miles, mostly along level bayirs, though the sandy isthmuses between them grew both higher and broader as we advanced. The only fault we had to find with our route was that it continued to go 35° west of south. If it persisted in that direction it would bring us into the very heart of the interminable ocean of sand and compel us to cross its entire expanse in a diagonal line to Niya, a task beyond the powers of any caravan, even under the most favourable conjuncture of circumstances possible. On the other hand, it would be folly to abandon the bayirs, for it would be impossible to imagine any ground that could be more suitable for travelling on than they were.

The sheer illimitable accumulations of sand which are spread out over this part of the interior of East Turkestan are arranged in a sort of net-work pattern, and the bayirs of which I am speaking lay inside the meshes. No matter what point on the river we started from, we should of necessity have got into an unbroken continuity of bayirs all running in the same direction, namely, towards the south-south-west. And yet these depressions are subject to important changes even now. As we advanced we found that their bottoms became firmer, and consequently more convenient for the camels, as well as drier, and covered to a greater depth with sand. Then at their edges clay began to show itself in the shape of oblong terraces or steps, four or five feet high, or even simple cornices projecting through the sand. These, however, did not owe their origin to the erosive force of the wind, but to the action of water; in fact they resembled ancient beach-lines, marking the different levels of lake or river. This view, that the bayirs indicated ancient lake-basins, was borne out by their basin-shaped formation, and the concentric arrangement of the terraces, the belts of soil impregnated with salt (*shor*), ringed round by zones of actual salt—precisely the appearance which the existing marginal lakes of Yanghi-köll, Bash-köll, Tana-bagladi, etc., would assume, supposing they were to dry up.

Nevertheless I was rather disposed to believe that we were travelling along the bottom of an immense inland lake or sea. This view was supported by the general level of the whole of the Tarim basin, by the direction in which the two rivers, the Tarim and the Cherchen-daria, flow, and by the position of the several chains of bayirs; for, as we shall see lower down, each of these chains curved like a bow, while all radiated from a point intermediate between the old Lop-nor and the existing Kara-koshun, or the point where the lowest depression of the whole of the Tarim basin occurs. But the problem is a complicated one, and too long to be properly discussed in this present book; it must be dealt with in a special scientific work.

From the seventh bayir onwards the ground was so firm that we were able to march wherever we chose, though the first six had been so soft and treacherous in the middle that it was quite impossible to travel anywhere except along their edges. In the fifth we discovered traces, about a fortnight old, of a stray antelope, which, however, had returned by the same way it came from the river; and in the eighth made the interesting discovery of bones of the wild camel, though they were now brittle and spongy. In bayir no. 3, by way of experiment, we had dug a well, and found water at a depth of four feet, plenty of it, with a temperature of 4°.8 C. or 40°.6 Fahr., though of an intensely bitter salty taste. Although the ground was moist right up to the surface, it was nowhere frozen, owing to its very strong impregnation of salt.

On the 23rd December we were again awakened by a veritable buran or black tempest, but it came from the north-north-east. The sky was cloudy and the atmosphere so laden with dust that the features of the landscape—if one may apply this description to that abode of desolation and torpor—became invisible at a few hundred yards' distance, and even those which were quite close to us appeared distorted and spectral owing to the haze. We, the only human visitants that this fearful desert had ever known, were amazed that the drift-sand, which is wont to be shifted in enormous quantities by the tempests of spring, had not long ago filled up these depressions and so raised them to the general level of the desert. But, as a matter of fact, every individual grain of sand seems to travel along its predetermined line with the same undeviating certainty with which the electrical current speeds through its wires. It is the wind which guides them; and the wind, moving close to the earth's surface, is compelled to accommodate itself to the relief of the dunes. Hence, the sand which these wind storms sweep up before them is constrained to avoid the bare places, and to deposit itself upon the slopes of the dunes at their side.

As the day wore on, we several times travelled over soft sand, and two or three times, after crossing one of the sandy isthmuses I have mentioned, failed to strike the next bayir. But it soon became evident that we had got off the proper route, and in the haze were wandering astray on the broad isthmus or neck of sand between the two depressions. We therefore came to a halt, and searched until we found the way back to the proper bayir.

The ninth, tenth, eleventh, and twelfth of these depressions were cauldron-shaped, but so small that they gave us little assistance, especially as they were threaded by a system of low dunes stretching from the north-east to the south-west. Fortunately the sandy isthmuses which separated the bayirs lay very favourable for us, in that they invariably offered an easy ascent, but a steep (33°) descent into the next following bayir.

After we traversed the twelfth bayir, matters began to look serious. We spent a long time struggling to the top of the next sandy lintel or isthmus, for the slope was exceptionally prolonged, and the camels kept stopping more frequently; but at last we reached the culminating crest, and were very agreeably surprised at the prospect we saw before us. Deep down below lay the thirteenth depression, its bottom entirely free from sand, and its farther end swallowed up in the haze. It looked like helping us a good distance on our road. In the middle of it were some solitary terraces of clay, horizontally disposed, which, when seen at a distance, resembled houses and walls. Here, between two of these clay deposits, we halted for the night; and during the time the cooking-pan and kettles were bubbling and boiling over the fire, we all sat crouching over it. After supper, while the Mussulmans were discussing the prospects for the next day, I jotted down my notes by the light of a candle. In order to make our firewood hold out for the fortnight we restricted ourselves to three billets for each encampment, two for the evening and one for the following morning.

During the night the storm subsided, and when at daybreak I peeped out of my furs, the moon was still bathing our slumbering camp in her silvery white sheen, and the long-drawn breathing of the camels was the only sound which disturbed the silence. It struck me that if the moon only possessed the power to see and reflect in the way man does, she would be not a little amazed at the insignificant insects she saw groping their blind way through that everlasting desert, and with boundless audacity forcing a passage across a part of the earth's surface where man was never meant to put his foot. And then, that night more than all nights again, I really envied her her commanding position in the firmament; for not only did it enable her to see a long way across that sandy ocean in the heart of Asia, but it enabled her to look down upon my home in the far North, whither mv thoughts were just then drawn with especial tenderness, for it was—Christmas Eve!

Wearied as we were with our strenuous march through the sand the day before, we all slept soundly, and the sun was already peeping over the crests of the sand-dunes when I at length awoke. Clouds and dust—both were gone as if by magic, and the sandy desert glowed all round us like a lava-flow. The camels always lay closely packed together for warmth's sake; and their sharp-cut shadows were now flung far out over the barren soil. And how strange a soil it was! Hardly like the soil of earth, more like the integument of some other planet.

Soon the camp awoke, the baggage was arranged afresh, though the thinning out had been so thoroughly done there was little else could be dispensed with, for Parpi Bai, Faisullah, and Khodai Verdi were now to return. It was originally intended that Kurban also should accompany them, but he was such a cheerful, pleasant fellow, Christmas without him would have been gloomy indeed, and so he received permission to stay. The men were as glad as I was: it was as though we were all under a spell. Each of them wanted to accompany me through the desert.

We gave the returning party two or three small lumps of ice, one billet of wood, and a few pieces of bread—not very sumptuous fare for Christmas Eve! But then they were to do the return journey in two stages, and were to make for the Seit-köll, the nearest point where water was to be obtained. To know they were in safety was both a relief to me and an advantage to the caravan. Our supply of water would last longer now that there were six lives less dependent upon it. On the other hand, our seven remaining camels would of course have heavier burdens to carry. Yet these would grow lighter with each succeeding day, and nobody was permitted to ride until the loads became very sensibly less.

We rapidly traversed the remaining portion of the thirteenth bayir, which helped us well on the way. The ground was granular, hard, and dry, and covered in places with a thin incrustation of salt resembling rime-frost, which crackled every time we trod on it. Upon digging eight or nine inches down we came upon a thick deposit of pure salt, evidently filling the bed of a desiccated salt-lake. The margins and side-terraces of the depression, which were seldom more than seven feet high, were coated with a perfectly horizontal layer of yellowish red clay, some eight or nine inches thick, and as hard as a stone. Underneath the clay was dust, grey and loose, and sloping outwards.

Bayir no. 14 was of a rudimentary character, and only gave us about one hundred yards that were free from sand; but the fifteenth was really a large one, and towards its lower end was bordered by terraces that called to mind the walls of Chinese fortresses. At its south-western extremity it was shut in by a lofty isthmus of sand. While the poor camels were toiling up this, the wind arose again in the north and soon packed the sky with heavy banks of cloud. The sunshine had brought out the features of the country in sharp relief; now, with its disappearance, the landscape appeared as gloomy as could be, and inspired in us a feeling of hopeless depression.

I led the way on foot, but failed to see any bayir on the other side of the sandy peninsula; and, finally, instead of the exceptionally large bayir which I hoped for as a Christmas box, I discovered that I had missed my way, and was wandering on another of those ill-omened promontories. Nor shall I easily forget the feeling of vexed disappointment which came over me, when from the top of the steep dune, fully 200 feet high, on which I stood, I looked down into bayir no. 16, gaping like a huge black cooking-pot down below. For the bottom of it was moist and wet, and edged all round by a narrow belt of salt, besides being shut in on every side by lofty sand-dunes. It was like the mouth of hell itself. However, after waiting until the caravan came up, I led the way down the steep sandy slope into the repellent pit at the bottom; and then on we struggled as best we might, keeping as much as possible to the outer margin wherever it would bear us. But after 9½ miles we had had enough, and encamped on the dune which terminated this hateful bayir on the south.

Yet no matter what the difficulties of the day's march had been, everybody's spirits rose the moment I commanded halt. Then, whilst Islam prepared my bed near the fire, Turdu Bai and Ördek unloaded the camels, placing the loads convenient for starting again the next morning. After that the camels were tethered close beside us, the two billets of wood were split up, the fire made, the pieces of ice put, some into the pot and some into an iron pail to melt. Meanwhile Ördek set about preparing the rice pudding. The water in which the rice was washed was afterwards given to the horse and the two dogs; we could not afford to waste one drop. If the camels did not grow too thirsty, the supply we carried with us was enough to last fifteen days, and the wood enough to last eleven.

I have never spent Christmas Eve amid gloomier or more desolate surroundings. The only thing in keeping with that season of gladness was the cold. We however sat crouched together, like bats in winter, round the niggardly fire, watching the last tiny blue flame or two which hopped above the embers. Then we wrapped our furs close about us, to take the sting out of the icy wind of the midwinter night; but the angel of Christmas went on past us, although all our doors stood opened hospitably wide. It was a desert Christmas, and could not have been more dreary had we been at the North Pole.

On Christmas Day the ground was favourable, and we travelled no less than 11¼ miles. Beyond the "Christmas pit" came three small bayirs, followed by a very long one (no. 20), which stretched almost exactly due south for as far as we were able to see. Being in the shade, owing to the steep and lofty wall of sand—close upon 300 feet high—which shut in the bayir on the east, all its features were sharply defined. Its floor was soft and slightly moist, and consisted of fine dark-brown dust, mingled with salt, without a single grain of sand in its composition. Had the east wind been the only wind which prevailed in that region, it would have been easy to understand the reason for this. But our experience went to show that the prevalent winds during the winter months are the south and north winds; hence it is safe to infer that with time they will fill up all these depressions. The only part of the Takla-makan in which we found firm bare ground during our former journey of 1896 was on the side next the Khotan-daria, that is to say those parts of the desert which lay most exposed to the east wind.

In a bed of hard gypsum in bayir no. 20 we observed the skeleton of a water-bird, which had succumbed whilst crossing this ocean of sand, as well as a dead day-fly (*Ephemeris*), which might well have utilised the brief moments of its existence to better purpose than getting lost in that desert.

At the further end of the bayir we again entered upon deep sand, which steadily led upwards. It is true there were two or three bayirs down below by the side of our route, but they profited us nothing. We meanwhile were marching along the culminating crest of the promontory, where the sand-dunes, running north and south, sloped on the east at an angle of 16°, and on the west at an angle of 32°. The reason we kept to the crest was because it was easier going, owing to the sand there being more tightly packed. All the same the track was in several places so unfavourable that we were obliged to use our spades and cut steps for the heavily-laden camels. Although every man of us was marching on foot to keep himself warm, we were all chilled to the bone by the cutting south wind, which met us in the teeth and never once slackened its energy. We were here witnesses of the effect which the wind has upon the summit of the dunes, in curling their crests over like hanging plumes. Everything was enshrouded in the yellowish grey haze. The sand penetrated everywhere, until it got to our very skin, and gritted between our teeth when we brought them together. Some grains of it even fell out of my old note-book when I wrote down these sentences, two-and-a-half years after the day on which I noted them down.

The men were beginning to lose heart; but I quieted their apprehensions, and assured them that they had nothing to fear. We encamped that night in a little corner or angle between two lofty sand-dunes.

On the 26th December we traversed no less than eight bayirs, but they were all small and gave us little real help, for every time we went down into one of them we had to climb up out of it again. It pained me to see how all this taxed the camels' strength. For the most part therefore we marched on sand, all on foot, except that I rode about a mile or so whilst traversing the harder soil of the bayirs. In the small depressions that we were now traversing we observed very distinctly various series of concentric rings or desiccation lines, like those which are left round a pool as it dries up.

The sandy isthmuses which separated bayir from bayir con-

A Loaded Camel.

tinued to grow higher and broader, and of course encroached more and more upon the hard, level ground of the depressions themselves. When descending on their southern side, the camels used to stiffen their legs and let themselves deliberately slide down the steep slope. The sand, being loose, gave way under their feet and poured down like a cascade, carrying the animals with it. To this manœuvre the camels soon grew accustomed, and learnt to balance themselves securely, being no longer afraid of the dizzy crests of the sand-dunes. Whether viewed from above or seen from below, the spectacle of the clumsy brutes glissading down in that way was unspeakably funny.

Islam, my experienced desert pilot, generally led the way, endeavouring as far as possible to steer a course that should keep our zigzag route at the same level. At the top of every crest we stopped to look around us, in the perpetual hope of discovering a fresh bayir; but more frequently we were disappointed, and consequently were obliged to advance as best we could along the crests.

Upon reaching Camp no. VII., I was able to comfort my men with the assurance that we were now well half-way to the old bed of the Cherchen-daria, which, according to the map of the Russian traveller, Roborovsky, lay some 40 miles north of the river's present bed. We still had 2½ camel-loads of ice left, and that would suffice. But there was just a doubt as to whether our firewood would hold out; if it did not, we should have no opportunity to melt the ice. We gave the camels the straw stuffing of one of the pack-saddles to eat.

On the 27th December we made an early start. The men's spirits were damped by the interminable desert; they thought it would be best to hasten on to more hospitable regions before our supplies ran too low. During the past night the thermometer had fallen to $-20°.0$ C. or $-4°.0$ Fahr., and in the morning when we started it still stood at -18 C. or $-0°.4$ Fahr. But there was a beautiful sunrise, and the sky was clear. Yet ere the sun climbed very high above the horizon, the usual banks of clouds gathered and intercepted his rays, thus keeping the earth cold.

A cup of hot tea and off I set, to lead the way. After traversing a considerable number of crests, I at length reached the culminating point of the isthmus, where I stopped to survey the country ahead of me, and examine it through my glass. In the distance, in the direct line of our march, I perceived a bayir, which at once arrested my attention, because of its unusual appearance; it was covered with little black dots. Curious to know what they could mean, I hurried down and was still further astonished to discover kamish leaves lying on the slope, whither they had been blown by the wind, as well as traces of some small rodent no bigger than a rat. Upon getting lower down and nearer to the bayir (no. 30), I observed, to my delight, that there were reeds (kamish) in it, although dry and shrivelled, and growing in thin, scattered bunches. Besides this, I also discovered, a little later, live yellow kamish, which I had failed

Descending the Steep Face of a Sand-dune.

to observe at first owing to its being of the same colour as the high dunes which crossed the depression diagonally.

Gladdened by this unexpected sign of life, I waited till the caravan came up and joined me. The men could not have been more delighted had they seen paradise opening before them, and the camels distended their nostrils, sniffing pasture. We called a council of war. Turdu Bai proposed to stay where we were and let the animals have a good feed; they had grown tired of living upon nothing but maize, and during the last day or two had brought up what they ate. But on the supposition that the next bayir would be still more favourable, I sent on Islam Bai to reconnoitre, whilst the rest of us followed slowly after him, letting the camels browse as they tramped along. Our pioneer signalled to us to push on, and we did so, and encamped in bayir no. 31, although in point of fact it was not really much better than the former one.

This was a most unexpected and astonishing discovery—to come upon vegetation in the middle of the desert, 70 or 80 miles from the nearest water. It could not possibly be an extreme outlier of the vegetable-belt of the Tarim, for it was separated from that river by miles upon miles of the barrenest sand, and soil heavily impregnated with salt. Nor could it in any way owe its existence to the Cherchen-daria, for that river was still 90 miles distant. Perhaps the river Kara-muran may at one time or another have flowed in this direction. Anyway we all took fresh heart, and the immediate future presented itself in quite rosy colours.

We now gave each camel a couple of pailsful of water, or about 6½ gallons, the ice being melted over a fire of kamish stalks, and they swallowed it like a cup of tea. This made a big hole in our ice supply; but, on the other hand, it lightened the loads we had to carry.

At sunset we turned the camels loose to graze. Then, as long as the light lasted, we gathered heaps of dry kamish, and so were able to economise with our wood for at any rate that occasion.

The sun set that evening with an unusually fine display of colour effects. The heavy clouds, which all day long had obscured the sky, parted asunder and revealed their upper sides—greyish violet, edged with vivid gold—and their under sides, a dun yellow like the sand-dunes. It was as if the image of the desert were reflected on the mirror of the sky.

CHAPTER XVII.

IN THE HEART OF THE DESERT.

THE disagreeable weather still continued. During the night of the 27th December, the thermometer sank to $-21°.0$ C. or $-5°.8$ Fahr. When we awoke next morning the wind was blowing from the east, the country was shrouded in haze, and the sky heavy with clouds, through which not one single ray of sunshine succeeded in penetrating all day long. We had chanced into the land of everlasting twilight, so that the opportunities I enjoyed during the journey of using my photographic apparatus, or making astronomical observations, were extremely few. As I experienced the same sort of hazy weather when I was on the Keriya-daria in the winter of 1896, I suppose it must be characteristic of the interior of the Takla-makan Desert. In such a haze you are easily deceived as to distance. You imagine the bayir you are just entering will be a long one, because you are unable to see the farther end of it; but before you have advanced very far, the inclosing sand-dunes rise up like ghosts in your path. The promontories immediately in front of you loom through the "smoke" of the dust like far-off mountain-chains. In fact, you get so confused as to both distance and direction, that you do not know which way to go. The wind was so piercingly cold that riding was out of the question; it was much better to walk and lead the horse.

The arrangement of the sand still continued to be subject to the same laws, the desert being swept by a power which with sovereign energy had modelled into plastic forms the peculiar volatile material that filled it, viz., that something intermediate between land and water. The shape of each individual sand-dune was copied in the promontories, and repeated again in the countless ripples which crumpled its slopes. The deepest part of the "hollow of the wave" was always close to the base of the steep sheltered side of the dune; and this was true also of the bayirs, the most developed form of the "hollow of the wave." The desert sand, after being originally ground out of the hard granite mountains, is compelled to obey the same laws as the highly unstable water. It breaks into waves, as does the heaving ocean, and like the ocean it keeps moving unceasingly onwards, only at a much slower pace.

In bayir no. 33 I was able to ride on a good distance ahead, and was led to do so by a certain black object I saw rising above the dead and withered kamish. This last was seldom more than eight or nine inches high, and had the appearance of having been grazed off. Yet that was not the case; the reeds had only begun to droop (and they would eventually die) after their roots failed to reach the ground water below. The black object which so greatly excited my curiosity turned out to be a tamarisk, the first we had seen for several days. It was still maintaining a precarious hold upon life; but round about lay its boughs and branches long since dead. These, however, made a welcome addition to our supply of fuel.

I rode on for yet another hour, without seeing the end of this friendly bayir, or of the kamish either. This last was still living, had even a tinge of green in it sometimes, especially close to the drift-sand; but it was quite dead on the level "dust-ground." It almost looked as if sand was necessary for its welfare or helped to preserve it alive. I saw no more tamarisks, and so, upon reaching a spot where the kamish was thicker, and furnished some protection from the wind, I dismounted, tethered my horse, and kindled a little fire.

It was quite dusk when the caravan came up. Here we lost our first camel, a magnificent male, the best of the fifteen which had tramped all the way from Kashgar. For the last four days he had been unwell, and therefore travelled slower than usual; indeed he had refused to eat anything, ever since we started from the Tana-bagladi-köll. Turdu Bai shed tears. He was extraordinarily fond of camels, and always found something to do for them long after the other men were resting beside the fire. This big fine fellow did not, however, die from weariness or want of food, like so many of his successors. The Mussulmans said, "Khoda kasseli värdi!" "God gave him an illness," and no doubt his death would have been just as inevitable had he been grazing on the Tarim steppes instead of trudging with us through the desert. All the other nine camels were keeping wonderfully well, and yet it was the ninth day since we started. In my former journey across the Takla-makan it was precisely on the ninth day that I was forced to abandon my two men, four of the camels, and the whole of my baggage; but then we suffered terribly from both heat and thirst. Now, however, we were chilled to the bone, owing to the intense cold, and had an abundance of water.

We had now reached that stage in a desert journey at which the difficulties lay behind us, and our attention was mainly directed to the discovery and observation of fresh signs of life and the presence of water. Leaving behind us these the first kamish and tamarisk we had seen, we marched on in the same long bayir (no. 33), with the high steep wall of sand on our left. Every now and again a low tongue of sand projected from the right, but after each such headland the bayir opened out again, and pointed on and on like a dry river-bed carved between the lofty sand-dunes. The ground was patterned in every direction by the tracks of hares; and here also we observed the foot-prints of foxes. Shortly afterwards we came across a few steppe plants, clumps of grass, and *chiggeh*, a variety of rush very common in the Lop country. At length there appeared also more tamarisks, some of them fresh and elastic, others dead, and still resting on their characteristic root-mounds.

The going was all that could be desired, for the ground was level. Who would have supposed we should be so favoured in the heart of that vast desert? But it blew so hard from the east, that I was sometimes obliged to dismount and walk, to prevent my hands and feet from getting frozen. At last I reached the end of this very helpful bayir, and found it terminated in an exceptionally high isthmus of sand. As the ground just below it was the lowest level throughout the bayir, and seemed to indicate that the "ground water" was not very far down, I collected an armful of dry tamarisk branches, and made a fire, and then waited for the others to come up. Islam and Ördek at once set to work and dug a well, while Turdu Bai looked after the camels, and Kurban collected more fuel. We reached water at a depth of 4½ feet; it was almost perfectly fresh, and had a temperature of 8°.2 C. or 46°.8 Fahr., but trickled out desperately slowly. That evening we gave two of the camels their full quantity, namely, half-a-dozen bucketsful, of water each.

Hence we were now amply provided with everything we needed—water, firewood, and grazing for the animals. It was a veritable oasis in the heart of the desert. We kept two big fires blazing all the evening, and their red glare played upon the tops of the dunes, from which the drift-sand came pouring over us like rain, as it was caught up by the wind. The men when following in my footsteps had come across yet another encouraging sign that we were getting into better regions, namely, a large black wolf, which fled over the sand-dunes westwards.

This day's rest was heartily welcome to both men and animals. The men had for the most part travelled on foot, the camels had borne heavy loads; and we all suffered more than usual from the cold and the wind, because we had not sufficient firewood to warm ourselves with. We made our camp as comfortable as circumstances would allow by converting the white felt carpet, which was generally laid underneath my bed, into a make-shift tent, and propping it up with two or three tamarisk branches. This sheltered us against the storm, which raged all day, and also allowed me to have a big fire. The men protected themselves in a similar manner.

In the morning the water which had gathered in the bottom of our well was frozen, and the earth we had flung out of it as hard as a stone. Each camel drank not less than nine bucketsful, two of them even drank eleven; you could actually see their skins swelling out as they gulped the fluid down. This wrought a remarkable change in their spirits. They grew quite lively, and began to jump about, and play, and afterwards ate away eagerly at the thin patches of kamish. Now curiously enough, whilst close to the ground, the storm blew from the east, higher up, in the sky, masses of black cloud were drifting from the west to the east. The last day of the eighteen hundreds—that is the last day of the year 1899—looked quite promising, even before it was fully light, for I noticed the stars beaming down upon our bivouac, while the tamarisk mounds stood out like black phantoms. However, when we were making ready for the start, the weather again came on as thick as ever. That winter was characterised by bright, still nights and windy, cloudy days, which made the earth all the colder.

The caravan quite distinguished itself that day by doing 15

miles, the longest day's march during the whole of that desert journey. Although one of the camels had perished, their burdens were now so small that the men were allowed to ride in turns, especially as the ground was for the most part level and firm along the bottoms of the successive bayirs.

There was still vegetation in bayirs nos. 34, 35 and 36, but the tamarisks were less frequent. From the neck of sand which bordered the southern end of the last of these depressions, a bayir extended towards the south-east, but as it did not coincide with the direction in which we wanted to go, we left it on the left hand. I saw the men considered it a mistake not to follow it, instead of striking off as we did for a high pass to the south-south-west. Nevertheless, I was as much surprised as they were, when we reached the top of the pass or isthmus and looked down into bayir no. 37, for it was broad and open like a field, quite different from the inclosed areas which its predecessors were. The pass that bounded it on the south resembled a very low "threshold" or cross-ridge, and beyond it we were unable to perceive any sand, a fact I attributed to the great distance and the thickness of the atmosphere.

Bayir no. 38 was equally extensive, and just as open as no. 37. It seemed as if some invisible hand had ploughed a gigantic furrow through the desert on purpose to serve as a track for our caravan. We encamped near its beginning, at a spot where there was plenty of good fuel. Islam wanted to use up our last camel-load of wood; but Turdu Bai, like a prudent general, proposed to take it just one day longer—a very wise suggestion.

Here we were then, that still and quiet New Year's Eve, encamped around two fires, under the open sky, and in a locality that was as peaceful as any forgotten grave beside an unused track in the heart of Asia. Our friends did not know where we were. The people we had left behind at Tura-sallgan-uy were no doubt uneasy about us, especially since their imaginations had been excited by Islam's sensational descriptions of our former journey across the desert in 1896, now no doubt enhanced by the account which Parpi Bai would be able to give them of the first three or four days' march of this present journey. The Cossacks saw for themselves what sort of a country lay before us in the reconnaissances they took part in, and afterwards admitted they were afraid we should find every road barred by the sand, and should perish of thirst, weariness, and cold.

The Interminable Desert "Ocean."

My four companions admitted also that until that afternoon, when for the first time we came within reasonable sight of a happy termination of the journey, they had been filled with anxiety. They could not, however, understand how I was able to determine with such accuracy the distance to Tatran. I suppose they thought my promises and assurances were simply so many well-meant attempts to allay their fears.

If the first day in the new year, to say nothing of the new century, could in any way be taken as an augury or prognostication of the future, then in all conscience the 1st of January, 1900, was as full of gloomy forebodings as it well could be. The sky was hung with a black shroud, and there was not a single glimpse of the red promises of morning. At seven o'clock the temperature stood at $-15^{\circ}.0$ C. or $5^{\circ}.0$ Fahr., and when I arose and dressed, it was, thanks to the big fire, even warmer still. The only circumstance which in any degree inspired us with New Year's feelings was, that bayir no. 38 seemed to extend to a vast distance, and we started with buoyant steps. The men even fed themselves with the foolish hope that this was the beginning of the steppes which stretched down to the bank of the Cherchen-daria. Vegetation still continued scanty—an occasional clump of grass, a few stalks of kamish, or a tamarisk. In the sandy soil were a number of small holes belonging to a species of rat, which the natives called *säghisghan*.

Upon reaching the isthmus which closed this bayir on the south, we started to cross it at its lowest part, thinking it was quite narrow; but in this we deceived ourselves, for it was the broadest we had yet encountered, and continued to increase in height as we advanced, until at last it merged gradually into a labyrinth of big sand-dunes.

Ascending to the highest point in the vicinity, we searched in vain for the next bayir; but this peculiar formation appeared to have now come to an end. As far as our gaze was able to penetrate southwards, the desert ocean predominated in every quarter, the lofty walls of sand which had hitherto been on our left hand likewise came to an end, and there were no longer any depressions—in a word, the architecture of the desert had all at once changed, though fortunately for us the dunes still continued to run north and south.

Up to this point we had made admirable progress, we had been like ships threading the sea-weed and drift-ice in smooth water; now we passed out into the open sea again. The waves of our "sea" were as high as houses, and we crawled along at a desperately slow pace, up and down, up and down, over the heavy dunes, first one camel stumbling and falling, and then another, and every time one did so, we had to unload the animal, get him up on his feet again, and reload him. Vegetation had now almost entirely ceased. I once more began to suspect that the oasis we had just crossed belonged to an extreme outlying bed of the Kara-muran. If that was the case, we might make up our minds to some exceedingly difficult country before we came in touch with the Cherchen-daria.

Eastwards in the far distance there appeared what looked like a continuation of the depressions, but they did not run in the direction in which we wanted to travel. Towards the south the elevations seemed to have been levelled down, with the exception of an occasional dominating dune with a sharp crest. In other words, the horizon line resembled a saw-blade with a notched edge. Occasionally a dead tamarisk came into view, perched on the top of its root-mound, amongst the sand-dunes, but the distances between them grew greater and greater. Hence, upon reaching a living tamarisk, with a litter of dead branches and some kamish about its feet, we halted, after a toilsome march of only 8½ miles.

Upon awakening at daybreak, on the morning of the 2nd January, I found we were enveloped on all sides by a perfect winter scene. It was snowing softly, the ground was perfectly white, and the dunes were indistinguishable from stupendous snow-drifts, every vestige of sand being smothered out of sight. Islam had thoughtfully spread a cloth over my box, for as usual I left my instruments and note-books lying on its lid the night before. It was still only half-light when the fire was kindled in front of my bed, and the falling snow glistened and sparkled like diamonds against the background of its flames. For it was descending, not in the usual form of soft flakes, but in delicate crystals, as though it were rime-frost. During the first few hours of that day's march the landscape was blindingly white in every direction. This was the first time I had ever seen the sand-dunes of the desert in this unusual attire, this funereal winding-sheet, and its effect was to enhance still more their corpse-like nakedness and desolation. But as the morning wore on, the slopes looking towards the south threw off the thin covering of snow, and shortly after noon the declivities on the other side also resumed their usual yellow tones, until finally all that remained of the snow was a tiny strip in the bottoms of the hollows.

The sand continued to grow more and more difficult, and no bayir appeared to ease our plodding footsteps; it was sand, sand everywhere. The steep sheltered sides of the sand-dunes looked now towards the south as well as towards the west, pointing to the fact of there being two systems of dunes intercrossing one another and so forming a network, the meshes of which were long ago sanded up. It was evident the winds were less regular here than in the northern half of the desert. It was a good thing we did not start from the south; we should never have got through, but should have been compelled to turn back, for no fires, however large, would have been able to pierce far through the haze with which, during that winter, the atmosphere was intermingled.

At four o'clock in the afternoon it began to snow, and this time the snow came down thick and fast. We were evidently not doomed to perish for want of water. It was a regular snow-storm, driven before a south-south-west gale. What a difference from the sand-storms of the Takla-makan! In half-an-hour the country was like a white sheet: the clouds were trailing their snowy draperies so low down as actually to touch the ground. Then down came the twilight, engulfing the chaos of sand and snow, and we began to look about for a spot where we could tie the camels for the night. At length we observed, about one mile ahead of us, a black point, and for it we resolved to make, let the cost be what it might. Nevertheless, it took us a good hour to get there, and was pitch dark when we arrived. The black object proved to be a tamarisk, and beside it we found some fuel.

The falling snow did not sizzle against the flames of our fire, it was converted into steam before ever it reached them; but it left more perceptible traces on my note-book. By this, the ordinary oases had entirely ceased, and wherever the eye turned there was nothing but sand, barren sand, yellow sand. For a couple of hours or so we followed the tracks of two foxes, an older one going north, and a fresher one, showing that the creature had returned to the Cherchen-daria. What was he looking for in the desert? Surely he could find a more fruitful field for his predatory instincts nearer the river.

Ördek felt ill at ease in this weird ocean of desolation;

it seemed to him to be without boundaries, without termination; the sun never shone there; and with each succeeding day we apparently got deeper and deeper entangled in the hopeless labyrinth of sand-dunes. And he began to talk with ecstasy of the banks of the Tarim, of its lakes, its canoes, and its fishing-grounds as of a paradise to which he would never return. He talked of the swans, those celestial and sensitive birds, which haunt the lakes of his native land.

The camels were now beginning to show the effects of the journey, and we felt it was necessary to give them a day's rest. We again dug for water, and found it at a depth of 3¾ feet; it had a faintly bitter flavour. Besides this, we had of course the snow. The ground was frozen to the depth of 13 inches. It snowed all day long, in thick blinding flakes, which hissed and sizzled when they fell upon the fire. The men made little exploring trips in the vicinity, and in the evening Turdu Bai came back with two big camel-loads of firewood, which he had gathered close by. I was almost dead-beat with weariness, and lay and read all day long in the midst of the snowstorm, the flakes dropping upon the paper I held in my hand, so that I had to keep shaking it, to prevent them from covering the words I actually wanted to read. Even at mid-day it was only half-light, so that in the murky atmosphere, sand-dunes, earth, and sky all melted together into one confused blend of whirling whiteness. It was still snowing last thing at night, when the sparks from the fire leapt up as if to encounter the snow-flakes, and turned them into water-drops, which flashed on the night like sprays of glowing iron.

Considering that the thermometer fell to $-30^\circ.1$ C. $-$or $22^\circ.2$ Fahr. during the night, it was a bit cool for sleeping out in the open air; while at seven in the morning it was still $-27^\circ.0$ C. or $-16^\circ.6$ Fahr., and when I got up at half-past eight, no less than -24° C. or $-11^\circ.2$ Fahr. Decidedly cold that for a dressing-room, for I always made it a practice to take off my clothes and sleep in night-attire. The worst part about it was washing and dressing with a temperature of $30^\circ.0$ C. or $86^\circ.0$ Fahr. on the fire side of you, and a temperature of $-30^\circ.0$ C. or $-22^\circ.0$ Fahr. on the other side of you. It continued snowing every bit as heavily all night, and in the morning, when I awoke, I was completely covered up, so that Islam had to fetch a spade and kamish broom to get me out. But the snow had helped to retain the heat inside my nest, so that I did not feel the cold.

However, I was more comfortable after I had struggled into my clothes and sat drinking my tea beside the fire, with a warm fur coat about my shoulders.

It was still snowing, and snowed on and on all day. The thermometer never rose above −13° C. or 8°.6 Fahr., which is far from pleasant when the wind blows straight into your face with a keen cutting edge to it. As some compensation for this, the ground was not altogether unfavourable. We were frequently able to make detours round the worst sand-dunes; and before the day was over we once more came into a string of small bayirs, which ran south-south-east and were filled with sand. In one of these, no. 43, we encamped for the night, although there was not a scrap of fuel of any description; but we still carried with us half a camel-load of our original supply, and let the consequences be what they might, we *must* have a fire that night, for we were all literally stiff with cold. The snow was unable to remain long on the slopes and declivities which faced south, because of the rapidity with which it evaporated. But it clung to those which faced north, and lay some inches thick in the bottoms of the depressions. Hence, upon looking northwards, the country was almost everywhere an expanse of bare sand, but upon looking south, nothing but snow.

At last, then, the black clouds, which had overhung the desert ever since we started, had been induced to part with their contents. All night long between the 4th and the 5th of January the snow went on falling, falling as softly as wool, and in the morning even the places where the fires had been were buried under snow. Everything we wanted, every single thing we possessed in fact, had to be fished out from underneath this soft white coverlet. The camels also were snowed up, and truly picturesque they looked in their be-powdered "wigs," like great lords of the Gustavian (or Georgian) period, with little snow-wreaths at their backs, and tiny icicles in their peaked beards and round their mouths. At nine o'clock it cleared up a little, although the fine snow needles still continued to flash their brightly glinting facets in the sunshine. However, it was nothing more than a temporary lull, for at the end of a couple of hours or so it began to snow again. When the camels moved, the snow crunched with quite a wintry sound under their feet.

By this every speck of sand had once more vanished from

sight. During the morning the steep slopes, which were turned towards the west, lay in the shade, and presented a magnificent spectacle, with their several nuances of steel-blue, the shades varying with the steepness, while above them glittered the white domes of the sand-dunes brilliantly lighted by the rays of the sun.

The high sandy promontories bore a striking resemblance to the crest of a mountain-chain clothed with perpetual snow. I fancied I had before me a reproduction in miniature of the Trans-Alai, with Peak Kaufmann: the pale blue colouring was precisely the same. The extent and brightness of the snow were very trying to the eyes, although I wore double snow-spectacles, and every one of the men had smoked glasses. Yet the atmosphere was nothing like so clear as it is in the mountains on bright days. It was too full of snow crystals to admit of our distinguishing contours and shapes at more than half-a-mile away. Beyond that everything was mantled by the opaque blurr of the falling snow. And so far it was an advantage, for the ground immediately in front of us was not very favourable—mountains of sand growing continually higher, not a patch of native soil as big as a square yard in area, no vegetation living or dead.

During the course of the day the snow showed certain variations. Notwithstanding the rate at which it melted and evaporated, it grew deeper the further we advanced towards the south, this being a natural consequence of our nearer approximation to the mountains. Sometimes there was a crust upon the snow, so hard that it would have been possible to skate upon it for long stretches together. Who would have believed that such a thing could be possible in the desert?

Generally speaking, the snow facilitated our march, for by keeping along the lines of contact between snow and sand, we were able to take advantage of the effects of regelation, which were strongest marked there. The crests of the dunes in particular were as hard as ice, and a single step on the steeper slopes sufficed to set a patch of twenty to twenty-five square yards slipping bodily down the declivity. The snow had the same effect upon the sand that oil has upon waves; it would have been impossible for even the fiercest *buran* (black desert tempest) that ever blew to have shifted it with that snow lying upon it.

On the 6th of January the desert ocean still presented the

same features, though, if anything, its "waves" ran somewhat higher. On the whole the ground rose a little towards the south; at any rate we had a far wider outlook in the opposite direction. The camping ground we chose that night was the worst we had hitherto had, namely, a mere hole in the sand, in a spot where there was not one single blade or leaf of vegetation to be seen anywhere. The temperature of my bed was nearly $-20^\circ.0$ C. or $-4^\circ.0$ Fahr. when I crept into it, and I had to wait patiently for some little time for my limbs to thaw and the blood to circulate before I found energy enough to stop up all the holes and crevices through which the cold night air penetrated. It was difficult to sleep that night on account of the cold and the wind, and in the morning we had nothing with which to combat these evils, except a handful of chips, and even then the thermometer registered over 43 degrees of frost (-24° C.) The men tried to keep themselves warm by lying in a lump all together. They were fast losing heart in this dim, weird country; we were like ship-worms penetrating into a sandy plank of the hull of Mother Earth.

It was ten o'clock the following morning before we were sufficiently thawed to continue our tramp across these strange hills of intermingled sand and snow. The atmosphere was, however, remarkably clear, and here we obtained our first glimpse of the outermost chain of the great Kwen-lun system, namely, the range of Tokkuz-davan. To the north the sky was pure and blue; but to the south it was streaked with low white clouds, very often scarce distinguishable from the tops of the snow-covered sand-dunes, so that the latter had the appearance of merging into level snow-fields which led directly up into the sky.

Meanwhile, from the top of a neighbouring sand-dune, I made a welcome discovery. Whilst examining the horizon with my field-glass, I caught sight, away towards the south-east, of something which looked like black stumps projecting through the snow; that could mean only one thing—a dead forest. Although the place where I saw it lay a little off our line of march, I ordered the men to make for it, and that night we encamped amid a grove of dead and withered poplars.

The men set to work with quickened energy and fresh courage. Shovelling away the snow, they began to ply their axes, and very soon had several piles of wood ready for kindling.

One huge poplar close to the camp was too big to be felled, so we set fire to it as it stood, and let it burn—a gigantic torch lighting up the white pall of the desert. Another poplar, with a hollow trunk, was flung across my fire, and the flames roared through it, as though it had been a funnel. It glowed, it crackled. The flames lit up the interior, making it gleam like rubies, until the bark burst, and curled and withered under the fierce advance of the devouring element. Gigantic columns of smoke soared up as if to greet the moon, which now for the first time for many days emerged from behind the screen of clouds. That night my men outwitted the cold. They dug holes in the sand, filled them with hot ashes, shovelled the sand back again, and slept on the top of it. For the last two or three days the camels had had nothing to eat, and there had been nothing to give the dogs except bread. On the other hand, we had no lack of water, for the ground was everywhere covered with snow to the depth of eight or a dozen inches.

The next day, the 8th of January, liberated us from the ban of that ghastly desert. Before we started, I comforted my men with the promise that they should sleep that night on the bank of the Cherchen-daria. We did not trouble to carry firewood with us, for we perceived other dead trees some distance ahead. Yet as we advanced, these grew fewer; however, before we lost sight of them altogether, we collected enough wood to make a camel-load. Upon reaching the top of a dominating sand-dune, I noted, towards the south-east, the first indication that we were approaching our goal, namely, a dark line on the horizon, contrasting very sharply against the universal sheet of snow. It could only be the belt of forest which bordered the Cherchen-daria.

An hour's march brought us to the first tamarisk cones. The dividing line between the desert and the forest was extremely abrupt. Not a bush marked the transition; the last slope of the sand-dunes swept straight down to the foot of the trees. The tamarisks stood so close together, that we had some difficulty in threading the narrow, winding avenues which formed the only pathways through them.

The men wanted to stop in a grove of mature poplars, where there was a superfluity of everything we wanted; but I assured them, that if only they would have patience a little longer, we should be able to encamp on the river bank itself. Another quarter of an hour brought us to the road which leads from Cherchen to the Lop country, where new-made tracks of cattle and sheep were visible in the snow. Following that road a short distance, we came to the river-bank, and there pitched our camp on a little hill overlooking the stream, which was here some 350 feet wide and covered with ice. It was quite a pleasure to rest at the foot of these big trees and enjoy the beautiful view. The mountains stood out sharp and clear, and the snow sparkled in the moonshine. But the best sight of all was to see our six camels and one horse revelling amongst the reed-beds; and well had they deserved their feast. My men were amazed that I was able to calculate the distance almost to a *gulatsh* (fathom), and declared that they would now, without a moment's hesitation, follow me wherever I chose to lead them.

According to my former map (see *Petermanns Mitteilungen*, Ergänzungsheft No. 131) the distance between the point where we struck the Cherchen-daria and the point where we left the Tarim at Tana-bagladi-köll was 177 miles. According to the measurements which I made during the march just concluded, it amounted to 176½ miles; which is as great a degree of accuracy as can be expected over such ground.

I had thus succeeded in crossing the broad Desert of Cherchen, at the cost of only one camel, and without putting an undue strain upon the others, which were all in good condition. The highest sand we encountered was in the north, but the most difficult in the south, owing to the fact that we were unable to get round the dunes. The happy issue of the expedition was due to the unexpected occurrence of the bayirs, which carried us over two-thirds of the distance, and to the circumstance that we hit upon water, fuel, and fodder (kamish) in the middle of the desert. What led me to attempt this long and dangerous expedition through the desert was, that an older edition of the map of the Russian General Staff, dealing with the region south of the Siberian frontier, showed a road crossing this desert from Tatran to a point a little to the west of Karaul. I considered that it would not be marked on the map unless there existed some warrant for it, and I am now of opinion that it is not impossible some such road may have run in that direction in former times.

The camels well deserved "a day off" amongst this luxuriant pasture, and it suited excellently, for I wanted to take an astronomical observation, which would occupy me a whole day. As the temperature did not rise higher than $-14°.0$ C. or $6°.8$ Fahr., while there was at the same time a slight breeze from the north, I was unable to use the theodolite without warming my hands at the fire after each observation. In the evening, when I took an observation of Sirius, the thermometer was down to $-25°.1$ C. or $-13°.2$ Fahr. and the tips of my fingers stuck to the instrument, which felt burning hot.

Ördek went out to reconnoitre, and managed to light upon a shepherd dressed from the crown of his head to the sole of his foot in sheepskins. He was greatly taken aback at finding visitors such as we intruding upon the peaceful solitude of his woods. But we soon became good friends with him. Not only did he sell us a sheep, which made a welcome variety in our bill of fare, but when he returned in the evening, he brought us a can of milk. The heavy snowfall of the last few days had been disastrous to the 400 sheep which he and two companions were in charge of. Several of them had frozen to death, and the rest had had great difficulty in getting at their food. The name he gave to that part of the forest was Kenglaika, or the "Broad Inundated Tract." The river had been frozen for 20 days, and would remain frozen another two and a-half months. Thus the Cherchen-daria freezes considerably later than the Tarim; but then it has a steeper fall and lies on a more southerly latitude.

We were only four miles from Tatran. According to my survey, I expected we were a good day's journey distant. The discrepancy was due to the variation of the compass, which amounts in those regions to 6°. In other words, if you steer your course direct south by the compass, you will in point of actual fact travel 6° west of south.

During the 10th and 11th of January we travelled on to Cherchen by the road which I had already traversed on the occasion of my former visit. About one month previously, a new beg had been appointed to Cherchen, and, to my delight, I learned that he was no other than Mollah Toktamet Beg, that is my old friend Togda Mohammed Beg, from Kopa. Accordingly I directed my steps towards his house, and received a hearty welcome. With his seventy-two years, he was the same pleasant old man, aristocratic looking, and polite, that I had known him before, and he placed his house at my disposal. I therefore took up my quarters in an inner apartment, while my men were accommodated in an outer one. This was the first occasion, and one of the very few occasions, on which, during the whole of this journey through the heart of Asia, I slept under a house-roof.

At Cherchen, which had grown into a place of about 500 families, we rested from the 12th to the 15th of January

CHAPTER XVIII.

A TWO HUNDRED MILES RIDE IN FIFTY DEGREES OF FROST.

TALES about towns and treasure said to be buried in the desert were incessantly being repeated to me, more especially a tradition about an ancient city supposed to lie near Andereh-terem, 100 miles west of Cherchen. But although I questioned the natives exhaustively, I was unable to obtain any definite or trustworthy information about it. They were afraid I should go to the place and discover all the gold which their wild imaginations depicted as lying hidden underneath the sand-dunes. It was, however, part of their tradition that the ancient town in question was haunted by ghosts, and—what is certainly strange—that it was a city which travelled. One man told me he had actually been to Andereh-terem, and seen a cylindrical tower of blue pottery, ten fathoms high, but it looked so strange and mysterious that he had not dared to approach it. Afterwards, having recovered his courage, he went back firmly resolved to look for the gold that was inside it; but when he arrived at the place, behold! the tower had disappeared. He could not, therefore, undertake to guide me to the spot, for he was convinced, that the tower shifted about over the desert, and would only mock all our endeavours to find it.

Now, as it happened, the region between Cherchen and Andereh was one of the few districts of East Turkestan which I had not hitherto visited. Hence, I resolved to make a trip to the latter place, although it meant a forced ride of over 200 miles there and back. In addition to the guide whom the beg compelled to go with me, I took three other men, namely, Ördek, Kurban, and Mollah Shah, the last-named an inhabitant of Cherchen, who accompanied Littledale in his journey through Tibet. I bought three new horses, and hired another three to carry our belongings. Islam Bai and Turdu Bai I left behind to look after the camels and my little white horse, and the dog, Dovlet II. The other dog, Yolldash, I took with me.

But before I quitted Cherchen I was destined to have a great pleasure. On the morning of the 13th one of Consul Petrovsky's jighits arrived from Kashgar, namely, Musa, the man who acted as my interpreter of Chinese at Khotan in 1896. He brought with him a well-filled post-bag, and I need not say I spent some right pleasant hours in devouring the contents of the letters and newspapers which it contained. How the man managed to find me so readily is to this very day a puzzle to me ; for it had been agreed between myself and Consul

On the Astin-yoll to Niya.

Petrovsky that the couriers were to travel to the Lop country *viâ* Aksu—that is, to the north of the great desert ; but Musa declared that he "knew it in himself" that I should be to the south of it. Islam Bai let drop hints about Musa having a sweetheart in Keriya, and it was the desire to see her which brought him that way round. If it was so, I give the girl my unadulterated blessing. Had Musa arrived two days earlier, I should not have got my letters until I returned to Tura-sallgan-uy, near Yanghi-köll, for neither the beg nor anybody else in Cherchen had the least idea that we were likely to emerge from the desert, and so Musa would have continued his ride to the east.

We began our little trip of over 200 miles on the morning

of the 16th January, having altogether seven horses, all of them small but active, and perfectly fresh. Two of them carried our belongings, and provisions sufficient to last 12 days. So off we set at a gentle trot along the *astin-yoll* or "lower road" to Niya, a route that had been traversed in 1889 by Captain Roborovsky, a member of General Pievtsoff's expedition. This, however, was practically the only time during the whole of these three years that I did not actually break fresh ground; on all other occasions I was the first European to traverse the routes which I selected.

We soon left behind us the last dwellings of Cherchen, and struck into the barren country to the west, travelling between clay terraces, which had been moulded by the erosive force of the wind, with a belt of sand on our left, and tamarisks, occasionally also poplars, on our right. We halted the first night at the well of Kallassteh or the "Hung-up Skull," though the well itself was frozen. When I was roused in the morning, there were 40 degrees of frost (−22° C.), and the sun and moon both stood at the same altitude above the horizon, namely, about 5°, and both had precisely the same reddish-yellow colour. Any one ignorant of the points of the compass would at the first glance have been in doubt as to which was the luminary of the day and which the queen of the night.

Up in the saddle and off again! A wretched west wind sprang up and chilled us to the bone. I assure you it is no light thing to ride against the wind, with 36° of frost (−20° C.) in the air. Your hands get so stiff and numb with cold that the only way to hold the pen at all is to grasp it as you do a hammer. It is not exactly encouraging to start in the morning with the prospect of a day like that before you. You can't keep in the saddle longer than half an hour at a time, but have to get off, and stamp and run, to prevent your extremities from getting frozen. The people of Cherchen told me they never remembered such a bitter winter, nor yet so much snow.

The route was perfectly straight, except when it crossed the tongues of sand from the desert, and there it curved to avoid the sand-dunes, which turned their steeper sides to the south-west.

When we reached the well of Kettmeh, we were all so done up that we stopped for a quarter of an hour, and made a little fire to warm ourselves at. Then on we went again at a smart pace over gently undulating ground to Yantak-kuduk, where we had to stop again for an hour to thaw ourselves. The same thing happened again at the well of Ak-bai. As a rule, all these wells were frozen hard into one solid mass to a depth of five feet. We met a small caravan of Tatars and *ishans* (holy-men) travelling from Keriya to Urumchi and a merchant with twenty asses, carrying *chapans* (cloaks), cloth, and 'kerchiefs to the bazaar of Cherchen. During the last part of the day's journey it snowed, and we began to look out anxiously for a place where there was plenty of fuel.

When we awoke the next morning, we were all snowed up. The new fall lay as light and soft as down upon the old and

Shepherds' Huts at Shudang.

now hardened snow-fall. The country was terribly monotonous and dreary. Not a hare, not a raven to be seen, nothing but the tracks of the former and of some wolves. Immediately beyond the well of Osmán Bai-kuduk, the sand became plenteous, and then followed a labyrinth of tamarisk cones, amid which the track twisted and twined as if it were playing at hide-and-seek. These cones or pyramidal accumulations of roots, on the top of which the tree stands, were like curled-up hedgehogs or porcupines, some of them like huge shaggy heads sticking up out of the ground.

The bed of the Kara-muran was now empty and dry; there was not even a single patch of ice in it. It was 250 to 350 feet wide, 3 to 6 feet deep, and was reported to bring down into the desert very considerable quantities of water, derived from the rainfall in the mountains to the south. The soil was yellow clay, deposited horizontally, and in layers of varying hardness, shaped into cornices, cubes, and terraces.

We encamped at dusk at Tokktekk, where there was a thick and luxuriant poplar wood, and did so because we observed fresh signs of the presence of shepherds. The only person we had met during the whole day's march was a solitary individual, a poor wretch, travelling on foot to Keriya, followed by a dog. The latter limped pitifully, was covered with blood, and had quite lost one ear, while the other hung by a small fragment of skin only. The man told us his dog had had a brush with some wolves during the night, and had got rather badly mauled. It must be a queer piece of work to travel from Cherchen to Keriya on foot, alone, and unarmed, in the depth of winter. But the man said, quite composedly, that at night he made a fire with flint and tinder, and the wolves did not come anywhere near him, whilst during the day they generally kept at a respectful distance.

During the night of the 18th January we had $50\frac{1}{2}°$ of frost ($-28°$ C.), and next day travelled by short stages, making fires at frequent intervals. The region we had now reached was more plentifully watered by the streams which come down off the northern slopes of the Kwen-lun mountains, and consequently richer in vegetation. All the same, we had unbroken sterile sand on our left, though to the right there were steppe-land and small groves of wood.

Upon reaching Pakka-kuduk we heard shouts proceeding from the north, and Mollah Shah soon found they came from a friendly brown-bearded shepherd, who led us to the airy hut in which the bai, his master, lived with his family. The man only dwelt there during the winter; in summer his home was at Andereh-terem, for at the latter season the whole of this region is fearfully hot, and swarms with gnats and mosquitos. The wolves cause the sheep-owners great losses, especially when they get so numerous that the dogs are unable to cope with them. The shepherds say, that if a wolf only just touches a sheep, the animal will die of fright; and once wolves set upon a flock they will destroy it to the last sheep, unless interrupted.

At the well of Shudang we encountered another shepherd, watering ten or a dozen asses. The well, which was situated in a depression, was 10 feet deep and yielded perfectly fresh water. Beside it stood a *lengher* or "caravanserai," built four years previously by the Chinese. Beyond Shudang the road led up on to a terrace, dotted over with tall and finely grown tograk woods. Here we pitched our quarters in the clay huts of the Shudang shepherds, and were warm and comfortable, especially after we killed two sheep, which the bai sold us in the evening. Here also we overtook another traveller from Cherchen, namely, a Chinese *siah* or "secretary," who was on the way to Keriya to report to the amban concerning his district. Like ourselves he stayed there a day to rest, and so we exchanged

Shudang.

visits. But on the following morning, when we set out, he had a fearful headache, brought on by over-indulgence in opium-smoking.

As I have stated in my former book (*Through Asia*), the river Mölldya or Möllja, at the point where it was crossed by the upper road, was a large river; but here on the lower road or *astin-yoll*, along which we were now travelling, it was hardly perceptible, owing to the fact that it was divided into a number of capricious arms, like an interlacing delta. This, of course, made irrigation more effective, and consequently the vegetation more luxuriant. The Kara-muran seemed, however, to be the bigger stream of the two, and no doubt it penetrates further into the desert, or did do so at one time, for it was pretty certainly this river which may possibly have given rise to the scanty vegetation which we noticed struggling for existence in the bayirs we had recently crossed.

The shepherds, who lead such lonely and monotonous lives in these terribly remote regions, far off the beaten tracks of the world, are a good-natured, friendly people. At first they are naturally shy of strangers, but so soon as they are convinced that the latter mean them no ill, they become at once accessible. They all speak in soft, gentle tones, not at all unpleasant to the ear, and give the impression of seldom mixing with their kind, and of being almost afraid of themselves. Our shepherd had a really beautiful voice, with a great many variations in it, and he used it cautiously, speaking in subdued tones, almost as if he were afraid to speak at all. Had you merely heard his voice, without seeing him, you would have believed you were listening to a man of a much greater degree of culture than he actually possessed, for his appearance stamped him at once as an undeniable barbarian. He was clothed in sheepskins, wore a woolly cap, and his foot-covering was also made out of sheep's wool and sheep-skin. He was as black as an Indian, owing to his never washing himself; and his eyes were narrow and oblique, his nose dumpy and shapeless, his lips fleshy, and he was destitute of beard. All the same he did profess some sort of religious faith, for as we rode past a *masar* (saint's grave), he recited a Mohammedan *dua* or "prayer," and drew the palm of his hand along his face, as the Mussulmans always do when they repeat their *Allahu ekbar*.

On the morning of the 22nd January we were again snowed up, the snow lying a foot deep. At this point we quitted the main road and struck across the trackless country straight for the "ancient city." A snowstorm was raging, and the going was bad, for the track led through a chaos of small disconnected sand-dunes, intermingled with tamarisk cones, the whole blurred by the fresh-fallen snow. At each step the horses sank in over the fetlocks. All this made it really hard work to get along, so that our progress was fearfully slow. At length we came to the ruins of a house, containing two square rooms. The walls consisted of clay, upheld by a skeleton framework of posts and spars, and were still standing to the height of 19 feet. They were extraordinarily thick and strong, and suggested that the structure must anciently have been a fortress. We encamped a short distance away, near the ruins of some very ancient towers. The snow still continued to fall, and was so deep as to render the examination of the ruins a matter of extreme difficulty.

In the evening, after the camp was ready, Turduk, our Cherchen guide, used to prepare his pipe. This was a highly original contrivance. Cutting two chips of wood, he used to stick them both together into the ground, one perpendicular, the other sloping towards it at an angle of 45°. Then he packed moist clay all round them, and drew out the chips of wood, and his pipe was ready. The vertical opening, or bowl, was filled with a pinch of the horribly sour tobacco grown in the country, and the sloping opening served as the pipe-stem. But the attitude which the man assumed when he smoked this primitive implement of luxury was neither very comfortable nor very elegant; for he was obliged to lie at full length on his stomach on the ground.

During the course of the evening the snowstorm increased so greatly in violence, that, having no tent, we deemed it necessary to take some sort of precautions for our own safety. My bed was prepared in the usual way, by shovelling the snow away and laying it on the bare ground, with the higher end next my little instrument-box. To this last, a felt was fastened, and stretched out so as to cover at any rate my head, and then propped up at its other end by a couple of tamarisk branches; my feet and lower extremities, however, became gradually buried under the falling snow. During the night I was awakened by feeling something like an icy cold hand touching my face. It was the felt, which, weighed down by the snow, had fallen in, and some of the snow had found its way along my neck into the bed. The snow melted close round the fire and made the felts sopping, as though they had been dipped in liquid mud, and in the morning we made a queer spectacle, and had no little difficulty in getting our clothes dry.

After that we went and examined the *kona-shahr* or "ancient town." It consisted of a remarkable massive wall, and several mounds and barrows. We also detected traces of a canal, which had clearly been connected with the adjacent stream of Bostan-tograk. The best preserved relic was a tower, 34½ feet high and 79½ feet in circumference, with an opening or port-hole high up on one side, inaccessible without a ladder, for the interior of the tower was solid. There were two other towers a little to the south-east, all three being in a line, probably alongside an ancient highway. Beside them we discovered a large quantity of red and black potsherds of burnt earthenware, but no traces of inscriptions or ornamentation. The whole were sadly battered and weathered; but unfortunately the depth of the snow prevented a closer and more exhaustive examination.*

In the evening we continued our journey towards the Bostan-tograk, the high, steep banks of which were lined with thin belts of poplars and reeds. The river had scooped out for itself a trench 26¼ feet deep and 463 feet broad, and at Andereh had a volume of 106 cubic feet in the second.

At Andereh and Baba-köll, which formed the end of our journey, we turned about and went back to Cherchen. On the way we met nobody except a caravan of asses, bringing down from Northern Tibet to Keriya a collection of wild yaks' and wild asses' skins. It was a bitterly cold ride we had. During the night of the 24th January the thermometer sank to $-29°.6$ C. or $-21°.1$ Fahr., equivalent to 53 degrees of frost, and the highest point it reached was only $-14°$ C. or $6°.8$ Fahr. Exposed to these intense degrees of cold, especially when accompanied by wind, you lapse into a state of apathy. As, however, we were returning by the same road we had gone out, there was no need for me to plot the route or take any measurements, and so I kept my hands wrapped inside the sleeves of my Sart wolfskin fur-coat.

During the night of the 26th we had 56° of frost ($-31°.2$ C. or $-24°.2$ Fahr.), and when on the following day, thanks to the stillness of the atmosphere, the thermometer rose to $-16°$ C. or $3°.2$ Fahr., we felt it relatively warm. We rode hard, crouching all of a heap in the saddle, and leaning forward against the wind, with our arms crossed, and left the horses to guide themselves. Thus we rode, hour after hour, the horses'

* During the course of the extremely interesting and highly successful expedition which Dr. M. A. Stein, of Rawalpindi, made in East Turkestan in the years 1900-1901, principally for archæological purposes, he visited, among other places, the lower Andereh-daria, and discovered there the ruins of an ancient town. One especially valuable find he made consisted of several MSS. I cannot too strongly urge all who are interested in the archæological problems of Central Asia to study Dr. Stein's excellent book *Archæological Exploration in Chinese Turkestan*, Preliminary Report (London, 1901), especially as the thorough investigations made by this inquirer throw a clearer light upon the discoveries which I made in the Lop-nor region. It may be added that Dr. Stein has also just published a more popular account of his journey in *Sand-buried Ruins of Khotan* (1903).

hoofs ringing monotonously thud, thud, thud on the frozen ground.

On the last night of our journey we registered 58° of frost (−32°.2 C. or −26°.0 Fahr.), the lowest record for the whole of that winter. The next day we were in the saddle ten hours; but we started so late in the morning that we had to ride several hours in the pitch-dark night. It was stinging cold, and to make things worse, the wind blew in our faces, not very strong it is true, yet quite strong enough to freeze us stiff as we sat in the saddle. I tried to protect my face with a neck-kerchief, but my breath froze upon it, until moustaches, beard, and nose all became one piece; still it did afford a certain amount of protection. The greatest difficulty was to protect the eyes. The wind made them water, and the water stuck the eyelashes together and froze into tiny icicles, which had to be thawed at intervals to enable us to see at all.

I cannot describe how glad I was to reach the shelter of the beg's house and warm myself at his roaring fire, while I enjoyed a good meal of tea, fresh eggs, bread and honey, and afterwards crept into bed and lay for a couple of hours reading Swedish newspapers, and revelling in the play of the flames upon the walls and roof of the little room. Meanwhile Yolldash lay stretched out in front of the fire, and snored, as well he might do after such a long cold run.

The results of this reconnaissance were less than I had hoped for. In fact, the journey was hardly worth the 13 days I sacrificed to it, though it was not entirely fruitless. I made several important geographical observations, especially with regard to the extent of the sand-belts in that part of the country, the development of the vegetation, the size and direction of the rivers. These last really have a more easterly position than is assigned to them on Roborovsky's map, in consequence of the gentle slope of the Tarim basin towards Lop-nor.

CHAPTER XIX.

AMONGST THE DRY RIVER-BEDS.

THE day we left Cherchen—the 30th of January—to return to Tura-sallgan-uy was anything but seasonable for the beginning of a long journey; wind, dense clouds, snowstorm, and an icy chilling mist, with the thermometer down to $-15^{\circ}.0$ C. or $5^{\circ}.0$ Fahr. at one o'clock in the afternoon. We made quite an imposing caravan with our six camels and five horses, especially as we were accompanied as far as the river by a crowd of the good folk of Cherchen. The camels were fat and well rested, and we were again plentifully supplied with everything we needed. I engaged Mollah Shah permanently; he would be a useful man to have in Tibet. He said adieu to his native town and his wife and six children as calmly as if he were only going off for a two or three days' trip. No European who knew he was to be absent for two whole years would have quitted his home in that easy unconcerned way.

Instead of following the usual route along the left bank of the river, we crossed over, and for the first two days travelled along the steppes on the right bank, our object being to reach Keng-laika, the position of which I had determined astronomically.

It was my intention to find out if possible where the old bed of the Cherchen-daria ran. According to Roborovsky, who, however, never saw it himself, it was situated 40 miles north of the existing bed. This was the problem I now had before me, a problem which formed part of my original programme. It turned out that the information which Roborovsky obtained from the natives was untrustworthy and required revision. For to my surprise the shepherds of Keng-laika told me that the more northerly of the two depressions which we had crossed in the desert rejoined the Cherchen-daria at Su-össghen, a day's journey down the river, and that below that point there existed no ancient river-bed to the north. Of this particular depression we had already taken accurate note during our journey southward across the desert.

On the 3rd February, 1900, we struck away from the Cherchen-daria at a little salt-pool called Shor-köll, and travelled across tamarisk steppes and through dead forest until we came to Chong-shipang, as the farther ancient bed was called. It was very plainly marked, having about the same breadth as the existing river, and formed an almost straight trench in the ground. Its banks were high and clearly defined, and were dotted with tama-

The Ancient Bed of the Cherchen-daria.

risks and scattered poplars, some living, others dead. Beyond this trench stretched the desert for as far as ever we could see to the north.

Further on this river-bed divided into two arms, of which the one on the right hand returned back to the Cherchen-daria, while the one on the left continued to the east-north-east, though it, too, gradually led back to the Cherchen-daria, until it struck it at Su-össghen, the point already mentioned. On the night of the 2nd February the wolves howled fiercely about the camp. They were no doubt hungry, as the intense cold still continued. At all events, we judged it prudent to keep the horses tethered close to our camp-fires.

Having thus proved that there existed no ancient river-bed

north of the Cherchen-daria, I preferred to travel along its right bank, where there was no recognisable route. And there we did discover a *kona-daria*, or "ancient river-bed," proving that the Cherchen-daria had not always shifted to the right when it changed its channel. Near this abandoned river-bed we encountered, standing isolated amongst the tamarisk groves, the most massive poplars I have ever seen in East Turkestan. They were not more than 20 to 24 feet high, but upon measuring two of them close to the ground we obtained a circumference of 15½ and 22⅓ feet respectively. The trunks proper were not more than 3 or 4 feet high, but upheld bizarre crowns of gnarled and shaggy

An Ancient Tograk beside the Cherchen-daria.

branches. The existence of such trees as these proved that the river must have flowed here for centuries. For, even though we do not accept the natives' computation of age, namely, that a tograk (poplar) lives for a thousand years, then stands another thousand years a dead trunk on its own roots, and finally lies rotting on the ground for yet another thousand years, it may at any rate be safely concluded that these veterans were at least some centuries old. Immediately beyond these ancient trees our guides conducted us to an old Mussulman burial-place, with several *gumbez* (tombs) and the ruins of some houses, the largest of the latter measuring 49¼ feet by 42½ feet. Close by were plain indications of fields having been formerly cultivated, amongst other things an arik or irrigation canal, now, of course, in great part destroyed.

That evening we encamped near two or three graves which our guides had told us about, and on the 4th of February we examined them more closely. They had been excavated some three years before by shepherds, who, of course, believed they would find gold and other valuables in them. When we came to the place, there were three coffins standing outside a tamarisk cone, within

A Poplar beside the Lower Tarim.

which they had been originally placed. Two of the corpses, an elderly man and a middle-aged woman, were well preserved. The skin sat close to the skeletons and was as tough as parchment. The woman's was especially interesting. The hair, which was in no way decayed and was of a reddish-brown colour, was caught up at the back of her head with a red ribbon. This tint of hair is seldom seen in any Asiatics who would be likely to visit these parts; besides, the women of Asia, at any rate of Central Asia, all wear their hair in long plaits hanging down the back. The skull was of Indo-European shape, with high cranium, straight eyes, very slightly projecting cheek bones, narrow Roman nose, with elongated, almost parallel nostrils. Beyond a shadow of doubt she was neither of Chinese nor of Mongol blood. Moreover, her dress was not Asiatic at all. It consisted of a coarse linen shift, with tight arms, and the lower part widening out like an ordinary gown. Now the Asiatic women always have loose sleeves and wide trousers, but never wear skirts, which would be a hindrance to them when they ride, for they sit the saddle in the same attitude that men do. Around the forehead of both man and woman there had been a narrow bandage of some thin material, though it was now almost completely rotted away. The woman had red stockings on her feet. In the case of both corpses the nails were cut—not allowed to grow long as is the Chinese fashion.

Of the man's clothing very little was left. His hair was neither partly shaved off nor yet gathered into a pigtail : he could not, therefore, be a Chinaman. Inside his coffin lay an ordinary wooden comb.

The coffins were simple and hastily made, each consisting of six poplar planks, the width being precisely the same as the height, the sides parallel, and the length slightly exceeding that of the bodies. Close beside the coffins stood the remains of an ancient hut, with walls of interlaced brushwork.

All the indications pointed to these people having been Russians, and I jumped to the conclusion, that they possibly belonged to the Raskolnikis (Nonconformists), who a little after 1820 fled from Siberia towards Lop-nor, and of whose subsequent history nothing further is known. The tamarisk cone, inside which the coffins were originally placed, must of course have presented precisely the same appearance then that it does to-day.

Amongst the actual inhabitants of East Turkestan at the present time one often meets types which, by intermixture of Aryan blood, have lost a good many of their Mongol characteristics. But these bodies could not very well be Mohammedan, because the Mussulmans of Central Asia do not bury their dead in coffins. The shepherds declared that several other tamarisk cones in the same neighbourhood were used as burial-places, but they were not able to lead me to any of them. It is possible a Raskolnik colony may have found refuge in this remote part of the world from the persecutions to which they were only too frequently subjected. Unfortunately the coffins were totally destitute of inscriptions.

Leaving these mysterious dead to their last long rest in the wilderness, we travelled on further, partly along the right bank, partly on the ice of the river. The Cherchen-daria did not present the same strongly-scarped outlines as the Tarim, nor was its bed so deeply eroded; but its banks were like those of the Tarim, in that they were bordered by poplars, tamarisks and kamish. The belt of vegetation on the right bank was, however, broader than that on the left bank, for on this side the desert approached nearer. From the river we generally saw the sand-dunes peeping over the shoulders of the forest.

It still continued cold. During the night of the 5th February

On the Bank of the Cherchen-daria.

there were 52 degrees of frost (−29°.0 C. or −20°.2 Fahr.), though luckily we were able to command an unlimited supply of excellent fuel. At the *lengher*, or rest-house, of Ak-ilek we crossed over to the left bank of the Cherchen-daria, the ice cracking ominously under the weight of the camels just over the line where the current still ran. Upon reaching the spot where the Charkhlik-Cherchen road crossed the river, a spot I had already visited in 1896, we had unfortunately to bid adieu to our guides, for they possessed no knowledge of the region we were now about to traverse. In lieu of definite information we had nothing to go upon except an inference from a story which Toktamet Beg, of Cherchen, told me. Once, when he was sitting in his own house, he was disturbed late at night by a knocking at the door, and in reply to his inquiry a well-known name was given. Thereupon he opened it, and in rushed seven robbers. One of them, who had a drawn knife in his hand, threatened to kill Toktamet if he offered any resistance. Having bound him, they plundered his house, carrying off everything of value they were able to discover, including 2,000 tengeh (about £20) in silver money. Then they fled, taking the beg, still bound, along with them, so that he might not rouse people to pursue after them. The part of this story which specially interested me was that the robbers, in the course of their flight, crossed the Cherchen-daria and travelled north to the Tarim down an ancient river-bed, which obviously must have been the Ettek-tarim. This was clearly not the first time that this particular river-bed had been used as a line of retreat by fugitive cut-throats.

On the 8th February we continued our course down the Cherchen-daria, keeping to the left bank, partly because I did not want to travel in Roborovsky's footsteps, partly that I might ascertain whether any other river-channels branched off or rejoined the principal stream. Thus our road led close along the edge of the forest, across steppe-land diversified with tussock-grass and reeds. The high sand-dunes advanced to within half a mile on the north. The river, it was evident, had often been swollen, for its terraces or scarped banks projected six or seven feet above the level of the ice. In one place, but only in one, the sand-dunes advanced quite close to the river, and terminated abruptly in a wall of sand, which went down some 30 or 35 feet straight to the water's edge. We encamped for the night in one of the few poplar groves we met with.

Young Kurban, who had at first promised so well, now seemed likely to turn out a veritable young rascal. This evening, for instance, as soon as it grew dark, he disappeared. All the animals were in camp, so that he could not be out with any of them, and he had also left his sheepskin behind him, although there were 32½ degrees of frost (− 18°.0 C. or −0°.5 Fahr.). As hour after hour passed and he did not come, we began to fear he had been attacked by wolves. Accordingly I sent men out to look for him. At last, although it was quite late, they came back, bringing him with them. It seemed that, during the march, the young rascal had lost a pair of boots off one of the camels. There was, of course, nothing wrong in his losing a pair of boots, but he ought to have told somebody he was going back to look for them. We were afraid he had fallen asleep somewhere, and would freeze to death during the night. I bade Islam Bai keep a sharp eye upon my young gentleman, and a good thing I did so, for he turned out eventually to be a full-fledged rogue.

That night offered the first indication that the severity of the winter was past. We had not more than 36 degrees of frost (−20°.1 C. or −4°.2 Fahr.), and during the following day, the 9th of February, the thermometer rose to −7°.6 C. or 18°.3 Fahr. It had never been so warm since the 28th December. The country we were now travelling through was painfully monotonous, and we looked in vain for the slightest trace of human beings. And so it continued on the 9th and the 10th; but at

On the Frozen Cherchen-daria.

last, on the 11th February, we met human beings at the sattma of Aralchi, on the left bank of the river, namely, a man, two boys, and two women, with 600 sheep, 6 cows, and some horses and asses. These people told us that an ancient watercourse which we had followed the day before disappeared at the extreme end of the desert, and in the opposite direction united itself with the Ettek-tarim.

By a lucky chance, Togdasin Beg, my old friend from Charkhlik, found us on the evening of the 12th at a place called Yiggdelik-aghil, having been commanded by the amban of Charkhlik to keep a look-out for me, and place his services at my disposal. He was consequently quite pleased to show me the way to the Ettek-tarim, along which he had already travelled twice, and he gave me a good deal of information about it, which on the whole agreed very well with what I was told by Kunchekkan Beg of Abdall in 1896. It was only about 30 years, he said, since the Ettek-tarim was abandoned by the current. Previous to that time one-half of the volume of the Tarim, *i.e.*, the Yarkand-daria, used to flow along that watercourse.

Togdasin Beg told me he had even rowed down it in a boat, although at this time there was not a single drop of water in it. The second time he saw the river was in 1877, when the notorious Niaz Hakim Beg of Khotan, the confidant, and later on the murderer, of Yakub Beg of Kashgar, fled from Khotan to Korla with a caravan of camels, asses, and mules, upon which occasion he, Togdasin Beg, was called upon to guide the fugitive down this *ogri-yoll* or "thieves' road," as it was called, because of its being frequented by those who had very good reasons for desiring to avoid the great caravan roads. The complaisant old beg accordingly acted as our guide, and it was amazing how well he remembered the way, although he had not been there for 23 years. The topographical sense of the natives of East Turkestan is often developed to an incredible degree of accuracy. This old man, for instance, would say to us, if you will go a couple more *yoll* (stages), you will come to a place where there is better pasture. And he was always right.

During their rutting season, which falls in February, camels are savage and dangerous. We had only he-camels in our caravan, and consequently care and vigilance were needed to prevent them from injuring one another. At the camp at Koshmet-kölli, however, two of the brutes got fighting. In their blind fury they beat their heads on the ground, twisted their necks round one another like a couple of snakes, and strained and wrenched, and bit and kicked with all the force they were master of, until the froth flew about them like soap lather. The stronger of the two pushed his head between the fore-legs of the other and tried to heave him over. Had he succeeded, his vanquished enemy would have been lucky if he escaped without serious injury. But before the former could get his opponent over, the men rushed in to the rescue. At such a time, when he is foaming with rage, it is no use tugging at a camel's nose-rope; he pays not the slightest heed to it. The men struck the pugnacious brutes over the nose with thick sticks, until they at last let one another go, and, bleeding and splashed with froth, and their eyes blazing with enmity, stalked off to graze again. After that we always tied up the fore-legs of the most ferocious when we encamped at night, and whilst on the march kept them muzzled.

On the 14th of February we made a very short march of only 9¼ miles, for as we were about to traverse a waterless region, three marches across, it was necessary to make a fresh start from Bash-aghiz, the last place where water was to be obtained. From that point the northern arm of the Cherchen-daria bent back to the south-east into the lake of Lop-kölli, the only name by which the Kara-buran was here known.

A Shepherd's Hut (Sattma) at Aralchi.

At one o'clock p.m. the thermometer recorded 0°.4 C., or 32°.7 Fahr., the first time since Christmas Eve that it rose above freezing-point. All the same, it sank during the ensuing night to −24°.0, or −11°.2 Fahr. Here, however, the snowfall had evidently not been so heavy, for we saw none except in sheltered places.

Carrying with us a couple of sacks of ice for ourselves and the horses, we directed our steps on the 15th February towards the north-east, and struck the Ettek-tarim at Yulgunluk-köll, or the "Tamarisk Lake." Thence it continued southwards, and formerly entered the Kara-buran, not far from the present fishing-station of Lop. But we followed it in the opposite direction, to the north, finding all day long an abundance of small wood, fresh and full of sap, although the ground was everywhere as dry as tinder. At Kutchmet, a day's journey due west of Shirgeh-chappgan, there was forest as fine as any alongside the Tarim. The bottom water was, of course, not very far down, as we found, for instance, at the well of Yulgunluk-kuduk, which happened just then to be sanded up. The well itself was dug in the bed of the river, in a hole about 16 feet deep, which had been scooped out by a powerful eddy. Beside it was a trough, the hollowed-out trunk of a tograk, or poplar, for horses and asses to drink out of, showing that this "back-way" was used sometimes, especially, as I understood, by men engaged in gathering *yiggdeh* berries. The sand-dunes which ran alongside the Ettek-tarim were at most 12 to 14 feet high, though later on they rose to 65 feet.

This former river-bed was uncommonly easy to distinguish; it could not well be more than about 30 years since it was abandoned. Not only was it a bare trench bordered by dense woods and thickets, but the last channel in which the water actually ran was clearly distinguishable as a winding grip lying even deeper; and occasionally some of the drift-wood still stuck fast in the bottom.

Here I may mention *en passant* two or three features of a physical geographical nature which tended to illustrate my views as to the migratory character of the lake of Lop-nor. In the first place, the circumstance, that the Ettek-tarim was accompanied by vigorous poplar woods, while the corresponding part of the course of the Tarim proper was destitute of forest, proved that the latter was of such recent formation that there had not yet been time for any forest to grow up. In the second place, the huge accumulation of drift-sand, which overhung our camping-ground that night, and which bore the significant name of Tagh-kum, or "Mountain Sand," proved that in ancient times there was no Tarim to the east of it; for if there had been, it would have been impossible for the dominant east wind to pile up such stupendous masses of sand in that situation. But this becomes no longer impossible, if we assume the Tarim to have entered the old Lop-nor, that is the lake, now dried up, which lay to the north of Kara-koshun; for there was at that time nothing to prevent it doing so. Thirdly, the sand between the Ettek-tarim and the lower course of the existing Tarim decreased materially in proportion as we travelled northwards from Tagh-kum; in other words, the drift-sand was unable to accumulate on the exposed side of the ancient lake of Lop-nor.

The belt of vegetation which accompanied the Ettek-tarim was about two miles wide, and was fenced on the east by high steep sand-dunes, whereas on the west the dunes had a gentle ascent right up to the immense promontories which we encountered in the interior of the desert.

Whilst the men were engaged in loading up on the morning of the 16th of February, I climbed to the highest summit of the Tagh-kum, some 160 to 200 feet above the woods, and from there obtained a splendid bird's-eye view of the surrounding country. North-east stretched a bayir of the usual type and with the usual characteristic concentric water-markings, or former lake-levels.

A Poplar Grove in the Delta of the Tarim.

On the east the depression was shut in by a wall of sand, which, however, was only half as high as the Tagh-kum, and sloped away east towards the right bank of the Tarim, distinguishable by the darker colouring of its forest-belt. Beyond that again was sand, with its steeper faces always turned towards the west.

It is a pretty obvious inference that these bayirs occur all over the desert, and owe their origin to the action of the wind. As yet the dunes which had managed to establish themselves in the bed of the Ettek-tarim were only insignificant, but in its accompanying forests they were 10 to 12 feet high. To this extent the ancient watercourse is still protected from the gigantic ocean of sand which is slowly approaching it and threatening to engulf it. Indeed the process of engulfing has already begun, for the Tagh-kum has actually invaded a portion of the bed of the Ettek-tarim, and farther north the latter was frequently hidden underneath the encroaching sand. The bayirs are not stationary, but travel westwards across the level plain of the desert, having their origin on its eastern boundary, near the Ettek-tarim, and disappearing in the far west, where the winds are less regular, as well as subject to other laws than the winds in the Lop country. Thus each bayir maintains its identity during the whole course of its existence, although the soil of which it is composed is renewed every century or so—assuming that the sand-dunes travel at the rate of 15 or 16 feet every year. Thus, though the "waves" of the desert sand obey the same laws as the waves of the ocean, there exists, nevertheless, a great dissimilarity between them. In the case of the latter it is only the wave-movement which is transmitted onwards, the water retaining its position; whereas in the case of the sand-waves the material travels as well as the wave-movement, being flung forward and then poured on over itself. And if the wind failed to bring up fresh material, the existing sand would be all swept away.

As we advanced farther towards the north the forest gave signs of dwindling away, as though its roots experienced difficulty in getting down to the bottom-water. Notwithstanding that, it was still thick, and some of the trees measured as much as 8 feet in circumference. The belt on the right bank was, however, beyond comparison more luxuriant than that on the left bank, owing to the greater protection it enjoyed against the wind; whereas the belt on the left bank was being gradually choked and smothered by the sand. Six swans, the first harbingers of spring, were seen flying towards the north-west, and the temperature rose to 4°.2 C. or 39°.6 Fahr. One of the localities we passed on this day was called Kulchak-kölli, pointing to the former existence of a lake, which has now disappeared.

During our last day's tramp along this instructive watercourse dead forest became quite as common as living, and the work of desolation was in general farther advanced, for the sands on both banks closed in to within 350 yards of each other. Indeed, in some places they had even flung bridges of small dunes across from the one bank to the other.

At length, at Bash-arghan, we once more struck our old friend the Tarim. How small and insignificant it appeared as compared with the mighty stream which had impressed us all so much in the autumn! Ice-bound and motionless, it resembled a narrow canal, without any alluvial formations. The sheet of ice which covered it was like a flat, shallow gutter, for the edges were higher than the middle, owing to the river having dropped since it became frozen. When it first froze it was 141 feet across; now, however, it only measured 77½ feet. As the camels had had nothing to drink for three days, we hewed a hole in the ice to get water for them, and found it was more than 20 inches thick. Thence we travelled through forest, thickets, and brushwood to Arghan or Ayrilghan, where we encamped for the night.

Sunday, the 13th February, we rested. We were now at the

Watering the Horses at a Hole cut in the Ice.

confluence of the Tarim proper and the Koncheh or Kunchekkish-tarim. The former was 194 feet broad, the latter 79 feet, and the united stream, which flowed into the Kara-buran, 252 feet wide. Our camp was pitched in the angle between the Tarim proper and the united stream. This spot I visited twice subsequently, and thus it became of importance as a fixed point for checking and controlling my topographical and astronomical observations. Here that fine old fellow Togdasin Beg took leave of us and returned home, but eighteen months later he again rendered us important services.

CHAPTER XX.

TURA-SALLGAN-UY—THE BURIAT COSSACKS.

I do not propose to weary the reader with a description of the network of waterways which we threaded on our way back to Yanghi-köll. A more intricate and labyrinthine hydrographical system it would be impossible to conceive. No river possesses a more tangled complex of waterways than the delta of the Tarim. It would be impossible to make it perfectly intelligible without a detailed map, and that it must be a work of the future to prepare. Names ending in *köll* = " lake," *choll* = " pool," *dashi* = " salt-pool," *akhin* = " stream," and *kok-ala* = " river-arm " occur repeatedly, even in those tracts which are now completely desiccated.

At the village of Sheitlar we observed an old woman beating rushes (*chiggeh, i.e., Asclepias*) until its fibres became as thin and soft as cotton; this material would then be woven into a coarse but strong material. She told me that her parents had lived beside the Chivillik-köll at a time when it was a much larger sheet of water than it is now, and even now it is the largest lake that the people of that locality are acquainted with.

Our route now lay to the north-west, across steppes and through woods, thickets, and fields of kamish. At Arelish the Kunchekkish-tarim split into two arms, the more easterly of which entered the lake mentioned just above, and the western one was the Kok-ala, which we skirted for some distance.

Although the thermometer dropped at night to –18°.8 C. or 1°.8 Fahr., the days were steadily growing more spring-like. On the 21st February we reached Dural, the headquarters of the amban, or Chinese governor, of the Lop country; and on the 22nd Tikkenlik, where we were met by Kirgui Pavan, the man who in 1896 showed me the way to the large lakes that lay to the east, and so furnished me with the opportunity of making the very important discoveries I then made. At Tikkenlik I again took up my quarters in the house of Naser Beg.

We experienced another stroke of luck at Turduning-söresi, for we found there, encamping in the forest, a man with eight camels, named Abdu Rehim, from Singher in the Kurruk-tagh. Now my next expedition was to be to the dry river-bed of the Kum-daria, and I wanted a guide. This river had been touched in a couple of places by both the Russian traveller, M. Kozloff, and by myself; but beyond that nothing was known about it. Now this Abdu Rehim was, it seemed, the same man who guided M. Kozloff to the well of Altimish-bulak in the Kurruk-tagh,

Reed Huts at Sheitlar.

that being, as it happened, the nearest well to the Kum-daria. In fact, he was one of the only two or three hunters in all that region who had ever penetrated as far as Altimish-bulak. But the man had a pretty high opinion of his own importance, and it was not easy to come to an understanding with him. I offered to buy his camels, but he asked an altogether unreasonable price for them, especially as they were not to be compared with ours. Islam Bai, who in his dealings with his co-religionists showed something of the arrogant despotism of Tamerlane, came to blows with Abdu Rehim over this matter. Now the latter did at first give the impression of being something of a freebooter and turbulent fellow. But when he was going off in a tempest of rage, I called him back, and we eventually came to terms—without assaulting one another. I agreed to hire six of his camels at the rate of half a sär (1s. 6d.) a day for each animal; and Abdu Rehim agreed to guide me by way of the Kum-daria as far as Altimish-bulak, after which he was to be at liberty to continue his journey to his own home at Singher. His camels were carrying no loads, for he was on his way home after taking his sister and her dowry to a beg at Dural. Islam Bai prophesied that I should have trouble with this man; but he was wrong, I had no trouble with him whatever. This was the first time I ever had occasion to find fault with Islam; but it was not the last.

After this acquisition—some of Abdu Rehim's animals were she-camels—it was no easy matter to control our own, especially a big Bactrian he-camel, which was very restless and kept trying to bite his companions. In fact, he turned quite wild, and the froth hung about his mouth as if it had been lathered by a barber. He screamed and wept in the most plaintive and melancholy way possible; and whenever we encamped we tied him to a poplar tree, not only by his nose-rope but by strong lashings round his feet.

During our last day's march, the 24th of February, we were met by troops of villagers from all over the district, by begs with their attendants, by scouts and couriers. They were all pleased, and even amazed, to see us come back again alive, after witnessing us disappear in the desert so silently, and without leaving a trace behind us. Then came, dashing up at the gallop on their black horses, three Cossacks in full uniform, a dark green colour, with high, black lambskin caps, and bright riding-boots, and with their sabres suspended over their shoulders. They were Sirkin and the two new Cossacks from Transbaikalia. In spite of their pronounced Mongol features, the new-comers made a fine show as they reined in their smoking horses, which they sat and managed with masterly skill. Compared with them, I was a perfect tatterdemalion. Pulling up in front of me, they saluted and presented their respective reports.

Sirkin, whom I had left in command of the camp during my absence, reported that one of the camels had run away, and that one of the greyhounds had been seriously hurt whilst in pursuit of a wild boar. Except for that, all was well.

The elder of the two new Cossacks reported that he and his comrade had been ordered by their commanding general at

Chita to come and join me in the country of Lop. They were both pure Buriats, and their language differed but little from Mongolian; but they could also speak Russian fluently, and during the time they were in my service they learned to speak excellent Jaggatai Turki as well. Their names were Nicolai Shagdur and Tseren Dorshi Cherdon, and both were 24 years of age. They belonged to the army of the Transbaikal Cossacks, a force which consists to a considerable extent of Buriats. Their term of service was four years, of which they had served only about the half when they received the welcome command which sent them half-way across Asia to serve me, in a country and amongst a people whom they had never seen before. They had been given their pay for the two remaining years of their term of service, namely, a thousand roubles (£106) in gold, for the Tsar desired that my escort should be no expense to me. However, I took charge of the money for them, found them in everything so long as they were with me, and at their departure gave them back their thousand roubles, besides other gifts, so that from the monetary point of view they did very well by the expedition. But they fully deserved all they received: their services were simply invaluable, and their conduct beyond all praise.

It had taken them four and a half months to travel all the way from Chita, using railway, diligence, post-horse, and Turkestan arba (cart). They carried passes dated "Chita, the 20th of September (o. s.), 1899, and being Cossacks in active service, they travelled free so long as they were in Russian territory. Their route had lain through Irkutsk, Krasnoyarsk, Ob, Barnaul, Sergiopol, Kopal, Jarkent, Kulja, and Urumchi; but there they had been detained two months by the great Chinese scholar (now dead) Consul Uspensky, who had lost traces of me, and did not know exactly where to send them on to.

The Buriat Cossacks, after completing their term of service, during which they become thoroughly Russianized in both speech and discipline, return to their stanitzas or settlements, resume their native dress and native manner of life, and live principally by breeding cattle. The stanitza of my two men was Ataman Nikolaievska, situated 130 miles north-west of Troiskosavsk, near the southern end of Lake Baikal. I believe that both these men, Shagdur and Cherdon, would have laid down their lives for me, and I became as much attached to them as I was to their comrades from the west. Shagdur, in particular, was the beau-ideal of a man, and a good and faithful servant.

Properly speaking, I ought now to have sent back the two West Turkestan Cossacks, Sirkin and Chernoff, to their quarters at Kashgar, for I was only authorised to keep them until the arrival of their Buriat comrades. But I had taken such a liking to them, and had learnt how honestly and conscientiously they carried out the tasks I set them, that I could not reconcile myself to the idea of parting from them. I wrote therefore to Consul-General Petrovsky, begging him to appeal on my behalf to the proper authority that I might retain the two men, and in the sure hope that my request would be granted, I kept them with me until I heard something further concerning them.

But to return to our last day's march back to Tura-sallgan-uy. Upon arriving there, which we did in the company of an imposing escort, we found, assembled in the "market-place," a large company of our neighbours and the remaining Cossack, Chernoff, for it was an inflexible rule that one of these men should always be on guard. During our absence the camp had been enlarged, and another tent put up. Everything was clean and tidy in honour of our return, my hut all in order, and a fire burning in the stove inside the tent. All the animals were in first-rate condition—the mules fat and plump, and both the camels and the dromedary had put on flesh. But these latter had grown wilder, the dromedary in particular. He screamed in a "ghostly" and rumbling voice, most painful to listen to; and gritted his teeth, and ground them till the froth dropped off in big flakes, and he rolled his eyes and tried to bite. He would not allow anybody to go near him except Faisullah. We kept him tethered by each leg to a stake driven into the ground, so that the poor beast was unable to move.

As soon as the men knew that one of the camels had run away, Parpi Bai set off after him. But although he followed his track for a whole fortnight across the Koncheh-daria, and along the Kurruk-tagh as far as Shinalga, and thence to Kuchar, he eventually lost him. Later on we heard that he made for the valley of Yulduz, and was there appropriated by some Mongols. At any rate, we never saw him again. This was the only time that a camel ever actually ran away from my caravan. But both Turdu Bai and Faisullah, who had had several years' experience of camels, and were perfectly familiar with their habits, told me that a camel will sometimes be frightened out

Chernoff, Sirkin, and Shagdur.

of his wits by a tiger or a wild boar, and, in a panic of terror, will flee as though the devil and all his imps were after him. Evidently something of the sort had happened to our camel. Tigers did occur in that district, for one of our friends, Mirabi, caught one in a trap not very far from our camp, and brought him just as he was, frozen and stiff as a wooden horse, and set him up in the midst of our market-place; and after he thawed in the spring, we flayed him and kept his skin.

About this time the number of my live-stock was increased by the addition of a cat and two new-born pups, which Pavan Aksakal gave us. They were called Malenki, or the Little One, and Malchik, or the Boy, because they were so small and so pretty; and these names clung to them after they grew up and became veritable giants of their kind. They turned out first-rate caravan dogs, and I and they were always the best of friends. Our poultry, too, had multiplied, adding yet another element to our rural prosperity. Besides these we had a falcon and the goose which travelled with us on the ferry-boat all the way from Lailik. The latter seemed to have entirely forgotten its former relatives, the wild-geese, and paid no further attention to them.

Ever since the middle of February the wild-geese had been returning. They were the same flocks we had seen travelling towards India in the autumn; only they were now going in the opposite direction, pursuing the same course, crossing the same rivers, the same lakes, flying over the same poplars and the same belts of forest, which they know generation after generation. Their great highway is the Tarim; it is extremely seldom that they take a short cut across the desert. We now began to hear them flying in vast numbers over Tura-sallgan-uy. We heard them screaming and chattering at all hours of the day and night and in all weathers. We saw them by day, in calm and in storm, equally whether the sun was hidden or whether he glinted out through the tempestuous skies. We heard them when it was pitch dark at night, and the black clouds prevented the light of the moon and stars from reaching the surface of the earth. And they were always driving along at the most desperate speed, never stopping, never resting. The Lop-men aver that the same colonies return year after year to the same breeding-places, and that they recognise certain laws and rights of possession, just as the Lop-men do themselves. Thus they are absent during the four months of extremest cold, during which all the rivers and lakes of East Turkestan are ice-bound.

There was no lack of game. The Cossacks went out shooting every day, and never came back empty-handed. They killed several wild boar, and brought home pheasants, wild-duck, wild-geese, and occasionally a roe-deer. We were kept well supplied with all sorts of country produce, such as eggs, milk, cream, mutton, poultry, hay, and so forth, and we always had a superabundance of fish. And in the forest there was any quantity of firewood to be had for the fetching; and for that purpose we had plenty of camels.

Our camp at Tura-sallgan-uy thus became an important market, well known throughout all the Lop country, and immediately outside its precincts there grew up a ring of small "suburbs," where tailors, smiths, and other handicraftsmen came and plied their several trades. In one of these establishments, that of Ali Ahun, a tailor from Kuchar, a little sewing machine rattled briskly all day long. Parpi Bai, who was a saddler by trade, took up his quarters near the stables, and kept himself busy making new pack-saddles for the camels and mules. Merchants came from Kuchar and Korla, bringing such wares as they believed we should be likely to want, *e.g.*, sugar, cube tea, Chinese porcelain, Russian tea-cups, cloth, and so forth. One of these men, a merchant from Andijan in West Turkestan, built himself a straw hut and hung its walls with red cotton stuffs from Russia, and had ranged about him stacks of cloth, chapans (cloaks), caps, boots, etc., exactly as in a store in a bazaar. This shop became immensely popular, and there were nearly always some of my men, Cossacks as well as Mussulmans, inside it, talking, drinking tea, smoking, or bargaining.

And then the throng of wayfarers who came that way! The great caravan road ran of course through Jan-kuli, but Tura-sallgan-uy proved to be a formidable rival to that place, and gradually travellers began to come our way. And when they did come, they all felt it incumbent upon them to stay the night; for it was quite a *tamashah* or "spectacle" for them to observe how we lived and what we did. Every day horsemen rode into the market-place, and offered their horses for sale, and some of them we bought.

Thus our little town grew with American rapidity, and there was an incessant coming and going, bustle and noise, until quite a late hour every night. The market-place was lighted by a single big Chinese lantern, which was never put out until our

Dragging the Canoes Overland (*viae* p. 397).

last visitor had gone; after that the only sounds were the tread of our sentinel and the barking of the dogs.

During my absence Sirkin had kept the meteorological register with exemplary correctness; and as it would be advantageous to have as long a series as possible of these observations taken at one place, I ordered him to remain and take charge of the camp during my absence on the forthcoming expedition, and at the same time continue his meteorological work. But I took Chernoff with me, for he excelled in the preparation of cutlets and *pilmen*, this last consisting of pieces of meat boiled in dough.

During the short time of our stay at Tura-sallgan-uy the weather was perfectly winterly. The first real *kara-buran*, or "black tempest," of the year came as early as the 25th February, and I felt how pleasant a thing it was to sit inside my own house-door and listen to the wind whistling through the reedy walls of our huts, and threatening the life of our only poplar. Drift-sand and dust swept down the Tarim and made the air so thick that we were unable to see the steep dune which faced us on the opposite bank of the river. On the 26th of February it snowed, the snow being hard, and round, and small, and it struck against the tent-cloth like pellets of shot. The country was once more white all over, and the dune, when we were again able to perceive it, looked like a snow-covered mountain range. At length, however, the weather cleared up, and I set about my astronomical observations; and also found plenty to do in developing negatives. Tura-sallgan-uy was the most important centre of all for controlling my cartographical work.

On the 4th of March the temperature rose to 7° C. or 44°.6 Fahr. The strong ice panoply in which the river had been so long held spell-bound, now began to turn soft, and not only did the melted water stand upon it, but it swept along it like a tidal current. Our big ferry-boat, which was frozen into the first ice, was listed over, so that her gunwale was level with the surface, and she gradually became half full of water.

Presently a rift appeared in the ice, showing first where the current ran strongest. We warned Sirkin and the men who were staying behind with him to be watchful and on the alert when the early spring freshets came. I especially directed them to have all my boxes on board the ferry-boat in case the camp should be threatened with an inundation; in that way they would be able to move to some safer place, should the danger become serious.

I now dismissed the unlucky young Kurban, who disappeared the moment he was in possession of his wages. I learnt subsequently that the young rascal had a "rare old time of it" on his way back to Kashgar. At Kuchar he went to the serai, or rest-house, of the Andijan (West Turkestan) merchants, and represented to them that he was travelling as my express courier to Consul Petrovsky, whereupon the good-natured traders gave my young gentleman everything he wanted. In Aksu he became too intimate with the young wife of a beg, and was beaten, but met with lenient treatment at the hands of the Chinese amban, who no doubt thought it would be only prudent to show politeness to the courier of a European. After that Kurban stole a horse in Aksu, and took his departure secretly on its back. But it was in Kashgar that his effrontery reached the greatest lengths; for he went to Consul Petrovsky and tried to put upon him a cock-and-bull story about his having been robbed. He pretended to be plunged in the depths of despair, and asserted that I had entrusted to him, for conveyance to the Consul, a packet of specially important letters, but that he had been attacked on the road by a band of robbers, who took away from him both the package and what money he had. But this was not the first time that Consul Petrovsky had heard these sort of tales, and before my fine gentleman knew where he was he found himself behind the bolts and bars, with plenty of leisure to reflect upon the untowardness of his fate. This was the sole reward he earned by his hardihood. As for the simpletons who let themselves be cheated by him on the road, they had to suffer for their imprudence, unless they managed eventually to get a *quid pro quo* out of young Kurban himself.

This time I left Islam Bai behind me in the camp to act as foreman of the Mussulmans, and I instructed him and Sirkin, as soon as I had started, to go to Korla and buy twenty-five horses and some mules, besides a stock of provisions for our use later on in the summer, when I proposed to make an excursion into Tibet.

IV.

Lop-nor and its Sister Lakes.

A Reedy Wilderness in the Desert.

CHAPTER XXI.

THE KURRUK-TAGH AND THE KURRUK-DARIA.

As soon as the weather began to feel spring-like, I sent Faisullah and Abdu Rehim on in advance with the camels and heavy baggage to Dillpar on the Koncheh-daria, instructing them to cross the river in good time, find good grazing, and then wait until we joined them. I started myself on the 5th March, accompanied by Chernoff, Ördek, and Khodai Kullu, a Loplik who remained in my service fully a couple of years, besides a perfect crowd of uninvited attendants. In addition to the ordinary baggage, I took this time two tents and a stove, a case full of scientific instruments, two cases containing the cooking appliances, and two sporting rifles. Khodai Kullu, who had the reputation of being a great hunter, carried his own weapon. The Osh jiğhit, Musa, also went with us for the purpose of taking back several of the horses, when we reached Ying-pen on the edge of the desert.

Our first stage in this new expedition led obliquely across the steppeland which stretched northwards between the Tarim and the Koncheh-daria. As is almost invariably the case when a caravan makes a fresh start, it was late in the day when we really got under weigh. There is always so much to arrange and settle, and a number of petty details to be seen to, just at the last moment. The three Cossacks who were staying behind, and all the Mussulmans, were drawn up in a line to say good-bye to me. As I was going off I warned Parpi Bai not to fall too deeply in love with any of the daughters of the land, for he had a reputation that way. He smiled as he stood there, straight and strong in his lusty manhood, dressed in that becoming blue chapan of his, and answered, that I might be perfectly easy on that score. And the poor fellow was right. His love affairs were over, for twelve days later he died after a very short illness, and was buried with great solemnity in the peaceful graveyard of Yanghi-köll, amid the sorrow and sympathy of his comrades and the native inhabitants of the place; and his grave is now marked in the usual way by an array of little fluttering flags and yaks' tails.

Thus Parpi Bai never had an opportunity to distinguish himself during this series of expeditions in the same way as he did during the former series, when he was in the full prime of his manhood; but for all that I have none but pleasant recollections of him, and shall not readily forget him. Some of those who have at different times been connected with one or

Bash-tograk.

other of my caravans I may indeed forget; but never the men who have died in my service. They will always have a warm place in my heart, for they have fallen faithfully at their posts, and have given me all they possessed—namely, their own lives. Peace be with thy ashes, my faithful Parpi Bai, and may thy last long slumber at the foot of the desert dunes never be disturbed!

It was quite dark before we saw Faisullah's fire flaring up between the poplars on the bank of the Koncheh-daria. We encamped on the left bank of the river among the woods of Dillpar, and stayed there all the next day, partly that I might measure the volume of the stream, although it was still frozen hard, and partly that I might take certain astronomical observations. In the morning I sent back the begs who had guided us thus far, and thenceforward we were left to our own devices.

The current, which was now flowing underneath the ice of the Koncheh-daria, had a volume of 1,353 cubic feet in the second, or very little more than one-half the quantity which always flows, summer and winter alike, underneath the bridge at Korla. The breadth extended to 118 feet, the maximum depth was 19½ feet, the thickness of the ice 1½ inches, and the transparency of the water 7½ inches. Luxuriant kamish-beds lined the right bank of the river; on the left bank stood a vigorous forest.

A Tamarisk Thicket.

We were once more on the move on the 7th March, steering towards the north-north-east. The *personnel* of my caravan consisted of the following:—Abdu Rehim and his two younger brothers, with eight camels, six of which were in my hire—the other two were ridden by their owners; Faisullah, with five camels; Chernoff, Ördek, Khodai Kullu, and Musa, each on horseback; and lastly myself, mounted on the same strong little horse which had carried me through the Desert of Cherchen. Yolldash and Mashka accompanied us to keep guard at night.

Shortly after leaving Dillpar we crossed three successive deserted channels of the Koncheh-daria. Beside the last of them three huts were still standing in a state of good preservation.

Turning our backs upon the woods of the Koncheh-daria, we rode across a hard plain, the surface of which was impregnated with salt, and covered with a thin layer of sand, which crunched under our feet. It was also dotted about with tamarisks. On the way we struck the little oasis of Bash-tograk, with some huge, but now decaying, poplars, some of them as much as 12¼ feet in circumference. West of that stood a *tora*, or "road-pyramid," towering conspicuously above the plain, and visible to a great distance. It marked the ancient highway, called by the inhabitants of Lop Kömur-salldi-yoll, *i.e.*, "the road where coal was spread," which ran from Sachow to Korla along the northern shore of the old lake of Lop-nor. In *Through Asia* I had occasion to describe that part of this great highway which extends north-west from Ying-pen to Korla. One of the objects of my present excursion was to examine its eastward continuation on the other side of Ying-pen.

No sooner had we turned our backs upon the last of the tamarisk mounds than the surface assumed the character commonly found at the foot of the mountain-chains of Central Asia—namely, in the native tongue a *sai*, that is to say, a gentle slope, almost imperceptible to the eye, but as hard as asphalt, utterly barren, and strewn with fine, thinly-scattered débris. The ground was furrowed by a dry watercourse, which came out of a side-glen of the Sughett-bulak. This was the point we were aiming for, as it would afford us a convenient path to the foot of the mountains. Although we were able to make out their outlines quite distinctly in the morning, the sun would rise again and set a second time before we could reach their actual slopes.

The desolate *sai* extended like a sea on every side of us. We were still just able to follow the outline of the Koncheh-daria in the south by means of its dark belt of accompanying vegetation. The only signs of animal life were a few timid deer, which made off the instant they were shot at. Gradually the ascent became more noticeable, though the ground at the same time grew more stony. The watercourse contained some drift-wood, fragments of tamarisks and willows, which had been swept down by the torrents after rain, the so-called *sils*. As we advanced, the sides of the Sughett-bulak, that is to say, the faces of its scarped terraces, approximated closer and closer together, and the bottom of the stream became more uneven and irregular.

Finally the mountains closed in on both sides; we were in

the mouth of the glen of Sughett-bulak, which takes its name of the "Willow Spring" from a solitary willow that stands beside it. The little brook which came down the glen, and which originated in another spring a day's journey higher up, carried 3 cubic feet of water in the second. We did 20½ miles that day, and the temperature rose to 13°.1 C. or 55°.6 Fahr., so that we had no need of overcoats or cloaks except in the evening. We were now within two days' journey of the nearest Mongol nomads. There are always some of them in the large valleys that lie embedded amongst the parallel ranges of the Kurruk-tagh, where excellent pasture is said to exist.

The Pool at Kurbanchik.

It was a splendid place to encamp in; a fresh breeze blew down the glen all night. This was the first night of the year in which the thermometer did not sink below zero; its maximum was only 1°.3 C. or 34°.3 Fahr.

Our next day's march led eastwards along the foot of the mountains and across an infinite number of dry watercourses. We saw hares, antelopes, and *arkharis*, or mountain sheep; but when Chernoff tried to get a shot at the last named, they disappeared into a ravine with great agility and ease. On our left we passed a continuous panorama of mountain scenes, peak after peak emerging and disappearing in endless succession. The most conspicuous of these were all entered on my map, their bearings being taken from divers different points. The summits of the main chain were, however, screened by the flanking ranges, and we only saw them in occasional peeps up the transverse glens. The colouration continually changed, shifting from brown to violet, then to red, grey and yellow in regular succession, and it was influenced too by the shadows cast by the airy clouds as they flitted in front of the sun.

On the right the surface fell away slowly towards the plain through which the Koncheh-daria meandered towards the lake of Kara-köll. But we were no longer able to discern its forest-belt. The horizon kept changing—it brightened, grew blurred, disappeared in the mist, melted with the sky. After crossing over several shallow rivulets, separated by rolling country, we came to the edge of the deeply eroded glen of Kurbanchik, some 130 feet down below our feet. To the north was the broad, wide-open glen-mouth; to the south the clay terraces loomed up like black walls. Behind a projecting shoulder of the mountain lay a pool of beautifully pure water, of an emerald green colour, and so deep that the bottom could not be seen in the middle. It was fed by a little brook, carrying 3 cubic feet in the second, which entered at its upper end, but left it again at its lower end. In fact the pool was a miniature Bagrash-köll—the lake near Kara-shahr over on the other side of the Kurruk-tagh. It was situated at the very extremity of a deeply eroded side-glen, and after rain the water must pour into it like a waterfall, because there was a big drop from above. Yet, as rain is a great rarity in these "Dry Mountains"—for that is what Kurruk-tagh means—it must have taken a very considerable time to scoop out this little gathering-basin, especially as the surrounding mountains were composed of diorite.

At Kurbanchik we were said to be two and a-half days' journey from the crest of the main range, by a track or mountain path which led up to a pass called simply Davan (Pass), or by the Mongols, Többveh. From the summit it was another one and a-half days to the Bagrash-köll.

On the 9th of March we travelled a good distance down the glen of Kurbanchik before we found a side-glen by which to climb up the eastern side. After that we pressed on towards the south-east over broken steppe-land, dotted with an occasional clump of grass; then, after threading a labyrinth of low hills, we descended into a dry ravine, which wound between rounded heights of some soft material, though further on this gave place to hard rock. Just before the ravine opened out upon the level and desolate *sai*, we encamped in a delightful little spot known as Tograk-bulak, which consisted of a poplar grove and a well, the latter being covered with thick ice pierced by a forest of reed-stalks. It was a spur of the Kurruk-tagh which we had just cut through by means of this ravine.

After that we continued towards the east, hour after hour, having the mountains always on our left. Although not trenched by any deep or large watercourses, the *sai* was nevertheless furrowed by an immense number of tiny runnels, generally

Tograk-bulak.

about one foot deep and filled with débris, which was anything but pleasant for the soft pads of the camels' feet. The sun set a ball of fiery red; it became dusk, and still we were a long way from the place where the next well was said to be. Our guide just now was Khodai Kullu, who had visited this locality before, and we continued to follow the directions which he shouted to us until far on into the night. At last we reached the margin of another big glen, and down its steep side the camels scrambled, or rather slid for the most part. However, when we got to the bottom there was not a drop of water to be found anywhere. We had mistaken the glen in the darkness; but as we had already done 26 miles we encamped where we were.

Next morning we discovered that we were not so very far out of our reckoning after all, for the spring of Bujentu-bulak was only half-a-mile farther on, and the animals were at once taken down to it. I was awakened at sunrise in rather an alarming way. Chernoff came in, and lighted the stove, as usual, whilst I was still asleep, but he failed to notice that the breeze which came down the glen was pressing the tent canvas against the heated stove-chimney. I was awakened by an unbearable warmth, and opening my eyes saw the tent in flames. At the same moment the men came rushing up and pulled over the tent, whilst Chernoff dragged out the packing-cases, papers, and other things that lay scattered about inside it. Nor was I idle; for, seizing a felt cloth, I set to work to smother the flames, and eventually got them out. After this misadventure my breezy domicile looked the reverse of comfortable. However, the men took a piece of sacking, and having clipped away the burnt edges of the canvas, sewed a patch on. Beyond that, fortunately, nothing was damaged.

The brook which came down the glen of Bujentu-bulak was divided into several arms, all rippling along underneath a broad covering of ice.

When we started again we turned our backs upon the mountains, and steered our course towards the south. In the distance was the *kona-shahr*, or "ancient town" of Ying-pen, standing out in relief against the blurr of the sandy desert behind it. The ruins of this ancient town were ranged on a line running due north and south, so that I was able to examine them, and measure and sketch them, without deviating from our line of march. The first we came to were two *toras*, or "towers of clay," each 14¾ feet high and 49¼ feet in circumference. Next, on a terrace, the outer face of which had been washed away by an inundation, was a *guristan*, or "burial-place," about 200 years old. The graves were marked by monuments of sun-dried bricks (adobe), shaped like cigar-boxes, and the position of the skeletons—the feet towards the south, the head towards the north, with the face turned in the direction of Mecca (*kebleh*)—proved that it was a Mussulman burial-place. Owing to the façade of the terrace having been swept away, several of the graves were open, and showed the skulls of their occupants, peeping out as if through loopholes in a wall. One skeleton, that of a youth of about 15, had fallen out altogether. Close beside this burial-place stood something which might have been indifferently a *mesjid*, or "smaller mosque," a *khanekah*, or "prayer-house," or a *gumbez*, or "domed tomb" of some person of consequence. It consisted of three walls without a roof, and the fourth wall had clearly been swept away by a flood, like the face of the terrace. The back wall was 19½ feet long and 13½ feet high. In close proximity to these ruins we picked up a quantity of fragments of red and black earthenware jars, on some of which a round ear still remained. After that we came to a *tora*, about 26 feet high and 103 feet in circumference, and then to seven others of smaller size, crowning an isolated hill. Either these last were intended as monuments

On the Way to Bujentu-bulak.

to mark graves of distinguished men, or they were Chinese *pao-tais*, or "mile-stones," which by their number were intended to indicate, as is still the practice at the more important road-stations of Central Asia, the distance in *li* to some other notable road-station in the same district.

But the most interesting ruin of all was a circular wall, precisely similar in appearance to those which I had formerly examined at Sai-chekkeh and Merdek-shahr. It was constructed of sun-dried clay (adobe), held in position by a framework of horizontal beams, and was pierced by four gates. Its diameter was 597 feet, the thickness of the wall 36 feet, and its height 21½ feet. The gates were situated at the four points of the compass. In the centre of the inclosure was a small pyramid of clay.

What object such a wall could be built for is not easy to say. It was too small for a town wall; besides, there were no signs of any dwellings having ever existed inside it. If it were a fort, the four wide gateways were surely unnecessary. Hence, I am disposed to look upon it as a kind of caravanserai or post-station, the inhabitants of which dwelt in tents or wooden houses. And no doubt the great Lop-nor highway ran directly through it, for the eastern and western gates lay exactly along the line it took. Indeed, old folk amongst the Lop-men still preserve a tradition that the great highway to Peking ran through Ying-pen, and so on to Dung-khan or Sa-chow.

Leaving these ruins, we steered east-south-east to Ying-pen, having on our right, though a long way off, a thick belt of fine poplars, marking the dry river-bed which it was the main purpose of our expedition to explore. The name given to that watercourse by all the native hunters who are acquainted with it is Kurruk-daria, or the "Dry River," though they also call it sometimes the Kum-daria, or "Sand River"; it was by this name that Kozloff knew it.

The *örtäng* or "hostel" of Ying-pen was a Chinese post-station, which at the time of our visit had stood empty and deserted for a whole year. The authorities had for some time past been endeavouring to revive the traffic on this the old route between Lop and Turfan, but without success; for the route *viâ* Korla is more comfortable as well as more convenient. Ying-pen was a true oasis in that it was surrounded by desert on every side; and during the two days' rest which we gave our animals there we had no fear of their running away. The place was frequented by wild-duck, wild-geese, and partridges; and fresh water was obtainable from a well. The post-station stood on a prominent terrace or platform, some six or seven feet high, immediately north of a salt marsh overgrown with reeds.

Geographically this was a point of the greatest possible interest, for it was soon apparent that the marsh in question lay in the elbow of an ancient river-bed, which had run between two belts of poplars, just as the Tarim does now. The fact was even patent to the natives themselves. But from this point eastwards the channel contained not a drop of moisture. All the way from Ying-pen, until it entered the desiccated basin of the ancient lake of Lop-nor, it was as dry as tinder. On the 12th of March the temperature rose to 21°.4 C. or 70°.5 Fahr., and the flies and spiders began to show signs of reviving animation. It was a warning to us of the uncomfortable days to come, when we should be tormented by the intense heat and swarms of insects, and should enjoy coolness only in the night-time. These indications of summer suggested, however, that we might with advantage lighten our baggage. It was now time for Musa to return with all the horses—except my well-tried, gallant little grey—and one of the camels, which was not eating very well. I therefore seized the opportunity to

A Ruin near Ying-pen.

send back with him my furs and ulster, my winter boots, the stove, and other things we could do without. But as it turned out, it was a premature and ill-advised action.

On the 13th of March we were once more in motion; but during the march, the wind, which had set in the day before, increased to a perfect hurricane. We were travelling eastwards, keeping to the left-hand scarped edge of the dry river-bed, which was plainly marked all along by groups of poplars. One of the loops which the river made was as fresh as if it had been carved out only a year ago. It contained a crescent-shaped pool of salt water, entirely free of ice, just like the *boljemals*, or "abandoned loops," of the Tarim, and on its left side was a group of poplars, some of which measured as much as 13½ feet in circumference at their base. This, however, was the last pool of water and the last patch of living forest we encountered along this dry and ancient watercourse, though we did find dead forests, the trees still standing on their own roots, like gravestones in a churchyard. The ground was covered with fine powdery sand, which whirled up and hung behind the caravan like a comet's tail. The men sat rocking on their camels wrapped in their chapans or cloaks. It was twilight as early in the day as two p.m., and as the storm still continued to increase, Abdu Rehim declared we must stop; it was killing work for the camels to struggle against the wind. Accordingly we halted, and set about seeking for a sheltered place in which to pitch camp. Just in this locality the clay desert showed peculiar modifications of relief, being carved by the wind into pyramids, and horizontal terraces, and flat benches or shelves, each rising, as a rule, six to seven feet above the general level of the surface. Branches of dead poplars lay scattered about in every direction.

Whilst seeking for a sheltered place to camp in, we nearly lost one another. I walked towards the south-west, or rather I was carried by the wind, and at such a rate that I did not observe how far I was being taken from the others. However, failing to discover a suitable site, I turned round to retrace my steps; and then it was I felt the full brunt of the tempest. For it drove right into my face with terrific violence, smothering me with sand and fine reddish-yellow powdery dust. I could not see a single glimpse of the caravan. It was like wading against running water or liquid mud, and despite my most desperate efforts, I was unable to make headway. My previous footprints were entirely obliterated—obscured the instant I lifted my foot. Eyes, mouth, nose—all were stopped up with sand and dust, and I was forced to stand still to catch my breath. Then I saw a spectre looming out of the haze, and discovered it was Chernoff coming to look for me.

As soon as we were able to get hold of the other men, we encamped just where we were. My tent was reared on the sheltered side of a tamarisk mound; but we did not dare put up more than the half-lengths of the side supports, and even then had to stay their upper ends together with ropes. The side-cords were wound round massive arms of the root, and heavy pieces of timber were laid across the folds of the canvas

A Sand-storm in the Desert.

which lay on the ground. When all was finished, the tent stood quite firm, and rode out the tempest successfully, though showers of fine sand penetrated through the canvas, and smothered everything in the interior.

Owing to the poles of the men's tent being in single pieces, they were unable to put it up at all, but lay on the ground, muffling up their heads in their cloaks. The camels knelt in a long row, with their necks stretched out flat on the ground in the direction in which the tempest was blowing. Close to the earth the wind had a velocity of 40½ miles an hour; but on the top of an adjacent mound, only six or seven feet high, it was some 18 miles an hour more, or 58½ miles in all, and I was only able to keep my balance when I knelt. The storm came from the north-east, and its violence enabled me to form some idea of the inconceivable quantities of sand and dust which are transported by this mighty agent towards the regions of the west and south-west. When we stooped down, we were well-nigh choked by the swirling cloud, which careered along the ground like a cataract, making little eddies of dust as it swept on. Branches, tufts of grass, grains of sand as big as peas were whirled into our faces with stinging force.

Just about dusk this black tempest seemed to tire a little; for the space of two or three minutes the sky lightened a shade, while the wind slackened and caught its breath as it were. This pause was very instructive; it showed how easy it was to be mistaken in our calculations of distance, both horizontal and vertical, when we were entirely swallowed up in a dense "sand-fog" such as this. For while we imagined ourselves to be en-camped in a depression or valley, we discovered that the adjacent country was in point of fact almost flat.

But the pause was soon over. The tempest returned in full blast, and went whistling, howling and roaring past my canvas cave, within which I hastily burrowed out of the all-engulfing sand-fog. Cooking was of course absolutely out of the question. I had to content myself with bread and water and the contents of a pot of jam. I set to work to write up my diary by the light of a candle, but the ink dried in the pen owing to the shower of sand that fell over me, and the pen itself scraped and scratched as it moved through the little heaps of sand which gathered on the paper. Within half-an-hour every object that was exposed to the air had completely vanished from sight. To undress amid such a rain of searching sand was extremely disagreeable, especially as my bed, too, was full of it. That stifling dust-laden atmosphere! It was enough to suffocate anybody and everybody.

Where, I wonder, did those millions of cubic miles of air come from, and where did they go to? What were the forces which started this torrential rush of air? Was it that the vast deserts of the western parts of Central Asia were already warmed so greatly in excess of those farther to the east, that the latter were called upon to fill the vacuum which was caused by the upward movement of the heated air? Or was all this stupendous pother nothing more than a merely local occurrence, a column of air pouring like an untamable flood down the sides of the Kurruk-tagh, and then returning again on the revolution of some imaginary wheel at higher altitudes, after simply brushing against the surface of the earth? It was not easy to tell; but this at any rate is certain, that it is the wind which is the most powerful physical agent in moulding the features of the earth's surface in those parts of the world.

The minimum temperature during the night of the 13th March was $-7^{\circ}.1$ C. or $19^{\circ}.2$ Fahr.; and although on the following day the tempest abated very considerably, it still remained bitterly cold—so cold, indeed, that we were forced to make up a gigantic camp-fire, and afterwards travel a good long distance on foot to get warm. I had made a great mistake in sending back my furs and winter clothing.

The bed of the Kurruk-daria was still moist in two or three places south-east of our camp, and in those spots a few tamarisks and patches of reed still struggled for life; but the forest along its bank was dead, some of the trees lying prone, others still standing on their own roots. After that we came to some exceedingly difficult country, namely, a perfect labyrinth of clay "terraces," with sharp-cut edges, which the natives called *yardang*; and as this is a very graphic descriptive word, I shall for the future use it when speaking of these scarped formations. They were originally formed by the agency of running water, but have subsequently been resculptured by the wind into the most fantastic and capricious outlines imaginable. Hence it was not always easy to trace out the continuations of the river-bed which wound amongst them; and travelling amongst them was not only wearisome, but also terribly slow work, for we were all the time unceasingly climbing up them and then down again on the other side. These yardangs of the Kurruk-

The Onset of a Desert Storm

Vol. 1—to face page 350

daria appeared to extend a long way towards the south; at all events they stretched as far as a couple of isolated sand-dunes which stood out above the dead level of the desert.

Farther on, we again passed two or three well-preserved river-bends, the bottoms of which were covered with coarse sand and gravel, the whole embosomed in dense woods, now dead. The tree-trunks which lay on the ground were as a rule more rugged than those which still stood upright; but then the latter were more exposed to the weather and the wind, as well as directly subject to the rasping, destructive effects of the drift-sand. These lifeless stems, standing like the embalmed mummies of ancient trees, gave the country the appearance of a stubble-field of Brobdingnagian dimensions. It was only alongside the dry bed of the Kurruk-daria that these dead forests existed; they had, of course, been once nourished by its fickle waters, and only died after the river changed its course and took a more southerly direction to the newly-formed lakes of Kara-buran and Kara-koshun.

The dry river-bed we were following wound along the foot of the extreme outliers and spurs of the Kurruk-tagh, and their lowest terrace—that is, the plain immediately to the south of them—afforded us a level and convenient road to march upon. One outstanding section of the mountains bore the curious name of Charchak-tagh, or the "Mountain of the Wearied Ones," the story being that a troop of Chinese soldiers who encamped there on their way from Turfan to the recently established post of Charkhlik discovered that their stock of provisions was at an end, so they flung away their weapons and other paraphernalia and returned to Turfan.

On our right we had the Kurruk-daria, and immediately on our left a parallel trench with a markedly scarped edge on the farther side. That is to say, we were travelling along a long narrow bank, as it were, between two river-beds, for the second trench, that on our left, was simply an older channel of the Kurruk-daria. This was evident enough even to Abdu Rehim, who knew that it continued for some distance towards the east. Sometimes the dead forests thinned out until their bare upstanding tree-trunks, when seen from a distance, acquired a remarkable likeness to telegraph-poles. We now observed for the first time traces of wild camels; they occurred in depressions sheltered from the wind.

Numerous *yiggdeh* bushes (*Elæagnus hortensis*) now appeared in the dead forests. The natives of that region affirm, and quite truly, that these bushes afford the clearest proof of irrigation having been formerly practised in the localities where they survive, for of all trees and bushes they are invariably the first to succumb after irrigation ceases, and they wither as soon as the water turns salt. Tograk (poplar) and yulgun (tamarisk) are far more tenacious of life, and will continue to survive a long time upon their own roots.

On the 15th March there was again a strong east wind. Although it only blew at the rate of 15¾ miles an hour, still the cold ($-1^\circ.1$ C., or $30^\circ.0$ Fahr., at seven a.m.) made us very sensitive to it, as it penetrated through our thin spring clothing. It was impossible to keep ourselves warm even when we walked half the time, for at one p.m. the thermometer only stood at $6^\circ.8$ C., or $44^\circ.2$ Fahr.; whereas at Ying-pen, with a west wind, it had recorded $21^\circ.4$ C., or $70^\circ.5$ Fahr. It is not inconceivable that these differences were in some way intimately connected with the varying degrees of calefaction or heating of the surface in different parts of the Asiatic continent. In the year 1897, just at this same season, I experienced stinging wintry cold with deep snow whilst travelling through Eastern Mongolia. Over the central parts of the desert region there was formed on the other hand a barometric depression, which acted like a suction-valve upon the colder regions all around. Now this inequality of atmospheric pressure is greatest in spring; but, as the summer advances, it gradually tends to disappear. It is owing to these causes that the Lop country is visited in spring by such furious tempests from the east and north-east.

We now left the Kurruk-daria, and directed our march towards the foot-hills of the Kurruk-tagh, in quest of a spring which Abdu Rehim knew of, and which we were anxious to reach. We were still separated from Yardang-bulak by a crest, built up of coarse crystalline rock and intersected by veins of diabase, the whole greatly weathered; but after crossing over yet another belt of barren country, we encamped in the little glen where the spring was situated. Here, on a very limited area, there was a luxuriant growth of reeds; and as this was one of the only two localities where pasture and water were to be met with, we decided to let the animals have two or three days' rest. In the same immediate neighbourhood were three other similar springs, though no vegetation worth speaking of anywhere near them. Our spring was called Achik, or the Bitter; the others, Yukarki, Tömönki, and Yakka, or the Upper, the Lower, and the Outermost respectively. The water of Achik-Yardang-bulak trickled forth in a natural channel between low elevations, but was covered with ice, three or four inches thick. Thus we had to thaw the ice before we were able to use it; but when it was thawed, the water was excellent, and entirely free from any disagreeable mineral flavour, although the areometer, when placed in the very throat of the spring, showed that the specific gravity of the bubbling water was 1.012.

Our guide, Abdu Rehim, was a mighty camel-slayer, and

Wild Camel Shot by Chernoff.

utilised his first rest-day to go a-hunting. When he came back, after an absence of fourteen hours, he said he had found a big he-camel at Tömönki-Yardang-bulak, and had wounded him severely, though the animal crossed the Kurruk-daria, and finally escaped amongst the sand-dunes. Abdu Rehim declared that when a wild camel is wounded it always makes for the open desert, and he also believed that when, in the natural course of things, these creatures feel the approach of death, they go in amongst the dunes to die. His reason for this belief was, that he had seldom or never come across a skeleton of the wild camel amongst the mountains of the Kurruk-tagh. Maybe their instinct tells them, that in case they have to make a long fight against death, they are more likely to be left in undisturbed peace in the desert than they would be amongst the mountains. Abdu Rehim reported further, that he had also observed fresh signs of a herd of seven wild camels, an old male, two females, and four *tailaks*, or young ones, which had been down to the "lower" spring to drink on the previous afternoon, and had possibly fled at our approach.

Chernoff was more fortunate. Very early in the morning I heard him speaking in an animated voice, but with extreme caution, bidding someone tie up the dogs. Then there was a dead silence, and then came five shots in quick succession, quite close to camp. A camel had come down the wind towards the spring without suspecting any danger. Chernoff and Khodai Kullu fired at him, but they only wounded him slightly, and he turned and fled back to the east. The Cossack followed him, and every now and again the animal stopped and regarded his pursuer with a certain amount of curiosity. Chernoff shot at him again at 500 paces' distance, and the shot struck him in the shoulder. The camel then went off at a slow run towards the south, fell two or three times, got up again, and finally fell for the last time about one mile and a quarter from camp.

It turned out to be a young she-camel, and her coat was covered with the finest and softest hair imaginable; and as this was the season when the wild camel sheds its coat, her hair came off almost of itself. The men gathered what there was of it for making into cords and ropes. After that they cut the camel up; and the meat was very welcome, for our supply of mutton, which, during the last few days, had been tasting very strong, was now quite at an end. Abdu Rehim asserted that the wild camel always shuns for a long time the locality in which one of its own species has been killed.

In the evening Chernoff shot a fine brace of partridges, which also proved very acceptable. During the hot weather, it was always a difficult problem in Central Asia how to supply ourselves with fresh meat. I had arranged with Kirgui Pavan and a couple of other hunters, who knew Yardang-bulak, to meet us there with five sheep, besides poultry and eggs. But we heard nothing of them, and could not afford to wait any longer. After we got back, we learned that they started all right, but lost their way in the desert, and during the storm three of the sheep also went astray. When they at length reached Yardang-bulak, the rest of the sheep were half-dead with fatigue, and as the men saw from our camp-fires that we had been and gone, they turned round and went back to Tikkenlik. However, their non-arrival was not a matter of any consequence, for, once we reached Kara-Koshun, we should be, relatively speaking, in the land of plenty.

CHAPTER XXII.

THE WILD CAMEL.

ABDU REHIM gave me a good deal of information about the habits and peculiarities of the wild camel, which agreed well with what I learnt in 1896 from the old camel-hunter on the Lower Keriya-daria. At the spring season the wild camel requires to drink once a week, though in the winter he can go a whole fortnight without. He can even go half a month without water in summer, provided he can get grazing with plenty of sap in it. The reason he cannot do without it for a longer period in winter is the dry nature of the food he eats at that season. The wild camel knows his way to the nearest springs as unerringly as though he guided his footsteps by map and compass. He will even drink water that has a decidedly salty flavour, and seems to like it. When there is a strong wind blowing, a hunter may approach within 30 paces of him, if he happens to be amongst tamarisks or kamish, or indeed if he is grazing anywhere where the hunter can conceal himself. As a rule he is not shot at when the distance exceeds 50 yards.

The wild camel's keenest sense is that of smell. Abdu Rehim asserted that he could scent a man at Yardang-bulak all the way from Oy-köuruk, a distance of 13 miles. The moment his suspicion is aroused, he takes to flight with the speed of the wind. The wild camel of the Kurruk region resembles his congener of the Keriya-daria, in his unspeakable horror of the smoke from a camp fire, and in the fact that he shuns every place that human beings visit, however seldom. And he has just as great a repugnance to the tame camel when the latter carries a pack-saddle; indeed even after the pack-saddle is taken off he recognises the tame camel by the unfamiliarity of his scent. On the other hand a young camel, not yet broken to work, had once or twice run away from Abdu Rehim's father, Ahmed of

Singher, and gone and joined itself to a herd of wild camels, and been received by them without hostility. On one such occasion Abdu Rehim's brother shot one of his father's own camels, thinking it was a wild one. Here I may mention that, according to Przhevalsky, the wild camel was common in the desert of Kum-tagh, to the east of the marsh of Kara-koshun. At the present time he is never seen there, or very rarely indeed; which may be owing to the desiccation of the lake, or is, perhaps, due to the fact that the pools of water which still survive in that quarter are situated too near to inhabited regions.

The wild camel will not approach the spot where a hunter has once encamped until after a very long interval of time has elapsed. As a rule, wild camels only remain two or three days at a time at each grazing-ground, and then move on to another. They only visit the springs to drink; they never stop there to graze, no matter how tempting the pasture. My informant persisted that the wild camel's instinct tells him it is at the springs he runs the greatest risk of being molested by man. As soon as it gets dark he lies down beside a tamarisk, where the ground is soft, and does not move again until the sun rises. He eats all sorts of green stuff, though his favourite provender is clumps of withered grass, which, having been separated from its roots, has been blown together by the wind. Hence he is fond of frequenting localities where the ground and the winds favour the accumulation of this tussock hay. He also displays a marvellous sureness of instinct in finding his grazing-grounds, travelling in a straight line from the one to the other, even when they are several days' distance apart, and even though there happen to be no prominent features in the landscape to guide him.

In the breeding season, that is to say, the months of December, January, and February, the males fight fiercely whenever they encounter one another, equally whether on their grazing-grounds, at the springs, or in the desert. The animal which is vanquished is often driven away by himself, while the victor will be followed by as many as eight she-camels. If two fairly well-matched males come into conflict, they do not stop fighting until one or both of them is put *hors-de-combat*. They mangle one another terribly with their teeth, and very often tear large pieces of flesh out of one another; in fact you seldom find a full-grown he-camel which is not disfigured by some nasty scar or other.

The wild camel is frequently seen quite solitary by himself, often also in pairs; but the general rule is for a troop of four to six individuals to associate together. Troops of 12 to 15 are extremely rare. The leader of a troop is always a big he-camel. The period of gestation in the case of the tame camel is one year; in the case of the wild camel it is reputed to be fourteen months. It is estimated that a tame she-camel can bear one young once every eighteen months, beginning with her third year and ceasing with her fifteenth. The young suckle forty days before eating grass, but even then still continue to suckle for more than a year. In fact the little creature can barely reach the ground with its muzzle until it is fully one and a half months old. These things are apparently true also of the wild camel.

The tame camel can be worked until it is twenty years old. The wild camel is said to live for fifty years; but this is more than doubtful, it is unlikely. Abdu Rehim, however, once found embedded in the rib muscles of an old he-camel a Mongol rifle bullet, which, from its shape, must have been at least forty or fifty years old, for it was something like that period of time since the Mongols had used bullets of that particular shape. According to his account the camels of the mountainous districts are more difficult to kill than the camels of the Takla-makan. Chernoff suggested that that is because the hunters in the mountainous districts use less effective charges of powder, and carry less perfect weapons. The consequence is the bullet does not penetrate sufficiently, and often stops without touching a vital organ, so that the animal escapes without suffering any real injury.

The wild camel is found everywhere between Yardang-bulak and the district of Khami; but he never goes west of the caravan-route from Ying-pen to Turfan. Our Camp no. VII. (13th March) may be regarded as his most westerly point in the bed of the Kurruk-daria. In the Kurruk-tagh he frequents principally the neighbourhood of Altimish-bulak, and to the east of it. He is, however, a restless creature, and leads a nomad existence over a wide range of country. A year subsequent to this I obtained further data for determining the range of his distribution.

Abdu Rehim had been a camel-hunter for six years, and during that period had shot fifteen camels, which shows that they are not an altogether easy game to bag. On one occasion his father tried to capture a young one, and rear it and tame it. But the moment the little thing was born its mother, having grown suspicious, caught it up between her chin and neck, and fled with it in such haste that it was impossible to overtake her.

Before I part with Abdu Rehim, I must say a word or two about his family relations. He was the son of Ahmed Pavan, who had dwelt forty years at Singher, and had had four sons born to him there, of whom three were married. That is as much as to say, all the inhabitants of the little village were members of Ahmed's family. The eldest son was the *karaulchi* or "station-keeper" in the village, and was appointed to the office by the amban of Dural. It was his duty to report anything that happened within his district in violation of the law, or indeed anything that was in any sense noteworthy. The father, Ahmed, was a native of Turfan, and owned some 200 sheep, which he placed under the care of a Mongol shepherd in the district of Asghan, the arrangement being that the lambs born every year were divided equally between the two, while Ahmed received as much of the wool as was required to weave three *kighiz* or thick felt rugs. And the Mongol shepherd himself owned large flocks of sheep.

Besides sheep, Ahmed possessed a troop of 27 camels, and trafficked in the animals, buying when they were cheap and selling, of course, when they were dear; also two horses and ten cows. At Singher he grew wheat, maize, melons, onions, and other vegetables, the soil being exceptionally fertile, so that he was able to count upon a return every year, whereas, in other districts, the people are some years obliged to leave the ground fallow He obtained his water for irrigation purposes from the spring-fed rivulet of Singherlik, which is about as big as the brook of Sughett-bulak. Ahmed and his family were passionately devoted to Singher, and would not exchange it for any other place in the world.

Abdu Rehim was a strong, handsome young fellow, cheerful of disposition, and very trustworthy; but what I valued most about him was his truthfulness, and the reliability of his information. When he was unable to answer a question I put to him he used to say he did not know. The usual practice of the Central Asian Mussulman in such cases is to invent some sort of an answer on the spur of the moment. Abdu Rehim managed his eight camels with admirable skill, attended to everything, helped to load up and unload like a slave, and found his way from spring to spring like a wild camel. He was as strong and agile as a tiger, and to see him swing himself up on the back of his riding camel with his heavy and clumsy-looking rifle slung over his shoulder was quite a treat. I generally summoned him every evening to my tent, and pumped him about his experiences. I tried to induce him to travel with me, but he was too anxious to get back to his home amongst the mountains.

When we started on the 18th March we took with us seven goatskins and two sacks all filled with ice, as well as two sacks stuffed with kamish, which we proposed to dole out to our camels when we came to the next desolate camping-ground. However, for the first night we decided to halt at Yakka Yardang-bulak, which was close at hand, so as to get what advantage we could from its kamish grazing.

All at once the advance guard halted, and Abdu Rehim slid down off his camel, and began to creep along the ground, with his rifle on his back. I stole up to him, and then through my field-glass saw a troop of wild camels, consisting of a big black *bughra* (male) and five other individuals of a lighter colour. The black one had just got up, and was stretching his head in every direction, sniffing the wind with keen suspicion. Three of the others lay and chewed their cud, while the other two were grazing. I and the hunters—for Chernoff and Khodai Kullu had also joined in the stalk—concealed ourselves in a favourable place about half a mile distant, whence we were able to follow every movement of the troop without being seen ourselves. Meanwhile Abdu Rehim stole along the yar terraces, whither the trail also led Chernoff. But the wind blew from us towards the camels, and the big he-camel plainly suspected something was wrong. He moved to where the she-camels were lying, stopped, sniffed and sniffed, keeping his head turned all the time towards us, and then went on a little further. Meanwhile the other camels, two full-grown females and three colts of a year old, noticed nothing amiss.

A shot echoed ; but it failed to reach its mark. The distance was too great. The bughra, however, alarmed by the report, set off in rapid flight. For one instant the she-camels hesitated, then they leapt up like a shot, and went off at full gallop, skimming up the dust behind them. The big male ran by himself, the others all in a cluster about a hundred paces to his right. I followed them with my field-glass, and saw how within a very few minutes they dwindled to tiny black dots, and after that the rising dust alone revealed which way they had fled. They travelled at a great rate and without once stopping, for they had got scent of the caravan, and fully realised the nature of their danger. At first they directed their flight towards the south-west, but gradually veered round in a semicircle to the south and the south-east. Abdu Rehim thought they would in all probability make eventually for Altimish-bulak.

At Yakka-Yardang-bulak the ground was trampled in every direction by wild camels, the little kamish oasis being evidently one of their chief feeding-grounds and stopping-stations in that part of the desert.

Next morning we had travelled but a short distance when our sportsmen stopped again and pointed towards the south. There we perceived a solitary camel meditating amongst the dead tamarisks. Three rifles were at once levelled at him; three shots echoed. But the distance was too great, and the beast trotted leisurely off towards the north-east. That is to say, he ran across our line of march, and thus came over on our left hand, after which he stopped short, and observed the disturbers of his peace. Chernoff had another shot at him, and wounded him, though only slightly, and although he pursued him on horseback, the camel managed to escape into the mountains. He was clearly one of those solitary males which had been vanquished by some stronger rival.

All this while we had the lower terrace of the Kurruk-tagh on our left hand; it was seamed by innumerable rivulets and ravines, all made by rain-water. On the right was the winding Kurruk-daria, with its dead forest and its yar terraces, its bed being 246 feet broad and 12 to 16 feet deep. From this point onwards the ground was littered with enormous quantities of snail shells (*Limnæa*); you could gather them up in basketsful; which goes to show that the river was formerly accompanied by marginal lakes. The matter admitted of no doubt whatever, for freshwater molluscs do not frequent swift running water, only tranquil lakes and lagoons where there is an abundance of vegetation.

Shortly after this we crossed the river-bed, and directed our steps towards the south-east, so as to get some idea of what the desert was like in that direction. The ground at the foot of the mountains was very granulated and difficult to travel on. The yardangs were, it is true, lower, and the watercourses not more than a foot or so deep; still there were so many of them, that the camels did nothing but stumble.

On the 20th of March we were favoured with exceptionally bright, fine weather. The continuous ridge of the Kurruk-tagh was plainly visible; and it steadily increased in height as we advanced east. As far as we were able to see, the country in that direction still continued to present the same characteristics; but in consequence of the mirage the lower flanks of the mountains appeared to be lifted a little above their true level.

We often lost sight of the old river-bed for hours together; then we would strike it at some bend or other. In all probability the existing relief is the result of several hydrographical epochs. The extraordinary sharp-cut terrace which runs along the foot of the lowest sai is in reality the shore of what was some time or other a large lake, which subsequently gradually contracted in area. The snail shells that remain indicate the extent to which the country was formerly under water. In proportion as the western shore of the lake travelled back towards the east, so did the river-mouth advance with it, flowing as it went through smaller lakes and basins, exactly as the Lower Tarim does at the present time; as we shall indeed see lower down. This explains why the old river-bed was distinctly traceable for short distances only.

As we advanced, the desert became more and more barren. We frequently crossed wild camels' tracks going towards the south. It is not at all unlikely that wild camels do visit the Avullu-köll, although the Lop-men seldom visit it themselves. Presently we were once more travelling along a portion of the river-bed, which was remarkably distinct. Here it was 308 feet broad, 21¼ feet deep, and still had dead forest on its banks. In other words, it was a "fossil" river. If you were to cut off a section of the Tarim and let its water flow away, and its forest wither and dry up, you would have precisely the same effect as in the river we were now following beside the Kurruk-tagh.

The aspect of the country changed but little. The mountains resembled a chain of low hills, with a scolloped crest. Dead forest grew less frequent, and trees that still stood upright rarer than ever. On our right was a "sea" of yardangs, strewn with myriads of snail shells. Ördek discovered an earthenware jar, a fragment of a large dish with glazed arabesque ornamentation, and a piece of a huge copper pot, with its edge turned horizon-

Cakes of Ice at the Oasis of Altimish-bulak.

tally downwards. The dish was of Chinese make. It was clear there had once been a dwelling or a settlement here ; at any rate the vicinity had plainly been inhabited at some time or other.

At length the bed of the Kurruk-daria came finally to an end, and we entered upon a tract of country which was formerly covered by the ancient lake of Lop-nor. The forest, of course, came to an end as well, but the snail shells were still more numerous than heretofore. The yardangs consisted now of ridges, five or six feet broad, and about three feet high, built up of tolerably firm, yellow clay, disposed horizontally, and following one another to infinity in a north-east and south-west direction ; and between them were an equal number of parallel trenches or hollows, of the same depth and the same breadth. The geographical disposition of this peculiar formation suggested that it was exclusively caused by the prevailing north-east wind, which uses the drift-sand as a file against the easily sculptured clay ; and the suggestion was confirmed by the surfaces of these long "benches" all showing unmistakable evidences of having been scoured or polished by the wind. There were of course no accumulations of drift-sand, owing to the quite recent date at which the lake disappeared. The exaggeration in Marco Polo's statement, that a man would require a year to cross the desert of Lop, is not so very great after all, when you bear in mind that in his day the lakes of Kara-buran and Kara-koshun did not exist, and consequently one unbroken desert might very well stretch all the way from Takla-makan to Manchuria.

At Camp no. XII. there were dead tograks still standing on their own roots—a little grove which had formerly existed on the northern shore of Lop-nor.

Not far from this camp we discovered some thick potsherds of a bluish grey colour, which had belonged to a large earthenware vessel with small ears. This made the third time we came across evidences of human beings amongst these dried-up waterways. The ground was covered in places with deposits of salt, pointing to the lake having become gradually saline as its water left it. Were it not for the wind planing off the surface, these deposits would no doubt be more numerous than they actually are.

Our next object was to discover Altimish-bulak, or the "Sixty Springs." Accordingly we directed our course towards the north-north-east, and in so doing ascended the extreme outlying spurs of the Kurruk-tagh, and of course left behind us the absolutely level, but locally irregular, surface of the desert. Towards evening a strong gale sprang up from the north, and the sky became thickly overcast, so that it grew dark early, before we were able to strike the springs. Hence after going 23½ miles, we came to a halt in a perfectly barren clay desert. This made the fifth day on which we had failed to reach water, and the little we had left in the goat-skins was polluted. As our supply of meat was also exhausted, we all got very short commons that evening. Next morning the wind was still blowing at the rate of 24½ miles an hour. When I stepped outside of my tent at daybreak, it was a very dreary scene my eyes rested upon—a low ridge stretching towards the north-east; south-east the contour falling away towards the "ocean of sand," with insignificant crests and long chains of low hills in the far, far distance; the earth everywhere covered with gravel, not a plant to be seen; everything weather-worn, cheerless, desolate! So insignificant were the distant chains of hills, that the Chinese have not even entered them upon their maps; the only thing they have depicted is the main range a long, long way to the north.

This day we were guided by Melik Ahun, Abdu Rehim's brother. And well did he pilot us, for immediately after passing an eminence, we became aware of an open expanse ahead, with a yellow patch in the middle of it. It was the splendid oasis of Altimish-bulak, and oh, how welcome a sight it was!

Abdu Rehim and his brother, their eyesight quickened by their open-air hunter's life, at once perceived a troop of wild camels grazing on the eastern edge of the oasis—but I, even with my field-glass to help me, was scarce able to distinguish the creatures. Directing that the caravan should make a detour and so keep behind a low ridge, the experienced camel-hunter, accompanied by Chernoff, hurried on towards the reed-beds of the oasis. I, too, followed them, intending to watch the issue of the stalk. Crossing the little rivulet, which drained the Sixty Springs, and which, as our guide had quite correctly foretold a month before, was covered with big cakes of splendid ice, we crept in amongst the reeds and tamarisks. The borders of the little oasis terminated quite abruptly, and we crossed over the greater part of it before Abdu Rehim stopped behind a couple of tamarisk mounds.

The troop we were stalking consisted, like the last one, of a big dark-coloured bughra and five other camels of a lighter skin.

A Wild Camel Shot at Altimish-bulak.

Perhaps they were the same we had seen at Yakka-Yardang-bulak. The old male and one of the others were busy grazing; the rest lay with their heads turned in our direction, that is, away from the wind. We were now within 300 paces of them, and the wind blew straight from them towards us, so that neither by scent nor hearing were they able to get any warning of our approach. We, of course, used the utmost precautions not to be seen. I could not help feeling how cowardly it was to creep thus stealthily upon these noble beasts, and attack them from an ambush.

I was most interested to observe as much as possible of their movements and habits in the state of nature; but I could not forbid the men to shoot them, for it would have caused discontent, and given dire offence in the caravan, and ultimately might have led to unpleasant consequences. Besides, camel-hunting was Abdu Rehim's calling. Mussulmans possess not an atom of sympathy for the feelings of the animal creation, and if I had forbidden the men to shoot the camels, they would have set it down as an act of malice against themselves. An occasion like this was, too, a solemn moment for a hunter, as I could easily see from the bearing of my men. Their eyes glowed with excitement, and they neither heard nor saw anything except the game they were stalking. But I always drew a sigh of relief when they missed. I confess my sympathies were with the camels, not with the hunters.

Bidding us wait where we were, Abdu Rehim made a long detour with the object of getting past a gap in the reeds without being seen. And then he disappeared in the bushes as silently as a panther; we neither saw nor heard which way he went. Meanwhile I made the best of the opportunity to study the camels' movements. The two which were grazing kept their heads to the ground, but lifted them occasionally when their mouths were full, and masticated slowly and with great power of jaw, so that the dry kamish rustled between their teeth, while their glances scanned the horizon. They did not, however, betray the least sign of uneasiness, and evidently never suspected what was about to happen.

Crack! went Abdu Rehim's rifle, and five of the camels came at a slow trot towards the bushes in which we were hiding. Then, thinking danger might lurk there, they suddenly wheeled about and went off up the mountains at a gallop.

It was the younger of the two camels that were grazing which fell. He had got a ball in the abdomen; a second struck him in the neck when he tried to rise and go after his companions.

When we came up to him, he was resting on all four knees, and chewing the reeds he still had in his mouth. He raised himself upon his hind legs, but his fore legs refused to support him, and he fell over on his side. His expression was that of calmness and resignation, without any trace of surprise or fear, and the only attempt he made to bite was when we stroked

Head of the Wild Camel Shot at Altimish-bulak.

his nose. He bore a remarkable likeness to the tame camels from Singher, and had just begun to lose his hair. After I had photographed him from various positions, Abdu Rehim, with one powerful sweep of his knife, cut his throat, the blood gushing out in a torrent. A few convulsions, and this son of the desert, who only a few minutes ago was grazing so peacefully and securely amongst the reed-beds round the spring, passed to the pasture-grounds of eternity. The other wild camels were long ago out of sight. Abdu Rehim was quite delighted at the prospect of having such a pleasant surprise to give to his old father as a large supply of camel-meat.

A Tame Camel, which Participated in my Journeys of 1896 and died in Tibet 1901.

The dead camel was a male, four years old. The appearance of his front teeth furnished, as they do in the case of the tame camel, a pretty safe indication of age. His presence in a troop which was led by a bughra was explained by the fact of his having an ugly bite in the neck and by his still tender age. Two or three months before he met his death he had had an encounter with a hunter, for we found a bullet under his anterior hump, and a clot of black coagulated blood hanging in his hair showed where it had penetrated.

We kept our Singher camels tethered at night, and had them watched during the day, otherwise they would have gone off and made their way back to Singher. For their sense of locality is very highly developed, and they are capable of finding their way home from a totally unknown district fully a month's journey away. Abdu Rehim declared it was his camels which led us straight towards the spring of Altimish-bulak the dark night we encamped in the stony desert, and had I not commanded a halt, they would have gone on until they actually reached the spring.

The number of wild camels along the foot of the Kurruk-tagh varies a good deal in different years, according to whether they are most pressed by the hunters there or in the district of Lukchin. The year of our visit they were plentiful in the Kurruk-tagh region.

CHAPTER XXIII.

THE ANCIENT LAKE OF LOP-NOR.

We pitched our tents among the tamarisks and reeds close to the spring. After our long tramp through the desert the place wore a most inviting and attractive aspect, and it was quite a pleasure to see how the camels and horses revelled in the luxuriant pasture, and kept returning again and again to nibble at the ice-cakes. But as we had another desert tramp before us we thought it well to let them have a few days here to pick up their strength. Unfortunately we ourselves were short of provisions. It is true we had a superabundance of rice and bread, but bread and rice alone, without anything else, get decidedly monotonous. The Mussulmans enjoyed the camel-flesh, but neither I nor Chernoff could prevail upon ourselves to eat it. Two or three flocks of wild-duck passed overhead, but did not settle at our spring.

The men from Singher were getting very anxious to set out for home, but I succeeded in making the following arrangement with them. Melik and his younger brother were to remain at Altimish-bulak with four of the camels, whilst Abdu Rehim and the other four camels accompanied me two days' journey to the south, to help our camels with their loads and carry sacks of ice. Further I could not induce him to go ; he had a horror of the desert, although he had never penetrated into it.

We remained at this oasis, the most beautiful I have ever visited, from the 23rd to the 27th March. Indeed, after our forced march from Yardang-bulak rest was imperative. Although the atmosphere was greatly disturbed, it occasioned me but little inconvenience. My tent was so hemmed in by a dense belt of kamish and tamarisks, that the wind might howl and whine as it liked outside, I hardly knew anything of it in my snug little shelter.

I spent my holiday in taking a series of astronomical observations and in reading. The air was beginning to have a touch of spring in it. On the 25th of March the thermometer registered 17°.2 C. or 63°.0 Fahr. at noon, although during the preceding night it had been as low as – 7°.1 C. or 19°.2 Fahr. Abdu Rehim gave me a good deal of geographical information about the region we were in, including the names of a great number of springs and their respective situations. A year later I had occasion to test the accuracy of his information, and found it quite reliable. To the east of Altimish-bulak he said he only knew of three springs, none of them named, and all within two short days' journey; he had discovered them whilst pursuing a wounded camel. Subsequently I found them all three, and, as it turned out, just at a critical time. He also described to me all the old routes he was acquainted with in the Kurruk-tagh, and told me they were marked by cairns of stones which he called *ova*, obviously the Mongol word *obo*. One of these ancient routes led to the south-south-west through Singher, and was probably identical with the route which the Chinese tax-collectors used to follow when they visited the Lop-nor country.

After completing our preparations, which included the collecting of a large supply of ice, packed in four *tagars* (bags) made of kamish, we started again on the morning of the 27th. It was my intention to cross the desert of Lop from north to south, so as to obtain a clear idea of the extent of the ancient lake, as well as incontrovertible proof of the existence of the lake basin. Our recent march along the bed of the Kurruk-daria, and the fact that it did eventually issue into a lake, had proved not only the accuracy of the Chinese maps, but also the correctness of Von Richthofen's and my own views with regard to this disputed question. It only remained to get a sketch of the contour-lines of the region which the lake formerly covered.

The desert journey which lay immediately before us was not likely to be attended with any danger. The distance to Kara-koshun, where we should find game, and, further to the west, Lop fishermen, could be traversed in a week, so that even though the supply of water we were taking with us should prove insufficient, we were not likely to perish from thirst. We crammed the *tagars* with clear ice, and although we afforded them the best protection we could against the sun, we lost fully a couple of bucketsful during the first day or two of the march.

Soon after starting we saw a flock of wild-duck settle in a little rivulet which came out of a glen on our left. Chernoff stole upon them with his double-barrelled gun, and managed to bag five. They were fat and tender, and made a most welcome addition to our scantily-furnished larder. The birds came from Kara-koshun, because, as Ördek and Abdu Rehim explained, that lake was so densely thronged with them, the late-comers were obliged to turn back and go to Bagrash-köll, which they did *viâ* Altimish-bulak and Singher.

We did 18½ miles that day, and emerged from the mountains into the uniform desert, where the clay formations were deposited at three different levels. The lowest level was the bottom of the watercourse we were following. The middle level, which covered half the entire area of the desert, was the ordinary yardang, some 6 to 8 feet higher. And the third level consisted of small plateaus, towers, and pyramids of red clay, reaching 50 to 60 feet above the ground; these were most numerous on the east side of the route we were pursuing. These peculiar features were arranged in long rows, and bore such a remarkably close resemblance to the ruins of fortified walls, that two or three times it was only an examination at close quarters which convinced us they really were not such. It is worth recording that the trenches which lay between the flat yardang ridges ran exactly parallel to the bayirs in the Desert of Cherchen. In both cases alike the depressions owed their existence to the action of the prevailing winds.

The Kurruk-tagh had no definite continuation towards the east. At the most there was merely an isolated mountain group. Thus I already saw reason to doubt the existence of the large range which is shown on our maps as running in that direction through the heart of Asia, and my investigations a year later established the fact that it really is an insignificant chain.

The desert was absolutely barren; there was not even so much as a decayed tree. Occasionally we came across snail shells, but they were nothing like so plentiful as they were further west.

On the 28th we travelled 13½ miles, going to the south-west. During the course of the day the lake-basin assumed a different aspect. The snail shells became more numerous, and amongst them were thin patches of sand not exceeding a foot in thickness, and dead forest again made its appearance at pretty frequent intervals. There were now only two levels in the clay deposits, indicating different periods and different water-levels of the former lake. As the wind eats its way into the clay, the snail shells drop lower and lower, until the ground becomes in places quite white with them. We picked up a small iron cup, and fragments of clay pottery were so common that we ceased to pay any heed to them. A belt of dead forest, which stretched in two directions, 60° east of south and 60° west of south, marked an important piece of the ancient shore-line of Lop-nor, showing as it did that the lake long remained stationary there.

Thus on we went between the ridges of clay, with the water drip—dripping in an alarming manner from our *tagars* of ice. About three o'clock in the afternoon Ördek and Chernoff, who were leading the way on foot, seeking out the easiest path to

Ruins of a House in the Desert.

travel by, suddenly stopped and shouted back that they had come to the ruins of two or three houses. The watercourse we were following had brought us straight to this remarkable discovery. Had we been travelling two or three hundred yards either to the east or to the west we should never have seen them. Indeed, so close was the resemblance which they bore to the ordinary dead forest that it was only a near inspection which revealed what they actually were, namely, human dwellings on the northern shore of Lop-nor.

We of course stopped and encamped at once, and I began a hurried survey of the locality. There had originally been three houses, but their immense beams and posts, their roof and boarden walls, had all fallen in ; the timber was greatly decayed through time and the effects of the desert storms, and was moreover partly buried in sand. The only portion of the structures which still remained in position were the beams of the basement, and from these I was easily able to draw up a plan of the houses and measure their dimensions.

There was one circumstance which pointed to their being of some antiquity, namely, the fact that they stood upon mounds or ridges of clay, 8¼ feet high, which had precisely the same outline and area as the plan of the house. Originally the houses were no doubt built upon the level ground, but after the surface dried it had been scooped out and blown away by the wind, leaving behind only those portions on which the house actually stood. Round about these buildings were a great number of earthenware vessels, and small cups, such as are wont to be placed in front of the images of Buddha and in other parts of the Buddhist temples. We also picked up some iron axes, as well as two or three Chinese coins.

Upon excavating the easternmost of the three houses, we brought to light some remarkable wood-carvings which had been used to decorate the walls. There were the picture of a soldier, with a helmet on his head and a trident in his hand, and another man with a chaplet. The other designs consisted of pattern devices and scroll-work, lattice-work, and lotus-flowers, all cut with artistic sense, but sadly injured by time. I selected specimens of the different patterns to take with me.

There was also another tora or clay tower standing 58° east of south from where we were. That also I visited in company with Chernoff and Abdu Rehim, to see if by any chance there were any discoveries to be made there. The mound was cupola-shaped, and part of it had fallen down ; it had probably served as a roadway sign-post or as a signal-mound. This tora, together with three others like it, standing at distances of three to four miles apart, made a figure disposed in the same way as the four principal stars are in the constellation of the Lion. But we failed to find any further remains of ancient houses. It was already dark when we wended our way back to our big camp-fire, and by the time we at length reached it we were thoroughly tired out by our three hours' tramp up and down the numberless yardangs which stretched at right angles across our path.

But, at all events, we had by a lucky chance hit upon the continuation of the Kömur-salldi-yoll, or ancient road from

Korla to Sa-chow and Peking, along the northern shore of Lop-nor.

At this point Abdu Rehim was to leave us. His pay amounted to 1½ yambas (£12), a big sum, but nothing like too big considering his excellent services and the valuable information he had given me. Along with him I sent Khodai Kullu to carry the wood-carvings we had discovered, ordering him by some means or other to take them from Singher to Tura-sallgan-uy —a task which he executed to my perfect satisfaction. On the following morning, then, Abdu Rehim and his companion set off to return to the north. They hoped to make Altimish-

"They Stood upon Mounds of Clay."

bulak in a single day, for we were unable to spare them one drop of the water we carried with us. Indeed, our supply was run so low that I dared not stay more than one day at this place, interesting though it was. By this departure the caravan was greatly reduced in numbers, for I had now left with me only Chernoff, Faisullah, and Ördek, with four camels, one horse, and two dogs.

It was very late when we started, for I went back to the ruins for a further examination, and this occupied a good half day. Amongst other things I took a couple of photographs, measured various dimensions with the tape, and made sketches of several details. The smallest building, to judge from the cups for offerings, as well as from its decorations, was a temple; its walls measured 18¼ feet by 21½ feet.

The ground-plan of the larger house measured 172 feet by 59 feet, and its longer wall lay along a line that stretched 22° west of south and 22° east of north. Its main uprights projected above the mound, and the latter was everywhere greatly eaten away by the wind. The building had been divided into several rooms of different sizes; one of the door-frames still remained *in situ*. Those parts of the timber which were buried underneath the sand were particularly well preserved, whereas the parts which were exposed to the atmosphere were greatly decayed, soft, and often frayed at the extremities. Round the square mortises of the upper beams into which the tenons of the corner uprights were fitted, we could still see in some cases the marks of the graphite pencil with which the outline of the mortise had formerly been marked. Several of these corner-posts were beautifully ornamented and turned in such a way as to resemble a number of globes and disks piled one upon the other.

One of the outer compartments had probably served as a sheep-fold, for its floor was covered with a layer of sheep-dung a foot thick. It is true the Chinese use sheep-dung as fuel, yet in a region so amply furnished with wood as the northern shore of Lop-nor, economy to this extent would surely be superfluous. The whole of the roof lay on the west side of the house, where it had been swept by the last east wind it was unable to withstand. The whole of the timber was poplar wood from the immediate neighbourhood. The principal beams measured 13 inches by 8¼ inches. Judging from the contours of the ground, these two buildings, together with a third which was almost entirely destroyed, had once stood on a peninsula that jutted out into a lake, or on an isthmus between two lakes. Whence we may perhaps infer that the outline of the former Lop-nor was quite as irregular and capricious as that of the present Kara-koshun.

What purpose did these houses serve, and who were the people who built them and dwelt in them? My first impression was that they had been an *örtäng*, or larger station, on the route to Dung-khan (or Sa-chow). These questions I will not, however, discuss here, but will leave them, as well as a fuller discussion of the problem they raise, to a later chapter; and the reason for this will appear presently.

Whilst I and Chernoff were measuring the houses, the other two men, from an early hour in the morning, explored the vicinity, though without discovering anything of importance. We therefore loaded up our camels and continued our journey towards the south-west. Indeed, we had no choice but to follow in that direction, because the yardangs, as well as the trenches which had been furrowed out by the wind, all ran that way. After a while the sills or "isthmuses" at the ends became lower, and rudimentary dunes made their appearance. Decayed forest was very common, though the trees occurred in clumps or grooves, without doubt marking the islands of the ancient lake. What a contrast to Kara-koshun, where there does not exist a single poplar! Milliards of snail shells littered the ground, and the hard, sharp stubble of the kamish and rushes was not at all pleasant to the camels' soft-padded feet. Some day when the

Chernoff and Abdu Rehim beside a Tora in the Desert.

Kara-koshun is drained dry it will in its turn show a similar kamish stubble.

The sand soon came to an end again, but it was nothing more than an outlying strip. Here, where water was formerly so abundant and vegetation so luxuriant, everything was now dead, desolate, and arid. After a march of 12½ miles we halted in a slight depression, where two or three tamarisks still struggled for existence, so that we hoped, consequently, to find water by digging for it. But when the men were ready to begin to dig their well, they discovered that they had left the spade at the ruins, and Ördek, who was responsible for having left it behind, at once proposed to go back and fetch it.

I hesitated to let him set out on such a perilous expedition alone, at a season of the year when there was the greatest risk of being overtaken by a sand-storm; but as we had only a short supply of water, and could not get any more without the spade, I reluctantly allowed the man to go, bidding him stick closely to our trail. Before he set out, I made him take a couple of hours' sleep, and instructed him that, if he failed to find us when he got back, he was to keep on due south, and he would sooner or later strike the shore of the Kara-koshun. We could not afford to wait for him; but with the view of helping him to travel faster I let him take the horse. After a thorough good supper of rice and bread he started, about midnight, on his lonely ride through the desert.

What I had feared happened about two hours after he left, for at two o'clock I was awakened by a gale blowing from the north-east; and it continued all the following day, whirling up the sand before it, and making the air thick with dust. It was impossible to see very far, and the worst was, our trail would very soon be obliterated. However, I trusted that, when the storm broke out, Ördek would have the good sense to turn back and leave the spade to its fate.

For us, however, who were travelling towards the south-west, the storm proved very welcome: blowing at our backs, it helped us on, as well as moderated the intense heat of the sun. The desert now became more desolate than ever, the decayed forest had almost entirely disappeared, and the sands were continuous except for an occasional small bayir; but the sand-dunes were as yet only 16 feet high, though we observed that they increased in height towards the west and south-west, the directions in which the drift-sand was carried by the wind. The dead kamish we passed was also bent in the same direction, as though it had been flattened down by a gigantic brush.

We pitched Camp no. XVIII. on a spot where we chanced to find two or three pieces of timber. Whilst we were still busy with our preparations for the night, we were overtaken by Ördek, who came walking, leading his horse, and carrying his spade. Both man and horse were utterly exhausted by their 36 miles' journey over difficult ground. After resting for about an hour Ördek came to me bringing news of the very utmost importance.

In the storm he lost our trail and got astray, but finally came to a tora, or landmark tower, in the vicinity of which he discovered several houses, richly decorated with carved panels. He also collected earthenware cups, iron bars, axes, pieces of metal, money, and several other things, some of which he had

Chernoff amongst the Ruins.

A Door-post still Standing *in situ.*

brought with him to show me. He also appropriated two of the carved panels, the best he could lay his hands upon, and then went in search of the place where he had previously discovered the three ruined houses, and at length found them. But he could not induce the horse to carry the panels, the animal stubbornly refusing to let him put them on its back; so he was forced to carry them himself. His shoulder was actually bleeding from the pressure of the rope by which he carried them. Upon reaching Camp no. XVII. he again tried to fasten them on the horse; but the creature broke from him and galloped off into the desert. After a great deal of trouble he managed to catch him again; but he was then so tired that he left the panels where they were, and followed after us on horseback. The camels' trail was still plain to see on the clay, although quite obliterated on the sand.

This report made one thing instantly clear to me—namely, that I must recast my plans for the following year. Meanwhile, I ordered the unfortunate Ördek to go back next morning and fetch the panels; which he did before we started. The panels were exceptionally well preserved, and had on them flowers and garlands carved in relief. I was strongly tempted to turn back at once, notwithstanding that it would have been the height of folly, for our supply of water would only last two or three days longer, and the hottest part of the year was rapidly approaching. No, I must alter my plans entirely. These ruins must be visited at all costs. That summer was, however, to be spent in Tibet; consequently I should have to return to the Lop country next winter. But there was one very important question: Should we be able to find the place again in such a terribly uniform region as this flat desert, in which there was not an object that could serve as a landmark? I did not doubt it, for I had the most implicit confidence in my map. Ördek declared that if only I would pilot him to Altimish-bulak, he was positive he should be able to find again the ruins he had discovered. How I blessed that spade, and, above all, Ördek for forgetting it!

The Desert of Lop is even more desolate than the Desert of Cherchen, for whereas we did find both grazing and water in certain parts of the latter, it would have been altogether useless to dig for water in the former. We still kept observing snail shells and old earthenware potsherds scoured by the wind. On the night of the 31st March we encamped beside a dead tamarisk, where the dunes were about 20 feet high, although latterly the sand had only occurred in belts. The camels had drunk no water for five days, and consequently were tired and listless. But we were still 35 or 40 miles from Kara-koshun, and should have to push on faster.

When we started next morning, I led the way as usual, and steered due south. In every direction barren dunes, the same dreary waste of desert which I had seen so many times before! However, a piece of a bird's egg indicated that we were approaching regions somewhat less God-forsaken. Having climbed to the summit of a high dune, I flung myself down to rest a bit, for I was tired, and scanned the horizon with my field-glass. Nothing but sand—ridges of sand! Yet, stay, what was that? Away to the south-east—wide sheets of water, flowing in amongst the dunes and yardangs! Water in the middle of the desert? I dare not trust my eyes—it must be a mirage!

The Scene of Ördek's Discovery—Photographed a Year Later.

However, I at once jumped to my feet and hurried on as fast as I could. No, it was no mirage, but verily and truly a lake, meandering into and around creeks, bays, inlets, islets, sounds, isthmuses in the most fantastic way possible—it was, in fact, such a labyrinth of waterways as could only be formed on perfectly level ground amongst a multitude of sand-dunes and wind-sculptured terraces. Except for a few young tamarisk sprouts, which had taken root in the soft, marshy ground, and a score or so of kamish stalks, the region was every bit as destitute of vegetation as the country we had just travelled through. It seemed as though it had only quite recently been overflowed. The contours of the lake were in great part determined by the yar terraces. In one or two places the dunes were broken down and had been carried away by the water.

I continued south-westwards along the deeply-indented shore. The lake soon contracted, narrowing greatly, but very shortly afterwards it widened out again. The water had a slight saline flavour; nevertheless, all our animals drank it and enjoyed it. After a while the shore-line wheeled away to the north, and we were constrained to follow it, for we failed to discover any ford thereabouts, and without something of the kind the camels would have stuck fast in the mud. The lake sent out several long "fingers" towards the north-east, each of which forced us to make a detour. On our right we sometimes had small self-contained lagoons and pools. The ground was moist, and "wobbled" unpleasantly under the feet of the timid camels. In fact, it was like walking on a sheet of indiarubber spread out over water, for the mud "billowed," as it were, in front of us as we walked.

The country was absolutely sterile. The lake appeared to consist, as it no doubt really did consist, of a great number of parallel bayirs and yardangs—valleys between the sand-dunes, and furrows ploughed up by the wind—all stretching from north-east to south-west. In many places the yardang ridges were easily perceptible under the water.

This lake could hardly mark the beginning of the Kara-koshun, otherwise it would have possessed a superabundance of reeds. Where, then, did it come from? The slightness of its salinity proved that it was tolerably new. Had it been long in that locality the kamish seeds would have grown up, for they follow the water with incredible rapidity. I could only surmise that it came from the new branch of the Shirgeh-chappgan, which Togdasin Beg had told me about.

But, interesting though this new discovery was as a contribution towards the solution of the complicated Lop-nor problem, it was of little profit to us in the meantime. What we wanted most especially just then was fresh grazing for our animals and meat for ourselves, for the only supplies we had left were rice and tea, meagre provisions to satisfy thirst and hunger upon. Instead of advancing well to the south, we had been stopped by this unexpected lake—a proper trick for the First of April!

As the water stretched away for ever so far towards the west, I resolved to wait and see whether we could not find a ford. It was evident we were confronted by a newly-formed branch of the

Tarim, which we must somehow get across. It is true there was no current perceptible; but there was a newly-made "beach-line," showing that the surface of the water had dropped about $3\frac{1}{4}$ feet in consequence of the subsidence of the Tarim in the winter.

Some of Ordek's Discoveries—A Meter-length (3.281 feet) is Shown on the Right by Way of Scale.

The large dunes which encircled the lake on every side, and sometimes even formed islets in it, were a proof that they were already there when the water first overflowed the district. Had it not been so, the dunes would have been arranged in a very different way, that is to say, they would have been absent on the south and south-west of the lake, where now, as a matter of fact, they were highest.

On the 2nd of April Chernoff searched and searched until he at last did find a ford, with a firm sandy bottom and about 3 feet of water over it. The camels delighted in the water. Once across, we pushed in amongst the high sand-dunes, and the lake very soon disappeared behind us. At one place we crossed over a bayir, the floor of which was strewn with cylindrical incrustations of lime, which had been formed round the stalks of reeds, as also crystals of gypsum, which adhered to our naked feet, for we often marched barefoot. The sand increased in volume. I measured the crests of some of the highest dunes with the levelling mirror, and found them to be 25 to 35 feet high.

My Mussulmans were discontented; they believed the lake we had left behind us was the Kara-koshun. Indeed, I began to wonder myself whether it was not so. If it were, we were lost. The poor camels, toiling through the sand, kept looking wistfully behind them, as though they too were wondering why we had left such a comfortable spot. The heat was intolerable, and the sun shone straight in our faces. However, we were not in quite such a perilous position as we supposed. The country soon altered its appearance again, and for the better, in that the sand grew less, and we came to a belt of dead poplars and then beyond that to another of living tamarisks. In front of us was a hill about 16 feet high. I invited Faisullah to follow me to the top of it, and have a look at the Kara-koshun. And, sure enough, there it was, in the south-west, the south, the south-east, and the east—a succession of sheets of pure blue water, some large, some small, and separated from one another by belts of yellow kamish (reeds).

We pitched the tent on a promontory that jutted out into the first large expansion of the lake we came to, putting it close at the water's edge, the entrance being turned towards the north-east, and as soon as my bed was arranged, I lay on it, and through my glass watched the flocks of wild geese and ducks and swans which swam about and disported themselves on its surface. For a desert-farer it would be impossible to imagine any sight more beautiful! Unfortunately the birds kept too far from the shore; but from the way in which they dived it was clear that the lake was not very deep. Its water was perfectly fresh.

Here was my tent canvas flapping in a fresh breeze that blew off the lake. What a difference from the desert wind, with its choking clouds of dust! The lapping of the water against the shore was perfectly delightful as I lay and listened to it whilst summing up the results of the expedition. We had established the existence of an ancient Lop-nor lake-basin ; we had discovered an ancient inhabited place, and met a new lake wandering through the desert—all without losing a single man or a single animal.

But the contour which I had obtained by marching diagonally across the lake was not sufficient. Boiling-point thermometers and aneroids are not of much use in a region where differences of level were so slight as they were here. This strengthened me still further in a resolution I had formed, to make a detailed survey of the lake-basin as the only means of determining accurately the small difference of level which existed between Lop-nor and Kara-koshun. After my former journey in Central Asia, I had maintained that Lop-nor must be a migratory lake, basing my inference on the fact of the almost uniform level of the whole of that region.

CHAPTER XXIV.

BOATING ON THE KARA-KOSHUN LAKES.

On the 3rd of April it blew hard from the north-east, until the wind attained a velocity of over 22¼ miles an hour. The lake possessed for me an irresistible attraction. After all the choking sand and burning heat of the desert, I should like nothing better than to be tossed on its crisply curling waves, and sound its depth ; but unfortunately we had no boat. Still we had goatskins; and out of them and the frames to which they were fastened, we ought to be able to construct some sort of a craft, that would at all events carry us if we drifted across the lake before the wind. The lake extended from the north-east to the south-west, so that all we had to do was to find a suitable starting-point. Accordingly, I set off along the shore, with Chernoff and Ördek, taking the materials for our " boat " on the back of a horse.

Upon reaching a little cape that jutted out into the lake, we stopped, tied the frames fast with ropes to two poles, and then floated the airy raft, thus fashioned, on six goat-skins, which Ördek inflated by blowing into them. Then Chernoff and I embarked, each astride a pole. When Chernoff took his seat, the whole affair very nearly capsized, and when I joined him, the goat-skins became entirely immersed, carrying the frames down a little way with them, and there we sat, half-naked, with our feet dangling in the water. Our own backs were our sails, and away we went straight for the camp, which was visible to good eyes in the far distance, 60° west of south. The wild-duck, terrified by such a strange object approaching, rose in hundreds, screaming and quacking. When the big waves rolled in upon us, we were forced to hold on to each other, to preserve our balance and prevent ourselves from being capsized. Every wave which came broke right over us, so that we were quickly wet through. The voyage lasted two and a half hours. The water was now neither perfectly fresh nor perfectly clear, for the wind forced it out of the stagnant reaches and blew it westwards. On the shore where we were encamped, the level rose 6 inches. The greatest depth we sounded was 12 feet.

Over against our camp the lake was very shallow, so that Ördek waded out a long way before he was able to haul us in. We were both so stiff with cold that we were hardly able to walk up to the fire, and upon reaching it I was at once seized with a violent shaking-fit, so that my teeth "dithered" and rattled together. Flinging off my wet clothes, I dried myself by the fire, and then crept into bed. But even with the help of a big cup of boiling hot coffee, and a change of warm clothing, it was a full hour before I was able to shake off the attack.

The sky at sunset exhibited marvellous colouring, especially over the dunes to the north, which were lit up with a yellowish red gleam. Meanwhile, the wind increased to a full-fledged buran. The waves drove so fiercely against the shore, that the spray was blown right over my tent, and I judged it expedient to move it further back from the lake. As the storm thus continued to rage, we let the camels have another day's rest. Both north and south of Kara-koshun the horizon blazed in a fiery yellow; but towards the north-east it was a dark steel grey, indicating not only that the water stretched a long way in that direction, but also that it was accompanied by an absence of drift-sand.

When we started again, on the 5th of April, I hoped we had no great distance to go before striking the first inhabited village beside the Kum-chappgan. The wind still blew strong, and as the thermometer registered only 8°.1 C. or 46°.5 Fahr. it was decidedly cool. But in the afternoon, it turned warm again, and the sun shone directly in our faces. The lake-side was bordered with reeds, and on our right the sand-dunes approached quite close to it. The waters were alive with wild-duck, wild-geese, swans, divers, gulls, and terns, and crows were numerous. Hares, too, and hedgehogs were not uncommon. The shore was literally net-worked with the tracks of foxes, deer, lynxes, and wild boar. About two months before, a couple of hunters had been out on the ice; their foot-prints were still quite plain to see in the moist clay.

Our route was intersected by a vast number of long narrow

arms from the lake, separated by belts of desert, and each of these compelled us to make a detour round it. Snail shells and dead kamish were present not only close along the shore, but also at a considerable distance away. Both alike belonged to a far distant past, and were older than the lake. Next we crossed a brook, which had a volume of 123½ cubic feet in the second and a maximum depth of 2 feet 8½ inches. It was steadily rising, a fact proved by the successive rivulets which broke off from it and poured themselves into the little depressions at the sides. At Camp no. XXII. we were for the first time annoyed by gnats.

The next day we continued our journey under the same conditions. I hurried on on foot, resolved not to stop until we met with human beings. Not that we were longing for company; but we wanted fish, we wanted poultry and eggs, and above all, we wanted a boat, that I might explore the actual extent of the lake. Towards evening I caught sight of a thick column of smoke rising from the middle of the immense marsh which stretched away to the south; and sent off Ördek to see if he could get hold of the men who made it.

He came back towards evening, bringing with him eight Lop fishermen, and a supply of urgently needed stores—wild-geese, two score eggs, a large quantity of fish, flour, rice, and bread.

On the 7th, the Lop-men guided us to Kum-chappgan. The wind again blew hard, at the rate of 31½ miles an hour. During the continuance of a storm such as that the variations of temperature are not very great, the minimum on this occasion being 12° C. or 53°.5 Fahr., at noon 14°.6 C. or 58°.3 Fahr. and at one p.m. 16°.6 C. or 61°.9 Fahr. We had no reason to complain of the heat, and the gnats were all blown away.

Upon reaching Kum-chappgan, we encamped in the bifurcation between that channel and the Tuzun-chappgan. The huts which we built in 1896 were still standing as we left them, and all the other surroundings of the spot were precisely the same. During the night, it rained heavily, the drops smiting the tent very audibly—a rare occurrence in this part of the world. The men who were lying out in the open were driven into the nearest *sattma* (reed hut).

The next morning there arrived two old acquaintances, namely, Numet Beg of Abdall and Tokta Ahun, son of that fine old fellow Kunchekkan Beg, who had died two years

View from the Northern Shore of Kara-koshun.

previously. Numet Beg proved himself a very useful man in a many ways. The first thing I set him to do was to take charge of the camels and horses, lead them to the pasture-grounds of Mian, watch them there, and finally return them in good condition when we were ready to start for Tibet. Besides that, I asked him to find us provisions and guides to take us back to Tura-sallgan-uy, a journey which I purposed to make by canoe.

A Chappgan or Reed-pass in Lake Kara-koshun.

We utilized the stay at Kum-chappgan by making two long boat excursions—the first to the same localities that I visited in 1896, the other through the Tuzun-chappgan, and along parts of the lake in the south which I had not hitherto visited. We set out in two canoes—Chernoff and I in a large one, with three men to paddle, and Faisullah in a smaller one, with the provisions and two boatmen. The reeds were wet after the rain, and gave us many a shower-bath, as we glided through them like eels.

During the four years since I last saw it, this alluvial region of water, reeds, and sand had totally altered its appearance; its features were no longer recognizable. Lakes which in 1896 were perfectly open and free from weeds were now completely overgrown with kamish, while new ones, with new names, had been formed alongside them. Names such as Kum-köll (Sand Lake) and Yanghi-köll (New Lake) fully explained themselves. The greatest depths we sounded during the trip were 16 and 17 feet, and these soundings, significantly enough, were made in a recently formed basin called Toyagun —a proof that deeper depressions may exist by the side of the Kara-koshun, while the older portions of the lake itself are gradually shallowing and becoming overgrown with reeds.

On the way back our boatmen caught with their naked hands a big, beautiful swan. We first observed it swimming in open water at the edge of the reeds; but when we approached it the bird dived. Then the boatmen just made their paddles spin, and we flew along to the spot where, judging from the dimples on the surface, the swan would in all probability reappear; and, sure enough, when it did emerge, we were so close to it that, in order to escape us, it was forced to plunge blindly in amongst the reeds. That was its doom, for amongst the reeds it was unable to spread out its wings to fly. After the swan darted the canoe. Overboard into the water jumped old Yaman Kullu, although it came up to his waist, and, seizing his victim with both hands, dragged it into the canoe. The swan was so terrified that it lay as if dead, with its neck limp and its head hanging down, but we killed it at once. Close beside us was a dead swan, entangled in the reeds. It had been wounded some few days before, and it was its mate which we had captured and delivered from its grief. The lake literally swarmed with wild-duck and wild-geese.

On the 10th of April I measured the volume of the Tarim at the point where it entered the marsh: it was 1,049 cubic feet in the second. At the same place and the same time of year in 1896 its volume was 1,784 cubic feet. This difference was, no doubt, due in part to the newly formed branch of the Shirgeh-chappgan, in part to a number of natural canals which had broken away from the main river above Kum-chappgan since my former visit.

The sand-dune to which Kum-chappgan owes its name was 33½ feet high. The maximum depth of the lake was 17 feet. This vertical altitude of 33½ plus 17 = 50½ feet may be regarded as the maximum for the whole of the lower Lop-nor basin.

On the 11th we started on our second canoe expedition to the southern parts of the Kara-koshun. These were essentially different from the northern parts; for instance, the maximum depth was 6¼ feet, but throughout the whole of the second half of the trip the depth was one foot and less. The bottom consisted of fine yellow mud, resting on black ooze or blue clay. A touch of the paddle made it boil up like ink. When the water grew too shallow to float the canoes, the men simply stepped out and dragged them after them with ropes; but even this method of progression soon proved impossible, and we were compelled to turn back. The black ooze was 4 inches deep, but underneath it was a hard though thin layer of salt. Immediately north of the desert-road which leads from Abdall to Sa-chow was an extensive but shallow sheet of water, called Sateh-köll. It contained few reeds, and no *algæ* on the bottom, and was frequented by neither bird nor fish. During the summer it dries up completely, and its bed becomes converted into a hard and cracked layer of clay. Another proof that the Kara-koshun is travelling back towards the north. The marks on the stalks of the reeds plainly showed that since the ice broke up, six weeks before our visit, the level had fallen nearly 10 inches.

The next day we rowed to Abdall, where the camels met us, and encamped on the left bank of the Tarim, which had there a volume of 3,295 cubic feet in the second. Thus the river had lost 2,246 cubic feet in the short distance between Kum-chappgan and Abdall. The delta of the Tarim was travelling back up stream, like the numerous lakes formed by the many arms of its delta. The river now stood at its highest point since the melting of the ice in the spring, the level being about the same as that to which it attains when the ice begins to form in the autumn. In summer the river is 9 feet lower.

A short day's journey north of the district of Abdall, the desert was ploughed up by a recently formed arm, which broke away from the Lower Tarim at Shirgeh-chappgan. As this had never been visited by anybody except the hunters of Abdall, I decided to map it. But it was only possible to approach it by canoe. The camels dragged (see p. 329) across the strip of sand that intervened between us and it a couple of canoes, drawing them like sledges. Then I took the instruments with me in one canoe, while Chernoff had the supplies and stores in another; but the latter was so heavily laden, that the gunwale was only $1\frac{1}{2}$ inches above the water, and in the opener reaches the waves washed over her. Tokta Ahun, old Yaman Kullu, and two other boatmen also accompanied us.

It was a difficult journey. The buran whistled and "shrilled" through the reeds, forcing us to keep as much as possible behind the shelter of the kamish beds. Out in the open lake, the least ruffling of the surface threatened to swamp our frail craft and send them to the bottom. In the dense thickets of reeds the daylight was little better than twilight. Every now and again a fish leapt to the surface. Swans and wild-geese darted away as we approached them, and on two or three occasions lost their eggs.

So long as we were able to make out the current, and kept to it, all went well. But at last we lost it, and soon got entangled in an impenetrable labyrinth of kamish beds, tamarisk mounds, alluvial formations, capes and promontories. Here we spent over three hours trying to find a passage, and in the end were forced to go back the way we had come. A second time we got lost in the winding channels, and were again obliged to turn back. Then by sheer force we drove the canoes through the crackling reed-beds. We got out, and dragged our craft across the reed-grown tongues of land which parted one basin from another. We climbed every sand-dune to see what we could make of the country; but the atmosphere was so hazy, owing to the storm, that all we could distinguish was an inextricable tangle of thicket and watery jungle.

Failing to discover a passage, we at last set fire to the kamish. At once a magnificent spectacle broke upon the hazy dimness of the atmosphere. The flames flung themselves upon the rain-dripping reeds. The reeds burst with loud reports, crackled, shot up dense clouds of black smoke. The storm seized them, whipped them to pieces, and tossed the trailing fragments like a tattered mourning-veil over the endless marshes with their labyrinthine reed-choked channels and water-ways. The air was thick with soot-flakes, so that, as we staggered about in the shallow water, hauling our canoes into the reedy lane carved by the flames, we got grimy as well as wet.

At length we found the current again, and it was now so swift and strong that the boatmen were forced to paddle with all their might to make headway against it. After spending some time in a vain search for a suitable spot to encamp in, owing to the moistness of the adjacent shores, we were at last obliged to put up with them, moist though they were, and make the best shift we could by spreading dry kamish at the foot of two or three tamarisks. The storm meanwhile lashed the river till it became specked all over with foam.

Next morning there were few inducements to continue the journey. To the north the sky was a blackish grey, owing to

Dragging the Canoes across a Tongue of Land.

the drift-sand, and the agitated surface made it difficult to see which way the current ran. It was 11 o'clock before we got started. We steered towards the north-west, across a series of elongated lakes, which took us again into what was decidedly a river-bed, for the channel narrowed to some 30 feet and the current flowed at the rate of two miles an hour. Then followed a complicated piece of the delta, called by the natives, Tokkuz-Tarim, or the Nine Rivers, from the number of arms into which the river was split.

The largest lake we traversed in the course of the journey luckily extended from north to south, and by keeping close to its eastern shore, which was shielded by high sand-dunes, we were able to obtain a certain amount of shelter. To have gone straight across it would have been perfectly impossible, for it was whitened with the breaking crests of the waves; and it was more by a lucky fluke than by any exercise of skill that we managed to hit the continuation of the river on the other side of it. After that, the channel turned, and the current, coming from the south-west, was neutralised by the wind. At Camp no. XXX. the river-arm which we had just ascended carried 374½ cubic feet in the second.

Our next day's journey was just as intricate, and the wind still continued to blow. During the night the thermometer fell to a maximum of $-0°.3$ C. or 31°.5 Fahr. We kept close to the bank, although that frequently took us into watery *cul de sacs*. A young shepherd, whom Tokta Ahun had somewhere got hold of, acted as our guide, until we reached a *sattma* or fisher's hut, where we exchanged him for an old fisherman, who led the way in his canoe. Without his assistance, it would have been impossible for us to find the mouth of the river, for it was completely masked by reeds. A little higher up he piloted us through a channel which was barely a yard wide, until we came to a cataract nearly two feet high. There it was necessary to land, drag our canoes after us through the reed thicket, and again launch them below the falls.

This and another small cascade, in the same locality, suggested that the arm of the Shirgeh-chappgan had a bigger fall than the principal river, which consequently must flow at a higher level. All this threw light upon the tendency which the river showed to travel towards the north and pour itself into the flat depressions which existed there. A difference in level of only a bare yard is a very important matter in a region which is everywhere almost perfectly horizontal.

At Yekken-öy we found a small village of only four sattmas, with a score of inhabitants, all of them old men, women, and children. The able-bodied men of the community had gone to Charkhlik to sow their crops and cultivate the ground. Their other chief means of subsistence were fishing and catching wild-duck, as well as collecting the eggs of the latter. The villagers owned also 150 sheep and some cows. They had migrated to their existing quarters four years before, coming from Chegghelik-uy. They told me, that the new river-arm which flowed eastwards out of their lake was only seven years old. On the 18th of April we, followed by a

The Branch of the River winding through the Reed-grwon Sands

Vol. 1—to face page 400

large flotilla of native canoes, steered south-west across a string of lakes, which had a maximum depth of only 15 feet. These lakes possessed one peculiarity, in that the water they contained flowed at one and the same time in two opposite directions—both east and west. While the main volume of the water went eastwards, a portion ran westwards and entered the Tarim at Shirgeh-chappgan. They were, however, situated 23½ inches above the level of the Tarim. Gradually we wormed our way into a *kok-ala* or small stream, which meandered into the Tarim, where its crystal clear water instantly became absorbed by the muddy current of the larger river.

A little distance down the Tarim we halted at Shirgeh-

The Tarim at Shirgeh-chappgan.

chappgan, whence we had a splendid view of the great river itself. It was straight and regular, and bordered by rows of shady and venerable poplars. Here two channels, flowing out of the lakes of Yekken-öy, restored to the Tarim 198 cubic feet of water per second; while the Tarim itself had a volume of 3,828½ cubic feet in the second, the greatest volume I had hitherto measured in this stream.

During the night of the 19th April the thermometer again dropped to $-4°.0$ C. or 24°.8 Fahr., a quite unusual thing at this season of the year. Picking up Faisullah and Ördek, with the dog Mashka, I now purposed to row back to Tikkenlik by the lakes which I discovered during my former journey. It was of course irksome to have to traverse the same ground again, namely, the two days as far as Kum-chekkeh ; but as the hydrographical relations had in the meantime changed, it would not perhaps be time altogether wasted. Hence, leaving the Niaz-köll on the left, we paddled across Chong-köll, which fully justified its name of the Big Lake. Indeed, in our frail canoes we did not dare to venture very far away from its shore. After that we penetrated up a large river-arm, which ploughed its way through an expanse of pure sand, and was called Lailik-daria. It carried a volume of 738 cubic feet, or 165½ cubic feet more than did the two channels (see pp. 400 and 401) which flowed out of the lakes of Yekken-öy. By taking a series of similar measurements along this eastern arm, I should be able to infer what its real character was, and ascertain what quantity of water it bequeathed to the lakes along its course, or lost by evaporation, how much was absorbed by the ground, and so forth.

During the four years which had elapsed since I last saw it, the Sadak-köll had totally changed its appearance ; not only was it choked with sand and alluvium, it was also overgrown with reeds, through which a strong current forced its way. The huts in which I had formerly taken shelter from a storm were still standing, and their inhabitants were for the most part the same ; they recognised me again, and gave me a most friendly welcome. They called their village, with its 26 inhabitants, Merdektik, because it was situated at the mouth of a new river-arm, which emerged from the Merdek-köll, and after passing through a considerable lake to the east, here discharged its 83½ cubic feet of water in the second. This again was another proof that the entire hydrographical system of the Lop-nor is moving northwards, back again towards its ancient basin.

A fisherman from this village guided us from his canoe against the swift current. The shores were lined with young tograk woods ; the trees, having just put forth their fresh, spring foliage, were very attractive, especially when compared with the yellow glare of the barren desert behind them. The velocity of the current varied with the depth ; sometimes it flowed at the rate of two and a half miles an hour, rippling and gurgling against the poplars which stood in the stream. We stopped for breakfast at Kulakchah, and found there the same five families whose acquaintance I made in 1896.

Since my last visit the shepherds of the neighbourhood

had built a permanent bridge across the river, consisting of beams, branches, and reeds, so as to be able to drive their stock over from the one bank to the other during the summer. It was, however, so low that a man in a laden canoe was only just able to pass underneath it. However, it made a picturesque feature, with its beams and timbers mirrored in the

The Arm of the Merdek-köll Entering the Desert.

A Bridge Over the Ilek.

inky black waters of the Ilek, which nevertheless were perfectly transparent.

Thus we paddled along at the rate of four miles an hour between the luxuriant woods and the impenetrable reed-thickets, and finally arrived about sunset at Kum-chekkeh, where we were again welcomed by old friends of 1896. Next day, one of these men accompanied me to the Merdek-köll, when I went to map it. This lake received 247¼ cubic feet of water in the second from the Ilek, and was in places 24¼ feet deep, that is to say, it was considerably deeper than the Kara-koshun.

Above Kum-chekkeh the river, with its borders of magnificent woods, made a picture of exceptional beauty, quite park-like in its intermingling of wood and water. The volume of the stream was 950 cubic feet in the second, and increased as we ascended, for lower down in the direction of Yekken-öy the lateral lakes and side lagoons levied heavy contributions from it.

Between the lakes of Arka-köll and Tayek-köll, both of which I explored, we obtained in the middle of the river the

Our Canoes on the Ilek.

greatest depth I sounded anywhere in the whole of the Tarim basin, namely, $41\frac{1}{6}$ feet. Arka-köll was in places as much as 23 to 26 feet deep. Tayek-köll—whose eastern shore we traversed with our camel caravan in 1896—was a perfectly open sheet of water, and gave in the middle depths of $18\frac{3}{4}$, $22\frac{1}{2}$, and 31 feet, or nearly double the depths of any part of the Kara-koshun. When I got back to camp my tent was so full of gnats that I literally had to smoke them out.

We left this inhospitable gnat-haunted place at day-break on the morning of the 27th April. We were still ascending our old friend the Ilek, which was less like a river than an open lane through the reeds. These stretched on the west as far as we were able to see, but on the east soon terminated in hard ground, whereon poplars were growing. Upon reaching the lake of Suyi-sarik-köll, or the "Yellow Water Lake," we

Poplars Growing Beside the Ilek.

Among the Reeds in Suyi-sarik-köll.

turned to the west, and plunged into another unconscionable tangle of kamish, through which we found our way by means of an ill-preserved *chappgan*, or channel. The interior of our reedy tunnel was dark and stuffy. The reeds, which were bent across the narrow waterway by the incessant storms, were, moreover, heavily laden with dust and drift-sand. In some places they formed a kind of bridge, on which a man could walk long distances. As a rule the water was six to seven feet deep, and percolated through the myriads of reed-stalks into the Ilek. That evening we encamped at the village of Sheitlar, which we had visited during the preceding winter, so that I thus secured a point of connection with the map that I made during my journey through the Desert of Cherchen.

Next day, taking two men with me, I made an excursion to the Kara-köll. A north-easterly gale of the worst description was blowing, and it was as dim as twilight, when we rowed round the biggest sheet of water, hugging the reeds or keeping just along their fringe, where the force of the waves was broken. On this lake were several floating islands, consisting of kamish roots matted together with clay, mud, and rotting *algæ* from the bottom; some of them floated on the surface, others were partly submerged. The natives called them *sim*; some of them looked big enough to bear a man. At all events, they proved that aquatic vegetation is one of the factors which help to level up these wide and shallow marshes.

The hydrography of this region is so complicated, that it cannot be clearly understood without a detailed map; hence I cannot dwell upon it longer in this place. With Chernoff for my assistant I measured every arm and every canal which conveyed water towards Arghan and Ilek, with, amongst other things, this interesting result, that the Tarim now poured a considerably greater volume of water into the system of lakes which lay to the east of it than it did when I visited them in 1896.

On the 29th April, with a fresh set of boatmen and fresh canoes, we travelled west and north-west across the large lake of Chivillik-köll. This, like all the other lakes in that locality, was in great part overgrown with reeds and sedge. It was so extensive that we were unable to see its western shore, even from the top of a high dune, though at the same time its waving reed-beds were swallowed up in a distant haze.

Next day we were joined at Kadikeh by my old guides, Kirgui Pavan and Shirdak Pavan, who brought me the first intelligence of Parpi Bai's death. Starting again on the 1st

May, with fresh canoes and fresh men, including Kirgui and Shirdak, we steered west-north-west on the Kunchekkish-Tarim. At Darghillik we discovered in the forest traces of a score or so of huts, which the begs of Turfan used to visit in the days before Yakub Beg, for the purpose of collecting tribute of otter skins for the Emperor of China. These Chinese officials used

Our Canoes at a Night-camp.

A Bridge at Tikkenlik.

to travel by way of Turfan-köbruk on the Upper Ilek, and used to bring with them, for the begs and inhabitants of the district, presents of flour, for this, before agriculture was practised in the Lop country, was a highly valued commodity.

At the camp of Dilghi we measured a current of 2,977½ cubic feet in the second, flowing *into* the Chivillik-köll, although only a few days before we had measured a current of 3,214 cubic feet in the second flowing out of the same lake. This [illegible]enon, at first sight so strange, was due to the fact that the inflow had already begun in the natural course of things to diminish, so that the lake, which acted as a reservoir and moderator, did for a time discharge more water than it received.

On the 4th of May we encamped near old Naser Beg of Tikkenlik, and from him heard good reports of our principal camp. The 5th of May we spent at Tikkenlik, for the first caravan had just arrived from Tura-sallgan-uy under the command of Cherdon. It consisted of Faisullah, Mollah Shah, Musa, Kutchuk, and ten Lopliks, together with an imposing array of 35 horses, 5 camels, and 5 dogs, all in excellent condition. Their orders were to take the main caravan

View from Kalmak-ottogo.

road to Abdall, thence strike direct for Chimen in Northern Tibet, seek out a suitable site for a camp, and there await my arrival, taking care in the meantime that the animals were fit for the laborious journey which awaited them in the summer. Cherdon still had a good deal of difficulty in making himself understood in Turki, the *lingua franca* of that region; but by dint of using it every day, he learned it rapidly.

Whilst I was staying at Tikkenlik, Jan Daloi, the amban of Charkhlik, passed the place on his way to his own town. He was an uncommonly well-bred, amiable, and polite Chinaman, who afterwards proved a very useful friend to me.

On the 6th of May we exchanged canoes and boatmen for

the last time, and started to force our way against the powerful current and formidable volume of 3,383½ cubic feet in the second to Yanghi-köll.

When we at length reached our well-known camp beside the solitary poplar, all the men were waiting to receive us. Sirkin told me everything that had happened during my absence, and handed to me his meteorological journal, together with the observations and records he had made as to the changes in the river. Whilst I was away, the men had set up in the market-place a neat little Mongolian yurt, in which I subsequently lived. The Cossacks lodged in the kamish hut; Islam Bai and Turdu Bai in the tent. My old friend the ferry-boat lay moored in her dock, but was soon destined to resume her travels.

CHAPTER XXV.

SOUNDING THE STORMY LAKES OF THE LOWER TARIM.

THUS I had forged a new link in the chain of my expeditions, and brought to a close a new chapter in my travels. The base at Yanghi-köll was no longer needed; it was time to transport my possessions, animate and inanimate, to a different region, where different conditions prevailed, namely, to the inhospitable uplands which lie between the Himalayas and the Kwen-lun, the most stupendous swelling on the face of the earth.

I spent ten days at my old headquarters, partly in much-needed rest, and partly in making various arrangements. For one thing, I settled with Khalmet Aksakal, of Korla, who had provided us with horses and a plentiful supply of provisions; and when he left me I gave him my packet of letters for Europe.

During these days the Cossacks were by no means idle. They made an exceedingly judicious alteration in the structure of the ferry-boat, which we were now about to use for the completion of our journey down the Tarim. On the fore-deck, in place of the tent, they built an ordinary cabin, precisely like my dark-room, except that the uprights were covered with white felt. Two hanging felt curtains formed the front, though the one on the right hand, where my writing table stood, used only to be let down at night. They also fixed up a little awning, just above the table, to shield me from the sun, for we should be travelling south. The long wall, next the larboard passage, was made entirely of planking, near the top of which we had various hooks fixed to hang clothes on and instrument cases. Here stood three of my boxes, one of them being used as my dining table. My bed was placed alongside the opposite wall, which consisted of one big hanging felt carpet. Otherwise the cabin was kept as airy as possible. The meteorological observatory was in the same place as before, and when I lifted the short felt curtain which was

The Ferry-boat after its Re-construction

nailed to the roof along the back I could easily read my instruments from the inside of the cabin. The roof consisted of seven stout spars, covered with a carpet. From one of them was suspended by a wire an exceedingly primitive " chandelier."

On the after-deck the Cossacks built for themselves a similar cabin of felts and planks, and packed it all round with their own things, such as their travelling-trunks, beds, and clothes. Here Sirkin had his own little work table, with his aneroids, a watch, his thermometers, the velocity instrument, measuring tape and writing materials; and all the way to Abdall he acted as my amanuensis.

As soon as the Cossacks had finished their work of re-constructing the ferry-boat, I gave them a new problem to solve. My friends, the Lop fishermen and canoemen, had with one voice declared it was impossible to travel by water in the teeth of the wind without the help of paddles or oars. I was therefore tempted to astonish them, and at the same time put before them a convincing proof of the correctness of my assertion to the contrary. Accordingly I carved a tiny model, and with that to guide them, the Cossacks hewed out of a poplar tree a sailing canoe, the hull of which was shaped with mathematical exactitude. I could not use my English skiff for the purpose, because tacking was just the one thing she would not do. Along the bottom of the new craft we fastened a false-keel, by means of iron clamps, and underneath that hung two or three bars of iron which had been bought in Shar-yar for a totally different purpose. Then we covered her with skins stretched as taut as a drum. A mast, which could be put up and taken down at pleasure, was fixed in crutches in the fore part of the boat, and she was rigged with a fore and aft sail. Our smith made a first-rate rudder, and swung it on a stern-post in such a way that it was movable between two thole-pins. To make the boat ride more steadily we fastened two bags of sand in her bottom. At the most she would only carry one man, and was so narrow that the "yachtsman" scarcely had room to sit behind; indeed, he was obliged to balance himself as best he could with his legs propped on the rail.

The natives sat and watched our proceedings with the greatest interest and curiosity, and when the boat was ready and tried in a hard wind in an expansion of the river, they were loud in their exclamations of amazement. She tacked easily, and readily obeyed the helm; but she was not a particularly dry craft, for she generally had her rail under water, so that to navigate her was pretty much like sitting in a bath.

On the evening of the 17th May all the Mussulmans paid a visit to Parpi Bai's grave to recite prayers by way of farewell to their old comrade. After that the inhabitants of the neighbourhood were called together, and all who had served as hewers of wood and drawers of water, as purveyors of hay, as shepherds, or in any other capacity, were duly paid and settled with.

Next morning when I stepped outside my cabin, there stood the nine camels waiting for their loads, which were already made up and lashed upon the pack-saddles. I had originally intended to send them on by night, in order that they might escape the gad-flies, which torment the poor beasts horribly, especially when they have just shed their hair, as ours had recently done; for they are then almost naked and exceedingly sensitive, looking like fledgling crows, with a tuft of hair on their heads and two or three tufts on their humps. But as they had had a long rest, and would probably be playful and sportive at starting, we thought it best to let them travel the first two or three stages by daylight, and afterwards, as soon as they had sobered down, to continue by night. The caravan was led by Islam Bai, Turdu Bai, Khodai Kullu, and two Lop-men; and Chernoff was commissioned to escort them to the mountains. The dogs Mashka, Yolldash, and the two pups, Malenki and Malchik, which had thriven famously, were all tied up to prevent them from going along with the caravan. These, being my especial favourites, I wanted with me for company on the ferry-boat. All the other dogs accompanied the caravan, and Yollbars, who had got badly torn in the side by a wild boar, was allowed to please himself. He lay in my old hut and licked his wound until it healed. Later on he went with me when I attempted to get into Lassa.

The camels with their towering loads, and the men with their parti-coloured attire, made a taking picture, as, surrounded by a crowd of spectators, and followed by mounted Lop-men and begs, they defiled through the reeds and bushes.

As soon as the camels' bells had died away, I, Sirkin, Ördek, and two or three boatmen set off in two canoes to explore Göllmeh-ketti, or the Lake of the Lost Fishing-net. Whilst we were sounding it the wind increased to a half gale, and clouds of dust and sand brought on a premature twilight. The dust-clouds hung down from the crests of the sand-dunes like tassels, and the waves broke over our canoes. We hurriedly dragged them ashore, baled them out, and resumed our journey. Owing to the shallowness of the lake we were forced to keep a good way out from shore, but then the waves beat in over the low rail and drenched us to the skin. All at once down went Sirkin's boat. Out jumped the men. A little later we saw them philosophically hauling their craft up on dry ground and wringing the water out of their clothes. Ere long we in the other canoe were in a very similar plight; for our light canoe was tossed about like a nut-shell. At length she shipped so much water that it became only a question of time when we should go down. Accordingly we turned

Children on the Bank of the Tarim.

before the wind and ran ashore in shallow water with a sandy bottom, where we waded out without getting wet above the waist. Then, taking off our clothes, we spread them and our other things out on the sand to dry, for it was still warm from the sun. The men lay down and slept; but I remained awake, watching for an improvement in the weather. As, however, the storm did not abate, and we had brought no provisions with us, and as, besides, it was imperative that I should get back to the ferry-boat in order to wind up my chronometers, I directed two of the boatmen to paddle the canoes close in beside the shore, and continued my mapping on foot.

During the night the wind blew so hard from the south-east, that the ferry-boat was almost careened as she hung at her moorings; for, guided by a fire which Shagdur made, we successfully found our way home, though the last part of the trip was in pitch darkness. During the past few days the river had risen a few inches. The natives told me that in addition to the great spring flood, caused by the melting of the ice, the river rises again, though not so high, at a subsequent period of the year, namely, when the *Elæagnus* bursts into flower and the young wild geese begin to leave their mothers. These fluctuations are probably connected with the distribution of the atmospheric pressure. So far as we were concerned, every addition to the volume of the stream was welcome; this, on the 16th of May, measured 2,592½ cubic feet, or about 790 cubic feet less than on the 7th of May. Once the great flood is past, the river falls with extraordinary rapidity. There was consequently no time to be lost. Hence on the 19th I bade the men cast off. My new boatmen, Ak Käsha, Sadik, Tokta Ahun, and Atta Kellghen looked decent, reliable men. One Loplik navigated my English skiff. The little sailing boat and the big canoe were lashed together, and put in the charge of another Loplik; but we gave the smaller commissariat boat, which we had brought from Lailik, and our other canoes, to the inhabitants of Yanghi-köll. The *kemi-bashi*, or "ship's captain," of the bigger ferry-boat was Ördek, while old Aksakal Pavan, who begged that he might go with us, was stationed just in front of my writing table.

The women of the neighbourhood gathered in our abandoned huts, and peeped out at us between the sheaves of reeds, and as soon as our ferry-boat got well started, the men accompanied us some distance along the bank, until at length they dropped away one by one, and returned their several ways home. They would certainly miss the bustle of our camp.

The whole of the first day, during which we were retarded by contrary wind, the river hugged the high sand-dunes. My object in this new expedition was to map the lower course of the Tarim, and as many of its lateral lakes as I possibly could manage. But although this would make my third itinerary in that region, the only points at which it would come in contact with the first two were Arghan, Shirgeh-chappgan, and Abdall. At Yanghi-köll there had been disturbing rumours rife with regard to the river. It was said to be deflecting into some new arms situated farther to the east, and there was also said to be scarcely water enough left to float our ferry-boat to the termination of the Tarim. But, whether or no, I was determined I would not abandon her until I was absolutely forced to do so.

On the 20th of May, with the same crew of boatmen as before, I made a trip to the Karunalik-köll, which turned out in every respect successful, the weather being splendid. I was consequently enabled to take my soundings along systematic lines, zigzagging backwards and forwards across the lake, and in this

Women and Children Looking on with Curiosity.

way obtained more than sufficient material for drawing out bathymetrical curves. In the very entrance to the lake I made one interesting observation, namely, that the lake drew off from the river 81¼ cubic feet of water per second, that is to say, the latter was drained by this one lake alone of over 7,000,000 cubic feet in the twenty-four hours. This will convey some idea of the vast quantity of water which is lost in the Tarim system by evaporation and absorption in the sand. The muddy river water spread out fan-like over the surface of the lake, for its own water was of an emerald green or ultramarine blue colour, although nothing like so pure or so intensely blue as the blue of the glacier lakes in the mountains.

The Lake of Karunalik-köll consisted of two elliptical basins. shaped like the figure **8**, a formation very common in these peculiar desert lakes, as well as in the dry-land bayirs. Thus the same common designations occurred in them all, *e.g.*, *bolta*, the strait or narrow channel which connected the two basins; *kakkmar* or little bays, lying beside the *mojuks* or projecting capes and headlands. Their deepest depressions occurred, as they do in the bayirs, immediately at the foot of the steep dunes on the eastern side. Thus most, if not all, of the poplars stood on that same side, and very often were so smothered in sand that it was a wonder they were not killed by it. But their doom was anyway sealed, for the dunes were being driven steadily and unceasingly westwards by the easterly gales. Tamarisks and *Elæagnus* occurred but seldom. Reeds grew almost everywhere along the western shore, though only on the dry land.

Measured by the levelling-mirror, the crest of the highest dune beside the lake was 293½ feet above the water; but at the same time I perceived several other points 30 to 50 feet higher still. Thus the sand-dunes on the right bank of the Tarim reached in this locality an altitude of over 300 feet. The loftiest summit which I measured went steeply down on the west to the next depression, which belonged to the Tograklik-köll and its bayirs. These, like the string of bayirs which we followed when we crossed the desert to Tatran and Cherchen, appeared to stretch towards the interior of the desert.

In the afternoon we continued down the river as far as the entrance to Ullug-köll or the Big Lake, and there encamped. The *acha*, or channel, by which the river water entered it, carried 236½ cubic feet in the second. The reeds along the shore showed plainly that during the last autumn flood the lake had risen 4½ feet higher than it stood at the time of our visit. That is to say, the lake had then been considerably bigger. Its waters were abundantly stocked with fish; but regular fishing would not be carried on until the river fell low enough to allow of the lake being cut off. Here the fishermen did not hang their nets in the chappgans, as they did in the reed-grown lakes. A drag-net of some 60 fathoms in length was drawn along the shallow parts by two canoes. First it was stretched out into a semicircle; then one of the boats turned inwards, making a sharp loop with the net; after which the other boatmen drove the fish into the loop by beating the water with their paddles. That done they hauled in the net, and killed the fish with a blow from a club. Fishing cannot of course be carried on in this way when the wind blows, for the canoes then drift too much. The fauna round the shores of Ullug-köll was represented by deer and wild boar, though the latter only visited the locality occasionally. Sirkin shot a male which was on its way to the river. The only birds we saw were eagles, terns, and a few small waders. There was no food for wild duck or wild geese.

The whole of this series of lakes, which hang like leaves on a stalk along the right bank of the Tarim, are parasites or out-

Sand-dunes on the Right Bank of the Tarim.

growths upon the river, in that they derive their vitality from it, and would die if it were to flow in some other direction. By the autumn they are half empty, and have to be filled anew. Thus every year the river is drained of enormous quantities of water, which but for these lakes would find its way into the Kara-koshun. It is not difficult, therefore, to conceive that at a time when as yet they did not exist, the Lop lakes were much more extensive than they are at the present day, and that their origination and expansion are one of the causes of the gradual disappearance of the lakes lower down.

Life on board was as peaceful and quiet as it had been during our long autumn drift down the Tarim. The Cossacks enjoyed themselves thoroughly. They sat outside their cabin and talked; they circled around the ferry-boat in their canoes; they rowed to shore and shot wild-duck in the quiet angles of the stream; and when their day's work was done they amused themselves with fishing. In fact, we lived almost entirely upon wild-duck and fish, although we were able to procure mutton and milk from the shepherds on the banks. Shagdur was my cook and *valet de chambre*. Ördek, our skipper, was rather noisy in issuing his orders, otherwise he managed first-rate. When we stopped for the night the Cossacks slept on board with me, but the Mussulmans always slept on shore. Every afternoon I had the two pups bathed, a performance which afforded immense amusement to the onlookers, though it was an abomination to the little wretches themselves.

On the 23rd of May we did an unusually long stage. In the afternoon, just as were about to measure the velocity, etc., Naser Beg, Kirgui Pavan, Shirdak Pavan, and Temir-shang-ya came paddling down the river in their canoes. The last-named was sent about his business at once, for he was an arrant rogue. Not only had he, by means of his own specially-trained ruffians, stolen some cloth and other wares from Khalmet. Aksakal, but he oppressed the people in his district. In fact, in spite of his entreaties to the contrary, I reported him to the amban of Charkhlik, who deprived him of his office and his rank.

Perhaps I shall not seem presumptuous if I add here that so long as we dwelt in the Lop country peace and good order prevailed, for I would tolerate no injustice or wrong to its poor, but honest inhabitants. Hence all who suffered from any wrong, and lacked the means or power to get themselves righted, used to come to me with petitions for help and redress. In this way Tura-sallgan-uy became famous as a court of justice, and so in a sense acquired the position of capital of the country, sometimes, to the prejudice, I am afraid, of the Chinese ambans of Dural, Kara-shahr, and Charkhlik. In the more serious cases I used to write to these gentlemen and remind them that if they failed to carry out my behests it might be the worse for them. Smaller affairs we used to settle ourselves. The fact is, the people of the Lop country suffer far more from their begs and ambans than they do from the gnats and gad-flies.

We now engaged a flotilla of nine canoes to clear a passage for us through the intricate net-work of new-formed lakes, choked with

Setting Fire to the Reeds

Vol. 1—to face page 420

kamish, which began at Keppek-uy. The lakes of Kurban-jayiri and Syssyk-köll, we crossed without any trouble, thanks to the wind which helped us along, and to our men, who, exchanging their punting-poles for paddles, paddled the ferry-boat across what was fairly open water. But on the other side of this we again steered into a tunnel, where the reeds fenced us in on each side like a hedge, 13 feet high. Here we were nearly stuck fast altogether, the ferry-boat being for some time unable either to advance or to retire. We began to fear that this was the end of her journeyings. As long, however, as we stuck there, we had one thing to comfort us : we were in the shade, and it was cool. On the other hand, the gad-flies (*kökkön*), of which the air was full, were a perfect curse. My ears were assailed with their never-ceasing buzzing. Down they banged upon my map-sheet ; they made themselves impudently familiar, they tormented me like imps of evil. I could, of course, have protected myself with a mosquito-net ; but I was really ashamed to use it, when the men, who were half naked in the water, never uttered a word of complaint. At sunset our tormentors disappeared, but their place was instantly taken by midges and mosquitos. At that season of the year in the Lop country you cannot obtain a single moment's peace throughout the whole round of the twenty-four hours.

It was no easy matter to get out into the lake of Tuvadaku-köll, for the passage was fully 6 feet too narrow, as well as shallow and crooked; and unfortunately this was the only way there was. It took a score of men working fully two hours to deepen the channel and hew down the reeds at the sides, and even then we were only able to move the ferry-boat slowly along, foot by foot. Time after time, with the view of lightening our labours, we set fire to the reeds, until the lake became edged with living pillars of fire, which volleyed forth dense columns of smoke. However, this method could only be employed on the sheltered side, for it was not unattended with danger to our own inflammable craft ; had her top-hamper caught, it would have burned like tinder. But at last, after a heavy day's work, we dropped anchor at the little island of Yekkenlik, situated in the middle of the lake of the same name.

On the other hand, the excursion which we made on the 25th May to Beglik-köll turned out an exceedingly lively trip. Although during the night the thermometer did not fall below 16°.0 C. or 60°.8 Fahr., the morning felt quite fresh. It is astonishing how the body accommodates itself to changes of temperature.

I have known it feel comparatively warm with the thermometer standing as low as $-10°.0$ C. or $14°.0$ Fahr. The Beglik-köll was so peaceful and still it was hardly possible to believe that it could be whitened with hissing waves. The sun burnt fiercely, especially during the three hours we were travelling due south. The only way I could keep myself tolerably cool was by sprinkling water over my white clothes. We spent the whole day on this lake, simply measuring two or three of its bays. One of these I mapped from the top of a sand-dune, whence I obtained a bird's-eye view of it. The sand was burning hot ; I could feel it through my shoe-soles. How refreshing, then, to sit afterwards with my feet hanging over the side of the canoe, whilst I enjoyed a smoke.

But my enjoyment was short-lived. My old friend, Kirgui Pavan, called also Kurban, pointed to the summits of the lofty dunes on the east of the lake, and ejaculated in a questioning tone, "*Kara-buran?*" (black tempest) A dark pillar was rising above the horizon and leaning over in our direction, and it was crowned by a capital of lighter cloud. Gradually other similar pillars mounted upwards on each side of the first one, until they made a long row, resembling gigantic hands with the fingers upstretched. Then they slowly drew nearer one another, melted together, formed one continuous wall with a serrated upper edge, and all the time still kept on mounting higher and higher. There could no longer be any doubt as to what was impending.

After weighing the situation, the Lop-men voted for staying where we were. But that course I could not agree to; not because we were short of provisions, nor because it was disagreeable to lose the comfort of my cabin, but solely because the chronometers must be wound up at the usual time. Kirgui Pavan thought it would be anything but pleasant to await the tempest on the west side of the lake, because that was the exposed quarter. Now Kirgui Pavan was a very cautious and prudent man; he did not know what fear was, and in moments of real danger never lost his head. After studying the position for a second or two, he proposed that we should seek shelter in the throat of the narrow channel which supplied the Beglik-köll with water, and which it had taken us two solid good hours in the morning to wind through. But to reach it we should have to traverse the greater part of the lake, crossing on the way the open end of a broad bay which penetrated the sand on its west side. The best plan would have been to cross straight over to the eastern side at once, where we should have been sheltered by the sand-dunes ; but, although the lake was still scarcely ruffled, all the men without exception were against such a course. The distance was too great ; we could not possibly get across before the tempest burst. There was consequently only one thing to be done : we must cross the mouth of the bay and creep along the northern shore of the lake, getting the best shelter we could amongst its small islands and holms.

The men plied their paddles with such energy that every moment I expected to hear them snap. The blades bent like bows, and the water foamed high off the bows of the canoes. We went at a terrific pace, close upon $5\frac{1}{2}$ miles an hour. The men were in a panic of fear, and continually ejaculated in hollow,

The Ferry-boat Fast in the Reeds of Tuvadaku-köll.

awe-inspiring tones: "Ya Allah! Ya Allah!" The atmosphere was still serene, but there was an unmistakable feeling in the air that we were on the eve of a convulsion of nature, and the tempest advanced rapidly.

"Now it's on the top of the dunes!" cried Kirgui Pavan. Even whilst he was actually speaking their crests became blotted out as though they had been rubbed off a slate. A moment later and their flanks were gone: then the shore-line was engulfed in the thick, greyish-yellow haze. "Row, children, row! There is a God above!" cried the old man, encouraging the paddlers. "Khodaim var" (There is a God above)! was his invariable war-cry in all critical moments of excitement or danger.

Down came the first gusts of wind from the east-north-east. We heard the swi—i—i—ish of the tempest as it swooped down upon the lake. Up flew the water, hissing and foaming, and in less than a moment the surface was all aboil with big black pitching breakers. The nearer the tempest advanced the harder the men paddled, until I verily believe we were travelling nothing short of six miles an hour. But there still remained nearly $1\frac{1}{4}$ miles to the northern shore. "We shan't do it!" cried the men. "Ya Allah!"

I put into my pockets the few instruments we had with us. I took off my shoes and socks, so as to be ready for the worst. "Here it comes!" cried our canoemen, and they tried to paddle still harder. Every man was on his knees, and the paddle-strokes followed one another so fast they seemed to be driven by steam. Just as the tempest was upon us, and our light craft would to a dead certainty have been capsized had we not tilted them to windward, we became enveloped in the dense fog of dust. The western shore was now hidden from us as well as the northern. The seriousness of the situation forced itself home upon us when we saw nothing but hungry waves all around us and the canoes dancing away into the fog like floating straws. But Kirgui Pavan and his canoemen were equal to the occasion; every time a high "curler" threatened to engulf us they switched the canoes a little into the wind, and so kept out the greater part of its breaking crest, though we all got drenched to the skin as the spray drifted over us.

At length we caught a glimpse of the tamarisks on the northern shore, looking like black blotches in the fog. Then a minute or so later we got under the shelter of a long, narrow tongue of land which served as an excellent breakwater. But we only just reached safety in the nick of time; a few minutes more and the canoes would have sunk.

Sirkin and Naser Beg, having become very uneasy on our account, the latter set off from Yekkenlik for the Beglik-köll with two big canoes to assist us. We met him and his flotilla near the entrance to the channel I have spoken of. He brought with him beds, warm clothes, and provisions, a complete outfit, in fact, which Sirkin had sent in case we should not be able to get back before evening. A capsize in mid-lake in such weather as that when it would be quite impossible to see where to swim to, could hardly fail to be attended with some fatality, although all except Shagdur were good swimmers. But the floating power of a Lop

On the Beglik-köll in a Sandstorm.

[VOL. I.—*To face page* 424.

canoe is insignificant, especially when once it gets full of water. My instruments would, of course, have been utterly ruined.

It was no easy matter to find our ferry-boat amongst the rank reeds of the lake of Yekkenlik-köll. It was pitch-dark when we entered it, and the tempest was just about at its climax. We literally saw nothing, though we felt very sensibly when the buran beat the reeds across the canoes and whipped them into our faces. I had to keep my arms up over my face the whole way, or it would have been cut to pieces by those long, sharp, ribbon-like blades. It was no use shouting out warnings; all sounds were swallowed up in the shrill howling of the wind through the kamish. How the canoemen found their way I do not know, but at last we caught a glimpse of the fire which Sirkin had lighted to guide us. We were, however, quite close to it before ever we saw it, for, although the flames were fanned to a white heat by the tempest, they were unable to penetrate the fog. The ferry-boat and other boats being securely moored both fore and aft, we were quite safe.

This was one of the most awful storms I have ever been out in. We did not get much sleep that night. A couple of the felts on the fore-cabin were torn loose and had to be fastened down with ropes and poles, and I had to bring the meteorological observatory in under shelter. All small, light articles which were lying about the cabins began to whirl about, and had to be picked up and put safely away. The sand and dust rained in through the felts, and penetrated at every orifice. But I was most concerned about the fire, for the ferry-boat was surrounded by reeds on every side. To guard against this danger, I appointed a man to keep watch all night, both on board and on shore.

CHAPTER XXVI.

FLOATING DOWN THE TARIM BY NIGHT.

The tempest raged the whole of the following day, keeping us prisoners at Yekkenlik. But towards evening it abated somewhat, and gave me an opportunity for a splendid sail across the lake in my new boat. The gnats and gadflies disappeared when the storm came; but on the 27th May, when it was again still and warm, they crept out of their hiding-places in myriads. On that day we traversed the remaining portion of the Yekkenlik-köll, until we reached the point where it discharged itself over cascades into the Tarim. Here a flotilla of 12 boats, manned by 30 men, met us, to help us over the rapids. Holding the big ferry-boat by ropes at both ends, we let her down gradually by working her from the shore, for the water in the middle of the cascades was broken and tumultuous, and so continued for some distance below. Step by step the big leviathan dropped from sill to sill, her fore part advancing until it was lifted by the tossing crests below. Everybody was greatly excited, and the men shouted deafeningly. But we steered her over quite safely, and then on she went again, calmly floating down the Tarim.

This part of the river, which carried only 547½ cubic feet of water in the second, was on the point of dwindling away, having been superseded by a new river-arm, the Lashin-daria, which branched off into the eastern lakes. The following day I dismissed all the men I no longer wanted, Naser Beg at their head, and thus, with a greatly diminished complement, our flotilla slowly drifted down the river. The weather was splendid. During the preceding night the thermometer dropped to 6°.9 C. or 44°.4 Fahr. and the insects were not so troublesome as usual.

At this period the day's routine was as follows. At daybreak I was called by Shagdur. Then I started to inspect the camp, greeting the Cossacks with a "Good morning, Cossacks!" which they answered with a salute and "Starovieh shelayim vasheh prevoshoditelstvo!" (We wish your Excellency (!) good health!) To the Mussulmans I gave the usual "Salaam aleikum!" (Peace be with you), and like an echo the phrase was repeated by each of them in turn. Next came breakfast, which consisted of fish, eggs, bread, and tea. During the day the tea-pot generally stood in my cabin, and the samovar was always kept warm in the Cossacks'. We had dinner at eight o'clock; it generally consisted of rice pudding (ash), fish, coffee, and milk. We worked all day so long as it was light, and the evenings were devoted to the writing up of notes and observations.

Shagdur answered excellently well; I became more and more attached to him and gave him my confidence. He had already learnt to speak fluently with the Mussulmans, and of his own accord persuaded Sirkin to give him lessons in taking the meteorological observations, as well as lessons in reading and writing Russian; and before our travels were over, he had made such progress that, on several occasions when we were separated, he was able to write me reports and letters in Russian. Had the Cossacks not been naturally men of good character, they would, I fear, have been spoilt during the time they were with me, for they enjoyed a very considerable amount of liberty. But their discipline never slackened for one moment, and they never forgot the respect they owed to their new chief.

The best of the Mussulmans was Kirgui Pavan, the camel-hunter of Tikkenlik, an old man of seventy, thoroughly upright and honest; it was quite a pleasure to have such a man about one. His place was at the fore, in front of my writing-table, where he looked after the starboard punting-pole; while Aksakal, of Yanghi-köll, a big, strong, white-bearded old man of sixty, looked after the punting-pole on the other side. I quite enjoyed listening to these two old worthies as they talked about the prospects of the voyage, and the gradually growing distance which separated them from their homes in the north-west. They wondered how in the world they would ever get back there; and several times I had to comfort them by promising that I would undertake to see them home again. Kirgui Pavan knew the river well, and it was a great advantage being able to ask him, every time I began a fresh sheet of my map, which way the current turned next; otherwise I should sometimes have run over the edge shortly after beginning it.

Ordek, who had proved himself such an excellent fellow, reported himself sick, and was sent home in a canoe. As soon as it was dark we moored the ferry-boat. I had had my dinner, and was busy with my diary, when the dogs began to bark, and a strange canoe came paddling through the darkness and pulled up alongside. I thought it was a Loplik come to pay me a visit; then I heard quick steps along the passage outside. The felt curtains were pulled apart, and behold there stood the well-known figure of Musa, the jighit. He had ridden from Kashgar, a 33 days' ride, with my letters, and finding the camp at Yanghi-köll empty and deserted had taken a canoe and followed us down the river. The arrival of a jighit, or courier, was always a red-letter day, for it again brought me into touch with home and the outer world. After the letters, books, and newspapers were stacked up on the floor, I closed the cabin, and lay and read till three o'clock the following morning.

My old pilot, Kirgui Pavan, told me as usual the names of all the outstanding geographical features, and all he knew about the river and its history. In connection with a lonely poplar standing on a hill, which he called Kamshuk-tyshken-tograk, or the "Poplar where the Kamshuks settled," he told me a strange story about a people of unknown nationality, who several *decennia* ago came from Korla, and floated down the Kontcheh-daria on rough rafts made out of poplar trees. They consisted of 50 families, with women and children, but relatively few old people, and travelled slowly, resting at intervals for two or three days at a time. They were very poor, dependent in fact on what they shot for the necessaries of life. Kirgui Pavan had himself seen them when he was young. He recollected that they were clever shots, and lived a good deal on fish and the flesh of the wild boar. Their leader was called Yiven (Ivan?), and had previously visited the country alone, for the purpose of inquiring whether it was suitable for colonising. Their manner of killing sheep was different from that of the Mussulmans; for they first stupefied the animal by striking it on the head with a club. One of the older men amongst them was called by the Lop-men Yeghalaghak, or "the Weeper." His wife died and was buried underneath the poplar just mentioned. After spending three years in the Lop country, where they penetrated as far south as Charkhlik, they were, by command of Ashur Beg of Turfan, driven back the same way they came. Travelling back by land, they were one dark night overtaken by a buran, during which a beautiful young girl, who was betrothed to a man named Everani, disappeared. The latter almost went out of his mind with grief, and spent several nights and days searching for his *fiancée*; but as she had evidently lost her way during the storm, her people were forced to abandon her to her fate. They all spoke fluent Turki, and described themselves as fugitives. This disconnected and fragmentary story was the only tradition about the Raskolnikis that I heard in the Lop country.*

On the afternoon of the 29th of May, the river again turned capricious and unsettled, dividing into several arms, amongst which we had to choose with the greatest possible care, and finally we encamped for the night beside a little island in the new lake of Sattovaldi-köll, the only spot of dry land which was visible. Here the gnats were more troublesome than usual, for the nights we spent amongst these reed-grown lakes were much more stifling than those passed on the open river bank.

The next day our route lay continuously through lakes and a labyrinth of narrow canals, which we couldn ever have threaded without the help of a native levy. However, at nightfall we once more encamped beside the Tarim, which had a volume of 840½ cubic feet in the second. But the river was becoming uncomfortably sinuous, and the wind, too, was against us. Paddling and punting made but little difference, so that it was the evening of the 2nd June before we reached Ayag-arghan, and pitched our camp on the same headland on which we had tented twice before. There we stayed two days. Whilst the Mussulmans thoroughly cleaned the ferry-boat, I measured the two rivers which at Arghan issued from the Chivillik-köll, and entered the Tarim. Their united capacity was 1,289 cubic feet in the second. Hence for yet a few more days there would be no occasion to complain of lack of water. The main stream, which from this point also bore the name of Baba Tarim, or Old Father Tarim, carried 2,147½ cubic feet in the second.

The stretch of river which we travelled over on the 5th June was winding and full of sharp turns, and took us between luxuriant forests, now in the full beauty of their summer foliage. The water was warmed up to 23 .5 C. or 74 .3 Fahr., and Sirkin often used to slip over the side and have a swim. For my own part, I only bathed at midnight and at 7 o'clock in the morning. But I always had a big tub of water standing in my cabin, so

* But see pp. 309-310 above.

that I might cool myself in the intervals between the taking of the compass-readings. The Cossacks, setting their nets every evening, kept us well supplied with fish. One morning the catch amounted to a score, each fish being big enough to satisfy a hungry man at a single meal.

The farther we advanced down the Tarim, the more the gad-flies, gnats, and mosquitos multiplied in number, and as they were fond of confederating together, there was not much pleasure to be got out of life. They were excessively social, and vied with one another in their attentions. It was no use fighting against them, we only got worsted. The gad-fly's bite left a burning sting behind it; and every morning the "varmints" generally lay so thick round my writing-table that I had to order one of the men to come in and literally sweep them away. The dogs waged desperate war against them, but the only time they obtained a truce was at night. Kirgui Pavan maintained that the incredible multitudes of insects in this particular locality were directly connected with the absence of other animal life. As a rule, all the huts we passed were uninhabited, nor were there any shepherds either: their flocks would have been destroyed by the gad-flies. Nor did we see any deer or wild boar. In fact the entire country was rendered absolutely uninhabitable by the insect plague. Merchants who have occasion to travel at this season of the year from Charkhlik to Korla only ride by night, and hide their horses or camels in the kamish huts during the day.

After stopping at Kyiyish for supper and to measure the river, we were off again at ten o'clock, and went on for about two hours by moonlight. But after the moon set it was pitch dark, except for the Chinese lantern that swung aloft on a pole on the pilot canoe. The night was perfectly still and peaceful; not a sound was audible, not a breath moved. The gad-flies had long ago crept amongst the grass and reeds to sleep. Every now and again a fish splashed softly on the surface, and occasionally we heard the water gently rippling against a reed-stalk.

The Cossacks sat on the "bridge" smoking, and started the musical-box, to keep the old men awake, as they said; though this was an unnecessary precaution, for, as a matter of fact, they were both apprehensive of coming into collision with some overhanging poplar or of running aground. Sirkin had lighted a big flaring naphtha lamp, which lit up the banks, so that he and Shagdur were able to tell me from time to time what they were like ; for instance, " on the right, thick forest close to the water's edge ;" " on the left, kamish fields, bushes, young forest, etc." The compass-bearings I took from the light in the pilot canoe.

Thus we glided down the never-ending river in the silence of the night. I whistled as I worked to the old well-known tunes of the musical box, while the Cossacks puffed away at their short clay pipes. At intervals, when old Kirgui Pavan considered a little extra care or vigilance was called for, he used to cry out " Khabardar ! " (look-out) We were now rapidly approaching the grave of the mighty river, and a feeling of melancholy began to steal over me, as I saw one loop after another disappearing behind us.

When the novelty of the music had worn off, the men grew drowsy and sleepy. The musical-box stopped ; the lamp went out. Sirkin nudged Aksakal, whose head was drooping with a suspicious nod, but was himself, a little while afterwards, caught with his back against the bulwark, his nose tilted skywards, and his mouth wide open, snoring his hardest. His cap slipped off his head, and was dropping into the river, but he just managed to catch it in time ; then for a little while he was as lively as a squirrel. At two o'clock I took compassion on the poor fellows, for of course they had not the same interests to keep them awake as I had. We moored the ferry-boat to the bank, and in less than five minutes dead silence reigned on board.

But before we had slept very long another buran burst upon us, and rent open the felts of my cabin. All the next day the tempest still raged, and prevented us from starting until ten o'clock at night, when it abated a little. Then we did three hours. On the 8th and 9th of June we were again detained by a furious gale from the east-north-east. Most opportunely, as if to give me something to do during the enforced wait, another jighit arrived, and I at once surmised that he brought important news, for he was an extra courier, not one of those I had arranged for. Consul Petrovsky informed me that he had received a telegram from the governor-general of Turkestan, to the effect that, owing to the disturbed state of the outskirts of the Empire in Asia, the two Cossacks, Sirkin and Chernoff, were wanted, and must be sent back without delay to Kashgar. This was a blow both to me and to Sirkin. We discussed the intelligence for a long time, and assumed that serious disturbances had broken out somewhere on the Siberian frontier ; for of what was at this time happening in China we had not the remotest idea.

I at once sent off an express messenger to the Chimen-tagh with a letter to Chernoff bidding him, without a moment's delay, return to Abdall. Sirkin had of course to wait for his comrade; they could not travel separately. Now that we were constrained to part in this unexpected manner, I was very glad I had written to the Emperor of Russia from Yanghi-köll, thanking him for sending me two such excellent men as these Cossacks, and telling him of the great services they had rendered me.

On the evening of the 9th June we were all very anxious about Shagdur, who went out hunting about five o'clock. At supper-time, nine o'clock, he was not back, so we kindled, at

A View of the Tarim at Shirgeh-chappgan.

different places along the bank, six big fires, which threw a lurid and picturesque glare upon the clouds of fine dust which still hung in the air. Still, however, Shagdur did not come. Then I sent off all the men, each in a different direction, with torches and lamps. I heard their shouts die away in the distance. I thought of the various dangers which might beset a lonely wanderer amongst those unearthly sand-dunes, of tigers, and of wild boars. It would have been hard to lose three out of my four Cossacks all at one blow. One after the other the searchers returned, but they came without Shagdur. However, about midnight Shagdur himself turned up, and told me that, having wounded a deer, which fled westwards into the desert, he had followed it for some hours; but when it grew dark and he turned back he lost his own trail. Yet by keeping straight to the east, he at length struck the river and then wandered up and down it looking for us, until at last he caught sight of one of our fires.

Resuming our journey on the 10th of June, we skirted, on our left, a district called Tuga-ölldi, or the "Camel Died," a name which it derived from the fact that a camel belonging to a band of Mongol pilgrims died here whilst they were on their way to Lassa. For in Yakub Beg's time they used to keep to the left bank of the river, so as to be safe from molestation by his men. Thus an unimportant event, itself long since forgotten, is perpetuated for years in the geographical nomenclature of the

Women and Children at Chegghelik-uy.

country. Nowadays the Mongols always travel by the great caravan road, which follows the right bank of the river.

We stopped in the afternoon at Shirgeh-chappgan, to measure the river at the same point at which we measured it on the 18th of April. The volume now amounted to 2,412 cubic feet in the second; the river thus dropped very rapidly at this season of the year. After sending back the special jighit to Kashgar, we continued our voyage by night, piloted by several canoes carrying torches. And truly a wonderful procession it was which thus drifted, through the stillness of the June night, down the Tarim by torch-light, to the monotonous accompaniment of the canoe-men's plaintive love-songs.

I had already mapped the stretch from Shirgeh-chappgan to Chegghelik-uy in 1896; and when we passed Ak-köll, on the 11th of June, I found that the river had deserted the big loop which it used to make there, and had cut out a new channel across the narrow intervening neck of land. But the loop was still full of water, and a couple of steep and ragged headlands bore eloquent witness to the violence of the breach.

During the course of the day the forest came to an end, and the country on both sides opened out flat. The air was still, although still subdued to a kind of twilight after all the dust-storms. Then we perceived several canoes coming to meet us. In the first of them was Temir Beg of Chegghelik-uy. I invited him on board, and amongst other things he told me that it would be impossible to take our ferry-boat beyond his village, for the next lake, the Semillaku-köll, was entirely overgrown with reeds. Now, although I was longing to get up into the mountains, and the boatmen were impatient to return home, I could not help feeling rather sorry that this was to be the old boat's last stage. Towards evening we saw fires gleaming in the distance, and late that night we moored our faithful old craft for the last time to the left bank of the Tarim, immediately opposite to Chegghelik-uy.

Early the next morning I sent off Kirgui Pavan through the lakes to reconnoitre. He came back with the intelligence that it would be impossible to take the big ferry-boat any farther; and by way of confirmation brought with him a big bundle of kamish stalks, which showed by their length how deep the water was in the shallowest places. He thought, however, that 25 men could cut a navigable channel in a few days; but I rejected his proposal, because it would only take us three days to get to Abdall. But before starting on that stage, I wanted to use my dark-room once more for developing my plates; hence I decided to stay a few days at Chegghelik-uy, especially as in the meantime two or three canoes could be getting ready to take us to Abdall.

At this peaceful fishing-station we spent a very pleasant and restful week. We were encamped on the left bank of the river immediately opposite the village, and had a good view of its kamish huts and open stables, and saw how the cattle and horses and asses were tormented by the myriads of gad-flies. The little children ran about the bank naked and played amongst the canoes. As a background to this homely picture there was, if one may so call it, a *memento mori* in the shape of the burial-place of the villagers, with its staves, and its fluttering streamers.

Every night I worked in the dark-room till four a.m., and Sirkin was my assistant, fetching me fresh water and drying the prints. During the whole of this week we were visited by uninterrupted storms from the north-east. After spending a whole spring exposed to these incessant burans, and witnessing what power they possess to mould and sculpture the earth's surface, I no longer wondered at the deserts, lakes, and rivers in this part of the world being subject to perpetual alteration.

A Stable at Chegghelik-uy.

We were obliged to paste paper all over the inside of the dark-room, to prevent the dust from penetrating in and spoiling our plates. As we worked the tempest howled and screeched outside. When we lay down to sleep the wailing of the wind and the splashing of the waves echoed in our ears; and when we awoke in the morning, the first things we heard were the same familiar sounds, and the first thing we saw was the same dust-laden atmosphere. But there was one advantage about this weather; it kept the gad-flies and mosquitos at a distance, and cooled the air delightfully. Before the storms began the temperature had twice risen above 40°.0 C., or 104°.0 Fahr., in the shade; but after they began, it was seldom more than 25°.0 C., or 77°.0 Fahr., and at night it even dropped to 9°.3 C., or 48°.7 Fahr., and 11°.0 C., or 51°.8 Fahr.

The Cossacks spent a good deal of time hunting and fishing, but otherwise had plenty to do in getting ready our new river craft, each of which consisted of three long canoes. First a flooring of planks was laid across them; upon the planks a framework of spars was erected, their upper ends meeting on a horizontal bar arranged parallel to the middle canoe; then the spars were covered with felts, making an oblong floating tent. After sunset on the 18th of June, as soon as I had finished my last dinner on board the big ferry-boat, she was given over to destruction. The cabins were taken to pieces, all the nails being preserved, and the felts were beaten to cleanse them from

Building the Tents on the Triple Canoes.

the loads of sand and dust which they had accumulated. My boxes were flitted over into my new floating "palace," which, as it was calculated to carry 26 men, was amply sufficient for me, my baggage, and the four boatmen it required to navigate it. We stowed away a portion of our provisions under the plank flooring; the rest were carried in separate canoes, which were to follow in our wake. I had of course less room than before, but my new apartment was very comfortable. The Cossacks lived in a similarly constructed vessel.

Before starting I dismissed Kirgui Pavan, Aksakal, and the other boatmen who had come with them. In the evening we had a joyous banquet in their honour, sheep being slaughtered and rice-pudding cooked by the potful. In addition to their stipulated wages, I gave them a couple of canoes, and rations to last them all the way home; in return for which they, in accordance with the custom of their country, read prayers for my welfare. Next morning at sunrise when I stepped out of my laboratory, where I had been at work all night, there they all were in a row, reciting their morning prayers. Then they stepped into their canoes, said farewell, and set off for their distant abodes; whilst I went in to sleep.

It was like saying good-bye to a beloved home, to leave the old ferry-boat, which for all these months had rendered me

Ördek in the Reeds below Kum-chappgan.

such excellent service. I left her as a present to the inhabitants of Chegghelik-uy, who were enraptured with such a splendid means of transport, especially useful as it would be for carrying their live stock across the river, and for conveying over both caravans and merchandise. I learned afterwards, that by command of the amban, she was transferred to Arghan, where the main caravan road crossed the Tarim, and where there had previously been only a very dilapidated ferry-boat. Before we handed her over, Shagdur chopped my name in her side in large Roman letters, together with the date, 1899-1900.

It was midnight on the 19th of June when our new flotilla started from Chegghelik-uy, accompanied by a number of boatmen and begs. We succeeded in crossing the lakes, and threading their narrow waterways without difficulty, though it would have been quite impossible to force them with the big ferry-boat. Next day we stopped at the mouth of the Cherchen-daria to take measurements. Although the river-bed was steeply scarped, deep, and full of water, it did not contribute to the lakes of Kara-koshun more than 141 cubic feet in the second. Except for a single small group of ten-year-old poplars, the country was perfectly open.

Our last day's journey on the Tarim was a short one. The wind blew from due east at the rate of 24½ miles an hour,

The Tented Canoes on the Way to Abdall.

and was fresh and splendidly cool. Although the boatmen received considerable assistance from the current, they were also compelled to ply their paddles well to make headway. The river was so ruffled, that the waves forced themselves in between the canoes, and splashed into them, so that we were obliged to stop to prevent them from filling.

At Abdall we were met by our old friends, Numet Beg and Tokta Ahun. The latter had accompanied both the horse caravan and the camel caravan to the Chimen-tagh, and reported that all was well in our new headquarters. The men also took with them up into the mountains the four camels which we left at Abdall the spring before, as well as my little grey saddle-horse, and they were all now in good condition, and thoroughly rested. Whilst crossing the desert between Abdall and the foot of the mountains two horses had fallen, and all the dogs, including Taigun, had died of thirst. My men also drove up with them a flock of fifty sheep, to serve us for food during the summer. My courier with the letter for Chernoff had reached the camp long ago, and within a few days the Cossack ought to be at Abdall, with the small retinue which was to escort me to the mountains.

During our stay at Abdall we had good weather at first; that is to say, wind, which increased to as much as 42½ miles an hour.

A Sattma or Hut at Abdall.

This kept me, as it were, a prisoner in my own tent on board the canoes, where I spent all my time writing letters. It was a good opportunity to send them, together with my finished photographic plates, to Kashgar by the Cossacks. During a lull in the storm I made astronomical observations. One day whilst thus engaged, I was surprised to see a horseman riding towards the huts of Abdall, but soon recognised in him the Cossack Chernoff. He had started the moment he got my letter, and had performed the journey in a marvellously short time. During the last 35 hours he had not slept a wink, but was every bit as active and wide-awake as he always was. I invited him to go for a sail with me up the river in a brisk breeze, and whilst we were out, he told me all about our new headquarters, which were to be the base of operations for the remainder of the year. He was very sorry at having to leave us just now, when we were about to begin a fresh chapter in my travels, and, after having looked forward to spending the summer in the mountains, did not at all relish the prospect of the long hot ride to Kashgar. Two or three days later Turdu Bai and Mollah Shah arrived with four camels and ten horses. Although they had only travelled by night since quitting the mountains, the camels' necks and legs were bleeding from the bites of the gad-flies, though the other parts of their bodies were protected by felt trappings. We gave the animals several days' rest, more especially the horses which the Cossacks intended to ride to Kashgar.

The weather now underwent a disagreeable change; the wind dropped and was followed by oppressive heat. We had to take the greatest possible care of the camels. With the view of protecting them from the swarms of gad-flies which literally blackened the air, I ordered a *sattma* to be specially cleared for them, thickened its walls with reeds, and bade two of the men stay beside them and ward off the pertinacious insects. At night, however, we let the poor beasts out to graze. One morning they were missing, and Turdu Bai, who knew the ways of his protégés, at once suspected that they were trying to run away from this horrid place. But the men went after them and fetched them back; for they were indeed returning to their companions in the mountains, where it was cooler, and there were no gad-flies to torment them. After that we gave them a bath in the river every evening, which they liked immensely. In this hot weather my tent on the canoes became unbearable; on midsummer morning it was like a Turkish bath. Outside it the air was filled with a never-ceasing murmurous hum, like a distant waterfall, and the moment I unfastened the flap, the tent became filled with gad-flies. I took my dip and dressed as fast as I could. Then, having moved the tented canoes over to the right bank, I ran as through a shower of bullets to Tokta Ahun's hut, which had been got ready for me. It was 10° cooler than in the tent, for the sun was unable to penetrate the thick bundles of reeds which formed its roof. To it I transferred all my boxes and carpets, my table and my bed. The dogs thought it a fine idea, and came and joined me; and they had a royal time catching gad-flies.

Meanwhile the days passed, and it was time to be on the

move again. We were only waiting for the next storm to deliver us from the gad-flies, for so long as the weather remained hot, we were literally besieged by these bloodthirsty insects. Once, indeed, we did try to make a start; but it wouldn't do. The camels flung themselves down on the ground in despair, and threw off their loads. I could not travel by night, because I should be unable to see to map the country. So I put off the moment of departure from day to day. As long as we remained where we were, we were well off. We had everything we wanted, and the people of Abdall could not do enough to serve us. We also had plenty to occupy our time. The Cossacks shot wild duck, and paddled about in their canoes. We measured the Old Tarim for the last time; its volume was 1,543½ cubic feet in the second. Thus in two and a half months the river had shrunk to less than half its size, and during the course of the summer it would dwindle still more.

CHAPTER XXVII.

THE POETRY OF THE LOPLIKS.

DURING these days I amused myself by jotting down some of the best-known songs which had been sung for a hundred years or more by the sons and daughters of the Lop country ; besides which, I also preserved some new ditties which were sung by the fishermen of Kara-koshun. They are simple, very simple and unsophisticated, these songs of the Lopliks, and bear witness to a restricted imagination and a naïve conception of life. But they prove that even these humble fisher-folk, who lead such monotonous lives in the heart of Asia, remote from the great caravan-roads and isolated from other races, are not without their love-poetry, and that they also, like men and women everywhere else throughout the world, are not insensible to the sweet impulses of the tender passion. These songs also furnish an indication of the limitations of their world of thought and knowledge. But, as usual, they lose a good deal in the translation, and sound immensely better in the original Turki, with its rugged, rhymed, and rhythmical cadences, sung to a monotonous tune twanged on the strings of a *dutara*. For my own part, I always enjoyed them : the melancholy note which runs like a red thread through both words and music well expresses the feelings of one who is lonely, and so paints his hopes in sharper relief. Here, then, are a few examples of this simple and homely poesy.

The first is a song which was sung by Jahan Beg, the father of old Kunchekkan Beg, and consequently is more than a hundred years old. The singer is a woman whose love has been despised :

"The spirits have created thee more beautiful than other men. When thou didst return to thy home, I would, had I had wings, have

flown after thee like a wild goose, and have screamed as the wild goose screams. Thou knewest not, that I waited for thee the whole space of one year, and whilst that I was waiting loved not any other man. I have waited for thee long, thou my other half, and I beseech all who journey to thee to greet thee tenfold. Thou receivest all that pass thy way, and all that come to thee, and thou playest to them, and singest to them; but when thou playest and singest I, alas! am not there to hear thee. Thy feet must of a surety be bound; otherwise thou wouldest come to me. Thy name is known throughout Alti-shahr. Do thou as Yulduz Vang did: take thine ease, and let others work for thee. Since thou wilt not have me for thy wife, behold! I will come and be thy servant, and I will serve thee all I may. All my friends and companions counsel me to go to thee. For the space of a full year I have not smiled for thy sake, for thou hast spoken untruth. I have had no joy of thee. My tears have flowed like a river. It is God's will, that we should not be united. O how beautiful are thy eyes, and the long lashes, and the arched brows which shield them—none more beautiful!"

The following song, with its mingling of bitterness and pensiveness, dates from the same time. It is by a lover who has been rejected by his mistress:

"Since thou didst ride away, oh! how have I sighed after thy black eyebrows. If only I may, I will, ere this month run out, journey to thee, and play and sing with thee, and beat the drum Thou art still young, and thy father and mother have given thee to a good man. Oh! thou art crueller than the Devil, Mistress Sahib! Thou art hard-hearted! Thou cruel devil, thou understandest not my words! Thou art like the weather—now cloudy, now sunny. Thy father and thy mother loved thee well, and clothed thee in soft and delicate raiment. Let me—oh! let me know, when thy wedding shall be, that I may come and witness it! Thy mother were better than Imam Pattmah, and pure as nephrite. Imam Pattmah loveth thee. Whenas we all were young, we played together and were friends. Now thou swayest to and fro like the feathered plume of the *okkar* bird, and thy fame hath flown as on wings to Chimen. When the autumn cometh, and we journey to the Tarim, then shall our eyes meet. Fatherless and motherless art thou now; but we all shall give thee more than father or mother can give. When thou puttest on thy attire, lo! beautiful art thou as the glow-worm!"

Kunchekkan Beg's father-in-law used to sing the next song. It must consequently be eighty years old, although it is very likely that it was by no means new in his day. The singer is a lover, who has not yet abandoned all hope:

"Sorely it grieveth me, that I took not my little sweetheart; I shiver like an otter that is frozen. O what a lovely *khalat* (dress) is thine; yet was I not strong enough to gain the same. And though I do not win thee to my wife, yet I shall go past thy dwelling and see thee. Very lovely is thy black hair! Had I won thee, thy lovely hair would have rested on my breast; but another won thee from

Eight Boys Sitting on a Canoe, at Chegghelik-uy.

me, and gave thee not to me. Had I known thou hadst the ring on thy finger, I would never have desired to know thee; but I will come in the tenth month. When I come in the tenth month, I will ask how it is with thee, thou bewitching angel, thou that remainedst alone in thy empty dwelling. Thy breast is as white as the flame of a lamp! When thou openest thy gown, lo! one beholdeth thy snow-white breast! The nails of thy fingers are like the day. Very warmly do I love thee, O thou that art like a star which wandereth in the track of the moon. When I prayed thee to abide awhile, then didst thou hasten away on thy swift-footed horse. Now that I am become a beggar by the roadside, I cannot have thee, O thou loveliest amongst women; verily, thou art lovelier than the sun! O Assan! go thou to her, and tell her the words I have said: I will beseech the begs to give thee to me. When I beheld thy footprints beside the lake, I wept big tears, so that the sand on the lake-bottom was dimpled with them. Thou art like a princess: thou drinkest thy tea from vessels of silver. I crossed over to Yachi * to see thee, yet found naught but the empty dishes of thy feast. Since thou hast been denied to me, I have lived as one that is dead in the world. But now will I pray God, that I may live yet a year or two; then shall I mayhap win thee at the last. I have sent away my former wife. May God bid thee come to me. Thou walkest as light as the falcon flies; but thy husband hath not abandoned thee, and I am waiting without."

Here is a song from Arghan, about ten years old, and sung by a man who had got himself into a fix:

"As Tayir Khan and Suyah Khan both died in one night, so, in like manner, have we two not won one the other. Tayir Khan died in his mistress's village, before that he married her. Kara Bater smote him three times with the sword, and now cometh he never more. Though not sorely smitten, yet must his sins have been many, seeing that he died. Even as no man avenged Tayir Khan's death, so no man careth aught, that I have not won thee. Yet now that I have known thee, doubtless there will come one and slay me too. Since then I have taken me another wife, and they may do with thee whatsoever pleaseth them. Yet now do I grieve me, that I bade not the beg and Ahun, give thee to me instead. And yet methinketh, if God suffereth me not to die, no man shall ever avail to kill me. Truly it had been better to contend against all the village, and be slain, than have been saddled with her I now have to wife."

The next song is the song of Agacha Khan, a girl of Kumchappgan, who comforted herself thus:

"Hither hath my beloved come, and all things are fresh and green. It is time thou sowedst thy wheat, thou who now diggest the ground with thy spade. Did I but know the wild-duck's speech, I would ask him how thou farest. Thou camest hither, yet didst thou not look in upon me. Thou journeyedst home again, yet did Agacha Khan not journey with thee. She mounted into the saddle, and rode away with another husband."

* A village near the former lake of Kara-koshun.

Next comes a love-song of a hopeless swain, composed some years ago in Tuzun-chappgan :

" Thou art like the white spirit. I would I might sleep on thy bosom. When thou dancest to the music of an evening, how beautifully thy ribbons flutter around thee. I sit in my home, thou sittest in thine ; but I know that thou thinkest of me. Send me the falcon thou bearest on thy hand. When I lay me down to sleep, I may not sleep, so sorely do I think upon thee. Thy parents will not give thee to me ; but they will give thee to a beg from Turfan. Men say, thy parents will not give thee to me, because they are not pleased with me. So sorely do I long for thee, that my head spinneth round ; it is as though the cloud whistleth about me. Thou hast a great man for thy husband, but I am deserted and lonely. Another hath wedded thee ; thou art not mine. Thy mother hath bread and seed-corn in plenty ; her store cometh never to an end. When thy mother baketh bread in the morning, lo ! the pot boileth ready for the noontide meal. Long, long is it since that I saw thee ! "

It is the same plaint which echoes through all these poetical effusions—the old, old story, which is always perennially fresh under whatsoever clime you meet with it. But the songs which have nothing to do with the tender passion are also of a melancholy cast. Here is the way a youth sang to his brother in the days of old Numet Beg (who was born about 1700). Both youths belonged to Kara-koshun, but had gone to Abdall :

" Return thou home, and see how things fare there. I will abide here and catch the fish. Should the fish be few, then will I, too, return home and fish there. I long to return home ; so greatly do I long that I cannot eat. All the people here, both good and evil, quarrel with me, so that I cannot eat. I came hither to see whether it was a good place ; but my wife and my little ones abode at Yachi. I will launch my canoe at daybreak, then shall I win me home ere the night cometh. Now will I return. 'Twas foolish of me to bring skins and gear which I needed not. Even though these Abdall folk should be minded to kill me, yet will I not turn back, but will go home. Like the seven stars in the sky, like the arkhari in the mountains, I went forth from my home, and now I weep. Yea, now will I return. Farewell, my only friend in this place. After that I have left thee, and gone away home, then shall we be as though a high mountain parted us."

A hundred years ago an old blind man in Tuzun-chappgan

Natives of Abdall. The Second from the Right is Tokta A… …ow.

gave utterance to his pain in the following song, which is still sung in the country of Lop:

"I, miserable that I am, have been stricken with blindness by God. Oh, how unhappy am I! Now see I no longer either the hut of reeds or the fields of the green kamish around it. 'Tis mine to sit lonesome at home in my sattma. Oh, how pitiable am I! Now see I not my friends; my bones are become soft as the grass. Since that I am blind, it is as though my whole body were eaten up with pain. Hard hath God punished me, in that He suffereth me not to see, neither the hut of reeds nor the fields of green kamish around it. Wherefore, O God, didst Thou suffer me to be born, since Thou hast now deprived me of the light of mine eyes? Since that I am blind, my heart is full of sorrow and desire. May God visit no other poor mortal with blindness! Since that I see not, I cannot walk, but grope my way with my hands. My children cry to me, 'What doest thou? Thou catchest not fish, thou givest us naught to eat.' Better were it God doomed me to die, than suffer me to be tormented thus in this world. Whenas I saw, I gained me money; but now I may not see it, and know it not, save whenas I smell upon it. Hard hath God punished me, in that He hath made me so wretched. Do I speak with my wife, straightway she answereth me with hard words. Whenas I saw, I had well dressed meats to eat; now she grudgeth me tea. Did I but see, I would fare forth upon the lake as heretofore, and put down my nets. Were I now to fare forth, verily I should not find the way, but should drift and be lost. Whenas I was a child, and sinned in some small thing, surely, then, my father and my mother must have cursed me, and wished I might be stricken with blindness. In the days that are past I was wont to put down my nets; but what skill hath a man that is blind in the catching of fish? Now I may not take fish for my dear ones to eat, and they are pinched with hunger. I trusted that thou, my son, shouldest help me in my old age, and feed me, but now hast thou thrust me from thee."

Formerly these people lived almost entirely upon fish. Hence it is easy to understand that they should sing about fishing and its small misadventures. I give one specimen of this artless "lake poetry," a description of an event which happened at Kara-koshun:

"I was out on the lake. Down came the storm. My canoe capsized. And here I lie, and my father and my mother know it not. The fish and the bread that were to feed me have gone to feed the maw of the lake. When my canoe overturned, lo! I lost all things, save only my cooking-pot, thanks be to God! What hard words spake I to one that is older than myself, or what offence have I done, that I am punished thus? My friend, that was out on the lake with me, behold! he hath lost nothing. It must be that God loveth him. Thirty fish had I in one parcel, and a dozen in another; yet went they all to the bottom. But let me now arise and hasten, then shall I reach home ere that the supper is done. I searched with my eyes the bundles of rushes that floated upon the lake, and then hastened I home. But whenas I came there, my parents spake reproachfully to me, saying, 'What hast thou done with thy fish?' And I answered them, 'Since ye set greater store by the fish than by my life which is saved, ye would do well to slay me.' Come, my friend, let us draw the boat up on land, that she may be dry."

It may not be without interest to see how the people who composed and sang these songs wrote their letters; fortunately I have preserved a few of them. In spite of their excessively servile spirit, they breathe much goodwill and a feeling of courtesy, and between the lines it is easy to perceive the great consideration with which our caravan was everywhere received. During the time I remained in the Lop country, I received a host of letters, so that I required to have a native amanuensis always at my elbow to answer them. My secretary read each letter aloud to me, and in a few words I indicated what was to be the nature of his reply. It is significant of the high respect with which I was regarded, though at the same time comical, that all these letters began with the formula "To the great king, the gracious lord, God's blessing!" The Cossacks were accustomed to call me, "Your Excellency!" and I thought that would have been a lofty enough title to satisfy anybody. But no, the begs of the Lop country thought that far too colourless; nothing less than *Ullug Padi-shahim*, or "Your Majesty," would suffice for them. Yet for some two hundred days I did feel almost as if I were the king of Lop-nor.

Whilst in Abdall I received the following letter from old Naser Beg, of Tikkenlik:

"We, your most unworthy subjects, Naser Beg, my son-in-law, and all, great and small, to our great Padishah! we wish that you, may God be gracious to you! may reach Chimen in peace and safety; and after you have arrived there, we should desire greatly to hasten and serve you, but that the amban is here, so that I cannot demand leave of absence. And yet it were very desirable that I came to see you, and bowed down before you. If you would let me know by a line from Chimen that you have arrived there in peace and safety, I should be very grateful. As a token that I still live, I send you ten ells of white linen. Be good and forget me not."

Mirab Beg, of Ullug-köll, wrote thus:

"Your humble slave and servant! Mirab Beg of Ullug-köll, and his son, Baker Shang-ya Seidullah Imam, Mahmet Baki Mazin, Sati Ahun, Allah Kullu, all, great and small, inhabitants of Ullug-köll, inquire by this letter after Tura's (the Lord's) health. We desired greatly to accompany you and serve you, but could not, since we feared the amban. God alone knows if we shall ever see you again. We hope we shall. When we know that you have happily come to the mountains, we shall, in truth, thank God, and we shall pray that you may come back hither, so that we may meet again."

This is how the amban of Charkhlik writes:

"To the gracious lord He-dani (*i.e.*, Hedin), who is well-affected to all, from Jan Daloi of Charkhlik. I pray that I may write and express my regret that the first time we met in Tikkenlik, we had no opportunity to show hospitality the one to the other. It was late when we met; you went your way and I went mine, but we shall never forget one another. God grant that we may meet again under happy circumstances. We ought to come nearer to one another, and know one another better, and become the best of friends. May we think but good of one another. Wheresoever you may happen to be, pray write me a letter and appoint a meeting with me. We beg to inform you that we have read the letter from Khalmet Aksakal, and are very grateful that you have asked us to have an eye upon the thieves and hold them fast. We have found the goods that were lost in the possession of the thieves, and have brought the matter to an end, in that it has been dealt with and settled according to the law. If there be aught else you desire, be so kind as to let me know it. Unfortunately, I could not come and meet you, but have been informed that you passed this way. Herewith I send you 100 *jings* (150 lbs. avoir.) of rice and two bottles of brandy, and pray you, forget me not."

According to the rules of etiquette, he had been unable to visit me, because I gave no sign of calling upon him. His brandy I sent back by the messenger which brought it. All spirits were strictly prohibited in my caravan. As a rule, the politeness of the Chinese, whether oral or written, does not mean much ; but so far as Jan Daloi was concerned, I had no ground for complaint. A year later he was removed by the Gove nor-General of Urumchi. This was said in Charkhlik to be because he had shown a too great willingness to serve a *yang-kwetsa*, or "foreign devil." Of the Boxer movement in China, with its murderous hatred of strangers, we heard not the slightest rumour in the middle of Asia.

V.

In Northern Tibet.

Mountains, Lakes, and Quagmires at High Altitudes.

CHAPTER XXVIII,

OVER THE ASTYN-TAGH.

But at last we grew tired of waiting for the storm which never came. I spent most of my time reading Selma Lagerlöf's and Heidenstam's* books, and studying Buddhist mythology. The gad-flies, however, did not relax their siege, and the wind failed to come and give us an opportunity to break through their investment. At last I lost all patience, and determined to start, let the cost be what it might, on the evening of the 30th June. Sending the caravan by land, by the seven hours' route round the marsh, I directed them to meet me at Yoll-arelish, the point where the road branched, one portion of it going on to Sa-chow, the other bending away to the mountains of Tibet. Meanwhile, I proposed crossing by canoe the same lakes which I had already traversed in April, and at Yoll-arelish, which I had already mapped on a previous expedition, I intended to resume my cartographical work.

The 30th June was a busy day, what with packing up, settling accounts, and getting the two Cossacks off to Kashgar. Besides commissioning the latter to carry my letters to Europe, I gave each of them two yambas (£16), and promised to recommend them warmly to their highest commanding officer, the Czar. They also carried a letter to Jan Daloi, amban of Charkhlik, asking him to send at once 3,000 *jings* (30 ass-loads, or about two tons) of maize to my new headquarters.

We began to load up at five p.m. The moment the camels emerged into the open air, they were surrounded by a swarm of buzzing gad-flies. However, they bore the infliction patiently; and as fast as each animal was loaded up, four men were told off to protect him with big kamish brooms. When all was ready,

* Two popular and distinguished Swedish novelists; the latter has also won great fame as a poet.

Turdu Bai mounted his horse, and putting himself at the head of the cavalcade led off at a good round pace.

Then it was the horses' turn; but they made a tremendous pother, kicking and even flinging themselves on the ground, so that we had to lash their loads with extra ropes to keep them on. At last, however, they too set off in the wake of the camels, conducted by Mollah Shah, Kutchuk, and Tokta Ahun, the son of Kunchekkan Beg.

The big and comfortable canoe which was to carry me to the rendezvous was already provisioned and equipped with felts, pipe, matches, etc., and lamps; and it only remained to say good-bye to my faithful Cossacks. I thanked them warmly for their services, and after a hearty shake of the hand saw them mount their black horses and set off along the road to Charkhlik, which town they hoped to reach next morning. They carried with them letters of recommendation to the ambans, begs, and aksakals all along the road, and intended to take the mountain route through Kopa and Sourghak, and after that travel by night to Kashgar *viâ* Khotan and Yarkand.

When I started with my boatmen it was pitch dark; but the current helped us, and we went down the river at a smart pace, leaving its dark banks rapidly behind us. At Kum-chappgan I only stayed to change my canoemen. When we started again, the moon had disappeared; but the night was clear and the stars glittered like diamonds above the wandering lakes. A faint, but refreshing, breeze flickered through the reeds, and happily, on that my last night on the waters of the Tarim, the gnats were not troublesome.

At eleven o'clock p.m. we left Tuzun-chappgan, guided by a man in a small canoe. It was perfectly wonderful the way he steered his course in the darkness through that labyrinth of high, dense reeds, across the lagoons and lakes, and through the chappgans and narrow, confined waterways. The other canoemen paddled on without a moment's hesitation and without once stopping, as though their canoes were running on invisible metal tracks, off which it was impossible for them to get astray. They did not talk, they only paddled—paddled unceasingly, and in good time together. But the breezes of the summer night failed to penetrate into those dense reedy wildernesses, and it was oppressively warm, close, and stuffy; and the miasmatic vapours rose from the tepid waters of the marsh. At intervals I slumbered, and on towards morning the men began to sing, to keep themselves awake. The lake of Sateh-köll was a good deal shallower than it had been in April, so that the men were obliged to get out and draw the canoes after them. Soon after that we were forced to abandon the big canoe altogether, and take to the smaller one. Yet even that soon ceased to float, and we had to wade ashore through the mud.

Then followed two or three hours of waiting in the silence of the dark, dreary waste. At length, however, we heard shouts in the distance; then they came nearer, and lighting our lamps we went to meet them. It was Shagdur and Tokta Ahun, with the horse caravan. They had travelled faster than the camels, so that we had to wait again for them. I thought I could not employ the time to better advantage than by having breakfast; but the Lop-men had to row a long way out into the lake to get a can of fresh water, as well as a few bundles of kamish to boil it with, before even that simple meal could be prepared, for the shore was absolutely barren.

The camels came up just as day was breaking. They had gone astray in the darkness, and, misled by an ass-track, had turned off too soon. They continued without stopping, and as soon as breakfast was finished the rest of us got to horse and followed them.

The country was a mere barren waste. On the north side of the marsh the sand-dunes gave at least some relief to the desert, and the dead forest witnessed to the existence of life at a former period. But here there was nothing: the ground was as level as a pavement, and consisted of hard, rough, saliferous clay, which had once been under water. The only break in the monotony was the winding track we followed.

We struck away from the shore at an acute angle; and when the sun rose, and poured a flood of light and warmth across the desert, we could just discern the last lakes of the Tarim system like a dark line hovering above the horizon behind us. The sun rose with unusual splendour. Its beams broke amongst the light and delicate clouds which hung like a veil before its face; so that their edges, lit up from behind, glowed like molten gold, while the middle parts were stained various shades of violet. The air was clear and still, and the sky a pure pearly, spotless blue.

But an even finer spectacle was presented by the panorama of the mountains which, in the oblique, almost horizontal, light, stood out in sharp and distinct relief. Their colouring varied from light blue to violet, shading off through silvery tints. The transitions were not at all harsh, being tempered by the distance, so that they formed a harmonious and enchanting background to the arid desolation at their feet, just as the sunrise is all the more beautiful when it follows a gloomy and stifling night.

But the sun was not without its shadows. No sooner did it show above the eastern edge of the desert than the air became filled with myriads of gad-flies, which, in clustering clouds, followed horse and rider as they moved. Long before noon the heat was oppressive, and we yearned for night to come to free us from our tormentors.

Just on the edge of the desert, where the outer skirts of the mountains began their slow ascent, we halted at the little oasis of Dunglik, or the Hills. Its altitude was 3,415 feet above the sea, and as Abdall lay at 2,750 feet, we had consequently climbed 665 feet whilst crossing the desert. The horses were put inside a shelter which had recently been built, but the camels were turned out to graze on the thin sparse steppe. We were all tired after our night march. As for myself, I dropped asleep under the first tamarisk I came to, and lay there until the sun burnt my head; after which I went inside the tent, and sat and worked, scantily attired. There was a well, 10¾ feet deep with brackish water, which, however, did not prevent the animals from drinking it. For our own use we had brought water with us from the lake, and sinking it into the well, which had a temperature of 14°.3 C., or 57°.7 Fahr., we kept it nice and cool, and every now and then I gave myself a douche from a pail. The temperature of the air rose to 40°.1 C., or 104.2° Fahr. in the shade.

I was awakened at three o'clock on the following morning, lamps and candles were lighted, and my breakfast of tea, eggs, and bread was served. We packed up and loaded the animals, and by the time that was done it was dawning in the east. When we started at 4.30 a.m. it was broad daylight, and the gad-flies had begun their strenuous day's work. They buzzed about us in myriads, and followed us a mile or so on our road, literally red with frenzy as the rising sun shone through their blood-swollen bodies. I myself killed two or three hundred which had got entangled in the camels' naked skin. Crack! went a whip, and crack! went the suctorian as his inflated body burst. But we soon got too far away from the vegetation, and they durst no longer follow us, so that for the rest of the day we had peace from them.

We were now marching across the open, gravelly *sai*, which sloped gently up towards the mountains. It was a perfectly barren and desolate region, without a single blade of grass, without an insect or any other sign of life, nothing but gravel and sand, thinly scattered over a soil as hard as asphalt. On the left was the narrow belt of vegetation which marked the oasis of Dunglik; while on the right were the mountains, gradually unfolding themselves, as their reddish-yellow outlines became shedded out into separate chains and valleys. I took the bearings of every conspicuous peak from several different points, and noted them all down on my map. Behind us on the distant horizon was the faint, dark line of the Tarim lakes, and beyond them a low diffused haze suggested the sandy desert of the Lop country.

At irregular intervals were a number of small stone pyramids, intended to mark the road during the continuance of the storms. Asiatics consider it their duty to show a certain amount of gratitude towards their roads and tracks, and they do it by adding one or more stones to these pyramids as they pass them. Without them, they could not find their way to the springs and grazing-grounds; and when a traveller is fortunate enough to escape the storms himself, he is grateful enough to think of those who may travel that same road under less favourable conditions, and so adds his contribution to help make the road plainer.

The heat of the day began to make itself apparent in warm exhalations and warm breezes. I knew it was a long way to the first spring of Tattlik-bulak, for at every point where I had previously crossed it, this gravelly slope at the northern foot of the Kwen-lun was excessively broad. But my hope, that we should soon get amongst the mountains, was doomed to disappointment, for when we reached two huge cairns, one on each side of the trail, Tokta Ahun gave me the very comforting intelligence that we were only half-way, and yet we had been tramping steadily on at the usual caravan pace for fully seven hours.

The little pups, Malenki and Malchik, which were only five months old, had tired very soon after we started, and were then stowed away in a basket on the back of one of the camels. When the sun began to burn, we covered them with a felt, and after that heard nothing more of them until we reached camp, when they jumped out of their hiding place as brisk and lively as possible, though a little stiff. Mashka and Yolldash were more sensitive to the heat, and when we began the second half of our day's march, they appeared thoroughly exhausted. Although we gave them water two or three times, they kept loitering behind and had to be fetched. Finally, we put them on the back of a camel. Yet they did not relish that method of travel, but struggled down as soon as the camel began to walk. Thus they dropped behind again, and Shagdur rode back to fetch them, taking some water with him. After a pretty long absence he came back with Yolldash, and reported disconsolately that Mashka was dead. When he found the dogs, they were both lying at the bottom of a dry ravine in the shelter of a shady terrace. He gave the whole of the water he had with him to Mashka, who gulped it down greedily. Then he put a cord round Yolldash and led him, while he took Maskha on the saddle in front of him. But before he had gone far, the dog turned very strange, bit the horse in the neck, and let her head fall hopelessly. Thus died the best of our dogs, and had to be left by the wayside. But we had not one drop of water, and I feared the worst for Yolldash. After several unsuccessful attempts, I managed to lash him fast on the top of a camel's load, where he lay rocking and jolting half dead with "sea-sickness."

But the rest of the animals and all the men bore the journey well. It was worth while making an extra push to escape from the killing heat in the lowlands. Getting tired of riding, I walked for several hours. The country was still the same, and the ascent imperceptible, while all day long we had the same peaks constantly on our right. But towards evening the ground became more broken, and we got amongst low hills of gravel-and-shingle, sand, and clay. Further on we could see the bare rock, a light green schist and granite, greatly weathered and brittle. Our path lay up a dry and steeply scarped glen, which was entered by numerous natural water-courses from both sides, and by numerous torrents, which, although now perfectly dry, had cut deeply down through the sides of the glen. The path wound away to the east across an infinite number of ridges, hills and gulleys.

Through the upper part of a narrow gap in the side of the glen we caught a glimpse of the brook, oasis, and refuge of Hunglugu, an especially welcome sight after such a day as we had had. The first thing we did when we reached the spot was to send the dogs off to get water. Their delight knew no bounds; they drank, they coughed, they rolled in the grass, they barked with delight, and then drank and drank again.

There was an abundance of vegetation, chiefly noble tamarisks, which attained the dimensions of trees, though there were also grass and kamish, and a great variety of herbs; while in an expansion of the glen stood a group of rugged old poplars. But we did not stop there. We pushed on farther up, the brook growing bigger and clinging to the mountain-wall which shut in the glen on the right. We found the horse caravan, which had been a long way ahead all day, encamped at Tattlik-bulak,

The Dogs Malenki and Malchik.

in a grove of magnificent tamarisks, besides a little caravan of seven asses and seven sheep, which Numet Beg had sent on from Abdall the day before, with a store of provisions for our use.

I know nothing more delightful, after a 14½ hours' march through a burning desert, than to encamp in a beautiful oasis like this, and here we had one of the most comfortable camps I have ever had anywhere. My little Mongolian yurt was put up, for the first time, on the outer margin of the tamarisk grove, and it was so neat and cosy and inviting, with its bed, and carpet, and boxes, that I did not really miss the old ferry-boat and its snug cabin. Shagdur, Turdu Bai, and Mollah Shah erected the white tent under the tamarisks, while the other men encamped in the midst of a bower-like thicket. At nine o'clock the temperature of the air was 20°.0 C. or 68°.0 Fahr. and of the water 12°.8 C. or 55°.0 Fahr., so that my usual wash-down was very refreshing after all the heat of the march. We were now at an altitude of 6,408 feet, or 3,658 feet above Abdall.

When I gave orders that we were to rest the 3rd July at Tattlik-bulak, or the Sweet Spring, the rejoicing was general. We no longer had occasion to complain of the heat; for, although the sun was hot enough at midday, it was tempered by a south-west breeze. This, however, came, not as the steady, continuous

Tamarisks at Tattlik-bulak.

blow of the lowlands, but in gusts, which were sometimes so violent that they threatened to bowl over my yurt, yet sometimes again so gentle that they died away into a dead calm. The left side of the glen was bounded by a perpendicular wall of gravel-and-shingle, and it was out of its crannies that the spring gushed; the water was quite fresh, as clear as crystal, and had a temperature of 10°.0 C., or 50°.0 Fahr. The rivulet it gave origin to ran straight into the glen brook, which was somewhat discoloured by dust and mud. The glen itself was from 50 to 200 yards wide, and after hard and long-continued downpours of rain appeared to have been filled from side to side. On the top of the wall above the spring was a cairn of stones, surmounted by two or three staves, on one of which I read "P. Splingaert, 1894," and "C. E. Bonin, 1899;" the former was the Belgian mandarin known as Ling Darin.*

The vegetation was luxuriant, although it consisted of but few species. The fauna embraced a few small birds, besides ants, spiders, flies, ticks, and beetles. We also saw two or three gad-flies; but they had no doubt been brought up by our own camels. Had we not lost Mashka, who was a general favourite with everybody, we should have been perfectly in clover. When we started again I had the canvas skiff sewn up in a felt, to protect it against chafing, and the yurt was carried

The Frame-work of my Yurt.

by one of the horses, because they travelled faster than the camels. Thus, from this time onwards, I always found my "house" ready for me when I reached camp in the evening.

The route led up the glen, beside the brook, between cliffs of black slate, which were often connected with the bottom of the valley by sheets of gravel-and-shingle. As we advanced, the vegetation gradually died away. The tamarisks were just in flower, and the pure violet tints of their clusters of blossoms imparted a touch of life to the otherwise monotonous brownish grey of the mountain landscape. We crossed the little

* See *Through Asia*, Vol. II., p. 920.

stream repeatedly; it was delicious to have it beside us when the day grew warm. In winter the entire glen becomes choked with ice, and travellers then avoid this route for fear their animals should fall and break their legs. In fact, we did observe one camel, which had belonged to a caravan of Mongol pilgrims, lying by the side of the brook.

The sky was cloudy, and we should have had a pleasant march had we not been pursued by swarms of mosquitos, which showed an unhappy predilection for our ears and nostrils as their chosen field of operations. Their incessant tickling and stinging made the skin sensitive, and irritated it until it itched intolerably.

That evening, when we reached the little pasture ground of Bash-kurgan, or the Fortress at the Head of the Glen, my portative hotel stood ready erected and furnished by the side of the track. But there were several things to be done before I could step inside and enjoy a much-needed rest. First, I unpacked my meteorological instruments; then I labelled and put away the geological specimens which I had collected during the day; then I drew my maps, and wrote my notes and observations. By this dinner was ready. Then at nine o'clock came the reading of the meteorological instruments and the boiling-point thermometer, and the winding up and comparison of the chronometers; after which I went out and played with my dogs, and fed them. My day's work was seldom over before eleven o'clock at night. When it was, I usually lay and read for half an hour, and then went to sleep, and the fresh, strong, healthy mountain air made me sleep the sleep of the just. At nine p.m. the thermometer stood at 12°.1 C. or 53°.8 Fahr. What a difference two days' journey made!

During the night the temperature dropped to 0°.1 C., or 32°.2 Fahr., and next morning we unpacked our warm winter wraps.

I had made up my mind I would not travel up to our new headquarters at too rapid a rate, and so we sacrificed another day to rest at Bash-kurgan. The place was named from the ruins of a small Chinese fort, crowning an isolated hill, and built at the confluence of three other glens with the long ravine of Tattlik-bulak.

As this trench or ravine pierced the lower range of the Astyn-tagh, or Astun-tagh, we were already on the other side of it when we reached Bash-kurgan. The next day took us up towards the main crest of the same system ; but we were unable to get over it in one march, and stopped for the night at Bash-yoll, a little grazing-ground with a splendid spring (temperature, 5°.8 C., or 42°.5 Fahr.), beside the ruins of a Chinese fort.

On the 8th of July we had a long and desolate piece of road before us, and consequently carried a supply of water. On both sides our path was overhung by steep, denticulated, irregular masses of rock ; but gradually it widened out, and eventually led up to an easy, flat-topped pass, which, strange to say, bore no other name than simply Davan (the Pass). Hitherto the road had run east ; now it turned towards the south, although a defile did lead on to the east between cliff-like rocks. There we saw two wild camels, but they were in full flight. This made the third region in the centre of Asia where I had observed these animals ; so that, with the information I gathered subsequently, I am now in a position to trace out a map of their distribution.

There was a slight dew on the summit of the pass ; but when we descended into the broad, flat latitudinal, or parallel, valley which separates the Astyn-tagh from the Akato-tagh, and were crossing it, it began to rain merrily, and the thunder rumbled amongst the mountains. The valley was a perfect desert, without a single sign of life. After a ride of 13 hours we reached a nameless steppe, where there was neither water nor grazing, though the teresken shrubs did afford a supply of firewood.

CHAPTER XXIX.

THE START FOR TIBET.

On the morning of the 9th July the sky was perfectly clear; during the previous night the temperature had fallen to 0°.7 C. or 33°.3 Fahr. Our order of march was as follows. The asses and the sheep started first. Then followed Mollah Shah and Kutchuk with the horses, which always arrived at the next camping-ground a long way in advance of the rest of the caravan. After them came Turdu Bai and Mollah with the camels; while I, Shagdur, and Tokta Ahun brought up the rear. The last-named, who was well acquainted with all that region, acted as my cicerone. Shagdur held my horse when I took the compass-bearings of the mountain-peaks, or collected geological specimens, though I left him to pack them up in newspaper. All this generally made us an hour or two behind the others in reaching camp.

To the south-west lay a magnificent mountain mass crowned with perpetual snow, called Illveh-chimen, and on this side of it were two small salt lakes, Uzun-shor and Kalla-köll. At the foot of the Akato-tagh we rested for an hour beside a small spring and pool, called simply Bulak, the water of which was beautifully fresh (12°.0 C. or 53°.6 Fahr.), and our thirsty beasts, which had had no water the day before, were allowed to drink their fill. There was also luxuriant grass around the spring, though its extent was limited. During our short halt the weather suddenly changed. The sky clouded over, and it began to rain heavily. It was evident we had already entered the zone of the characteristic Tibetan weather, in which sunshine, rain, and wind alternate incessantly at intervals of only a few short minutes.

Leaving the spring, we followed a dry ravine towards the south-west, and were met by a violent storm from that direction. It was not rain, but wind, which made the dust and sand spin, and drove them with cutting force into our faces, till the skin felt quite sore. The storm advanced upon us like a compact, yellowish-grey wall of spinning whirlwinds, and enveloped us in an impenetrable haze, which completely blotted out every feature of the country. We could see nothing except the path in front of us. It was as much as I could do to sit in my saddle, and when I tried to jot down my notes, it was like tearing the paper to pieces. But after two hours the hurricane stopped quite as suddenly as it began. It was as if we had waded through a river of rushing wind. And no sooner was the storm past than the air cleared at once, and became as pure and transparent as it was before. A very different storm from the storms in the lowlands! But we soon had convincing proof that these violent mountain hurricanes really do carry drift-sand with them; for on the top of the double easy pass of the Akato-tagh we found a number of sand-dunes in miniature, which had been formed there by the south-west wind.

The southern flank of the Akato-tagh, which we crossed to the south-east, was a repetition, in point of orographical relief, of the northern flank of the Astyn-tagh. The *sai*, or hard gravelly slope, descended gradually to a broad valley, which ran from west to east, and on the south was fenced in by another mountain-range, the Chimen-tagh. This gravelly formation was succeeded by *kakir*, or a horizontal deposit of argillaceous mud laid down in water after rain. There we found the skeletons of the two horses belonging to Cherdon and Faisullah's caravan, which had died on the way up. At length we caught sight of the yurt standing on the shore of a small lake, which we had seen in the far-off distance from the *sai* above. It was known simply as *köll*, was about one-third of a mile in diameter, and surrounded by grass.

Strange to say, the gnats and gad-flies again honoured us with their company even at this altitude; the former even kept with us until after we left the main camp in the Chimen-tagh. The moment the wind dropped, out they came in swarms. The horses and dogs suffered the most; the camels' skin was too thick for their delicate probosces to penetrate. The gnats haunt the mountains for about two and a half months in the summer. You would think it impossible for their larvæ to survive the bitter cold which prevails in those altitudes in the winter; but they do.

On the 10th of July we still continued towards the south-east, striking obliquely across the valley, over several deep gullies, which, when in flood, helped to swell the large stream that, farther east, emptied itself into Ghaz-nor (or Gaz-nor) on the frontier of the country of the Tsaidam Mongols. We halted beside some springs, surrounded by fresh grass, on the edge of a gully called Temirlik. To take my astronomical observations next day was a veritable baptism of fire, because of the gnats. They used maliciously to wait until I had both hands engaged with the screws of the instrument, and then opened fire.

At a subsequent stage of my travels, Temirlik (9,715 feet above the sea) became a very important centre. Even now several visitors came to our camp. Simultaneously with us there arrived four gold-hunters from the mines of Bokalik, who had been two or three months in the mountains hunting for gold, but had discovered nothing worth speaking about, and were now returning discontented to their homes in Khotan. Here, also, we were overtaken by the maize caravan, which I had ordered from Charkhlik, led by five men, who brought a polite letter from the amban. And, last of all, came a couple of messengers from my principal camp, from which we were still two days' journey distant, who reported that all was well. One of these messengers was Khodai Värdi, whose name means "the God-given," but who, as a matter of fact, was a disagreeable individual from Yanghi-köll, who subsequently tried to play me an unfortunate practical joke. The other was an Afghan named Aldat, from Cherchen. He had spent the winter in the mountains shooting yaks, the skins of which he sold in Keriya. He was a fine, handsome young fellow, who lived the life of a real Nimrod amongst these wild mountains. Coming up in the autumn with a good stock of ammunition, his musket, and his furs, he used to spend the whole winter hunting, carrying neither tent nor provisions, but living on the flesh of the yaks he shot, and drinking of the springs which are fed by the everlasting snows.

In the summer his brothers used to come up with a train of asses, collect his stock of yak skins, cut out the serviceable parts, and carry them down to Cherchen. He had been engaged by Islam Bai because of his knowledge of those mountainous regions right away to the foot of the Arka-tagh, though he had never been south of that range. I took a great fancy to Aldat, and proposed he should accompany us on our first expedition

The Headquarters Camp at Mandarlik—Looking Down the Glen.

into Tibet, and he closed with the proposal without hesitation. His manner of life struck me as being remarkably strange, and yet, at the same time, as very fascinating. I asked him what he did when he had no luck, and failed to kill any game, and so got nothing to eat. "I go hungry till I do find a yak," said he. Where did he sleep? In crevices and ravines, sometimes in caves. Was he not afraid of wolves? No, he carried tinder and flint with him, and always made a fire in the evening to cook his yak steak, and trusted to his musket. Did he never lose his way? Oh, no, he couldn't lose his way! He knew every pass, and had hunted every valley times without number. As for being alone, he thought nothing at all of that. There was nobody he cared anything about, except his old father and his brothers.

What a restless, wandering spirit! I can hardly conceive a more dreary country to be alone in than Northern Tibet. The desert could not be worse. One might get through the days—but the nights! When the cold freezes you to the marrow, and the dark mountain ranges shut you in and menace you with all sorts of imaginable evils! Aldat's life was, of a truth, "dangerous, poor, and great," and even now, when he has long been dead, I cannot understand how he stood it; he remains a mystery to me down to this very hour. I was surrounded by everything I needed—servants, a bodyguard of Cossacks, night-watchmen and watch-dogs—and yet, when the snowstorms raged around my yurt and the wolves howled in the mountains, I often felt a sense of utter loneliness steal over me.

Every one of the men who accompanied me on this expedition to the Chimen-tagh was destined to distinguish himself in some way or other. Turdu Bai was the best Mussulman I ever had in my service; and when the camels were under his care, I was always perfectly comfortable about them. Shagdur was above praise; I do not know how to describe sufficiently the services he rendered me. He learned to do everything; he never forgot anything, and wanted no reminding; life was very pleasant in his company. There was a something about him which was very sympathetic. I especially admired his bold and impetuous courage in moments ot danger, and the calmness with which he received commissions of real difficulty. Twice, subsequently, he had occasion to show that he was ready to lay down his life for me. It was elevating to have about one a man who exhibited such a degree of disinterested fidelity; no wonder, then, I became attached to this Buriat Cossack. In his own country he worshipped the idols of Lamaism ; but now he turned his back contemptuously upon them. This was not my fault, for I did not consider it my business to shake the faith of any Asiatic ; but there was much that went on in my caravan that gave Shagdur, and indeed all the other Asiatics as well, occasion for a good deal of thought—things they had never even dreamt of.

Tokta Ahun of Abdall was a thorough honest good fellow, a man of sound understanding, who proved himself exceedingly useful. I have already said, that he accompanied both the horse and the camel caravan to Temirlik, and he now went with us for the third time when we started for our new head-quarters at Mandarlik, whither they had recently been flitted from Temirlik, because of the gnats. As he will play a conspicuous part in a later expedition, I will say nothing more about him here. With Kutchuk, also, the reader will become better acquainted later on. He, also, was a fine fellow, and uncommonly useful, a sort of Asiatic "Sven Dufva." * Mollah Shah was also with us in Northern Tibet. It only remains to mention Mollah, the "Doctor," a comical little fellow of fifty, a thin wrinkled old man, without a trace of beard or moustache ; for which reason we sometimes asked him in jest, whether he were not really an old woman, or at all events a Mongol—an appellation which the faithful of the Prophet do not regard as altogether flattering. His voice was shrill and piping, and he was fond of talking to himself, especially of an evening. He was very full of fun, however, and knew what he was about, and everybody liked him. With Mollah, too, we shall become better acquainted, for he accompanied me on my second expedition to Lop-nor. This man must be distinguished from Mollah Shah, previously mentioned, for he also took part in this expedition.

The evening was celebrated by a furious tempest from the west, which threatened to batter in my yurt, until we stayed it down again all round

On the 12th of July, our course being eastwards, we were not long before we turned our backs upon the zone of vegeta-

* The type of the man of "poor brains" who shows a "good heart" in a heroic fight. He figures in the *Fänrik Stål's Sägner*, by Runeberg, the national poet of Finland.

View of the Main Crest of the Chimen-tagh from above Mandarlik.

tion, in that we rode across hard, barren, gravelly ground, though we had all the time on our left the light-coloured belt of grass-land, which stretched away to the débris which muffled the foot of the Akato-tagh, whence two or three troops of *kulans* (or wild asses) watched us with curiosity. Just after we passed the spring of Kumutluk, which filled up the greater part of the valley, we caught a glimpse of the large lake of Gaz-nor to the north-east. At its west end the lake was broad and rounded, but gradually narrowed towards the north-east, until finally it issued in a little brook. Owing to the treacherous marshes which surrounded it, it was only approachable at a single point. Its shores were in places as white as snow, and its water as salt as brine. In front of it was a little freshwater

Our Headquarters Camp at Mandarlik—Looking Down the Glen.

pool called Ayik-köll, because bears were said to visit it for the sake of the berries which grew on the bushes near it. This pool was overgrown with kamish, and abounded in wild duck, which winter in that district; but Gaz-nor was entirely destitute of vegetation. The *boghana* bushes, kamish, and rushes which grew at Chigghelik (9,768 feet), or the "Place of Rushes"—the Mongols call it Dundu-namuk, or the Middle Spring—south of Gaz-nor, were the cause of the air there being literally thick with gnats and mosquitos, which tormented us worse than they did anywhere along the Tarim; for their bites produced an eruption of the skin like eczema.

We had now only one day's journey to go to reach our head-quarters camp. It took us up the glen of Mandarlik, deeply trenched between gravel-and-shingle terraces twenty-five feet high. Higher up we met a bubbling brook of bright crystal water. When we entered this transverse breach in the northern face of the Chimen-tagh, we left behind us the northernmost outcrop of the rocks and came amongst the granite, which thrust out its fantastic craggy buttresses nearer and nearer towards each other from both sides. Looking backwards, we saw as through a wide gateway the lake of Gaz-nor, and beyond it in the distance the Akato-tagh. Upon reaching an expansion of the glen, we turned our horses, mules and camels loose to graze. Cherdon, Islam Bai, and Faisullah came to meet us on foot, and an hour later we were snugly housed in our new quarters.

Before starting on our first Tibetan expedition, we granted ourselves a week's rest in the glen of Mandarlik (11,277 feet). It was a splendid place, with plenty of grass. Our camp stood

A View Just Above Mandarlik.

on a terrace on the left bank of the brisk little brook, which sang as it danced down the glen, except after rain in the higher regions, when it swelled to a considerable torrent. The Cossacks and Ali Ahun, the tailor, whose hands were never idle, lived in the big Mongol yurt, behind which Shagdur made a fence of planking, to protect the meteorological instruments from the attentions of the camels. Some of the Mussulmans lived in two spacious tents, others behind the sheltering barricades made by the maize sacks and the camels' pack-saddles when ranged round in circles. My own quarters were in the smaller Mongolian yurt; and in front of it stood all my big cases, stacked up close together, and covered with a white felt, to protect them against the frequent showers. The view up the glen was magnificent, the background being formed by the main crest of the Chimen-tagh, with its glittering snow-fields. Those of the camels which had already been grazing two months in the

The Start from Mandarlik.

mountains were as fat as could be, and in the pink of condition; indeed, all the caravan animals looked well. Only 42 of our 50 sheep were left, and we had acquired three fresh dogs from the nearest Mongol camp at Jurkhak.

Shagdur went over to see the Mongols there, and had a very friendly reception. They promised to sell us any animals we required, and hoped that I should visit them. One day Cherdon rode up the glen and fell in with a herd of 50 yaks, one of which he killed, a fine fat cow. As for me, I took astronomical and other observations, made little trips in the neighbourhood, and got ready for the next big expedition. We told off provisions to last seven men for two and a half months, and then fastened them ready on the pack-saddles. Two cases accommodated the instruments and my own personal belongings.

At the headquarters camp I left behind Islam Bai as caravan-bashi, or head-man; Faisullah, to look after the four camels from Abdall; Khodai Kullu, Kader, and Khodai Värdi, to attend to the horses; Ali Ahun, to do tailor work, and Shagdur as guard and meteorologist, it being his duty to take the observations three times every day. Musa, from Osh, was to go with us as far as the lake of Kum-köll, taking six horses for the purpose of lightening the loads of the other animals; but from Kum-köll he was to return in company with Tokta Ahun. The last-named begged that he might spend the summer at Mian, where he was growing wheat; but I asked him to join us again at the end of two and a half months, and at the same time bring with him half-a-dozen fresh camels.

I bestowed great care upon the selection of the caravan I was to take with me in my projected expedition. It was composed as follows: Cherdon, as my right-hand man, body-servant, and cook, as well as tent-man; Turdu Bai, caravan-bashi of the seven camels; Mollah Shah, for eleven horses and one mule; Kutchuk, to act as boatman in my boating trips across the lakes. One Niaz, from Keriya, a gold-seeker, whom we chanced to meet in the mountains, was to act as hodman to the other Mussulmans, and Aldat, the Afghan, was to be our guide as far as his topographical knowledge extended. Yolldash, of course, went with us, and generally slept in my tent. But we only took two of the other dogs, Malchik and a big yellow Mongol dog resembling a wolf. We were also accompanied by sixteen of the sheep, which Niaz, the gold-seeker, drove and guarded in the wake of the caravan.

CHAPTER XXX.

OVER THE CHIMEN-TAGH, ARA-TAGH AND KALTA-ALAGAN.

ONCE more we turned our backs upon the abodes of men, and set our faces towards the unknown parts of the world which were still a *terra incognita*. We soon left the principal valley on our right, and struck into a smaller glen without water, but studded with isolated grass-grown hills, backed by high black rocks, with a serrated edge. Thence, after crossing a secondary pass, we followed a path, frequented by hunters and gold-seekers, which led towards the south-east across extensive undulating pasture-grounds. On our right we had magnificent mountain scenery, with almost vertical cliffs. Then over another pass, and we began to descend the glen of Dung-sai, the brook of which never dries up, because it is fed by perennial springs. But although we zigzagged up and down over hills and passes, we were all the time gradually ascending to higher regions. The declivity which led down from the second of the two passes just mentioned, although as easy as possible for the horses, was steep and difficult for the camels, which made a glissade down the gravel.

The mountains began to assume a more Alpine character in the glen of Kar-yakkak (the Glen of the Falling Snow), which had an altitude of 13,072 feet above sea-level. A clear brook bubbled amongst the waterworn granite blocks which strewed it, while small and pretty flowers grew amongst the moss and grass. We had plenty of fuel in the shape of the droppings of wild yaks and kulans. Two or three yaks' skulls, which we came across, proved that the district had been visited by hunters, and ashes in a cave close by showed where they had spent the night. In several places the ground was burrowed by marmots (*davaghan*), and we often saw these nimble and wideawake little rodents sitting at the entrances to their runs as we approached. The partridges called busily to each other on the mountain sides, and Cherdon brought in a brace for my supper.

We pitched camp in the upper part of this fascinating glen. It is true, we had not made anything like a full day's march; but fresh animals, carrying big loads, ought not to be overtaxed at the start. As time went on, however, the loads would naturally grow lighter, for the geological specimens which we gathered, although amounting to a goodly collection, did not really add much to the total weight of baggage.

Towards the afternoon a north-easterly gale sprang up, and a perfect cascade of heavy black clouds came pouring down the glen; farther on, they condensed into a continuous downpour. When we left Mandarlik the sun was burning hot, and the air thick with dancing gnats; now it was already bleak autumn. And on the following morning, when I stepped out of my yurt, it was quite wintry: the snow fell in thick flakes and the ground was everywhere covered with snow. The depth of winter in the middle of July, and that in the heart of Asia! If the summer was like this—well, we could not help feeling a certain sense of respect for the winter.

We thought we would wait for better weather; but the snow did not stop, and the day was lost. Sometimes the snow ceased to come down in flakes, and took the form of hail, which rattled noisily against the coverings of the yurt. The temperature, however, kept just above freezing-point, and at midday the snow began to melt, causing the water to trickle in at every seam. The clay soil around the camp became slippery and sticky; you felt as if you were paddling about in the mud of a duck pond.

A slight acquaintance with this, the fourth of the parallel ranges of the Kwen-lun system, was sufficient to show that it differed very greatly from the preceding three ranges. Whereas they were bare, possessed no perpetual snow, and exhibited rounded and weathered forms, this range, the Chimen-tagh, was Alpine in its character, and had a copious precipitation, with a resulting abundance of vegetation. A short distance back we had been obliged to tramp 13 to 14 hours to get from one spring to the next; here we found water at every step.

Although it was still snowing on the 22nd July, we decided to wait no longer. By noon, most of the snow had melted, though the mountain-tops still glittered white. In the depressions the snow fell in the shape of big moist, feathery flakes, which disappeared the moment they touched the ground, leaving it wet and slippery; but on the heights above it was granular, light, and round. This last variety was more pleasant for the equestrian, for the hail readily rolled off; whereas the flakes stuck to us, and wetted us. There was a constant drip, drip, from our caps, our hands got wet and numb with cold, and my mapping sheet wrinkled up and was spoiled. We were unable to see far ahead, and could obtain no general view of the contour and arrangement of the mountain peaks. To the north, however, the weather lifted once or twice, affording us glimpses, as through a tunnel, of the dome-shaped. flat-arched ridge of the Akato-tagh.

Our day's march described a wide curve from the south-east to the west, round a massive knot of the Chimen-tagh, crossing over innumerable gulleys on the way. We were all glad to stop when we reached Yappkaklik-sai (13,117 feet), where there were teresken shrubs, but poor grazing. Yet it was not very pleasant sleeping on the ground with nothing but a carpet between one's ribs and the mud. As the temperature during the night fell below freezing-point, the snow did not melt, but lay very much thicker, especially as it came down faster than ever the whole of the evening. Strangely enough, it was sometimes so clear immediately above our heads that we saw the stars glistening, whilst all around us the snow was tossing its huge flakes in every direction. It was, however, a good thing it no longer melted, but lay as it fell, thus making a warm blanket for the yurt. The thermometer went down to $-4°.8$ C. or $23°.4$ Fahr.

Next morning I was awakened at daybreak by a fearful commotion in the camp, and upon hurrying out I learned that the shepherd Niaz, and all the sheep except four, were missing, and tracks in the snow plainly showed they had been visited by wolves during the night, which had been pitch dark. I at once sent out all the men after the marauders, Cherdon riding with his rifle in his hand; and about ten o'clock they came back with Niaz and one sheep. They found nine others torn to pieces amongst the hills, and one was missing entirely.

Niaz's story was as follows: He slept as usual under a felt carpet close beside the sheep, which were all loose except four; for if you prevent a few of them from straying, the others will remain beside them. In the middle of the night he was awakened by a trampling in the snow and by the bleatings of the sheep;

but owing to the howling of the storm he could not hear very distinctly. However, he at once jumped up, and saw three wolves, which had crept up against the wind, on the very point of attacking the sheep and driving them out of camp. Niaz stupidly never thought of calling up the other men, but rushed off after the sheep, and had kept on after them all the rest of the night, though he only managed to save one. The wolves had planned their attack so cunningly that the dogs heard nothing of it. Our Mongol had already run away; Yolldash was sleeping in my yurt; and the inexperienced Malchik lay curled up like a hedgehog behind the men's tent. The men cursed and swore at every wolf in existence. But what good did that do when we had lost more than one half of our supply of meat?

Soon after we left this ill-omened camp, and were striking up into the pass, we were amazed to see the missing sheep coming running through the hills, terrified, and beside itself. Upon perceiving us, it stopped, and looked at us narrowly, evidently wondering whether we were friends or enemies; yet seeing its five companions, it no longer hesitated, but hastened to join them. It had no doubt been wandering about all night, having, luckily for itself, got separated from the others that were killed.

The day turned out clear and bright, and the snow melted fast. We were now close to the summit (14,007 feet) of the principal pass of the Chimen-tagh, and upon surmounting it a magnificent panorama opened out before us. Right across our field of vision from east to west stretched another mountain-range, the Ara-tagh, entirely sheathed in snow from top to bottom, although only a few of its peaks, in the south-west, actually bore perpetual snow. Between the Chimen-tagh and the Ara-tagh was a broad, latitudinal or parallel valley, called by the simple name of Kayir (the Clay Mud Valley). It was traversed by a small river, which flowed towards the west; later on we explored where it went to. Beyond the stream to the south were wide grazing-grounds, dotted over with troops of wild asses and herds of antelopes.

With regard to the orographical structure of the Chimen-tagh, I will only say now, that it is asymmetrical. The valley of Chimen lies at an altitude of 9,715 feet above the sea, but the valley of Kayir at 13,731 feet; thus we had ascended another of the huge steps which lead up to the plateau of Northern Tibet. Seen from the north, the Chimen-tagh wore the appearance of a gigantic mountain-chain; seen from the south, it had quite an insignificant appearance, owing to the slight difference in the relative altitudes.

At this camp, too, we had a little mishap with the sheep. When I as usual made the round of the camp after taking the meteorological observations, I found that only two out of the six sheep were tethered, but as wolves were probably prowling about in this quarter also, I ordered that they should be all tethered. But when they tried to fasten up the four that were loose, off they went in a mad panic. Although it was now quite dark, off went the men after them, and their shouts soon died away amongst the hills. At length Cherdon returned, bringing two of the sheep, which he had caught with a lasso. But the other men did not come in until two hours later; they had been obliged to drive the poor brutes down the glen and there catch them in traps. After that we always kept them fastened up, until we gradually killed them off.

The next day, favoured by beautiful weather, and a blue sky, without a speck of cloud to mar its serenity, we prepared to storm the next barricade in the border-ranges of Tibet, namely, the Ara-tagh, or Middle Chain. The ascent was by a little ravine, traversed by a rivulet from a natural spring. The top of the pass of Ak-chokka-aytuseh (14,348 feet), or the Pass of the White Cliff, afforded us a repetition of yesterday's panorama, except that the range we now looked upon was a fresh one, namely, the Kalta-alagan, from which the Aratagh was separated by another latitudinal valley, which farther west was connected with the one previously mentioned. There the two rivers which flowed down these valleys merged together, and the united stream then broke through the Chimen-tagh into the Chimen valley.

The transverse valley which led down from the pass was very deeply scarped between its erosion terraces.

My caravan always outstripped me and got a long way ahead, for I was continually delayed, taking observations in the passes and at the entrances of the glens on both sides, collecting geological specimens, photographing, sketching, etc. The road still went up and up, until we reached the top of a rounded pass; then down it dipped again into another glen, deeply trenched in the mountain side. It began to get dusk, and cold, and we were longing for a glimpse of the column of smoke, which generally announced that the caravan leaders had discovered a suitable place for camping in. But on and up went the trail, without our being able to perceive the least sign of a tent. The vegetation came to an end, and we ascended to colder regions. It was evident the caravan had pushed on over the next pass; although the large river which flowed beside us seemed to indicate that the pass over the Kalta-alagan must still be a long way off. We wondered why the men had gone on, and not stopped where fuel and grass were plentiful. Eventually the trail swung round a projecting elbow of the cliffs, and entered a little side-glen, which plainly led up to a nearer pass, where, however, except for two or three pools amongst the stones, there was no water. But it was now dark and I could not see to work any longer. What was to be done? We could of course easily ride on; but I could not leave a gap in my map, and least of all at such an important point, where we were about to cross a pass of the first magnitude. I therefore simply stopped where I was, and bade Tokta Ahun go on until he overtook the caravan, and then return with my yurt and boxes.

In the meantime, Cherdon and I did not have a particularly lively time of it in the cold and darkness, at an altitude of 15,263 feet above the sea. At nine o'clock we took the usual series of meteorological observations, and the reading of the boiling-point thermometer, which, owing to the strength of the wind, occupied us a considerable time, and was only taken at all after we had screened the lamp with a cloak. That finished, we had nothing to do but wait. We crept close together to keep one another warm, and mutually related our experiences of similar situations. Cherdon had not much to boast of in that way from the manœuvres in Transbaikalia, but I had spent the night amongst jackals in Persia, had been nearly frozen to death on the shores of the lake of Kara-kul, and many a night had lain awake in the weird desert of Takla-makan.

It was too cold to sleep, and the frost grew keener; as we had no furs, we were forced to keep moving about to prevent ourselves from freezing. But we had been in the saddle 11 hours besides doing a good deal of work during the time, and nature at last asserted her rights, and we grew heavy and drowsy. Then we again crouched together between two big stones, which afforded us a certain amount of shelter. Before many minutes passed, we were both startled by the long-drawn howl of a distant wolf. We at once sprang up and fastened our horses, which were impatiently scraping the ground close beside us, and Cherdon held his rifle in readiness. If only we could have made a fire, the situation would have been very much less disagreeable, but although we hunted all over the neighbourhood we failed to find either yak-droppings or teresken scrub. Besides, it was so dark that we had to feel where we were going with our hands. The only way to keep the blood in circulation was to stamp our feet and flap our arms together.

After waiting five weary hours, we at length heard a rattling amongst the gravel. It was Kutchuk and Tokta Ahun, with two horses and the yurt. Half-an-hour later they were followed by Turdu Bai, with my cases and the dinner service on camels. The men blamed Mollah Shah for going on with the horses after Aldat told him there was good grazing near a little spring on the other side of the pass. As they also brought fuel with them in a sack, we soon had a fire alight, and I can assure you that when at last I did get my dinner at three o'clock in the morning it went down famously after the seventeen hours' fast. Day was already breaking on the barren mountains when we retired to rest.

Wearied by the exertions of the preceding day and night, we did not get started the following morning until ten o'clock. After traversing the remainder of the distance to Camp no. XIV. we picked up the rest of the caravan, and proceeded up the gentle slope to the pass of Avras (15,703 feet), by which we crossed the Kalta-alagan (Kalta's Hunting-Ground). Here a view o immense amplitude and sublimity unrolled itself in the south. It was no longer a single definite mountain-range, but a whole world of mountains, which it would take months to unravel. Far off in the south-east were gigantic mountain-masses covered with snow, which seemed to belong to one of the usual east-west ranges. More immediately south of us, and forming a continuation of the foregoing, was another stupendous isolated group, or mountain-knot, also mantled with perpetual snow. In the south-south-west we saw the white shimmer of yet another mountain-range, clearly situated to the south of the valley stream which picked up the Kum-köll. Along the line of the southern horizon were snow-fields and glaciers or fleecy clouds, it was difficult to tell which. I inferred, however, that they were the tops of the Arka-tagh, the culminating range of the Kwen-lun system.

A dry transverse valley led down from the pass to the open flat country, and there, beside a spring situated amongst low hills, we found the caravan encamped. I gave Musa and Mollah

Shah a good wigging for making such a long march the day before.

On the 26th of July we turned due west, and travelled at right angles to the route which we had been pursuing during the past few days; that is, we struck off in the direction of the upper lake of Kum-köll, which was visible in the distance through a field-glass, though it was afterwards hidden from us by lower hills and undulations of the surface. Our route thus lay down the broad and spacious latitudinal valley which ran along the southern foot of the great range of the Kalta-alagan. This range not only thrust out several spurs and ramifications across the valley, but overtopped it in occasional snowy peaks. On the opposite side of the valley was a wide belt of sand, which I at first took for a smaller range of hills running parallel to the bigger ranges; but when we approached nearer to it, I perceived that it consisted of pure sand-dunes, of the same yellow colour as those of the Takla-makan, and very nearly as much developed. Thus the general conditions for the formation of an "ocean of sand," like that which existed down in the desert, obtained here also, at an altitude of 12,000 to 14,000 feet above the level of the sea. The transition from the soft or gravel-strewn valley bottom, with its scattered teresken scrub and other combustible vegetable growths, to the belt of sand was extraordinarily sharp. The crests of the dunes ran from north to south, and appeared to have been built up by predominant westerly winds.

With the sand continuously on our left and the Kalta-alagan on our right, the day's march was extremely monotonous, although vast numbers of kulans were grazing and frisking all over the steppes, which sloped gently westwards towards the lake. Marmots were common, and used to sit up with their fore paws crossed over their breasts until the dogs got near them, then they darted into their holes. Hares, too, abounded, and wild-duck flew overhead on their way to the lake. Once more the gnats came and assailed us, but retired shortly after sunset. It was summer weather all day. The temperature rose to 20°.0 C., or 68°.0 Fahr., and it felt oppressively hot, because of the stillness of the atmosphere. We were only reminded of the great altitude by our shortness of breath and the beating of the heart which ensued upon even very slight exertion.

Aldat and Cherdon rode towards a troop of wild asses (kulans), 34 in number, which, however, fled at their approach, except a she-ass and her foal. But as the men still continued to press on, the mother finally deserted her offspring, which proved to be only four days old. The little creature made no attempt to escape, but stood quite still, until the two hunters picked it up. Aldat placed it on the saddle in front of him and brought it in. We then packed it in a felt, and hoisted it upon a camel's back—a method of travelling to which it took quite kindly. We also captured another kulan foal at Camp no. XV. in precisely the same way.

When we encamped, we let them both range at will amongst the tents and stores, and they showed no fear when we patted them. I was anxious to rear them on milk porridge, until they could shift for themselves, which, it was said, they would be able to do three weeks after birth. But when I consulted Tokta Ahun about the matter, he said they would not live longer than five days; he had no less than eight times tried to rear wild asses, but on every occasion had failed. Upon this, I ordered that they should be taken back to the places where they were captured, so that their mothers might find them again, and Cherdon and Aldat were already mounted to carry out my order, when Tokta Ahun said it would be useless. His experience was that once a young kulan had been touched by the hands of man, its mother fled from it as from the pestilence. Nor did she appear to miss her offspring or grieve for it, but kept with the troop she belonged to, and shunned the place where she lost it.

Had we had a brood mare with us, I dare say we could have managed to rear our two little captives. The men told me that a great number of kulan foals perish every year in the Chimen valley, because, during the first few days of their existence, they are unable to accompany their mothers on the approach of danger. When thus deserted, they die of hunger, or are torn to pieces by the wolves. The older kulans are no doubt able to protect their young, so long as the latter are with them, otherwise their numbers would not increase.

In the meantime we took the greatest possible care of our captives, which readily learned to sup up their sloppy porridge. But they were doomed, and as in the evening they showed signs of pining away, and were longing greatly for their mother's milk, I ordered them to be killed. The Mussulmans took possession of their skins, and ate the meat, which they declared to be particularly tender and tasty. But before the little creatures were killed, I photographed them from various positions. One stood $35\frac{1}{2}$ inches high, the other $35\frac{3}{4}$ inches. The head was disproportionately large, and the legs absurdly long in com-

Two Views of the Wild Ass Foals.

parison with their body; but then the latter are in their case the limbs which are first used, as well as those which are of the greatest importance to them. The body was very short and compressed, and gave scarce any indication of the noble and harmonious lines which distinguish the full-grown kulans. The little ones we had in captivity were too young to be afraid of human beings, or of the camels or the tents; but had they been a week older, they would neither have let themselves be captured nor would they have been at liberty without making attempts to escape. When we gave them a finger, they sucked at it greedily, a proof that they were hungry.

During the night of the 26th of July the temperature fell to only 1½° above freezing-point, though the following day was beautifully warm. These latitudinal or parallel east-west valleys, which of course are, relatively speaking, the lowlands of the elevated regions, have, as a rule, a more temperate climate than the higher mountainous parts.

Next day we still continued westwards, riding close to the edge of the belt of sand, and having on our right all day long an unbroken succession of marshes, morasses, and pools, all more or less connected, or, at any rate, linked together, by small channels or watercourses. They were surrounded by luxuriant grass, but the ground was extremely treacherous, and even dangerous; it would not bear so much as a man's weight. Some of these depressions were a couple of hundred yards long. All of them were fed by subterranean springs, which trickled underneath the sand, and lower down they became united into a single stream, which entered the Kum-köll at its eastern end. Six of these rivulets were of considerable size, and one of them carried as much as 70 cubic feet in the second, the water, after filtering through the sand, being as bright as crystal.

We kept a good look out for the lake, and at last saw it gleaming like a silvery ribbon in the west. The day was warm and still, and the mosquitos troublesome. Moreover, a species of gad-fly called *ila* tormented the horses, and made them nervous and restless by getting into their nostrils. The kulans protect themselves against these insects by keeping their nostrils close to the ground when they graze, the orongo antelopes by spending the hot part of the day deep in the belt of sand, and by coming down to the grazing-grounds in the evening only. The yaks protect themselves in the same way, but go higher up in the sand, so that we did not get a glimpse of them all day, although we observed their foot-prints and droppings everywhere. At four o'clock a violent squall of hail and rain came on, and the yaks, which knew this would banish their enemies, made their appearance in little companies on the crests of the dunes. First appeared a cow with her calf, glissading down the steep slope; but upon catching sight of us, she turned tail about and went back. After that a herd of over 30 arranged themselves in a line on the top of a high sand-dune, and fearlessly stood watching the caravan. I stopped and observed them for some time through my field-glass. The wild yak is in truth a magnificent animal. The herd stood out with remarkable distinctness, black as coal, against the yellow background of the sand. They were on their way down to their grazing-ground beside the lake, when they found themselves thus cut off from it by our caravan. We could almost see them literally rejoicing in the refreshing rain, which patter-pattered on their shoulders. The yaks that live in this region always graze all night, but at sunrise return up amongst the sand-dunes, where they remain until it gets dark, or a storm tempts them down again.

The slopes of the sand-dunes were deepened in colour by the rain. You would think that a violent downpour such as that was would convert them into soft mud from end to end; but it did not even affect the sharp outlines of their contours, and only formed little shallow pools on the surface. The sand gradually decreased in height as well as swung back from the middle of the valley. We now had the lake on our right; its southern shore extended 60° west of north. Here 14 big yaks were already grazing. Cherdon, who rode with me, could not take his eyes off them, and at last begged that he might try his luck. He crept as stealthily as a cat towards a powerful bull, which simply stood still and looked hard at him without showing the slightest trace of fear. Cherdon did not like the look of him, and thought discretion the better part of valour. I had warned him to be careful when hunting yaks, and not to go after them alone if he could help it; for when a yak is wounded, he will often turn and attack his hunter.

A little bit further on Cherdon caught sight of a solitary wolf-cub, four months old, and galloping after it, managed to catch it. Upon reaching camp, he tied up his captive; but the dogs showed the greatest possible indifference to it. The men, however, bestowed upon it all the most endearing epithets they could think of; they had not forgotten the nine sheep which the wolves tore to pieces. Tokta Ahun warned me to keep good watch upon the sheep; for the she-wolf, which no doubt had her lair somewhere close by, would not lose sight of her cub, and if any harm came to it, she would take her revenge upon the sheep. He had twice caught wolf-cubs himself, and on both occasions the older wolves had killed an ass of his. Wolves will not try to meddle with full-grown kulans, because they could never catch them; but they will sometimes chase the young ones into soft marshy ground, and then bite their throats till they kill them. We intended to take our young wolf-cub with us, and try to rear it; but it proved too cunning for its captors. During the night it gnawed the rope through, and ran away with a piece of it round its neck. The Mussulmans hoped that as the beast grew the rope would throttle it; but I thought it more likely that its mother would gnaw the rope away before that.

Camp no. XVI., beside the Upper Kum-köll, which lay 12,737 feet above the level of the sea, was all that could be desired. We had plenty of grass, and plenty of fuel, and the water in the lake was fresh. On the north the imposing range of the Kalta-alagan stretched its rugged sharp-cut spurs down into the valley, and itself extended as far to the west as we could see. The mountains on the south were, on the contrary, entirely enveloped in clouds. The next morning my little boat lay ready screwed together on the shore; so taking Kutchuk with me I sailed across the lake before a steady breeze. We carried with us the yurt and such instruments as I required for my cartographical work, for taking soundings, and so on. But before we got very far from shore, a sudden squall snapped the sail yard, and we were forced to row back and mend it, by lashing the ends together and strengthening the fracture with pieces of tamarisk wood. Then we steered for a snowy peak which lay 13° east of north. This lake was shallower than I had expected to find it; its greatest depth only measured 12¼ feet. We landed on a little gravelly island about 35 yards in diameter near the northern shore.

The sky in the east now began to assume a threatening aspect, and the valley filled with dense clouds, while columns of rising sand were driven like smoke across the sand-dunes. Accordingly, we thought it best to wait a little; and sure enough, down came the storm. We sheltered ourselves as well as we could against the driving rain by crouching behind the boat. But although the lake was alive with big, foam-crested waves, I could not resist the temptation of dropping the sail and pushing off. We had, however, to exercise the utmost vigilance, for the flat valley acted like a funnel for the wind, which thus swept the lake with unmitigated fury. We kept as well as we could to the crests of the waves, so as not to get filled with water. But the gale increased in violence, and the mast threatening to break, I at last called to Kutchuk to furl the sail; but even under bare poles we went along at a spanking pace before the wind. I was only able to get an occasional sounding, we travelled too fast; but I easily managed to obtain the velocity and also took my compass bearings.

In this way we soon reached the western end of the lake, and found that it contracted into a little stream, which carried off its superfluous water, and emptied it into the big salt lake of Ayag-kum-köll, or the Lower Sand Lake, which lay further to the west, and which we shall encounter again on another excursion. Here the Kum-köll was very shallow, its depth seldom exceeding 3¼ feet; while the shelving southern shore was continued by mud-banks, over which the water was stained black after being stirred up by our paddles. This part of the lake swarmed with wild-duck and wild-geese. The latter were sitting on their eggs, and unwilling to fly far; but they were all the cleverer at diving, as we soon found out when we tried to row down a flock and attack them with our paddles.

But our return was nothing like so glorious as our departure. We paddled our hardest; but the wind freshened again, and after a while it began to rain, so that we got wet through, a result to which the waters also contributed by occasionally washing over us. At length, however, we perceived the tents, though still a long way off; in fact it took us two or three hours longer to reach them. I was always unlucky in my lake excursions; no matter how fine the weather was when I started, it always came on stormy before I got back.

CHAPTER XXXI.

ACROSS THE ARKA-TAGH.

ON the 30th of July I sent Tokta Ahun and Musa, with six horses, back to the headquarters camp, although this made the loads somewhat heavier for the animals that remained behind. Besides myself, our strength now consisted of six men—Cherdon, Turdu Bai, Mollah Shah, Kutchuk, Niaz, and Aldat—seven camels, 11 horses, one mule, five sheep, and two dogs. The day's march ran to the south-south-west through open monotonous country for a distance of 23 miles. In the morning the basin of the Kum-köll was enveloped in a moist, impenetrable mist, and the range of Kalta-alagan had entirely disappeared. The air was warm and still, and full of mosquitos, which faithfully followed us all day. We longed to reach altitudes where these wretched creatures could not live, and once there we should not return to their native habitat until they were all perished in the winter cold.

The surface of the Kum-köll glittered like plate-glass, but we soon lost it in the mist behind us. In between the dunes, which jutted out like headlands into the valley, we found firm ground, and a series of small basins, each containing a pool of saltish water. When the sand-belt came to an end, we travelled over a gently undulating surface, with patches of grass here and there, until we reached the stream known as Pettelik-daria, which was enclosed between scarped terraces of loose yellow earth. This stream, which flowed due north-west and issued into the lake of Ayag-kum-köll, had a volume of about 353 cubic feet in the second, and a maximum depth of 2½ feet. But Turdu Bai and Mollah Shah, in trying to find a suitable crossing-place, nearly perished in the mud at the bottom, man and horse together. Barely a tenth part of its bed was now under water, but the moisture still clinging to its sides showed that it had recently been full to the brim. It would then have been quite impossible to ford it.

The next day's march, our fourth at these sublime altitudes, took us to the south-south-east, and was equally as long as the preceding stage. After fording the river once more, we found our road blocked by a minor range, probably a spur of the Arka-tagh. The atmosphere was again clear, and in the east-south-east we saw the glittering, snowy mass of Chullak-akkan, which we had first observed from the pass of Avras. The belt of sand still continued on our left hand. These dreary steppes were haunted by innumerable orongo antelopes; but in spite of all their endeavours our hunters failed to bring one down. This country was sometimes visited by gold-seekers and yak-hunters, and this had taught the animals to be on the alert, so that they took very good care not to let us approach too close to them. We were now at the end of Aldat's geographical knowledge. He had never been so far south before, nor any of the other men either; so that for the future I had to take the responsibility of guiding the caravan myself.

We directed our course towards a notch in the mountain-chain, up to which a promising glen appeared to lead. But when we entered it, we found it was destitute of water. However, on the right hand, that is to say, the west side of the glen, in an elbow or recess, we discovered a little fresh green grass, and a small spring, which yielded enough water for our wants.

On the 1st of August we did eighteen miles to the south-south-east. On the whole we travelled towards the south, because I was anxious to cross these successive mountain ranges at right angles, and, in addition to geographical observations, to gather also material for a geological profile. My plan was to get as far south as I possibly could, and only turn back when our supplies were half exhausted. In making this calculation I deliberately left one important factor out of account—namely, that on the return journey the animals' strength would become so reduced that they would travel very much slower, and consequently take a longer time. I did not overlook this; but the main thing was to penetrate as far south as I could possibly get. We could somehow or other manage to pilot the caravan home, and if the worst came to the worst we could walk ourselves. I hoped we might have to turn back in a region where there was plenty of grass, so that the animals could obtain a good rest before starting. But I had no conception what a strain the return journey would put upon them, and what trouble it would cost us to get the remnants of our caravan safely home again.

It proved no easy task to force a passage over the granite wall which now towered up across our path. Although it took the whole day, we managed it successfully at last. It was a parallel range of the Arka-tagh. After groping our way up to the watershed of this new range through winding gorges and glens, over spurs and secondary passes, we beheld, upon reaching the main pass at the top, a stupendous range, black as ink, but capped with snow. This I took to be the Arka-tagh, the same difficult mountain-range which I encountered in 1896; and I feared we should have as tough a job to get over it now as we had then. We pitched camp beside a little brook in the longitudinal valley at the foot of this new mountain-wall, at an altitude of 15,217 feet above the sea.

It had been a splendid day, and we had not been molested by either mosquitos or gad-flies. But at seven o'clock the rain began to patter on the yurt; and when I stepped outside, the whole landscape was steaming with rainy mist, and not a mountain visible. The horses stood tied together in pairs, with their heads hanging down; they were half asleep, and the raindrops ran down their sides and drip—drip—dripped from their pack-saddles and manes. The camels crowded together in a clump, to keep themselves warm, and in spite of their heavy breathing they seemed to enjoy the rest. The camp-fire was smoking in front of the men's tent, and whilst Cherdon prepared my dinner, Mollah Shah got the men's ready. After a while Kutchuk and Niaz turned the horses out to graze. We left them out all night, but told off a watchman to give an eye to them, to see that they did not stray too far. The camels could not see to eat before day-break, and therefore lay where they were all night; but we gave them a few pecks of maize for their supper. Yolldash took very good care not to venture out in such very disagreeable weather, but lay curled up inside my tent. Malchik had a sore foot, and during the last day or two had been packed on a camel's back, where, with the skill of an acrobat and a certain degree of elegance, he adapted himself to the cradling movements of his "steed." With the rain falling like slanting arrows in the darkness outside, I was very glad to creep back into my well-lighted yurt.

We stayed where we were all the next day, for I wanted to take an astronomical observation—a process that is very trying

The Caravan Resting whilst Cherdon was Looking for a Pass (3rd August, 1900).

to the patience when you are continually interrupted by passing hailstorms and flitting clouds. The morning did not look very promising. It had snowed ever since midnight, and continued snowing until about nine o'clock, burying what little pasture there was under a white sheet, so that, although our animals were groping about all day, they came home at nightfall only half satisfied. The mountains exhibited a variety of colouring: sometimes the snow-fields glistened intensely white against a background of dark clouds; sometimes the sky was clear in the distance, and the snow-fields assumed a cold, steel-blue tone, while heavy black clouds obscured the sun. Yesterday the perpetual snow, with its rudimentary glaciers, stood out in very sharp relief; to-day it and they were alike hidden under the white mantle of the fresh-fallen snow.

The night of the 2nd of August was the coldest we had had for some time; the thermometer dropped to $-5°.2$ C. or $22°.6$ Fahr. In the morning every pool and rivulet was covered with a thin sheet of ice, which, however, thawed in the splendidly bright weather that ensued, although in sheltered crevices it did not melt at all. To-day the animals showed the first symptoms of fatigue; one horse was allowed to go without a load, and one of the camels turned sluggish soon after the track began to ascend. We penetrated the next range at a point where it appeared to be lowest, and came eventually into the expansion of a glen in which were hundreds of orongo antelopes—big, beautiful animals, with horns that stuck straight up like bayonets. They sped swiftly and easily up the mountain sides, it apparently costing them no effort at all to exert themselves in the rarified atmosphere.

From this expansion two glens led off, one to the south, the other to the south-west. We chose the former, for it had a little brook running down it. But it soon narrowed and grew steep, and at the head of it a snow-clad mountain towered up like a wall directly in our path. As our advance in that direction appeared barred, I sent Cherdon on to reconnoitre, and whilst we were waiting for him to return, I took a couple of photographs. He soon came back, however, and said that it would be impossible for the camels to get through that way; so we tried the other glen. Then, whilst the caravan was making a detour round a steep spur, I rode over the top of it with Cherdon, and found it equally steep on the other side. From the top we perceived forty or fifty antelopes grazing on an acclivity not very far away, and made signs to the men with the caravan to drive them into the corner where we were waiting. But they were too knowing for us, and going off up the glen, were speedily out of sight.

The glen soon turned to the south-south-west, and ran up towards a pass which was free from snow. I rode on ahead. The ascent was dangerously steep, and on the top of the pass—the highest point we had hitherto reached, namely, 16,280 feet—I had to wait half-an-hour while the rest of the caravan struggled slowly up the débris-strewn slope towards me. The prospect on the other side was anything but encouraging, a chaos of rocky pinnacles, mountain-spurs, and snow-capped crests extending away to the south. It was plain we were not yet at the summit of the Arka-tagh—we had merely crossed one of its many parallel chains which run from east to west, and consequently still had the worst obstacle to surmount.

At last the others scrambled up to the top of the pass beside me. The poor camels, their legs actually trembled under them! Their nostrils were widely distended, they wanted more air; and their eyes turned with a weary and indifferent look to the south, as if, amid this universe of barren, naked mountains, they had abandoned all hope of ever getting a good feed of grass again. From the summit of the pass we zigzagged down between the craggy headlands into a gorge which led to the south-south-west, and was itself cut through solid rock of black slate, porphyry, and diorite. Moss was the only thing that grew beside the brook which traversed it, until we came out upon the broad longitudinal valley into which it issued. There there was some *yappkak* scrub, which the men gathered for their evening fire. This valley was drained by the biggest stream we had encountered since we left the Tarim; it was 213 feet broad, had a maximum depth of 23½ feet, and carried 954 cubic feet in the second. It appeared to have its source in three large rounded mountains, which stood side by side like three-cornered hats in the east-south-east, and flowed towards the west-north-west. Its left bank was twenty-five to thirty-five feet high, and vertical—an obstacle which we should have been unable to surmount had it not been for a little side-ravine which led up to the top of it. After that we struck into a transverse valley, and, entering a glen on its southern side, encamped in open ground beside a little tributary of the big river, at an altitude of 15,693 feet. A little higher up we saw thirteen big black yaks grazing.

View from the Pass, Looking 80° East of North (3rd August, 1900).

They did not at first perceive us, but as soon as we stopped and began to pitch the tent, the leader of the herd caught the alarm and off they all went in a body towards the Arka-tagh, whose main crest did now really loom up before us in all its gloomy majesty. Once safely over that, the country beyond ought to be fairly open.

The next day we decided to rest, so as to give Cherdon and Aldat an opportunity to reconnoitre the nearest glens leading over the Arka-tagh. They reported that the glen in whose mouth we were encamped was impassable; and so, on the 5th of August, we proceeded a good bit down the latitudinal

One of the Parallel Ranges of the Arka-tagh—Seen from Camp no. XIX.

valley, until we came to a deep-cut watercourse, with a large stream flowing down it. Here, where we turned south again, I stopped for a short time to enter the main geographical features on my map. From that point the latitudinal valley extended as far west as I was able to see. But some distance down I observed a transverse valley or breach, where the river probably cut through the range which we had crossed over the day before. My point of observation was situated a long way above the bottom of the valley, and offered a panorama that was overpowering, both because of its gigantic dimensions and its sublimity. The river, split into several arms, wound through the light grey mountain débris, interrupted occasionally by large sheets of ice.

I could just hear the murmur of the water. The spurs of the Arka-tagh lay like sphinxes looking towards the north, with their stony paws just hanging in the stream. But the desolate beauty of the landscape was soon veiled in clouds and steaming rain. Turning our backs upon the scene, we resumed our toilsome march up the glen, the air in which was cold and raw.

The east side of the glen was bounded by a range of snow-clad mountains, but the opposite side was more open. However, it soon came on to rain and the wind blew hard. Then while we made haste to run up the tent as fast as we could, Mollah Shah rode on further to ascertain where the glen went to. If there was no practicable pass, we should only tire the animals to no purpose by proceeding with the whole of the caravan. Even as it was, our animals were beginning to lose flesh. Cherdon's black horse refused to eat, and looked in a bad way, which distressed the poor fellow a good deal, for he was passionately attached to the animal. He had trained him splendidly. When he called him by name, the horse came and put his head over Cherdon's shoulder. The little Buriat Cossack was quite an acrobat. Whilst his horse was moving, he would stand on his hands on the saddle, play at leap-frog over his hind-quarters, and turn somersaults across him without the animal being in the least degree startled by these performances. No wonder, then, Cherdon tended him as the apple of his eye, and was very much distressed to see him ailing. Our four remaining sheep were extraordinary animals. They followed the caravan like dogs, climbed the steepest slopes with ease, and appeared to be perfectly satisfied with the scanty and miserable grass we found for them.

By this we had become accustomed to the extraordinary altitude. So long as I sat still in the saddle or the tent, I did not notice any difference ; but the least exertion, such as chipping at a rock with a geological hammer, occasioned shortness of breath and accelerated action of the heart. It was, however, a great advantage to be freed from the attentions of the mosquitos and gad-flies. In place of them we had a species of gigantic humble-bee, which, when the sun shone, came out and sailed through the air, humming like the bass notes of an organ. It was specially equipped for the intense wintry cold of these regions, being clad throughout in coat and greaves of thick yellow hair.

As there was not a scrap of pasture at this camp, it was

The Pass of 3rd August, 1900, Looking North.

useless to turn the animals out. Although it was scurvy treatment, all we could do for them was to give them a shower bath of commingled water and ice, instead of food.

Mollah Shah came back after an absence of six hours, and reported that the pass in which our glen terminated was practicable. But what it was like on the other side he did not know, for the view was obscured by a driving snow-storm. And, indeed, when we left that inhospitable camp next morning, the whole country was once more shrouded in snow. But as the morning wore on, the sun peeped out, and the snow began to melt. The glen led by a slow, gradual ascent up to the pass. Its bottom was strewn with black, slaty débris, which crunched under the horse's hoofs; and down its middle ran a bright, cheerful little brook, picking up a number of smaller tributaries on each side as it proceeded.

The pass formed a rounded, flattened saddle, which even the camels surmounted without any special difficulty. With the help of the camera-stand I made a little temporary shelter for the boiling-point thermometer, and found the altitude was 16,996 feet—thus we were standing on the highest *mountain-chain* on the face of the earth. At our feet stretched the latitudinal valley which I traversed in 1896. Immediately on the other side of it was a stupendous mountain group crowned with perpetual snow and *névés*, with short glacier arms radiating in every direction; seen from a distance it might be compared to a starfish. On its northern face were three broad truncated glaciers, with enormous terminal moraines of black débris. Of the naked rock itself there were only a few black and brown pinnacles visible; all the rest was buried under ice and snow. Each glacier-arm gave birth to a little rivulet, which ran down and joined the river that drained the valley from east to west.

After we had thus for several days been struggling up to higher regions, it was quite a treat to go down again. The animals travelled more easily, and we were buoyed up by the hope of finding grass in some hollow or other. Thus we swung at a good pace down the transverse glen which led from the pass to the next valley below. Near its lower extremity Aldat surprised an orongo antelope, and brought it down with his clumsy, primitive muzzle-loading musket. It proved a welcome addition to our larder, and enabled us to grant our three remaining sheep a few days longer reprieve.

Instead of continuing right down to the river at the bottom

of the valley—its banks looked grey and sterile—we turned to the west, and encamped on a gentle declivity where there was a little thin grass. Here Aldat managed to bag a big orongo, which put us all in better humour, for this supplied us with meat for several days. At these high altitudes rice did not make a very appetising dish ; the "pudding" baked into a tasteless dough, and we did not want to kill our sheep until we were really forced to do so. Unfortunately Cherdon had only brought a small supply of cartridges with him, and had used them up too lavishly at first ; so that for the future we were compelled to rely upon Aldat's gun. He, fortunately, had a sufficient supply of ammunition.

On the Summit of the Arka-tagh, 16,996 feet above Sea-level.

CHAPTER XXXII.

ON THE TIBETAN HIGHLANDS.

THUS we had at last climbed the gigantic wall which Nature has built up like a bulwark to guard the secrets of Tibet on the north. We had long left behind us the paths of the half-civilized yak-hunters and fatuous gold seekers, and plunged into a region which was an absolute *terra incognita*, except that I should cross my own former route, Wellby's, Rockhill's, and Bonvalot's each at a single point. As I had now exhausted the topographical knowledge of my guide, Aldat, my map from this point embraced only a narrow belt on each side of our actual route; but I hoped in the future, that other routes which I proposed to take would enable me to obtain a clear conception of the orographical structure of the region.

I had always plenty to do from morning till evening. Leisure moments were few, and such as I did get I spent in reading Geikie's *Great Ice Age*, Hann's *Klimatologie*, and Kern's *Bhuddismus*. Although we led the lives of dogs in this country, which was as desolate as the moon is supposed to be, yet we reaped more than an equivalent reward in the discoveries and observations which we made from day to day. It was a delicious feeling, to know that we were the first human beings to tread those mountains, where there existed no path, where there never had been a path, and where there was not a footprint visible, except those made by the hoof of yak, antelope, or kulan. It was a no man's land; rivers, lakes, and mountains were all nameless; their shores, banks, and snow-fields had never been seen by any traveller's eyes but mine; they were mine own kingdom of a day. It was delightful—it was a great thing, to cruise, like a vessel that leaves no track behind her, amongst those upswellings of the world's "high sea," to make our way over those gigantic mountain waves. Only the waves which roll across the Tibetan highlands are petrified ; and all distances and dimensions are cast on such a gigantic scale, that you may march for weeks at a time and still find the situation unchanged—still find yourself the centre of a universe of mountains. And it was just as wonderful to live up amongst the eternal storms, those insurgents of the atmosphere, which drive across the howling mountain wastes and set their swift-moving batteries—namely, showers of clattering hail—to play upon the mountain sides.

That night when I stepped out of my tent the sky was mantled with clouds, their edges tipped here and there with the silvery rays of the moon. The wide-spread glaciers, out in the open, were flooded with the pale, frigid moonshine. The men were all asleep, the caravan animals safely tethered, the fire extinguished ; and the only sound that disturbed the solemn hush of the night was the little brook murmuring its pensive song amongst the flaky shales. The night was keeping its silent, solitary watch over the mountain wastes, and all around it flitted the ghosts of a multitude of questions and problems craving their answers. Far away in the south I pictured to myself the crests of the snowy Himalayas, and beyond them again India with its stifling jungles. In the west our mountains linked themselves on to the Pamir highlands, and by the time the sun rose here, he was already pouring a flood of brilliant light over the kingdom of the Middle and its mountainous western borders. With the north, where lay the heart of Asia, we were to some extent familiar ; but, here in Tibet, we were alone in an unknown land. In vain did we strain our eyes for a glimpse of a fire or the footprint of a human being ; we had reached an uninhabited and uninhabitable part of the earth. I felt like an atom of dust in the midst of the illimitable wastes, and fancied I could hear the swish of the planet as it rolled without rest, without cessation, along its everlasting orbit.

On the 7th of August we went on down the latitudinal valley, in the hope of finding one of my lakes of 1896. It was now all over with Cherdon's horse : he kept falling, and had difficulty in getting up again. But, as his appetite remained good, we did all we could to save him. Cherdon treated him in the Mongol fashion ; that is, he bled him at the tips of the ears, and cut away a couple of pieces of glandular connective tissue in his eyelids. This seemed to revive him a little, and he managed to go longer stretches at a time. At first I thought

Camp no. XXVII.—A General Drying. The Men, going from Left to Right are—Aldat, Niaz, Kutchuk, Mollah Shah, Turdu Bai, and Cherdon.

it would be best to kill him; but as Turdu Bai was of opinion that he might be saved, I ordered Mollah Shah to lead him slowly after us, whilst the caravan pushed on at the usual pace. As we failed to find a lake, I determined to wheel south again, and cross the mountain-chain which stretched west from the glaciated mountain group already spoken of. The latitudinal valley we were traversing was rather narrow, its stream very nearly dry, and on the south side, immediately underneath the moraines, was a belt of drift-sand, piled up precisely as it was beside the Kum-köll, into big dunes, which were very often detached from one another. They were regularly formed, and crescentic in shape, with their steep concave slopes toward the east. Within the arms of two or three of them were small crescentic pools formed by the melting glacier-arms. We forded several of these little brooks, the water of which was red and muddy. One of them had a volume of as much as 106 cubic feet in the second. The water in the pools, however, was transparent, and of an intense ultramarine blue colour, making a striking contrast to the yellow sand. We encamped beside one of these little brooks, close under the western shoulder of the glaciated mountain group, which we were thus half-way round. The grass, however, was worse than usual.

Mollah Shah came up five hours later. He had left Cherdon's horse a couple of miles from camp, neither better nor worse than in the morning. But when Cherdon went to look after him the animal was dead.

Turdu Bai rode up a transverse valley through the range which we were now about to cross, and returned in the evening with the report that the pass was not dangerous, and there was a big lake over on the other side of it; but he had not seen any grass. The ascent next day was smooth and gradual, and the pass occasioned us no exceptional difficulty, although one of the camels gave up, and had to be relieved of his load. From the top (16,805 feet) we had the same characteristic scene which our eyes had so often rested upon before—namely, immediately below us a latitudinal valley running east and west, backed by a mountain-range covered in part with perpetual snow. This latter was, I concluded, identical with the Koko-shili mountains. The bottom of the new latitudinal valley was in great part filled with a new lake, prolonged both east and west. The caravan had, as usual, a good start of me; but instead of going straight down to the lake, they swung off a good deal to the west of it. This they did, not only in the hope of finding grass, but also that they might avoid the soft and treacherous strip of alluvium which encircled the lake. We encamped for the night at its western extremity, our Camp no. XXIV. (alt. 16,497 feet), counting from Abdall, being the very worst we had yet chosen. There was not a blade of grass, nor a scrap of fuel of any description; and we could only obtain a little hot tea at the cost of breaking up a packing-case. All that the beasts got was a handful of maize each. Scarcely was the camp settled down when a furious tempest burst upon us from the west. It began as rain, then turned to hail, and finally came down a regular deluge, until the felting of my yurt was sodden, and the rain dripped through upon me. Then during the night it changed to snow. The camels were just shedding their coats, and shook with cold, so we threw two or three felts over them. It was interesting to note that the new hair grew faster up here in the mountains than it did down in the warmer lowlands. Thus wonderfully does nature adapt herself to her surroundings.

The new mountain-range appeared to be low and easy to cross at a point south-west of our camp. Indeed, in comparison with the many which we had already crossed, we believed it would be a mere trifle. Its northern slopes were not even hard rock, but consisted only of low, rounded hills, which we never anticipated would occasion us the slightest trouble; but in reality this proved to be the most difficult bit of country we had yet encountered. In the first place, it was by no means easy to reach the foot of the hills, for the ground was everywhere marshy, necessitating the utmost caution to keep the horses out of the worst pitfalls, into which they sank up to their withers. But we assumed that, once we did reach the foot of the slope, the ground would be hard, and would bear us as usual. And at first the going was indeed not bad: the surface consisted of yellow clay, littered with stones and flakes of shale, and the ascent was easy. The only difficulty we experienced was with one big camel, which had a rooted antipathy to passes of all kinds, and which simply lay down at the foot of this. We left Turdu Bai to bring him on. Upon reaching the top of the first ridge, we continued along its crest to the south-east, having a deeply-eroded escarpment on each side of us. I led the way in the tracks of a wild yak, which went at first over firm ground, but higher up disappeared into the soft rain-drenched mire, which splashed at every step my horse took. At last he dropped in to such a depth, that I thought it better to get off and lead him. I ought, of course, to have turned back; but the next ridge looked so enticingly near. When, however, one of my boots stuck fast in the mud, I thought it really was time to stop, and wait for the others. The men came up panting. The camels, patient and submissive, as they always were, struggled along in their wake, sinking in a foot or more at each step; and yet their broad, flat pads were better than the horses' hoofs. One of the former fell, and we had to unload him, get him up, and reload him.

Walking on a veritable quagmire like this, at such a high altitude, completely took our breath, and made us feel quite giddy. Nor did we get on any better when we used as stepping-stones the big pieces of flat slate which lay scattered over the bog. For when we stepped upon them, they too sank into the ground, leaving a little pool of water where they had been. We could hear the water bubbling and trickling under the débris; so that I almost fancied we were walking over a subterranean river, which might suddenly open and engulf the entire caravan. I could not help thinking that the whole bunch of hills would, like a viscous fluid or thick porridge, gradually flatten themselves out to a uniform level. This conformation was caused by the incessant precipitation searching into the ground and making it like a sponge; for only a very small quantity trickled into the superficial brooks and rivulets, and so flowed away. The absence of vegetation with its interlacing roots also contributed to the same result. In two or three places the shales stuck up edgewise and cut the camels' feet. In one place two of the horses would have been literally smothered in the oozy mire, but that we hurriedly freed them from their loads and hauled them up. As the situation became at last absolutely intolerable, I sent Cherdon on to reconnoitre. He came back and said that this ridge was the first of a whole series, which extended a long distance to the south, and that all were flecked with melting snow, which of course would make the going even still more difficult.

This was the signal to return. We had lost more than four hours over this wretched piece of road, besides climbing up to an altitude of 17,219 feet to no purpose whatever; but the worst was that we had taxed the animals' strength severely, and all to no avail. After a little search we found a natural watercourse, or gully, and descended actually in the brook which traversed it—the only direction in which the ground was firm enough to bear us. But upon reaching the latitudinal valley at the bottom, the ground there proved to be not a whit better than it was higher up. Several other brooks poured into the one we were travelling down, until the united stream swelled to a volume of 283 cubic feet in the second. Coming at length to a patch of grass on its right bank, at an altitude of 16,441 feet above sea-level, we encamped, and decided to give the animals—what they sorely needed—a good two days' rest at Camp no. XXV.

A queer sort of rest it was, too! The morning, it is true, was promising enough; but just as I was going to take an observation of the sun, the sky clouded over. A little while after that the men carried out my bed, and felts, and carpets, and had just got them hung on the ropes to dry, when the sky blackened in the west. In we bundled all our belongings again as fast as we could, and had barely finished when down came the hail, rattling and crashing about our ears like bullets. This over, I managed to obtain my solar observation, but had scarcely finished when I saw a new storm advancing, quite as black as the former, but seven times more violent. It was preceded by furious squalls, upon which followed hail and wetting snow. I have seldom seen worse weather in Tibet. It thundered and lightened several times in the minute, and both thunder and lightning were quite close to the surface of the earth, immediately above our heads. The reverberations of the thunder were like mountains being cleft asunder, or mountains crashing flank against flank. The dazzling lightning made us involuntarily flinch, and we actually felt the ground trembling under our feet when the thunder crashed. It was a solemn and awe-inspiring sensation to be in the very centre of such a convulsion of nature, exposed to its uncurbed violence. We stopped working, we watched it, we listened to it, we wondered. The dogs howled pitifully. The men's tent was torn open, and it was as much as they could do to get it fastened again. The landscape was sheeted with hail and snow, underneath which the poor hungry horses had to seek their niggardly sustenance.

The second day proved, however, better: the sun came out and melted the snow, and the hail-storms kept off until five o'clock in the afternoon. One camel and one horse showed signs of exhaustion; and when, on the 12th of August, we continued, towards the south-east, over the "mud-range," Turdu Bai went on ahead, with the two sick camels carrying no loads; although this of course made the loads of the others all the heavier. In spite of that, however, we soon passed him, for he was travelling terribly slowly, owing to the big pass-hater wanting to lie down and rest so frequently.

On our left we now had a chain of mud-hills; in the far distance on the right a string of reddish eminences, while the ground between the two ascended imperceptibly towards the south-east; but there were no high mountains immediately in front of us. The ground we were travelling over was, however, abominable—one gigantic morass of yellow plastic mud, saturated through and through like a sponge. Although covered in places with a thin sprinkling of gravel, which looked tolerably firm, the animals nevertheless sank in up to their knees at every step, and as each foot had to be drawn in turn out of the tenacious, adhesive mire, it was very exhausting work to get on at all. The surface was, in fact, so soft that no sooner was a deep footprint made in it than the ooze closed round it and filled it in again. It was a piece of exceptional good fortune when the animals did not sink in more than four inches, and we were glad for their sakes when we came to comparative oases like this in the midst of that interminable slough of despond. But our joy was always short-lived: they were soon in again up to the knees, stumbling, falling, so that we had to unload, haul them up, and reload time after time. Truly an accursed land! That grass and fuel should be wanting at an altitude of 16,000 feet above the level of the sea was easy to understand; but why on earth should the ground not bear us? Why should it threaten to engulf the entire caravan? There was not a patch of dry ground as big as a threepenny-piece; it was everywhere saturated, sodden, through and through. In fact it was like the muddy bottom of a lake just after the water has been drained out of it. To tell the truth, I was astonished that our animals were willing to face it at all. I should have expected they would lie down and absolutely refuse to budge an inch. The big camel, that had such a rooted objection to passes, was quite right in refusing to exert himself. The heart of the Takla-makan Desert was not more destitute of organic life than were these truly abominable mountain wastes. Everyone of the men was obliged to walk. Our hearts beat as if they would burst, and we literally gasped for breath; while to climb into the saddle was like bringing the horse down over his own head. He moved as if he had a stone's weight of sticky soil adhering to each foot, and was unable to complete his pace until he had kicked it off. I rode on in advance to see what the country turned to. But the baggage animals were shy of stepping in the actual foot-prints of the animals which preceded them, and preferred to strike out a fresh track for themselves, though this was really no positive advantage to them.

Thus we plunged on hour after hour. This country threatened to be our doom! Our advance was like that of an invading army, which has burnt its bridges behind it, and is in the midst of the enemy's country, surrounded by dangers on every side. And yet there was a peculiar charm in a rash undertaking such as this. The farther we went the greater obviously grew the difficulties we should have to encounter on our return; but it was just these difficulties which enticed us on. We kept wondering. Shall we overcome them? Yet never for one moment did we think of turning back.

It is a remarkable thing, that in such a relatively short distance as that which intervened between the Akato-tagh and this region there should be such a striking difference in the natural conditions. There we might travel a whole day before we came to a miserable spring; here we had only to stamp on the ground in any spot we chose, and instantly the print of our foot was filled with water.

In the south-west stood a small, conical, detached eminence, and between it and the muddy ridge on our left was a low saddle, the water-parting of this particular district. On the way up we met a solitary wolf, which, however, took to flight the moment it saw us. Here we lost the big camel which hated passes: he failed to reach the top of the saddle, and died before morning. We had just reached the summit (16,769 feet) when the usual storm came on, and the thunder rumbled like the rolling of the ball in a giant's skittle-alley, or like the firing in the bombardment of a distant fortress. Although it was only four o'clock, it was as dark as an autumn evening. The horses walked sideways to avoid the hail. We ran up our tents hurriedly on the south side of the conical hill, where, although the ground was muddy, there was nevertheless a little grass (16,654 feet); but before we had finished our work, we were all wet to the skin. The storm lasted two hours, then the sun peeped out; but we were in the shade, and the sunshine played on the hills in the east as if in mockery of us. As the earth was relatively warm,

The Glaciated Mountain-mass seen South-west of Camp no. XXVII.

the hail soon began to melt, and the men dug a trench round my yurt to draw off the water.

At last, on the 14th of August, the sun shone out. During the night preceding the thermometer fell to $-3°.2$ C., or $26°.2$ Fahr., so that in the morning the ground was frozen hard, and the holes made by the animals' feet were covered with thin coatings of ice. But our mutual congratulations were short-lived. Before noon the surface turned as soft and spongy as ever. This day, however, we managed to turn our backs upon this abominable range, which had cost us so much trouble. From the easy rounded saddle by which we crossed it, we saw below us yet another latitudinal valley, shut in on the south by yet another lofty range. In the south-west was a vast glaciated mountain-mass; in the south-east a lake, and behind the latter the contours rose up into snow-clad heights of great altitude. The lake was fed by a stream which came from the west. Higher up the valley, that is towards the south-west, the ground assumed a green tinge, and accordingly we steered our course towards it; for grass was the thing we now needed most.

Upon reaching the place, we at once halted, for the ground was dry, firm sand, and it was quite a pleasure to see how the animals brightened up when they found themselves amongst the grass. Thin and sparse though it was we spread out all our bedding and every felt we had on the sand to dry in the blazing sun; but the tent and the yurt dried best erected in the usual way.

The next day, the 15th of August, it was exactly fifteen years since I started on my first journey to Asia, and I thought that the best way to celebrate the anniversary would be to take a day's holiday in this hospitable spot; and I was glad we did, when I saw how the animals picked up. Although it rained for a couple of hours, the weather was, on the whole, fine, and the thermometer went up to over $15°.0$ C., or $59°.0$ Fahr. This was a veritable oasis in the dreary mountain wastes, and as both animals and men visibly gathered strength, I agreed to give them yet another day. The men really had nothing else to do except bake bread, wash their clothes, and collect fuel, which they obtained from a little plant called *yer-baghri*, which put forth bunches of leaves on the top of a dry stalk.

On the 17th of August we started to climb over the next mountain-range, fording on the way the stream which flowed down the valley from the glacier in the south-west, and which carried from 250 to 280 cubic feet in the second. We began the ascent in a transverse valley, which our animals soon began to feel. After crossing three secondary passes, we reached the main pass, which was flat, and had two pools on the top. On our right, that is in the west, was the mountain-mass sheathed with glaciers and snow-fields; in the east, a flat-topped mountain, the edge of which was as straight as if it had been drawn with a ruler. It was probably capped with the porous tuff which is so common in these regions. From the summit of the pass we descended by an easy watercourse through the red, rounded sandstone hills; but the glen soon contracted into a veritable ravine, which in two or three places was so narrow that we were obliged to scramble up out of it and climb over the hills at the side. Finally, we came out upon a glacier stream with a volume of 350 cubic feet in the second, the water of which was muddy, and reminded me of 'hip' (*nypon*) soup. As there was a little scanty grass beside the stream, and the sandy ground was at least dry, the caravan halted for the night. Here Aldat, in shooting at an orongo antelope, had the misfortune to break his musket by bursting off a screw, which nearly struck him in the face. But, fortunately, he found it again, and was able to fasten it on with wire and a leather strap, so that, in case of need, the weapon could still be used.

During the greater part of the next day it rained again, and rained all night until seven o'clock the following morning, when we again started down the valley. The stream flowed almost due south-east, at the rate of nearly 3¾ miles an hour, and we followed it for over 18½ miles. We did not care where it took us, provided we got down to a lower level and found grass. Early in the day the men made a very unexpected discovery—namely, a piece of an old shirt, of Mohammedan make, a piece of rope, and a wooden pin with notches in it, such as is used in fastening a pack-animal's load. Whether these things were left by a caravan of Mongol pilgrims, or by Captain Wellby, I could not say. The latter, however, is not unlikely. Wellby and Malcolm crossed Northern Tibet from west to east—that is, from Ladak to Tsaidam—at the time I was in Tibet in 1896, their route running along the valley which lay immediately south of, and parallel to, my own route. A few years later Captain Wellby fell in the Boer war; where Lieut. Malcolm also was seriously wounded.

On the 20th of August we did 17 miles in a due south-easterly

View towards the South from Camp no. XXVIII.

direction, over slightly undulating country, with a gentle fall, where the going was excellent. In fact, the ground was, on the whole, so level that the water, instead of flowing off by any sort of distinct watercourse, collected on the surface in a vast number of little muddy pools. The grass gradually improved, until it was better than any we had hitherto found in Northern Tibet, and mingled with it were patches of luxuriant wild garlic, a herb which the camels ate greedily, and which also made a welcome flavouring in our soup.

The aspect of the region now changed entirely: it was open right away to the horizon. On the horizon there were, it is true, one or two mountain crests; but they appeared quite insignificant. The country assumed in fact a plateau-like character, and consisted of immense table-lands. Three big black yaks, grazing beside a pool, set off in a heavy gallop after us, thinking no doubt that we were somehow old acquaintances. But when they arrived within a couple of hundred yards of us, they perceived their mistake, and swinging round, went off at a clumsy jog-trot. Before us were two smaller lakes; but when we attempted to march between them, we were stopped by the channel which connected them, for it was 6½ feet broad and 5 feet deep. Skirting the more southerly of the two lakes, we became aware of a third lake of great area, farther towards the south-east, backed by low, dome-shaped hills. As there was good grazing on its nearer shore, we stopped there and pitched Camp no. XXX.

The 21st of August was devoted to rest and astronomical observations. The weather was splendid, beautifully warm, and the flies were buzzing about in the sunshine. We pitched our tents a little bit back from the lake shore, on some sandy hills, which absorbed the rain without making the ground soft and muddy. The strip of shore itself was low, and strewn with gravelly débris. The water of the lake was salt and bitter; but, fortunately, we discovered a fresh spring close by. And we had no lack of fuel, for yappkak bushes were very plentiful, and grew larger than usual. Two or three of the men, who came in carrying big armfuls of it, were a good deal disturbed in their minds by an uncanny howling they had heard, and asserted it was men shouting. But Aldat, who had been out hunting, explained that the noise was made by wolves. It was getting high time we did have fresh meat, for we were living almost entirely on rice and bread, although I still had a few tins of preserved food left, and every day Cherdon made me a good, nourishing soup of green peas, wild garlic, and Liebig's extract. This last I found of immense service during the journey; it was light of weight, went into small space, and possessed relatively great nourishing value.

CHAPTER XXXIII.

ADVENTURES ON A SALT LAKE.

On the 22nd of August I made the following arrangements. Kutchuk was to row me across the big lake, in a diagonal direction, towards a dominating peak which lay 50° east of south. Meanwhile the caravan would march west and south round the lake, until they came to the foot of this same peak. As their road might possibly be stopped by the considerable glacier-stream which we had followed a couple of days ago, and which entered the lake at its south-west corner, I sent on Mollah Shah on horseback to find out. He came back in the evening, and assured us there was no hindrance; but at the same time he reported another lake farther to the west, and equally large, which no doubt received the melting waters of the glacier. I assumed, therefore, that the caravan would have no difficulty in reaching the rendezvous before us, for we should spend a good deal of time in taking soundings and other observations. I ordered Cherdon on arrival to light a big fire, to serve as a beacon for our guidance.

It was a warm, bright day, the lake was like glass, and the turquoise-blue of the sky was only flecked by a few light, fleecy clouds. Whilst the caravan was loading up we got the skiff ready, putting into her the sail, the oars, and the life-belts, as well as the necessary instruments. We got started some time before the caravan, which we subsequently saw skirting the lake in a long string.

The bottom of the lake was covered throughout with a layer of salt, from $\frac{3}{4}$ to $1\frac{1}{2}$ inches thick quite close to the shore. The salt rested upon red mud, and broke under our naked feet; for we had to drag the boat a good mile before it would float. Even at that distance from the shore the lake was barely 20 inches deep. First we directed our course towards a little island in the east-south-east, Kutchuk punting, not rowing; and every time the oar touched the bottom, it produced a sound as though it struck against a stone. This extensive lake was nothing more than a gigantic salt-pan, utterly destitute of life—not an aquatic bird, not a lacustrine animal, not an alga. The very shore itself was barren as far as the water washed up it. The grass only began on the sandy hills several feet above the water. On its west side were some peculiar islands of rocky débris, semicircular in form.

The little island we were making for was shaped like a pear, with its stalk pointing towards the north, and its maximum height above the lake did not exceed 16 feet. It was a peaceful fragment of virgin soil, carpeted with excellent grass; but the only indication of organic existence it bore was the skeleton of a bird. Nevertheless, it afforded me a splendid view all round. Both east and west the country was perfectly open right away to the horizon. To the north-west was the massive mountain-knot, covered with glaciers, beside which we had encamped two or three days before. On the south the principal features were low, softly rounded ridges; in the north, the range we had last crossed, overtopped here and there by snowy peaks. The island was encircled by a narrow belt of blue clay; but beyond that was the layer of salt, all the irregularities of its surface being visible through the transparent water. After a while Kutchuk was unable to punt, and had to take to rowing, which of course made our advance somewhat slower.

The soundings of this lake gave a result I did not at all expect. Its floor was almost perfectly level; the maximum depth only slightly exceeded 7½ feet, or one-half the depth of the marsh of Kara-koshun. The difference of depth given by the various soundings did not exceed one inch. Thus the water formed a thin layer upon the top of the salt deposit. I had brought with me a sounding line several hundred fathoms long, but we found our seven-foot oar, which was accurately graduated to scale, quite sufficient for our purpose. Towards the east the lake appeared to extend to an immense distance, but this was only an optical illusion caused by mirage; for the eastern shore came into sight, though not very clearly, late in the afternoon.

It was altogether a remarkable day that I spent on this salt lake. The weather was splendid, the air perfectly still,

Turdu Bai and Kutchuk, with the Skiff Folded up, the Sounding-line and Lifebuoys (from a Photograph taken at Temirlik).

and the few white clouds which hung about the crests of the adjacent mountains were every one reflected on the surface of the lake. The sun, that rare visitant in these unfavourable regions, was very warm; we were delighted to get a glimpse of summer, and dream of its fleeting pleasures. It was delightful, too, to bathe our faces in its hot beams, and feel that we were dry after the many wettings we had had in the Arka-tagh, and at the same time delightful also to escape from the poisonous insects which, in lower regions, were such devoted associates of the summer sun. All around us was the silence of the grave, not a fly buzzing in the air, not a fish leaping in the water, the lake as lifeless as a chemical solution. The restless spirits of the air were taking a holiday, though doubtless only to prepare themselves for fresh outbursts. It was, in fact, as tranquil and peaceful as a Sabbath-day.

Viewed through the pure and rarefied atmosphere, there was something light and evanescent about the landscape. I can only liken it to a bride in an "Empire" robe of white and sky-blue silk; it was the airiest *aquarell* in diluted colours; everything was ethereal, transparent, like a *fata morgana* or a half-remembered dream. The water, except in the immediate vicinity of the skiff, where it was green, reflected the light blue colouring of the sky.

After the slow, dragging pace of the caravan, it was delicious to travel in this way. My place in the fore was as comfortable as an easy chair, and there I made my observations and sketched, precisely as I had done some months before on the big ferry-boat on the Tarim. I had no need to trouble about steering; a glance at the mountain we were making for was sufficient to control our course. Kutchuk sang and hummed as he rowed; or rather he did not row, he paddled. The mast and sail were lashed across the boat amidships, so as to be out of the way. I had brought no overcoat or furs with me; if I turned cold, I could of course take a turn at the other oar. But I was perfectly warm; the temperature of the air was 14°.0 C., or 57°.2 Fahr., while the temperature of the water was 17°.1 C., or 62°.8 Fahr. I revelled in the enjoyment of existence, and forgot all about the showers of hail.

The water was so heavily charged with salt that the drops which fell into the boat stiffened like stearine; after the water evaporated, there was left a thin, chalky-white hollow ball, which generally collapsed. The oar with which we took the soundings looked as if it had been painted white, our hands got white and rough, our clothes were spotted white from top to toe, from the sprinklings of the spray, and the velocity-instrument glittered all over with crystals. The bulwarks and bottom of the boat looked as if she had been recently employed in transporting flour. For the first few hours we saw the caravan duly marching along the western shore, and after that I saw it from time to time through my glass, plodding along in its usual orderly fashion. It was making a detour, whilst we were going in a straight line towards the rendezvous. Thus at first our routes diverged, until the caravan disappeared behind the hills, and after that I lost sight of it.

Mile after mile the depth remained constantly six feet. Hour after hour Kutchuk paddled steadily on, and yet we seemed to get no nearer to the southern shore. Towards the afternoon light clouds began to gather in the sky, and the bright surface of the lake became as it were marbled over. The lap—lapping of the water against Kutchuk's oar was the only sound that broke the brooding silence of this Tibetan Dead Sea, which lay at an altitude of 15,634 feet above the level of the sea.

At four o'clock the sun peeped out again, and now the lake appeared to extend farthest to the west, this effect being, of course, due to the low angle of the sun's rays as he was setting. I failed to see the caravan; but then the distance was great, and they might be hidden behind the hills. Further on in the afternoon the surface of the lake clouded over along the southern shore, and we heard a rushing noise, which gradually approached nearer. Kutchuk thought it was a stream entering the lake somewhere close at hand; but it soon became evident that it was a tempest rising. The wind blew from the east, and made it hard work to paddle; but it soon grew stronger, and we hoisted the sail and turned to the south-west. Then away we bowled at a glorious pace across the high waves, which, with a hollow roar, lashed themselves into white foam against the gravelly beach. We were afraid the sharp gravel would cut the canvas hull of the boat; but we managed to get the sail down in time. Kutchuk jumped out into the water, and helped her up, whilst I pushed with the oar, and in that way we got her beached without damage.

It was now dusk, and we hurried to the top of the nearest hill to look for the caravan; but not a trace of either man or animal! The whole region was silent, uninhabited, almost weird in its loneliness. It was like entering the ruins of a monastery in which no man has put foot for a thousand years. Whilst Kutchuk gathered an armful of yappkak fuel—the shrub grew plentifully just there—I penetrated farther up amongst the hills, but was stopped by two or three creeks and lagoons, in which the salt lay like ice, merely covered by a thin film of water. On a hill-side was the bleached skull of a kulan, and not very far away we noticed the foot-prints of a bear. I shouted, I listened, I shouted again, but no answer. The caravan was nowhere within hailing distance.

When I got back to our landing-place it was already dark. Kutchuk had gathered together a big pile of fuel, and as I had nothing else to do, I set to work and helped him to make it bigger. It was abundantly clear that some unexpected hindrance had arisen to prevent the caravan from reaching the rendezvous. Otherwise they would at least have sent a mounted messenger or two to tell us where they were, and—what was to us more important still—bring us food and water and warm clothing. Our first idea was to make use of the favourable breeze, and sail on to the west; but second thoughts showed that would be very risky in the darkness, especially as the wind was still increasing in violence. And, after all, the circuit round the lake might be a good deal longer than we anticipated, so that there really had not been time for the caravan to get round.

The best thing, therefore, was to make ourselves as comfortable as we could for the night. Choosing a level space, we stacked up our fuel, lifted all the things out of the boat, and took the boat to pieces; then, raising the two halves on end, we made, as it were, two sentry-boxes, which sheltered us capitally against the wind. Scarcely had we finished our preparations when it began to rain. Then we tilted each half of the boat at an angle of 45°, propping it on an oar, and in this way procured a roof over our heads as well. Converting the life-belts into pillows, we each managed to get a short nap. At nine o'clock I wound up the chronometer, and took a meteorological observation, whilst Kutchuk lighted the fire. Then we sat and chatted for a couple of hours; but it would have been much more enjoyable if we could have had a cup of warm tea and a slice of bread, or even a cup of water. From this I learned never to embark again without taking food and extra clothing with me.

When we had used up all our fuel, it was time to think of going to bed, and here the two halves of the skiff again came in very handy. We spread the sail on the gravel, though that did not make it very much softer. Then half burying the life-belt in the ground, and doubling myself up, I lay down, while Kutchuk tilted the half-boat over me. After that he stopped up every crevice with gravel and sand, using the oar blade as a spade. The bottom of the boat was only an inch or two above my head, and I was packed into it like a corpse into a coffin —an idea which was a good deal strengthened by Kutchuk's digging and scraping outside. Inside it was as dark as the grave, and the space was so confined, that I had the greatest difficulty in turning myself round.

After spending a whole day on the water, and getting no supper, I naturally felt cold; but in my cosy "tent" I very soon grew warm. Kutchuk made himself comfortable in a similar way. Capital thing that boat! First she carried us all day across the lake, then she sheltered us all night on shore, and when, a little afterwards, it began to pour with rain, and the heavy rain-drops rattled like drum-sticks against the taut canvas, we only felt all the more comfortable. We chatted for a little while, Kutchuk's voice sounding through the double canvas walls like a voice from the grave, and my own hollow and sepulchral. But Nature soon asserted her right, and we slept as sound as the dead, oblivious alike of wolves and bears and our own faithless caravan.

I was awakened two or three times by the insidious cold, but at length daylight blinked in under the bulwarks, and I was astonished to find it was already seven o'clock. I called Kutchuk, who came and helped me to open my coffin lid, and, sure enough, there was the sun high above the horizon. We were both stiff with cold, and made haste to gather a fresh supply of fuel, which we lighted with our last two or three matches. The fire put fresh life into us. As there was a fresh and steady east wind, and we neither saw nor heard anything of the caravan, I decided we would go and look for them. We put the boat together again, rigged her up, launched her, manned her, and shook out the sail, using one of the oars as the boom and the other as the rudder, and away we skimmed like a swallow, hugging the southern shore. The wind blew hard, and the lake rose high, so that the skiff rolled a good deal, and Kutchuk, who sat in the bow, was seasick. I was busy taking soundings, measuring the velocity, and mapping the route. At the end of an hour or a little more, I saw through the glass two white objects at the western end of the lake, surrounded by a number of small black dots. The former I took to be the yurt and the tent, the latter the men and animals of our caravan.

At the end of another three hours we reached our destination. Cherdon and Aldat waded out and hauled us carefully ashore. It was as I supposed: the caravan had been stopped by a broad river, which was too deep for them to ford, and which flowed out of the large lake farther west. Turdu Bai had tried it in several places, but always found the water so deep, that his horse lost his feet and began to swim. After that they turned back and encamped beside the spring where we found them. They had kept a fire burning all night on a hill, to serve as a beacon to us, in case we should be driving about on the lake. As they were in urgent need of fresh meat, Aldat had managed to shoot a kulan or wild ass. During my absence our young wolf-cub was so generously fed that he died from over-eating himself.

Directly we landed, Cherdon brought me coffee and breakfast. The rest of the day I spent in making up arrears of work. The next question was, which way were we to go? If we turned to the west, it would take us three days to get round the new lake; and to the east lay the big salt lake which we had just crossed. On the south we were stopped by the river, which ran from the evidently fresh-water lake into the salt-water one. To turn back was not to be thought of. I would not go back until the miry high ground had frozen sufficiently to bear us. Finally I resolved to convoy the entire caravan across the river with the aid of the skiff.

Whilst I and Kutchuk rowed round to the mouth of the river, which was about 325 yards across, the caravan went down to the spot where it was narrowest. Just outside the mouth we found a ridge or bank, with only about 20 inches of water on it; this would have made a first-rate ford, except that there was a gap in the middle of it 8½ feet deep. At the spot where the animals were being unloaded the water, notwithstanding there was a strong current flowing out of the fresh-water lake, was intensely salt. We saw the two waters blending together—turning thick, and giving rise to eddies, as when a spoonful of sugar is put into water.

Both banks consisted of hard gravel. The place where the

Towing a Camel Across the River.

Firm Ground under Foot.

crossing was to be made was 190 feet wide. The principal difficulty was getting a rope stretched from one side to the other. Having tied together the greater part of the ropes

The Salt Lake at Camp no. XXXV.—Seen from the North-west.

with which we lashed on the loads, we made one end fast on the left bank and dragged the other end up stream; then, whilst I rowed across as hard as I could pull, Kutchuk stood up in the bow with the end of the rope in his hand ready to jump ashore. But we failed to hit the little headland on the other side; the rope was too short. Back we hauled ourselves, joined on another piece of rope, and repeated the manœuvre again—this time with a better result. Thereupon we made the rope fast on the right bank and tightened it until it hung clear of the water.

We tried to drive the horses across, but they refused to

A Camel which has just Swum Across the River.

enter the river until after we had towed one of them over. But the worst business was with the camels. As it was impossible to get them to swim across themselves, there was nothing for it but to tow them over with the boat one by one. Having forced a camel into the river, we slipped a rope round his neck, with which Turdu Bai, crouching in the stern, supported the animal's head above the surface. Meanwhile I hauled the boat across the river by pulling on the rope. But as the camel did not condescend to exert himself in any way, but simply lay and floated like a log, I had his entire weight to bear as well as the full force of the stream, and was obliged to exert myself to the uttermost; if I had let go, the whole bag of tricks would have drifted out into the lake and the camel been lost.

However, I managed to get him far enough to feel firm ground under his feet, and he then condescended to help himself.

After we had in this way ferried across the third camel, the rope grew so slack that it dipped into the water. Whilst we were doubling it, and tightening it up again, the first rope broke, and so we had to do the whole thing over again. As my hands were by this time badly blistered, Cherdon hauled across the remaining three camels. Our last surviving sheep, which was accustomed to keep beside the camels, swam over of its own accord.

We carried the baggage across in 14 journeys, and encamped on the spot where we landed. This river was the largest I had hitherto seen in Middle or Northern Tibet. It carried a volume of 1,678 cubic feet in the second. In all probability it had its sources a long way to the west, and gathered into its basin all the glacial streams of the region. Several small aquatic animals were carried by the current from the fresh-water lake towards the salt-water lake; but they would of course perish as soon as the infusion of salt grew too strong for them.

As two or three of the horses and one of the camels had chafed backs, we allowed them to travel for the next few days without loads. My favourite grey also needed rest, so I rode another horse. It was my custom to train my saddle-horse to stand when I wanted to take a compass-bearing; and the moment I put my hands into my pocket to get my compass, my good grey used to stand perfectly still until I had finished.

We now climbed the hills, consisting of soft material, without a trace of hard rock, which bordered both lakes on the south. At intervals we found excellent grass on the hill-side, which, added to the springs and the abundance of fuel, tempted us to stay; but the animals were still tolerably fresh, and so we kept on. After crossing a low ridge, we came upon another lake, which, although without visible outlet, was nevertheless fresh.

Amongst the hills south-west of the lake, we observed 18 yaks grazing, and higher up a herd of above a hundred, young and old together—in fact, the ground was black with them. Whilst we were watching them, the sky darkened in the east and west simultaneously, and the rumbling of the thunder—a warning, like the lion's roar, for us to be on the alert—announced that a storm was approaching. Down burst a hail-shower with overpowering violence. The yaks disappeared in the

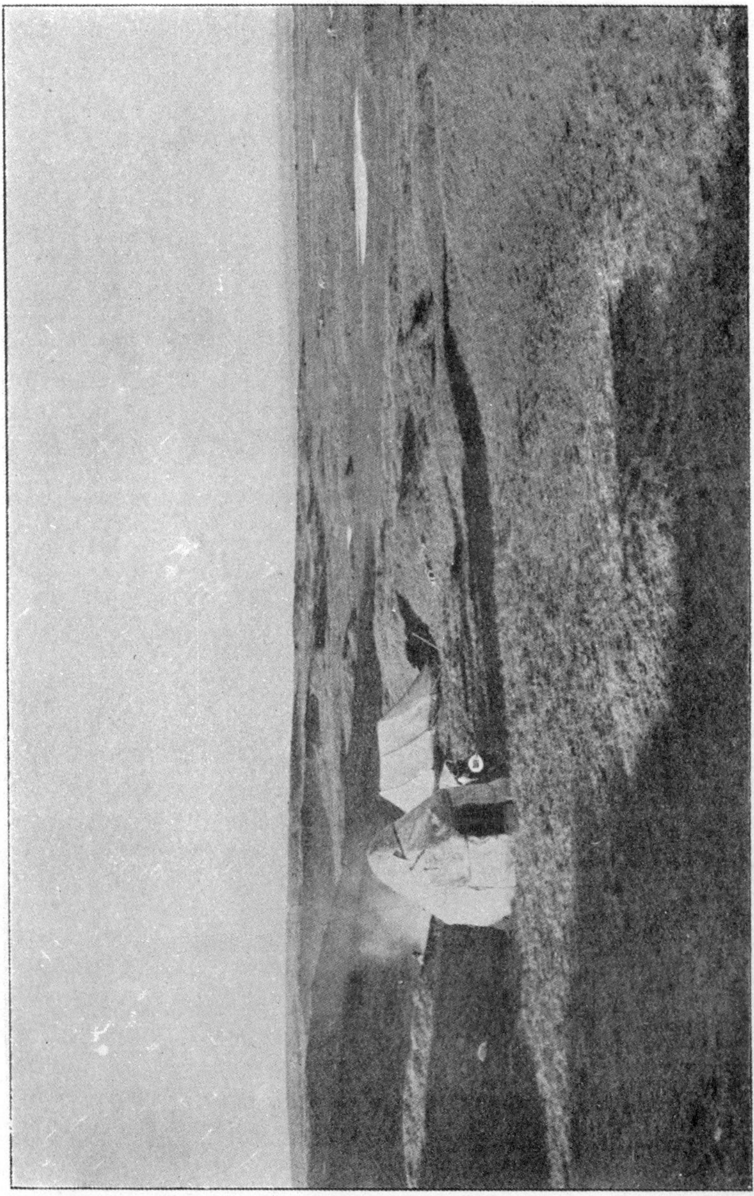

My Yurt at Camp no. XXXV.—Looking North.

thick downpour, as also did Aldat, with his gun on his shoulder, as he hurried up the slopes on the other side of the valley. Leaving him to look after himself, we continued along the lakeside, and encamped beside a little pool a mile or so from its southern shore. About nine o'clock we heard shouts in the darkness, and two or three of the men, whom I sent out to see what it was, met Aldat utterly wearied out, staggering under the load of a big lump of yak-flesh and a yak's tail. Aldat's victim was a well-grown calf, which had dropped at the first shot.

The next day, being Sunday, was devoted to rest. Aldat and Kutchuk rode back to the place where the former had killed the yak, and fetched in a whole load of meat—an invaluable addition to our scanty larder. Cherdon cut me some cutlets, which were not at all bad; but then it was a young animal, whose flesh was tender.

On the 27th of August we steered due south, and soon crossed a little brook, the water of which had a temperature of no less than 20°.3 C., or 68°.5 Fahr., and contained an extraordinary number of small crustaceans. That evening, too, we encamped on the shore of a large lake, where the grass was too good to be passed; in fact, the hills on its western side were overgrown with what I may describe as luxuriant grass. The water of the lake had a specific gravity of 1.021; but there were springs of fresh water not far away. The next day we skirted the south-west corner of the lake, crossed over a ridge of flattened hills, and were again stopped by a labyrinth of creeks, pools, and other sheets of water. One of these was of considerable size, and had a strong muddy red current. Mollah Shah tried in two or three places to wade across it, but it was too deep, and he was forced to turn back. So, here we were again stopped by an impassable river, and were just on the point of turning up along its northern bank in search of a fordable crossing, when we perceived our old, all too familiar enemy threatening us. Although there was an east wind blowing, the western horizon was darkening rapidly. Masses of cloud, heavy as lead, came rolling across the country, with the sweep of an immense seine-net. Or rather it was like an army advancing both wings at once to the attack with irresistible *élan*. The clouds of the left wing had blood-red edges, but those of the right wing were black as ink. The advanced skirmishers were packed together in the most extraordinary formations, as they raced before the tempest. All this time the country in the east was basking in bright sunshine ; but the terrible net of the west was drawing in closer and closer around us. We hastily decided to encamp where we were, though not too close to the stream, for the violent downpour might perhaps cause it to overflow its banks. Every man gave a hand with the framework of the yurt, and we had just got two or three felts stretched across the top spars when the storm burst. The hail-shower literally swept along the ground. Every pellet stung, for they came as if discharged from a pea-shooter. There was quite a race for shelter.

The next morning the weather was not very promising, and it was noon before we got the boat ready for measuring the stream and exploring the intricate network of water-ways which stopped us. To the north lay the big salt lake, which I and Kutchuk had sailed across, while to the south was another lake of very respectable dimensions, which, like the fresh-water lake I have mentioned before, discharged itself into our special friend, the salt-water lake. In its lower course the new river expanded into two or three broad basins. Not knowing in which direction the stream flowed, we entered one of these side arms, but were of course soon turned back. At its inner end was a flock of about 50 wild-geese, presumably resting on their way to India for the winter. But at our approach they all flew off, except one, which took to the water. We made for him and pursued him for nearly an hour, his divings growing shorter and shorter, until at last we got within about 12 yards of him, when I began to harpoon him with the oar, the only weapon I had at hand. He was several times embarrassed by the blade, and at length succumbed to a well-directed shot. He made a welcome change in our bill of fare.

We eventually discovered, that the new stream joined the broad river which flowed from the fresh-water lake to the salt-water lake. Landing on the other side of it, we climbed a hill, and perceived we were almost entirely surrounded by large sheets of water. We were standing at the very extremity of a neck of land which ran due east, and had to the north of us the big salt lake so often spoken of, and on the south the fresh-water lake we had just discovered. About half-way down the neck of land was a low range of hills, with apparently plenty of good grazing and abundance of game at its southern foot. On our way back to camp, I made up my mind to have a sail on these new lakes.

The Salt Lake at Camp no. XXXV.—Looking to the North-east.

CHAPTER XXXIV.

A TIBETAN LAKE-LAND.

CAMP no. XXXVI. was now the base for further operations. Leaving Turdu Bai, Aldat, and Niaz there with the camels and four tired horses, I, with Cherdon, Mollah Shah, and Kutchuk, besides seven horses, our one mule, and the dogs, went off on the new excursion. We were provisioned for a week, and took with us only such things as we absolutely needed, in addition to felts and furs. The boat, of course, was indispensable in this land of lakes. I packed my instruments in the big camera case. Of the yurt we only took one-half—that is to say, the lower part of the framework, and a couple of felt rugs to cover it. The men made a shelter in bad weather out of a few of the roof-spars and two or three felts. After the horses had waded across the river, getting only the lower half of their pack-saddles wet, we easily carried our loose luggage across in the boat.

Before we advanced very far we were stopped by the sound that connected the two lakes, and had to unload, swim the horses across, and ferry over the baggage in the boat. As soon as we were once more loaded up, we got started in real earnest, skirting the northern shore of the fresh-water lake. Very soon, however, we came to a place where the hills plunged steeply down into the water—nay, actually hung over it—so that we were forced to climb right over the top of them. Extensive sheets of water stretched both right and left of us.

We put up our temporary yurt beside a little brook that issued from a side glen, about 300 paces up which a herd of big black yaks were peacefully grazing. As they made not the slightest attempt to flee, I was inclined to think they were tame yaks, and must belong to a band of nomads somewhere in the neighbourhood. But when we turned our horses loose to graze, and they slowly made their way up to the richer grass where the yaks were, the latter sniffed and turned and steadily examined us, and then went off at a gentle trot over the crest of the hills towards the salt lake.

My quarters were so confined that Cherdon had to make the bed first, and then fix the lattice framework round it. It was like creeping into a dog-kennel; but once inside, I was very comfortable and warm, especially after I let Yolldash come in beside me.

Although during the night the thermometer fell to $-5^{\circ}.2$ C., or $22^{\circ}.6$ Fahr., the next day, the last of August, turned out a splendid summer's day, without a speck of cloud or a breath of wind. The lake was as smooth as a duck-pond. A kulan came and had a look at the horses with as little concern as if he knew perfectly well that Cherdon's cartridges were all exhausted long ago. On the southern side of the lake were two peaks, crowned with glittering white snow, which, with the flawless sky above them, were reflected with photographic distinctness in the lake. A few hours' further march took us to the end of this lake, but a new neck of land, only a few hundred yards broad, separated it from yet another lake, which extended still farther to the east. This also we followed along the northern shore.

For a short distance we travelled on the top of the cliffs, which hung some 230 feet above the surface of the lake, following a kulan path, which ran so near the edge as not to be altogether pleasant. Away below in the water we could see a shoal of very large black-backed fish, which greatly excited Kutchuk's interest. So we stopped, to see if we could not catch some. We made hooks out of the metal in Yolldash's collar by heating it in the fire and hammering it out. At the same time we contrived a bow out of the ribs of our tent; if we came across wild-duck we might perhaps hit them with arrows. You see, we were living like Robinson Crusoe, and had to do the best we could with such scanty materials as we possessed.

The evening was raw and windy, and the prospects for the morrow not very promising. My yurt stood as firm as a rock, but the interior was so confined that to dress and undress was attended with a certain amount of difficulty. Early the next morning I walked to the top of the nearest hill, and thence obtained a splendid view of the entire vicinity, in which water was decidedly more abundant than land. The lake, which sent off a wedge-shaped arm towards the north-east, lay spread out below my feet like a map. It was situated at an altitude of 15,906 feet above the sea. We had thus come down to a relatively lower level, but were still higher than—the top of Mont Blanc! In the meantime Kutchuk had launched the boat and got her ready, and as soon as I returned we rowed in under the perpendicular cliffs of red sandstone where we had seen the fish.

Meanwhile the caravan continued its way round the lake, having instructions to stop on the south side, immediately underneath a peak, which I have indicated on my map by the sign O1. We anchored the boat quite close to the shore, with big segments of the mountain wall hanging over our heads, as it were, by a hair, and threatening every instant to topple down and crush us. Although we felt nothing of the north-west wind, because we were in shelter, we nevertheless heard it swishing along the crest of the precipice.

For a fishing-rod we used one of the spars of the boat, our bait consisting of small pieces of yak flesh, while an empty matchbox served capitally as a float. The *asmans*—the fish—bit splendidly, yet we only caught four medium-sized fellows. We were not fishing for amusement, but because we wanted food, and our catch was barely sufficient for one meal. However, skimpy though that meal was, it was a great change, and the fish was tasty.

But whilst I sat in the boat thinking and enjoying the sunshine and the rest, the hours flew all too fast, and it became time to start for the rendezvous. But it was darkening in the west; the sky was rapidly clouding—a storm was brewing. We had to choose between staying where we were until it was over—which would hardly have been worth while, for it was now two o'clock, and the caravan no doubt by this already arrived at its destination—or we might take the risk of crossing the lake. I preferred the latter course. Before Kutchuk had rowed very far we began to feel the north-west wind, which helped us along first-rate. Right ahead the leaden, grey clouds were trailing long fringes of hail across the mountains, gradually blotting them out. Behind us the sky was thickening in the same way. The storm approached nearer, the lake went higher, its waves hissing white-crested around us. Down came the hail-burst, peppering the water with its big round pellets. In a moment or two the inside of the boat was as white as chalk. Water and hail, water and hail—everywhere! Shores and mountains alike vanished! We had to keep a sharp watch upon the water, for, as the wind went on increasing in violence, the waves broke higher and higher. Still, as they were several times longer than the boat, we had only to keep her head straight before the wind, and we rode on beautifully, up and down, up and down, with the spray dashing from our bow. Immediately south of the red

The Fish Mountain.

The Fish Mountain Seen from the Middle of the Lake.

sandstone cliffs the sounding-line had given a depth of 159¾ feet, the greatest depth I ever sounded in Tibet, but this rapidly decreased as we approached the southern side, until I began to fear the lake would shallow to such an extent that our light craft would be dashed like a nutshell against the beach.

The hail ceased, but not so the wind. It, on the contrary,

View Down the Lake—The Storm Disappearing in the Distance.

The Sun Setting on the Lake.

raged still more fiercely, for the further we proceeded from the cliffs the more we became exposed to its fury. Still there was one thing in our favour: we were now at any rate able to see where we were going to, and found we were not yet half-way across. We now steered for a headland, behind which we hoped to obtain some shelter. The waves meanwhile rose so high that they hid the shore from us when we went down into the trough of the "sea," and when the sun peeped out through the clouds, as he soon did, they were almost weird-looking: they glittered like the backs of dolphins, changed from blue to green and from green to blue, and were capped with hissing foam, which sparkled like jewels where the sun's rays tipped them. The canvas covering of the skiff was indented every time she pitched, and was strained so tight that a single powerful side-blow would have been sufficient to burst it; hence we had to manœuvre her with both oars so as to shield her against the onset of the waves. To be brief, this voyage again ended happily. The storm passed over, the wind subsided, the features of the shore came out distinctly, and we altered our course, making straight for the camp. The sunset was magnificent. The sun himself was hidden behind a dense black cloud, but his reflected rays glittered like quicksilver as they streamed across the ruffled surface of the lake.

We were now a long way from our base-camp under Turdu Bai's charge, and it was time to think of returning to it. According to my reckoning we could not be very far from the sources of the Yang-tse-kiang, and I had not given up all idea of trying to discover them. But one thing was clear: the three large lakes which we had discovered in this region had plainly nothing whatever to do with the Yang-tse-kiang, but formed a self-contained basin, possessing no outlet; but as I was not yet absolutely sure of this, I resolved to sacrifice the 2nd of September to a ride farther south. This led us over undulating tablelands, with scanty grass and dangerous, yielding ground. After going 16¾ miles, we stopped on the bank of a stream, which entered the next lake—a small salt pool lying south-east of the preceding. Beyond this we were unable to proceed, because of our fast diminishing supplies and our exhausted horses. Next day we turned back, but struck off to the west. We again very nearly got stuck fast in the treacherous quagmires, the horses sinking in nearly two feet. A large stream, which issued from the mountains on our left, flowed due north, and emptied itself into the lake in which we had fished. We travelled along its bed, for it was there we got the firmest ground to ride upon.

Game was extraordinarily plentiful thereabouts. We saw fully half-a-dozen herds of orongo antelopes (*Pantholops Hodgsoni*), each consisting of a score of individuals, though the yaks and kulans occurred either singly or in small troops. Rats, marmots, and hares were very common, while wild geese and gulls made the lake shores noisy with their screeching. We rode in two divisions, with a gap of about 50 paces between us. Yolldash was very busy amongst the game. Once he drove three kulans at full gallop through the gap between us, but before I could get my small camera ready to snap them, they were gone. About an hour later he went off after a herd of orongo antelopes, and when he came back was covered with blood; he had evidently had a royal time of it. Wolves and foxes frequented the uplands to the south. During the latter half of the day's march heavy snow drove straight in our faces, so that I could barely see the horse which marched immediately in front of me. We were all sheathed in white armour of soppy melting snow, which kept peeling off in big strips. Mollah Shah led the way, following a yak-track, which, fortunately, in spite of the snow, was pretty easy to see.

I had intended next day to row across the lake from south to north, so as to take a second series of soundings, but when we woke the weather was, to say the least, peculiar. The sky was perfectly clear, the sun shone in all its splendour, but a strong half-gale was blowing from the north, and the waves broke noisily on the flat shelving beach. Of course, crossing it by boat was out of the question. We rode west along the shore, which was nothing but a mud bath, a very slough of despond! What a wonderful—what an utterly God-forsaken region this was! The ground seemed to be as thin as the air; the very mountains themselves as soft as pumice-stone. Everything was in a state of disintegration. The weather the most unreliable it is possible to conceive. To embark on the lake was to put your life in direct jeopardy. In some places, although the ground did bear, it nevertheless quaked under the horses' feet, and undulated before them as though it were an indiarubber sheet.

At length we reached the end of the lake, and found that it, too, emptied itself through a broad, and considerable stream, into the lower fresh-water lake. The latter was black with wild geese, trying their wings after moulting, flying round in short, quick circles, in preparation for their long journey to warmer climes. They were being closely watched by a solitary golden eagle. We pitched camp (no. XLII.) beside the embouchure of the river into the lower lake. From this spot it could not be more than a day's journey to the place where we had left Turdu Bai. Whilst Mollah Shāh and Cherdon led the horses along the southern shore of this the lower fresh-water lake, I and my trusty boatman, Kutchuk, started to cross it diagonally. When we started it was glorious weather, with a favourable wind, but we had not got very far when the wind freshened, and drove us out into the open, where, however, the depth nowhere exceeded 10 feet. After about an hour the wind changed, and the usual forerunner of a tempest, the black clouds, loomed up in the west. They divided themselves into two sections, one of which went off over the mountains to the south, leaving a trail of white snow behind it, while the other hastened across the lake to meet us, once more churning up the never-resting waves. The most prudent course would have been to run before the storm, except that we should then have been carried away from our men, who were cut off by the broad channel which connected the second fresh-water lake with the first salt-water lake. We therefore resolved to try and row against both wind and waves. In the distance, to the west-north-west, stood the little hill from which I first saw this lake. Our boat was already pitching in such an uncomfortable manner that I, who was sitting in the fore part, was drenched by every billow that broke. A pelting rain came on and helped to make the situation more disagreeable still. Although we each strained at our oars we made no headway. Very often one-half of the boat would hang over on the top of a wave; then down she would plump, threatening a rent in her fragile covering. Soon another ill-omened change took place in the wind, for it swung round to the south, and blew with unparalleled violence, setting up a second system of waves, which ran at right angles to the first. This caused them at the points of intersection to rise to double their former height. All our efforts were now required to avoid these watery pyramids, and to keep to the relatively level spaces between them; but before we were aware of it, the skiff was hovering on the summit of a wave, and had we failed to balance her there, over she would have gone. Of course, I had now abandoned all idea of taking soundings. We might esteem ourselves lucky if we escaped with our lives, and we kept wondering whether it was to be the next wave or the one after it which was to bowl us over. In this way we toiled for an hour and a half before the storm subsided. But even then the sky wore a threatening aspect, being streaked in every direction by storm centres resembling waterspouts, with

A Struggle for Life.

hanging draperies of black cloud. Most of them went past us on one side or the other; but some of them drifted right across our lake. We were not a bit nearer land when the second storm came and shook out its heavy load of snow and hail over our heads. Although it drove straight in our faces, we could do nothing to ward it off, for one moment's unwariness and over we should have gone. Throughout the whole of that day we toiled like galley-slaves.

During the respite which followed the second squall we made haste to win headway, for the sky was already darkening for the third time; and down charged the third storm upon us with its pouring torrents of rain. The second had painted the inside of the boat white with snow and hail; this half filled her with water, which lapped backwards and forwards as we rode up and down the heaving waves. But this squall, too, passed, and pursued its solitary way across the inhospitable mountains and impressionable lakes which stretched to the east.

After eight hours' hard work we at length came to land, and I was never more delighted to put foot on *terra firma*. Climbing a little hill, I perceived Mollah Shah waiting for us on a headland with the four horses. We paddled round to where he was, and then stopped to take the volume of the stream which we had crossed a week before. We also measured its breadth and sounded its depth, and took three measurements of its velocity, when down came the fourth squall. Although the sun was still above the horizon, it was as dark as midnight, except when the dazzling flashes of lightning lit up the weird chaos of lake and barren mountain. The hail came down from the sky and swept along close to the surface of the earth; the spray rose from the lake and mingled with it. We happened to be just then on the east side of the channel, and it was only by the most desperate efforts that we were able to push our boat over to the other side, although it was not more than 200 feet across. This, however, was the farewell greeting of that day of storms, and I need not say we had had enough of it. We unscrewed the boat, packed sail, mast, oars, and life-belts into the one half, loaded up, distributed the instruments amongst us, mounted, and set off at a smart trot for home.

It was a pleasant change to ride after the long stretch of strenuous rowing. The moon shone through the breaking clouds, mingling her light in a fantastic manner with the incessant flashes of lightning, which seemed to turn her white crescent yellow every time they flamed out upon it. At length we reached camp, and found all well. Aldat had shot four orongo antelopes, so that we were well provisioned for two or three weeks to come. The camels and ailing horses had gathered flesh during their rest. Even after we lay down to sleep, utterly tired out, the storms still continued to chase one another unweariedly over the earth. We rested all the next day, the 6th of September. The afternoon was like a winter's day, without a single glint of sunshine, while one hailstorm followed another without intermission. Whilst Cherdon and Kutchuk went fishing, the other men prepared the skeleton of an orongo antelope, and I was kept busy recording the results of our recent excursion.

Possibly I often dwell upon events, and describe incidents, which may seem to the reader trivial and insignificant, but I do it for the purpose of conveying some idea of the life which the solitary traveller leads in those desolate, uninhabited wastes. Taken as a whole, they will give a consistent picture of how the days passed month after month in our little community. We were not a large company, and we lived under monotonous conditions, the same occupations recurring with uniform regularity, and our lives strictly governed by the clock. It was only the country we travelled through which, with its never-ending variety and change, kept our interest awake.

With regard to my choice of servants, I had every reason to be satisfied. With stoic serenity Turdu Bai tended the camels as if they were his own children. Cherdon was attentive, alert, and punctual, and yet at the same time a comical little man, with his own peculiar philosophy of life. Mollah Shah watched over the horses with irreproachable care, but was somewhat taciturn, abrupt, and reserved. When on the march, one-half of the horse-caravan was led by Kutchuk, a young giant of two or three and twenty, always happy and contented, but especially so when he was afloat, for most of his days since he was a child had been spent on the water. Without Aldat our situation would have been very critical indeed; he kept us supplied with fresh meat, and was always after the game. But both in camp and whilst on the march he preferred to be left to himself, and spoke but little. Niaz did all the heavier work, carried water, gathered fuel, drove in the animals of a morning, and gave a hand with loading them up. The dogs had the best time of it, for they had plenty of meat to eat, nothing whatever to do, except to keep watch, and that was a sinecure. And they had a playmate in our last surviving sheep, which nobody had the heart to kill. The creature consorted faithfully with the camels, grazed with them during the day, and at night found a warm and cosy lair beside them.

CHAPTER XXXV.

THE LAST DAYS OF ALDAT THE AFGHAN.

Camp no. XLIII. was the turning-point of the expedition. Our supplies would not allow us to proceed farther south. We were only provisioned for two and a half months, and we had already spent six weeks on the tramp. Although we still had a plentiful supply of rice, we were obliged to husband our flour with the utmost care, having used too much of it in attempting to save the camel that died. Winter would soon be here, and we ought to return, making a wide detour, first west, then north, then east, back to our headquarters camp in the Chimen valley.

But before leaving this part of Tibet, I wished to cross a particular east-west range, which culminated in the south-west in a vast mountain-mass, capped with perpetual snow. After a rather short day's march to Camp no. XLIV. (16,038 feet), I decided to divide our party, sending on the larger portion of the caravan, under command of Turdu Bai, down a latitudinal valley which opened out to the west-south-west. I ordered him to wait for us somewhere in the open country to the north-west of the culminating mountain-mass, while I myself skirted its left flank. This excursion would, I estimated, take only four days, and I selected Cherdon and Aldat to accompany me. We had only six horses, and carried the small temporary yurt, provisions for a week, and fuel enough to last two days. There *was* a certain element of adventure in the plan, for the Mussulmans might lose their way. But in case our trail should be obliterated by hail or snow, I instructed Turdu Bai to wait for us one week, and if at the end of that time he failed to hear anything of us, he was to abandon all further search, and make his way back as best he could to our headquarters camp in the Chimen valley. Their provisions could be made to hold out at a pinch; and as for ourselves, we relied upon Aldat to keep us supplied with meat.

Both sections started simultaneously on the 8th of September, and after leaving the upper course of the river, which some days before had stopped our southward march, our routes diverged, and we were soon hidden from one another by a cluster of low hills. Our own course was towards the south-south-west, through fairly open country, except that it was a little diversified on both the right and the left. The contours rose slowly as we advanced, and the ground became barren, except for a few patches of moss. After riding smartly for several hours we reached a chain of flat hills, with small basins of crystal spring-water between them. Each of these last was surrounded by a belt of short, thick, vivid-green grass, soft as an Oriental carpet. Here, as there did not appear to be any grazing towards the south, while there was good spring water, as well as plenty of fuel, for the district was much frequented by yaks and kulans, we halted for the night, our camp being 16,316 feet above sea-level. Apart from a couple of big wolves, the only traces of animal life were two or three ravens. The weather was, of course, unfavourable; this made the eighteenth day that we had hailstorms and snowstorms from the west. But the night was as usual bright and still, with a clear moon, and as early as nine o'clock in the evening the thermometer dropped to $-2°.0$ C., or 28.°4 Fahr.

On the 9th we continued in very nearly the same direction, the surface being a good deal more broken; we were now approaching higher regions. Before we turned due west we were forced out of our way by a watercourse, which issued out of the flank of the big snowy mass in front of us, and which was filled with soft ooze. We were all drowsy and stiff with cold when we stopped at a patch of grass. As soon as the camp was pitched Aldat came and begged permission to stalk a big yak which he had seen grazing not very far away. I went out and watched him, creeping like a cat along the hollows towards his unsuspecting prey. Thanks to the strong wind that was blowing against him, he was enabled to get within thirty paces of the yak. He fixed his gun on its fork, and fired. The yak jumped, making the earth fly all around him. Then he ran a few yards, stopped, staggered, tried to keep his balance, but finally fell. Then he rose again, and went through the same series of movements. This he repeated several times; but at last tumbled down all of a heap and lay without moving. All this time Aldat lay behind his gun, motionless as a statue, lest he should draw the attention of the dying animal to himself. Cherdon and I now joined him. It was difficult walking; we could only take two or three steps at a time, and then had to stop, for the least effort in this extraordinarily rarefied air brought on quickened action of the heart. The yak was a bull of fifteen years. Out came the knives, his head was cut off, his entrails taken out, and then we left him till the following morning. His fat was the part about him which we desired most. It cost Aldat a real pang to leave behind the magnificent skin, which would have brought him in a good sum at Cherchen; but we could not carry it with us, as we had only three baggage horses. However, I promised to give him full value for his masterly shot.

The 10th of September was a hard day. Before the sun rose, Aldat drove in the horses, which had wandered a long way down the valley, and then went to fetch the head and fat of the yak. That morning our bitterest enemy, the west wind, overslept himself, and did not get up until nine o'clock; but afterwards he took his full revenge for the delay. Our camp was in a bad situation at an altitude of 16,874 feet, and fully exposed to the wind, which blew as it had seldom blown before. We now perceived immediately in front of us the pass on the south flank of the snowy mass which we had to cross over. We trembled as we thought of it; it was so high, and yet it looked innocent enough!

As Aldat did not turn up, I sent Cherdon to look for him; but it was eleven o'clock before they came back. Cherdon found the young hunter lying beside his victim, ill and unable to continue his work. The Cossack helped his comrade down to camp, and also brought some of the yak fat. And, in truth, poor Aldat looked in a very bad way: he was bleeding at the nose and had a violent headache; so I made him sit still, while Cherdon and I took down the tent and loaded up the animals.

The ground was hard; there had been nearly eleven degrees of frost, although at one period of the night the thermometer dropped as low as $-10^{\circ}.7$ C., or $12^{\circ}.7$ Fahr. This was clearly an indication that winter was at hand. Aldat was so unwell that he was unable to get into his saddle without help. On our way up towards the detestable pass which we were about to cross we had on our right, one after the other in succession, the snowy peaks which we had seen at a distance, though now of course they were close beside us; while on our left was a black mountain-ridge, overtopped farther south by yet another snowy mass. As soon as the sun gathered power, the ground thawed, and then began our struggle with the mire. Hour after hour we plodded on up the acclivities, flattering ourselves time after time that we were now quite close to the pass, but time after time we were deceived. We crossed one saddle after another, but always found there loomed yet another ridge in front of us, hitherto unseen.

The horses sank in up to the fetlocks, and the fragments of slate which were embedded in the soft ground caused the poor animals to slip and cut their legs against the sharp edges. There were blocks of stone fully a cubic yard in dimensions, and two or three were as large as cottages. Under the shelter of one of these last we stopped for a quarter of an hour or so to thaw our stiffened limbs. About fifty yards or so north of our track hung two small transverse arms of the glacier, and along them two yaks were travelling at about the same pace we did. Yolldash went after them, and barked himself hoarse, but they paid not the slightest attention to him, though they stopped and regarded us. But, finally making up their minds that we were harmless, they turned and climbed a precipitous moraine, with an enviable ease and agility, which, considering their size and weight, the yielding nature of the foothold, and the intensely rarefied air, impressed me greatly. On the top of the pass the aneroids showed an altitude of 17,803 feet, or precisely half the thickness of the atmospheric envelope which surrounds the earth.

During the day the thermometer never rose half a degree above freezing-point ; but the wind searched us to the very marrow—skin vests and furs were no use at all against it. Had we been able to walk, we could easily have kept ourselves warm ; but we could not walk—we could only stick to our staggering horses and long for a tolerable spot to camp in. The sole consolation we had was that, having now at length reached the summit of the pass, we should next go *down*. The glen by which we descended led to the south-west, and was filled with débris, through which trickled a little rivulet. A short distance beyond its exit from the mountain we encamped at 17,268 feet above sea-level, or nearly 1,500 feet higher than the top of Mont Blanc ! We had only a handful of fuel left, while the animals were forced to be content with the few blades of miserable grass which grew there. Aldat was now unable to stand. We left him lying where he reeled off his horse, after wrapping him up well with felt rugs. We could not persuade him to take anything; he refused to drink even a cup of warm tea, but lay moaning all night. As early as nine o'clock the temperature was at $-3°.6$ C., or $25°.5$ Fahr., and during the night it dropped to $-11°.9$ C., or $10°.6$ Fahr.

Next morning we crossed the hills towards the north-west. A long way off in the south-west there was yet another snowy mass, the south-eastern continuation of which took the form of a line of snowy pinnacles; beyond a shadow of doubt, it was the range of Tang-la. However, we soon came to a main valley extending east and west, which gathered into itself all the streams, brooks, and rivulets of the region. In order to avoid the necessity of crossing all these watercourses, we decided to travel along the bottom of the valley. But on a small detached hill at the foot of the mountain Cherdon's sharp eyes discovered some small black objects, which he took to be either human beings or yaks. We stopped and regarded them through the glass. They were alive that was certain, for they moved. But one of the objects seemed disproportionately big; perhaps after all it was only a yak cow with a couple of calves.

Encouraged by this, we made direct for the hill where we perceived the mysterious objects. Poor Aldat was now so bad that we had to lash him on his horse to prevent him from falling off. He talked incoherently; his mind was beginning to wander, and he kept begging us unceasingly to leave him behind. After advancing some way down the mountain-side, we made out that the mysterious objects on the hill were two men collecting stones and piling them up into a pyramid, or cairn. An hour later our doubts were cleared up. They were our friends, Turdu Bai and Kutchuk, who had climbed to the top of the hill to look for us. Finding no traces of us they were on the point of returning to camp, but before they did so resolved to build up a conspicuous landmark. The cairn, which was over six and a half feet high, and occupies a conspicuous position, will easily be recognised by any future exploring party.

After giving ourselves a much-needed day's rest at Camp no. XLVIII. (16,645 feet), we resumed our westward journey on the 13th of September. It was repugnant to me to travel when one of our number was sick; but our scanty supplies would not allow us to linger. Aldat's mind had wandered all night; and he moaned, shouted, and sang songs in Persian. The treatment I adopted had produced no effect; he had no longer any command over either body or mind, and sat as limp as a rag, his eyes fixed in a distorted stare. We carried him on an improvised litter fixed between two sacks on the back of a camel, giving him a cushion for his head, and covering him well with felt rugs, and lashing him on to prevent him from falling off.

After crossing over a low saddle or threshold (16,756 feet) of the valley, we travelled along the sandy bed of the stream, a welcome change to the animals after miry ooze. Cherdon caught sight of a herd of twenty *arkharis*, or wild sheep; but when he tried to stalk them with Aldat's musket, they disappeared like a puff of smoke. The valley we were following led out upon a tableland of soft red sand, overgrown with grass, and open

Making a Sick-bed for Aldat.

towards the north-west. Here we encamped beside the first fresh-water pool we came to, at an altitude of 16,087 feet. From this time onwards I had my yurt heated both morning and evening; that is to say, one of the men brought in some glowing embers on a bed of ashes, carrying them on the lid of our cooking-pot, or when that was in use, in my hand-basin. Artificial heat of some kind was certainly needed in the incessant winds which cut across those ugly highlands.

Thanks to a favourable country, almost level and with firm ground, we were able on the 14th of September to travel eighteen and a half miles. The characteristic feature of the landscape was a countless number of small pools, each the centre of a self-contained drainage basin, with no outlet, and very often without any visible contributaries. After a long search for fresh water, we stopped beside a small spring, surrounded by sparse thin grass. In the early part of the day the weather was splendid; but in the afternoon we were visited by the usual storms of hail and lightning, though now, by way of a change, they came, not from the west, but from the east. Just as we were pitching our tents (altitude, 16,044 feet) it began to snow, and come down it did with a vengeance, much heavier than we had ever seen it before, so that the grass was very quickly hidden. Then the wind veered round to the north-east, and quickened to a velocity of twenty miles an hour. The snow was wreathed up to a great height on the windward side of my yurt. At nine o'clock it was no easy task to take the usual meteorological observations, for not only was it pitch dark, but the snow whirled and blustered so tempestuously that it was quite impossible to see an inch before our faces. Unfortunately my lantern was *hors de combat*: three of its panes were broken and the glass replaced by pasteboard, while the fourth was cracked in a dozen directions, and only held together by strips of paper and gum. The snow crunched under our feet, and after being but a few minutes in the open air, we might easily have been mistaken for snow men, such as children make. The men's tent was only two or three yards from mine, but I literally could not see it, because of the driving snow, and I only knew where it stood by hearing the wind whipping and lashing its cords. Truly a strange experience to be snowed up in a region where there existed nothing but water. Nor were the prospects for the future any brighter; for the melting of all this snow would make the ground like a quagmire. At nine o'clock the thermometer went down to $-2^{\circ}.1$ C. or $28^{\circ}.2$ Fahr., though at one p.m. it had stood at 11° C., or $51^{\circ}.8$ Fahr. But we were now so deeply buried in snow that the inside of both the tent and the yurt were kept warm all night. Outside, the storm howled dismally, and the fine snow pattered, pattered against the frozen felts as if it never meant to stop.

Our spirits were still further depressed by poor Aldat's condition. He was attacked by a serious illness which I confess I did not understand. He complained of pains in the heart and head, and his feet turned black, and were as cold and hard as ice. I rubbed them for some time, hoping to restore the circulation, but it was without effect. They were as if dead, and he had quite lost all feeling in them, even when I pricked them

Turdu Bai Beside a Mountain at Camp no. LIV.

with a pin. This moribund condition gradually crept up his legs; although late that evening I gave him a hot foot-bath, which seemed to do him good. But what surprised us most was the way his mind wandered. Whilst on the march he chattered incessantly, and kept shouting to his camel to lie down, and for a good hour after he was comfortably tucked up in bed inside the tent he kept on beseeching the other men in the most moving tones to let his camel stop. Mollah Shah, who had known him in Cherchen, told us that he had once been out of his mind, but had been cured by a certain Abdurrahman Khoja, an *ishan*, or "holy man," who went to his father's house and repeated certain prayers over him, making him at the same time swallow slips of paper written all over with texts from the Koran. It was heartrending to hear this young fellow of four-and-twenty, who had so recently been in the full strength of manhood, rambling in the delirium of fever, and talking of his old father and his brothers in Cherchen. We kept watch beside his bed all night, and did all we could to help him; but the prospects were anything but favourable for a dying man, to be thus carried on the back of a camel through icy snowstorms, and over mountains which almost scraped the sky.

The horses, impelled by hunger, wandered astray during the night in search of grass; and it was late in the morning before we managed to find them again. The snow lay nearly a foot thick, and owing to its dazzling whiteness was painful to the eyes. Although the sun was warm, the day remained cold and raw, for a cutting westerly wind swept across the snow-fields. Once, when it stopped for a breathing space, the sun actually burnt, but within a few minutes we were once more being buffeted by the blinding snow. This soon passed over, and the sun once more peeped out; but the wind still continued chilly. It was winter and summer in fraternal alliance—in a word, thoroughly typical Tibetan weather!

We were now travelling consistently north-west, over a tolerably open country, and consequently had no big mountain chains to cross. The temperature never rose above freezing-point all day, and the ground remained hard; but the snow hid the marmots' holes, which literally honeycombed the ground, and caused the horses very often to stumble and fall. The order of our itinerary was now three days' marching, the fourth rest. On the 16th of September our camp lay 16,395 feet above sea-level. Cherdon had carefully kept a few cartridges, but now expended them upon a young yak, which furnished us with a good load of excellent meat. Yak beef is not good; but when you have nothing else, you cannot afford to be over nice. He also shot a wolf, which was evidently meditating designs upon our last surviving sheep. When we stopped, Aldat begged to be left all night between two camels in the open air; for the Mussulmans believe that the bodily warmth of these animals will restore health and strength to a sick man whose own vitality is slackening. So we made him comfortable amongst the camels, and left Mollah Shah and Niaz to keep him company.

Early on the morning of the 17th of September I was awakened by a terrible din in the camp: men were shouting and dogs barking frantically. I looked out, and there was a big bear slinking off, not fifty paces from the tent. His tracks in the snow showed that he had minutely examined the camp, and made a complete circuit of my yurt; but when the dogs attacked him, he thought it best to sheer off.

The weather was now fine, but the going abominable: the surface undulated and was littered all over with nasty sharp-edged pieces of tuff of all sizes and shapes. There was not a square foot of bare ground between them, and every tiny patch that happened to be free from stones was burrowed into by rats or marmots. Our animals stumbled incessantly on the sharp-pointed stones, or in the treacherous holes, and two of the camels cut the pads of their feet until they bled. After this followed a stretch of soft ground, which at first was frozen on the surface sufficiently to bear the weight of a camel, but later on it gradually thawed. At one place the last camel went through with both fore legs, and in spite of all our efforts to help him sank deeper and deeper into the mire. At last I hit upon the device of slipping felts underneath his feet as we got them up one by one, and by this means we lifted him into his usual attitude when he lay down. Then, after he had rested a bit, we induced him to make a desperate effort, by which he succeeded in scrambling on to firm ground, where he stood with the ooze dripping in clots down his legs and sides. He was literally sheathed in mud—we scraped it off with knives—and stood trembling in every limb, breathless and bewildered.

We now approached a peculiar glen, which stretched east-north-east towards a lake about six miles distant. Beyond the latter was a huge mountain-knot, draped with snow, which we had had on our right all day long, and which was clearly the

The Wild Yak Shot by Cherdon, with Mollah Shah, Turdu Bai (Standing), and Kutchuk Beside it.

same gigantic peak which I called King Oscar's Peak when I skirted its northern flank in 1896.

The bottom of the valley consisted of low-terraced table-

Another View of the Wild Yak Shot by Cherdon.

The Head and Side-fringes of Cherdon's Yak.

lands, covered with layers of tuff fifty to seventy feet thick, while blocks of tuff were scattered around in every direction. About an hour later we reached the steep edge of a second similar glen, and so precipitous was the descent that it occasioned us a long hunt before we were able to find a suitable place by which to get down. Kulans and orongo antelopes were here numerous, and we counted a herd of forty-two yaks. The next day the sun asserted his supremacy, and we were not harassed by storms. The patches of snow that were left from the last downfall now melted and evaporated. At one o'clock the temperature rose to 12°.0 C., or 53°.6 Fahr.

In this way we plodded on day by day across the barren, inhospitable uplands of Tibet. It was two months since we had set eyes upon a human being except ourselves, and we were growing anxious to get back to our headquarters camp. But every day's march that I plotted on my map only showed how slowly we advanced, and how great was the distance we yet had to go: we were still over 240 miles from Temirlik.

Our spirits always rose with our third day's march, for everybody knew that "to-morrow we shall rest." Thus the 20th of September we spent in Camp no. LIV., at an altitude of 16,133 feet. Cherdon, using Aldat's gun, shot a fifteen-year-old yak, which I photographed in various positions before he was flayed and cut up. In the evening Cherdon came in with an orongo antelope, and we tried another Mussulman cure with Aldat. Undressing the invalid, we wrapped him in the antelope's still moist warm skin, pressing it close to his body all round. I confess I had not much faith in the remedy, and felt sick at heart at being so powerless to do anything for the man. The last evening or two I gave him a few grains of morphia; except for that he never slept a wink.

At our next stopping-place westwards down the valley, the ground was literally honeycombed with marmots' holes. One old fellow, who was basking on a hill-side in a comically killing attitude, being stretched out like a man, or at least like a monkey, was pounced upon by Yolldash. The men kept him two months and tried to tame him, but he was just as wild at the end of the time as he was at the beginning: whenever anybody went near him, he used to sit up on his hind legs ready to lay hold with his sharp fore-teeth, which were endowed with a very respectable amount of power. The marmot's bite was said to be dangerous, and the wound very hard to heal.

Where *davaghan* or marmots occur, you are almost certain to find bears; for the Tibetan bear lives almost entirely on these rodents, which he devours bones and skin and all. He doesn't

View Looking South from the Camp where Aldat Died.

stalk them down, as Yolldash did, but visits one hole after another, until he finds a victim at home ; then with his powerful claws he scratches away the soil until he is able to seize his prey. He gets, at all events, plenty of exercise before his meal, for you can always see where a bear has been by the big heap of soil he makes. Several small troops of kulans were galloping about the bottom of this broad valley. There was great natural beauty in the elegant forms and perfect shape of these animals. They would gallop in a half circle, lying over at an angle of forty-five degrees to the ground, then suddenly wheel and halt in a straight line a little distance away. Their evolutions were as regular and as well executed as if they had been ridden by invisible Cossacks.

To-day Aldat was able to sit on horseback, although he had to be tied on fast and well looked after. We all hoped that he was improving, but in the evening he grew worse again. Every breath was accompanied by a groan, and he breathed at the rate of fifty-eight gasps a minute, which even at the height of 15,873 feet above sea-level was abnormal. On the other hand, his temperature was remarkably low, and the most strained attention failed to detect the least sign of his heart beating, and his pulse was correspondingly weak. His intellect still continued clouded : he kept talking about wanting to go out and shoot yaks. Although it was a violation of the order of our itinerary, we halted for a day for his sake, notwithstanding that we had only bread to last two or three days longer, and a dozen more shots would completely exhaust our ammunition.

Although on the morning of the 23rd the invalid's condition was scarcely changed at all, except that he now took his breath twenty-four times in a minute, we resolved to continue. It was evident he could not last very much longer, but we were unable to wait. We packed him in between two bags of fuel, putting soft felts underneath him, and wrapped his feet in carpets, and rolled up a fur and put it under his head for a pillow, then lashed the whole fast with ropes on the back of a camel.

Just as the camel was getting on to his feet to start, Aldat ceased to breathe. His broken eyes—beautiful grey Afghan eyes they were—were fixed afar off upon a country which our glances were unable to reach. He who formerly had ranged over these stupendous uplands with light and hurrying footstep on the trail of the wild yak had succumbed to the hardships of his calling, and closed a life which had been exceptionally lacking in pleasure. "Ghetti!"—*i.e.*, "He is gone!"—whispered the Mussulmans, as they stood in silence round his strange death-bed. But Turdu Bai, looking at the matter from the practical side, asked me what we were to do with the body. I was reluctant to bury him in unseemly haste, and all the men were quite satisfied when I gave the order to start. The camel had carried him several days, and he was not a heavy load. I had promised the men that they should be at Temirlik in eighteen days, which would allow us six rest days, if we travelled at the rate of fifteen miles a day. Consequently, they counted them with growing interest, and were anxious not to lose a single hour.

CHAPTER XXXVI.

STRUGGLING BACK OVER THE TIBETAN BORDER RANGES.

WHEN we started again, making for a large lake lower down the valley, our caravan was converted into a funeral procession. The men no longer talked, but were silent and grave. Kulans and yaks grazed unmolested near our line of march. The ravens of death hovered around us in wide circles. The lake shore was hard and afforded excellent going. The water was salt and bitter, and had a temperature of 16°.6 C., or 61°.9 Fahr., which was abnormally high when compared with the mean temperature of the air at that season of the year. It was, I dare say, partly a consequence of the high temperature of the lake, combined with the absence of wind, that this day, at one p.m., the temperature rose to 17°.5 C., or 63°.5 Fahr.

After passing the lake, we continued, still towards the north-west, over a gently-rising, undulating tableland, furrowed by numerous watercourses, with treacherous mud at the bottom. Beside one of these we came across a small piece of wood belonging to a Mongolian pack-saddle. It was as soft as cork, and must have been dropped either by a pilgrim caravan which had strayed this way from the north, or by Captain Wellby and Lieut. Malcolm's caravan, the route of which we crossed somewhere this same day. When we stopped, Mollah Shah and Niaz dug a grave for Aldat, whilst the other men were about their usual duties. After putting in one skin underneath and another on the top of the corpse, they shovelled in the soil, and made an oblong mound above it; and so we left the dead man to his last long rest in the moist and treacherous earth. It was the simplest burial I have ever been present at—no ceremonies, no tears, no prayers, except those I silently breathed for the peace of the dead man's soul. Beside the grave we set up one of the tent spars, and fastened on the top of it, by way of *tugh*, one of Aldat's own hunting trophies, namely, a yak's tail; for this is the usual headstone to a Mussulman tomb. But I scratched on a small piece of wood, in Arabic and Latin lettering, the dead man's name, as well as the date, and my own name, in case destiny should lead any traveller to the spot before Aldat's burial mound becomes finally levelled down.

Later on I was able with my own hands to give to Aldat's brother, who met us in the Chimen valley, the dead man's gun, the wages which were due to him, and his clothes and furs. His old father, Eisa Ahun, son of Dill Mohammed Khan, visited me a year later at Charkhlik, and it was a relief to me to know that Aldat's mother was dead, and so spared the grief of losing such a handsome and splendid son.

On the 24th of September the men were ready to start at an unusually early hour, being anxious to get away as soon as possible from so sorrowful a spot. After the Mussulmans had repeated a *dua* or prayer over his grave, poor Aldat was left alone with the mighty silence of the hills; no pilgrims, except the wild beasts of the wilderness, would hereafter visit his grave. The last we saw of it was the black yak's tail fluttering in the breeze as we dipped below the hills in the west.

We now set ourselves resolutely towards a yawning ravine or gateway in the mountain-range in front of us. But it was no easy matter to reach it. The ground consisted of loose red sand, furrowed by a great number of deep trenches, 100 to 150 feet deep, with precipitous sides and a treacherous morass at the bottom of each, in which we should of course have perished, man and mouse, had we once dropped into them. The glen, which we finally reached after very great difficulty, led gently up to a double pass, beyond which we halted for the night.

The following day we threaded a series of small passes or gaps in a number of minor parallel chains; but when at length we were gratified by the sight of open country, namely, a broad atitudinal valley, stretching as usual east and west, all vegetation had come to an end. Although we had done a good day's work already, we nevertheless pushed on diagonally across the valley, riding for several hours on its hard floor before we reached a fresh-water pool, with a few blades of grass beside it. That day we did 19¼ miles.

As we approached the Arka-tagh the country grew more and more desolate. On the 27th of September we did not see a blade of grass anywhere, nor a single trace of any other kind

Camp no. LX., 16,769 feet Above Sea-level.

of vegetation, or the least indication of organic life. Up and down we went, over the mountains and across the valleys, traversing them all at right angles. No sooner did we get down to a stream than we had to begin to work our way up on the other side of it, and although the difference of elevation did not exceed 350 feet, the climb proved a tremendous strain when it was repeated time after time without variation. After many tiresome detours and halts we at length reached the summit of the new range, situated 17,071 feet above the level of the sea. Immediately north of it was a solitary ridge, which we were forced to double either east or west. I preferred the latter, and rode on a long way in advance of the caravan, until it grew dark, when I stopped and waited for them at an altitude of 16,769 feet. They came in in small parties, all dead beat, and reported that they had left behind, in a hopeless condition, a white horse which we had brought from Yanghi-köll. Besides this, two camels and one horse were suffering from some affection of the eyes; they nodded their heads when they walked, as if they were suffering from want of sleep.

The next morning we were again in the midst of winter; but the clouds soon disappeared, the wind dropped, and the sun came out and proved scorching hot. At such moments the black bulb thermometer used to register up to 70°.0 C., or 158°.0 Fahr. When we stood and watched the patches of snow attentively we could actually see them dwindling before our eyes. Kutchuk went back to fetch the white horse; but although he was still alive, he fell down and died on the way to camp.

We descended into the next latitudinal valley through a narrow gorge shut in by red cliffs, consisting of sandstones and shales. The brook which flowed along the bottom of it had frozen during the night. As long as we were in the deep cutting, we were in shelter; but as soon as we emerged into the open the caravan was caught by the full force of the gale, which was just beginning, but rapidly increased to a westerly hurricane of the worst description. We had to sit tight to prevent ourselves from being actually blown out of the saddle. Horses, men, and camels—all bent over and literally lay *upon* the wind. The entire caravan was blown sideways. Horses' tails and loose ends of clothing flapped and fluttered like streamers down the wind. It was hard work to get our breath: we were nearly choked. The camels were blown from side to side as they lurched along. The valley in front of us was shrouded in mist, so that we were unable to see which way to go. But the first bite of grass we came to should, I resolved, be the signal to stop; for it was impossible to travel far in such a gale. Those who have never been in one can form no conception of what it is like. It was as though the entire volume of the atmosphere were concentrated into this great trench of the earth's surface and forced through it like a roaring tide. The clouds drove overhead at racing speed; drift-sand—nay, actually small stones were caught up from the ground, and hurled point-blank into our faces. In the more exposed situations the wind had a velocity of over 55¾ miles an hour; but after we got in the shelter of some low hills, beside a little brook at the bottom of the valley where we encamped, it dropped to 31½ miles an hour.

Owing to this fickle weather, and these abrupt and violent changes of temperature, our skin grew very sensitive. The nose and ears suffered most, the skin peeling off time after time. Our nails turned as brittle as glass, and split and cracked; and there was constant pain in the finger-tips.

Several of our horses were now in a bad way, and as we had only maize enough to last two days more, I directed one of the men to see if we could not spare some of the rice for them. Our smallest mule very nearly gave up at this camp, No. LXI. (16,100 feet), but was saved by Cherdon, who treated her according to a practice of the Buriats. She was swollen up to an enormous size, and lay writhing on the ground. The Cossack took an awl and with a powerful push thrust it into her side up to the hilt. The gas streamed out, but not a drop of blood. Then we forced her to stand up, flung a rope round her hind quarters, and whilst one man pulled at her head, another whacked her with a staff. Every time she kicked out behind, two other men pulled away at the rope, so that in this way she was forced to move forwards, swinging from right to left. People may say what they like about this method, but it certainly proved a sure cure in her case. She recovered, was with me when I rode towards Lassa, took part in my journey westwards across Tibet to Ladak, went over the Karakorum Pass, and when I last saw her in Kashgar, at the end of May, 1902, she was in first-rate condition.

After a day's rest, we set to work in earnest, on the last day of September, to scale the entrenchments of the Arka-tagh. Following the eastern shore of the lake of Camp no. LXI., we made for what appeared to be a suitable pass, but were compelled to circle round a creek or bay, which the lake sent out towards the east, and which was entered by a stream at its extremity. This bay was almost a separate lagoon, and contained fresh water sheeted with ice, whereas the ice itself was strongly saline, and when melted yielded water with a specific gravity of 1.0225. The west was shut in by vast snow-capped mountain-masses belonging to the Arka-tagh. We found a good road up to the top of the range in a deeply scarped watercourse, the bottom of which was littered with hard débris, while numerous small lateral glens entered it from both sides. I led the way with Cherdon and Mollah Shah. At three o'clock it clouded over, and became almost dark. The pass was easy to ascend from the south, and we had no difficulty in reaching the summit ; but the north side, where the strata cropped out along the strike, was fearfully precipitous.

This range, which overtops almost all others on the globe, resembles a colossal springboard, from which you might take a leap into the void spaces of the universe. Just as we reached the summit, the snow-storm was raging its worst. I thought we were lost. The altitude was 17,071 feet, and I had scarce strength to make the necessary observations ; my hands were stiff and entirely destitute of feeling. As the caravan lingered I sent the two men back to see what had become of it, and sat down with my back to the storm to wait for them. The snow whirled about me in huge plumes or tassels, while the abyss at my feet was a seething caldron of tossing snow-flakes. The wind howled and whined and whistled, as it swept over the sharp-cut summit of the pass. At last I heard the camels' bells close beside me—the animals flitted past like spectres—I did not hear a footstep. Turdu Bai marched leaning far forward, with one arm raised as if to protect his face: he walked as a man does when he forces his way through a dense thicket. But how to get down on the other side of the pass ? It was like plunging headlong into a black abyss, the bottom of which we were unable to see.

All the men went on foot, so as to be ready to help and support the camels. Kutchuk went first, feeling the way. He took the descent zigzag and at hap-hazard. At every ten or a dozen yards we were forced to stop and rub our faces with snow to prevent them from freezing. We slipped, we slided, carrying the snow with us. One of the camels stumbled, fell, turned half a somersault, but, luckily, lay in such a position that he was able to get up again without being unloaded. The snow whirled madly around us; we gasped for breath; everything danced before our eyes. By this the day was well advanced and it grew dark; nevertheless we persevered until the slope began to grow easier. It was pitch dark when we stopped on the flank of the mountain, at an altitude of 16,330 feet. Here there was not a blade of grass, nor a handful of fuel, though of water we had plenty in the shape of snow and ice. Indeed, we had more than enough, for the ground was as white as could be, and the skies were emptying out showers unceasingly upon our devoted heads.

When the sun rose on the 1st of October, we were enabled to see what sort of a place it was where we had stopped in the darkness of the night before. It was still snowing, and the landscape wore a decidedly wintry aspect. The animals were stiff with cold, and hungry, when we started down the chilly valley. As soon, therefore, as we reached a patch of scurvy grass we stopped, at an altitude of 16,074 feet, although we had only gone a very few miles. I gave the order to slaughter our last sheep; but it was like a stab into my own heart. I felt as if I were committing murder.

On the 2nd of October we travelled 18½ miles north, our track at first going downhill, until we reached the hard gravel at the bottom of the valley. We were still unable to see much of our surroundings, because of the blinding snow. The valley, with its gentle fall, gave us friendly help for yet another day. When the air cleared, we perceived the Chimen-tagh a good 60 miles away. But before we started on the second morning, the usual westerly storm was once more on its way to freeze us as we sat astride our wretched beasts. We saw the forerunners of the storm racing each other a long way off across the open spaces behind the projecting cliffs and in the throats of the glens.

We were following a little brook, and ought to have stopped as soon as it came to an end; but, perceiving a lake, the Achik-köll, further north, we hoped to reach it and find fresh springs there. The poor animals were thoroughly exhausted. The horse I had ridden to Andereh lagged behind with Niaz, and another horse, a white one, was left on the road in charge of Kutchuk. It grew dusk, and then dark; but the moon soon came out, and shed her pale spectral light over the frigid waste. As we failed to discover water, we passed the lake, leaving it a good bit on our right. Turdu Bai was leading the way on foot, and we were all overjoyed when he at length stopped and shouted that he had reached a stream which flowed into the lake. We had marched 23¼ miles, the utmost that our animals were now capable of doing in a day. The sick horses did manage to reach Camp no. LXV. (13,948 feet), but it was well on the next day, for the men had been obliged to leave them some way back all night. We tended them the best we could, feeding them with rice.

The basin of the Achik-köll was of very considerable extent, especially to the east and the west. From the latter direction it received a large stream, on which, when we forded it on the 5th of October, a good deal of drift-ice was floating. The basin lay ensconced between the Arka-tagh on the south and a smaller range on the north, the latter of which did not appear particularly difficult to cross. On the morning of the 6th, the whole basin was shrouded in a peculiar cold, moist, clammy mist, and through it the picturesque outlines of the range on the north were but faintly and dimly seen, painted, as it were, with evanescent colours on the canvas of the sky, with the snow etched in more strongly higher up. Owing to these subdued tones the range appeared to be at least a day's march distant.

The caravan was dying, and we breasted the new slopes at a funereal pace. The district was dotted over with hundreds of kulans, and more particularly with orongo antelopes. Yolldash managed to catch one of the latter, and held it fast by the nose until Cherdon came up and killed it. Its meat was very welcome as a change in our monotonous diet. The ascent grew steeper. We crossed an endless number of ravines and passes, where we had to make frequent halts to let the animals recover breath. A man came to tell me that one of the horses was unable to go any farther. No sooner was it slaughtered than down went another, never to get up again. This miserable pass would have been a mere trifle for animals in good condition; but before we surmounted it we lost two more horses, one of them being the faithful grey which had carried me to Cherchen, and then to Altimish-bulak. And when we did at last surmount it, the prospect was not a whit more encouraging. To right and to left were glacier-arms, in front of us a chaos of mountains. Just over the top we halted in a recess of the rocks, although there was not a scrap of firing or food for the animals. Next morning one of the horses was lying dead, his neck stretched out, his eyes fixed, his body stiffened with frost. It was evident we could not go on long in this fashion. Our marches were growing shorter and shorter, and the animals were getting utterly exhausted and worn-out.

Curiously enough, all the camels struggled over this fateful pass without any damage. In the morning we found them lying motionless, and with marvellous resignation, in the same attitudes in which we left them the night before. They were powdered with rime-frost, for the thermometer had not risen above $-3°.8$ C., or $25°.2$ Fahr., and there was an icy, cutting wind. We followed the valley towards the north-east, the country remaining absolutely barren and totally destitute of game. The only sign, I will not say of life, but simply of movement, was the stream breaking against the water-worn blocks of granite, some of them as much as a cubic yard in dimensions, which littered the watercourse at the bottom of the valley.

The night of the 8th of October was still and cold and bright, and the thermometer went down to $-18°.3$ C., or $-0°.9$ Fahr. An icy current of air, the usual night breeze, swept down the valley. From this sharply-defined valley a fresh caravan would have made Temirlik in four days; but it would clearly take us a good deal longer than that. We had only six small pieces of bread left, though our rice would last for three or four days longer. It looked as if we should have to do the last stage or two on famine rations. A little fuel, too, would have been extremely welcome; but, unfortunately, this region was never visited by yaks.

We resumed our way down the valley in a howling snowstorm. Very soon the valley contracted to a gorge, the bottom of which was impeded by cumbering masses of rock, in part water-worn, which had toppled from the heights above. In fact, we were threading a deep transverse glen cut through the granite, and the scenery presented all the characteristics usual in a granite region—rugged, pinnacled forms, at once capricious and picturesque. The stream was for the most part frozen over, although at the cascades we could see it rippling along underneath the transparent bridges of ice. We crossed it a great number of times, our object being to keep as far as possible along the same level on the erosion terraces between which it flowed. Very often the ice was strong enough to bear even the camels; but where it would not bear them, we broke it up with poles and stones. The veterans amongst the camels traversed this difficult piece of road in a wonderful way, especially as they now carried bigger loads, in consequence of the horses having died.

The name of the glen was Togri-sai, or the Straight Glen; and it was very well known to the gold-seekers of Cherchen and Keriya, for it contained a gold-field, which we passed in the course of that day's march. The miners seemed to have been there only about a month before; but there were no indications of the valley having been visited since. About half-way up the glen we came to the first three huts, built of granite.

Our Camp at Togri-sai on the 8th October, 1900.

Close beside them were a great number of pits in the gravel beds, surrounded by mounds of sand and gravel, which the miners had dug out. There were several hundreds of these pits, very few of them, however, more than eight feet deep. Most of them were abandoned long ago, but others appeared to have been worked that very summer. The huts were merely temporary affairs, four square, the sides 6 to 10 feet long, the walls composed of unhewn blocks of granite, without any sort of binding material. The roof consisted at the best of a piece of linen or felt flung across a spar. Lanes and alleys wound in and out amongst the gravel-heaps of this Asiatic Klondyke; and beside some of the mines there hung an antelope's skull or a kulan's skin, fastened to a stake, in sign of ownership. In some places the owner of a claim had surrounded his property with a low wall of unhewn granite.

Some of the huts contained primitive ovens for baking bread, for the miners bring flour with them; but for the rest of their food they depend upon the hunters who accompany them, and who for a trifle sell them the flesh of the yaks, kulans, and antelopes they shoot. The miners convey their paraphernalia on the backs of asses, which they then send down into the valleys to graze during the two months that their work lasts. We found household utensils in only two of the huts—namely, a few rough rakes, used in separating the gravel from the gold-bearing rock, a wheelbarrow, two or three ridge-spars, and a trough for baking or washing gold. We had no scruples about appropriating this excellent material; it would keep us warm for two or three days.

One of the camels here gave up and was left behind, until we should find an opportunity the next morning to fetch him in. We advanced terribly slowly in the bitterly cold weather, with snow falling and 3° C. (=5½° Fahr.) of frost. At a steep place one of the camels stumbled and rolled down the face of the slope, turning over several times, but happily he took no further harm. This misadventure cost us an hour, for we had to make a road up the cliff to get him back again. It was 11 o'clock at night when we encamped (14,814 feet) after this long and tiring, though interesting, day, and the moon was already shining out of the snow-clouds.

CHAPTER XXXVII.

BACK TO HEADQUARTERS AT TEMIRLIK.

THE camel which we had left behind died during the night. Of our original caravan there were now left only six camels, three horses, and one mule; and even they were all in a pitiable condition.

The valley widened out again, and ascended by three broad, step-like terraces, twenty-three, forty, and fifty feet high respectively. It was no use pushing on in the hope of finding grass, the animals were dead beat. We were forced to let them rest where they were, feeding them upon the stuffing of the last of our pack-saddles. The next day, the 10th of October, we continued our slow and weary tramp north-north-east along the same valley. I also went on foot now, so as to spare the one horse that was fit for duty. The river was frozen, for the temperature had fallen to $-18°.8$ C., or $-1°.8$ Fahr. At starting the sky was clear, but it was not very long before the everlasting westerly wind began to make itself felt. Happening to cross over to the right-hand side of the valley for the purpose of examining the lay of the strata, I lighted, by pure chance, upon some exceedingly interesting rock-drawings. They were made on the surface of what had once been a light-green slate, though it was now stained dark brown, and polished bright by wind and weather, and as the outlines had been cut through the outer laminæ of the rock with a sharp instrument they were very conspicuous, owing to the light incised lines showing against the dark background. They must have been of considerable antiquity, because portions of the pictures were obliterated.

They represented scenes from a hunter's life, and he must have been an enterprising fellow. He would seem to have hunted yaks, kulans, orongo antelopes, and wolves in the mountains, and wild duck, wild geese, and tigers beside the lake of Lop-nor.

One especially noticeable fact in connection with them was that the hunter represented carried in every case, not the Central Asiatic musket, with its forked rest, but bows and arrows, and the long arrows had their barbs pointing forwards, like the trident of Neptune.

Although consisting of a few strokes of bare outline, the animals were drawn in a characteristic and easily recognisable manner. The hunters were represented in different positions, standing, creeping, kneeling, and the one who was aiming at a tiger considered it safest to keep to his saddle. The rock faces on which this work of art was engraved were three and a quarter feet and five feet high, and the pictures very nearly a foot in length. There can be little doubt that they date from a period when Mongols still dwelt around Lop-nor, and probably spent a portion of the summer in the mountains. And at our next camp (13,344 feet), on the left bank of the stream, where the grass was tolerably good, I found strong confirmation of this assumption in a Mongol *obo*, or cairn, built of flat slates and inscribed all over in Tibetan lettering with the fundamental dogma of Lamaism: "On maneh padmeh hum"—which means, "O jewel of the lotus flower!"

These traces of human occupancy invested the place with a certain degree of interest, and we spent the next day beside the *obo*. But before that day came to an end, our position underwent a great and joyful change. Cherdon, with Aldat's last charge of powder, had just brought down a young kulan quite close to camp, when Mollah Shah came running to me to tell me breathlessly that he had seen, a long way down the valley, two hunters on horseback. I at once ordered him to go off after them, and bring them back with him at all costs. At first the men were rather shy, but soon recovered confidence, and told me that they had spent three months in the mountains, supplying the miners with kulan meat. But they had not been to Temirlik, so that we were still ignorant as to how our headquarters had fared during our absence.

This unexpected meeting with human beings, after being isolated from our kind for eighty-four days, put fresh life into us all. The first thing I did was to buy their two horses, which were as English thoroughbreds in comparison with ours. A small parcel of wheat flour also proved an exceptionally welcome acquisition. But what interested us most was the palaver which was held that evening round the camp-fire. Mollah Shah

An Obo at Camp no. LXXI., the Lower Togri-sai.

had already offered to tramp all the way on foot to Temirlik, and send a relief caravan to our assistance. But there was now no need for him to do so. Togdasin, one of the hunters, knew the mountain paths better than he did ; so I gave him his own horse, which I had just bought from him, and sent him to Islam Bai with a message. He promised to be there in two days, and was instructed to tell Islam Bai to meet us with fifteen horses and a goodly supply of provisions at the springs of Supa-alik, two days west of Temirlik, in the Chimen valley. Togdasin set off at eleven o'clock at night, taking with him two empty preserved fruit tins by way of credentials, to show

A Young Kulan (Wild Ass).

that he was an express courier from me ; they would also serve as a hint to Islam Bai to bring with him a fresh supply of the same kind. Togdasin took nothing with him to eat, except a small piece of kulan flesh. I did not envy him his night ride, seeing that the night before the temperature had fallen to $-20^{\circ}.2$ C., or $-4^{\circ}.4$ Fahr. ; but I promised him a handsome reward if he executed his commission well.

The next two days took us to the end of the Togri-sai, and a good bit along the Chimen valley. Into this latter the Piazlik, the imposing mountain-chain which overhung the valley on the south, and thus formed the continuation of the Chimen-tagh, thrust out across our path a long series of rectangular spurs *en échelon*, consisting of sharp-pointed irregular rocks of a brown, grey, or black colour. Our spirits rose high when we started on the 14th of October, nor were they in any degree damped by the fact that we all had to walk, for according to our calculation we should meet the relief expedition at nightfall.

The stream which descended the valley carried about 177 cubic feet in the second, and we kept to its left bank. On our left rose the Illveh-chimen, with its snow-capped peaks. Its flanks were scored by an endless number of dry ravines, each of which we had to cross over, and this occasioned us an infinite amount of trouble. But after we crossed the last of them, the ground became perfectly level, and the going first-rate. Mollah Shah assured me, that about twilight, and before it was dark, we should reach the springs of Supa-alik, the appointed rendezvous; but it was evident he did not know the country, and the second hunter who had only accompanied us for two days had now left us. It grew dark—it grew pitch dark—and yet we failed to find any springs. On the contrary, the path we had hitherto followed gradually came to an end, and although there were yappkak bushes at intervals, there was not a blade of grass. But, thanks to the splendid hard surface, the animals held out well through this long tramp.

However, at the end of about another hour and a half, Mollah Shah and Niaz, who were leading, stopped and shouted that they saw a fire in the distance. This news electrified us, and we quickened our pace. It was as though all our toil and privation were suddenly come to an end, and we had no further need to exert ourselves. We pushed on through the darkness straight towards the fire, which drooped, then flared up again. I walked beside the camel that carried the skiff, and held on to it, until my hand got numbed with cold; then I went round to the other side of the beast and held on with the other hand, whilst the first thawed and got warm. Then for a long time we failed to see the fire, and our hopes drooped, and we became doubly sensible of our weariness. Perhaps, after all, the fire belonged to some gold miners. We stopped and shouted. We gathered a bundle of yappkak and made a big blaze, but there was no answer to our signal. We fired two or three shots from a revolver, but the sound died away into space, without awakening so much as an echo. We held our breath and listened. The night was as silent as the grave, and the fire went out.

When we started again away from our own fire, around which we had warmed ourselves for half-an-hour, the darkness seemed even intenser than before. In fact, I involuntarily glanced up at the stars to convince myself that I had not been suddenly smitten with blindness. Hour after hour we plodded on, dragging our weary animals after us, which, as they did not refuse to follow, probably scented grass.

Again the fire flared up. The men, who had been plodding along in dogged silence, once more became lively and talkative. Soon after this we came to some *malgun* bushes, a sure indication of the vicinity of water. Then the deceitful fire faded once more, and finally it disappeared for good. Every five minutes or so the men shouted all together as loudly as they could, but their

The Illveh-Chimen Seen from the Chimen-tagh.

voices died away in the night unanswered. I was beginning to believe we were being deceived by a will-o'-the-wisp, which flitted on in front of us and disappeared just before we reached it. Our patience had been too severely tried; as the fire died out, so did our interest, and then fatigue finally got the upper hand. As soon as we reached the next belt of bushes, I commanded halt, to the intense satisfaction of everybody concerned. But although we had been on foot for over twelve hours, we had not accomplished more than 26¾ miles.

We were all completely done up, men and animals alike, and were in a truly pitiable plight; too far gone, in fact, to arrange camp. The men just sat down on the ground, on the very spot where each happened to stop. We had only one can of water left, which we had brought from the last river, and with this each of us got one cup of tea; that, and a bit of kulan meat roasted over the fire, was all we had left. On the off chance that relief might be in the neighbourhood, we kept up a big signal fire for about an hour and half. Then we dropped off to sleep, in a kind of swoon, with the frosty stars glittering above our heads. We had by this got down to 11,388 feet above the sea.

Next morning, the 15th of October, the men found a fresh-water stream not more than two hundred paces away, and as the situation was all that could be desired for a camp, there being an abundant supply of rich tall grass and plenty of fuel, we decided to stay there over the day and see what would happen. Mollah Shah, who had been out to reconnoitre, came back and said that the deceptive fire of the night before had been made by a party of hunters, who were on their way back to Cherchen with a load of skins, and had deliberately kept out of our way, not knowing who or what we were. Here we were, then, once more thrown back upon ourselves. What were we to think about the relief caravan? and how far dare we trust to our messenger, Togdasin? Cherdon, who had got from him a handful of powder and a little lead, spent the whole morning looking for an antelope, but returned at two o'clock empty-handed. This region was frequently visited by hunters, and the animals were shy and difficult to get near, but he said he had seen a dark-coloured something moving a long way off in the west, which he had at first taken for a troop of kulans; but he now believed that they were horsemen, and that they were approaching our camp.

I hurried out with my field-glass, and sure enough there was a troop of mounted men galloping towards us in a cloud of dust. Running to the top of a little hill we watched them with bated breath. They were still a long, long way off; but we could see them distinctly over the tops of the thicket. Owing to the mirage, they seemed to be travelling a little distance above the earth, but their bobbing movements showed that they were riding at a gallop. They disappeared amongst the thickets, but the cloud of dust which they sent up showed which way they were coming. It must be our friends, who, having failed to observe our signal fire, had started at daybreak, and pushed on until they came across our trail, and had then turned back and followed after us.

Our Headquarters at Temirlik. In the Background my Yurt and the Terrace with its Caves, and in the Far Distance the Akato-tagh.

Our excitement reached a climax when we saw two mounted men emerging from the bushes. Then appeared two others, driving a troop of horses in front of them—all coming at full gallop. But I soon recognised Islam Bai by the skin hood of his cloak. He was leading on a white horse. He quickened his pace, and soon outdistanced the others, and, dismounting a little way off, saluted. He looked well and pleased, and announced that all was well at headquarters. The other three men were Musa from Osh, Khodai Värdi, and Tokta Ahun from Abdall. It was, after all, their fire which we had seen ; and they, as we supposed they would do, had pushed on westwards during

A Dead Kulan.

the night, until they came to our trail, when they at once understood that we had gone past each other in the darkness.

Islam Bai brought with him fifteen fresh horses, all in splendid condition, and a good stock of provisions, and at three o'clock we had a thorough Lucullan feast. He brought nothing but good news. The post-jighit Yakub had arrived from Kashgar, and in an instant I was tearing open letters and newspapers from my home in far-off Sweden. Shortly after we left Mandarlik, Islam Bai had shifted camp to Temirlik, pitching his quarters beside some Mongol caves or grottoes. The *amban* of Charkhlik had been to visit me in state, and so had the Mongol chieftain of Pshui in Tsaidam ; but both had, of course, returned without seeing me. The former brought with him thirty ass-loads of maize. For the last two weeks Islam Bai and the others had been in a state of the greatest anxiety about us, for we had promised to be back in two and a half months at the outside, and they knew our supplies must be exhausted. Thus question and answer flew backwards and forwards for hours, and it was late when I got to bed that night. But the men sat and talked long after that, around a rousing big fire, which there were now plenty of hands to feed. Kader Ahun, Aldat's brother, had come to Chimen to meet him. He surprised me by saying that he was fully prepared for the sorrowful tidings; for some little time before he had dreamt he was riding across a broad tableland and met my caravan. But when he looked for his brother amongst the men, he could not find him, and when he awoke he knew that some misfortune had overtaken him. We made out that he had the dream precisely at the time of Aldat's death, and Shagdur was in a position to prove that the man's story was not invented. For Kader Ahun told his dream to the Cossack long before they had any intelligence of our return, and Kader Ahun added at the time, that he believed Aldat was dead. This was the only instance of telepathy which has come under my observation throughout my journeys in Asia.

After two days' rest, during which I took an astronomical observation, we rode, on the 18th of October, thirty miles to the east, across barren deserts and sand-belts, leaving the camels and surviving horses of our caravan to follow slowly on in our wake, but without loads. It was delightful to have a good fresh horse to ride on; and I was also glad that our surviving animals would now have a good six months in which to rest and graze at leisure. And well they deserved it!

On the 19th we rode along the right bank of a stream which bathed the southern foot of a small detached mountain group, and then shortly afterwards disappeared amongst the sterile gravel at the bottom of the valley, without reaching any of the lakes which lay further east. Upon reaching a wretched little oasis in the midst of this desolate region, called Bagh-tokai, or the Orchard Wood, we met eight men returning from Bokalik to Cherchen, carrying with them the skins of eleven yaks, four kulans and two orongo antelopes, which they had shot. We gave them what rice we could spare, for they had lived all summer on yak and kulan meat, and we knew how pleasant a thing it is to have a change in a monotonous bill of fare.

Our caravan had once more increased to an imposing cavalcade, when, on the 20th of October, we at last turned our faces north-north-eastwards towards Temirlik. But we were not to reach headquarters without a final salute from our all too pertinacious friend, the west wind.

Shagdur met us half-way, and pulled up and saluted in military fashion, as if he and his horse had just been cast in bronze. We were both glad to meet again, and he had a good deal to tell us. He had kept the meteorological records with exemplary care, and the self-registering instruments had never once failed. It was getting dusk when we at length reached the

Turdu Bai Guiding the Camels.

spring of Temirlik. There I was met by Faisullah and Kader, both of whom had been with me on the ferry-boat, and they pointed out to me the six camels which had been out at grass all summer. On the right bank of the little brook which issued from the springs several fires were scattering their sparks into the air ; it was the tented village of our new headquarters camp. Besides the big Mongolian yurt there were two tents, a hut made of reeds and branches, long rows of maize sacks, and all the heavier baggage. Here I was greeted by Ali Ahun, the tailor, and Yakub, the post-jighit, as well as by a crowd of old men, chance visitors, whom I had never seen before.

Over on the other side of the brook was a two-storied loess

terrace. On the lower platform my little yurt was already put up, with the stove lighted inside it. In the vertical face of the upper platform the Mongols had, in time past, hollowed out a number of caves or grottoes. One of these Shagdur had converted into a very convenient dark room for photography, and got everything ready for developing the plates which he knew I should bring back with me.

Thus ended this toilsome journey, and we could now with a good conscience indulge ourselves in two or three weeks' rest. The expedition had resulted in geographical discoveries of very great importance, but it had entailed a considerable amount of hardship and suffering and loss of life. Of the twelve horses we started with only two were now left, and of the seven camels only four ; and of these four, one stood like a bronze statue for two days amongst the long grass, and on the third day lay down and died, without having attempted to bite a single mouthful. And last, though by no means least, it had cost the life of one man.

END OF VOLUME I.

Central Asia and Tibet

Towards the Holy City of Lhasa

Vol. 2

Curzon. 1902

Frontispiece to VOL. II.

Central Asia and Tibet

Towards the Holy City of Lhasa

(In Two Volumes)

by

SVEN HEDIN

With 420 Illustrations from Drawings and Photographs, Eight Coloured Illustrations from Paintings and Five Maps

Vol. 2

Low Price Publications

2012

First Published 1903
Reprinted in **LPP** 1997, 2012

ISBN 10: 81-7536-101-8 *(Set)*
ISBN 13: 978-81-7536-101-0 *(Set)*
ISBN 10: 81-7536-103-4 *(Vol. 2)*
ISBN 13: 978-81-7536-103-4 *(Vol. 2)*

Published by
Low Price Publications
A-6, Second Floor, Nimri Commercial Centre,
Ashok Vihar Phase-IV, Delhi 110052 (INDIA)
tel.: +91.11.27302453 fax.: +91.11.47061936
url: www.Lppindia.com e-mail: info@Lppindia.com

Printed at
Salasar Imaging Systems
Delhi

PRINTED IN INDIA

Dedication.

THE ENGLISH AND AMERICAN EDITIONS
OF THIS WORK ARE DEDICATED BY SPECIAL PERMISSION
TO
HIS EXCELLENCY
LORD CURZON OF KEDLESTON,
VICEROY OF INDIA,
WITH GRATITUDE AND ADMIRATION
BY THE AUTHOR.

CONTENTS.

VI.

ACROSS THE DESERT OF GOBI.

MOUNTAIN DEFILES AND A WATERLESS DESERT.

VII.

THE RUINED TOWNS OF LÔU-LAN.

A VANISHED COUNTRY.

VIII.

A SURVEY OF THE LOP DESERT.

A WANDERING LAKE.

IX.

ACROSS TIBET FROM NORTH TO SOUTH.

TRAVELLING AMONGST THE CLOUDS.

X.

A DASH FOR LASSA.

THE FORBIDDEN LAND OF THE HOLY BOOKS.

XI.

ACROSS TIBET TO LADAK.

A CHAIN OF HIGHLAND LAKES.

XII.

TO INDIA, KASHGAR AND HOME.

LIST OF ILLUSTRATIONS.

LIST OF ILLUSTRATIONS.

MAP.

KEY TO THE TRANSLITERATION OF THE MAP-NAMES.

a on the map is rendered by o in the text.						
ch	,,	,,	,,	kh	,,	
dj	,,	,,	,,	j	,,	
e (final)		,,	,,	eh	,,	
g (final)		,,	(sometimes)	gh	,,	(e.g tagh)
gi	,,	,,	rendered	ghi	,,	
j	,,	,,	,,	y or i	,,	
s	,,	,,	(generally)	z	,,	
sch	,,	,,	rendered	sh	,,	
tj	,,	,,	,,	ch (as in "church")		
tsch	,,	,,	,,	tch or ch		

VI.

Across the Desert of Gobi.

Mountain Defiles and a Waterless Desert.

CHAPTER I.

A TRIP TO THE AYAG-KUM-KoLL.

As soon as I was settled down in my yurt beside the springs of Temirlik, my day was spent in the following manner: After a good sleep and breakfast, I spent several hours making clean copies of my scientific observations and journals, so that I might have a double set to send home. I also wrote letters to friends in Europe, and then sat down beside the fire to read my Swedish newspapers, using a sort of home-made arm-chair which Islam had contrived for me. When it got dark, I had a fire lighted in the cave, and developed photographic plates until a late hour of the evening, and finally, when this was finished, went back to the yurt and had my dinner, or supper, whichever you please to call it.

I paid the men their wages for the time I had been absent, and bought four more excellent camels, thus increasing the number to fourteen. I dismissed Musa of Osh and young Kader, both of whom were very anxious to return home. To the former I entrusted my big budget of letters for posting in Kashgar. Several of these were of great importance. We had been through what remained of my money, and found it was not enough. I wrote therefore to my father and to the Swedish Ambassador at St. Petersburg, Count Gyldenstolpe, begging them to send a considerable sum in Russian bank-notes to Consul-General Petrovsky, who would change them into Chinese silver money, and send it on to me at Charkhlik by the following summer. I also wrote to Colonel Saitseff at Osh, asking him to send me a fresh supply of preserved foods.

Between the 25th of October and the 4th of November, the Cossacks, accompanied by Tokta Ahun, Mollah, and Togdasin Beg, made a hunting excursion to Kum-köll. As I should have no opportunity myself to cross over the Chimen-tagh and Kalta-alagan in that direction. I commissioned Shagdur to draw me a sketch map of the route they took, to make meteorological observations throughout the trip, and—what I was chiefly anxious about—to note the altitude of the pass. This task he executed in a faultless manner. His map agreed beautifully with the calculations which, by way of check upon his work, I afterwards made from the compass bearings and distances. At all events, Shagdur's map bridged over an important gap in my own cartographical observations. The Cossacks killed and brought back with them a large number of deer, but had had a rather raw, cold time of it in the mountains, which were now one unbroken sheet of snow from summit to base.

Our new camp at Temirlik was as busy a centre as Tura-sallgan-uy on the Tarim. All the gold-prospectors and hunters who were on their way back from Bokalik naturally dropped in to pay us a visit, while several men came up from the low-lands seeking employment. I however lived peacefully and quietly on my terrace, having a good view of the camp over on the other side of the brook, which was crossed by a little bridge. My idyllic peace was perfectly undisturbed except for the hoarse cawings of the ravens, which housed in the caves, and which had to be frightened away with half-a-dozen shots when I wanted to begin my series of astronomical observations.

By the 11th of November, however, everything was ready for a fresh start. My first object was to explore and map a part of the Chimen-tagh and Akato-tagh which had never before been visited, and thus fill up a big lacuna which existed on my map of Northern Tibet. I did not enter upon this new expedition, which would last about a month, with any anticipations of pleasure, starting as I did towards the middle of a bitterly cold winter; but the work had to be done, and the best thing was of course to go and do it.

I selected the following men to accompany me: Cherdon, Islam Bai, Turdu Bai, Tokta Ahun, Khodai Värdi, and Togdasin. The last-named knew the region we were going to as intimately as he knew the country close around his own dwelling. Kutchuk and Niaz went with us for the first few days, to help lead the horses, which, after their thorough rest, were rather lively, and danced about a good deal with their loads. There were thirteen of them, and we also had four mules,

Our Headquarters Camp at Temirlik.

though no camels. I had promised myself that I would not be inconvenienced as I had been on my last trip, and therefore took a sufficient supply of tins of preserved food, and also the heating-stove. I appointed Shagdur chief of the camp at Temirlik, bidding him continue the meteorological observations. Before starting I packed away into one of the caves all the baggage I left behind, so as to secure it against the risk of fire, and directed that the entrance to the cave should be guarded day and night.

As the country we now explored was very similar to the regions I had visited during the past summer, I shall cut my

The Cossacks Cherdon and Shagdur.

narrative short. We traversed the 84 miles to the lower lake of Kum-köll in six days. The first day we marched diagonally across the valley of Chimen, over its level, sterile clay bottom, through a belt of sand-dunes 40 to 50 feet high, and then, by a gigantic gate-way, as it were, of granite cliffs, entered the Chimen-tagh. The glen, or rather gorge, of Savugluk was threaded by a brook, now, however, cased in ice as bright and transparent as glass. The path ascended all the time, and when we encamped for the night we obtained a splendid bird's-eye view of the whole of the valley behind us, right away to the dome-shaped mountains of the Akato-tagh, the crests of which were entirely free from snow from the one end to the other.

When next morning I was awakened out of my dreams after a beautiful night's rest, I had at first some difficulty in realising that we were again on the march. My short holiday had flown all too quickly. But there was no time for reflections ; breakfast came in, was despatched, and off we went. We were now to traverse a mountainous region, in which granite of every conceivable variety was the prevailing formation. Togdasin led us across one of the foot-hills of the Chimen-tagh by an easy pass, where the snow lay in an unbroken sheet, completely covering up the marmots' holes. But the animals themselves were snugly curled away in their nests for the winter. Wise little creatures ! Northern Tibet is raw enough in all conscience, even in summer.

The main pass by which we crossed the Chimen-tagh was remarkably easy, and consisted of a gently-rounded saddle, where the hard rock nowhere cropped out. On its southern side we went down into the same latitudinal valley which we had crossed higher up—that is, farther to the east—in July. The district a little beyond our camp bore the name of Att-attgan, or the " Shot Horse " ; and was thus named because a hunter, who had had a long run of ill-luck, and was on the point of perishing of hunger, was at last forced to shoot and eat the horse he rode. The spot where we encamped was called Mölleh-koygan, or the "Flung-away Saddle," because it was there the man abandoned his riding-saddle. Here the temperature dropped during the night of the 13th of November to $-21°.9$ C., or $-7°.4$ Fahr.

Shortly after entering, on the south side of the valley, a narrow glen which led up to the summit of the Kalta-alagan, we disturbed a herd of yaks, which were peacefully grazing on the mountain-side. In their flight they carried with them a troop of kulans, which were also grazing a little higher up.

We descended the pass on the other side by a steep water-course strewn with blocks of granite and gravel, and shut in on both sides by reddish granite cliffs. Those on the left consisted of a series of sharp detached peaks and pinnacles, while the crest on the right, although quite as serrated, was more continuous. The strong sunshine, combined with the clear pure atmosphere, accentuated the shadows in every cleft and ravine and behind each cliffy headland, making them almost perfectly black, and causing the immense rocky wall to stand out in strong and fascinating relief.

Our Camp on the South of the Kalta-alagan (15-16 Nov., 1900).

The view southwards across this broad upland basin was unlimited; the mountain-chains along the horizon were mere narrow braidings, the outlines of which were only just perceptible in the strong sunlight. The stream which flowed from the upper to the lower lake of Kum-köll glittered like a silver ribbon. Upon emerging from the trumpet-shaped valley, we directed our course towards the south-west, and went along the foot of the mountains, the spurs and ramifications of which were sculptured into divers fantastic shapes by wind and weather. They resembled tables and chairs; they resembled cups; they resembled necks and heads. Indeed, in some places, where the

The Northern Face of the Kalta-alagan.

erosive power of the wind had wrought with the greatest effect, the thinner sections were completely cut through.

The lake of Ayag-kum-köll flashed like a gigantic sword-blade in the south-west. But as it was too far to do the distance in a single march, we halted in the barren waste, where we obtained water by digging down about 4½ feet.

The next day, which was a rest day, I granted Cherdon, Togdasin, Islam Bai, and Turdu Bai permission to go in quest of game. They divided into two parties; but only the two last-named returned in the evening. We of course wondered what had happened to the others; and when the evening passed, and the night became far advanced without our seeing anything of them, we began to fear they had lost their way. Nor did they turn up until ten o'clock the next morning, and then in a truly deplorable condition. They had ridden up several rugged glens in pursuit of a flock of arkharis, until, the ascent growing too steep, they had been compelled to leave their horses behind them and scramble on over the rocks and screes without them. As they were trudging along, Togdasin all of a sudden collapsed, complaining of acute pain in the head and heart. He was unable to do another step, and even after Cherdon fetched up the horses was unable to keep his seat in his saddle. Under these circumstances they were forced to spend the night on an exposed gravelly slope, without either shelter or water. The sick man besought the Cossack to return and leave him where he was. He would soon die in any case, and it didn't matter much where it happened; but Cherdon stayed beside him all night, and every now and again shook him to prevent him from freezing to death in the bitter cold. As soon as ever day broke they were on their feet again, and dragged themselves slowly down to the camp. And Togdasin really was in a most pitiable condition. When we started again he had to be tied on his horse.

That night we encamped beside the Ayag-kum-köll, or the lower lake of Kum-köll, although the only accommodation consisted of a few scattered clumps of yappkak and small patches of ice along the shore. On the morning of the 18th of November we got the boat ready for a trip across the lake. My boatman was Tokta Ahun, and we carried a considerable load, as, in addition to the sail, oars, life-belts, sounding apparatuses, and other instruments, we also carried supplies for two days—meat, bread, preserved foods, and coffee—as well as cooking utensils, a *chugun*, or copper vessel, filled with water, and a little bag packed with pieces of ice. And when to these we added furs and felts, there was very little room left in our skiff. Once launched, I held a straight course for a prominent rocky headland in the south-west. The weather was magnificent, the lake still and calm, its surface just moved by a scarce perceptible swell. Every quarter of an hour I measured the velocity and sounded the depth. The latter increased as we approached the middle of the lake, where it amounted to 64½ feet. Soon after leaving the shore we encountered a thin sheet of ice, which, however, as it was also soft, we easily cut through. It extended on our left all the way

Our Camp on the South of the Kalta-alagan (continuation of Illustration on p. 9.)

to the southern shore, to which it was firmly attached. These patches of ice, which were from a quarter to half an inch thick, glittered in the sunshine with such intense brightness that it was impossible to look at them without smoked glasses. The wavelets which our boat made in passing set them rocking and grinding together. It appeared to me as if a thin layer of fresh water, coming from the stream, had spread itself over the salter water of the lake, and that the former then froze. Towards the west, however, there was no ice. The surface water had a temperature of $-0^\circ.3$ C., or $31^\circ.4$ Fahr., so that it was very cool work using the sounding line. Every time it came up it was quite stiff and frozen, and it was as much as I could do to get my hands warm between the successive soundings.

The hours flew rapidly, and yet we did not seem to get any nearer to the rocky headland; but then we were crossing the lake diagonally. Towards the latter part of the afternoon we noticed eddies of dust and "sand-spouts" curling up along the southern shore. These soon became fused together into a greyish-yellow cloud, which drifted rapidly overland. It boded nothing good. Soon afterwards we began to feel the strong north-west wind which was blowing. Not long after that there came a rushing noise from the west. The first puffs of wind struck us. The surface of the lake, lately as smooth as a fish-pond, began to ripple all over. The ripples curled higher and higher, and soon grew into waves; and these again became bigger and bigger in proportion as we became more and more exposed to the full force of the gale. However, we held steadily on until the pitching of our heavily-laden boat compelled us to turn to the south and south-east. It now seemed only too likely that the wind would increase to a furious tempest, which might fling us on some inhospitable part of the shore, where our fragile craft would be rent to tatters. We must make haste and get to land as soon as we possibly could. It was already twilight, and it would be extremely hazardous to land in the dark, even at a favourable spot, when the lake ran so high behind us.

Before starting I had ordered the caravan, after marching for five hours along the northern shore, to stop for the night, and there light a big signal fire, to serve as a beacon to us in case it should be dark before we got to land. But we never saw their fire, and accounted for it partly on the ground that the distance was too great, and partly that the air was heavily charged with dust.

Meanwhile our little skiff was pelting bravely along her dangerous course. Fortunately for us the wind and waves played havoc with the ice-sheets along the southern shore, otherwise their sharp edges would have cut our boat to pieces. After a while we detected a white line gleaming through the darkness ahead; it was made by the waves breaking against the beach, which, luckily, at this spot consisted of sand, and shelved steeply down to the lake. Before we knew where we were, we were amongst the "breakers." We were flung on shore, but the next moment were drawn back again by the recoil of the wave. Again we were flung on the sand, until the framework of our boat creaked ominously, and the canvas swelled as if it would burst. However, Tokta Ahun jumped nimbly out, and by our united exertions we got her up on to dry land, though not before two or three hungry waves had leapt into her, drenching the baggage in the after part.

We encamped quite close to the lake, behind a little hill, where we found plenty of *köuruk* plants, a species of low, woody steppe "grass," which made excellent fuel. The only signs of life apart from this were a few goose feathers and the kulan tracks. What the country was like we could not tell, for we were surrounded by pitch-dark night on every side; indeed, we were only able to find fuel by the aid of little fires, which we made here and there at intervals. As soon as we got together a sufficient supply, we crouched beside the fire, with our skin coats over our shoulders, and set to work to prepare a luxurious supper. Mine consisted of ox-tail soup, cheese, bread, and coffee, while Tokta Ahun munched a leg of mutton and washed it down with tea. After that we sat and puffed away manfully at our pipes, and discussed the projected journey which I intended to make across the Desert of Gobi to the marsh of Kara-koshun. Tokta Ahun knew the latter intimately.

After the wind died away, and the sky cleared, it gave promise of being a cold night. At nine o'clock the thermometer was down to $-14°$ C., or $6°.8$ Fahr., and as our fuel was all done, we thought it time to think of bed. My worthy boatman received my proposal, to convert the two halves of the boat into a tent, with a look of polite scepticism; but he very soon realized the ingenuity of the idea. Rolling ourselves up inside our kennels, we prepared, with a certain amount of trepidation, for

The Author in the Skiff on the North-west Shore of the Ayag-kum-köll ; Tokta Ahun holding it.

a bitter night. Indeed, after sleeping a few hours, I was awakened by the intense cold ($-22°.1$ C., or $-7°.8$ Fahr.). Thereupon I called my companion, and he helped me out of my nest, which was anything but adapted for light summer dreams. By this we were half-frozen, and I had lost all feeling in my feet, although they were protected by four pairs of woollen stockings and a pair of huge boots, lined with sheep-skin with the wool still on, which Ali Ahun had made for me. Our first business was to collect enough fuel to make a big roaring fire; then I peeled off some of my integuments, so that I might restore the circulation by massage. But having got the night cold into our bones, we could not get it out again all the next day—in fact, it was not until we returned to our usual conditions of comfort that we thoroughly recovered.

When we launched again the temperature was $-19°$ C., or $-2°.2$ Fahr., but the weather was magnificent as we started to row back across the lake towards the spot where the caravan were, or ought to be, waiting for us. The maximum depth was 78¾ feet; the surface water had a temperature of $-0°.5$ C., or $31°.2$ Fahr., and the bottom water a temperature of $-0°.3$ C., or $31°.5$ Fahr. Between the two was a layer which stood at $-0°.0$ C., or $32°.0$ Fahr. Before we had gone very far, we thought we could see what we were in quest of—namely, the tent, yurt, and horses; but when we came near enough to distinguish clearly through the glass, the tent and yurt turned out to be two little hills, and the horses a troop of kulans.

After that we continued along the shore until in the far distance we perceived a column of something rising against the setting sun, though we could not quite make out whether it was smoke from a fire or a cloud of dust raised by a troop of kulans. In the twilight we doubled one rounded headland after another, until Tokta Ahun eventually ran aground in shallow water. All this time I sat in the fore part of the skiff, numbed with cold; but my boatman kept himself warm by paddling, whilst he sang a plaintive song about the reed-huts of Abdall. At length, however, we saw the light of a fire gleaming through the darkness; but these night fires, however encouraging at first, were apt to prove deceitful. So on the present occasion, as for three hours we rowed towards the firelight; then it disappeared. However, we still continued, shouting loudly at intervals, and at last were answered by the barking of dogs. Again the fire leapt up, this time quite close beside us, and a man with a lantern came down to the lake to meet us.

Togdasin, whom we first fell in with up in the mountains, just as we did with Aldat, seemed destined to meet with the same fate as the Afghan. His illness was evidently taking a bad turn. The man crouched, as the Mussulmans do when they are not well, on his knees, with his body leaning forwards and his head touching the ground. We could not persuade him to touch a mouthful of food, though he continually craved for cold water, and was delirious, groaning every time he took his breath.

Tokta Ahun told me that this illness, which was unquestionably a very aggravated form of mountain-sickness, was very common amongst the hunters and gold-miners of those mountains. According as the individual attacked was a man or an animal (horse or camel), the Mussulmans called it *tutek* (or "shortness of breath"), or mountain-sickness ; or they simply said, "Is allup ghetti"—that is to say, "He has got the mountain sickness." If a man had suffered from one attack previously there was little likelihood of his pulling through a second. When the attack first comes on, the sufferer has an intense desire to get down to the lowlands, though he never does get down unless he recovers in the mountains. (That very summer two gold-miners had died near Temirlik whilst on their way home.) But after the disease has made headway, the patient is said to be no longer able to appreciate his own condition. He does not know that he is ill, and is unable to describe his symptoms. These consist in the body swelling, the lips turning black, sleeplessness, and an entire want of appetite ; and there is pain in the head and heart, combined with thirst, weakened heart-action, and falling temperature. According to Tokta Ahun's experience, smoking was the best remedy, and that was why we always saw him with his pipe in his mouth. For my own part, I have never felt any trace of mountain-sickness, not even when travelling at 15,000-17,000 feet above the level of the sea. The essential precaution is not to over-exert yourself.

However, it seemed as if death was going to be busy amongst us again ; and the worst of it was I was perfectly powerless to combat the evil, for such treatment as I was able to prescribe seemed to be of no avail. Both the sick man and we who had been across the lake urgently needed a day's rest.

Islam Bai and Kutchuk Pushing Off. In the Background the Isolated Mountain Group at the North-west Corner of the Ayag-kum-köll.

Accordingly the next day I sent Islam Bai, with Kutchuk to row him, across the lake to take another series of soundings, which I required for the completion of my map. Unfortunately, Islam could not write, so that he was reduced to working mechanically, like a self-registering instrument. He did, indeed, understand a watch, and he also knew how to take the soundings at every quarter of an hour. The device he adopted was at the first sounding to tie a piece of string with one knot round the sounding-line ; at the second sounding to tie another piece of string with two knots ; and so on. These distances I could of course afterwards measure with a tape ; and I already knew the mean rate at which the skiff travelled. That night it was extraordinarily dark, the sky being covered with clouds of such inky blackness that it was impossible to tell the difference between land, water, and atmosphere. When I opened the yurt a thin stream of light cleft the darkness ; but, except for that, the only object the eye found to rest upon was the fire in front of the men's tent. The interior of my dwelling was fitted with every comfort. The floor on which my cases stood was covered with a Khotan carpet ; my bed rested on the ground, and so served me for a divan as well. There I used to sit cross-legged and make my notes and draw my maps. At intervals Cherdon came in with a brazier of hot embers, without which it would have been difficult, if not impossible, to work in — 20°.0 C., or — 4°.0 Fahr.

When I now, surrounded as I am by all that I value most, recall those long, cold, silent winter evenings in Tibet, I am almost amazed that in that terrific loneliness—a loneliness which never changed day, month, or year—I never found the time hang heavy on my hands. But then I always had plenty to do; sometimes more than enough. I was surrounded by faithful and trusty servants, and I carried with me a little book containing Bible texts for every day in the year, which I knew was faithfully read in my own home in Stockholm. But it was always very depressing to have a sick man in camp, and Togdasin's ejaculatory supplications to his God—" Ya, Allah ! " " Ei Khodaim ! "—made me very uneasy. I could not get them out of my thoughts, even though I took out and tried to read Kipling's glorious songs in *The Seven Seas*.

CHAPTER II.

CROSSING THE PASSES OF NORTHERN TIBET.

THE return journey to Temirlik, which we begun on the 22nd of November, occupied 12 days, and led us across the mountain-ranges of Kalta-alagan, Chimen-tagh, and Akato-tagh—the last range twice.

The first day's march was a dogged piece of work. We were travelling west, and the wind—a half gale—was dead against us; while at 1 p.m. the thermometer stood at $-2°.0$ C., or $28°.4$ Fahr., and at 2 p.m. at $-10°.0$ C., or 14 .0 Fahr. Seldom have I felt so exhausted and incapable. The ice on the Ayag-kum-köll was broken up by the storm, and driven to the eastern end of the lake. The lake itself looked fearfully grim; it was cold and dark blue, and edged round with white foam. To have attempted to cross it in our small craft would now to a dead certainty have been disastrous. The entire eastern half of the lake was only six or eight inches deep, and the boat would infallibly have been forced against the hard, jagged edges of the ice, and been rent to pieces. The bottom of the lake consisted of ooze, and had we been stranded in it, there would have been no help for us. The Cossacks, whilst out hunting, tried to cross on horseback the mouth of the river that connected the two lakes, but the first horse dropped into the quagmire up to the neck, and was only extricated with the utmost difficulty.

At the point where we now crossed the range, the architecture of the Chimen-tagh was of a highly remarkable character. The glen, by which we climbed up to the pass, was itself so high that its threshold or culminating point was scarcely distinguishable. On the northern side, however, the descent was correspondingly steeper, dropping step by step down a succession of rocky platforms or declivities, through a ravine squeezed in

Our Baggage Horses on the Shore of the Ayag-kum-köll

between naked walls of rock and craggy promontories. We had already made a long march, and when I reached this mountain gorge the caravan was on in front. It was dark, and Islam Bai came back to meet me with a lantern; but all the same my horse stumbled every time he stepped from one platform to the next. The camp fire was a long way below our feet, in the deep glen of Kum-bulak, the springs of which, fenced round with sand, were sheeted with a thick panoply of ice. With very considerable difficulty we at length reached my yurt, which was set up on the brink of a rocky shelf, with a deep precipice immediately underneath it; though it was not until we were ready to start the next morning that I realized in what a dangerous position it stood. For it had been pitched right in the throat of a funnel, by which the rock avalanches that thundered down all the surrounding precipices made their way into the glens below. During the night I had, indeed, occasionally heard landslips and falling avalanches; but, happily, my yurt escaped uninjured.

Nor was the rest of the descent through that gorge any easier. In two or three places the ravine itself was choked with granite, which formed a giant staircase, the faces of the steps being each a dozen or fifteen feet high. Here we had to unload each of the animals in turn, and cautiously help it to slide down the steep slope. In another place, the gorge was covered from side to side by a thick sheet of ice, which penetrated every crevice and hole, and presented a surface as hard and slippery as porcelain. We had to strew sand on it before we durst think of leading the horses across. It was a real relief to emerge from this difficult ravine, and drop down into the Chimen valley, and encamp on the same spot where we were met by the relief caravan a month previously.

From this place I sent Kutchuk back to headquarters in charge of Togdasin, who was now somewhat better, and of the boat, whilst the rest of us continued our way north over the Akato-tagh. The night of the 27th of November was the coldest we had hitherto experienced that winter, namely $-24°.6$ C., or $-12°.3$ Fahr.

We crossed the Akato-tagh by the pass of Ghopur-alik (16,162 feet), up to which we climbed by a steep, gloomy granite glen. As we should be unable to do the whole distance in one march, we halted near the bottom of the glen, amid a chaos of fallen stones, without water, without grass, and without fuel.

Next morning we set ourselves to scramble up the steep acclivity. The horses breathed quick and with great difficulty, so that we had to let them stop incessantly, or we should have lost some of them. The summit of the pass was as sharp as a knife-blade, and the ascent on both sides precipitous. We all, of course, went on foot. I got some assistance by holding on to my horse's tail. The loads kept slipping off; the horses kept falling. We had to be constantly on the alert, and prompt in going to their assistance, for fear they should roll down the precipices and be smashed to pulp hundreds of feet below. Mules being surer footed than horses, I directed that one of them should carry my cases of instruments. The west wind was howling like a

The Glen leading up to the Pass of Ghopur-alik.

monsoon; and with the thermometer down to $-15°.0$ C., or $5°.0$ Fahr., it was what you might call decidedly fresh. Nevertheless the sky was bright and pure, and the mountains were bathed in sunshine. At length we reached the summit of the pass, and from its sharp crest obtained a sublime view. We beheld those stupendous mountain-ranges linked together as in a single panorama, each covered with snowy armour, which glittered dazzlingly in the sunshine; while an inextricable chaos of rugged heights shut in the west. Looking back, we saw the gorge by which we had ascended winding down the mountain side like a steep dry rivulet shrouded in gloom, and were amazed that we had been able to climb it. On the north the view was bounded by the immense snowy mass of the Illveh-chimen, with its crowd of eccentric peaks, a group we had already made acquaintance with during our previous excursions.

Having taken the usual observations, I longed to fill my lungs with less rarefied air, and to get some shelter from the wind. We descended by another magnificent gorge, which was joined by numerous secondary glens from both sides. To stand in the throat of one of these and look up, was like gazing through a gigantic gateway, with perfectly perpendicular walls of rock, at one of Nature's most eccentric efforts in the way of cliff formation, with the snow hanging like friezes and patterned reliefs from every projecting shelf. These snowy draperies, tinged as they were by the soft purple glow of the afternoon sun, were not unlike the decorations in a Tibetan temple.

There was again no grass where we encamped, at 13,311 feet above the sea. The wind still continued unabated; the thermometer registered –12°.0 C., or 10°.4 Fahr., inside my yurt, and the brazier of hot embers was not sufficient to keep the ink from freezing in my pen. Owing to the cross draughts, which we were unable effectually to shut out, a stearine candle burnt down in three hours, guttering fearfully before it went out. Cherdon shot a yak bull, and I heartily pitied Turdu Bai, Tokta Ahun, and Khodai Värdi, when at 9 o'clock at night they went out in the stinging cold to cut him up. As long as the body was warm, they were able to keep their own hands warm. They returned at midnight, each man carrying a load of meat, frozen as hard as stone. When they chopped it up with their axes the pieces scattered in all directions like broken glass.

Our next camp was somewhat better; the hard frozen tussock grass of the highland steppes made excellent fuel, and the snow gave us a supply of water. The next morning the sun tipped the rocky pinnacles of the Illveh-chimen whilst we were still shrouded in gloom; but there was no wind. We soon got started; but did not travel very far, for in a glen which ran up into the mountain-mass just mentioned, we discovered exceptionally good grazing, and could not afford to go past it. I was just putting up my theodolite stand when down came the westerly storm, and put an end to all work out of doors. Whipping up the men's tent, it carried it clean away, and dropped it on the ice on the bottom of the glen.

Shortly afterwards we perceived a man riding along the

flank of the opposite mountain on a camel. Thinking that he was possibly a messenger looking for me, I sent Tokta Ahun to find out who it was. But the man turned out to be a Mongol, belonging to a train of pilgrims on their way from Kara-shahr to Lassa. The rest of his caravan had gone by in the morning, and he had lingered behind because his camel had grown tired.

Every year large numbers of Mongol pilgrims travel from the tributary states of Russia and China, in the north of Asia, to the holy city of Tibet, *viâ* Temirlik, Ghaz-nor, and Tsaidam. They always make the journey out during the late autumn or winter, and return at the same season in the following year. They never pass through Abdall in the warm season, lest their camels should be tormented to death by the gad-flies. By the time they return they are always in a sad plight, only a few of their animals are left, and most of the men are reduced to travelling on foot. Upon reaching Abdall they generally try to exchange their exhausted camels for horses, so as to be able to reach their distant homes before the season gets too far advanced. One poor camel is considered equivalent to a horse, three camels in moderate condition as equivalent to one perfectly fresh camel, and a thoroughly emaciated beast as equivalent to one ass. The pilgrims carry their food in boxes and sacks, and on their way back usually replenish their supplies at Abdall. When going to Lassa, it is their habit to leave their camels behind them, with their kindred by race, the Mongols of Tsaidam, and perform the rest of the journey on horses, which they there hire. In this way several of the Tsaidam Mongols earn a considerable income every year.

These people must be animated by an intense conviction of the truth of their religion, when they sacrifice an entire year, with the fatigues, privations, and expenses incidental to it, for the sake of visiting the holy city, and taking part in its temple festivals and processions. They always arrange to be accompanied by a pilgrim who has been to Lassa before, and at Tsaidam they pick up a guide who knows where all the suitable camping-places are. The journey to Lassa takes them four months; for they travel leisurely and comfortably, using *argussun* (*argol*), that is yak-dung, for fuel. The evenings they spend round their camp-fires, drinking tea and eating *tsamba*. And when at length they catch sight, from the last mountain rampart they cross, of the white temple façades of Lassa, their hearts are, I daresay, as full of holy reverence as those of the Mecca

The Cossacks Cherdon and Shagdur, and their Trophies—Ali Ahun, the Tailor, on the right.

pilgrims, when, from the top of Mount Arafat, they for the first time set eyes upon their holy city.

It was a curious experience to find these pilgrims in our immediate neighbourhood following the trail that led to Lassa. For one moment I was tempted to disguise myself as a Buriat, and, taking Shagdur with me, go and attach myself to their company. But, upon second thoughts, I saw it would not do; I had other plans for the winter, and it would be inconvenient to alter my arrangements.

In the meantime we followed the trail of the Mongols' camels —that is to say, the light-coloured indentations which their soft pads had made in the sand. The prospect towards the north was arrested by the Astyn-tagh, which stretched right across from east to west. Towards evening the atmosphere assumed a light blue tint, although there was a white shimmer immediately overhead: in all probability this last was caused by the rays of the moon breaking into delicate pencils of light. The mountains wore a pinky colour, and gave a decided impression of wintry cold. No matter how warm we were personally, we could not help "seeing" that this region suffered from the disintegrating power of frost.

Travelling east, we at length approached the salt lake of Uzun-shor, lying close to the northern foot of the Akato-tagh; indeed the latter thrust several small spurs out into it. The lake was surrounded by luxuriant kamish (reeds) and bushes. As we crossed over these ramifications, we observed a great number of fresh-water springs bubbling out of the ground, and, lower down, uniting together into a single stream, before they entered the lake. Although there was ice at the embouchure, the salt water of the lake itself was quite free from ice, notwithstanding that its temperature was $-7^{\circ}.9$ C., or $17^{\circ}.8$ Fahr. In places the layer of salt which covered the bottom of the lake was so thick as to project above the water in the form of ridges and small hills.

We were all glad to reach "home" again, on the evening of the 5th of December, especially as everything was quiet and in order. The springs of Temirlik were now hidden under big pyramids and domes of ice. Togdasin had, it was evident, experienced a serious breakdown, for he was no better. The men had lodged him in a cave next to that which I occupied, and, as long as I remained in camp, I nursed him myself with every attention. When, at the end of December, the headquarters camp was flitted down to Charkhlik, he was taken with it, and I did not see him again until April of the following year. He was then a cripple ; both his feet had literally dropped off bit by bit ; but he was nevertheless cheerful and contented, and I gave him what I could spare for his support.

As for the Mongol caravan, Shagdur told me that it consisted of 75 men—all lamas—and 2 women, and that it rested one day at Temirlik. One of the lamas, or priests, was a man of distinguished rank, for the others treated him with the greatest possible respect. Of these about 25 were so poor that they were travelling on foot, and had only been allowed to join the caravan on condition that they acted as servants to their more well-to-do countrymen. The Mongols had with them money to the amount of about 10 yambas (£75–£100) ; besides which they had about 120 yambas (£1,000–£1,200) of tribute for the Dalai Lama. In other words, they brought money with them to pay for the all festivals, ceremonies, and solemnities in which they were to take part. It is upon this "Peter's pence" that "the Pope of Lassa" lives. The band was well-armed against Tangut robbers and other enemies, having about 30 Mongol muskets, 2 Berdan rifles, and 1 Winchester. Shagdur invited two or three of them to go out with him to shoot kulans, but they replied that blood-shedding was absolutely forbidden so long as they were on pilgrimage. The man who lagged behind was a lama, who had spent ten years in Lassa, and was now going to stay there another three. I just wondered whether he would recognise Shagdur again, in case we should, later on, be so fortunate as to reach the holy city. The caravan consisted of 120 camels and 40 horses, and, in addition to these, they led seven other horses of exceptional value, intended as a present to the Dalai Lama. Their rations consisted of minced meat, dried and frozen into small lumps, roasted wheat-flour (*talkan*), and tea.

The pilgrims manifested the liveliest curiosity in our camp, and asked no end of questions as to what I was doing in that part of the world. I have not the slightest doubt that on arriving at Lassa they related to the authorities all the information they succeeded in picking up concerning us, and that this was one of the reasons why the northern frontier of the country was afterwards so jealously guarded.

Shagdur on his side, also, extracted some useful information from them. The Mongols told him that a strict watch was kept upon all pilgrims who approached Lassa. As soon as they reached the borders of Nakkchu everybody was stopped and examined, and compelled to state his name, the place whence he came, the over-lama under whose authority he lived, as well as to show his passport, which must not only set forth which temple or monastery he was ascribed to, but also clearly explain the real object of his pilgrimage. After all these formalities had been complied with, a report was made to Lassa; but the pilgrims were not allowed to proceed until a special pass arrived for them from the authorities of the city. But once they got there, they were subjected to no further control. These precautions were said to be taken with the object of preventing "Russians"—that is to say, any Europeans—from smuggling themselves into Lassa. For the same reason orders had been sent a few years previously to the Turgut (Torgod) tribes, who are Russian subjects, that no pilgrims from their country would be admitted to Lassa; but just recently the inhibition had been cancelled, and their pilgrimages had been resumed. One of the lamas of the caravan said there existed a prophecy in an ancient and holy book at Lassa, which said that the Tsagan Khan, or White Emperor, would some day rule over the whole world, conquer Tibet and destroy Lassa, and that the lamas would then carry the holy things up to the top of an inaccessible mountain in the south of Tibet. The same man invited Shagdur to travel with him; he said he would have no difficulty, especially if he gave out that he was a Turgut Mongol. In the evening, when the camp was quiet, I discussed these things with my faithful Cossack, who was intensely interested in all he heard. From his boyhood he had heard speak of the holy city, and was consumed with eagerness to visit it. He had, of course, no idea that it was my intention to try my luck along the prohibited roads. But, as I have already said, Patience! I had more important matters to attend to first. The very idea of trying to enter Lassa in disguise was one of those perilous enterprises which never tempt a man except when he is young.

I spent six days in our headquarters camp at Temirlik. The ice volcanoes continued to grow around the springs, and the temperature went down to – 27°.0 C., – or 16°.6 Fahr. I was supposed to rest; but there were a thousand things to attend to. Once more I took a complete series of astronomical observations, to determine the position of this important point of cartographical control. I also developed the negatives which I had recently taken; got ready a new post-bag for Kashgar, and paid up all arrears of wages.

One sunny day we carried Togdasin out into the open air, and the Mussulmans gathered around him, and sought to banish his sickness by all sorts of ritual, including the sacrifice of a he-goat to Allah.

I naturally spent a good deal of time, too, in preparing for my forthcoming expedition through the Desert of Gobi. Provisions and stores, sufficient for a journey of over 1,200 miles, were selected and put on one side, divided into loads, packed up in boxes and bags, and lashed to the pack-saddles, ready for lifting on the camels' backs. My little yurt was repaired and renovated, its sides being re-covered with white felt, and the top or dome with red. Then I gave Cherdon lessons in the art of taking meteorological observations, although he had already made a beginning during our last trip to Kum-köll. He was to attend to this business during my absence, and generally to read and look after the self-registering instruments.

The men I left behind were Cherdon, Islam Bai, Turdu Bai, and Ali Ahun. I also engaged, temporarily, five hunters and gold-miners to help them down to Charkhlik, where the amban (Chinese governor) and native begs promised to look after them. In fact, all they had to do during our absence was to take care of my cases and other belongings, and see that the animals were in good condition, ready against when I should want them in the spring. I also ordered Islam Bai to send from Abdall two canoes, with paddles and fishing-nets, to the lake of Chöll-köll in the marsh of Kara-koshun; and he was to instruct the men who took them that they were to set up a *nishan*, or "landmark," on the top of some high and conspicuous sand-dune, so that we might know where to look for them. I saw distinctly that we should not get down there until after the ice had broken up.

CHAPTER III.

A JOURNEY TO ANAMBARUIN-GOL.

MY new caravan consisted of the Cossack Shagdur and the following Mussulmans—Faisullah, who acted as caravan-bashi, or leader of the caravan; Tokta Ahun; Mollah from Abdall, who was to guide me to Anambar-ula; Kutchuk; Khodai Kullu; Khodai Värdi; Ahmed; and Tokta Ahun, the hunter, whom we had recently engaged, and who, that we might distinguish him more easily from the other man of the same name, we called Li Loyeh—he spoke Chinese and Mongolian, had stolen horses at Bokalik, and was not quite right in his head. The animals embraced eleven camels, to carry the baggage, and eleven horses, to ride on. This left only one reserve horse; but if we required more, we could buy them from the Mongols. Three dogs accompanied us: Yolldash, Malenki, and Malchik. As it was my intention to sound Lake Ghaz, I took Turdu Bai with me for two or three days in charge of the boat. He wanted to go the whole journey, but after all the exertions he had undergone, I thought he needed rest.

On the morning fixed for starting, the 12th of December, I was awakened before it was light; the men drove in the horses, and the camels stood all ready tethered beside their loads. The day broke bright and clear, the atmosphere being still and the sky serene; in fact, it was a perfect spring day when we set off. All the men were eager and cheerful at the prospects of the trip. For my own part I was longing for the comparative ease of a journey across the desert. This time we should have nothing to fear from driving snows and sleet of hail. Cold, indeed, we might expect, for it was the middle of winter; but it would be a dry cold, which we could fight if we had plenty of fuel. It was also gratifying to have three full months of winter before us; we ought to get most of the problems of the trip settled before the warm days began again in spring. Nevertheless we did not neglect the precaution of taking light summer clothing.

After a friendly farewell to poor Togdasin and those I was leaving behind, I gave the order to march. Tinkle, tinkle said the bells, as the long dark train of camels stalked away with lordly gait from Sum-tun-buluk,* or the Three Hundred Springs; for thus Temirlik was also called in a combination of one Mongolian and two Tibetan words. All the camels behaved themselves well. But the foam clung like soapsuds about the dromedary's lips, and kept dropping to the ground in big clots; he would have made a fuss if he could. One of his forelegs was chained to his pack-saddle, so that, though he was able to walk well enough, he could not run away. He was fastened to his predecessor in the string by both a rope and a chain, and had a muzzle on to prevent him from biting his neighbours. Truly a magnificent brute, this veteran from Kashgar, with his wild, coal-black, flashing eyes, especially when he rolled them so as to show their gleaming whites, as he always did when in a bad humour.

Every animal in the caravan was in the pink of condition; indeed, two or three of the camels had been idle ever since they arrived at Yanghi-köll, more than a year ago. All had got their winter coats, as thick and fluffy as wool. The two biggest and quietest camels were selected to carry my personal belongings. The bulk of the loads consisted of flour, rice, maize, and *talkan* (roasted flour); but the weight would diminish every day, so that by the time we reached the regions where it became necessary to carry ice and fuel, we should have animals to spare for the purpose.

Our programme for the present journey was as follows:—First, I proposed to cross over the Astyn-tagh, and then skirt its southern flank, so as to clear up its orographical structure. This would take us to the north-east, into a region called by the Mongols Anambar-ula,† or by the Mussulmans Khan-ambal, the latter word being a corruption of the former. The distance was 240 miles. Thence I proposed to strike to the north, across an unknown part of the Desert of Gobi, until I reached the mountain ranges on its northern confines. After that we intended

* The Mongolian *buluk* = the Turki *bulak* = Eng. *spring* (of water).

† Or, with the genitive suffix, Anambaruin-ula.

to turn west, until we came to the springs of Altimish-bulak, whence I hoped to explore the ruins which Ördek discovered in the Lop Desert. Finally, we should cross the desert itself to Abdall, and thence to Charkhlik, our next rendezvous.

The journey to Anambar, which I will now briefly describe, took seventeen days. The first two took us across a hard frozen marsh, with hard crisp deposits of salt and sharp-edged laminæ of clay, to a spring that lay north of Lake Ghaz. The 14th of December I made a little excursion to the lake, thinking to row across it and sound it; for I had been told that it was so salt

The Camels Loaded up.

it never froze. We readily found the way to it by following a kulan path; but the ground at the lake-side, despite the frost, was so soft, that the horses dropped in up to their knees. In a few places the ice formed arches or bridges which we crossed, but many of them were so thin that the horses' feet went through and down the poor beasts came. It was no easy matter to cross this treacherous belt; but we did manage it at last, and we encamped near the mouth of the stream which collected all the spring-fed rivulets of the Chimen valley, to pour them into the lake. A little distance away we saw five yaks, and were just starting to hunt them, when Tokta Ahun observed that one of them was spotted, consequently they were tame yaks, and had probably run away from some Mongol camp in the neighbourhood.

A sail on the lake was not to be thought of; it appeared to be ice-bound throughout. But, as we had the boat with us, we converted one-half of it into a sledge, its wooden framework making capital runners. Seated in this light equipage, I was drawn by Tokta Ahun and Khodai Kullu a merry race across the frozen surface. The ice was uneven, sometimes hummocky, sometimes covered with a thin layer of water, sometimes cracked and fissured. But the sledge rode easily over all obstacles, and I was just beginning to think that I

Camp in Northern Tibet.

might obtain a second series of soundings right across the lake, when the ice-sheet began to crack and wobble. Tokta Ahun went through, and would have had a cold bath had he not clung to the edge of the boat.

After a quiet, uneventful night on the shore of this salt marsh, we rejoined the caravan next day at Yulgun-dung, or the "Tamarisk Hill." Here we rested one day; and I sent Tokta Ahun up the glen which penetrated the Akato-tagh north-east of our camp, to see if there was a practicable road. His report, when he returned in the evening, was to the effect that the glen led up to a pass, and that on the northern side of the range, a similar pass led out upon the table-lands immediately south of the Astyn-tagh. On the 17th of December we started therefore to follow his track. The previous night was the coldest we had experienced so far that winter, namely, $-29^{\circ}.6$ C., or $-21^{\circ}.3$ Fahr. Turdu Bai went back to Temirlik with the boat.

Turning our back upon the scanty vegetation from which the Tamarisk Hill derived its name, we started to cross the sterile, gravelly, gently-rising ground which led up to the mountains; and entered them by means of a rocky gateway, about 120 yards wide, with a seven foot deep gully at the bottom, which sometime or other had carried off the rainfall of those now arid

Glen Leading up to the Pass of the Akato-tagh.

regions. All day long the glen ascended, its floor being as level as an asphalted street, though it wound backwards and forwards round several sharp elbows. Thus I had to take fresh compass bearings about every three minutes, as one rocky buttress after another hid the next angle of the glen from my sight.

The substance of which the Akato-tagh was built up in this locality consisted of fine yellow argillaceous rock, but so soft that I was easily able to break off pieces with my naked hand. No wonder, then, the precipitation had worn the surface into the most fantastic and extraordinary shapes. On both sides an endless number of narrow gateways and dark arches were cut sheer down through the perpendicular walls, affording exit to a host of small torrents, streams, and dry ravines. The entire region was singularly barren, cold, and arid. The main glen was in places so narrow that two or three men were required at each projecting angle to prevent the camels' bulky loads from jostling against it. Every now and again this extraordinary "hollow" road opened out before us a fascinating perspective of views, the precipitous—sometimes overhanging—buttresses standing one behind the other *en échelon*, like the side scenes in a theatre. The bottom of the glen was choked with masses of stone of every conceivable shape and size, while others seemed to hang over our heads, as it were, by a mere thread. It was

Making a Road over the First Pass.

difficult to understand what kept them in position; the first gust of wind, or the first gentle shower would seem to be enough to send them hurtling down. My heart always came into my mouth when the caravan was passing these dangerous places. Pyramids, walls, towers, terraces, corridors, grottoes followed one another in never-ending succession. However, the caravan steadily and quietly pursued its course along the bottom of the smooth watercourse. Fortunately it was dry; otherwise the camels would have slipped and slided as badly as if they had been travelling on ice. As it was they marched confidently along, and left no impress of their footprints behind them. In fact, it was not easy to see the trail of the iron-shod horses.

But by degrees the relative altitudes decreased, and the glen lost its character of a deep-cut gorge. However, we did not quite reach the top of the pass, but encamped just below it, having brought up with us sufficient ice in *tagars* or sacks to last four days. Early next morning we said adieu to this silent, desolate camp, fully convinced that we should nevermore see it again. The last part of the ascent just before the summit of the pass was reported to be steep and difficult ; and Tokta Ahun and two or three others started early to level it down with spades. But when we reached the spot, I was amazed to find that, instead of continuing up the main glen, they had turned off to the east, through a side-glen, which was so narrow that when a camel stopped at an angle it was impossible to get past him. Still, our guide knew what he was about ; and there they were, working with their spades amid a cloud of dust. By dint of a good deal of hauling and pulling and pushing, we managed to get the first of the camels up. Two or three of the animals fell, and had to be unloaded, and their loads carried up by the men. But the beast which carried the fuel had the worst time of it, owing to the bulky character of his load ; however, after coming down on his knees once, he succeeded in pulling through all right.

Upon reaching the top of the pass (11,372 feet), Tokta Ahun turned to the south-east. This struck me as being wrong ; but our guide had reconnoitred the road himself, and now assured me that the glen we were striking into, a deeply-scarped gorge like that by which we ascended, would soon curve round to the east and north-east, and eventually lead out into the open country. However, down we went, zigzagging backwards and forwards in the most surprising manner. There was only one difficult piece of road to face, he said, where the gorge was so deep and so narrow that there was scarcely room for a man on foot to get through ; but the camels could be led over the declivity at the right.

A little bit further down the whole caravan came to a dead stop. The men hurried on to the front. The gorge was so narrow that the camels' loads touched the rocks on both sides, and the beasts were unable to advance until the rocky walls had been pared down with axes. Whilst the men were doing this, I went on a little way ahead, until I eventually came to a spot that was ten times worse than anything we had yet encountered. The gorge literally merged into a tunnel, which ran close in underneath the precipices on the left. Indeed, the rocks overhung it, and were cracked and riven in a highly dangerous way. There was no road over the top of this natural tunnel; the only path led through it. But just at its narrowest part the passage was choked by an avalanche of stones, which had come down quite recently. Some of the blocks we were fortunately able to roll aside by all of us putting our shoulders to them together. Others which were too big to be moved bodily were hewn to pieces with spades and axes. After widening the passage by cutting away the rocks on both sides, we first led through the horses, and then along the path which they made cautiously guided the camels one by one. The camel with the fuel, however, stuck fast in the middle, and in the midst of the desperate efforts he was making to force his way through, his load crashed to the ground, bringing down two or three big fragments of rock on the top of it. My heart turned over when I saw the caravan disappear in a cloud of dust. Had a fresh avalanche of stones fallen just then, whilst we were in the tunnel, we should have been buried alive.

Tokta Ahun cut a sorry figure, and lamely confessed that he had not ridden to the end of the dangerous gorge. Hitherto he had always been so very accurate in the information he gave me.

I have never seen a more peculiar glen formation than that was. It really consisted of two glens, or rather was a glen constructed in two storeys. The lower storey plunged down from the floor of the upper one to a further perpendicular depth of over thirty feet. The sides of the former were cut into terraces or shelves to which there was no possible access. Further on, the upper glen, too, grew so narrow, that the two storeys, the upper and the lower, merged into one, forming a tremendously deep fissure carved right through the argillaceous rock. The bottom was shrouded in gloom, and subject to frequent rock-slides of the most dangerous character.

However, on we went, stopping time after time, now to cut away some projecting angle, now to shovel aside the fallen débris which impeded our path. At last the caravan stopped in dead earnest. Tokta Ahun came and reported that there was no road. The ravine was choked with rock and stone, which had shot down the mountains from several hundreds of feet above our heads. However, a stream of water had forced a passage underneath the rockslide, and the only way to advance

The Cul-de-Sac where we Turned Back.

was over the top of this "glacier" mouth, as it were—that is, if it would bear the weight of the camels. Before deciding anything I preferred to reconnoitre myself. A little way past this pre-

The Two-storied Glen.

A Vault in the Glen.

carious and perilous arch the lower valley narrowed to a mere crevice of not more than two feet in width, with a depth of from forty to fifty feet, while the stream issued from an underground cavern. Thus the gorge became a vault, or a cave passage, so dark that a cat could hardly have found its way through it.

The situation was now clear: we must turn back. But the caravan was so tightly wedged in between the rocky walls that we had to back the last of the camels some distance before we could get room to turn him round in, and we had to do the same with each of the others. By this it was quite dark, and we were forced to encamp in a small expansion of the glen, where we were safe from being crushed by an avalanche of stones, though there was nothing to give the animals, either to eat or to drink. How dark, how silent, how weird it was in that rock-lined trough so distant from the busy haunts of men! Especially when the camels shook their heads, causing their bells to tinkle with a thin metallic sound. The voices of the men, chattering around the fire, were multiplied tenfold by the echoes. It was like talking in a dim wide cloister, or in the empty banqueting hall of a feudal castle.

It was irksome to return in our own footsteps, and not least so that our path lay along the bottom of a ravine, where tons upon tons of rocks hung, as it were, by a thread above our heads, threatening to crush us and our camels like beetles. If a big rockslide had taken place during the night, we should have been caught like rats in a trap. It took us a whole day to get back to the point where the main glen bifurcated. In the meantime Tokta Ahun and Mollah rode on ahead to the top of the main glen, and when they came back in the evening, assured us that this time they really had discovered a road through the intricate labyrinth of the Akato-tagh.

On the morning of the 20th of December I was awakened while it was still pitch dark. It was stinging cold, and I made haste to dress, wishing I had a cup of boiling hot tea.

Long before it was light some of the men had hastened up to the pass to level down the road and make it easier. This time we were on the right path; but the last bit of the ascent was dangerously steep—the camels would never have got up without help. But, once we were at the top, the extensive view which opened out before us proved that we were at the summit of the range (12,133 feet). On the north was the long-drawn ridge of the Astyn-tagh; on the south Chimen-tagh; south-east the desolate wastes of Tsaidam; while to the east was something which might have been a mountain, or a cloud, or dust haze, or merely a reflection of the desert.

The Akato-tagh is unlike any other mountain system of

Taking up the Camels one by one to the Main Pass.

The Spring of 22nd December, 1900.

Northern Tibet, in that it consists of an inextricable chaos of rounded domes and flattened tops of argillaceous rock, cleft by narrow ravines and unfathomable fissures, driven in every conceivable direction. A gloomy and lifeless region! The only indications of animate existence the skeleton of a kulan and the track of a bear! But when we got down to leveller ground, we came across a path which must have been made by human travellers.

Owing to our getting entangled in this defile, we lost so much time that our supply of ice was now rapidly running out. So, for safety's sake, I sent back two or three of the men in the morning, with six horses, to fetch a fresh supply from Yulgundung. Fortunately also, close beside the spot where we encamped, we found a few snowdrifts in a sheltered crevice.

Tokta Ahun had spoken about a pass, Kara-davan, which would have to be crossed on the way to Anambar, and after we had traversed in a north-easterly direction the broad, flat valley which intervened between the Akato-tagh and the Astyn-tagh, it began to be time to look about for his pass. We soon discovered again the track which we had noticed the day before, at the bottom of the Akato-tagh, but it was now considerably broader. Continued use had made it deeper and more conspicuous, even where the ground was hard. The hills and projecting crags on both sides were crowned with *ilehs* or "landmarks," consisting of small heaps of stones. In places there were several parallel tracks, showing that a large company had travelled over the ground in separate columns. It was clear that this route had been employed by Mongol pilgrims on their way to and from Lassa, when the usual roads were either unsafe or in a disturbed condition. We lost it, however, amongst the hills. Nevertheless we pressed on up the valley until we came upon what we least expected to find in this indescribably barren region, namely, a little spring bubbling up in the midst of excellent grass. Though the spring itself was salt, the patches of ice which formed immediately below it for about 160 yards down the valley, were perfectly fresh. When they stopped, so also did the vegetation.

When, however, we at length came out upon the plain, we found that it was a thousand times worse than the labyrinthine defiles of the mountains. The surface consisted of saliferous clay, crumpled into ridges and folds and steps as hard as brick, and all running at right angles to the way we were going, that is, they stretched from north-west to south-east. It was just as though the integument of the earth had shrivelled up, and thus become covered with wrinkles like a withered apple. The

Cooking and Washing at Anambaruin-gol—Looking North-west.

interior of the ridges, which were three to four feet high, was hollow, and, as we could see through their innumerable cracks and crevices, perfectly black. The spaces which intervened be-

Grass at the Spring of 22nd December.

Gravel-and-Shingle Terrace at the Spring of 22nd December.

tween the ridges were only three or four yards across. Two or three of the men, who went on in advance, were kept hard at work levelling them down with spades.

The next evening, too, we were lucky enough to find a spring, with grass around it. Whilst we were pitching camp amongst the thickets of reeds, Shagdur stalked a solitary wild camel. Upon hearing the muffled echo of the shot, I rode out to see what he was doing. The animal, which was wounded in one of its forelegs, was vainly trying to escape ; but Khodai Kullu, coiling a lassoo, flung it round its neck, and dragged it to the ground, whereupon it was soon despatched. This supplied the men with fresh meat for several days ; nor did we omit to take possession of the valuable fat in its humps. To judge from the tracks and droppings, this spring would appear to be frequented by large herds of wild camels in the summer.

The next morning, after collecting a supply of fuel, and filling a couple of sacks with ice, and cutting up the camel skin for pillows, we started along the track before mentioned, which we lost up in the hills, but had now found again at the springs. Here there were no less than twenty parallel tracks. Perhaps they were made at a time when the Mongols, who dwell farther east, used to drive their flocks to Temirlik to graze. It was quite dusk when we reached the foot of the Astyn-tagh, and pitched our tents at the entrance of a glen between two subsidiary ranges, in a spot that was absolutely destitute of organic life. Considering the bleak and desolate character of the region, the Christmas Eve we spent there was all that could well be wished. The air was still, the sky clear and blue. As soon as the camp was settled down, we kindled a big roaring Yule fire, though that was the only thing to remind me of the festivities at home. Wishing to banish the melancholy reflections which that day always brought to me when in the heart of Asia, I called in Shagdur, and unfolded to him my idea of trying to reach Lassa. He was immensely interested, and thought that we could manage it, if we travelled in the prescribed garb, and secured trustworthy Mongols to travel with. After this we often discussed this adventurous project of an evening, though we generally spoke in Russian, so as not to let the Mussulmans know what we were talking about.

During the last days of the century we threaded the valleys which lay between the parallel chains of the Astyn-tagh. It was very cold, and the wind still continued, bringing with it snow, though it only remained in sheltered hollows and corners. Whenever the clouds broke, the mountains peeped out in their white shrouds. The track was easy to travel : we crossed over

View looking S.E. from our Camp at Anambaruin-gol.

a succession of small, self-contained basins, which, after rain, would be converted into miniature lakes, though the water would of course soon evaporate again. The thin steppe tussock grass, with the teresken and yapptak scrub, furnished us with ample fuel. The only evidences of wild animals which we noticed during these days were the tracks of wild camels and a few ravens which accompanied us for short distances. Tokta Ahun, who was a far less trustworthy guide in these regions than amongst the marshes of Kara-koshun, never managed to hit the pass of Kara-davan; however, I found my way through the mountains without his help.

When I peeped out of my yurt on the morning of the 27th of December, it was stinging cold, and the ground was covered thick with snow; in fact, it continued snowing all day. However, the snow was welcome, as it gave us a supply of water for the horses; they, poor brutes, had had none for two days! On the 29th of December we went to sleep in a storm. We awoke the following morning in a storm. We rode the whole day through tempestuous squalls; and at night, when we again encamped, it was once more in a storm. It was impossible to keep the draughts out of the yurt; and we had to pin it down well all round, to prevent it from blowing over, which might have been fatal, for I had a lighted stove inside it. Oh, that we were in the desert! The atmosphere there during the cold months was never in this state of infernal uproar!

Some of the springs beside which we encamped bore Chinese names—Lap-shi-chen, Ku-shu-kha, Ya-ma-chan. The last-named perpetuated a bloody episode in recent Chinese history. In the summer of 1896, during the time that I was in northern Tibet, the scattered remnant of the rebellious Dungans,* who had been driven out of the district of Si-ning, arrived at this spring. The Chinese despatched an army against them from Sa-chow, and an engagement took place. The Dungans were defeated and very many of them killed, while others were taken prisoners and carried to Sa-chow. A large number of skeletons were still lying in the immediate vicinity of the spring. About 500 of the Dungans, including women and children, escaped, taking with them a number of camels, mules, and horses; but, being totally destitute, they were forced gradually to consume all these. At the height of this commo-

* See my former book, *Through Asia*, vol. II., pp. 1175, 1203-9 and 1247.

tion, a deputation was sent from Abdall to Sa-chow, consisting of one Chinaman, one Dungan, and two Mussulmans, namely, Islam Ahun, a relative of Tokta Ahun, and Erkeh Jan, the elder brother of Niaz Baki Beg, one of our friends at Kum-chappgan. These four men, when on their way back, fell in with the fugitive Dungans amongst the Astyn-tagh mountains, and were all killed by them at this spring of Ya-ma-chan. The 500 Dungans continued on to Abdall, where they were met by a Chinese force, which compelled them to capitulate. They were then taken to Kara-kum, a newly-founded colony to the south of Korla, where they are living peacefully and unmolested at the present day, a proof that the Chinese do not always deal barbarously with their rebellious subjects.

A stone pyramid, five feet high, which stood beside the spring of Ya-ma-chan, bore a plate with a Chinese inscription; but whether it commemorated this wretched victory over a handful of weary fugitives, or whether it merely indicated that this remote and valueless region belonged to the Celestial Empire, I do not know.

Some thirty years ago Dungan hunters often used to visit these regions, though they left no memorials behind them, except some fox-traps, which the Mussulmans called *kazghak*, for at that time fox skins were worth a good deal of money. These Dungan traps looked exactly like churchyard graves, or oblong heaps of stones, but were hollow inside, like a tunnel. A piece of meat was placed at the far-end to serve as bait, and just above it a heavy stone, fixed in such a way that, when the fox crept into the tunnel, the stone would crash down upon him and kill him.

During the night of the 30th–31st December the tempest raged more fiercely than ever, and brought the roof-spars of my yurt to the ground. New Year's night was, however, bright and biting cold; and the moon glittered like an electric light. I read the Bible texts and psalms which are sung in every church in Sweden on the last night of the year, and so entered upon the new century, alone, solitary, though of good heart, in the centre of the vast Asiatic continent. It was a solemn moment. Although not ushered in by the glad pealing of the bells, the wind, which knows nothing of the change of centuries, nevertheless sang a funeral dirge to the crashing of its own organ notes. On the 1st of January, 1901, the tempest still raged with unabated energy, inexhaustible cascades of wind being

Our Mongol Guides when Returning to Anambaruin-gol.

poured through the rugged defile. We got our first glimpse of the stupendous mountain-mass of Anambaruin-ula across a low saddle, by which the river Anambaruin-gol broke through the Astyn-tagh, to enter the sandy desert, where it speedily died away. This region was, we knew, often visited by Mongols, especially in the summer. Hence, no sooner did we catch sight of a solitary horse grazing in the distance than we jumped to the conclusion that we should soon be in touch with these people; and yet, even whilst we were pitching our tents in an expansion of the glen by which the river emerged, we noticed that the animal regarded us in a shy sort of way. Next day I sent off small parties of the men in different directions in search of the Mongols; but they all returned without finding them. Evidently it was a long time since they had visited that locality. This was a stroke through our reckoning, for we had counted upon gleaning a good deal of information from their knowledge of the local topography. Still, as we had plenty of time, I decided to keep steadily on until we did find them, although it would mean a detour of nearly 200 miles—in fact, it meant making a complete circuit of the Anambaruin-ula.

Thinking it would be a pleasant surprise for the first Mongols we met, we went out to catch the horse that had escaped from them; but it proved a very much harder task than we had anticipated. We tried to lassoo him; we tried to drive him into a corner. But it wouldn't do; he took to his heels, and galloped up the valley. He had grown as wild and as shy as a kulan.

CHAPTER IV.

AMONGST THE SÄRTÄNG MONGOLS.

FOR several days after this we travelled due east. The first day took us up a magnificent gorge, deeply trenched between naked walls of rock, at the bottom of which the Anambaruin-gol lay bound in fetters of ice, blue, shimmering, slippery. Our path was rendered difficult by reason of the masses of rock and débris which had plunged down the mountains on each side. A few solitary stone huts proved that the glen was occasionally visited by Mongols. We stopped below the pass which fenced in the gorge on the east. Just as we were pulling up, a flock of arkharis, or wild sheep, scrambled with the agility and sureness of monkeys up the crags beside the path. But, when they stopped to regard the caravan, Shagdur crept in underneath them. A shot awoke the sleeping echoes of the glen, and down crashed a big ram from a height of 160 feet or so. If these wild sheep chance to slip or slide along their craggy pathways, they are said always to fall on their horns; and certainly Shagdur's victim proved the truth of the observation, for he came down on his horns amongst the rattling gravel. We had had a long march, and there was a good deal to do when we stopped, so that it was midnight before the men came in, bringing the arkhari on a camel.

It turned out a frightfully cold night, namely, $-28^\circ.5$ C., or $-19^\circ.3$ Fahr. With the sky clear and the moon shining bright and high above the snowfields on the mountain flanks, we almost fancied we could actually see the cold vibrating in the night air. Next day we crossed another pass, and reached a part from which numerous streams descend in the summer southwards to the sandy basin of Tsaidam. In one place we caught, between two detached groups of mountains, a glimpse of that desert. The snow formed one unbroken expanse all around us. A party

Our Camp in the Glen of Jong-duntsa.

of Mongols had recently been there—the ashes of their camp-fires were still lying amongst the stones.

On we went through that wild mountain region, fighting against the wind, suffering from the cold, for we had no fuel, except what we obtained by the sacrifice of our pack-saddles. Nor were the camels any better off than we were; for, not only was the pasture scanty, it was also of miserable quality, and springs of water were few and far between. It does no harm to camels to go several days without water, but horses must have it. Ours, for want of anything better, nibbled at the snow as they passed along. When it dawned on the 6th of January, the mountain-mass of the Anambaruin-ula lay on our left, and

Up the Gorge of the Anambaruin-gol.

on our right, that is, to the south and south-east, stretched open table-lands, while before us lay the highland basin of Särtäng, inhabited by the Särtäng Mongols, who are tribally akin to the inhabitants of Tsaidam. Still farther to the east we caught glimpses of the little lake of Bulunghir-nor, and of the streams which fed it. The excellent grazing for which these table-lands were famous was pretty certain to be withered; still, such as it was, we resolved that our animals should have their fill of it. Although it was already twilight, we determined to make an effort to reach the pasture-grounds that night. In the distance we observed some black dots, which we took to be huts and herds, though they were too far away for us to make them out distinctly, and very soon the landscape was wrapt in darkness. Then Shagdur and Mollah galloped on ahead, and about an hour later we saw a fire flaring up through the night. This was a signal that they had reached the edge of the steppe. However, owing to the slow pace at which the caravan travelled, it took us a good two hours to get up to them ; but, once there, the animals were turned loose to graze all night : there was no fear of them running away from a spot like that.

Before I was called the next morning, the men had already hunted out two or three Mongol encampments farther on. Accordingly, making for them, we came first upon three yurts, with large numbers of cattle, horses, and sheep grazing in the vicinity. An old woman came running to meet us, without showing the least trace of fear ; indeed, all the time she was talking to us, she went on with the work she was about—namely, plaiting a cord. But she begged us not to stop there, for all the men were absent. Accordingly, we proceeded towards three other yurts, from which two men came forward and welcomed us, and said that we might pitch our tents beside theirs. We were quite at home amongst these friendly Mongols of Sando, as the place was called. They readily sold us what provisions we wanted, but, unfortunately, they had no caravan animals to spare. As a matter of fact, the district was very thinly inhabited; there were but a few yurts altogether, and quite recently one big caravan had started for the temple of Kumbum in Kan-su, and another for Sa-chow. However, what Mongols there were soon came to visit us. This gave me an opportunity to freshen up the Mongolian I learnt during my former journey, although I already had an excellent interpreter in Shagdur—in fact, Mongolian was his mother-tongue.

After a few days' welcome and agreeable rest, during which, however, the temperature went down to $-32°.5$ C., or $-26°.5$ Fahr., we started to return to Anambaruin-gol, but now on the north side of the mountain-mass. The next four days were spent in crossing this, the eastward prolongation of the Astyn-tagh. Our first station was Bulunghir-nor, where the wolves howled all night. The principal pass, Sho-ovo, or the "Little Obo," was a sharp-cut lintel or crest, extraordinarily steep on its northern face ; indeed we were obliged to lead the camels down one by one, lest they should topple headlong down the precipice. The transverse glen beside us was evidently traversed in summer by a large river, which had left behind it unmistakable evidences

Our Camels at Jong-duntsa.

of its excavating energy. Partridges were very plentiful; and although we had an abundant supply of mutton, I lived upon nothing but game throughout the whole of the Anambar-ula expedition.

From the little *aul* or "tent-village" of Sho-ovo, at the northern foot of the mountain, we directed our course to the west, although we were only a single day's journey from the large town of Sa-chow on Tung-khuan, called by the Mussulmans Dung-khan. It was probably fortunate that we did not visit that city whilst the disturbances were in progress in China, for of these we were quite ignorant. Tung-khuan is interesting as the definitive termination of the important journey which Count Béla Széchenyi made in company with two others, MM. Lóczy and Kreitner, in 1877-80. Our guide was a nice old Mongol, who knew the country intimately; he let me hire from him five camels as far as Anambaruin-gol, and sold me as much corn as we were able to carry with us. The surface was covered with snow, yet not sufficiently to prevent the animals from grazing; it was also grooved by an infinite number of trenches and ravines, some of them as much as 35 feet deep, and all of them deeply scarped. The second station was called Davato. There a most trying wind blew straight down out of the mountains. It appeared to be a sort of local *föhn*, for it ceased the next day immediately we crossed over a low secondary pass, and so long as we felt its influence it raised the temperature to $-16^{\circ}.0$ C., or $-3^{\circ}.2$ Fahr.

On the 18th of January we approached the gorge of Jong-duntsa, a very broad trench scooped through thick beds of boulder clay to the depth of some 160 feet. A countless number of similar deep trenches radiated northwards from the mountain-mass of Anambaruin-ula, until they gradually converged into a smaller number of water-courses, which penetrated the desert, and eventually disappeared in the sand. The only way by which we could get down into the gorge just mentioned was by a little side ravine. The gorge itself was like a gigantic railway cutting, with perpendicular sides driven through the gravel-and-shingle, and echoed like a corridor. It was pretty steep, and grew narrower and darker as we advanced; but upon turning a projecting angle, it opened out into a sunny glen, clothed with vegetation, and traversed by a now ice-bound river. We encamped on the left bank of the latter amid scenery which was at once fantastic and sublime. On both sides were the lofty vertical walls of gravel-and-shingle, with their sharply accentuated lights and shades, and black, gaping portals, that is to say, the mouths of the side glens which opened out upon the main

Stone huts at Lu-chuentsa.

One of our Mongol Guides.

glen. On the south was a chaos of wild, snow-capped mountain peaks.

The lower extremities of the glens which streamed down

Looking North from Jong-duntsa.

from the stupendous mass of Anambaruin-ula were in truth both grand and charming. In one of them, called Lu-chuentsa, there was a grove of small willows surrounding big sheets of ice, and themselves encircled by belts of excellent grass; while stone huts and cornfields showed that Mongols had dwelt there not very long before. On the other hand the country was all the more difficult to travel in, owing to the gigantic ravines just mentioned, and the countless number of small gulleys which ran into them. These with their vertical sides made, as it were, a choppy sea of detritus very picturesque, but difficult to traverse. Often the caravan, dipping down into one of these huge trenches,

The Mouth of the Ravine of Jong-duntsa.

became quite lost to sight, until it began to climb up again on the opposite side.

The wild camel was very common in the neighbourhood of Gashun-gol. We frequently saw troops of 15 to 20 individuals, sometimes on the right of our march, that is to say, on the outermost slopes of the mountain next the desert, sometimes, strange to say, well inside the higher valleys on our left, where one would think they ran a risk of being driven into a *cul-de-sac*.

Leaving Gashun-gol on the 24th January, we travelled the remainder of the way to Khan-ambal, where we encamped on the same spot that we occupied three weeks before. Close to this place we encountered the only caravan we met during the whole of the four months this expedition lasted—namely, two

Chinese with ten camels laden with dry and frozen fish for Sachow. They told me they came from Lovo-nur, that is, Lop-nor. I wanted to buy a parcel or two of their fish, but they stubbornly refused to sell me any. My men proposed that we should simply help ourselves to what we wanted, but I objected to use violence, and let the Chinamen go on their way unmolested.

In thus returning to Camp no. CXXXI., that is counting from Abdall, we had made the complete circuit of the Anambaruin-ula ; and yet we had not attained the object for which the detour was deliberately undertaken. We had procured no camels, we had not even bought a single horse. All we had done was to tax the strength of our own animals to no profit. The camels, it is true, were still in good condition ; but several of the horses already showed signs of exhaustion. And yet the expedition had not been altogether wasted ; we had traversed a region which, from the geographical point of view, was one of singular interest.

As we still had vast stretches of unknown country before us, I thought it advisable to make a change in the caravan before we started again. In the first place, we weeded out half-a-dozen horses, which did not seem strong enough to stand another two months of hard work, and then put aside as much of our baggage as we could conveniently spare, and such as was no longer necessary, *e.g.*, skeletons of animals and geological specimens, and thus made up a little caravan, which Tokta Ahun and Ahmed were to conduct back to Abdall. I also gave the first-named another commission, namely, to continue with the horses as far as Charkhlik, and there obtain from Cherdon and Islam Bai a number of stores which we should subsequently want. With these he was to return to Abdall, and there await our arrival, bringing with him at the same time the post-jighit who, according to my arrangement with Consul-General Petrovsky in Kashgar, ought in the meantime to have arrived at Charkhlik. Each jighit had been strictly ordered to deliver his post-bag into my own hands with the seals unbroken. After that, Tokta Ahun was to take three fresh horses, and travel along the northern shore of Kara-Koshun, a good three days' journey from Kum-chappgan, and then in some suitable locality make a permanent camp. At the same time he was to take with him some of the fishermen of the neighbourhood, with two canoes. Next they were to build a hut, and lay in a supply of fish and wild-duck, so that when we came in from the desert, we might

Our Camp at Lu-chuentsa.

find both shelter and good food after our privations. They were to be at their rendezvous not later than 45 days after the 27th of January; and as soon as ever they arrived there, they were to find out a hill that was visible for a long distance to the north, and on the top of it light a big signal-fire twice every day—at noon and again as soon as it was dark, and so continue until we arrived. Tokta Ahun did not like leaving us; but I consoled him by telling him that if he executed his task well he should be handsomely rewarded.

Having sent off the little caravan to Abdall, we started on the 27th of January to cross the Desert of Gobi, from south to north. In the beginning we followed the glen which the Anambaruin-gol had carved through the Astyn-tagh. In a bend of the stream we came across three stone huts, surrounded by patches of cultivated ground, belonging to the Mongols. But the glen soon widened out, the mountains on each side of it forming detached groups, low hills, and swellings, which finally merged in the desert. At the same time the river dwindled, until eventually it became a mere trickling rill, while its enclosing terraces grew lower, and its patches of ice thinner. The snow also became less frequent as we advanced. Upon reaching the last patches of ice, we made a critical pause. When should we next find water? We did not know—we had no means of knowing. I therefore ordered the men to break the ice, and fill five sacks as full as they would hold. This would keep us supplied for ten days—that is to say, one sack was considered sufficient for men and horses for a period of 48 hours.

In proportion as we travelled away from the mountain-chain, the details of its conformation grew fainter; but, on the other hand, the two main ridges began to stand out with increasing distinctness. The more distant, which the Mongols called Tsagan-ula, or the White Mountain, lifted its magnificently modelled, snow-capped crest with imposing and majestic grandeur to a lofty height; but the nearer range to the north, that which was pierced by the Anambaruin-gol, was black, and drawn in soberer, modester outlines.

But both the scenery and the surface now underwent a total change. The gravelly débris, over which we had struggled for a month past, thinned away, until it disappeared, and the ground became soft; at the same time by riding round the patches of snow, we were able to spare the horses the disagreeable balling of the snow under their feet. At intervals the steppe vegetation, consisting of teresken and tamarisks, was really luxuriant. To the north the view of the desert "ocean" was as yet cut off by a low, reddish-coloured mountain. We found a suitable stopping-place beside a little hill, where the dry clumps of vegetation furnished not only food for the camels, but materials for firing; while a lingering snow-drift in a crevice close by enabled us to husband still longer our stock of ice.

The next day a gale sprang up from the west, driving before it the cold, grey, heavy clouds, and carrying in its arms an immense quantity of dust. The gigantic barrier of the Astyn-tagh was obscured by the clouds, and only the extreme edges of the low desert range were visible through the dust-haze. Following the dry river-bed we gradually approached the foot of the nearer desert range. The steppe vegetation, still in places plentiful, consisted of the berry-bearing bushes and scrub akin to the ordinary tamarisk, which the Mussulmans call *chakkandeh* and *köuruk*. Some of these were withered, and so made excellent fuel. Soon we came to a broad but shallow river-course running towards the west-north-west, in the direction of the Lop-nor basin, the common termination of all the water-channels in the vicinity, both those that came down from the Astyn-tagh and those that flowed out of the desert range. Crossing this big water-course we scrambled up the opposite side, which was rather steep, and soon came to the low pass that led over the red and grey granite of the desert range. Over on the other side of it we put up our tents amongst the low, dry sand-dunes, which had drifted up against its northern foot. Below the pass *suk-suk* or *saksaul* (*Anabasis Ammodendron*) made its appearance for the first time.

During the 29th January, whilst threading our way through a chaos of insignificant hills, we came upon an ancient, but unmistakable, highway; though there was no trace of it whatever on the surface, it was obliterated ages ago. Every hill, however, and every headland—there were at least a score of them—was crowned with a cairn of stones by way of landmark. As a rule they consisted of two flat stones, one large and the other small, propped one against the other; but sometimes of a square stone supporting two round ones, one on the top of the other. These cairns could not possibly indicate a hunter's track, for hunters neither follow fixed routes, nor do they build landmarks of stones such as these were. It was probably a continuation of the road we had formerly seen in the Astyn-

The Caravan on the Ice at Lu-chuentsa.

tagh, and had undoubtedly been used by pilgrims, though it must have been many ages ago; for the cairns were beyond all question very old. The stones could not have been affected by anything except weathering; it would have been impossible for any storm to have worn them down in the way they were, or to have displaced them from their positions.

One more pass and there was the yellow desert stretching out before us, its ridged dunes looking weird and repellent. We halted in the throat of the last glen on the coast as it were of the desert "ocean." Here the saksaul grew very luxuriantly, attaining a height of over ten feet.

The extreme outliers, which embraced this glen between them, were half buried in sand, for the dunes climbed half way over them, and they themselves dipped down to an unascertained depth under the desert waves. It was evident that this elevated tract on the edge of the desert was sometimes visited by rain, for there were a number of dry rivulets winding in and out amongst the sand-dunes, until finally they united to form a dry channel, which gave signs of carrying at times a considerable volume of water. First it ran towards the east; then, striking against a sandy hill, turned to the north. Then again, it went towards the west, until it was once more deflected at a sharp angle towards the desert by another lofty dune. It was amazing to find that the downfall here was strong enough to contend successfully with the sand. Anyway, without this natural "road," we should have experienced considerable difficulty in making our way through the belt of formidable drift-sand.

Owing to the icy wind I preferred to walk all day and serve as guide, the post I usually filled when our march lay across the desert. Yesterday the tracks of the wild camels and antelopes were exceedingly numerous; to-day they entirely ceased. The saksaul only survived in an occasional plant half buried under the sand. In places pieces of granite as big as a man's head were lying on the sand at a distance of several miles from the foot of the mountains. How did they get there? Why were not they too buried under the drift-sand? I could only account for it by the direction the wind took. They looked wonderfully like pieces of wood floating on water.

Gradually the water-course became less distinctly marked, and the sand invaded it in several places. The sand-dunes were now nothing like so high as they were at the foot of the mountains. The little desert range, which we had twice crossed, acted as a sort of breakwater, and not only prevented the drift-sand from travelling farther to the south, but also protected the belt of steppe which lay along the northern foot of the Astyn-tagh. At length the water-course terminated amongst the dunes in an expansion which resembled a small lake, although now absolutely dry. Here sacksaul bushes grew very luxuriantly. The little depression was bounded on the north by a steep sand-dune, and beyond it stretched the real "ocean" of the desert in all its stupendous desolation, though locally differing in no respect from several other regions in which I had crossed the Desert of Gobi. Its boundary was drawn with marvellous sharpness: not a single plant crossed the line. East, north, west—nothing but sand—sand—sand! That day we encamped in the middle of the desert.

Next day the dunes gradually decreased in height, and eventually were succeeded by the underlying clay, disposed in a succession of terraces that looked towards the north. On the 1st of February this formation became still more developed, the terraces pointing like fingers towards the north-north-east, and presenting vertical faces of as much as 170 feet in height. A keen wind shrouded the desert in clouds of dust, so that we were unable to see more than a mile ahead. Towards evening we experienced a very pleasant surprise in another belt of steppe, where kamish and tamarisks grew luxuriantly, and the tracks of wild camels, antelopes, and wolves were very numerous. We dug a well, and at a depth of 3¾ feet obtained saltish drinking water; but it trickled so slowly out of the sand that it did little more than whet the camels' appetite for more. This belt of steppe-land lasted for a whole day. We followed the wild camels' tracks that led across it towards the north, passing an occasional clump of venerable and ragged poplars, all, however, withered, with the exception of one, in which there was just a spark of life.

At Camp no. CXXXVIII. on the edge of this steppe-land we had everything we wanted, and thoroughly enjoyed two days of much-needed rest. Whilst I took an observation of the sun, the men baked bread, and had a big wash, for we were staying beside an especially copious well. The camels had a thorough good drink, each swallowing about seven bucketsful. The water was almost perfectly fresh, and by pouring it out into a little pool, and letting it freeze, we were able to secure a fresh stock of ice.

Our Camp in the Middle of the Sandy Desert.

Beyond this belt of steppe-land we again plunged into the desert. Here the clay was carved and sculptured by the wind into cubes, pyramids, and obelisks, some of them more than 25 feet high, and often bearing a confusing likeness to the ruins of houses and town walls. That evening we struck the *astin-yol*, or "lower caravan road," leading from Abdall to Sa-chow. Here Mollah's topographical knowledge came into play, for on two or three occasions he had travelled that road with caravans, and knew where all the wells were situated and their names. It was

Watering the Camels at Camp no. CXXXVIII.

beside one of these, Achik-kuduk, or the "Salt Well," that we pitched our tents; and well it deserved its name, for the camels positively refused to touch the water it yielded. The moist saliferous ground around the well showed, that not long ago a caravan had passed that way from Abdall to Sa-chow. It was no doubt laden with fish, a food upon which the Chinese set great store. Amongst the footprints we recognised the footgear of both Mohammedans and Chinese.

This desert route had been already traversed by M. Kozloff and M. Bonin, and possibly also by Marco Polo. It had been my intention simply to cross it on my way north; but prudence dictated that it would not be wise to enter upon an absolutely unknown stretch of country without a sufficient supply of ice.

Mollah told me that the next well to the west, Tograk-kuduk, or the "Poplar Well," yielded good water. Accordingly we proceeded thither, and rested a day beside it; and, as the thermometer went down to $-27°.5$ C., or $-17°.5$ Fahr. during the night, and the next day was only two or three degrees higher, we experienced no difficulty in filling our sacks. Thus when, on the 8th of February, we began our long and extremely risky journey towards the north, we carried with us sufficient ice to last men and horses for ten days. The camels drank as much

Sand-dunes of the Middle Gobi.

as they could hold at the well before starting, and they had also done full justice to the kamish beds.

We now bent our steps through the dry yellow reeds, which rustled and snapped in the intense cold, towards a region about which we possessed absolutely no knowledge whatever either from European or Asiatic sources. I, as usual, led the way. The tracks of wild camels and antelopes ran in endless number in every direction; but there were no signs of kulans—the atmosphere was doubtless too heavy for their spacious chests. All of a sudden the vegetation came to an end, amid a labyrinth of clay mounds, each crowned with a dead tamarisk. Upon reaching a depression where the ground looked damp, I thought it might pay to dig a well, especially as we had in front of us a terrace some 230 feet in height, resembling a gigantic ornamental

The Terrace seen from the Last of the Oases.

frieze. The grazing was good, and I thought it a pity not to let the camels have a good feed. We dug our well; it gave tolerably good water. As for the bitter cold—we did not mind it much after we got our rousing big fires made.

Next day we penetrated the clay terrace by a cleft or glen, which we followed till nightfall, and which had a scarce perceptible ascent. Now, according to the existing maps of the centre of Asia, there ought to have been a considerable mountain-range across our path; but such elevations as we saw were so insignificant as scarcely to deserve the name of mountains at all. Here, in a little cranny, I found fragments of a very ancient iron cooking-pot, of a spherical form, and a tripod with a ring hanging from it. Chinese or Mongols had clearly visited the spot at some time or other. Was this, perchance, a further continuation of the road which we had seen in the Astyn-tagh, or did it indicate some ancient route to Khami? That we were in a region where anciently means of communication did exist was proved beyond a shadow of doubt next day. We were following a broad depression, which led straight north, and all alongside it was a string of cairns and landmarks of stone. Finally, in a flat undulating expansion of the valley, the old road bifurcated, one branch going west-south-west, the other north-west. The former led, no doubt, to the ruins which we had previously discovered on the northern shore of the old Lop-nor basin; the other, which we now followed, appeared to lead to Turfan. The track soon took us over a low ridge of reddish, weather-worn granite. Beyond it our view was obstructed by a somewhat higher range in the far distance. The country was strangely silent, desolate, and deserted. As the traces of man were here of great antiquity, and only survived in the landmarks of stone, so also the mountain-ranges themselves were on the point of disappearing off the face of the earth. After the stupendous mountains of Tibet, I almost doubted the propriety of applying the term "mountains" to these comparatively low swellings. In point of fact they were the crumbling remains of primitive foldings of the earth's surface, which are now being broken down bit by bit under the influence of the atmosphere.

In a sheltered nook on the north side of the range we discovered a snow-drift, which came in very opportunely for the camels. Perhaps it actually saved them from perishing of thirst, for, as it turned out, we had a very long way to travel before we came to water again.

CHAPTER V.

SEARCHING FOR WATER IN AN UNKNOWN COUNTRY.

We now began to observe the first premonitions of spring. The winds were not quite so bitingly cold as they had been. The temperature seldom dropped below −20°.0 C., or −4°.0 Fahr. And it was indeed time that our long winter did come to an end, for it had begun in July of the previous year, and had continued ever since without a break.

On the 11th of February we crossed a swelling that was relatively insignificant in height, though the pass which led over it was exceptionally difficult. Here the tracks of the wild camels were extraordinarily numerous, and many of them appeared to lead to the snow-drift which we had just left. But on the 12th we traversed, north-north-east, an unspeakably desolate country, where there was scarcely a wild camel's footprint to be found. The prospect was open in every direction, though low scattered hills shut in the horizon, and for some time it was impossible to tell in which direction the contour fell. The surface was, it is true, seamed with shallow, winding water-channels; but they were all as dry as tinder, and most of them looked as if they had not contained a drop of water for dozens of years. On the 13th, as no change took place, and the hope of discovering springs or snow appeared to be desperate, we once more changed our course back to the north-west and west. The going was now capital, and we thought 18 miles by no means a long day's march. At 1 p.m. the temperature went up to 4.°5 C., or 40.°1 Fahr.

The two following days we turned south-west, steering by the compass direct for Altimish-bulak. After the détour we had made to the north-east, our position was now become critical. We still carried with us a sufficient supply of ice to last men and horses for several days, but we could not afford

Shagdur and Khodai Kullu Digging a Well at the Last Oasis. In the Background the Extreme Outlier of the Kurruk-tagh towards the Desert of Gobi.

a single drop for the camels, and all our efforts were now directed towards the necessity of saving those untiring veterans. I began to enter on my map every wild camel track we came across, for I thought that the directions in which they ran would afford some clue as to the whereabouts of springs and grazing. Most of the tracks, I soon ascertained, ran towards the north-west or south-east. In the latter direction were the kamish steppes of the astyn-yoll which we had recently crossed; in the former there were no doubt springs which the camels knew of, and they only. I now spent most of my time walking, for when things begin to look serious I have no longer patience to ride. The camels remained immovably calm and patient, and lay perfectly still all night. But then there was not a blade of grass to be obtained in this unspeakably sterile region. All we had to give them was a little of the corn we had bought from the Mongols.

On the 16th of February I was forced to the conclusion that the only way to avoid disaster was to strike straight for the south, and try to reach once more the salt wells of the astyn-yoll. We were engaged in an exciting hunt for water, and in vain did we look and strain our eyes for a single surviving snow-drift. No, there was nothing else for it; we must go down to lower ground where we could at least try to dig a well. Upon climbing to the top of a pass in an insignificant range the view I obtained was anything but encouraging. Low swellings in every direction—the same moon-like landscape as heretofore—the same arid hills, without a trace of grass, or any other indication of moisture.

In a broad watercourse close by I perceived the fresh tracks of no less than 57 wild camels. They radiated inwards from every direction until they converged into a single main track. A little bit further on we counted 30 other tracks, all uniting with the same highway. We stopped and called a council of war. That these numerous tracks all led to a spring nobody doubted for one moment; but the question was, how far off was it? Perhaps several long days' marches? Would it not be better, then, to keep straight on to Altimish-bulak, the position of which we did at least know? Finally, we decided to ignore the tracks, tempting though it was to follow them; for, though they had been quite recently made, strange to say there was not a glimpse of the camels themselves to be seen anywhere about. The principal track led towards the north, perhaps towards Pavan-bulak, a spring which Abdu Rehim told me the year before he knew of by hearsay, though he had never visited it.

On the 17th of February our position began to look most serious. It was ten days since the camels had had anything to drink, if we except the few mouthfuls of snow they picked up a week ago. Their strength would not hold out for ever. During the course of the day we passed successively the two desert ranges which we had crossed over on our way north. They ran towards the west, and both alike disappeared in the sand, and consequently could not be directly connected with the Kurruk-tagh, although they belonged to the same orographical system. We saw the chains of the Kurruk-tagh a long way to the west, but they were higher and altogether bigger than these. As there was far greater likelihood of our finding water near them than in the desert, we decided to make for them. Turning my back on the outliers of the mountains, I soon reached the level plain, composed of saliferous clay, but diversified by ridges and swellings not more than six feet in height. The desert was perfectly open both south-west and north-east, and resembled the long, narrow bay of an ancient sea. After tramping for five hours, I stopped to wait for the caravan. The country now changed, and became worse than any sandy desert I ever traversed. It consisted of *yardangs*, or "clay ridges," like those which I have described in an earlier chapter, only here they were 20 feet high and 30 to 40 feet across the top. North and south they stretched in endless succession. Had it not been for the small gaps broken through them, we could not possibly have progressed, for their sides were perfectly perpendicular. An advance of ten or a dozen yards sometimes necessitated a sweep round of a furlong or even of a quarter of a mile. At length, however, I succeeded in finding a way out of the wearisome labyrinth, and we halted amongst low, flat hills, absolutely destitute of every trace of organic life.

Next morning, when the Cossacks came to call me, I seemed to have had a precious short sleep, for I had been desperately tired the night before when I turned in. At daybreak there was already a half gale blowing; and on towards the afternoon it quickened into a regular *kara-buran* (black tempest). The surface was abominable; we crossed one low ridge after another, up and down, up and down, and all at right angles. I was still leading the way, and trudged on for over a score of miles. Our fuel was exhausted some time previously—

The Caravan Marching through the Desert of Gobi.

[Vol. II.—*To face p.* 94.

we had not a splinter left. We were in a veritable rat-trap—stones, gravel, and sand—these and nothing else! The mountain-range for which I was making, and at the foot of which I hoped to find a spring, seemed to recede as if in mockery when I approached it, until at last it vanished altogether in the dust-haze. It grew afternoon, and our goal seemed further off than ever. In spite of the forced march, our camels were keeping up magnificently, despite the fact that they had not a blade to eat or a drop to drink; they nevertheless marched steadily on with a long, swinging stride and head aloft. The wild camels' tracks were now all directed towards the north-east, evidently making for the mysterious spring which we no doubt left behind us a few days ago.

It grew dark. We encamped in an open gulley, with no shelter whatever against the storm. My yurt was covered with a triple layer of felts, but I could not have the stove lighted for want of fuel. The only sources of warmth were my own body, my faithful travelling companion, Yolldash, and a flickering candle which would keep going out in the gusts of wind. The men banked up the sand all round the lower edge of the yurt, but in spite of that, its interior was like a cellar. Our ice was all done except a few small fragments. The unfortunate men had to content themselves with bread and a few fragments of ice for their supper, and then made haste to creep in underneath their sheep-skins. I managed to get a cup of tea, although at the sacrifice of one of the spars of the yurt.

The storm raged all night, but I slept well and peacefully. Next morning, the 19th of February, after a mug of tea and a piece of dry bread, off I started tramping again. Water! water! was the one thought uppermost in everybody's mind. Somewhere, somehow, we *must* find a spring, for it was now twelve days since the camels had touched a drop of water. Our situation was very serious indeed. If we failed to find water the camels would drop and die one after the other, just as they did in that awful march through the Takla-makan Desert. Here, however, we had certain advantages—the air was cold, and the ground hard and level, so that we were enabled to do long stages.

I was taking a bee-line for Altimish-bulak, the position of which I knew from our visit the spring of the year before. But according to what Abdu Rehim told me, there should be three springs somewhere to the east of Altimish-bulak; it was upon them my hopes were fixed. And yet how easily they might lie hidden behind some slight swelling of the surface, or be screened by a low ridge. The storm, also, occasioned us great inconvenience, for it obscured the country, except in our immediate vicinity, to such an extent that the map which I had made the year before was of little use. When crossing the Takla-makan, we knew that if we kept advancing east we were bound the strike the Khotan-daria somewhere; and again when travelling down the bed of the Keriya-daria, we had only to keep steadily to the north, and we were bound to strike the Tarim. In both these cases we were aiming to reach a line at right angles to our course; but here we were aiming for fixed points, which we might only too readily miss in the dust-clouded atmosphere. If we did miss them, one thing was certain, we should never reach the marshes of the Tarim.

We studied with strained interest every wild-camel track we came across. Although obliterated on the loose sand, they were plain enough to see on the clay. We all knew that they led to water or from water, and that, if we followed them in one direction or the other, we were quite certain to reach a spring; but then it might be days—it might be weeks—before we got to it. These tracks I was continually tempted to follow, and several times did follow them, until, without either rhyme or reason, they suddenly turned away at right angles. On the whole, they ran generally north and south. But in the former direction we were confronted by a reddish-brown mountain-barrier, while south there was nothing except the boundless waste of the desert. After all, it was best to keep pegging away west until we struck one or other of Abdu Rehim's springs.

Driving ahead for dear life, I soon left the caravan a long way behind. My native-made boots barely held together after the 180 miles tramp, and my feet were sore and blistered. Shagdur, who generally kept with me, and led my saddle horse, was nowhere to be seen. I had made up my mind that I would not stop until I did find water. That day (19th of February) was my 36th birthday, and I meant to have a pleasant surprise before it was over. The camel tracks were now more numerous, and they led towards the west. I seldom went two minutes without coming across one.

At last I reached a low ridge which forced me to turn to the south-west and south-south-west, and in the dry watercourse which skirted it I counted the footprints of no less than 30 wild camels which had passed quite recently. A little bit further, and I observed a tamarisk, then the tracks of hares and antelopes. I stopped. These animals were not wont to travel a tremendous distance from water. Shagdur came up. We took counsel. There were several tamarisks to the south, and we made for them. The ground thereabouts was decidedly moist, although covered with a thick layer of salt. At length the caravan arrived, and we dug a well. The water was undrinkable; it contained a concentrated solution of salt. We again resumed our march. The storm, being now at our backs, helped us up the slopes, though down them we went rather

Altimish-bulak or Sixty Springs.

faster than we liked. I and Shagdur hurried on in advance, my white horse following me unbidden, like a dog. Yolldash was scouring the neighbourhood, hunting and sniffing everywhere. At length we got on the track of a troop of 20 wild camels, which brought us opposite to a glen or opening through the 10 to 15-foot clay terraces on the right, with the crest of the range showing four or five miles back at the head of the glen. All the camel tracks converged into one principal trail, which turned up the broad, trumpet-shaped glen. I followed it, and before I had gone ten minutes I saw Yolldash drinking beside a white patch of ice-water. We were saved!

The spring itself was, as usual, salt; but the sheet of ice, which was not more than 12 to 14 yards across, nor more than four inches thick, was perfectly fresh. Strange to say, the only vegetation it supported consisted of two tamarisks. Shagdur was quite amazed when he saw the ice; he thought I must have had some secret knowledge of this hidden spring, seeing that I had marched straight to it. The cornice of the clay terrace on the left of the spring was crowned by a crescent-shaped wall, like a rampart or breast-work—evidently a hunter's ambush, for the spring was frequented by wild camels.

Here, I need hardly say, we encamped. Faisullah and Li Loyeh went up the glen to reconnoitre, and brought back each an armful of withered tussock grass, and with that the camels had to be content. We did not think it wise to let them touch the ice until they had recovered a little from the strain; but we let the horses try their teeth upon it at once. When the camels were at length watered it was quite a pleasure to give them small pieces of ice, which they crunched between their strong teeth like children eating sugar-candy. The weather still remained cold; but although at 1 p.m. the thermometer did not rise above freezing-point, the ink no longer froze in my pen, for I was now able to have the stove lighted again. The ice-sheet proved more enduring than we thought it would; for it more than supplied our wants, and when we started again on the 22nd of February we took several sacksful with us.

The scenery changed but little from day to day. It was terribly monotonous; the ground hard, often a good deal broken and furrowed by the watercourses all running out into the desert. The spurs of the Kurruk-tagu stuck out like short, truncated ribs. We now knew for certain that these ranges grew lower and more insignificant as they advanced towards the east, while at the same time the country became more sterile and the springs fewer, as well as more saline. Silence, desolation, and waste on every side! Absorbed in my own thoughts I mechanically followed another camel track, and it led me to a new spring, likewise with a conspicuous patch of ice about it. Upon this too all the camel tracks of the locality converged, as they had done in the case of the previous spring. Whilst our animals rested here a little to graze, I continued towards the south-west, and was threading some low hills when I caught sight of a handsome camel, which, however, did not observe me, owing to the wind blowing in the wrong direction for it. I stopped and waited

The Author Testing his Levelling Instruments at Altimish-bulak.

for the caravan, so as to give Shagdur a chance of a shot; for not only were we in urgent want of fresh meat, but I was also anxious to get a complete skeleton and skin of a wild camel; but the dogs put him to flight, and he escaped. At another similar oasis which I soon came to I observed no less than 18 camels grazing. But Shagdur, who came up at a run, was too hasty, and fired prematurely. Here, however, we found an abundance of everything we wanted—fodder, fuel, and water. This was the third of Abdu Rehim's springs, so that his information was perfectly reliable. According to my reckoning, Altimish-bulak ought to be about 17¼ miles from this oasis, in the direc-

The Wounded Wild Camel.

tion 60° west of south. Hence on the 24th of February I led the way towards it, though I was soon forced by a mountain-spur to keep a more westerly course. It was, I concluded, the range at the foot of which Altimish-bulak was situated. Had the atmosphere not been so obscured by dust, we ought to have seen it a pretty long way off. But my lucky star guided me right. I saw the yellow kamish glittering through the haze, and I also saw the outlines of five camels over the top of the thickets. Flinging off his cloak and cap, Shagdur crept stealthily towards them. I watched him through my field-glass. At the report of his rifle they moved off—at first slowly, but afterwards more swiftly. Their dark silhouettes flitted across the kamish, and disappeared at the edge of the oasis. There were fourteen of them. After another shot Shagdur came to me and reported triumphantly that he had brought down two camels. One was a young she-camel, which I photographed as she stood; after which we slaughtered her for food. The other was a big *bughra* (he-camel), which died instantaneously. His skeleton and skin eventually found their way to Stockholm. The Mussulmans were tremendously impressed by the fact that I succeeded in finding Altimish-bulak in the dust-haze. Our last day's march was 19¼ miles. Altogether I was less than two miles out of my reckoning, which, considering that my itinerary

The Dead Wild Camel.

extended over a total distance of 1,200 miles, was not so very bad. Here, then, I linked on my present series of astronomical and topographical observations with the series which I took the previous year. After that it ought not to be difficult to find the ruin we were come in quest of.

My yurt was put up between the same clumps of tamarisks and patches of kamish as the year before, and the camels and horses were turned out to graze. This had been quite a red-letter day.

We spent the remaining days of February beside the springs of Altimish-bulak. What cared we now for the never-tiring wind, or the never-lifting haze in which we were enveloped?

We were encamped in a sheltered spot, and we had everything we needed. There was an inexhaustible supply of fuel, and I kept my stove going without cessation, except in the middle of the night. The Mussulmans found the young she-camel's meat first-rate eating.

One whole day was occupied in testing the levelling instruments, and in instructing the men who were to help me. We measured the circumference of the oasis, and the vertical error in that distance of 3,014 yards amounted to no more than a millimètre (0.0394 inch), a result which promised well for our great levelling across the desert, a line of more than fifty miles long.

Cleansing the Camel's Skeleton at Altimish-bulak.

Here is a little story about Khodai Kullu, who hitherto had not played any important part in the caravan. He was reputed to be a skilful hunter, and possessed a gun of his own; but during the fourteen months he had been with us nobody had ever seen him use it. So far as we knew, he had not killed so much as a hare. The men came, therefore, to believe that he did not know how to shoot, and consequently it excited no surprise when one day he sold the weapon for a mere trifle to Li Loyeh, in whose hands it was just as harmless as in his own. But when Khodai Kullu got back to Yanghi-köll, he asserted that he had shot a camel at Altimish-bulak—as, indeed, he really had—and now that we were come to Altimish-bulak again, his comrades challenged him to show them the skeleton of his victim. But Khodai Kullu prevaricated, and swore that the feat had been performed at some other spring in the neighbourhood. The others refused, however, to be put off in that way, and chaffed him unmercifully. Now, Khodai Kullu was a harmless, phlegmatic man, clumsy yet jovial, and with a very comical expression of countenance. One morning he disappeared from camp before sunrise, and the other men, who were busy most of the day cleaning the skeleton of the camel which Shagdur shot, had no idea where he had gone to, although they suspected he was out hunt-

Our Camp at Khodai Kullu's Spring.

ing, because one of the guns was missing. About dusk he came waddling back, and whilst still some distance away began to shout loudly in triumph. Anybody that liked might go with him, he said, and see the skeleton of the camel which he had shot the year before. The spring was now dry ; but the skeleton was there right enough beside it. Then he went on to relate how he had discovered another spring, with abundant vegetation, and a plentiful supply of ice. There he had surprised four camels, and shot a bughra. In consequence of this feat Khodai Kullu, whose face beamed like the rising sun with genial good nature, rose considerably in the estimation of his fellows, and they became heartily ashamed of themselves for having mistrusted him.

An Ice-Sheet below Khodai Kullu's Spring.

We decided to remove to the new spring which Khodai Kullu had discovered; it would be a more convenient as well as a nearer base for the operations we contemplated amongst the ruins of the desert. Next day, the 1st of March, was Khodai Kullu's great day. He marched along bravely at the head of the caravan, full of importance, singing his loudest, with an air of self-satisfied complacency, as if he were sovereign of all the deserts and oases, and of their inhabitants, the wild camels, whilst the rest of us followed meekly and submissively behind him.

After passing some small low greenstone hills, greatly

Khodai Kullu and his Wild Camel.

weathered, there, sure enough, was the oasis in front of us. But it was so well masked by the configuration of the ground that it would have been impossible to find it, had we not known where it was, or hit upon it by mere chance, as Khodai Kullu did. Khodai Kullu's victim lay a few hundred paces from the edge of the oasis. As is usual with the wild camel, upon being wounded it had tried to escape into the desert. It was a fat and handsome male, and his head lay turned towards the spot where the bullet had entered his body. As soon as his blood turned cold, the ticks, which were in his coat, hastily deserted him. It was now getting warm enough—15°.0 C., or 59°.0 Fahr. at noon—for these inconvenient Acarids to begin creeping about the bushes and reeds. They frequent the borders of the small oases in vast numbers, and are carried from one oasis to another by the camels.

The water at the new spring bubbled up at a number of points, and fell into a deep trough; its temperature was 1.°7 C., or 35.°1 Fahr., and its specific gravity 1.0232. It was so salt that our camels would on no account touch it; but as the sun was now warm enough to melt the surface of the ice-cakes, we experienced no lack of fresh water. The ice was thick and clear, and we filled nine *tagars*, or "bags of reed," to take with us.

This oasis was, in fact, quite a God-send to us. It was, as I have said, 7½ miles nearer to the ruins, and as it afforded plenty of grazing, we were able to leave there all three horses, as well as three ailing camels, under the charge of Khodai Värdi, whilst we went in quest of the ruined village. For his own support we left with Khodai Värdi, out of our now terribly scanty stores, a matchbox, a small cooking-pot, and a handful of tea. He had plenty of water, and he could get what meat he liked from the dead camel; the matches would help him to make fires for boiling his tea and cooking his steak. As he told me afterwards, only one mishap befel him in his loneliness. The first morning, when he awoke, all three horses were gone. From their trail he saw that they had returned to Altimish-bulak, where there was better grazing. However, he fetched them back, and kept closer watch upon them in future.

On the 2nd of March I started with seven camels, carrying the whole of the baggage and nine sacks of ice. In some respects it would have been better to follow the route we took the previous year; for one thing it would have been easier to find the ruins. Three ancient cairns, or landmarks, showed that this little oasis was known to the people who once inhabited the region. Before we had advanced very far we came across traces of the northern margin of the desiccated lake. First we observed numerous fragments of earthenware; then dead tamarisks, standing on their own mounds on the tops of little hills; then brush-like stubble of ancient kamish-fields; and, finally, snail shells, in some places in vast quantities. Here we were, then, once more in the wind-sculptured clay desert.

VII.

The Ruined Towns of Lôu-lan.

A Vanished Country.

CHAPTER VI.

THE RUINS OF ANCIENT LOP-NOR.

THE morning of the 3rd of March was fresh and cool, and, thanks to the easterly wind, the heat during the day never grew oppressive. According to my survey, we had 8¾ miles to go to reach the ruins we were in search of. We travelled slowly, keeping a good look-out in every direction, so as not to miss them. Immediately on our left, Shagdur eventually lighted upon the remains of two houses. The one on the east was 21¼ feet square, and its walls, 3¼ feet thick, were built of square bricks or burnt clay. The other house was constructed of wood, now much decayed through lapse of time; still enough of it was left to show that it had been 85¼ feet long, and of the same breadth as the other house. In the bigger enclosure we discovered a small cannon-ball; an object shaped exactly like a rowlock, but made of copper; some Chinese coins; and two or three red earthenware cups.

A little bit further on, where my map indicated that we were quite close to the locality we were searching for, I stopped, and sent all the men off to explore the neighbourhood, except Faisullah, who stayed behind to look after the camels. They were absent several hours, and towards sunset I resolved to go and encamp at the foot of a clay tower, which stood about one hour east of the spot where we then were. But, owing to the steep and difficult ridges and yardangs which lay across our path, it was quite dusk when we reached the place. Having helped Faisullah to unload the camels, I took a rope and an axe, and climbed to the top of the tower. It was built round a framework of beams, branches, and kamish. On the top of it I lighted a fire as a beacon for the men.

Thereupon they began to return, one by one. Two of them had discovered another high *tora* (clay tower), surrounded by the ruins of several houses, and brought with them, as evidence of their discovery, some corn, a rusted cable chain, a copper lamp, coins, fragments of pottery, and a pitcher or jar. They recommended that we should make that our base of operations. Accordingly at sunrise next morning we went across to the new tora, and encamped on its south-west side, so as to obtain some sort of shelter if a storm should come on. We piled up the sacks of ice on a framework of timber under a clay terrace that leaned over towards the north.

As soon as the camels were sufficiently rested, they were to be led back to Khodai Kullu's oasis. This important task I entrusted to Li Loyeh, instructing him to spend the first night just where the ground began to slope up towards the mountains. The following day he was to go to the oasis, and was to stay there two days; and then, having loaded up all the animals with ice, was to take two more days to return to us. This left us deprived of all means of transport, and allowed us six days in which to pursue our investigations; for as soon as the camels returned we should have to resume our journey.

The first day I devoted to an astronomical observation, whilst the men roamed about the neighbourhood, hunting and investigating. Meanwhile I also took from the top of the tower two or three photographs, which are here reproduced (pp. 116, 117*), and which give a clearer idea of the locality than any amount of mere description. The view was broad and open, and altogether *sui generis*. The desert presented a uniform dreary aspect, with its sharp-edged, broken terraces and "tables"—yardangs of yellow clay. At intervals stood a house, more or less mutilated by time; but the entire region was absolutely uninhabited except for myself and my dog Yolldash. As I surveyed the scene, a feeling of solemnity and of expectation stole over me. I felt—I knew, that I was face to face with a great problem, and its solution. Would this niggardly soil, which, beyond doubt contained many secrets hidden in its bosom—would it reveal to me something that was known to no other human being in the world? Would it yield up to me some of its treasures? Would it grant me an answer to the host of questions which thronged in upon my brain? Anyway I meant to do my level best, to make those silent ruins speak. I had changed my original plan simply and solely that I might

* See also Vol. I., pp. 379, 385.

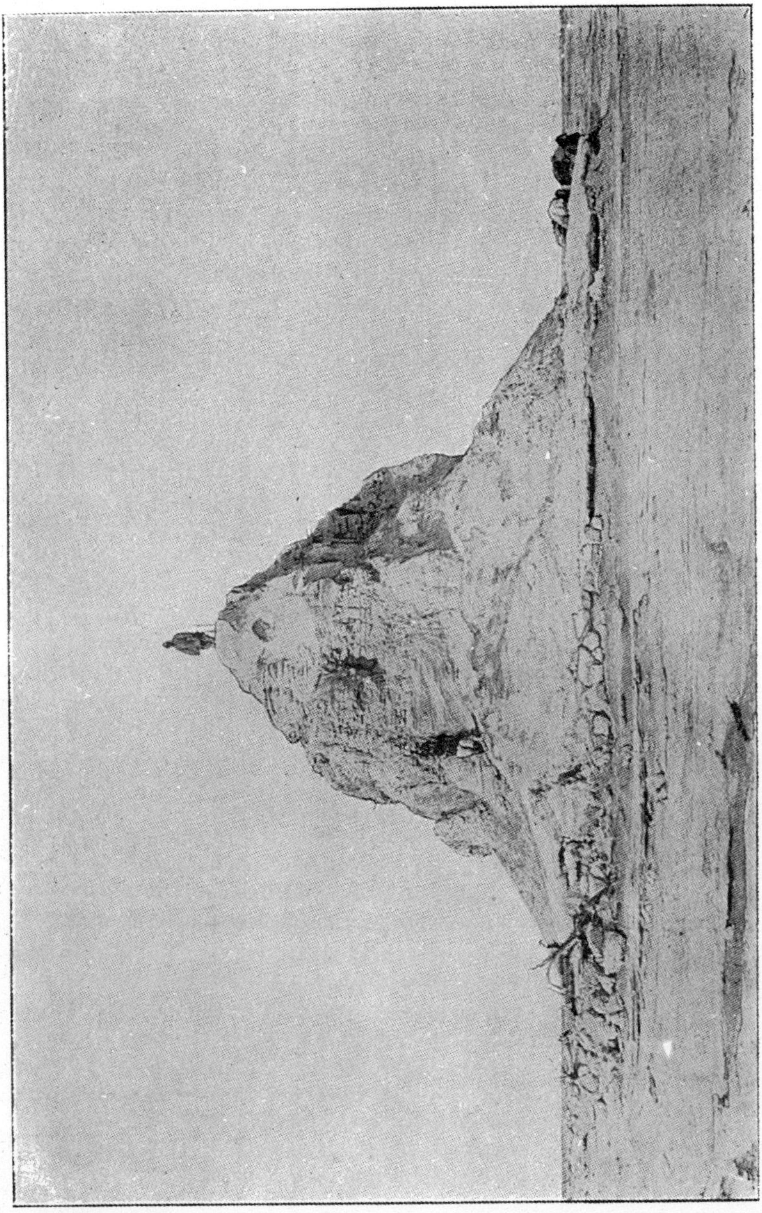

The First Clay Tower.

come back here. Surely it was not to be a mere waste of time! Surely my pains were not to be thrown away!

On the 5th of March, whilst my people were busy digging away with all their might, I took a morning walk amongst the ruins. In a little while they turned over the interior of a house, but without finding anything of importance beyond the wheel of an *araba* (Turkestan cart), and some nicely-turned pilasters. At the same time they unearthed a few trifles of no value, except in so far as they suggested inferences as to the manner of life of the ancient inhabitants. Amongst them were pieces of red cloth, precisely like that which the lamas wear at the present

A Copper Lamp from Lôu-lan.

day, felt rags, tufts of brown human hair, bones of sheep and cattle, soles of Chinese shoes, a leaden utensil, remarkably well-preserved pieces of rope, shards of clay pottery with simple ornamentation, an earring, Chinese coins, and so forth, and so forth.

In one enclosure, which had probably been a stall or fold, they came across a thick layer of manure, showing that horses, cattle, sheep and camels had been sheltered there. Its preservation was due to the fact that it had been buried under a thick layer of sand and dust. But there were no inscriptions, not a single letter to throw any light upon the mystery. The only fragment of paper the men picked up was a small yellow strip, without any writing upon it. Close beside our camp stood the framework of another house, but inside it we discovered nothing.

The circumstances here were altogether different from those of the ancient towns which I discovered during my former journey beside the Keriya-daria. There the ruins were smothered in sand; here the ground was perfectly bare. Everything that the former inhabitants left behind them or forgot was exposed

A View to the South-west from the Tora at our Camp. (In the Foreground is my Yurt, protected by Beams against a Landslide. In the Background the Clay Desert with its Wind-sculptured Yardangs.)

to the destructive influences of wind and weather. There was no sand whatever, except a thin layer on the sheltered side of the clay terraces, which nowhere exceeded ten feet in height.

The most imposing edifice still standing was the tower. This had for me an especial attraction, and I ordered the men to begin work with it. It might, like an ancient Northern burial mound, contain valuable finds in its interior. But, before they could start upon it, a big piece had to be pulled down off the

The Ruined House nearest to our Camp.

top. Down it crashed like a waterfall, sending clouds of dark brown dust scudding across the desert. Then the men dug down into it, making a vertical hole like a well. To have made a tunnel in from the side would have been too dangerous; for the walls were already full of big cracks, and the dry, loose material might easily have fallen in. The tower, however, was massively built, over 28¾ feet high, and held together by horizontal beams. Up to the height of ten feet the sun-dried bricks had a reddish tinge, as if they had been slightly burned. Altogether there were in this immediate locality nineteen houses, stretching in a long line from 30° east of south to 30° west of

The Clay Tower seen from the North-East.

north. I made an accurate chart of them; but to enter into a detailed description of them here would occupy too much space. I must confine myself, therefore, to a few brief general observations.

Some of the houses were built entirely of wood, the planks which formed the walls being morticed into a foundation framework of beams, resting immediately upon the surface. In others the walls consisted of sheaves of kamish, lashed by means of withes to poles and spars. A few of the houses were built of *adobe*, or sun-dried clay. Most of these ancient dwellings were, however, razed to the ground; but several of the beams and posts still stood upright, although greatly decayed through wind and sand. It was impossible to draw from the woodwork any inferences as to their age. It certainly looked very old, and was of a greyish-white colour, cracked, and as brittle as glass. One would have thought that such material, exposed as it was to storms, to drift-sand, and the enormous difference of 175° to 200° between the maximum summer temperature and the minimum winter temperature, would have been destroyed within a comparatively short space of time. Three door-frames still remained *in situ*, and in one of them the door itself was still hanging,

The Top of the Tower Falling.

wide open, just as it had been left, probably, by the last occupant, but it was now half buried in the sand.

The whole of the buildings stood upon elevated ground; but a single glance was sufficient to show that they had originally been placed upon the level ground. For the earthern platforms were of precisely the same shape as the ground-plan of the houses; while the soil all around, in so far as it was not protected, had been scooped out and blown away by the wind. As the trenches at the side were fully ten feet below the former level of the district, it was pretty evident that a very long time must have elapsed since these dwellings were deserted. The poplars, bushes and reeds also grew upon relatively elevated ground.

When I awoke on the morning of the 6th of March, I found all five men had disappeared, and I had to light my fire and

The Clay Tower seen from the South.

get my breakfast as best I could. We had agreed the night before that we would spend a whole day looking for a better place, and the men had now gone off in different directions to make a thorough hunt for other ruins. Before they started, they had gathered a heap of wood, and if they were not back by dusk, I was to recall them by a signal fire. I described to Shagdur where our camp had been the year before, and where he was to look for the ruins which Ördek had discovered.

Everything was as peaceful as a Sabbath morning, reminding me of the hours I spent in the leafy huts beside the Khotan-daria in 1895, after the shepherds had driven their flocks into the

Ruined House with its Doorway still Standing *in situ*.

woods to graze. I photographed several of the ruins; I took a meridian altitude, finished my plan of the locality, and examined various strata of the clay deposits. These were six in number, and of varying thickness. Some of them contained snail-shells and vegetable remains; others were without any, showing that they had been deposited at different periods and under different climatic conditions. Possibly the layers which were destitute of organic life were laid down in salt water.

The day passed quietly. Towards evening my scouts came back one by one, recalled by the signal-fire I lighted. It was nine o'clock before Shagdur came in. He had been on foot the whole day without resting; the others, I knew perfectly well, had slept through the middle of the day. He had had a good many tumbles in the dark down the clay terraces ; for the depressions or trenches between them were perfectly black, it was impossible to see how deep they were. He was just making up his mind to stay where he was till morning, when he caught sight of the fire. But he had been successful : fine fellow that he was, he had persevered, until he did find, not only our previous camp, but also the scene of Ördek's discovery.

The 7th of March we devoted to the investigation of the latter site. I set off at 8 o'clock, taking all the men with me, except Kutchuk, whom I left behind to look after the signal-fire. It was a beautifully bright day, with a cool north-east wind, which moderated the heat at noon. Guided by Shagdur, we proceeded due south from the clay tower of the 3rd of March. At intervals we observed beams lying on the ground, pointing to the sites of former dwellings. One of these measured 25½ feet in length, its other dimensions being 13¾ inches by 6½ inches. Thus the poplars which once grew there must have been as fine trees as any that now stand in the primeval forests of the Tarim. We crossed on the way a deep depression resembling an old canal, and saw yet another tora ; in fact, every village or "town" in this locality seemed to have had its clay tower.

The country we were traversing was of exceptional interest, and deserves a word or two of description. We were marching west-north-west, and consequently had to cross the clay terraces in a zig-zag line up and down them. A few small clumps of primeval poplars were still standing, the arrangement being precisely similar to that of the existing poplar groves beside the Kara-köll and Chivillik-köll, and the lower arms and connecting channels of the Tarim. That is to say, they sometimes stood in rows, sometimes were concentrated in clumps, plainly showing the outline of lake shore or river bank. Evidently in the places where they were wanting, there had been expansions of the lake or connecting river-arms. Kamish stubble was abundant everywhere, though it was only eight or nine inches high. The stalks were so loaded with sand and dust that they crumbled like clay at the least touch ; but the long-bladed leaves, which, however, were far seldomer preserved, still retained their flexibility. In fact the very timber of this region was so heavily charged with sand that on being placed in water it sank.

At length we reached the site of our camp of the year before, easily recognizable by the heaps of ashes left from our fires.

Another mile and we reached the scene of Ördek's discovery. Here we found eight houses ; but of these only three were sufficiently preserved to admit of being measured. They were arranged on the same plan as a Chinese *yamen* (or offices of a Chinese administrator) ; that is to say, a main building flanked

Carved Poplar Wood. On the right an Image of Buddha ; underneath it a Fish. The Vertical line on the left measures one metre (= 3.281 feet).

by two wings, with a courtyard between them. The south-east side of the latter was fenced in by palings or a plank fence, with an open gateway, the side-posts of which were still standing. The main building, which was rather small, had clearly been a Buddhist temple. This was the actual spot where Ördek had made his discoveries. The tracks of his horse were still discernible in a hollow close by.

The spades were soon at work amongst the sand, and after a while out came Buddha himself, though not altogether in the most graceful form of incarnation. The image was made of wood, and the head and arms were still intact. But this, it was clear, was only the foundation or backing of a clay idol, which had been painted and decorated in the usual way.

The accompanying photographs (pp. 125, 127, 133, 135) will convey a clearer idea of the carved woodwork which I brought home with me from this place than any amount of description in words. However, I may just dwell for a moment upon one or two of them. On one beam were depicted a row of images of Buddha, standing; on another a similar row of Buddha, sitting, each individual figure being surmounted with an aureole, shaped like a rounded arch. One ornamental device consisted of a fish surrounded by leaves and scroll-work, the gills and scales being perfectly distinct. Now, the artist would never have thought of using such a poor decorative object as a fish, unless it had been a creature of peculiar importance in the locality, and, we may also say, unless it had constituted one of the most important items in the food of the inhabitants; otherwise it would have been contrary to all rhyme and reason to combine fish instead of birds with leaves and garlands. Even if there existed no other incontrovertible proofs that these villages formerly stood on the shores of a lake, we should be quite justified in inferring the fact from the use of the fish as a decorative device in these wood carvings. Taking the country as it is now, a fish would be the very last creature in the world you would ever think of in such a connection.

The lotus flower also formed a conspicuous and pleasing device in these wood carvings. It occurred in long rows on some of the thickest planks, as also on panels, nineteen or twenty inches long, fixed in between them.

In this same place we also made another important discovery. Shagdur was digging and poking about with his spade, when he turned up a small tablet of wood, covered over with writing in a script which I was unable to decipher. This, however, Shagdur had not noticed, for he had flung the piece of wood on one side as a thing of no value; but I happened to be standing by, and thought how well-preserved it was, and so by mere chance stooped and picked it up. Every letter was sharp-cut and distinct, and written in India ink, but the script was neither Arabic, nor Chinese, nor Mongolian, nor Tibetan,

Carved Pieces of Wood from the Ruins.

What could be the purport of these mysterious words ? What was the information locked up in them ? I at once took care of the little tablet, and preserved it as if it were a precious stone. Hence the reward of ten *sir* (about 30s.), which I had promised to the first man who discovered a piece of writing of any description fell to Shagdur. And as I offered a similar reward for the next find of the same character, the men redoubled their efforts, and without the slightest scruple literally turned the interior of the temple inside out. They sifted the sand through their fingers ; they pounced upon every scrap of wood, and turned it over and examined it from every side—but without success.

Excavating the Buddhist Temple.

The only things that came to light were the string of a rosary, some Chinese copper money, and a heap of small earthenware cups or bowls, which had clearly been placed in front of the images of the gods to hold the offerings of the faithful.

How different, how exceedingly different, this region was now as compared with what it must have been formerly! Here was now not a single fallen leaf, not a single desert spider ; the scorpions, which are very fond of withered poplars, would have sought a hiding-place in vain. There was only one power which brought sound and movement into these dreary, lifeless wastes—namely, the wind. Unless we had had touch with a spring, we could not possibly have stayed there a week as we did.

The great number of wood carvings, small as well as great, which we excavated, plainly proved that this little temple, with its tasteful and minute ornamentation, must have been a perfect gem of artistic construction. I can imagine how beautiful a spot it was—the temple, with its elegant façade, which was probably painted as well as adorned with wood carvings, embowered amid shady poplar groves, with an arm of the lake touching it, and the green or yellow reed-beds spread all round it, except where they were interrupted by patches of cultivated ground, irrigated by the water of the winding canals! Round about it were the scattered villages, their clay towers

Clay Tower near the Buddhist Temple.

peeping over the tops of the woods, and high enough to show their signal-fires to their neighbour-villages when danger or war threatened, but in times of peace marking the great highway which passed near this sacred spot. Southwards stretched far and wide the bluish-green waters of Lop-nor, set about with forest groves, and bordered by immense expanses of reeds and sedge, swarming with fish, wild duck, and wild geese. The background of the picture to the north would be, then as now, in clear weather, the Kurruk-tagh, where the people were in touch with the springs and oases, and across which a road undoubtedly led to Turfan. In other words, it was plain to us pilgrims of a later age that this region had once been more beautiful than any now existing in East Turkestan. For at the present day one could nowhere find in that part of Asia houses decorated with such tasteful and artistic feeling as these were. And it requires no great effort of imagination to conceive how effectively the dense masses of foliage and their vivid greenness would show up the architecture.

Look upon that picture and then look upon the picture of the scene as it is now! An endless array of cenotaphs! And why is this? It is simply because a river, the Tarim, has changed its course, and now empties itself into new lakes farther to the south. The ancient lake would seem to have dried up very

The Ruined Building in which the MSS. were Discovered.

quickly, perhaps in the course of a few years, though the forest and the reeds subsisted for a long time upon the moisture which had been absorbed by the ground, but afterwards they gradually withered away, the trees which had the deepest roots being, of course, the most tenacious of life. Now, however, they were all dead, and the country resembled a cemetery; the inscriptions on its tombstones alone perpetuating the memory of its former luxuriant vegetation.

We were well satisfied with our day's work, when towards sunset we suspended operations, and started back for camp. The wind freshened, the sky in the east was grey and ominous, the haze deepened; it looked as if we were going to have a hard blow, and we made haste to get home before dark. The wind swept through the gulleys, or depressions between the clay terraces, driving rivers of sand before it. We could distinctly perceive their destructive effects in filing away the sides and edges of the terraces. At length we caught sight of Kutchuk's signal-fire, and succeeded in getting home in time, although completely tired out by our seventeen miles tramp. It was not, however, so much the distance, as the difficulties of the surface, which wearied us. And I can tell you that the big flagon of ice-cold water, flavoured with lime juice and sugar, was simply delicious, for we had had nothing to drink all day.

The next morning, the 8th of March, the buran was still raging, and the air was thick with dust. It would have been impossible to find the ruins of the temple; but the men, their zeal quickened by the hope of the promised reward, dug everywhere all round the camp, working like niggers, and this time their efforts were crowned with a success such as I had scarcely dared to dream of. After ransacking the sand in a number of wooden houses without finding anything, they turned their attention to a building of sun-dried bricks, which resembled a stable with three stalls; at any rate, it was apparently the least promising in the entire village. Nevertheless here Mollah unearthed, in the highest stall, a fragment of crumpled up paper, with several perfectly distinct Chinese script-signs written upon it. It would certainly be no exaggeration to say that every grain of sand inside those walls was riddled, as it were, through a sieve. Two feet under the surface, buried under the accumulated sand, we came across what may best be described as a dust-heap or "kitchen-midden," containing a number of precious rarities, such as rags of carpet, pieces of shoe-leather, sheep bones, grain and stalks of wheat and rice, vertebræ of fish, and underneath all this rubbish—over 200 strips of paper, containing writing, and 42 tablets of wood, resembling small flat rulers in shape—these also covered with writing.

This was quite a triumph. Perhaps you will think that an exaggerated expression for a few fragments of old paper. Not at all! I at once realised that these insignificant pieces of paper contained a little piece of the world's history, perhaps hitherto unknown, and that they would, at any rate, furnish me with the key to the Lop-nor problem. The purely geographical and geological investigations had disclosed the actual facts with sufficient clearness: that is to say, they proved that here where all was now desert, there must formerly have existed the basin of

A Signal Fire at the Tower of Lou-lan.

[Vol. II.—*To face p.* 132.

a large lake, and that here amongst these ruins human beings had once dwelt. But these fragmentary documents would now put the crown upon my toilsome investigations, the object of my study and attention for so many years, by telling me in plain black and white, *when* this lake existed, and *who* the people were who lived here, under what conditions they lived, with what parts of the interior of Asia they had been connected—nay, perhaps the very name which their country bore. This land which had, as it were, been wiped off the face of the earth—these people whom history had long forgotten, whose fate had perhaps never been recorded in any annals—

Some of Shagdur's Discoveries.

upon all this I hoped that light would now be shed. I held in my hands the story of a bygone age. I hoped to re-awaken it to life. Even though those people were a small people, and an insignificant community, my find would at any rate serve to bridge over a gap in the scheme of human knowledge. The Mussulmans had hoped, us usual, to find gold; but I would not have exchanged these scraps of torn and dirty letters for untold gold.

I inferred that this was a rubbish-heap from the fact, first that the space was too small for a dwelling, and secondly, that almost every piece of paper was a fragment, pointing to the originals having been torn up and thrown away. But this very circumstance led me to hope that they consisted only or chiefly of local letters, in which case their contents would probably deal with local circumstances, and consequently, for my special purpose, would be of far greater importance than huge folios about any other locality.

After my return home, I sent all this written material to the learned Chinese scholar, Herr Karl Himly, at Wiesbaden. This he is now studying, and he will in due course publish the results of his investigations. But his first preliminary scrutiny resulted in several interesting observations with regard to which he wrote me as follows :—

"The data, and other indications of date, point to the period between the middle of the third and the beginning of the fourth century A.D. The place where the discovery was made seems to have belonged to a well-to-do Chinese merchant, who carried on a sort of livery business, for he let out carriages and beasts of burden on hire, undertook to deliver letters to Tun-huang (Sa-chow), and so forth. People and goods were conveyed to that town by horses, carriages, and horned cattle. One document speaks of a military expedition, though without giving a date. Amongst the geographical names we find the name of the country in question—Lôu-lan. The inhabitants must have carried on agriculture, for the documents make frequent mention of weights and measures of seed-corn, and some of them indicate different kinds of seed-corn. Very possibly at the place where these pieces of paper were excavated there formerly stood a sort of treasure house or species of seed-corn bank, where seed-corn was bought and stored, or received as security for debt. These documents show one peculiarity : they are written on both sides, a practice which does not now obtain in China, either with regard to writing or printing.

"In any case the collection, which is of great interest even for the Chinese themselves, is of such a character that for a long time to come it will be certain to claim the attention of European savants. Some of the sheets consist simply of exercises in writing. Others are fragments, differing but little in their script from that which is now in vogue. The wooden tablets have this advantage over the pieces of paper, that each, as a rule, contains one or more complete sentences, and conveys some real information, *e.g.*, an antelope has been delivered, so much seed-corn has been brought in, so many people have been provisioned for a month or more, and so forth.

"To judge from the following sentence, the governor, who had his residence here, would seem to have governed a not inconsiderable province: 'Forty officials are to receive the army at the frontier (or shore ?), and the farms are numerous.' He seems also to have had two native princes at his court.

"Most of the documents date from the years 264–270 A.D.

Carved Wooden Ornamentation from a House in Lôu-lan.

In the year 265 A.D. the Emperor Yüan Ti, of the Wei dynasty, died, and in the north the Tsin succeeded to power under Wu Ti, who reigned till the year 290 A.D. Most of the copper coins which can be deciphered are what are known as *wu-tshu* pieces, and thus date from the period 118 B.C. to 581 A.D. Besides these there are numerous coins known as *huo-thsüan*, which date back to Wang Mang, who flourished between the years 9 and 23 A.D.

Consequently the dates on the coins agree with those of the letters and wooden tablets."

Even this short preliminary statement by Herr Himly makes it sufficiently clear that important information is to be derived from the collection which I brought home. For one thing it throws an unexpected light upon the political relations in Central Asia during the early centuries after Christ; and, in the next place, it shows what extraordinary changes have taken place in that part of the world within the last 1,600 years.

A learned mandarin at Kashgar, to whom I showed the manuscript, told me that the region round the existing Pichan near Turfan, was anciently called Lôu-lan. This and other historical data, to which reference will be made in the next chapter, taken in conjunction with my investigations into the physical geography of that part of the world, and with my enquiries as to the shifting character of the lake of Lop-nor, are undoubtedly of inestimable value. Not only do they give us information about the country of Lôu-lan, on the northern shore of the ancient Lop-nor, but they also throw light upon several other unsolved problems of that part of Asia. They tell us, for instance, that there was a regular postal service between Lop-nor and Sa-chow, and thus that there existed an established means of communication through the Desert of Gobi. This discovery invests with a totally different meaning the ancient highway from Korla along the Koncheh-daria, where on a previous occasion I noted a chain of clay towers (*pao-tais*) and fortified posts. In a former chapter of this work I have had occasion to speak of the ruins of Ying-pen; * they, too, without doubt, mark an important station on the same ancient highway.

That agriculture was carried on in Lôu-lan is a piece of information of the greatest possible interest. How was it possible? Not a single rivulet now flows down from the Kurruk-tagh; not a drop of rain now falls from the sky. Yes, but the climate may have altered, some one will perhaps say. Not at all. In the heart of a vast continent the climate does not undergo, even in the course of fifteen or sixteen centuries, such tremendous changes as that would imply. No; canals must have been led off either from the Tarim or the Kum-daria, and from them again irrigation *ariks* (channels), such as are now found all over East Turkestan. Seed-corn banks, of the kind here indi-

* See Vol. I., p. 344.

cated, are found at the present day in every town in East Turkestan. They are under the control of the Chinese authorities, and serve to secure an equal distribution of food amongst the native inhabitants. It is true, I only found four towns, the largest of which consisted of nineteen houses; but the desert may quite easily contain several others. And the mention of "armies," "40 officials," and "numerous farms" suggests that Lôu-lan was thickly inhabited. Perhaps the people lived, as they do at the present day, for the greater part in perishable huts of reed. In that case the ruins which we discovered would be those of the official centres, and the dwellings of the more

On the Left an Earthenware Vase, in the Middle a Wheel, on the Right the MSS. House, and in the Distance the Clay Tower.

distinguished men; and it is also likely that these stood near the watch-towers, while the huts of the fishing population would be built along the lake side, and would naturally perish long before the more durable buildings.

We had still one day left to spend at this—I was going to say holy—place. In any case, it was a locality which awakened feelings of sadness at the perishableness of earthly things, and at the thought that cities and races are swept off the face of the earth like chaff before the wind. When I awoke on the morning of the 9th of March the men had already been at work two hours, and came and brought their several finds to my yurt. These consisted of fragments of paper and wooden tablets like those of yesterday, all of which had been picked up in the north-east stall. Nothing was found in the other two stalls. Amongst the "treasures" the men displayed were fish-bones, bones of domestic animals, including those of the pig, rags, two or three pencils, a whip, a skeleton of a rat, and so on. Perhaps the most important of all was a red clay vase in perfect condition. It was 2 feet 3½ inches high and 2 feet 1½ inches in diameter, but had no handles. It was probably carried in a sort of willow basket with handles to it, which the men turned up beside it; shards of similar pieces of ware were extraordinarily plentiful. We also dug out a smaller vase; it, too, in perfect condition.

I spent a large part of the day in sketching architectural details, especially in noting carefully the manner in which the beams, posts and planks, which formed the framework of the houses, were put together. The tallest of the posts still remaining *in situ* was just one inch above fourteen feet.

In the afternoon the caravan arrived from the spring, bringing with them ten *tagars* (reed-bags) and six *tulums* (goatskins) all filled with ice.

CHAPTER VII.

LÔU-LAN.

As it may possibly be of interest to learn something further about the country which bore the name at the head of this chapter, I will add the substance of two papers by competent authorities as to what it said about it in ancient Chinese sources. The first is a paper entitled, "*Sven Hedin's Ausgrabungen am alten Lop-nur*" (*i.e.*, "Sven Hedin's Excavations beside the Ancient Lop-nor"), by Herr Himly, in *Petermanns Mitteilungen* (1902 Part XII., pp. 288-290); the other is a paper by Mr. George Macartney, of Kashgar, in the *Geographical Journal*, March, 1903.

After a short introduction, Herr Himly writes thus: "The name Lop-nur is not an invention of the present (Turki) inhabitants, for the word *nur*, meaning a 'lake,' is a Mongolian word. Previous to the middle of the 18th century the boundary between the Khalkha Mongols and the Kalmucks, or Western Mongols, ran just here. . . . . According to Hedin's statements in *Petermanns Ergänzungsheft*, No. 131 (1900), he regarded the lake of Kara-köll, which lay further to the south-east, as a surviving part of the ancient lake. But this was known to the Chinese long before the Mongol era, and bore several names, some Chinese, some native—Yen-tsö, a Chinese word meaning 'Salt Lake'; Puthshang-hai, 'hai' being a Chinese word meaning 'sea'; Yao-tsö; Lôu-lan-hai, etc. Now Lôu-lan was the name of a country which, by reason of its situation between the great northern highway and the great southern highway from China to Europe, played, in spite of its small size, a very important part in the wars between the Chinese emperors of the Han dynasty and the Hiung-nu [Turks or Huns] in the second century before our era, in that it acted as a kind of buffer state between the two powers. The famous pilgrim, Hüan-Tshuang (*i.e.*, Hwen-thsang), when on his way home from India, touched this country in the year 645 A.D., after crossing the desert from Khotan. Even at that time the inhabitants were being driven out of the towns, and their dwellings buried under the sand; indeed, several of the cities north of Khotan were then in ruins. But the shifting sand was not the only danger the people had to fear: they were also in peril from vast accumulations of water. According to the *Shuêi-king-tshu*, the waters were gathered in a basin of the lake north-east of Shan-shan (*i.e.*, Lôu-lan), and south-west of Lung-thshöng (Dragon Town), which was destroyed by an inundation in the Tshi-ta epoch (1308-1311). But the ruins still remained. Perhaps this was the ancient site which Hedin rediscovered on the occasion of his last visit to the Lop-nur district. . . . . Amongst his finds were small covers, which were docketed, and for the most part bore little grooves for the strings by which they were tied. That these covers were intended for "envelopes" to hold documents might be inferred, partly from the dockets themselves, partly from similar discoveries which were made near the Niya river by Dr. Stein in January, 1901; see Plate IX. of his *Preliminary Report*, where similar covers are very distinctly shown. . . . . Amongst the smaller objects unearthed, the copper coins are of especial interest. With one exception they are Chinese, and belong to a definite series of centuries. All have the familiar square hole in the middle, by means of which they are wont to be strung together by the hundred. Inscriptions such as generally characterise Chinese imperial coins of the period beginning with the year 376 A.D., and which are without exception present on those subsequent to the year 621 A.D., do not occur on a single coin in Hedin's collection. His coins generally bear the number of the *wu-tshu* (5 *tshu*, or $\frac{5}{24}$ *liang*, or 1 ounce) in ancient sphragistic script, in which the 5's resemble the Roman ten (X); this style was used between the years 118 B.C. and 581 A.D. Some of the coins bear the inscription *huo-thsüan* (according to Endlicher's translation = 'medium of barter'), well known from the Wang Mang epoch (9-22 A.D.). One coin, in which the central hole is oblong, bears an inscription which has not yet been interpreted.

"Amongst the remaining objects a small cut gem is of especial interest. It shows clearly a Hermes, who, as the deity

Excavating a House in Lôu-lan. In the Foreground the Big Earthenware Jar.

of travellers, found his way through Bactria to Central Asia. Skilfully made triangular arrows, and others smaller and flat, perhaps intended for shooting birds, and both of bronze; distaffs; an ear-ring set with pearls; copper wire; iron nails; cowrie shells, with an opening at the top made by some sharp instrument; copper and brass bells (for horses?); fragments of small bronze hand-bells; amber and amber beads; copper rings; various kinds of domestic utensils or fragments of the same made of different kinds of stone or semi-precious stones, such as nephrite, alabaster; ornamented green glass, etc.—all these convey an idea of the degree of development to which either the native handicrafts had advanced, or of the value which the native inhabitants attached to the products of other people.

"As to the question of the period at which the place perished,

"Finds" from Lôu-lan. The Clay Desert in the Background.

and what it—whether town or country—was called, here the documents which Hedin discovered speak more clearly. The name Lôu-lan occurs both on the wooden tablets and on the fragments of paper, and in such a connection as to leave no doubt that this was the name of the place to which the letters were addressed, or at which they were preserved. One of the tablets speaks of letters which were sent to Tun-huang and Tsiu-Thsüan (Su-Chow). On the same tablet, but below this statement, the 15th day of the 3rd month of the sixth year of the

Thai-Shi epoch—that is to say, the sixth year of the Emperor Tsin Wu Ti (265 A.D.)—is given as the date on which a letter was received in Lôu-lan. On one of the covers, which exactly resembles the covers shown on Plate IX. of Dr. Stein's *Preliminary Report*, except that it is smaller, the Prince of the Lake Concerns and his wife (Tien-shî Wang Hu) are named as receiving the same in Lôu-lan. The first date given is the year 264, when the Wei dynasty ruled over the northernmost of the 'three kingdoms.' Other dates are the years 266, 268, 269, and 270. The name Lôu-lan occurs twice on the paper fragments, which seem to have been deliberately torn. One of them contains an insignificant statement, to the effect that a certain Ma, of Lôu-lan, need not present himself on the sixth day of the sixth month; here we have the year 310, in connection with the town of An-si.

"The contents of these various documents are of very divers kinds. Some of them speak of deliveries of seed-corn; some are communications from Tun-huang; some speak of communications with Kao-tshang (ancient Turfan); some of judicial proceedings, etc. The wooden tablets clearly served, partly as diaries, partly for giving instructions to subordinates. One of the latter, which is broken, relates that 40 of the leaders of the army which has reached the border (*pien* (?) = 'frontier' or 'shore') are to be lodged in the farms near the dams. One small wooden tablet bears a non-Chinese inscription; it resembles the Kharoshthi script of Dr. Stein (see Plates IX., X., XI.).

"From all this there can scarcely exist a doubt that this was the site of the ancient Lôu-lan, and that Lou-lan stood beside the ancient lake of Lop-nur. The town would seem to have been destroyed by a desert storm or by an inundation, or by both, in the beginning of the fourth century. The people would then seem to have built in the same neighbourhood another town, the so-called Dragon Town, which in its turn was destroyed by a storm and flood in 1308-11."

My old friend, Mr. George Macartney, of Kashgar, a profound scholar of Chinese, has a paper in the March number, 1903, of the *Geographical Journal*, which I here, with his kind permission, repeat *in extenso*. It is entitled, *Notices, from Chinese Sources, on the Ancient Kingdom of Lau-lan, or Shen-shen*, and, when read in conjunction with Herr Himly's, furnishes a very clear conception of that kingdom of nearly 2,000 years ago.

The actual name of Lau-lan is well known to modern Chinese geographers, but hitherto, apparently, neither they nor savants in Europe have been able to fix with anything like accuracy the position of the country anciently called by that name. Mr. A. Wylie, a Chinese scholar of eminence, in 1880 had computed this position to be 39° 40′ N. lat. and 94° 50′ E. long. Now this would show an error approximately of 250 miles if we are right in understanding that the place where Dr. Hedin found the Chinese manuscripts, bearing the name Lau-lan, was in about 40° 40′ N. lat. and 90° E. long. The more accurate localization of Lau-lan, now apparently possible, may, it is hoped, lead to some useful results in the identification of other neighbouring countries whose ancient names are known, but whose positions are still a puzzle to modern geographers.

If the *Tsien Han-shu* (" History of the First Hans ") and the records left by Fa-Heen and Hsian-Tsang were consulted, we should find many places mentioned therein, with their distances given with reference to Lau-lan. Thus, the *Tsien Han-shu* (written roughly between B.C. 100 and A.D. 50) mentions the following distances: From Wu-ni (capital of Lau-lan) to the Yang barrier (evidently in the direction of Tun-huang), 1,600 li *; to Chang-an, 6,100 li; to the seat of government of the Chinese governor-general (name not given) in a north-westerly direction, 1,785 li; to Si-an-fu, 1,365 li; to Keu-tse (Ouigour) in a north-westerly direction, 1,890 li. Fa-Heen (fifth century A.D.), in the record of his travels, gives the following distances: From Shen-shen or Lau-lan to Tun-huang, about 17 marches, 1,500 li; to Wu-e (Urgur ?), 15 marches on foot in a north-westerly direction. From Hsian-Tsang we learn that Lau-lan, which he also calls Na-po-po, is situated 1,000 li north-east of Chémo-tó-na, also called Nimo. It will be seen from this that the site of Lau-lan can serve as a point of reference for determining the position of several other places. Perhaps the indications given above may prove to be of use to subsequent archæological surveyors.

But this is far from all that can be learnt about Lau-lan from Chinese records. The *Tsien Han-shu* tells us that China began intercourse with this country in the reign of the Emperor Wu-ti (B.C. 140–87), at whose time the western boundary of the empire would seem to have extended no further than the Yang barrier (possibly Tun-huang) and the Yu gate (modern Chia-Yu-kuan ?). The vast country lying beyond these places was designated by the Chinese geographers of the epoch under the vague term of Si-yu (western region), which they supposed to be divided into thirty-six different kingdoms. We are told there were two roads leading from China to this region. " That *viâ* Lau-lan, skirting the river Po (lower Tarim ?), on the north

* A li = ·358 mile.

of the Southern mountains (Altyn-Ustun-tagh ?). and leading west to Sa-chê (Yarkand) is the southern road. That by the Palace of the Anterior at Keu-tse (Ouigour kingdom ? 1,890 li from Lau-lan), following the river Po in the direction of the Northern mountains (Tian-shan) as far as Su-leh (Kashgar) is the northern road."

The watercourse in the Tarim basin is described in the following terms: "The river (Khotan-daria ?) runs northwards till it joins a confluent from the Tsung-ling (Onion range, in Sarikol), and then flows eastwards into the Pú-chăng-hai (lit. Calamiferous Lake), which is also called the Salt Marsh. This is over 300 li from the Yu gate and the Yang barrier, and is 300 li in length and breadth. The water is stationary, neither increasing nor diminishing in summer or winter, The river is then said to run underground and issue again at Tseih-shih, where it becomes the Yellow river of China."

The following is a *précis* of the account found in the *Tsien Han-shu* of the political relations between China and Lau-lan during the first century B.C. The Emperor Wu-ti, we are told, was desirous of cultivating intercourse with Ta-wan and adjacent countries, and repeatedly sent ambassadors there. These had to pass through Lau-lan; but the people of Lau-lan, in concert with the Keu-tse, harassed the officials on the high-road, robbed and attacked Wang-Kuei, one of the envoys. Moreover, the Lau-lans made themselves objectionable to the Chinese by acting as spies for the Heun-nu or Hiung-nu (Huns), and on several occasions aided them in the pillage of Chinese travellers. All this was not to be tolerated. Wu-ti, therefore, prepared an expedition against the disaffected state. Chao Po-nu was sent with an army of 10,000 men to punish the Keu-tse, while the envoy Wang Kuei, who had suffered several times at the hands of the Lau-lans, received orders to act as Chao Po-nu's lieutenant. The latter, advancing at the head of 700 light horse, seized the king of Lau-lan, conquered the Keu-tse, and, relying on the prestige of his army, overawed the states dependent on Wu-sun and Ta-wan. The Lau-lans soon submitted, and sent offerings of tribute to the Emperor Wu-ti. But their submission gave offence to their allies, the Huns, who lost no time in attacking them. On this, by way of satisfying his two powerful neighbours, the king of Lau-lan sent one of his sons as hostage to the Huns, and another to the Emperor of China. Thus ended the first episode in the relations between China and the kingdom in question.

But more troubles were in store for Lau-lan. The Emperor Wu-ti, for some reason or other, had to send another punitive expedition against Ta-wan and the Huns. The Huns found the Chinese army so formidable that they deemed it prudent to avoid any direct encounter with it; but this did not prevent them from hiding troops in Lau-lan, the inhabitants of which did not cease to be in league with them. These troops constantly harassed the army of Wu-ti. The Chinese soon got wind of Lau-lan's secret coalition with the Huns, and accordingly the general, Jen-wan, was sent to chastise them. Jen-wan proceeded to the city gate, which was opened to him, and reproached the king for his treachery. The king, in excuse, replied, "When a small state lies between two great kingdoms, it must perforce make alliances with both, or it can have no peace; but now I wish to place my kingdom within the bounds of the Chinese empire." Confiding in these words, the emperor re-established him on the throne, and commissioned him to keep watch over the movements of the Huns.

This king died in B.C. 92. Then a question of succession arose. It will be remembered that one of the sons of the deceased king was a hostage at the Chinese court. Now the Lau-lans made a petition to the emperor for the return of the hostage prince, in order that he might succeed to the vacant throne. The prince had not, however, been a *persona grata* with the emperor; in fact, all the time he was in China he had been kept in honourable confinement in the Silkworm House Palace. It therefore happened that the petition from Lau-lan was not favourably received by Wu-ti, but the answer returned was that of a diplomat. "I am tenderly attached," said Wu-ti, "to my attendant prince, and am loth to allow him to leave my side;" and the emperor suggested to the petitioners that they should install the next son of the deceased king in the royal dignity.

This the Lau-lans accordingly did. But the new king's reign was a short one, and on his death the question of succession again came to the front. This time the Huns, who, it will be remembered, had also a hostage prince from Lau-lan at their court, thought their opportunity had come to regain in that state the influence they had lost. They therefore sent the prince back, and established him on the throne. This successful *coup* alarmed the Chinese, who endeavoured, by bribery and intrigue, to recover their ascendancy. They made no direct attempt to dethrone the Huns' *protégé*, but sent an envoy requesting him to pay a visit to the Chinese court, where, the envoy said, liberal gifts would be bestowed on him by the emperor. But the emperor and the envoy little suspected that they had to reckon with a woman's cunning. The step-mother of the king was at hand, and she advised him, saying: "Your royal predecessor sent two sons as hostages to China; neither of them has ever come back, and is it reasonable that you should go?" The king thereupon dismissed the envoy with the words that, "having newly acceded to the throne, the affairs of the kingdom were engaging his attention, and that he could not attend the Chinese court before two years."

So far there had been no open hostility between the new king and the emperor, although, undoubtedly, relations between them were strained. But now the event which was to put an end to Lau-lan as an independent state was imminent. It appears that on the eastern border of Lau-lan, where this kingdom was contiguous with China, there was a place called the Peh-lung mound. This place was on the high-road, *viá* Lau-lan, from China to the western regions, and it suffered from drought, and had no pasturage. The Lau-lans were frequently called upon by the Chinese to furnish guides and carry water and provisions to this spot for passing officials. In the discharge of these duties the inhabitants were often exposed to the brutality of the Chinese soldiery. Friction was thus created; but the situation was

Reloading on the March.

made worse by the Huns, ever secretly instigating the Lau-lans against the Chinese. Finally, the Lau-lans resolved to break off friendly relations with Wu-ti, and forthwith murdered some of his envoys whilst passing through Lau-lan territory. This act of treachery was reported to the Chinese court by the king's younger brother, Hui Tu-chi, who, having made his submission to the Han monarch, was scheming to oust his elder brother from the throne. Accordingly, in B.C. 77, the Chinese general, Fu-keae-tsu, was sent to put the king to death. Fu-keae-tsu hastily selected a few followers, and, having spread a report that he was going to a neighbouring state on a mission of friendly inquiry, and had presents with him for the king, he journeyed to Lau-lan. On Fu-keae-tsu's arrival, the king, who suspected nothing, invited him to a sumptuous feast. Whilst the king was intoxicated, Fu gave the signal to his followers, and the king was stabbed in the back. His head was severed from the body and suspended over the northern gate of the city. Hui Tu-chi, as a reward for his treachery, was set up as king in the place of his brother, and the kingdom was re-established under the new name of Shen-shen, for which a brevet of investiture was prepared. That nothing might be wanting to the prestige of the new ruler, one of the ladies of the imperial court was bestowed on him as consort, and on Hui Tu-chi leaving the Chinese capital for his kingdom, he was accorded a send-off marked with every honour. Thus was he established. But he did not feel himself secure in his new position. Being a Chinese *protégé*, he was looked upon with suspicion by the people over whom he had been called upon to rule. Moreover, the late king had left a son, and Hui Tu-chi lived in fear of assassination by him. Hui Tu-chi therefore petitioned the emperor to establish a military colony in Lau-lan, in the city of E-tun, where, he said, the land was "rich and productive." This was done, and the emperor sent a cavalry leader with forty subordinates "to cultivate the fields at E-tun and soothe the people." Thus was the rule of the great Han monarch extended over the state of Lau-lan, or Shen-shen.

At the epoch when these chronicles were written, which, presumably, was about the time of the birth of Christ, the kingdom of Shen-shen, we are told, contained 1,570 families, forming a population of 14,100, with 2,912 trained troops.

On the physical features of the country, the *Tsien Han-shu* says (translation by Mr. A. Wylie): "The land is sandy and salt, and there are few cultivated fields. The country relies on the neighbouring kingdoms for cereals and agricultural products. The country produces jade, abundance of rushes, the tamaria, the *Clœcocca vermicifera*, and white grass. The people remove their cattle for pasturage wherever they can find sufficiency of water and herbage. They have asses, horses, and camels. They can fabricate military weapons, the same as the people of Tso-kiang."

So much, then, for the information contained in the *Tsien Han-shu.* Here is what Fa-Heen says regarding Lau-lan, which he passed through in the fifth century A.D. on his way from China to India to procure the sacred books of Buddhism. The translation is that of Dr. J. Legge: "After travelling for seventeen days, a distance we may estimate of about 1,500 li (from Tun-huang), the pilgrims reached the kingdom of Shen-shen, a country rugged and hilly, with a thin and barren soil. The clothes of the common people are coarse and like those woven in our land of Han, some wearing felt, and others serge or cloth of hair. The king professed our law, and there might be in the kingdom more than 4,000 monks, who are all students of the *Hinayana* (small vehicle of salvation). The common people of this and other kingdoms in this region, as well as the *sramans* (monks), all practise the rules of India, only the latter do so more exactly, and the former more loosely. Here the pilgrims stayed for about a month, and then proceeded on their journey, fifteen days' walking to the north-west bringing them to the country of Wu-e. In this there were more than 4,000 monks, all students of the *Hinayana*."

Hsian-Tsang, or Hwen-thsang (629–645 A.D.), passed through Lau-lan on his return from India, two centuries later than Fa-Heen, but his notice on this country is extremely meagre. We are merely told that, after leaving the walled but deserted town of Tche-mo-to-na, or Nimo, "he travelled 1,000 li in a north-easterly direction and reached Na-po-po, which is the same as Lau-lan."

All this goes to show that in its day Lôu-lan was a country of some importance. It is very probable that further excavations in the same neighbourhood would result in discoveries even more important than those which I made.

VIII.

A Survey of the Lop Desert.

A Wandering Lake.

VIII

A Survey of the Lop Desert

CHAPTER VIII.

SURVEYING THE LOP DESERT.

THE camp was astir early on the morning of the 10th March; we were to leave the silent ruins to their millennial peace. Would any European pilgrim ever set foot within the walls of Lôu-lan again?

We gave the camels three sacks of ice, and let them eat as much corn as they liked; even then their loads were too heavy. The carved woodwork and other finds were tied up in bundles and the baggage rearranged, for I was now going to divide the caravan into two parties. Myself, I intended to cross the desert southwards to Kara-koshun, taking with me Shagdur, Kutchuk, Khodai Kullu, and Khodai Värdi, my object being to make an exact levelling of the ancient basin of Lop-nor. We only had four camels, three to carry ice, and one to carry our baggage; for we took with us nothing but food, clothes, the levelling instruments, one-half of the yurt, and one-half of my bed. The men slept in the open air. Our provisions, which consisted of rice and bread only, were divided into rations calculated to last eight days. The other half of the caravan, consisting of six camels, three horses, three dogs, and all the heavier baggage, besides ice and provisions for four days, was to pursue another route. This detachment I put in charge of Faisullah, and gave him Li Loyeh and Mollah to assist him.

Faisullah, who had crossed the desert with me from Altimish-bulak the year before, was instructed to proceed direct to Kum-chappgan, and there await our arrival. To make quite sure, I gave him a thorough lesson on the compass, and impressed it upon him that he was to stick to the south-west. I had every confidence in his prudence and good sense; but all the same, I thought it best to keep in my own hands all my map sheets, the MSS. and wooden tablets from Lôu-lan, my diaries, and my scientific observations. Faisullah, before starting, was to help Khodai Värdi, whom I left behind to bring on the four camels.

Meanwhile I began the levelling, almost by pure chance, at the foot of the clay tower where my yurt had stood. There the levelling-pole, which was about 13 feet high, was set up for the first time; it was always fixed on a plate, so as not to sink in when we gave it a half turn. This instrument I put into Shagdur's hands, and he managed it capitally all through. We carried the levelling-tube 100 metres (110 yards) to the south, and I took my first reading; then Shagdur carried the levelling-pole another 100 metres to the south of me; and so on, turn about, day after day, all the way to Kara-koshun, a distance of 50½ miles. The distance between the tube and the pole was measured by Kutchuk and Khodai Kullu with a fifty-metre tape. Kutchuk also carried the levelling-tube and its stand, whilst I noted down the readings, took the compass bearings, entered the route, and made notes of the contours.

All this was absolutely new work to the men, and at first we made slow progress; but they soon learnt what was required of them, and after that everything went without a hitch.

Travelling south from Lôu-lan, we easily distinguished when we crossed the shore-line of the former lake. The dead trees, bushes, and reeds came to an end quite suddenly, and we stepped, almost at a stride, upon the dreary greyish-yellow clay, destitute of even the smallest trace of vegetation, which filled the bottom of the ancient lake. We moved the tube and pole ninety times, the total distance travelled being 5 miles 1,196 yards, before we stopped for the night. It was then rapidly growing dusk; but there were no signs of Khodai Värdi and the four camels. We went to the top of the nearest hill; no camels in sight! What was become of them? Had Khodai Värdi misunderstood my orders? Had he followed Faisullah? Had he stayed behind at the ruins? or—had he got lost? We made a big signal-fire as soon as we could find enough material. Shagdur went off into the darkness to look for him. I was a prey to the keenest anxiety. If Khodai Värdi had lost his way, his fate was sealed. He had never been in this quarter before, and had no idea as to the direction of Kara-koshun. If he failed to turn up, our position, too, would be highly critical, for we had neither water nor food with us. The distance to the lake was so great that we should scarcely be able to reach it, and a return to the little spring was not to be thought of. What made me most uneasy was the thought of losing the results of four months' labour, and all through the stupidity of a servant.

We piled up the fire; we listened; not a sound! The desert was as dead and deserted as though it belonged to an uninhabited planet. We were parched and tired after our hard day's work; and instead of quenching our thirst, we had this gloomy disquietude to fight against. It only wanted a desert sandstorm, and our cup of misery would have been full. However, things were not so bad as we imagined. Towards midnight we heard shuffling sounds in the darkness; it was Khodai Värdi

The Caravan for the Levelling Expedition.

with the camels. I was so glad at seeing them that I forgot to give the fellow the rounding-up he deserved. He explained that it was the clay terrace which had forced him to deviate too far to the right, and he had been unable to hit upon our track again. Towards evening he had caught sight of a fire, which he knew to be Faisullah's, in the south-west, and then he understood where he was, and turned back. Eventually he perceived our fire, but it was a long way off; however, by keeping it steadily in sight he had at last found us. It was a wonder that in the dark none of the camels broke their legs in crossing the deep, gaping hollows between the terraces. We made haste to get up the tents and boil the kettle. Even to this day I cannot understand how a man who generally showed common sense, could spend twelve hours wandering backwards and forwards over a tract of country which measured (along the straight line we followed) less than six miles, especially as even from our camp that night the clay tower of Lôu-lan was distinctly visible.

But now Shagdur was missing. I sent out Khodai Kullu to fire a succession of shots by way of signal, and for some time we heard them gradually dying away in the distance. Eventually, however, Khodai Kullu came back without finding Shagdur, and we went to sleep, for I was under no uneasiness on Shagdur's account. I knew that he could, in case of need, readily find his way to Kara-koshun; besides, he always carried a compass with him, and knew how to use it, and was familiar with my maps.

Next morning I was awakened by a violent storm, which swept dense clouds of fine sand through the depression in which we were encamped; it was like a river pouring in full flood down a newly-made channel. Surveying was, of course, quite out of the question: we must just stay where we were. Having nothing else to do, I spent a good deal of the time with the camels, patting them and talking to them. They were calm, contented, and dignified, as they always were, and appeared to think that it was part of the inevitable day's work that they should tramp backwards and forwards twenty or thirty miles through the desert. Regardless of the consequences, I ordered the men to give them a sack of kamish, and another of ice, which we had brought from the spring. Poor beggars! all except one died later on in Tibet!

About midday I was perfectly amazed to see Shagdur emerge out of the thick dust haze with a light, elastic step. Fine fellow! he was worth a dozen Mussulmans any day! He had been on foot since five o'clock the previous afternoon, having during the night visited Faisullah's camp, attracted by his fire. For, by way of experiment, I had requested Faisullah to keep up a good fire, that we might ascertain whether it was possible to see such a signal twelve miles across the desert; but it wasn't. Obtaining from Faisullah a small supply of rice and ice, Shagdur, notwithstanding that the storm was even then coming on, at once set off to return to us. Fortunately, he had kept a note of his compass-bearings. But that he ever did find us I regard as a remarkable feat. Nobody but a Buriat, who had spent his life in the open air, and who was a Cossack to boot, ever could have done it. For, you must bear in mind, the distance between the two camps was fully twelve miles, the contour as level as a billiard table, and, owing to the sand-storm which was raging, it was impossible for any man to see fifty yards in front of him; while the wind soon obliterated entirely every footmark we left behind us.

I had not contemplated losing a day like this; but what mattered it, seeing that I had escaped the heavy loss I feared? We made an attempt to continue; but it would not do. The wind was blowing at the rate of 24½ miles an hour, and the pole would not stand firm, nor the tube either; so we just had to exercise patience, and spend yet another night in that dreary place.

The 12th of March, however, was a splendid day, and we made an early start, and worked on until sunset, only stopping for about ten minutes at one p.m. to take the readings of the meteorological instruments. I now made Khodai Kullu lead the camels, and keep close behind us. Our course lay towards the south-south-east; but as the depressions, eroded by the wind, ran towards the south-west, we had, of course, to cross each successive ridge or "table" at right angles. Not that this mattered much to those who were on foot; but to the camels it was very tiring, as they had to make long detours. One of these depressions was no less than 400 feet wide and 26¼ feet deep. This must have been one of the deepest places in the former lake, or possibly it was part of an ancient river-bed. That evening I examined, with the keenest interest, the results of the day's work: they showed that the contour had fallen eight feet in just under seven miles. I should never have been able to continue this tiresome and wearisome labour had I not expected it to yield important results.

The next day, although the country was depressingly monotonous to the eye, it was, on the other hand, all the easier to survey, and we made rapid progress. Upon seeing five successive flocks of wild-duck passing northwards overhead, Kutchuk shrewdly surmised that it was our relief expedition under Tokta Ahun which had frightened them up from the northern shore of Kara-koshun. It is probable that the wild-ducks spend the winter on these marshes, but go to Bagrash-köll for the summer. During this day's survey we ascended nine feet, and consequently were now only about six inches higher than our starting-point at Lôu-lan. To be accurate, in twenty miles we had ascended a little over four and a quarter inches! This day's work gave me the key to the Lop-nor problem. The first two days we had descended, and the third ascended; thus we had manifestly crossed a depression, and that depression was the basin of the former Lop-nor. No matter what the results of the next day's work might be, this conclusion could not be upset. No matter what the level of Kara-koshun might be, as compared with our point of departure, we had, as a matter of fact, crossed a basin; and that this basin had contained water was conclusively proved by the snail-shells, and by other circumstances which I have already mentioned.

Just on the stroke of seven o'clock we heard a shrill whistling in the north-east, and, two or three minutes later, down came a black buran. We hurriedly took all necessary precautions—damped down the fire, saw to the fastenings of the yurt, and so forth. At nine o'clock Shagdur came into my yurt and fixed the boiling-point thermometer, and then set out to return to his own sleeping-place. Half an hour later, hearing a faint call in another direction, I shouted at the pitch of my voice—and Shagdur appeared at the opening of the yurt. He had lost his way, although his sleeping-place was only fifteen paces from mine. But then it was pitch dark; and it was impossible for any man to stand. Shagdur had been on his hands and knees the whole time. And now he was only able to reach his own quarters by creeping backwards with his eyes fixed on the light which streamed through a chink of the tent-cloth I held open for him. Only those who have been out in such a storm can form any conception of what it is like. You get bewildered, and want to keep going, without knowing where. Your sense of locality is paralyzed, and although you think you are going in a straight line, you are in reality describing a circle. It is a kind of desert-storm sickness, more nearly resembling the panic which seizes a person on the edge of a precipice than sea-sickness or mountain-sickness, because it affects the brain. If Khodai Värdi had been caught by a storm like that, he would infallibly have been lost.

Next morning the effects of this grim desert tempest were very easy to see; the sand was heaped up all round my yurt, and there were little mounds on the sheltered side of the camels. Thus, as soon as the drift-sand meets with a hindrance, it begins to form dunes, otherwise the wind carries it westwards. Fortunately the wind dropped at eleven o'clock, and we were able to resume our survey. The desert was painfully monotonous: the ground consisted of what the natives call *shor*, *i.e.*, sand, dust, lime, and salt—all fused together and baked as hard as a brick, though sometimes the salt lay in a thin layer on the top. After the water left it, this mass would appear to have expanded, for it was crossed in every direction by a countless number of little ridges, some of which were as much as two to three feet in height. Of course there was not the slightest sign of organic life, not even so much as a snail-shell. There could be no question about it—this was the bottom of a salt lake; and we know that the Chinese did anciently call Lop-nor by a

A Gully in the Shor (Salt) Desert.

name which signified salt lake. In Kara-koshun, too, there are basins cut off from connection with the main lake, in which the water is salt; and on the south side of that lake the district which was formerly under water now presents precisely the same appearance as this locality along the southern shore of the ancient Lop-nor.

The contour still continued to rise, although only two feet in the seven miles. Thus, when we encamped at the end of the fourth day, we were two and a half feet above our point of departure. It was beginning to be too much of a good thing! At this rate Kara-koshun would soon lie higher than Lôu-lan!

On the 15th of March shor, shor all day long. It was abominably monotonous. The weather, however, was beautiful, and at one p.m. the temperature was not higher than 11° C., or 51°.8 Fahr. But our position was becoming rather serious, for we had scarcely anything left to eat. Our rice was all done; and we had only one little bag of *talkan*, or roasted flour. Except for that, and tea, for the men, and coffee and sugar for myself, we had literally nothing left. The camels were all right as yet; they could eat up their pack-saddles. We still had plenty of water, though it tasted objectionably of goatskin. However, there were a few pieces of ice still swimming in it, and these were not amiss.

We searched the horizon in vain for the smoke from Tokta Ahun's signal-fire. Towards the end of the day we came across trunks of poplar trees, half buried in the shor. They were drift-wood, which had been carried there when the country was formerly under water. The result of the day's measurement was a drop of barely one foot in ten miles. It would be impossible to find a flatter, leveller region on the face of the earth. Thus we had already passed the watershed—if there was one—and in all probability the contour would now fall away to the southern lake basin.

According to our itinerary of the preceding year, we had barely twelve miles left to Kara-koshun when we started on the morning of the 16th March. Soon after starting we came upon the first indication that we were nearing the shore of this desert ocean, in two or three dead or dying tamarisks. After a while they became more frequent, and were attended each by its favourite associate, a sand-dune, three or four feet high, on the sheltered side. Numbers of wild-duck were out; but, strange to say, they were very erratic in their movements. Sometimes they flew towards the north, sometimes towards the south; then again they came from the south-west, and, after circling round, disappeared towards the south-east. What could be the meaning of this? The result of the day's work was a fall of 7⅛ feet in exactly ten miles. We were thus well down into the basin of Kara-koshun, the southern depression of the Lop desert.

We awoke on the 17th in high spirits: we must now be near our journey's end. The wild-ducks were flying from east to west to the south of us; we even observed two or three hawks. At the seventeenth pole, which was planted on a sand-dune, the men stopped and pointed southwards, shouting, "Water—water everywhere!" In fact, we were so near to it that the nineteenth pole was planted actually in the water itself. How different this northern shore of Kara-koshun was from the place where we struck it the preceding year! The beach was absolutely bare and barren, and bordered by a narrow belt of sand. The lake was perfectly open: there was no kamish, except in the far, far distance. Although the water was decidedly salt, it was at any rate better than the nasty thick "soup" we had in the goatskins.

As soon as we stopped, I sent off Khodai Kullu to the south-west, with instructions to push on day and night without rest until he found Tokta Ahun, who must be somewhere not very far away. There was no sign of a trail beside the lake; consequently he could not have gone past the spot where we struck it. My scout disappeared in the thick haze, taking nothing with him to eat, though there was no fear of his suffering from thirst. Meanwhile we were to remain where we were till he came back.

Once more we lived *à la* Robinson Crusoe. Our first aim was to get hold of something to eat. Shagdur went out with the fowling-piece, and brought back a couple of fat ducks, which we shared in brotherly fashion amongst us. Kutchuk, anxious not to be behind his comrade, said he would try his luck at fishing—if he had a boat. Now I was, as you know, an experienced boat-builder! My water-tight instrument-case, with one-half of the levelling pole and some goatskins lashed on each side of it, formed the principal part of Kutchuk's venture. Then with a spade for his oar, off went Kutchuk paddling across the lake. But he got no fish—the water was too salt, and there was not a scrap of vegetation for the fish to live on.

Whilst Kutchuk was thus risking life and limb, I worked out the results of the day's survey, and found that we had dropped another 21½ inches. Hence, the northern shore of Kara-koshun lay 7½ feet below our point of departure at Lôu-lan. That is to say, in the entire distance of 50½ miles, the fall did not exceed 7½ feet. I had, therefore, not only proved from the relief that a lake *could* have existed in the northern part of the Lop district, but I had proved that one actually did exist there. My survey line was not, of course, absolutely trustworthy; for I ought to have returned to the place of departure, and checked my readings again, until their errors amounted to nil. But the season was too far advanced, and I could not afford the time. My main object—proof of the existence of a depression—was sufficiently established even by this simple survey.

Here, towards evening, the fourth storm burst upon us; it was a good thing it did not come on at noon, and stop our work on the eve of completion, for it proved a long-winded storm, and kept us prisoners for two days and three nights, the air being all the time as thick as muddy water. I was very sorry I had let Khodai Kullu go, especially when the second day came, and we heard nothing of him. Something was clearly amiss. I began to be uneasy. Fortunately Shagdur shot five wild-ducks, which went down capitally, although they were over-plentifully peppered and salted with drift-sand. The time hung fearfully heavy on our hands, and I was consumed with impatience, especially when I thought of the mail-bag which Tokta Ahun had with him.

On the 19th of March our supplies were completely exhausted, and we were ravenously hungry. I had never been on such short commons since those terrible days in the Takla-makan Desert in 1895. Shagdur, when taking a stroll, made an unexpected discovery. A short distance to the west of where we were encamped, he stumbled upon a lake, stretching to the north-west and north, and alongside it observed Khodai Kullu's footsteps. This threw light upon the matter: we were entangled in a labyrinth of shifting lakes. Possibly Tokta Ahun had encountered the same obstacles. Something must be done. How would it be, if we left the others to their own devices, and made our way independently to Abdall, keeping to the east and south of Kara-koshun? But no; we had no provisions, and in two or three days we should be in the most desperate straits. All the same I sent Kutchuk east to reconnoitre. After going about seven miles he came back and reported that he had found some kamish huts, abandoned years before, had climbed a hill, and seen the water disappear in the haze at his feet, and that was all.

CHAPTER IX.

A WANDERING LAKE.

On the morning of the 20th it was perfectly clear to me that we could not any longer count on Khodai Kullu. He had pretty certainly failed to find the others; indeed, he might esteem himself lucky if he succeeded in reaching human beings before he perished of hunger. Accordingly we made haste to quit this inhospitable shore, which we had first beheld with such high hopes. The sky was grey and heavy; the diffused light cast no shadows; the surface of the water was crumpled by a slight south-south-westerly breeze. A narrow fringe of ice, about three-quarters of an inch thick, had formed along the beach; and of this we took half a sackful with us; it would be better than having to swallow down the unpalatable contents of the goat-skins. The camels were well rested, and had light loads, and we travelled pretty fast. The water on our left, the biggest expanse I had seen since I left Kara-koshun, forced us to the north-west and north. But it was shallow; the ducks—thousands of them—were busy a long way out from the shore. On our right was the desert.

After going a few hours I climbed to the back of the riding-camel I had used the year before, so as to command as wide a view as I could, that I might warn the men of any marshes and water-courses that lay in our way. About 80 or 90 paces from the edge of the water we again perceived, amongst a narrow belt of dunes, traces of the presence of human beings—two kamish huts, buried up to the eaves in sand. Against one of them leant a canoe, the fore end projecting some two feet above the sand. This discovery was not without its interest. The huts, the canoe, and the household utensils which were left showed that two or three fishermen's families had lived there, probably twenty or thirty years before. My first thought was, why not make use of the canoe ? So at it the men went with their spades; but when they got about six feet of it clear, they found a gaping hole in its side, so we left it to rot where it was.

Shortly afterwards we turned sharply to the west. Here there were reeds near the edge of the water; and Shagdur, creeping up behind another abandoned hut, let drive at a flock of wild-duck, and managed to bag no less than seven. His return was greeted with shouts of triumph; we were safe for two days longer. But this lake appeared to have no end; its south shore was not visible. For the greater part of the day we followed Khodai Kullu's track, until the lake allowed us to turn to the south-west. Here we found, before we had gone very far, that Khodai Kullu had swung off to the north-west. What on earth was the matter with the man ? Had he gone out of his mind ? Why should he want to go back into the desert again ? At length, upon reaching some salt pools, where there was plenty of kamish for the camels and for firing, we halted for the night.

When, late that night, the haze lifted a little, we again made up big fires of dry tamarisks. They flared up; they crackled; they glowed; they died out—no answer. The night was peaceful and still—not a sound, suspicious or otherwise. No horseman came galloping up to the camp with happy tidings. My impatience and uneasiness grew hour by hour. We no longer counted upon Khodai Kullu. Faisullah was by this, no doubt, safe at Kum-chappgan. But why did we hear nothing of Tokta Ahun ? When he left us at Anambaruin-gol he was ordered to meet us here, and ought to have arrived several days ago. Why was he not here ? I knew that I could implicitly trust him. I began to wonder if any accident had happened to him, and he had never got back to Charkhlik at all ? Or was it nothing more than these strange wandering lakes, which alter so from year to year, that were baffling him ? Who could answer these perplexing questions ?

The next day we continued in the same direction, skirting the borders of lakes and doubling creeks and bays, the ground all the time being bare steppe. Shagdur went after the wild-duck, and again brought in a couple. At length we reached a fresh-water lake, where the reeds stood thicker than usual, and found ourselves stopped by a narrow watercourse. It was only two or three yards wide, and not at all deep, but the bottom consisted of ooze, so soft and dangerous that we could not dream of trying to take the camels across; and in attempting to go round it by the south we soon became entirely surrounded on every side by water, except along the narrow path by which we had approached. We wanted to go to the south-west. Nevertheless, the next morning we were forced to turn back and travel towards the north-north-east. Never before had I so distinctly had the impression that Kara-koshun was nothing more than a gigantic marsh—not a real lake at all, but merely a series of wretched depressions, covered with water.

During the night fresh arms were formed, and we had to be up and off in a hurry to escape getting shut in on an island. That would not have inconvenienced *us*, but it would have been fatal to the camels. That strange shore, as hard as brick when it was dry, became as soft as pap when it got under water. Upon reaching a broad channel we again saw Khodai Kullu's footprints; evidently he had swum across it. I wondered what had become of the poor fellow, for it was now five days since I sent him away. Even if he were alive, which I greatly doubted, he would not—indeed, he could not—now return to us; for I had told him that if he delayed too long we should go in the opposite direction—east and south round Kara-koshun.

On the 23rd of March we were still travelling north-east, beside a chain of lakes united by small channels. I rode on a long way in advance of the others, and saw—actually saw with my own eyes—that Kara-koshun was feeling its way back north and north-east towards the basin of the ancient Lop-nor. Could I have a clearer proof of the correctness of the theory I had formed in 1896? It was becoming more and more evident to me that both Tokta Ahun and Khodai Kullu, and possibly also Faisullah, had got completely bewildered by the changes which were now taking place throughout the whole of this region. Its features did not in any way agree with the descriptions which I had given them. Tired and dispirited, I stopped at a point where the creek contracted to seven or eight yards in width, just before it entered a lake. As the bottom of this watercourse consisted of hard blue clay, I thought it a good opportunity to get the camels across. But before beginning the business I sent Shagdur to the north to have a look round. After a good hour's absence he turned up on the east side of the next lake, and with the most excited gestures began to beckon us to go over to him. But I preferred to hear what it was before moving. Shagdur then set off running, and as soon as he came within hailing distance, pointed to the south-west and cried, breathlessly, "Horsemen! horsemen!"

And sure enough there were two mounted men galloping towards us amid a cloud of dust, as hard as their horses could put hoof to ground. We watched them through the glass in a state of the utmost excitement. But I soon recognised them. They were Tokta Ahun and—Chernoff! We were saved!

My good Cossack was so delighted to see me again that he actually trembled, and his cheeks were red with eagerness, he was so anxious to tell me all he knew. Chernoff! Yes, it was Chernoff. As I have already said, the summer before a messenger arrived to tell me that, owing to the unsettled aspect of affairs in Asia, my two West Turkestan Cossacks, Sirkin and Chernoff, were to return at once to Kashgar. But about two months after they arrived there a telegram came from St. Petersburg to Consul-General Petrovsky, commanding the two Cossacks, in the name of the Czar, instantly to report themselves to me wherever I might happen to be. This order arrived on a Saturday afternoon. The Consul summoned the Cossacks, and bade them buy horses and set off next morning. They asked if they might not stay over the Sunday; but, no, an order from the Czar admitted of no delay. Accordingly, early on Sunday morning, they were in the saddle, and rode *viâ* Aksu and Korla to Charkhlik, which they reached after a ride of 48 days, in the end of December. But not finding me there, they had taken the matter quietly, and set about doing something useful. Sirkin took charge of the meteorological observations. Chernoff, meanwhile, went down to the delta of the Lower Tarim and prepared a series of maps of the latest changes which had taken place there. As he was unable to write, he took with him a *mirza*, or scribe, who prepared the drawings. This proved of immense service, the information being most valuable.

As for Tokta Ahun, he also executed his commission to the utmost satisfaction. He had ridden from Anambaruin-gol to Charkhlik, losing on the way only one of the six worn-out horses; had given my letters to Islam to forward; then, after being supplied with provisions and fresh horses, had travelled in company with Chernoff *viâ* Abdall to Kum-chappgan, and so on north-east along the northern shore of the Kara-koshun. There was only one point in which he had not implicitly obeyed my orders. He had only gone two days' journey from Kum-chappgan instead of three; but he was fully exonerated, because he had been hindered by the newly-formed lake which occasioned us so much trouble.

The two men encamped near the fishing-station, where we

Our Camp Beside one of the New Arms from the Lake of Kara-koshun.

struck the lake the year before. There they built a hut, snared wild-duck and caught fish; thus we were plentifully supplied with sheep, poultry, eggs, flour, bread, and maize. Every night after dark they used to light a big fire on the hill, from the top of which I first saw the water of Kara-koshun in the year 1900. But we had been prevented from seeing their fires, and they from seeing ours, by the dust-haze. And yet the distance between their camp and the point where we were first stopped by the water was only two miles. But two miles though it was, it had taken poor Khodai Kullu five days to get to them. The fact was, the two camps were separated by the new, deep, broad arms which were flowing northwards, out of the Kara-koshun; and Tokta Ahun's camp could only be reached either by going right round them or by swimming across them.

For twelve days Chernoff and Tokta Ahun, whilst waiting for our arrival, led an idyllic life—walking, rowing, hunting, and fishing, until one fine day our good Khodai Kullu suddenly emerged out of the desert and put an end to their easy-going existence. The very hour he arrived they packed up and set off, with Khodai Kullu as guide, to look for us—and now they had at length found us.

After talking over and discussing everything that had happened since we parted, we moved towards a pool quite close to our camp of the 20th March, picking up Khodai Kullu on the way. He sat on a clump of grass, and, upon catching sight of me, began to weep bitterly; he was so overcome by the recollection of the adventures he had gone through during the five critical days. On and on and on he had walked, and at last in sheer despair he had set to and swum across several lakes. On the third day he was sitting tired and dispirited on the margin of another lake, when a flock of wild-duck flew over his head. As if by a miracle, one of the ducks dropped just at his feet, with its wing either broken or injured. Like a wild animal he flung himself upon it, and ate it up, bones and feathers and all, alive just as it was. Strengthened by this meal, he pushed on two days longer, until he at length found those he was in search of.

In several places he had come across the trail of Faisullah's caravan, from which he inferred that they were all alive, including the three horses and the three dogs. But at length the trail had turned away from the lake into the desert, as though old Faisullah had suddenly lost his bearings. Where he was gone to we were completely ignorant, and I became exceedingly anxious about him. His caravan carried everything that was of value to me, except my maps—all my scientific collections, photographic negatives, wood-carvings, and a great part of the MSS. which we had discovered at Lôu-lan. Were all these to be lost? Tokta Ahun, however, assured me that the two parties which he had sent out into the desert in search of Faisullah, one from Kum-chappgan, and the other from Abdall, would be sure to find the old man. Besides, Faisullah was a clever and prudent man.

I gave Khodai Kullu a gratuity in silver for the courage and resource he had shown. He told me, quite calmly, that he was fully determined the whole time that he would *not* turn back, but *would* accomplish what he was bidden do, even though it cost him his life. Ever since he had killed the wild camel, Khodai Kullu's prestige had been rising. After this he was never called anything but *Batir*, or "the Hero." These are the sort of men you want about you; but amongst the Mussulmans they are, at any rate, rare.

We were now at the end of our long wanderings. My good star had not deserted me. My anxiety with regard to the various sections of the caravan was at an end. How delightful it was to rest beside this fresh, translucent water! We stayed there two days, and fared right sumptuously on the ample supplies of the relief expedition; they had brought even tea and tobacco with them. But the best of all was the mail-bag from home. It kept me chained to the inside of my yurt, so that it actually required a special effort to go out and take an observation for latitude. My letters were full of news; but it was very strange that I should be told about the Boxer movement in China in a letter from Stockholm. His Excellency the Swedish Minister for Foreign Affairs warned me of it, so that it was probably fortunate we did not go to Sa-chow when we were so close to it.

This camp, no. CLXX. on my map, was one of the very best throughout the journey. I shall not readily forget it.

This peculiar northerly extension of the Kara-koshun may also to some extent have been caused by the hydrographic relations of the Tarim basin taken as a whole. All the streams of East Turkestan had been unusually high during the preceding summer and autumn, this being no doubt caused by exceptionally heavy falls of snow on the encircling mountains. This circumstance, again, can only be explained by a more comprehensive view of the broad factors of the problem, such as the distribution of the atmospheric pressure and the extent of the winds, especially the monsoons. In consequence of the more copious flood in the streams, the terminal lakes of the Tarim system had naturally swollen to greater dimensions than usual.

On the 26th we turned our faces towards the north. Both this day and the next the going was difficult. The clay ridges and grooves, or trenches, were all directed towards the north-east, so that we had to cross them each and all in turn diagonally, and the creeks of the new lake all ran like fingers in the same direction, compelling us to turn to every point of the compass to get round them. When at length we had doubled the last of these hindrances, and were able to turn finally to the west

An Offshoot of the Travelling Lake—the White Patches on the Surface of the Water are Foam.

and south-west, we were half-way back to Lôu-lan. Had I had a conception of the way the water was behaving I might have confined my survey to the first half of the distance. About the point where we turned dead forest was quite common; and some of the poplars and tamarisks still stood upright. Here we were probably skirting the southern shore of the ancient lake of Lop-nor.

In two or three places in this quarter I was surprised to come across old camel-droppings. That these could only be attributed to wild camels was perfectly clear. It showed that those animals were in the habit of crossing the desert, and knew of the existence of the lakes farther south, though for such swift-footed creatures the distance was really but a trifle.

After we turned south-west we travelled more easily and more quickly, for we were now able to follow the wind-scooped trenches; indeed, for long distances we actually trod in Faisullah's footsteps. If we had had any doubts as to its really being his caravan we were following, they were finally dispelled when we came across Shagdur's brown horse lying dead on the trail. The animal had been opened, and its intestines removed, and the tenderer and better parts of the meat taken away; which showed that the caravan was at the end of its resources.

We stopped on the edge of a newly-formed stream, where the water flowed quite strong towards the north-east. This was pretty certainly the more northerly depression which we crossed when making our survey, and the slight rise between the northern and the southern basins was here totally wanting, or broken down.

On the 28th we continued along the edge of the capriciously wandering water. Here we observed a very interesting phenomenon on the edge of a pool which had formed since Chernoff made his sketch-map of the locality seven days before. The pool was now quite cut off, and was fed by water which trickled out of the ground. Its surface, about twelve acres in extent, was like water boiling in a pot; it bubbled and gurgled as if there were a hot blaze underneath it, and threw up bubbles of air, each of which became the nucleus of a patch of white foam. Sometimes the welling water gushed up several inches high, like a miniature geyser, and the pool splashed as if big fish were rising to its surface. The specific gravity of the water was 1.0036, and to us, who were accustomed to a greater infusion of salt, it tasted almost fresh. The greatest depth of the pool was 7¼ feet, and this little lake had been entirely formed in the course of—one week. Even whilst we stood and watched it, the water lapped over on both sides, giving rise to fresh runnels, which trickled away, penetrating into every cranny and depression of the ground. How far would these new lakes travel before the year was out? Would they get all the way to the ancient Lop-nor? These questions can only be answered after a fresh visit to the locality.

Thus we travelled west, south-east, and east round the lakes, where poor Khodai Kullu had floundered along so bravely with nothing to eat. When we reached the spot where Faisullah had struck out into the desert, I thought the action looked so hazardous that I sent Shagdur to see where the trail went to. With the help of his compass he jotted it down on a piece of paper for about six miles, and ascertained that the old man had merely made a detour, after which he had continued in the original direction. Had he stuck to the lake side, one day more would have brought him to Tokta Ahun's camp. Next, at the first salt lake beside which we had encamped the year before, we came upon two or three empty preserved food tins. On that occasion we thought it owed its origin to the Shirgeh-chappgan, for it was only a narrow arm, which we waded across without difficulty; but it was now so swollen that we could have readily drowned ourselves in it and the camels as well.

During the night the gulls screamed on the lakes, heralding a storm; and we got it at daybreak. The widespread sheets of water were whipped into foam. Our last day's march around this tiresome lake brought us at last to Tokta Ahun's camp, where we found Tokta Ahun himself quite comfortable, but alone. All the men from Kum-chappgan had returned home, under the belief that we had gone the other way round Kara-koshun. Fortunately they had left behind them two canoes. As we had plenty of provisions except fresh fish, Tokta Ahun, taking his horse, at once went off to fetch some of the latter from Kum-chappgan.

On the 30th of March we were kept indoors the whole day by the storm; but on the following day, although it still continued to blow, we were able to measure the volume of the water which was returning to the ancient lake of Lop-nor. The surface was, however, too rough to venture out in a single canoe; so we lashed our two canoes together side by side. Chernoff and Khodai Kullu were my boatmen. The former, during the time the men were waiting for us, had explored this reedy labyrinth in every direction, and knew exactly where to steer. In spite of that, however, the trip was a very ticklish piece of work. Six days previously Khodai Kullu and Tokta Ahun, when on their way to the hut, had swum across eight considerable streams; but I only succeeded in measuring six, each of them distinct and clearly marked. Their united volume amounted to 1,130 cubic feet in the second, a figure which is certainly too low, for a good deal of the water percolated unseen through the dense reedbeds without my being able to measure it. At any rate, we ascertained that enormous masses of water were on their way to the north. In view of the unexampled flatness of the region, a volume of 100,000,000 cubic feet of water in the 24 hours is sufficient to form a very respectable lake. In the swiftest current the water flowed at the rate of 1¼ miles an hour. Now it is undoubtedly strange that the lake had not advanced more than two days towards the north-east; yet it must be remembered that enormous quantities were being absorbed by the arid ground. The deep sand must first be moistened, then fully saturated, before the restless element was able to secure for itself a sufficiently firm channel along which to flow.

However, I was beginning to feel that I had had enough of these marshes, and began to turn my eyes longingly towards the mountains.

During the last few decennia—that is, since the time of Przhevalsky's visit—Kara-koshun had clearly shown a tendency to dry up. The reeds encroached upon it more and more every year, and the marsh grew less in area. I am convinced that in a few years' time the lake will be found in the locality where it was formerly placed by the Chinese cartographers, and where Baron von Richthofen proved by an ingenious deduction that it must once have been. I have said above sufficient to show that the actual facts are in agreement with Baron von Richthofen's theory. Nor is it surprising that such should be the case in this desert, which my survey proved to be almost perfectly horizontal. While the lake of Kara-koshun, which had existed a long time in its southern half, was being filled up with mud, drift-sand, and decaying vegetation, the arid northern half was being excavated and blown away by the winds, and thus being hollowed out to a deeper level. Now these changes of niveau are determined by purely mechanical laws and local atmospheric conditions; consequently the lake which serves as the terminal reservoir of the Tarim system must be extremely sensitive to their influence. It is a matter of mere physical necessity that the water should overflow and run towards the relatively lower depressions. Then vegetation and animal life, as well as the fishing population, inevitably accompany the water as it migrates, and the old lake-bed dries up. In the future the same phenomena will be repeated again, but in the reverse order, although the laws dictating it will be precisely the same. It will only be then, however, when there exist more abundant materials to go upon, that the length of the period of oscillation will admit of being determined. All that we now know for certain is that in 265 A.D., in the last years of the reign of the Chinese Emperor Yüan Ti, Lop-nor lay in the northern part of the desert. In fact, Lop-nor is, as it were, the weight which hangs on the pendulum of the Tarim river, and even though a single oscillation should stretch over a thousand years, still, measured by the clock of geologic time, that is comparatively speaking little more than one of our seconds.

On the 1st of April we struck into a part of the country which I already knew from the year before. The only interest attaching to it was the comparison I could now make between my present map and my old map. For instance, the new stream which came from Shirgeh-chappgan now carried a volume of 335½ cubic feet, as compared with a very insignificant quantity in 1900. On the 2nd of April we were met by Niaz Baki Beg, Numet Beg, and our old Mollah, who told us that Faisullah was safe at Abdall, and all the caravan with him.

Upon reaching the lake of Ak-köl, we stopped at sunset to wait for boats. It was a beautiful afternoon, peaceful and cool. Not that we had any cause to complain of the heat, but eight months of winter had made us rather sensitive on this point. At last we heard the splashing of oars and the voices of the boatmen, and up glided a flotilla of five canoes. By means of these we carried our baggage across the Ak-köl, and a tangle of lakes beyond it, and finally emerged upon the big river immediately opposite to Kunchekkan Beg's former dwelling, Kona Abdall, where I visited him in 1896. From there strong arms paddled us up the Tarim. There was a glorious moon, and by its light I continued my mapping. It was one of those enchanting, never-to-be-forgotten trips by moonlight on still, silvery water, like a lovely night in Venice, which I had enjoyed on two or three occasions before on that peaceful stream. It was late when my swift canoe pulled up amid the fierce barking of our dogs, which, however, soon changed to transports of delight when they recognised us.

The next day I measured the volume of the river ; it amounted to 5,517 cubic feet in the second, the greatest volume I have recorded anywhere throughout the Tarim system ; it was due, as I have already explained, to the cold, snowy winter and the unusually thick formation and long continuance of the ice.

Faisullah gave me an account of all that had happened to him from the day we parted at the ruins of Lôu-lan. He had been seventeen days on the road, and had made several unexpected hydrographical discoveries, which, however, I cannot now stay to dwell upon.

At ten o'clock in the morning a black storm of the usual character burst upon us like a clap of thunder, sweeping before it everything that was not securely fastened down. The next day was wasted; it was impossible to face such a howling tempest. That was the desert's last lingering good-bye to me, and it lasted 41 hours. When it at length ceased, the air was thick with fine dust. We bought, however, three good camels, making seventeen in all.

Three more days' march through another of the inevitable storms brought us to our headquarters camp at Charkhlik, where we were received on the evening of the 8th of April by a large escort of mounted men, and were by them conducted through the scattered orchards to our serai.

CHAPTER X.

PREPARATIONS FOR TIBET.

I NOW enjoyed a delightful and much-needed rest in the little town on the edge of the desert. And yet rest I can hardly call it, for I went on working from morning till night. There were endless things to arrange, endless preparations to be made, for the last and most difficult part of my programme, the journey right across Tibet. I took up my quarters in a very comfortable serai, near the Chinese *yamen*, or residence of the Governor, on the left bank of the Charkhlik-su.

A public gateway led off a street of grey clay-walled houses into a courtyard, with partly open, partly covered, stalls for the horses and mules. In the opposite wall of the courtyard another gateway opened into a large apartment where the Mussulmans lived, and from which a passage led to the Cossacks' quarters. Beside this last was a smaller room, which Sirkin had already converted into a photographic dark-room. Behind this house lay a large walled-in garden, planted with mulberry trees, poplars, and willows. Here, in a shady spot, the big Mongolian yurt was set up for my use. We always had a watchman posted at the gates of the serai during the night, and another in the garden. In this peaceful retreat, where I was secure from inquisitive eyes, my only companions were the two dogs, Yolldash, and the big black savage Yollbars (tiger), which had been so severely wounded by a wild boar at Yanghi-köll. No stranger durst ever go near him, though with me he was as quiet as a lamb. There was yet another inhabitant of the garden, namely, a stag, a beautiful animal, with big brown eyes, which had been caught young in the forests of the Cherchen-daria, and had been presented to me by Jan Daloi, the Governor of the place. The stag was quite tame, and let me feed him with bread. The first two or three days, but only the first two or three, I did rest in the armchair which Islam Bai had knocked together for me whilst at the grottoes of Temirlik. And yet even then I was not idle: I spent my time reading the big budget of letters which the jighit, Yakub, had brought me a little while back from Kashgar. The first to be devoured were, of course, the letters from home, from those near and dear to me; then came a pile of Swedish newspapers, and, lastly, some books by my favourite authors—Selma Lagerlöf, Rudyard Kipling, and several others. The evenings were devoted to the development of the negatives which I had taken during the last four months. In this work Sirkin proved exceedingly useful, in getting the

The Stag. On the Left a Chinaman, Chernoff, and Turdu Bai, and on the Right Islam Bai.

dark-room ready, and in tidying it up afterwards, in mixing the different chemicals, and in drying and printing the plates. Besides that, he looked after the meteorological observatory, which was placed on the flat roof, well protected against the sun. Meanwhile it was Chernoff's duty to look after everything that concerned the caravan, as well as to provide and cook my meals, though Cherdon was my body-servant.

But this was only until the 12th of April, when I gave the two Buriat Cossacks a special and important task to perform. When I made my big journey across Tibet, I intended, if possible, to try and get into Lassa (Lhasa), disguised as a Mongol. For that purpose it was necessary that I should have a complete

The Yurt in the Orchard at Charkhlik.

outfit of Mongolian clothes and appurtenances of travel—in fact, an outfit including everything that the Mongols are accustomed to take with them when they pilgrimage to the holy city. Shagdur was the only man in my caravan who had any knowledge of my plans, so I sent him to Kara-shahr to buy what I wanted. It was a long journey, and would take him a month to go there and back, so I let Cherdon go with him for company.

The days slipped past, and yet there still remained plenty to do; but I soothed myself with the thought that it was too early to go up into the mountains. For one thing, the grass was only just beginning to sprout down here, and it would be fully six weeks later before it showed in the higher regions. In the meantime our animals were all resting, and gathering strength for the hard times which almost certainly awaited them. We gave them as much kamish and maize as they could eat, and they were capitally looked after by their attendants. Turdu Bai was the captain of the camels, and answerable for their condition. This, the *élite* corps of the caravan, was increased by a score new camels, which Islam Bai bought in Charkhlik; so that, when we at length started, we had no less than 39, of which, however, three were young ones. The last of these was born on the 6th of May, and I at once went to see it. The little creature could scarcely stand on its long, tottering legs, and gazed about it with an air of observant curiosity at the restless bustle of the scene into which it had been thus suddenly transported. Yet, within a few days, it was running about the stable courtyard, playing, and quite at home, and soon became a general favourite. During the day the camels were taken out of the town to graze, but at nightfall were driven back to an open square just outside the serai, and given a good meal of maize, poured out on mats. At the same time the horses and mules had their corn in their mangers. On warm days we gave them a bath in a big pond, surrounded by shady willows, which was immediately outside the entrance-gate to the serai, a proceeding which was always witnessed by a crowd of curious onlookers.

The support of my now numerous and continually increasing caravan soon began to cost a good deal of money. I had to feed all the men whose names were enrolled on my caravan, and make them advances of wages. Every day we killed at least one sheep, and rice, bread, and eggs disappeared wholesale. But, on the other hand, it was an important matter that we all, men and animals alike, should be well set up for the hard days before us. I will introduce the new members of our company as I go along. Even before our return to Charkhlik, Islam Bai had laid in stores sufficient to equip the caravan for a ten months' journey, consisting of rice, flour, and *talkan*. This last, burnt flour, when mixed with water, is eaten like porridge. For flesh meat we intended to rely upon the weapons of our hunters, but all the same I resolved, when we started, to buy a flock of sheep and drive them on with us. For my own use I had a couple of hundred tins of preserved food, which Colonel Saitseff had sent me from Osh. But I soon grew so sick of them that I turned over the greater part to the Cossacks, except preserved fruits, vegetables, and soups, which were always good.

We bought a large supply of maize in sacks for the camels and horses ; it was a heavy load to carry. I thought at first of buying asses, for they were cheap in Charkhlik, only costing ten sär, or 30s. each. There was, however, one objection to this : an ass caravan big enough for the purpose would require at least half-a-dozen men to look after it, and after the poor beasts were all dead, we should have these men hanging about our necks with nothing for them to do, and yet should have to feed them. I decided, therefore, to hire 70 asses for two months. They cost me, it is true, five sär each the month, or practically as much as if I had bought them ; but in this case the ass-drivers would have to find their own way back to Charkhlik when I had done with them. I arranged this business with an honest old fellow named Dovlet Caravan-bashi, from Bokhara, who did excellently well, though he made very little money out of the transaction, for nearly all his animals died before they got back.

On the 28th April my old servant Mollah Shah, arrived from Cherchen. I could not possibly do without him, for he had accompanied Mr. Littledale in his journey to Tengri-nor and Ladak, and consequently knew more about the country and its resources than anybody else. Every day men came to me in the garden asking me to employ them, but my company was already made up. I did not want too many men. Indeed I had made up my mind that as soon as we were across the Arka-tagh, and the animals had become accustomed to their work, I would send back some of those I had already engaged. Amongst others who came to visit me was Aldat's old father ; I gave him a present of money. Jan Daloi, the

A Corner of the Stable-Yard in our Serai. Sirkin seated on the Rice-Sacks, Turdu Bai standing in Front of the Dromedary.

Amban or Governor of Charkhlik, had gone to Kara-shahr on official business, but his little six-year-old son often used to come to see me. Both in speech and bearing he showed that refined, elegant breeding which is characteristic of cultured Chinese. I gave the boy sweetmeats and illustrated newspapers, besides a number of trifles, with which he was immensely delighted, and in return he used to bring me fruit or send bundles of fresh clover for my horses. But in the beginning of May the little chap died of the measles, and his poor father reached home just one day too late.

The weather was splendid: there were storms almost every

Sirkin and Chernoff with the two Baby Camels.

day, which kept the air fresh and cool. Even as early as the end of April the temperature went up to 25°.0 C., or 77°.0 Fahr., and down to 12°.0 C., or 53°.6 Fahr. The atmosphere was so thick with dust that we could not see the sun, and of an evening it sometimes grew so cold that I had to have a brazier to warm the yurt. But during the day I enjoyed listening to the wind whistling through the mulberry and plum trees. This stay in Charkhlik recalled vividly to my mind the month I spent in 1896 in the peaceful garden at Khotan, just before I started for my journey through the north of Tibet. But by the beginning of May it was decidedly warm; on the first of the month the thermometer registered 32°.7 C., or 90°.9 Fahr., in the shade. The atmosphere was still and bright, so that we were able to see the snow-fields which crowned the loftiest summits of the Astyn-tagh.

But the days were slipping past, and it was getting time to start. The baggage was divided and packed into boxes and sacks, which were lashed to the pack-saddles and placed ready to be lifted on to the animals' backs. When these were all arranged in a long row, I was quite dismayed at the sight; but Turdu Bai assured me that the animals could easily carry them. With the view of lightening the load as much as possible, I had already weeded out everything that could possibly be spared, including the scientific collections, such as the geological specimens, skeletons of animals, botanical specimens, and archæological finds from Lôu-lan. These things, which made up eight substantial camel loads, were to go to Kashgar, to be taken charge of by Consul-General Petrovsky. Who was there I could put in charge of such an important caravan? Should I entrust it to the tender mercies of the Chinese? No, not for worlds. I was thinking of writing to Khalmet, the aksakal of Korla, when the difficulty was solved in a very simple and quite unexpected way. One afternoon, when I was alone in my yurt, Islam Bai came to me and begged that he might take my collections to Kashgar. I was quite taken aback at his wanting to leave me just then, when the real difficulties and dangers of the journey were beginning, but answered without more ado, "Yes." He urged, as a reason for wanting to go, that he was getting old and tired, and was afraid he could not be of so much use to me as I should expect. It was very hard to part from him; but I had already found out that he did not like the Cossacks, and was pretty stern with the Mussulmans, amongst whom he maintained an exemplary discipline. I had a great deal to thank him for, and as a proof of my confidence, made the following arrangement with him. He was to take my collections to Kashgar, through Korla, Kuchar, and Aksu, as far as Korla by camels, and the rest of the way by *arabas* (Turkestan carts), and was to spend two months on the road. In addition to paying him the wages due to him, some 300 roubles (about £32) in gold, I defrayed all the expenses of his journey, both for himself and the animals, and gave him letters of recommendation in each of the large towns he was to pass through. From Kashgar he might go back to his home in Osh, and stay there five months, then return to Kashgar and do something for me which Consul-General Petrovsky would tell him about. This

In the Shade of the Willows beside the Serai Reservoir at Charkhlik.

was to meet me at Ladak with a large sum of money and my post-bag, which by that time would, no doubt, be a large one. This mark of my confidence not only flattered Islam, it reconciled us both to the bitterness of parting.

Old Faisullah accompanied him to Kashgar. He was tired and afraid of the rarefied atmosphere up in the mountains. He had served me faithfully, and in an exemplary manner, for two years, so I gave him a large sum of money and a riding-horse. The other men tried in vain to induce him to go with us, for he was a general favourite. Islam's departure, however, was viewed with nothing but the liveliest satisfaction.

They started on the 5th of May with eight camels, three horses, and three extra men, who were engaged to accompany them as far as Korla. It was a very stormy day, and at the end of the very first lane their caravan disappeared in a thick cloud of dust. During the past year I had not seen much of Islam Bai; he had always remained as caravan-bashi at headquarters whilst I was absent on the different excursions. Nobody had lodged any complaint against him; but now that he was gone I soon noticed a difference. The men were cheerful, and went about their work with pleasure, and were happy and contented.

I sent with Islam Bai a very heavy post-bag. One letter, to my father and mother, was no less than 216 pages long, quite a book in fact. Besides which there were long letters to Oscar, King of Sweden, and to the Czar of Russia. I also wrote to several of my friends at home, amongst others to Baron Adolf Nordenskiöld. The letter reached him a few days before he died. He was one of those friends whom nothing but death can take from you. Another important missive was addressed to Lord Curzon, Viceroy of India, to be forwarded by Mr. Macartney from Kashgar. I told his Excellency that I expected, towards the end of the year, to be at Leh in Ladak, and begged that I might be allowed to lift in that town a sum of £200. I also hinted at the possibility of a short visit to India, and asked permission, in that case, to take one of my Cossacks with me. The kind answer which I received to this letter belongs to a later chapter of this book.

CHAPTER XI.

THE LAST OF ISLAM BAI.

THE route I chose for reaching the Tibetan highlands led up the narrow gorge of the Charkhlik-su, a road which no European had ever tried before, but it was a road that was absolutely impossible for camels and extremely difficult for pack horses. Hence, I had to make this arrangement. The big caravan, led by Chernoff, Cherdon (when he returned), and Turdu Bai, was to go by way of Tattlik-bulak and Bagh-tokay, until it reached the west shore of the Lower Kum-köll, whilst I, followed by only a few men, ascended by the nearer, but more difficult, route up the glen.

On the 8th of May everything was ready for the start; the loads, some eighty in number, were arranged in long rows outside the big gate, and were soon swung up on to the animals' back. It was an immense caravan, the biggest I have ever led, the biggest, in fact, any European has ever led into the interior of Tibet. It was divided into several sections, which filed off one after the other. First, my boxes and trunks, then the men's belongings, then the tent and the boat, and after them the different stores. How much easier it is for an expedition by sea, or one that starts not very far from the coast, to get its collections home; but in the interior of Asia, every single object, from the very beginning of the journey, has to be carried many hundreds of miles, and under the most unfavourable conditions, on the backs of camels or horses. The loads have to be taken off and put on again every morning and evening, week after week, and month after month. And had it not been for the great kindness of the Dalai Lama, I never should have got out of Tibet the collections which I made during this, the journey that was just beginning.

I sent on with the caravan the big, roomy Mongolian yurt,

At Charkhlik the Day before the Start.

and so had to make shift with a smaller one, which consisted of a score of staves, the smoke-ring at the top, and a few white felts. This was my " house " all the way to Ladak. When the men moved my things from the one yurt to the other they found underneath one of the boxes a big, ugly scorpion, of a straw-yellow and grey colour. It had probably been keeping me company the whole time, but, strange to say, never did me any harm. On the other hand, once when one of the men was giving straw to the horses, he was severely bitten by a scorpion, and had to keep his bed for a couple of days.

Away went the caravan then. The older camel-foals followed their mothers, but the youngest was packed in felts, and hoisted up between two boxes on the back of my old riding-camel. His mother followed immediately behind him, and was very uneasy until she discovered where he was. The horses, which had put on flesh whilst resting, played fine pranks when they got out upon the road. They flung off their loads, and broke loose, and galloped away; but as they only carried sacks of maize and such like, no harm was done. The long train of baggage animals, winding away from our quiet serai, and the shade of the willows, to the tinkling of their own bells, the shouts and cries of the men, the screaming of the camels, and the neighing of the horses made quite an imposing spectacle. As I stood and watched them I was uplifted with pride at being the owner of such a magnificent caravan, and yet my mind was full of melancholy and sorrowful reflections, for I feared—I feared this would be a fatal march for most of them! And in point of fact it did turn out to be the hardest and most difficult journey that I have ever performed. Two or three of the men died, and all the rest, myself included, were utterly worn out when we reached the other side of Tibet. In fact, I was, myself, two or three times nearer death's door than when I so nearly perished of thirst in the Takla-makan Desert in 1895. Then my sufferings did not last more than a couple of weeks, but in Tibet it was a matter of daily occurrence for weeks together. I would rather cross the Desert of Takla-makan ten times than make another journey like that through Tibet.

Chernoff was in supreme command of the caravan. Turdu Bai was head of the camel caravan. Their instructions were to go first to Abdall, and thence follow the well-known trail up into the mountains. At Abdall they were to buy fifty sheep, and wait for Cherdon, who was on his way back from Kara-shahr. The stag went with them, following the camels like a dog. And they had seven dogs, amongst them Malenki and Malchik, both of which had crossed the Desert of Gobi with us.

After they were gone the courtyards were empty, and the serai felt quite lonely and deserted. Sirkin now acted as my body servant, and Li Loyeh was cook, while Mollah Shah looked after the horses. These were the only three men I retained with me. Yolldash was, as always, the faithful protector of my yurt.

It only remained to send off the ass caravan. They were to travel across the Ovraz-sai, by way of Kara-chokka, and meet the big caravan at Bagh-tokay. On the morning of the 13th old Dovlet, Caravan-bashi, was ready, his seventy asses laden with maize, and his ten subordinates supplied with provisions and pelts. And so off they went, too, the *tross*, or camp-followers. My forces were now more broken up than they had ever been. Here was I in Charkhlik; the big caravan was on its way to Abdall; the ass caravan on the way to the Astyn-tagh; Shagdur had not yet returned from Kara-shahr; and Islam Bai was to spend the hottest months of summer carrying my collections to Kashgar. I felt like a general who has to keep his finger on each detachment of his army.

At noon on the 14th of May, a man from the village of Lop arrived with a message from Shagdur, reporting that all was well, but that Shagdur's horses were exhausted. Accordingly, Sirkin set about getting three fresh horses ready to go and meet his comrade; but before he got outside the gate Shagdur and his little caravan rode in. Cherdon had received my orders at Chegghelik-uy, and, taking a canoe, had hurried to Abdall. Shagdur had performed his task splendidly. Not only had he brought a complete Mongol equipment for our pilgrimage to the holy city, but he was also accompanied by a real living lama, Shereb Lama, twenty-seven years old, a native of Urga, but belonging to a temple outside Kara-shahr. He was dressed in his red, priestly garb, most like a long nightgown, held together round the waist by a yellow girdle, and on his head wore a Chinese skull-cap. I gave him a very friendly greeting, so that from the first moment he might feel himself at home, and I at once began to brush up my rusty Mongolian, and before many weeks were past I was able to talk quite fluently with the Lama, as we generally called him. This man became the most interesting figure in our company. In the course of two or three days he grew quite confidential, and always used to bring his little worries to me. Indeed, he was ready to lay down his life for me—in fact, it was a miracle he did not lose it for my sake. He had returned from Lassa only the year before, having spent some time there studying the holy books in two of the temples. He had been accompanied by another lama from Kara-shahr, and on the way there had seen Kozloff's expedition in Tsaidam. This was the only time in the course of my journey that I heard anything about my Russian friend.

Upon being approached by Shagdur, Shereb Lama had at

Shereb Lama on Golden Ears, with Yollbars on a Cord.

once shown himself ready to accompany the Buriat Cossacks to Lassa, and had talked in such a high strain of the glories of the holy city that Shagdur was simply dying to get there. All the same he had not been free from suspicion, and asked whether a "Russian" was going with them; because, if so, he could have nothing to do with the expedition. It would be as much as his life was worth. In reply Shagdur had protested that no "Russian" was going with him. Putting Lassa on one side, our Lama was quite ready to go wherever I wanted him, and would be satisfied with a salary of two yambas (£20) for as long as I liked. At different times our Lama told me various things about the holy city and the pilgrimages to it. Amongst other things he said that at a distance of ten days' journey, it was surrounded by a ring of frontier guards, who minutely examined every caravan, as well as every solitary horseman, that arrived. In short, they stopped everybody, allowing nobody to proceed until their passes had been examined at Lassa, and permission given for them to do so. The big Mongol caravan which had passed our camp at Temirlik the year before had been detained ten days, solely because of a rumour that our caravan was on the border of the country of the Tsaidam Mongols, and the Tibetans were apparently afraid some undesirable person might be with them.

Shagdur also brought two other travellers with him, both of them old acquaintances. One was Ördek, the man who discovered the temple in Lôu-lan; the other was Khalmet Aksakal from Korla. Thus our little company was increased by a very interesting quartette, and our spirits again rose. Shagdur gave me an account of his mission, presented his accounts, and returned me the balance of the money I had given him, which was about one-half. Any other Asiatic would of course have put it in his pocket; but Shagdur was an honest and an honourable man. The very idea of stealing would have seemed to him utterly absurd. Ördek was now quite well again, and begged in the most touching way that he might go with me wherever I was going, and under any conditions I chose. When he left me the year before, he had done so under the pretext that he was suffering from a malignant disease; but he now told me that that was not true. The real cause was Islam Bai had threatened to kill him if he dared to show himself at Temirlik. The clouds seemed to be gathering about poor Islam now that he was gone! However, I engaged Ördek on the same terms as before, and ordered him to follow after the asses to Kum-köll.

Then it was Khalmet Aksakal's turn; but before he began, I asked him if he would do me a great favour, and of course he was quite ready to do it, namely, lend me ten yambas of silver, which at the existing rate of currency was equivalent to £100; and at the end of an hour he counted out the silver pieces in my tent. Without this augmentation of my "treasury," my position would have been extremely awkward when I reached the south of Tibet. At my dictation Khalmet Aksakal wrote a letter in Jaggatai Turki to Consul-General Petrovsky, and I signed it. This was a bill upon him for the amount named, to be repaid at the time stated upon it.

At last everything was ready, and we were to start the next morning, the 15th of May; but fate decreed otherwise. At five o'clock in the morning it began, by way of a change, to pour with rain, and the thunder rumbled in the mountains—a suitable background to the sad surprise that awaited me that evening.

Fresh clouds were gathering round the head of the unfortunate Islam Bai. Khalmet Aksakal complained that Islam had borrowed twenty-seven sär (about £5 5s.) of him in Korla, and when he reminded him of the debt, Islam had abused him and jeered at him. He then went on to say that he had good reason to believe that I also had been cheated. I did not understand what he meant. Islam Bai! Impossible! The man who had shared my destinies for five years, who had looked death in the face at my side in the desert, who had exhibited so many proofs of devotion, who had been the recipient of so many favours, who had higher wages than any of the rest, who wore my king's gold medal for his fidelity and honesty—impossible! I could not, I would not believe it. But upon my making cautious enquiries at Charkhlik certain things came to light which I durst not ignore. At Temirlik Shagdur saw him buying 165 sär (about £33) worth of gold from the gold hunters of Bokalik, but had not interfered, for he naturally assumed it was done by my command. Sirkin and Ördek had been cheated, the one out of 16 sär (about £3 3s.), the other out of 10 sär (£2); but neither had cared to worry me with complaints. The real truth of the matter may be said to have been brought to my knowledge by a mere accident. I had commissioned Khalmet Aksakal to buy sugar and other commodities, and send them to us. When I got back to headquarters and examined his account, it struck me as being excessively high, and in spite of all Islam's explanations, he was bound to admit that it was 23 sär (£4 10s.) too much. Thereupon I sent for Osman Bai, Khalmet Aksakal's brother, who was a merchant in Charkhlik, and gave him a bit of my mind, telling him that his brother was a dishonest man. Osman defended him, and besought me by all that was holy not to believe the slander. When he found he could not move me. he sent a special messenger to his brother at Korla, advising him to come without loss of time, or he would suffer very serious injury. So here he was, come back with Shagdur. When the little party met Islam near Tikkenlik, Islam was greatly disconcerted, and said that he had been ordered to tell the Cossacks that I had altered my plans, and that they must take the road through Abdall and Chimen if they wanted to find me. If they had believed him, they would not have met me until they reached Kum-köll, in the beginning of June. Islam's idea was, of course, to get a good start on the road to Kashgar; but the Buriats, like true soldiers, had obeyed orders. They knew that they were never to do anything without written or verbal orders from myself, and, fortunately, as it happened, I had sent a letter to Shagdur a few days before through the Chinese post, and so he took no notice of Islam's intrigues, but came straight back to Charkhlik.

The preliminary investigation which I now made into all these things delayed us two or three days longer, and when we did at length make a start, the Aksakal accompanied us the first day out. Upon his return to Korla he took with him a letter to the Consul-General, requesting him to arrest Islam Bai, who was a Russian subject, immediately he arrived at Kashgar, and have all his effects examined. He would, of course, seize all the Chinese silver, as well as all the gold, he found amongst them.

But before relating what happened to Islam in Kashgar, I will first show that he fully deserved the punishment he brought upon his own head. As soon as I reached Kum-köll, and joined the caravan, I called my men before me and examined them one by one. With only one exception they had all been cheated out of money, some more, some less; altogether they had been done out of 12 yambas (£120). Chernoff was the only one amongst them who had not been cheated. It also came out that Islam Bai had robbed me of about 9 yambas (£90), the greater part of it when he bought the last batch of camels. At Yanghi-köll, too, I had bought a large supply of *chapans* (Turkestan cloaks), furs, and boots to give to my men. These things had certainly been distributed to them; but Islam had, I found, made them pay for them, and had put the proceeds into his own pocket. It is, I confess, strange that I never observed I was being deceived in this rascally way, but the matter is easy enough to explain. In the first place all payments from my exchequer were properly booked, and nothing was ever stolen from me directly. Islam was too clever for that. But the payments for every big purchase of stores, camels, and horses, as well as the men's wages, went through Islam's hands, so that he had an opportunity to make deductions, and give the purveyors less than they were entitled to. There was never any leakage in my exchequer. I always knew how much was paid out and how much was left in, and the amounts always tallied. It was the poor natives who suffered.

You will perhaps think it inconceivable that none of the men who were cheated ever complained to me; and, indeed, I am myself astonished, when I look back, that they did not. But Islam was a big, strong fellow, and the Mussulmans stood in great awe of him. In fact, they feared him as they would an Asiatic despot, and never dared to say a word, but held their tongues and accepted whatever he chose to give them, especially as, I heard at Kum-köll, he threatened to break the head of any man who dared to complain to me. As long as he was amongst them, therefore, they were afraid to speak, but now that he was gone the truth came out. "Oh, God! how many there are," they cried, "who have had to weep because of him!"

On the ferry-boat, and across the Desert of Cherchen, the only occasions when Islam Bai worked under my own eye, he was the same steady, trusty servant that he had been all through my journeys in 1893-97. It was for this reason that I chose him to take charge of my headquarters camps, and did not take him with me on my long excursions. When I returned from them nobody made any complaints, everything seemed to be in the best of order. The circumstance that we were generally separated will explain to a large extent why it was I never noticed any irregularities. Besides, I should never have suspected Islam Bai. I placed the very highest confidence in him; to that extent I am answerable for his misfortune. Psychologically, I soon unriddled the causes of his fall. For three years he had always been the chief man in my caravan. From being a simple groom with a horse-caravan that plied between Osh and Kashgar, I had promoted him to be caravan-bashi, and out of gratitude for this he had served me with exemplary devotion. During this present journey also he had been my right-hand man until the arrival of the Cossacks. They were, of course, much more useful than Islam, and I naturally valued their society more. Hence, while the Cossacks were employed on more personal services to myself, Islam looked after the Mussulmans and superintended the harder work of camp-life. He was piqued at being thrust into the background by "unbelievers," and I have no doubt he reasoned within himself in this way: "If I am to give way to them, I will at least have some recompense." And so he began his peculations at Yanghi-köll, and continued them all the time we were at Charkhlik. I was very sorry for the poor fellow, and made up my mind that I would endeavour, as far as possible, to mitigate his punishment, especially as Mussulmans generally exaggerate in their accusations. Yet, even though only the half of what they charged him with were true, it was sufficient so send him to Siberia. But I did not forget that in the Takla-makan Desert he had saved for me 23 yambas (say over £200), and on numerous other occasions had rendered me great and invaluable services.

But in the meantime several other disagreeable stories came to light, which made me completely indifferent to his fate. At Yanghi-köll he had taken three young "wives," one of whom, a daughter of Mirab, had cost him 100 sär (£15-£20) at a time when he had not received more than 30 sär of his wages. During the twelve days he stayed in Cherchen, whilst I made my forced ride to Andereh, he had taken another wife, and now again in Charkhlik he had "married" yet another. These ladies he had dismissed from favour one after another, as he moved from place to place, and now that he was starting finally for Kashgar, he washed his hands of them all. The worst side of this hateful business was that all the time he had his own lawful wife and five children at home at Osh. Now it is an expensive business to maintain five wives. In the first place, the lady had to be bought for ready money; then she had to be dressed, and her taste for Chinese silks and so forth had to be gratified; and, finally, she, and perhaps also her parents, had to be supported. This last would of course be readily accomplished with the aid of my stores, so that it would seem to have been I who paid the piper, and not Islam.

Perhaps I had better give here the end of his story. As soon as he arrived at Kashgar, Consul-General Petrovsky examined his effects, but failed to find much ready money. Such as he did find, however, was restored to those from whom it had been taken. Islam was allowed to retain his freedom, but was forbidden to leave Kashgar. When I arrived at that city in May, 1902, he was still unemployed. He came out as far as Yappchan to meet me, and flung himself at my feet, bathed in tears. I was heartily sorry for the man, he looked so pale and haggard, and realised that he had ruined his life. I earnestly besought him, at his trial, which was about to take place in Kashgar, to keep strictly and faithfully to the truth. If he did so, he should escape punishment; but if he lied I should without further consideration leave him to the tender mercies of the Russian law. He promised he would follow my advice. Had he behaved as well on this journey as on the former, he would have been a man of consequence in his own native town. His name was already known throughout the whole of Central Asia, but now it would be synonymous with reprobation. When the trial came on, and the witnesses were examined, Islam was cold and hard, and stubbornly denied every point of the accusation. He could not be brought to admit even the most obvious peccadillo, but swore that it was all a base calumny from beginning to end. I reminded him that it was in his own interest to confess, but all to no purpose. Not a voice was raised in his defence. He was ordered to report himself to Colonel Saitseff at Osh, the town where, according to the Russian law, the sentence was to be pronounced. He arrived there shortly after I did, but again denied everything. As by his thefts he had offended against the Russian Criminal Code, and by his loose conduct transgressed against the *Sheriet*, or customary law of the Mohammedans, he was declared worthy of banishment to Siberia; but his actual punishment was reduced to three months' imprisonment. At my special intercession, this was still further reduced to 14 days, for he still had his co-religionists to reckon with. The Russian authorities had promised to allow him the privilege of wearing a gold embroidered *khalat*, in honour of the services he had rendered to me; this, and all other dignities and honours, he had forfeited by his arrogance and folly. This was the end of Islam's saga. I never saw him again.

The moral of the whole story is—never trust a Mussulman. You would think that after a man had served you faithfully for so many years, and been the recipient of so many favours you could trust him with untold gold. But not so the Mohammedans; they never forget they are serving an "unbeliever." From the moral point of view, these Central Asiatics stand at a low level; but they must not be judged too severely; their conditions of life are exceptionally hard. The Mongols stand incomparably higher than they do, and when you have the good fortune to be accompanied by an escort of Cossacks, you need only employ Mohammedans for the more laborious tasks. Several of my Mohammedan servants, however, such as Turdu Bai, Kutchuk, Khodai Kullu, and Ördek, were first-rate fellows ; but they were never exposed to severe temptation.

IX.

Across Tibet from North to South.

Travelling Amongst the Clouds.

CHAPTER XII.

ACROSS THE BORDER RANGES TO THE KUM-KÖLL.

ON the 17th of May I was at last able to take the saddle again for a full year's further wandering through the vast wastes of Central Asia. I set forth with fresh courage and high expectations to explore the most inaccessible regions of the continent If I succeeded in my plans there would remain, relatively speaking, little of that part of the world which I had not visited. I hoped much from this journey, but was fully aware that it would prove to be the most difficult of any I had yet undertaken. Yet somehow difficulties have their attractions. In the midst of the hard and unremitting labour which each day brought with it I was stimulated by the thought of the adventures which awaited me "Over de höje Fjælde" (across the mountains high).

But before we left the hospitable little town on the edge of the desert we made an unpleasant and disconcerting discovery. On the afternoon of the day before we were to start there arrived a caravan of ten Mongol pilgrims from Tarbagatai, with eleven horses and twelve camels, who pitched their tents in the grove a short distance from the bazaar. Shagdur and our Lama had met them in Kara-shahr, and knew that they were bound for Lassa, and the Mongols, too, were fully aware that there was a big caravan somewhere in the neighbourhood, for two or three of them spoke Turki. We could not of course start without being seen. When Sirkin rode past their camp with the pack-horses, they asked him point-blank where he was going to, and he answered that he was on his way to Ladak and Kashgar. Shagdur and the Lama and I were most anxious not to be seen. The first two started early in the morning, and made a wide detour to the west, while I struck up the river-bed, accompanied by Khalmet Aksakal and that worthy old gentleman Togdasin Beg, of Charkhlik—he who had guided us through the bed of the Ettek-tarim. As soon, however, as we got out of sight of the trees of the oasis we joined forces with Shagdur and the Lama. The Mongols had not, at any rate, seen me, so that if we should meet again under critical circumstances, they would be unable to identify me.

But why all this needful precaution against a band of peaceful Mongols, who would not harm even a cat? The reason was they would reach Lassa before we did, and would unfailingly report that we were coming. It is true, their camels were very much done up, and it would take them a long time to get to Tsaidam, where they would, as usual, exchange their animals for horses. But, even allowing for that, they would travel easier and faster than we should, for we were intending to cross the very worst parts of Tibet. And, in spite of our precautions, my forebodings proved true.

The caravan with which I now crossed the northern ranges of the Kwen-lun system consisted of Shagdur, Sirkin, Mollah Shah, and Li Loyeh, together with the Lama and a guide, and we had twelve horses and the dog Yolldash. The mountains towered in front of us in overpowering majesty; south-east was the throat of the glen out of which the Charkhlik-su emerged, and to the south stretched the Kurruk-sai and the Korumluk-sai, which we had first to traverse. The glen by which the river pierced the northernmost range of the Astyn-tagh was too deep and rough to be ascended. The sun burned, and the gnats were hungry; but they disappeared as soon as we reached the barren, desolate country which ran up to the foot of the mountains. In the distance, on the left, we perceived a few solitary horsemen watching us: they were Mongols.

The first place we camped at was called Yiggdelik-tokai, on the left bank of the Charkhlik-su. The water was a muddy red, and foamed along at the bottom of a trench 130 feet deep, hemmed in by precipitous cliffs of gravel-and-shingle. We reached the stream by means of a break-neck path down the cliffs. Here, in spite of the violent storm which came on in the afternoon, accompanied by a considerable drop in the temperature, Khalmet Aksakal and Togdasin Beg, who had hitherto been our guides, turned back and left us.

Next morning it was fresh and cool, and we found it expedient to don warmer clothing. Soon after starting we entered the echoing gorges of the Stony Valley, having on either hand

Our Camp in the Glen of the Charkhlik-su.

cliffs of granite, striped black or red, and hard, dark-coloured schists. The prospect was for the most part bounded by bare, jagged peaks, though every now and again we obtained, up the successive side-glens, a magnificent panorama of mountains, rising higher and higher, one behind the other—a chaos of pinnacles, summits and mountain groups, with picturesque snowfields hanging at intervals from their shoulders. The bottom of the glen was littered with blocks of gravel-and-shingle, and fragments of granite of various sizes, which made riding irksome. Tamarisks and wild briars abounded, and at one place, Tograk-bulak, there were a few solitary, but beautifully green, poplars. The rain during the night had given rise to a rippling brook. I was completely fascinated by the bold and sublime features of the landscape. After our long winter amid the monotonous and sterile deserts, it was perfectly delightful to let our eyes rest again upon the ever-changing variety of the mountains, to hear our voices flung back by the echoing cliffs, and to feel our lungs expand with the pure crisp mountain air, free from all admixture with the everlasting dust and sand.

Sometimes the glen was so narrow that we had to climb over the low buttresses which jutted out at the side. We were now travelling east, and after riding over a detached group of heights, we turned into the main valley of the Charkhlik-su. The river was considerably swollen from the rain, and in a sharp bend, near the end of the gorge, we pitched our tent for the night under a solitary poplar. Here we had to wait a whole day for ten asses which I had hired to accompany us to the Kum-köll with maize for the horses. But nobody objected to the delay in such a beautiful locality, for we had plenty to do, and there was quite as much grazing as we wanted. But besides that, there was no need to hurry. We should any way reach the rendezvous before the slowly-moving camels.

The asses came up before nightfall, and next day we resumed our journey. It was a stiff march we had before us, up the deep-cut glen, in which the grey granite cliffs, in places undermined by the tumultuous flood, hung over like a vault or roof. We knew we had to cross the Charkhlik-su no less than sixteen times, and consequently would have to keep a sharp look-out. A shepherd whom we met gave us anything but encouraging news. His horse had fallen in the middle of the stream, and he had lost the whole of its load of bread, maize and clothes. The river, which had a volume of 318 cubic feet in the second, was churned into foam as it thundered amongst the water-worn rocks. But, thanks to our care, we suffered no mishap. The Mussulmans, lightly clad, tried every ford before we ventured to cross, and the horses which carried the most valuable loads were led cautiously across one by one. At one of the fords, one of two mules which we had with us refused to follow the other animals, but thought she would go over a little at one side. But she lost her footing and was swept away by the stream, and flung upon a bank of gravel a good bit lower down. The Cossacks dashed in with their clothes on, and got her upon her feet again; but the whole of her load, which luckily consisted of flour and bread, was lost. Unfortunately we were now enveloped in a thick mist, and in the dim afternoon light the mountain peaks disappeared like the roof of a temple amid clouds of incense. Indeed, the spot where we encamped was known as Mesjid or Meschit-sai (the Mosque Valley).

On the 4th day we turned our backs upon the Charkhlik-su, and struck up a side-glen, narrower and wilder than even the preceding. So steep indeed did it become at last that we preferred to get off and walk; in some places we had literally to clamber up hand over hand. To get pack-horses up these steep places was a decidedly awkward business: their loads kept slipping off behind them, or turning round underneath them, and we were incessantly putting them to rights. There was seldom any track visible on the stony, gravelly surface—in point of fact, the route was very seldom used. On a projecting crag above our heads we once caught a glimpse of three *arkharis* or wild sheep; but they were too far off for the Cossacks to get a shot at them. At length we reached a deep notch in the next range, called Yaman-davan, or the Bad Pass; and a suitable name it was, for its summit was so sharp and difficult that there was only room for one horse to stand on it at a time. On both sides the pass was shut in by wild and lofty cliffs. On the east the descent was very much less steep, and the surface was covered with earth and overgrown with grass. The air was now clear again, and the view magnificent. Nor could we complain of the heat, for on the summit of the pass the thermometer registered only 2°.6 C. or 36°.7 Fahr.

Next day we continued up a new gorge, which at first was so narrow and difficult that in one place, where it was completely choked with granite débris, we were forced to unload the animals, and by our united efforts haul them one by one

The Last Sharp Turn in the Transverse Glen of the Charkhlik-su. Immediately Below the View Shown on p. 207.

up a rocky step or threshold, twelve or thirteen feet high. But, beyond that, the glen widened out again, and the going was easier. We observed no signs of animal life except partridges and "mountain swallows." Two or three of the horses and one of the mules were going stiff and lame in consequence of the hard and stony character of the path. That evening we encamped at a place called Tölkölik, where the thermometer registered only 5°.4 C. or 41°.7 Fahr., though during the night it fell to −6° C. or 21°.2 Fahr. Winter in the middle of summer! That year my summer lasted little more than six weeks in all.

On the 23rd of May a long and tiring march led us out upon open plateau-like uplands (*vidder*), a highland steppe in fact, carpeted in places by the yellow withered grass of the year before. We had crossed the last of the border-ranges, and were on the Tibetan tableland. The kulans now began to show themselves by ones and twos. And our arrival was greeted by heavy, dark clouds which at intervals shook out their contents over us in the form of rain and snow. Towards evening, when riding down a scarped ravine, we came, at a place called Hashek-lik, across our old friend the Charkhlik-su. Here its volume was less, and its water of a peculiar milky-white colour, evidently caused by its springing out of or passing through some species of disintegrated white rock.

Shereb Lama, in his red robe, his yellow girdle, and his blue cap, which he protected in rainy weather by a Mongolian *bashlik* (hood), was the most picturesque member of our caravan. He was already on a footing of intimacy with both Shagdur and myself; but he made little acquaintance with the others, for as yet he could only speak a few words of Turki. But he was quick at learning, and soon began to pick it up. During these long marches he was very thoughtful, though what he thought about I do not know, unless it was about the strange company he had got into. It was an awful business to initiate his priestly reverence into the utility of astronomical observations and map-making. He evidently regarded me as a wonderful person, and he clung to me with unshaken confidence, even showing a degree of affection that was touching. He understood perfectly well that, though we were strangers, we should do him no harm. Every afternoon he gave me a lesson in Mongolian. I wrote down lists of words and phrases, and learnt them ready for the next day, and I have seldom had a pleasanter teacher. He was most anxious that I should make haste and learn his language sufficiently to be able to discuss with him the subjects in which he was most interested.

We gave the horses a day's rest on the meadows of Hasheklik, but we had raw wintry weather, with snow and hail, so that it was impossible to work in the open air. I therefore called in the Lama for a talk, for, whatever might happen in the future, I did not wish him to think or believe that I had deceitfully led him on into any crazy-brained adventure. I wanted to give him an opportunity of returning, if he were so minded, to his own country before his reputation was compromised, and so I thought it best to tell him now, before we went further, that I intended accompanying him and Shagdur to Lassa, disguised as a Mongol. The news filled him with consternation, and he tried to convince me that it was utterly impossible. Nobody would dare to touch me and Shagdur; but he, being a lama, would be sure to lose his life. He was not afraid of the Dalai Lama, or of the Mongol or Chinese pilgrims in the city; but he was afraid of the Tibetans who watched the roads to it.

"If they do not kill me," he said, "they will destroy my career as a lama; I shall be looked upon as a renegade and traitor, who guided a European to Lassa."

Yet even now his resolution wavered, and he proposed that the whole caravan should march straight for the city. The worst that could happen to us would be that we should be firmly but politely turned back. He could then disguise himself as a Turk, and none of his friends in Lassa would have the least suspicion that he was with us. But when I stuck to my plan he proposed that I should call myself a Urankha—a people dwelling in the Altai Mountains, who are adherents of Lamaism, but speak a Turki dialect, resembling Jaggatai Turki, in which I was perfectly at home.

We spent the whole day discussing this matter, and by the time we had done, the Lama was greatly disturbed and upset. He agreed, however, to accompany us as far as the Kum-köll, whence, I promised him, if he were so minded, he might return home. Some of the ass-drivers, who would be no longer needed, were in any case to return from that lake, and he might go back with them to Charkhlik. He was, he said, afraid of the summer in the lowlands, and would prefer to go to Chimen. I at once saw through him: he meant to go and join the Mongol caravan and accompany them to Lassa, where in some unguarded moment he would be led to betray my plans.

Our Camp at Unkurluk, Looking up the Side-Glen.

That must be prevented at all costs. Whether we tried to get into Lassa or not, there was one very important service that he could render me. I needed an interpreter in Tibet. If my long tramp through unknown Tibet was not to lose half of its value, it was of the utmost importance that I should be able to converse with the people I met in the course of it. I explained all this to the Lama, and he at once saw that I was right. Finally, I proposed to him that he might remain behind with the caravan whilst I and the two Buriat Cossacks went to Lassa But this again did not suit him : he was not without his ambition, and he was no coward, as he proved on several subsequent occasions.

The following days he was silent and depressed, and rode by himself, thinking, no doubt, that he had drifted into queerer company than he had at first imagined. After this he was never quite friendly with Shagdur : he considered, and rightly too, that Shagdur ought to have acquainted him with my secret purpose before they left Kara-shahr. I explained to him that Shagdur had acted by my express order, and that, if he had let it be known that a European was thinking of going to Lassa in disguise, there was not a single lama from one end of Mongolia to the other that would have accepted his offer. Every day after this, both when we rode along the valleys and when we stopped in the twilight, we discussed our plans about Lassa. Shereb Lama underwent a veritable martyrdom of the spirit. I found great pleasure in his company : he was one of the best men I have ever associated with. For piety, resignation, and genuine goodness he would bear comparison with his colleague in *Kim*, one of the best characters Kipling has ever drawn. For the present, then, the arrangement stood thus : he was to accompany us to the Kum-köll, and there make his decision. He would then be like Hercules at the parting of the ways : on the one hand he could return to his quiet and peaceful cell in the monastery at Kara-shahr ; on the other hand, he would have to make up his mind to face many remarkable, if not perilous, experiences.

During the next few days we crossed several of the contributories which flowed north-west to join the Charkhlik-su. Upon reaching the big cauldron-shaped valley or corrie of Unkurluk, which we did in a heavy snowstorm, we saw several herds of sheep scattered over the surrounding mountain slopes ; but though the Cossacks scoured the neighbourhood, they failed to find any traces of human beings. A little higher up we stopped at the entrance of a side-glen, where there was good grass, though no water; and as soon as the air cleared a little, we perceived two tents and ten or a dozen men. The Cossacks rode to the mountaineers to buy from them fuel and milk, and a dozen or so of sheep. They learned that there were eighteen shepherds settled there, in charge of sheep and horses from Cherchen, spending the winter in wretched earthen caves, partly covered with felt mats. The district abounded in game and other animals—arkharis, ibexes, yaks, bears, and wolves. But since the autumn before the shepherds had seen no yaks: those animals frequent higher altitudes in the summer. Partridges were calling to one another all over the mountain-sides; and the Cossacks went out and shot a few brace. That afternoon it snowed thick and fast, and we were again in the midst of winter.

It was cold and wintry weather when we left the Valley of the Earth-Caves on the 27th May. Here we dropped the guides from Charkhlik and five of the asses, whose loads of maize were consumed, and took in their stead three of the shepherds, and a dozen rather poor sheep, without fat tails. We were now at a considerable altitude (12,458 feet), as was evident from our difficulty in breathing, though as yet nobody showed symptom of mountain-sickness.

The following day we crossed four easy secondary passes, and after traversing an undulating country covered with snow, reached the Valley of Kar-yaggdi, and a spring, from which gushed the brightest of sparkling waters. Snow-clad mountains shut in the view on the south and south-east. The glen ascended by an easy, pleasant gradient, and down its middle meandered the several arms of a brook, which issued from the fresh-fallen melting snow, and was tinged red by the finely disintegrated sandstone of the locality. Shortly afterwards we crossed over a pass, which, although quite easy and gentle, was yet one of great geographical importance, in that it formed the water-shed between East Turkestan and the valley of Chimen. Its altitude was 13,383 feet, and the snow lay quite thick upon it.

We reached the broad valley of Chimen by an open glen, which ran towards the south-east, having the snowy ridge of Piazlik spread out in a glorious panorama before us. It was now colder and more wintry than it was in the previous October, and, summer though it was, all the mountains, except the top-

Buying Sheep from the Shepherds of Unkurluk.

most pinnacles, were wreathed in snow. We encamped on the left bank of a stream, which lower down joined the Togri-sai.

Here Shagdur suddenly became very ill; his pulse went up to 134, and his temperature to 38°.6 C. or 101°.5 Fahr. I may say that my own temperature, even at 13,000 feet and above, seldom exceeded 36°.0 C. or 96.°8 Fahr. Here we had to stop a day to nurse the sick man. Sirkin went out with his gun and brought back two orongo antelopes, so that we were able to give our sheep a few days' longer reprieve. At this season the antelopes were very lean, for the new grass had not yet sprung up. They were fatter and better in the autumn. On the 30th Shagdur was better, and positively insisted that we should go on. We crossed the broad stream of the Togri-sai, and penetrated the transverse glen which cut south-east through the mountain range of Piazlik. The weather was splendid, not a shimmer of cloud marred the pure turquoise blue of the sky, and the fresh-fallen snow for the most part melted and evaporated.

After advancing for a good bit up the glen, we missed the invalid and the Lama, and I sent back Li Loyeh to see what had become of them. When a little later they all three came up, Shagdur was faint and giddy, and scarcely able to sit in the saddle. I took some alcohol out of one of the flasks for zoological specimens, and made him a stiff glass of hot grog, and packed him in felts till he perspired. Towards evening he was decidedly better; his temperature dropped to 37°.2 C. or 98.°9 Fahr., and his pulse to 112. Except for this alcohol, I carried no spirits with me; and I will say, to the honour both of the Cossacks and the other men, none of them seemed to miss them. Spirits are an intolerable nuisance in a caravan; they slacken discipline and undermine the men's strength. Here, again, we rested a full day, to give the invalid an opportunity to get thoroughly well; and by the time we reached the lake of Kum-köll he was quite recovered.

It was the 1st of June when we struck the lake. We were travelling south-east across excellent ground, when in the distance we first caught sight of its immense, bright, ultramarine blue water. In the east the range of Kalta-alagan presented its vast dimensions to us in shortened perspective, its crest showing up dim and white. Every watercourse and ravine was dry; the lake had just then no active contributories. Hence it cost us a long search for water. At length one of the shepherds showed us a place where he thought we might obtain fresh water by digging a well, and his surmise proved to be correct. The district abounded in kulans and orongo antelopes.

Here, according to agreement, we were to wait for the caravan. We waited the 2nd of June, we waited the 3rd of June; but no caravan turned up. The surface of the Kum-köll was ruffled with pretty big waves by a strong east wind, whose monotonous whining was the only sound that broke the silence of the wilderness. At times there was a mist; but even when it was clear we were unable to see the eastern shore of the lake. The wind was fresh and cool, like a sea breeze; in fact, when it brought with it squalls of hail or snow, it was a good deal too cool. The shepherds, who had now accomplished their task, were impatient to go home. After stowing beside the Cossacks' tent the three ass-loads of maize which were still left, they set off to return. I cannot imagine anything more tedious than month out, month in, to wander amongst those mountains, watching other people's sheep. And yet the shepherds were happy and contented enough; a very small thing delighted them down to the ground. For my own part, I found it a sufficient trial of patience to have to wait over two days for the caravan. I began to wonder if anything had gone wrong with it, although I knew it was in the trusty hands of Chernoff, Cherdon, and Turdu Bai.

Meanwhile Shagdur was treated with massage and cold bandages, and gradually recovered. Sirkin rode to our camp of the year before, on the north-west side of the lake, to measure a line for controlling my itineraries. And there he left a sign-post—a piece of wood with a hand drawn on it, pointing towards our camp in the west—in case the caravan should strike the lake on that side.

The 4th of June was a beautiful day, the atmosphere being perfectly clear, so that we were able to follow the Kalta-alagan right away to its outermost extremities. Its crest appeared to vanish to a needle point. The lake presented a fresh play of colour—light green, striped with white foam. The horses were grazing some distance from the camp, and most of the men were asleep; but our Lama maintained an incessant look-out for the caravan. He was greatly interested in my telescope, and very fond of using it. I was working in my yurt, when he came and said he thought he could see them coming. I took the telescope, and sure enough there they were at the foot of the mountains—a long black line, followed by several small dots.

Nothing more was done that day; we were all too much interested in watching the progress of the caravan.

The distance was still too great for them to be able to see our tents; but instead of steering directly towards our camp, they were travelling due east. Then, to our great surprise, they stopped, unloaded, and turned the camels loose to graze. I sent Mollah Shah to them. At length we saw a horseman ride out and meet him, and both continued to their camp. Then the camels were again driven together, and the caravan once more got under way, the long line curling round like a railway train circling round the end of a valley. Then from behind a detached

The Camel-Loads Stacked Beside the Kum-köll.

group of hills in the east there emerged a solitary rider, approaching at a good hand-gallop. It was Kutchuk. Chernoff, the caravan leader, had sent him off two days before in advance, to report their approach. Kutchuk had seen Sirkin's sign-post on the north side of the lake, and had at once understood its meaning. He rode my old Kashgar horse, and brought nothing but good news.

Meanwhile the caravan was approaching in good order. The two Cossacks galloped up and, saluting in military fashion, reported that all was well. Men and animals were alike in first-rate condition. One mule, however, had been left behind at Baghtokai, as unfit for work. I gave her to some of the men who were returning, to see if they could make anything of her. Next came the ass caravan, with Dovlet Caravan-bashi at its head; and in the rear of this motley company appeared a kulan, galloping amid a cloud of dust straight towards our camp. But when he perceived he was running into danger, he turned tail and went off towards the west.

Next arrived Turdu Bai, leading his camels; they were fat and in excellent condition, and full of play, evidently well content with the cool mountain air. And no wonder they rejoiced at being freed from the oppressive heat and murderous insects of the lowlands. During their rest-days on the march the men had made *chapans*, or "white felt rugs," to protect them against the extreme changes of temperature. The three little ones with their white coats were a pretty sight as they trotted at their mothers' heels—in fact, the youngest of them skipped and jumped about without showing the least signs of fatigue. He was only a few days old when he got up into the rarefied mountain air, so that his lungs became adapted to it in good time; it was to this circumstance, I feel sure, that he showed a greater power of endurance than the other two, and long survived them both. Even the stag, which generally accompanied the camels, had put on flesh. He had only one fault; he would eat too much maize, and refuse to touch the yellow mountain grass.

Last in the procession came the horses, with their loads and drivers. Each detachment defiled in front of me and the Cossacks, who were standing beside me, and as they marched past the men saluted politely. It took some time for the full cavalcade to pass in review. Then they pitched their tents and stacked their baggage immediately south of our camp, arranging the loads so as to make an enclosure or fold for the sheep. Of these we had quite a flock; on the march they obediently followed Vanka, a ram from Kuchar. This animal had been with us ever since the autumn of 1899, and was the only one out of all the animals of the caravan which was still with us when, a year later, we returned to Kashgar.

When the camp was all ready, the shore of the lake resembled a lively *corso*, with groups of men chatting round the fires, the animals scattered all over the niggardly steppe, trying to pick up what they could. Meanwhile the water beat—beat against the shore, for the lake was again churned up by a regular easterly gale, and down came the rain thick and fast until our settlement was drenched.

The Camels on the Shore of the Lake of Kum-köll.

A whole day was spent in making arrangements for a fresh start. For the first thing, I re-packed my own travelling cases, so that I might have ready to hand in the two which always stood inside my yurt such instruments and other things as I should want every day. The meteorological observatory, which Sirkin took charge of, was kept in a special box, under his own eye. Then the preserved foods which would be required in the immediate future were also packed up separately.

The time was now come for our Lama to make his final decision as to whether he would accompany me or return, and his decision was already made—with the help of Li Loyeh. The latter, who had performed his duties irreproachably for close upon a year, now wished to leave me, alleging that he had learned his old father had died in Keriya, and he must go home to look after his own interests. But I did not take him seriously, for twice before, when we were in the middle of the desert, he had dished up the same story. Had he not been paid half a year's wages in advance at Charkhlik, it would not have mattered much. In fact, it was strange he had not simply run away, for he rode his own horse, and it was one of the very best in the caravan. Now our Lama had made up his mind to go with Li Loyeh, his intention being to find out the Mongol caravan in the Chimen valley or Tsaidam. But, when he learned that Master Li Loyeh was not to be allowed to return, even though we had to keep guard upon him, he changed his mind, came to me in my yurt and declared that, let happen what would, he would follow me to the end of the world. The only condition he made was, that in case he fell ill, I would not desert him ; but I soon convinced him that he had nothing to fear on that score, for we never deserted even our animals until their case was absolutely hopeless. This matter therefore was soon settled. Without the Lama we could scarcely have made our way through the inhabited parts of Tibet ; and Li Loyeh, whose real name was Tokta Ahun, although a little bit "dotty," was a general favourite. He told funny stories and related comical anecdotes, and did his work splendidly all the way to Ladak.

Finally, I called together all the Mussulmans, and formally nominated Turdu Bai *tugachi-bashi*, or "leader of the camels," while Hamra Kul, a big, strong man from Charkhlik, who had his son, Turdu Ahun, a lad of 16, with him, was appointed *att-bashi*, or "leader of the horses." The other men were straightly enjoined that in everything which concerned the animals they were to render implicit obedience to these two. Mollah Shah, on the other hand, was not promoted, because, on the way up to the Kum-köll, when set to guard the horses, he did not know when they all ran away. By evening, it is true, he managed to recover them all except five, which did not turn up till the following morning. The Cossacks ranked, of course, above the Mussulmans, and each had his own special duties to perform, besides looking generally after all the rest.

CHAPTER XIII.

FRCM THE KUM-KÖLL TO THE ARKA-TAGH.

THE next day was the first, since I began my tramp through Central Asia, that I had the whole of my caravan collected together in one place. We were now to march in a solid body south through Tibet. The work of striking camp and loading up proceeded pretty smartly, for each man had his own appointed duty to do. Whilst some of them took down the tents, and re-packed the boxes which we used every time we stopped, others lifted the loads upon the camels and horses, and as each section got ready it started off by itself.

First went the camels in five different groups, each with its leader, Turdu Bai himself riding at the head. Amongst the animals, as amongst the men, some possessed special features of interest, *e.g.*, the three young camels which trotted at their mothers' heels. The youngest, although only a little more than a month old, easily did his 23½ miles without being distressed. Amongst the bigger camels, the tall, handsome *bughra* (male), which helped me through the desert of Keriya in 1896, and which we had bought again recently in Charkhlik, was especially noticeable. Nahr, the dromedary, which had crossed the Gobi with us to Lôu-lan, always wore a muzzle, to prevent him from biting the others. The two *artans* (castrated males) which had taken part in all three desert journeys, and one of which I had ridden, being the quietest, carried my instrument cases. My old riding-camel was one of the nine which survived to Ladak

The horses and mules, to the number of 45, were also led or driven in separate groups, each accompanied by men on foot, to see that the loads rode level, and did not fall off. The sheep followed Vanka, and scarcely required looking after. We had eight dogs, which ran and frisked about the animals, as if the whole were a huge joke. As for the stag, the very first day he turned unwell and was unable to keep up, nor could he eat his maize. When I saw that he had not strength to travel with us, I gave orders for him to be killed, although it was with an aching heart I did so ; but I preserved his skeleton.

The asses were always the last to be ready, and we soon left them behind ; in fact, they did not reach camp at all that day. Although they numbered now about 60, only two or three of them lived to the end of the journey.

This long caravan of animals, laden with boxes, cases, tents, yurts, bundles, and sacks, made a picturesque, and even imposing spectacle, as, with slow, heavy tread, they wound through the desolate landscape beside the blue-green lake. Cossacks, Russians, and Buriats, in their threadbare uniforms, and their felts strapped behind them on the saddle—Mohammedans in their chapans and skin caps—ass-drivers, more like a band of banditti and tatterdemalions than anything else—the Lama, in his red robe, turning up, now here, now there, in different parts of the caravan, like a good-natured Puck—all these contributed to make up a varied and lively picture. It put me in mind of an army marching to conquer a new country. And, in truth, that is precisely what we were ; but it was to be a peaceful conquest, namely, to subdue unknown countries to human knowledge. All the men, as well as all the animals, were now in splendid trim ; but how long would they remain so ? Experience had taught me that it was only a question of time before they would begin to melt away. I knew perfectly well that the journey would not be accomplished without victims. I had 30 men, but several of them were to return when we reached the Arka-tagh, including all who attended upon the ass-caravan.

My place was sometimes in the van, sometimes in the rear of the procession ; but my own special work, of which plotting the route was the most important, generally took up the greater part of my time.

At first we travelled south, close beside the lake, but were soon turned south-east by the treacherous marshes and morasses, and then followed the foot of a ridge, having on our left a large lagoon, with intensely salt water. We reached the other side of the ridge over a little pass, which consisted of soft, loose earth, that made it difficult and tiring for the heavily-laden camels. On the other side we were led straight down into a brook, which trickled along a veritable ravine. The bottom was nothing but brick-red mud, in which we should have been smothered, had we not kept to the middle of the brook. Even though the stream was flowing, it was nevertheless in places intensely salt. The camels kept slipping and falling to their knees. With the view of escaping out of this wretched hole, we struck up the first side-ravine we came to, surmounted another pass, crossed another valley, and climbed up to a third pass. This last was hemmed in by steep banks of soft, reddish-brown earth, sculptured into fantastic towers and bastions, so that it was like riding through the ruins of an ancient town.

At sunset we encamped (No. XII.) in the dreariest region it is possible to conceive. We had not indeed expected to find either pasture or fuel; but we did expect to find water. Fortunately about 9 o'clock it began to snow quite briskly. We at once put out all the cups and dishes we had, and in that way gathered sufficient to make a few mouthfuls of tea for each man. The animals were allowed to have as much maize as they could eat; for it was clear that the asses would not be able to go very far, and it was better to use up their loads in this way than to leave them behind or throw them away.

As soon as it stopped snowing we set to work, although it was then late, and dug a well; but, after getting down 3¼ feet, we gave it up as a bad job. Next morning, however, there was a pretty large pool, big enough to supply all the men, and all the dogs as well. Dovlet came up with half of his ass-caravan. That day we did a short journey, so as to give the rest of it a chance to catch us up.

Chernoff had already reconnoitred the country ahead, and now led us south-west, across hard, firm ground, with scanty clumps of yappkak, networked in every direction by kulan tracks. We could still make out the range of the Kalta-alagan to the north; but the lake which lay on this side of it was hidden by the hills we crossed the day before. By this we were quite familiar with the characteristic Tibetan weather—violent hail-storms, followed immediately by sunshine, or a bright sky above head, with black, gravid clouds ringing round the horizon.

The same order which governed the march prevailed also when we stopped for the night. Every evening the camp was arranged on the same plan, so far as the varying contours of the ground would admit of it. At one end of the long row of loads stood Turdu Bai's tent, which he shared with Hamra Kul, Mollah Shah, and Rosi Mollah. The last-named, the Mohammedan priest of the caravan, was a pleasant, trustworthy man from Charkhlik, about 40 years of age, who was able to write. Like Li Loyeh, he rode his own horse, and was paid the same wages as most of the Mussulmans, namely, 8 sär (about 30s.) a month.

The tent at the other end of the baggage was occupied by Kutchuk, who used it as a kitchen for myself and the Cossacks. Cherdon was my own steward, with Kutchuk for his assistant. Chernoff cooked for the Cossacks. In this way our kitchen was separated from that of the Mussulmans, who object to eat with "unbelievers," and have a mortal horror of any cooking-pot into which, by any chance, a piece of bacon might happen to find its way. On the other hand, the Cossacks had just as decided an objection to pollute their cooking-pot with the flesh of the wild-ass, for which the Mussulmans have a special fondness.

The next in the arrangement was the big yurt, occupied by Sirkin, Shagdur, and the Lama. Each man had his own bed, consisting of felts and skins, besides a pillow, and kept his private effects in a box. The natives' personal belongings were not very bulky: in most cases a *kurchin*, or "double knapsack" of leather, was sufficient to contain them all.

Although I issued strict orders to Shagdur to abstain from hard work after his illness, before many days he was hard at it again, lifting boxes and sacks with the best of them. As for our Lama, I had given him to understand that, being a "Doctor of Divinity," he need not perform any of the harder work incidental to caravan life, for that belonged to the Mussulmans. His sole duties would be, I told him, to give me lessons in Mongolian, and afterwards, when we got into Tibet proper, to act as my interpreter of Tibetan, or Tangut-kälä, as it is called in Mongolian. These instructions I repeated several times, but it was all to no avail; there was no work which the Lama thought too rough for him, although his soft hands were far more accustomed to handling the holy volumes. He would rush in and lug off the heaviest boxes, or hoist them up as ably as any man in the caravan. Old Turdu Bai just laughed, and chuckled to himself at getting such a useful hand. By this means our Lama earned a certain degree of popularity in the caravan, and piqued the Mussulmans' ambition. A believer could not, of course, allow himself to be beaten by a *Kaper*, or "heathen," who ate swine's flesh. The Lama was a keen observer, and had a wide knowledge of men. Before very long he had taken the measure of every man in the caravan, and grouped the Moham-

Turḍu Bai's Tent.

medans in a double series, one according to their value as workers, the other according to their intrinsic worth as men.

The next tent was Chernoff and Cherdon's little yurt. Chernoff's business was to superintend the actual labour of the caravan; he was held responsible for everybody doing his duty. Cherdon was, as I have said, my body-servant and cook.

At the extreme end of the opposite wing stood my yurt, guarded by Yolldash and Yollbars, whose zeal was often too lively with regard to imaginary enemies—that is to say, our own horses and camels, when they happened to be peacefully roaming about the neighbourhood. For sometimes, when the latter failed to find anything to eat, they would go up to Turdu Bai's tent and beg for maize.

The rest of the men had to content themselves with tents of a more temporary character, such as felt carpets stretched between the camels' loads. They cooked their meals over fires lighted in the streets and market-place of our tented town. Some of them were on duty every night, keeping watch upon the animals, to prevent them from straying too far. In this irksome duty they of course took turns, while Chernoff saw that nobody shirked his turn, sometimes even riding out in the middle of the night to where the animals were grazing, to convince himself that the guards were not asleep. As for the sheep, they were always folded at night, because of the wolves.

Every evening, as soon as the tents were pitched, the camp presented a busy scene of life and movement. The men talked and argued in Jaggatai Turki, Russian, and Mongolian, for about an hour. Then Turdu Bai led off the camels, and Hamra Kul the horses, to pasture, and issued their orders to their subordinates. After that any pack-saddles which had burst open were mended; while the camels or horses which were not up to the mark were kept in camp, and specially looked after. Our fuel consisted now almost entirely of *argol*, or the dung of wild yaks and kulans; although we had a valuable reserve in the strong wooden frames to which the baggage was lashed. As the loads grew gradually less, these saddle-frames became no longer necessary, but were gradually used up, though at first only for starting the other fires. Whilst supper was cooking, the men gathered in groups round the fires, talking or resting. When, as was the case to-day, the usual westerly storm burst over the camp, with a heavy fall of snow, making the country white and wintry in the course of a few minutes, the men simply flung felt carpets over their shoulders, and without further concern, continued the preparations for their supper.

The felts and skins, which made my bed, were placed, like those of the men, immediately upon the ground. As soon as my yurt was up, and my bed ready, I sat down and wrote up my diary for the day. After supper or dinner, call it which you like, I plotted out my map, reckoned the compass-bearings and distances, and marked the situation of the new camp on a general or key map. Thus, I always knew exactly where we were, and could avoid approaching too near to the routes of Mr. Littledale and M. Dutreuil de Rhins on the west, or that of Prince Henri d'Orléans and M. Bonvalot on the east, and at the same time was able to direct our course towards Lassa.

The ass caravan camped separately, close beside ours. As yet only 30 asses had turned up, and we knew nothing of the rest. Next morning, the 8th of June, I sent back the old man Dovlet to see what was become of them.

Meanwhile we continued our journey up a dry ravine, carved through soft disintegrated clay and sand of a red colour. The sky was everywhere clouded, grass was scanty, hares the only animals. After a while the country became difficult. Hundreds of dry watercourses gathered into a glen that pointed towards the north, and was pretty deeply trenched through the hills. We descended into it, and followed the bed of the brook; but it was so soft and loose that the camels splashed the mud about them at every step, and soon began to sink in. Shouts of warning—shouts of encouragement arise every moment. A camel has capsized—a horse has flung off its load—a mule is stuck fast in the mire! The most malevolent imagination could not invent a more irksome and tiresome surface to travel over. Sometimes these deep, but intermittent runnels were no bigger than mere gutters a foot wide. Thousands of them ran together at steep angles to form bigger rivulets, and these again gathered into others still bigger, until, finally, they issued into the main valley which ran down to the Kum-köll. Hence to march along the bottom of the main valley was like walking with leaden soles or heavy weights attached to our boots; for, of course, on ground like that everybody went on foot. In one pool that I stepped into, I left my boot, and dumped into the mud up to the knee. The paths which led to Dante's hell could scarcely be worse than this seven-fold, accursed highway. And the worst of it was, it was taxing the animals' strength to no purpose; in fact, two camels soon became exhausted, and had to be released from their loads. Yet in the distance these heights had looked so easy and innocent that the men had asserted we should have almost level ground to travel over.

At last things grew so bad that we were brought literally to a standstill. Out of this horrible quagmire we must get somehow, and that soon. Turdu Bai proposed to climb up the bank on the left, and summoned a dozen men with their spades and set them to work to prepare a sloping pathway up. Whilst they were doing this, Chernoff rode on to reconnoitre, but soon came back, and said that it was impossible for a man even on foot to advance further in that direction. I at once gave the order right-about-face, and immediately the long procession turned about, each animal on the ground where it stood. This, however, was no easy thing to do, owing to the narrowness of the space. But if going up the ravine was bad, going down it was ten times worse, for the ground was now trampled into mire. After numberless small mishaps, we eventually managed to struggle back out of this treacherous trap. Next we tried another glen, which led up to another pass on the west, and which Sirkin had already examined. The middle of the glen was occupied by a dry watercourse with vertical sides. This we had to cross two or three times, and as the sides consisted of red soil, as loose and soft as flour, it cost us a good deal of spade labour to get up and down. Upon reaching the top of the little pass, I sat and watched the caravan file past me, down into the more open country on the other side. Of the two camels which had given up, we were only able to get one over, and that not without five men bodily pushing him up. He, I saw, would be the next to give in.

Upon reaching a little meadow beside a fresh spring we halted, and for four reasons. In the first place, the pasture was exceptionally good, better than beside the Kum-köll. In the second place, the animals were exhausted. In the third place, we still had to wait for the asses, which were now a long way behind, and were going very badly; several of them had, in fact, perished during the last two days. And, lastly, it was necessary to send scouts to look for a practicable road south, for it was a sheer waste of time to take on the whole of the caravan until we had ascertained what the country was like ahead. Mollah Shah and Li Loyeh were the men chosen for scouting duty, and they were instructed not to return until they had found a decent road.

At three o'clock we had a storm from the west, accompanied by snow, and at nine o'clock a storm from the east. I sat and worked in my furs, half leaning over a brazier, and this was in the—middle of summer, 16° south of London ; but then we were at an altitude of over 13,000 feet above the level of the sea. I felt sorry for the poor camels, being brought into such a cold climate just when they had shed their coats, though we protected them as well as we could with thick felt rugs. All the next day it snowed fast, except that at noon it cleared sufficiently to let me take an observation for latitude. In the afternoon the scouts returned and said they had found a practicable road. Upon this I decided to start at once ; we could wait at the next camp for the asses to catch us up, as well as send out fresh scouts to prepare for the following day's march. It is by no means such an easy thing to travel through Tibet as some people would have us believe ; it requires a very great deal of forethought and study. During the night the temperature fell to $-13°.0$ C., or 18°.6 Fahr., and during the day seldom rose above freezing-point.

Our scouts now led us due south, and although it was good travelling, we soon had to leave behind two of our camels, one of them being the individual which had such a rooted objection to passes. At length we approached the left bank of a considerable stream, the biggest we had seen for some time ; it was full of water, and there were large, thin sheets of ice floating on its surface. We stopped on a hill slope about 100 yards from its margin, at a spot where the first blades of grass were just shooting up. I walked towards the stream, and found myself on the edge of a precipice of loose, vertical gravel-and-shingle, about 76 feet high. Places like that were dangerous for the camels, their heavy weight causing the ground to give way under them. During the course of the evening Dovlet arrived with his 30 asses.

As this was a suitable camping-ground, we remained three days, but led the camels to a safer valley to graze. Six more asses arrived with their burdens intact ; but as we heard nothing of the rest, I sent Cherdon back with some of the mules and horses to help them up. It was three days before he returned, but he brought with him all their loads. One day nine of them had perished, and thirteen on another day, so that only two or three now survived, and they were no longer fit for use. Of the two camels that we left behind Turdu Bai succeeded in bringing in one, the other I entrusted to the care of the ass-drivers, who were returning, desiring them, if possible, to get the animal down to a warmer climate.

The Cossacks spent their time hunting, and shot several orongo antelopes and wild-geese; the latter were resting on their journey north. In the evening Sirkin used to read aloud to his comrades Przhevalsky's *Fourth Journey*, in which they were greatly interested.

Sirkin and Mollah Shah were appointed guides, and went off

View at Camp no. XVI.

with provisions and heavy coats, in case they should not be back before night. This was the 14th June. We had a favourable start, up a broad, open valley, with a gentle ascent, although in places it was dangerous in the lowest parts. Once Chernoff nearly disappeared, horse and all. Wild-geese swarmed everywhere; the men asserted that they were a peculiar species, and were not found north of the upper lake of Kum-köll. One which the Cossacks shot at and wounded, fluttered down into the bottom of the valley. With marvellous agility Ördek scrambled down the steep bank and ran after it; but he forgot where he was, and nearly fainted for want of breath and the violent beating of his heart. After killing the goose he lay flat on his back for a long time motionless. I sent two of the other men to help him, and at the end of an hour he was all right again. Shagdur shot three partridges, and a little bit further on Sirkin shot another orongo antelope. Kulans also abounded, the troops generally numbering about a score. But we saw no wild yaks, although their droppings were abundant.

On and on plodded the caravan to the dull jangle of the big bells. We were directing our steps towards a glen which penetrated the formidable mountain-range that lay across our road. At the entrance of the glen the grass was thick, though short, and the glen was nearly filled with a big sheet of ice. It was just the place for a camp, much too good to be passed by. But hardly was the tent up, when an unexpected incident happened. We had stooped on the very edge of the ice sheet, and on the far side of it the men soon perceived a black object, which they took to be a stone. But it moved. Then they thought it was a young yak deserted by its mother. I heard the Cossacks whispering earnestly together. Presently Chernoff stole towards me with the telescope, and whispered in a state of great excitement, "There's a bear! It's making straight for the camp!" And, sure enough, Bruin, taking not the slightest notice of either the tents or the camels, was marching calmly towards us as though he belonged to us. The dogs were hastily coupled together and led away out of sight, so as not to spoil sport. The Cossacks ran for their horses, for they thought that the bear would soon get scent of us and run away. But I advised them to stay where they were and wait quietly; it was so enjoyable watching the animal's movements through the telescope. Nearer and nearer came the shaggy recluse. He must have been both deaf and blind. He was now actually on the ice, barely 200 paces away. He advanced diagonally across it, making straight for the camp. He moved extremely slowly; evidently he was tired. Every now and again he stopped and sniffed the ground, though all the time he kept his head down. Then he dipped down into a hollow of the ice, and stayed there some time to drink. I advised the hunters to creep close up to the edge of the ice, and there wait for him.

Bruin came on again, marching straight to his doom. The three shots rang out as though they were one. Bruin did not stop, but went off at a gallop up the slope past the camp. The horses were standing ready. In a moment the hunters were in the saddle and after him. Another volley and down

The Tibetan Bear.

tumbled the brute, rolling like a ball to the bottom of the steep declivity. Picking up my big camera, I went to the spot where he lay and took two or three photos of the hermit of the mountains—the Tibetan bear. Then the men flayed him, for I wanted to keep his skin and skeleton. He was well riddled by the bullets. His teeth showed that he was an ancient male, for they were full of gaping, big holes. He must have suffered horribly from toothache, but it was now radically cured. In his stomach we found a marmot, which he had just devoured, and several herbs. The former he had swallowed whole, skin and all, although he had been unable to crush its bones. But he had exercised great ingenuity in making his meal as palatable as possible; for he had skinned the marmot down to its toe ends, rolled the skin up into a ball with the hair inside, and gulped it down whole.

The next day Sirkin and Mollah Shah returned, and undertook to guide us for two days. We had intended to start on the 16th June; but when the men called me in the morning, they told me a violent snowstorm was raging. It had snowed all night, and the snow lay several inches thick on the ground. In face of this, we decided to wait a bit, and we did. It snowed all day, and kept us there all the next night. But on the following day the weather atoned for its own bad behaviour; the sky was pure and bright, and the snow soon disappeared. With Sirkin as our guide, we ascended a very broad, waterless valley, leading up to the Arka-tagh. Except for green sappy moss, the pasture came to an end, and when we at length struck a little spring, we thought it best to halt. Again it snowed, coming on in the afternoon with a north-north-west wind, and the yurts were soon white.

The following day Sirkin again led the way up to a flat, easy pass, and at the end of an hour or so we reached the summit of the range, which for some days past had blocked our road. Then to the south-west there again rose before us another mountain-range, mantled from summit to foot in snow: that could be no other than our old enemy the Arka-tagh. Between the two ranges, but nearer to us, was a basin of self-contained drainage, with a little freshwater lake at the bottom, which was completely icebound. As there was grass beside it, we decided that that should be the place for a stop. Early next morning three men went off to reconnoitre again, with instructions that they were all to return if they discovered grass within about six miles; but if they found none, then one of them was to come back and tell us, whilst the other two went on. At noon, one of the three returned, but it was two days before we saw the others again. They reported that they had discovered a pass, though not a very easy one. From this camp (No. XVIII.), which was 15,529 feet above sea-level, I sent back several of my company. The few asses that survived were in such a pitiable condition that it would have been cruel to take them over the Arka-tagh. I therefore gave Dovlet Caravan-bashi permission to return. At best he would only be able to save half-a-dozen of his animals. I packed up the skeleton and skin of the bear and the stag, and entrusted them to the old man to send on to Kashgar when he got home, for he had horses with him as well as asses. At the same time I sent back three of the men I had engaged at Charkhlik—namely, Niaz, Kader, and Kurban. None of them wanted to go, but we had three men too many, and these were the least useful.

Thus reduced in strength, we resumed our march on the 21st June towards the south-south-west, the ground being in every respect favourable—a gentle ascent, just hard enough to bear the animals, and overgrown with scanty grass. When I speak of grass, I do not wish to suggest an exaggerated idea of the reality. Generally speaking, the region was perfectly barren, except for a few small patches of hard, sharp yellow blades, one or two inches high; this was called grass. I would not advise anybody who was wearing thin summer clothing to fling himself down on "grass" of that description for a siesta; for it was as hard as whalebone, and pierced like a needle through even thick clothes. Yet in that inhospitable country this was the only fodder obtainable.

Shagdur and Sirkin shot two antelopes. When the latter was riding to pick up his game, his horse stumbled head over heels with him, flinging his rider, who rolled for some distance. The horse lay stone dead; either he had broken his neck, or had a stroke. Strange to say, Sirkin, who came limping back, was little the worse for the mishap. He was very sorry to lose his favourite; it was a beautiful and powerful animal, with a long mane, and reminded me of the war-horses of Charles XII.'s time.

Once more our friend the pass-hater failed to come in, and Turdu Bai, who remained behind with him, turned up at night alone. Next morning I sent two men back, with orders to kill him if he refused to follow. But when we got over the Arka-tagh I learned that they had not killed the beast, their hearts having failed them. The camel was strong and well, and they left him to find his way back by the way he had come.

At Camp no. XIX. my old riding-camel, Chong-artan, was seized with some peculiar affection. His hind legs were as if paralysed, and he was unable to move them, except as the men lifted them each in turn. I was always sorry to lose my veterans, and had them looked after with extra care. But even thus early there were no less than nine camels that showed signs of exhaustion. Every evening we gave them a big dose of flour —in fact, we used up that important commodity at such a rate that our supply, which was originally calculated for ten months, was reduced to scarce sufficient for six. On the other hand, the diminution in the number of carriers—the tired camels—made the burdens of the survivors all the heavier, and rather than leave anything behind, we thought it best to use it up a little recklessly. The lame camel was massaged, and released from duty whilst crossing the Arka-tagh ; and he recovered in an amazing way, and was, as I have said, one of the nine survivors which marched into Ladak. His place was always in the van, and he carried a big bell.

The day we reached Camp no. XIX. we did twenty miles ; but it was a long time before we ever accomplished as much again.

CHAPTER XIV.

ACROSS THE ARKA-TAGH IN A SNOWSTORM.

On the 22nd of June I was called at daybreak. The morning was cold and raw, and the yurt but badly warmed, and I made haste to get into my clothes. The caravan, too, was promptly ready, and off we started, keeping as close together as possible, to storm the Arka-tagh. But we had barely got a stone's-throw from camp when one of the camels gave up. We took off his load; he got up, and went on a bit; then he fell headlong on a slope. He was evidently done for, and a slash with a knife put an end to his sufferings.

The sky at starting had not been very promising, and when we were half way up the valley the storm burst—one of the very worst I have ever experienced in Tibet. It was brought by the north-west wind, and shook out tons upon tons of snow and hail over men, camels, horses, mountains—everything. The snow melted on our clothes till we were wet through and stiff with cold. It was in vain we sought shelter against the cutting blast. Although the ascent was nothing worth speaking of, it was nevertheless killing work at that altitude, and in such weather. First one camel and then another stopped exhausted, and refused to advance further. One after one we uncoupled them and left them behind, each in charge of a man.

So blinding was the snow that it was utterly impossible to see where we were going to. At noon it was twilight, and at twilight it was pitch dark. And the snow tumbled down incessantly, until everything was dazzling white, except the stream, which tinkled with a sharp metallic sound as it rippled like a dark winding ribbon down the middle of the valley. I sat leaning forward in my saddle, trying to protect my map as well as I could. Where we were going to I did not know. I simply followed blindly the nearest caravan-bell. Slowly, like snails, like tortoises, we crawled up that wretched pass, the ascent gradually growing steeper as we advanced. Time after time the air was rent with the hoarse scream of the camels. Time after time came the warning shout, "*Tuga kalldi*," *i.e.*, "A camel has stopped!" Then one of the men would take compassion upon the poor beast and draw him aside, and let the others pass, and afterwards follow slowly on in their wake.

The snow grew deeper and deeper. Taking the Lama with me, I pushed on to see if the pass was practicable. In itself it presented no difficulty; but the altitude! the snow! There we sat waiting, waiting, wrapped in our cloaks, seeking what shelter we could behind the horses. The sharp, keen snow crystals cut our faces. We shook and dithered with cold, and gasped for breath. We were 17,025 feet above the level of the sea! Through the howling of the tempest—and it was fiercer than ever up here upon the top—we heard the shouts of the men and the mournful jingle of the bells; but it was a terribly long time before the first emerged like spectres from amongst the "pillars" of driving snow.

Thank God! I thought to myself when I counted the thirtieth camel go past. That was all except four. Two of them had given up at the foot of the last descent, and the other two almost on the very summit of the pass. Amongst them were the oldest of the three young ones and its mother. The horses stood the strain capitally, and the mules were very little the worse. The sheep, too, came through the ordeal splendidly.

On its southern face, the Arka-tagh offered a long, gentle slope, a sort of wide, open rotunda, surrounded on all sides by relatively low mountains. But under foot it was abominable: the fresh-fallen snow was converted into slush, which splashed and "sucked" at every step. We had to make long detours round the worst places. Camping on such ground was, of course, not to be thought of. We should have lost all our camels and packages in the mire. We were now possessed by only one desire, and that was for a dry, firm spot on which to pitch our tents. Grazing—fuel—these were luxuries we did not dream of asking for. At last we reached a gravel slope with moisture trickling through it; and there we pitched our tents.

Turdu Bai and several of the men did not turn up till ten o'clock that night. They had been obliged to leave the four camels behind them, but at daybreak on the 23rd of June they returned, taking horses with them to bring in the camels' loads and the hay in their pack-saddles, if they could not save the animals themselves. But their hopes were deceived. The camels were too far gone, and had to be killed, though we never took the final step until we were perfectly sure the case was hopeless. Thus in one day we lost no less than five camels, the biggest loss I ever had on any of my journeys, even counting that across the Takla-makan in 1896. The main body of the caravan having been thus reduced one-sixth, the loads were too heavy for the survivors. Accordingly I gave orders that both horses and camels should have as much flour and maize as they could eat. Next day we only travelled seven miles.

The principal thing now was to find a suitable camping-ground, so that the animals might rest after their strenuous exertions. This we eventually found on the farther side of a little brook, where a few miserable blades of grass were sprouting. It was as much as ever one of the other exhausted camels could do to reach the spot. A horse, which looked perfectly fresh and well, dropped dead all of a sudden right amongst the tents. This was, however, but a beginning. Every day we lost at least one of our animals. This part of our route could easily have been traced by the dead animals we left behind us. A lugubrious road, when skeletons stand for the milestones! I have frequently observed that a camel will begin to shed tears when it feels death imminent and the blood stiffening in its veins.

The weather now took a turn for the better; the sun was quite warm, and soon dried us after our soaking on the Arka-tagh. This diminished very appreciably the weight of our loads. On the morning of Midsummer Day, although the sky was clear, the country looked decidedly wintry. As soon as I had had my breakfast I went and thoroughly inspected the caravan animals, During the day Hamra Kul, the leader of the horse caravan, was reported to me as being seriously ill; and the man did indeed look wretched. He complained of pains all over his body; but I gave him quinine, and let him ride, for all the Mussulmans had been constrained to walk the day before, after the camels' loads were transferred to their horses.

The next on the list was my favourite riding-horse. He was scarcely able to stand. Our Lama, who in addition to his priestly dignity, was a medico by profession, and lugged about with him a whole chestful of more or less efficient drugs from Lassa, took him in hand, and promised that he would cure him. He opened the arteries in both fore-legs, so that the black blood gushed out by the cupful. Then he bound up the wound, and the horse tottered after us into camp. Several camels were out of sorts; all were tired, and two or three carried no loads.

Midsummer Day passed without any further mishap. We zig-zagged south, in and out, round the countless little fresh-water lakes and pools which lay embedded amongst the low hills, and most of which were sheeted with ice. After a while we saw another imposing range peeping up from behind the hills. Turdu Bai, who always led the way, wanted to cross it by the first pass we came to; but I said, "No; let us follow this wide glen which runs to the west-north-west." We did so, and

Fording a River in Northern Tibet.

stopped at the first pasture we came to, and were there greeted by a stinging shower of hail. Our first care was to examine and classify the animals. Those that were in good condition were let out to graze, but those that were not up to the mark were kept beside the tents. The Lama again bled my horse, and then gave him a long, icy-cold foot-bath in the nearest brook. After this the horse soon grew better, and grazed a bit, and then crunched a handful or two of maize. As we had still six camel-loads of rice left, I gave orders that in future the animals should have rice and maize mixed, partly to keep up their strength until we reached fresh grass, and partly to lighten their loads.

It was now two years since I started on this series of travels, and as I looked back upon the work I had accomplished, I felt I had every reason to be satisfied and thankful.

It was a long time since we had come across any fuel, and the wooden frames of the pack-saddles had been used up as fast as the camels died. I could not work without a little brazier in my tent. It was stinging cold of a morning, and during the night the thermometer generally fell below freezing-point, so that for a couple of hours after daybreak the ground was hard.

On the 25th of June we travelled almost due west, following the latitudinal valley which ran parallel to the Arka-tagh on the south. We did less than twelve miles. I was making for the camp where we had rested on the 28th and 29th September, 1900, the position of which I had determined astronomically, and I now wanted to control it by a fresh series of observations. As is usual in these broad, desolate, sterile main valleys of the northern Tibetan mountain ranges, the scenery was absolutely monotonous, with scarce a trace of animal life. It was an important event when we caught sight of an orongo antelope scuttling across the valley. The surface was undulating, and the view not very extensive. We would see our guide sitting on his horse like a sharp-cut silhouette on the summit of the next ridge, and were led to think that the man had a boundless panorama spread out before him. But nothing of the kind. His road was stopped by another similar ridge, only a short distance in front of him. And so it went on, ridge after ridge, all day long, until we halted beside a tiny lake, ice-bound, but with open shores.

At dusk I inspected the camp as usual. It was seldom I now found everybody well. Hamra Kul was better, but instead of him Rosi Mollah, the priest, had sore-throat, and Mohammed Turdu, the old camel-man, complained of pains in the chest. I gave both of them some medicine, which, thanks to their own imaginations, soon made them better. In the meantime they were exempted from duty. Several of the other men complained of headache, and I gave each of them an antipyrin powder, and comforted them with the assurance that in those high altitudes nobody escaped without signs of *tutek*, or "mountain-sickness." For my own part, fortunately I never felt the least symptoms of it.

My horse was now out of danger, but several of the camels were wretchedly lean. As the two little camel foals were unable to get as much milk as they wanted, I had them fed with flour made into a paste; this they swallowed greedily when we put the balls into their throats. At nine o'clock a storm came from the north, and the temperature went up to 8°.9 C., or 48°.0 Fahr.

We were evidently the first to penetrate amongst those mountains, for we failed to discover the slightest indications of previous visitors. We had long ago burnt our bridges behind us, and we were now entirely dependent upon ourselves. But—in proportion as we advanced amongst those barren and desolate mountains, so were our animals dying one by one, and those that still survived were growing every day weaker.

On the 26th of June we had very peculiar weather, gloriously bright in the morning, with warm summer airs; but it was not long before the wind began to blow with such violence from the west that we, who were riding in its teeth, literally gasped for breath. Even without that, our animals had quite enough to do to struggle along in the rarefied air, and an adverse wind tried them terribly. You might almost speak of a west monsoon, so consistently did the wind blow from one direction. It was precisely the same sort of furious gale, whirling the sand and dust high into the air, and threatening to buckle up tents and yurts alike, that we had encountered at Camp no. LVI. of the autumn before. Our present camp, no. XXIV., thus coincided with Camp no. LXI. of the preceding year, and gave me an invaluable point of control for my map. All that remained of our previous visit were the ashes and embers of our fires. We pitched our tents on the same spot, on the left side of the little brook.

The lake was still, for the greater part, coated with soft ice; it would be the middle of July before the ice all melted, and then early in November it would freeze again. The tendency of the different lakes to freeze, and the periods during which they remained frozen, naturally varied with the size, salinity, and more or less exposed situation of each lake. The little freshwater pools close to the Arka-tagh remained frozen for the greater part of the year. We had, as I have said, summer weather, and at one p.m. the temperature, in spite of the tempest, rose to 20°.0 C., or 68°.0 Fahr. In fact, it was a warm current of air, a sort of *föhn*, which was sweeping across those lofty, icy uplands—a summer wind crossing the ice-bound lakes!

Here we rested a day, and I took advantage of it to fix the position astronomically. Meanwhile Sirkin and Turdu Bai reconnoitred the country to the west, and found no hindrance in our way. The Cossacks, with the view of marking this important point, built a double-headed landmark of slates, on which Sirkin and Shagdur cut their names, whilst on another big slab our Lama engraved his everlasting "*On maneh padmeh hum.*" The *obo* stands on rising ground on the right bank, and will be easy to find should any traveller in the future chance to direct his footsteps into that region. In fact, if he carries my map with him, it is so detailed that he will be able to march straight to our camp. The Mussulmans, not to be outdone by the "unbelievers," built up a bigger pyramid for themselves.

On the 28th we continued south-west along the lake side, and soon came to another lake, which turned us to the south-east; although we were aiming in the former direction, so as

Our Landmark.

to avoid the difficult and mountainous country which we hereabouts got entangled in on our journey of the previous year.

On the 29th June we travelled 16¾ miles, making at first for a low pass, which, like the region in general, was free from snow. Its summit afforded a magnificent view of a fresh latitudinal valley, broad and flat, and studded with lakes. Of these the biggest lay in the south-west, and as it was free from ice we concluded that it was salt. On the farther side, that is the south, it was backed by softly-rounded hills of a fiery-red colour, which contrasted sharply with the glorious, pure ultramarine blue of the lake, especially as both were set in a landscape of monotonous grey.

Our chief want now was water. The watercourse which ran down to the lake contained a brook, but it was salt; nor was there any spring near the left shore. So Shagdur rode on a little bit, until he found a fresh-water spring. At sunset it was a dead calm; but at eight o'clock a gale set in from the north, blowing at the rate of 38 miles an hour. Its somewhat plaintive wail drowned every other sound, except the shrill shouts of the men when anything chanced to break loose or threatened to blow away.

Next morning we crossed the red heights beyond the lake without any trouble, but after that we had an extremely difficult march, for we had to climb over three passes, all cut through the soft red soil, plentifully sprinkled with bright crystals of gypsum. At last we struck a stream, which we soon recognised as the upper course of the one we had recently encamped beside. Had we had the least suspicion of the fact, we should, of course, have avoided the passes, and travelled up the bed of the stream itself, for it ran over hard ground. But, then, we were travelling in an utterly unknown part of the world, and it is just the discovery of these things that constitute the pleasure and fascination of travel.

On the 1st of July we covered almost exactly 17 miles. Before us rose an imposing mountain-chain, its upper reaches capped with snow which glittered like ice. This we had of course to circle round, either on one side or the other. While Chernoff tried it on the west, Cherdon and the Lama went to see what it was like on the east. The former soon came back, and said it would be impossible for the camels to get round that way; the latter reported that we could advance, but must prepare for a stiff climb.

Up we went, at a slow pace, towards the dizzy heights. The path grew steeper. The nearer we approached the snows the bigger waxed the stream, for it was fed by countless rivulets gushing out of every crevice. The water was thick and red, and poured, a heavy sullen flood, down the glen.

Vegetation ceased; there was not even a scrap of moss amongst the gravel. At length we conquered the last steep slope—we were on the top. The camels breathed hard; you could distinctly hear them labouring for breath. Some of the men, who had climbed the ascent on foot to look after the loads, flung themselves down on the ground. Everything danced before their eyes. On the top of the pass stood the Lama, waiting for us, his red robe now rather less conspicuous than usual, owing to the predominant colouring of his surroundings. The rock was red conglomerate, and the whole landscape was tinged with its colour.

Although five of the camels were in a bad way, and three came up minus their loads, they all managed to reach the top of the pass, which was 17,511 feet above the level of the sea, a good deal higher than the Arka-tagh. But the pass was, fortunately, free from snow, and, again fortunately, we were spared the inevitable snowstorm. Leaving the snow-field, a thousand feet or more above us, on the right, we struck down the bare southern face of this dominating mountain-knot. There again we found a considerable stream, which curved away to the south-east, and disappeared amongst the rugged hills. As so often happened before, we were unable to ascertain where it went to; in all probability it emptied itself into some hidden lake. We pitched Camp no. XXVIII. on its right bank.

It had now become part of the established order of the day for the medicine chest to make its appearance at every camp, Chernoff had a splitting headache, Turdu Bai had a sore eye, and when I gave him cocaine its effect produced a profound impression upon the other men. The same result had been produced the day before, when I cured Hamra Kul of toothache with some "drops." Probably it was curiosity rather than actual need that now brought me three fresh patients; one of them, Islam Ahun of Charkhlik, in especial, complained of toothache. The truth was they wanted to see if the effects of the medicine really were in agreement with Hamra Kul's description. The worst case was Mohammed Tokta, who complained of his heart, and suffered from sleeplessness. I gave him morphia occasionally to make him sleep. For a long time past he had done no work, and he was destined never to do any more. My medicine chest was thus looked upon as a miraculous talisman. As soon as I produced it, all the men who were disengaged used to gather outside my tent. Many were the supplicating glances directed towards its brass lock during those long months. For my own part, I was only too glad never to have occasion to make trial of its contents.

On the 2nd of July we also had a good day, doing 16½ miles. The country consisted almost entirely of red sandstone. The worst of it was that the camels, in consequence of the insufficient pasture, were growing thinner and thinner, and were fast using

A Wounded Orongo Antelope.

up their strength. We had only three sacks of maize left. Should we—this was now the all-important question—should we reach better regions before it was too late?

At last we hit upon a valley that descended towards the south, but before long it contracted into a disagreeable, winding gorge, the bottom of which was choked with slabs of sandstone that hurt the camels' feet. To escape this we were forced to turn up over a low rounded pass, where Sirkin shot a little antelope. Yolldash rushed blindly upon the wounded animal, but was greatly taken aback upon being met by a pair of sharp horns. The men never indulged in hunting for the sake of mere sport, only when we were in need of food. Besides, we had to think of the ammunition. Each of the Cossacks had only 142 cartridges left—quite sufficient if it were well husbanded; but we did not know what the future had in store for us, and it was best not to waste it.

After crossing a flat saddle, we perceived beyond it a small lake, and its farther side was—green! An hour later we were amongst it; it was, it is true, very thin and short, but it was fresh and tender. And, to crown our good luck, there was an abundant supply of kulan droppings for fuel.

All day the weather was everything that could be desired—much too warm for winter clothing. There was one characteristic of the winds of this region which I had for several days observed. Almost invariably the west wind dropped at sunset. Then, whilst twilight lasted, it was a dead calm, so that I used to dine with a light burning and the door open. But shortly after eight down came the gale from the north, and in a few moments the camp was all confusion. The men rushed off in all directions, to fasten their tents, and hurry under shelter any things that chanced to be lying outside. The sparks from our fires whirled up like comets' tails, and we had to keep a good look-out to see that nothing caught fire. That evening the wind had a velocity of nearly 36 miles an hour. As a rule the storm continued as long as I was awake, or, say, until midnight; but when I was called in the morning, just before seven, the atmosphere was again in equilibrium. Thus there were two prevailing winds in those regions, a westerly and a northerly, the former blowing by day, the latter by night. Wherever accumulations of sand were formed, it was always on the west side of the north-and-south valleys—that is to say, on the side that was sheltered from the west wind.

Just before the storm burst that afternoon, our camp and its immediate surroundings presented quite an idyllic picture, if one may ever use the word "idyllic" with regard to a Tibetan landscape. The sun had set, but its purple afterglow still lingered in the heavens. In the east the moon, pale yellow and of a frigid aspect, slowly sailed across the dark blue sky, and filtered its rays through the thin white haze, throwing everything into magic relief—softening the harsh tints, and obscuring the sharp angularities. Across the moon hung a narrow, coal-black strip of cloud, like a black ribbon flung athwart a silver globe. It made me fancy that Saturn and his ring had somehow wandered astray in the heavens. The sky was in places fringed with light, fleecy clouds. The caravan animals were scattered over the hill-sides, eagerly plucking the scanty grass. Such camels as were not up to the mark lay huddled together beside Turdu Bai's tent; and close by were the two little ones with their mothers.

Here we stayed yet another day. According to my reckoning this was the valley in which we had buried Aldat the autumn before, though his grave lay nearly 20 miles farther to the east.

On the 4th of July we travelled almost due south, over a gently undulating surface, with thin grass, numerous salt pools, and an abundance of game, especially kulans and antelopes. Yak dung was very plentiful too, and, what was more to our purpose, it was dry. The ground also was in general remarkably dry, as compared with what it was the autumn before, when we were several times very nearly engulfed in the mire. But then it was a long time since there had been any downfall. When the wind blew, clouds of dust hung over the track of the caravan.

Once more we were approaching a fresh pass, which we reached by a steep, gravelly ravine. On the way up we dropped one camel. On the summit, 17,094 feet above the sea, the only vegetation was yak moss. Thence we had a most extensive view: for fully four days ahead there appeared to be no serious difficulties to encounter. But, looking back, what a very different view! Range behind range, crest overtopping crest, until the high-pitched horizon was closed by the mountain knot we had climbed round, with its lofty pass and its perpetual snow! The landscape was for the most part dressed in light shades, red predominating. Faint tinges of yellow and green revealed the pasture-ground we had recently left. In places the eye caught

The Veteran of 1896. Sirkin Holding Him.

the gleam of snow. The whole scene suggested a flat desert picture, and above the whole stretched the turquoise-blue canopy of the sky. We pitched our tents on the slope going down from the pass, at an altitude of 16,582 feet. We obtained water by digging a well in a dry watercourse, but next morning discovered a spring. Sirkin and Cherdon shot six brace of partridges; and in another place they bagged two yaks. Although we thus fared sumptuously, the poor camels looked wretchedly thin and miserable. Nor were the horses much better; here at Camp no. XXX. one had to be killed, and we were obliged to give the others a day's rest.

On these rest days Shagdur and the Lama were busily employed getting my Mongolian dress ready. A very remarkable change had by this come over the last named: his courage had grown, and he was now actually longing to get back to Lassa. All this while my lessons in Mongolian went on without interruption, and the Lama drew me plans of the holy city, its temples, and its squares. The enterprise, as a whole, now presented itself to him in rosier colours, and he was wont to express his views in the following pregnant sentence: "Mo bollneh ikkeh mo bollneh gué, sän bollneh ikkeh sän bollneh," *i.e.*, "Goes it bad, it goes not *very* bad; but goes it well, it goes *very* well."

Every evening, on the stroke of nine, I used to pay a visit to the big yurt inhabited by Sirkin, Shagdur, and the Lama, to examine the meteorological journal kept by the first-named, as well as to take the reading of the self-registering thermometer, a duty I always performed myself. Then I used to sit and chat with them for an hour, while Turdu Bai and Hamra Kul came and made their reports about their respective animals. That evening they told me there was scarcely a sack of maize left, and whatever the consequences might be for ourselves, we must give up all the rice and flour we could possibly spare for the animals. Turdu Bai considered it absolutely essential that we should hurry on in search of grass, and then allow the camels at least a month to recover.

Another item of news they brought me was less satisfactory, namely, that during the day nearly all the sheep had run away. They had not been missed until dark, but most of the Mussulmans had gone off in quest of them. Chernoff also joined in the search on horseback, taking some of the dogs with him. I was afraid it would prove a repetition of what had happened the preceding year, and was rather dreading the scolding I should have to give to the offender. The plain truth of the matter was, the flock had been left to the tender care of Vanka, the ram ; and indeed he had managed his business as well as any Mussulman. At ten o'clock the searchers came back tired, but without the sheep. They said they would wait an hour until the moon rose, and then go and look for them again. It was midnight when they finally returned ; but luckily they brought all the sheep with them. They had found them in a side ravine, lying at the bottom of its deep watercourse.

As the animals' strength declined, so did our marches grow shorter and shorter. We seldom managed more than 12 miles a day now. But on the 6th of July they were slower than usual. I used to take the Lama and ride on in advance, and wait for them at the top of some pass ; but that day our wait was a very long one.

We were now surrounded by primeval nature in its most desolate and deterrent aspects. Never before had a human being set foot in those wild tracts. Days, weeks, months passed, and we were the only human beings to impart life to the region. Orographically the same parallelism of the mountain-ranges obtained which we had observed the year before. Every chain and every latitudinal valley between them, as well as every individual summit, stretched from east to west, and as we were travelling south, we had necessarily to cross them all one after the other. Scarce a day passed without our climbing over some pass, and very often we had two or more to our credit in the day. Yet it was very strange how seldom the bare rock cropped out. Both that day and the next the surface consisted of soft, sandy material, dry and tolerably firm, though in the bottom of the valleys there was generally some gravel. Gradually the grass, too, improved. When we stopped, two of the camels lagged, as usual, behind ; one of them was the veteran of 1896 ; his days were now plainly numbered. But before he died, I took the accompanying (p. 259) portrait of him.

CHAPTER XV.

FIRST CONTACT WITH THE TIBETANS.

On the 7th of July the going was unusually favourable; we had no pass to surmount, and the ground was firm. Our journey lay down the sloping side of a flat, open, cauldron-shaped valley, with an almost circular lake at the bottom. Its water was pure and intensely blue, girdled by a broad band of crystallized salt, which in the distance glittered like ice or snow. The western shore was overhung by heights of a brick-red colour. The strip of shore consisted of moist saliferous ooze, and it was no easy matter to obtain a canful of the water, to see what it was like. In fact it was only after Kutchuk had devised a pair of makeshift *ski*, or snow-shoes, that he durst venture to cross the dangerous margin. But the water contained such a heavy solution of salt that the areometer refused to sink by the half of its height. Of course the scale was no use at all, and we were forced to make a special mark on the glass. Fortunately, this treacherous strip of mire was sharply marked off from the slopes around by a distinct swelling. Passing the lake, we steered to the south-east, making for the mouth of a valley which led up to the next pass. We now began to look for water, for it was nothing like so plentiful hereabouts as in the Arka-tagh. I rode on first, to see whether there was a spring at the bottom of the valley. There we eventually dug a well, and at a depth of nearly two feet obtained cold, fresh water.

On the 8th of July, although we travelled no more than 8¾ miles, only 27 of the camels managed to reach camp—no. XXIII. (16,540 feet). They were now so far gone that we preferred to make a long detour round even insignificant passes, rather than risk losing one or two of the animals by crossing over them. But the pass which lay before us, 16,600 feet in altitude, could not be avoided, and our Lama, who had reconnoitred it, assured us that it was not difficult. Nor was the ascent, indeed, of any account; still, it was hard work for our exhausted beasts. On the other side the contours were more intricate and unfavourable. There were several crests which would have to be got over by some means or another; and at our feet were four fresh-water pools, each embedded like a saucer amongst the hills. Shagdur went on in advance to examine the country, and came back and reported that the next pass would be too high for the camels. Already three were lagging behind, and, sooner or later, we should have to wait for them. This we did beside a fifth pool, although the grass was thin and poor. Next day two out of the three laggards managed to get up to the camp, the third lay stiff and cold on the spot where he had been left.

It was clear things could not go on in this way much longer. A change must be made in the order of our march. The best thing seemed to be to weed out the weak animals, and leave them to follow on slowly after, whilst with the rest I pushed on at a faster pace. The first step was to reconnoitre our position, for we were now, as it were, in a sack, from which we could not get out until we found a hole somewhere. Chernoff rode to the east; the road was blocked by steep cliffs. Mollah Shah, who tried the south, reported that the two or three low passes he had crossed were not particularly difficult.

Then we picked out eleven camels, five of which had carried no loads during the last two or three days, and six horses, and left them to get a few days' rest, after which they were to follow on our trail by short, easy stages. This important task I entrusted to Chernoff, and told off five men to help him—namely, Rosi Mollah, Mollah Shah, Kutchuk, Khodai Kullu, and Almaz, the last-named an old man from Charkhlik, whose euphonious name means the same thing as "jewel." I also left with them four of our dogs—Malchik, Hamra, Kalmak, and Kara-itt—as well as half of our surviving flock of sheep, now reduced to about a dozen. The selection of the animals was made with great care and circumspection by Turdu Bai and the Cossacks. At first only ten camels were picked out; the eleventh was added just as we were starting. Eight camel-loads of baggage, consisting exclusively of provisions, were left for them to bring on; but all the instruments and other important things we carried with us.

It was not at all convenient to divide the caravan in this

way just then, when we were approaching inhabited regions, and might perhaps require the whole of our strength undivided. But we had no choice in the matter, and I left the rear-guard well armed with two rifles and several revolvers.

I arranged with Chernoff that on hard ground, more especially when we kept to the watercourses at the bottoms of the valleys, or crossed hard gravel, we would leave heaps of stones to mark which way we had gone. I could not of course tell him where the main caravan would stop, for the simple reason that I did not know myself. It would all depend upon circumstances, principally upon the presence of grass, and the chance of encountering human beings.

A change in the weather occurred at Camp no. XXXIII. The morning was bright and clear; but at noon the hail was dancing a witches' carnival on the hill-sides; and the first squall was soon followed by a second. After that there was a drizzling rain for the rest of the day, and at nightfall it turned into a good, steady downpour. We did not derive much satisfaction from listening to the monotonous patter-patter of the rain, for we knew that every drop would only add to the weight of our loads by making tents and yurts as heavy as lead, and would at the same time convert the ground into a quagmire.

We said good-bye to the rear-guard on the 10th July. Chernoff understood that it would be a feather in his cap if he brought in the greater part of the eleven camels I left in his charge. After a big snowfall during the night the ground was heavy and slippery. Amid these dreary surroundings the caravan we left behind looked even more forlorn and wretched than usual. Only one or two of the animals thought it worth while trying to hunt for a bite in the slushy snow; the others just lay still and rested. The Mussulmans wished me a successful journey, and at parting I gave Chernoff a hearty grip of the hand. I should not see him again until after I returned from my pilgrim journey to Lassa—that is, if I did return.

All day long the weather was terrible. One burst of hail was so fierce that we simply could not face it, but were compelled to stop, wrapped in our cloaks, until it passed. Next moment the sun shone out, and dried us, until the sky opened its ready sluices again. I and the Lama rode on in advance to choose a spot to encamp in. We did 14½ miles; for although the caravan, having got rid of the worst animals, went better and travelled faster than usual, we still had to wait a long time before they came up. This was too good an opportunity for the weather to neglect: it rained again—pouring down in torrents. The Lama sat repeating, with philosophic patience, his never-ending "*On maneh padmeh hum*," and let the 108 beads of his rosary trickle through his fingers as he recited.

On the whole, the day's march had been across favourable ground, especially after we had surmounted two low passes. On the southern slope of the second six wild yaks were grazing, and as we had for some time been without fresh meat, Sirkin and Shagdur took their rifles, and each brought down one. Then Turdu Bai and Ördek went with their knives and axes to fetch in the best pieces of the meat.

Meanwhile from the top of the pass (17,015 feet) I was enjoying the delightful prospect of open, level country for at least two days ahead. But my joy was short-lived; for right across the horizon, from the south-east to the south-west, stretched an unbroken chain of immense snow-fields, which, clearly, there was no avoiding. What scanty pasture there was in the broad, latitudinal valley, which, as usual, stretched from east to west, consisted chiefly of moss and wild garlic. This last was most welcome. It made nice flavouring for my soups. The Mussulmans chewed it raw, alleging that it was a preventive of mountain-sickness. The camels ate it greedily, preferring it to everything else. When there was nothing better to do, Turdu Bai used to set the men to collect this herb, and even on the march he used to stop occasionally, when it was plentiful, to give the camels a taste of its juicy and aromatic leaves.

Our next camp stood 16,346 feet above the level of the sea. The 11th of July was the anniversary of two events which have to do with altitudes. It was just four years since poor Andrée made his daring and in every respect successful ascent from Spitsbergen, and started on the journey from which he was never to return. I say deliberately "successful ascent," because the plan was so bold and grandiose in its conception—no other nation is able to boast of anything equal to it. It was also on the 11th of July, but eleven years ago, when I climbed to the top of Mount Demavend in Northern Persia. Then I had a hard day's work to do my 18,750 feet; but on that occasion I had only a single peak to climb, and it was surrounded by laughing valleys on every side; whereas here before me stretched a boundless expanse of barren uplands, across which we should have to drag ourselves with heavy, weary feet.

Our Camp of 13th July.

Our march ran east-south-east, and although we met with no obstacles, still we did not seem to approach perceptibly nearer to the snowy range which lay hidden behind its dark foot-hills. The rainfall was copious; the showers came too quick together for the ground to be able to dry between them. Consequently the surface was converted into mud, causing the camels to slip. Our Lama said it was the rainy season begun, and it would last two months. "At least, it is so in Lassa," he added. There is no need for me to describe the pelting showers we now encountered. They were in every way typical of the worst features of the worst Tibetan weather, and nothing could well be more villainous. The march was tiring and disagreeable. When we spread our beds on the ground they turned damp, and the yurts stunk vilely. It was seldom that I got an opportunity to use my camera or astronomical instruments, and the sheets of the map, upon which I was working, used soon to get wet, and then curled up.

The next day, after travelling east till noon beside the stream near which we had encamped, we turned south-east across gently undulating ground. But we failed to discover good water. The first pool we came to was salt. We dug a well; its water was salt. Then Shagdur took a couple of copper vessels, and went off on horseback; about an hour later we saw him riding back at full gallop. We wondered what he was in such a desperate hurry about. He said he had been attacked by a wolf, which had twice flown at him. Having nothing but the two copper vessels to defend himself with, he had flung them at the beast, and then taken to his saddle. Through the telescope we saw the big brute, almost white, following in Shagdur's tracks; but when Shagdur and Sirkin rode out to meet him with their rifles, Mr. Greylegs thought it best to show a clean pair of heels. That night we penned up the sheep more carefully than usual, and appointed men to watch the horses and mules.

Continuing in the same direction the following day, we traversed a region of rounded hills and ridges, with numerous salt-pools embedded amongst them, and crossed six insignificant passes before we reached a pretty large stream. But again we were disappointed. The water moved with painful slowness, and emptied itself into an elongated lake, with a belt of crystalline salt all round it. But whether the water from the lake was blown back up stream, or whether the stream itself originated in a formation impregnated with salt, anyway the water was intensely salt. However, a little way further on we at length found a small pool of good water, so that at last the poor animals were able to drink their fill.

On a hillside near by the dogs set upon a big black yak bull; and for some time it was quite comical to see them and the yak dancing round and round one another, the yak snorting, puffing and blowing, with his tail in the air and his horns lowered, ready for a lunge. Yolldash, the cunning rascal, kept hanging on to his fringes. The yak's attention was so engrossed with the performance that I was able to photograph him; but unfortunately the negatives were not satisfactory. I almost thought it was a tame yak which had escaped from some Tibetans, he was so nonchalant.

In the middle of these proceedings Turdu Bai came and pronounced the yak's death sentence; we were in want of meat. The dogs were called off, and very soon two shots rang out simultaneously. But the yak seemed not to take the slightest notice of either reports or bullets. The dogs were let loose upon him again. But by this the yak had got his dander up, and he charged them in dead earnest. Up the hill they went; but all at once down came the yak headlong, and when we reached him he was quite dead. He was a magnificent bull; and the tips of his horns were worn and frayed from ancient battles with his rivals. After taking the best pieces of the meat and the fat, we left the rest for Shagdur's friend, the wolf.

It was a strange thing that we should go two whole days without finding water, especially as it was the rainy season, and there were pools in every direction. We certainly travelled ten or twelve miles from one fresh-water supply to the next. It was now a daily question—a question of the utmost, of vital importance—where we should find good grass, and make our headquarters camp. We were still very nearly 240 miles from the north-west corner of Tengri-nor; but we could scarcely expect to come across human beings before we reached the other side of the lofty range, which occasionally showed its snowy peaks above the hill-tops. The wild yak we had just shot had clearly never been in contact with human beings; otherwise he would never have allowed himself to be photographed at the cost of his own life. And yet, curiously enough, the skeletons and skulls of kulans and orongo antelopes were scattered all over the locality; these must have belonged to animals which died a natural death, or were killed by wolves, for the Tibetans never meddle with kulans.

On the 13th we kept to the latitudinal valley, so as to spare the camels crossing any pass. The grass, however, was of the scurviest description, although we now came across a new species, which our Lama called *buka-shirik*, or "yak grass"; it was, he said, very common in the neighbourhood of Lassa, and along the routes the Mongol pilgrims take to that city. The whole region abounded in game—yaks, kulans, orongo antelopes, hares, and partridges. Upon reaching a brook which carried 177 cubic feet in the second, we thought it wisest to stop.

The Camels Fording a River.

During the course of the day it rained, snowed, and hailed, sometimes in succession, sometimes all three together.

On the 15th of July the temperature rose to 11°.1 C., or 52°.0 Fahr., although the night before it was down as low as −3°.4 C., or 25°.9 Fahr. We still continued our south-east course, keeping a sharp look-out all the time for a gap or depression in the lofty range which parted us from the secrets of the Holy Land of the Lamaists. Once on the other side of that gigantic natural wall, which it was very probable was of climatic importance, and we should find it warmer, and meet with better grass, and no doubt human inhabitants as well. Up to the present we had not seen the slightest trace of human beings. About the middle of the day's march we crossed the biggest river we had encountered since we left the Tarim. It flowed north-west into a very large lake, which we had only seen in the distance, as it glinted between the hills. The stream, which was divided into about a score of big arms, and the same number of smaller arms, had a volume of upwards of 810 cubic feet in the second, a velocity of two and a quarter miles an hour, and a maximum depth of just under two feet. Had the current been confined to one channel, it would have been impossible to get across without the boat. As it was, it took us a good half-hour to reach the opposite bank. Its bottom consisted of fine gravel. I was strongly tempted to unpack the boat, and sail down with the current into the lake; but upon second thoughts decided it would be wiser to postpone all such ventures until after my hazardous trip to Lassa was over.

In the far distance, up the broad open valley we were traversing, there appeared a tall, upright object moving towards us. We took it for a man, but could not be quite sure by reason of the distance and the reflection of the atmosphere. Sirkin, the Lama, and Turdu Bai, who examined the object through the telescope, were all positive it was a man; the Lama added, that he was gathering *argol*, or "yak dung," and that there were two black tents behind him. A little way back the hills on the left bank of the river we had just crossed were dotted over with yaks, numbering about 75. Tibetans with their yaks thus early! It was a stroke in our reckoning to be surprised in this way whilst on the march; it would make our Mongol disguise useless, and so upset all our plans. I also watched the approaching wanderer through the telescope; then we waited some time to let him come nearer. Finally, our man became transmogrified into a kulan, which we had seen in perspective. The black tents were nothing more serious than the shadows cast by the high banks of an eroded gulley, and the yaks were wild ones.

A little bit farther on Yollbars started a young hare, which, however, managed to escape into a hole. But even there poor puss was not safe, for Shagdur put in his arm and pulled her out. I took the timid little beastie, and stroked it and patted it, and when the caravan was safe past with all the dogs, I set it at liberty. Away it scuttled, overjoyed at its unexpected release; but before it got very far a hawk, which we had not observed, swooped down upon it. Shagdur hurried after it with his gun, but arrived too late. The leveret was dying, with its eyes picked out. *Incidit in Scyllam, etc.* It was little incidents like

Scanty Grazing in the Great Latitudinal Valley.

these that formed the only break in our otherwise monotonous marches.

Soon after this we came to the western bank of another river, which, a little farther down, obviously joined the one I have recently spoken of. Here the pasture was better than it had been for a very long time, and as there was also an abundance of fuel (yak dung), we decided to stop. The weather was glorious; flies even were buzzing about. A little higher up the hillside was dotted over with yaks, and there were more kulans and antelopes than we could count. Even partridges and wild-geese, with their young ones, were denizens of this uncommonly hospitable region.

Here, on the 16th July, we rested all day. I sent Turdu Bai and Hamra Kul to the head of the valley, to see if we could advance with the whole of the caravan: I did not want to turn back again. Just as I had got my theodolite set up for an observation, down came a terrific hailstorm. The sky turned black in the west, and the thunderclaps followed one another so swiftly that the earth literally shook. I was glad to creep under cover again. The hailstones rattled like peas on the canvas, and the ground was soon white.

Then we heard excited shouting. Cherdon, who was on duty for the day, announced that the other two Cossacks had routed out a big bear, and it was at that moment lumbering at a smart trot towards the camp. But, suddenly turning, Bruin plunged into the river, splashed across it, and clambered up the opposite bank, followed by the two horsemen at full gallop. Scarcely had they disappeared when crack went Cherdon's rifle. A huge whitish-grey wolf had sneaked close up to the camp, but now paid the penalty of his rashness.

An hour later, or a little more, we saw the two Cossacks coming back at a smart trot. They rode straight towards me, and even before they pulled up, it was plain that they brought important news. The bear, after a parting shot, managed finally to escape, though not before the two Cossacks rode plump into the middle of a Tibetan camp. At their approach a man, armed with a gun, disappeared behind a neighbouring hill, and there were horses grazing in the vicinity. Perhaps the score of yaks which we had seen the day before were *tame* ones after all. Then the Cossacks, who were not able to talk to the man, hastened back to bring me the news.

Now that he found himself face to face with realities, our

Lama was filled with consternation. So long as we were travelling through uninhabited regions, my plan, no doubt, appeared to him somewhat vague, and he had failed to realize it thoroughly. Now, however, the crisis was come. Having obtained touch with the natives, it was time for the caravan to halt, and for us to think of starting on our adventurous expedition. Perhaps, after all, the kulan we saw the day before was a man; at any rate, it was a warning, an indication that we were approaching inhabited regions.

We called a council of war. But there was no time to lose; the Cossacks were under the impression that the Tibetans had at once set to work to collect their yaks and horses, with the intention of striking camp. They must not escape. By hook or by crook we must get hold of them. In the first place, they would be able to give us valuable information about the routes and other circumstances. And it would be a good thing to try and win their confidence, and induce them to keep company with us, so as to prevent them from spreading the news of our approach; for, once it got wind, the tidings would, we knew, travel like wildfire all the way to Lassa.

The distance to their camp was, Sirkin said, not more than two miles. They must infallibly have seen us, for we had been where we were since the day before. Yet, were they Tibetan nomads, or were they Tangut robbers? Probably they were nothing worse than peaceful yak hunters, carrying meat and skins to the south. I had not expected to come across human beings thus early. It was strange, because we had not hitherto perceived any traces of old camp-fires.

In the meantime I ordered the Lama and Shagdur to ride to the Tibetan encampment as fast as they could, and detain the men in conversation. Before starting, however, my Cossack put on his Mongolian attire, and he looked the real thing in it. Indeed, that is what he was, for the Buriats are closely akin to the Mongols. I gave him some money to buy horses with, in case the Tibetans should have any to sell, and also let him take some tea and tobacco for presents, to convince them that they had to do with people who meant them no ill. The two men ploughed their way through the river, and disappeared in the twilight.

The moment which I had wished to postpone as long as I could was come quite unexpectedly. It would be an obvious advantage to have our main strength advanced as far south as

A Young Kulan Wounded.

possible, so as not to be cut off from it by too great a distance. We had already made up our minds to stop as soon as we came in contact with human beings, even though we should actually be on the march. The idea was that when we first perceived them, we pilgrims should don our disguise, ride back unseen, and approach the Holy City by a different road, so as to disarm any suspicion which might arise of our being connected with the big European caravan.

Some two hours later our horsemen returned; it was then pitch dark. The Tibetans were, however, already gone, their trail leading to the east; but their argol fires were still smoking when Shagdur and the Lama reached their camp. Shagdur thought that the first shot at the bear must have aroused them, and that they had begun to pack up on the instant. According to the Lama, they were three yak hunters; two or three heads and some hoofs were lying about in the vicinity. Our first idea was to pursue them; but, as they would probably travel all night and all the next day without stopping, we were forced to give up the idea; our horses were not fresh enough.

CHAPTER XVI.

QUAGMIRES AND SKY-SCRAPING-PASSES.

FROM this day on there was no peace in our camp. Sentinels were posted at night, and the caravan animals were never let out of our sight. We lived pretty nearly as if on the war-path; indeed, I began to wonder whether it would not be too risky to leave the caravan at all. It would soon be well known that a caravan was approaching, and after I left them my men might be exposed to an attack. On this ground, therefore, after talking the matter over with Shagdur, I decided to leave Cherdon behind with Sirkin to defend the camp. Later on, when Chernoff arrived with the invalids, he, too, would materially strengthen the defence. Yet, as there was now no prospect of our reaching the Holy City before the news, exaggerated and no doubt perverted, of our arrival got there, there was the less need for us to make our headquarters camp where we were, especially as our horses were anything but fresh. To Lassa and back would have been a ride of over 650 miles, and that was certainly too much for our horses, especially if we attempted, as we should, to do the thing by forced marches.

However, we had to stay another day at Camp no. XXXVIII. to await the return of Turdu Bai and Hamra Kul. This delay we utilized in getting our Mongolian equipment ready, in case we should be compelled to slip away from the caravan at a moment's notice. Inside one of my Mongolian top-boots I contrived a sort of pocket for a thermometer, and made other pockets in the lining of my overcoat for my watch, aneroid, and note-book. Our two scouts turned up at dusk, and announced that as far as they had gone up the valley they had encountered no hindrance to our advance. In two or three places they noticed the remains of old camp-fires, which indicated that the valley was pretty well known to the yak hunters.

On the 18th of July we resumed our journey to the south-east, and crossed the river three times. During the day one of the camels, although apparently perfectly well—indeed, he was rather fatter than the others—barely managed to crawl into camp. Next day, as we could not induce him to move, we decided to leave him. It was only incorrigible laziness, and he would be picked up by Chernoff and his men. The Mussulmans said he would be quite safe from wolves, for, fierce though these animals were, they had never been known to attack a camel carrying a pack-saddle. All the same, we stuck up a spar of the yurt on a little hill close by, and tied to the top of it an empty preserved food tin, containing a strip of paper with the following message written in Turki: "We have left a camel here. If you don't see him, follow his trail till you find him." For we thought that, after he had rested a little, he might follow us in quest of his companions.

This was the first of the 18 to drop out of the ranks. The last we saw of him he was bending down his head to graze, and none of us ever saw him again. As it happened, Chernoff, who always encamped on the same spots that we did, made just here a detour, and never saw the camel at all. This was the only camel I ever left behind me alive without learning what became of him.

We now began to ascend, keeping on the left bank of the river. But the country soon changed, becoming bare and barren, and the weather changed too, for the summer warmth and the flies of the day before were succeeded by wintry snow and hail.

One day more and we should be in the heart of the snowy range which we had so long had on our right. The camels still held out, but their strength was fast sinking. The dromedary seemed as if he would be the next to go; he was nothing but skin and bone, and used to weep pitifully when we stopped. For supper we gave him a good bucketful of flour balls, the hay out of a pack-saddle, and two or three lumps of raw mutton-fat, which was said to be especially strengthening.

But the sun, as well as the alpine features of the landscape, was soon hidden behind impenetrable clouds. We were now going south-south-west, and the tempest—one of the very worst I have witnessed—drove directly in our faces. *Bashliks* (hoods) were no use whatever. The hail and snow met us horizontally, stuck fast inside the collars of our overcoats, and, melting, ran down inside our necks. Every now and again we had to turn our back to the storm so as to catch our breath. To ride and write under such circumstances was no easy task. We felt—we could not see—that we were gradually ascending ; but when the tempest lifted a moment we were disagreeably surprised to find that we were apparently no nearer to the snowy group. Still, we kept doggedly at it, gradually rising, but so gently, so slowly. In fact, the ascent was so imperceptible that at times I thought we were travelling over perfectly level ground ; the rivulets alone showed that it was not so. But the poor camels ! They slipped, and their feet sank in ; and one actually went down with such a thud that the earth shook under him. What made the path so difficult was not only its loose consistency, but its saturated condition. Several glacier fingers stretched down towards the pass from both sides. All were completely buried under the snow ; but from each of them trickled a rivulet. The margin of the glacier was literally black with yaks. We counted considerably over 300, many of them quite little calves. Cherdon shot one of these last to replenish our larder. As we approached them they gradually moved over to the south side of the pass.

Down the middle of the broad depression by which we were climbing up to the summit of the pass trickled a brook some two or three yards wide, and not more than three and a half feet deep. It was bordered with thick, moist yak-grass, and contained small fish. Yes, fish at an altitude of 16,500 feet ! As usual I took specimens in spirits.

At length, however, brooks and rivulets came to an end, and the ascent grew steeper. With the Lama I pushed on to the summit. We were 17,921 feet above the level of the ocean, the aneroid registered 394 mm. (15.5 inches). The caravan was still struggling up the slope. The descent on the other side was blocked by a big yak, which looked very wild and threatening ; his tail was curling backwards and forwards in the air, his horns were lowered, and he gave no sign of running away. We thought it wise to wait for the rifles ; but when the first of the camels showed above the crest the yak lumbered off.

Meanwhile we examined, through the telescope, the country which unrolled itself on the other side of the pass. It was a chaos of mountain peaks and ranges, threaded by a tangled labyrinth of glens. A little way down we struck a pretty big stream, and decided to follow it. Here seven old yaks were attacked by the dogs. Four took to flight at once. Three stood their ground; but when their enemies concentrated their efforts upon one of the three, the other two slipped away. The survivor had a lively time of it with his assailants, until he hit upon the ingenious tactics of taking his station in the middle of the river, where the water foamed about him, greatly bothering the dogs. After a while two of the other yaks returned to see how their comrade was getting on; but by that time the dogs had grown tired of the game, and were sitting on their haunches, with their tongues out, watching their victim.

Just as the men were taking the loads off the camels for the night, one of the Cossacks let fly with a shot-gun at a partridge which sat motionless right out in the open watching us. Then as she fluskered about in her dying agony, we saw that she was brooding three young ones, which ran about cheeping anxiously for their mother. Had it not been that this was a stingy land, and we were in absolute need of food, I should have felt like a criminal at disturbing the idyllic peace of such an innocent creature. As it was, it was a very long time before I got that cowardly shot out of my mind. The only thing that consoled me was that the partridge would, in any case, have been disturbed by the dogs.

After the heavy downfall of the day the ground was soft and spongy, and as the grass was not only scanty, but tough and hard, it came up by the roots when the camels pulled at it. Even then they had to browse a long distance before they gathered a mouthful big enough to chew.

The Lama, who was an intelligent fellow, observed quite correctly, that this stupendous mountain-range filled the same place in the Tibetans' regards that the Arka-tagh did in the case of the people of East Turkestan, in that it served as a frontier wall to shut out the unknown and the uninhabited, and formed a dividing line which was seldom crossed except by the yak hunters. Between these two ranges lay the highest, the barrenest, and consequently the most inaccessible parts of Tibet. We were now barely 170 miles distant from the northern shore of Tengri-nor, and we might expect almost any moment to stumble across the camping-grounds of the nomads.

When I awakened on the morning of the 21st July the snow was falling fast. Heavy clouds, almost black, hung about the crest of the snowy range; in fact, it was shrouded in them, and there would have been nothing to reveal its existence had it not been for two glacier arms which, like the paws of a gigantic polar bear, stuck out from underneath the cloak of the clouds. I estimated that the limits of perpetual snow ran at about 350 feet above the pass, or say, 18,250 feet above sea-level. In spite of this stupendous altitude, we had no actual case of mountain-sickness, although Cherdon, who had been out after the yaks, complained of headache.

We followed the river due south, having the hail and rain in our faces all day. The wind blew up the pass with cutting keenness. A little way down our stream was joined by another from the right, and afterwards was deflected to the south-east. At the confluence two or three thick sheets of ice still survived, although with big cracks in them, through which we could see the water flowing on underneath. It amazed me that these fragile bridges did not collapse under the weight of the camels; but their surface was soft and decomposed, so that the animals walked as safely as they would have walked on gravel or sand. After a while the ice became thicker, and formed a continuous bank, with vertical or overhanging edges on each side of the glen, while down the middle between them flowed the river. We were marching on the right bank, but at a turn in the glen the ice was broken, and we were forced down on to the gravel at the bottom. The drop was 6½ feet down, so that we had to get out our axes, crowbars, and spades, and cut out a sloping path. This took a long time. Meanwhile Shagdur rode on to reconnoitre; for, to my eyes, this looked an extremely hazardous sort of road, especially as the gorge narrowed rapidly. After strewing the ice with sand, we cautiously steered each of the animals in turn down to the bottom, which was 60 to 120 feet wide. Then we travelled very often in the stream itself, the water splashing all about us. As the thermometer was a few degrees above freezing point, there was a continuous drip, drip from the edges of the ice. Altogether our surroundings were pretty moist.

After proceeding in this way for a good while we met Shagdur. He said we might go three or four miles farther; but then the ice came to an end, and the river was forced into a deep ravine, which it would be impossible to get through. If we did not look out we should be penned in both up-stream and down-stream. If the water came down upon us from above—and the river would very likely go on increasing in volume until a late hour of the night—we might not be able to turn back, and the glen contained no bays or expansions into which we could lead the camels safely out of harm's way.

Right-about-turn, then, and back through all the pools and the river, and over the ice! It was water, water everywhere —water all around us, and the ice was cracking and crumbling fast. No doubt in winter the entire glen was sheeted with ice from side to side. It may appear amazing that such huge masses of ice as these should survive till the middle of July, but it was partly explained by the altitude and partly by the fact

The Two Ice Margins.

that the glen was screened from the southern sun by a precipitous cliff.

Upon reaching the confluence of the two streams, we turned up the tributary, leaving at the apex, between the two rivers, a cairn of stones, with an arrangement of other stones like an arrow pointing south-west, to show Chernoff which way we had gone. Thus, instead of descending, as we had hoped, into warmer regions, we were now led up a perfectly sterile glen to still higher altitudes. The hail came down more fiercely than ever, but we were now beyond caring what happened. We were dead beat, and as it was perfectly evident that we had another pass before us, and there was no hope of reaching pasturage until we got over it, we decided to stop.

Towards evening the sky cleared; the setting sun coloured

the clouds brownish red, and at dusk heavy rain-drops pattered against the yurt. I went to Sirkin's tent for a chat. We wondered how Chernoff was getting on with his exhausted camels. Then we discussed our expedition to Lassa. I suggested that we might smuggle two or three heavy and bulky articles with us in the stuffing of a mule's pack-saddle.

"No," said the Lama decidedly; "you are never safe in this country. They would perhaps steal the mules with their saddles and all."

Next day the country showed no improvement. Having built up another cairn, we proceeded to breast the pass. In the distance it looked a mere bagatelle; but in reality it was more difficult than the one we had crossed last. I rode on with the Lama up the river-bed, for that was the only strip of firm ground there was. Two paces out of the water and in dropped the horse above the fetlocks. The slope consisted of a gigantic sheet of mire, of the consistency of porridge, and to judge from the cracks which ran across it and all round it, the entire mass was slipping slowly, though imperceptibly, down the mountain-side. The immense altitude and the steepness of the slope, combined with the shifting and insecure foothold, were enough to play havoc with any caravan. And then, to make matters worse, a terrific hailstorm came on and drenched us all to the skin. It took the camels two hours to get to the top, and only fifteen of them turned up. Two were left behind, each in charge of a man. But the southern declivity was ten times worse than the ascent. There was not an inch of firm ground, and it was absolutely impossible to ride. One man went on first to pick out the way. Turdu Bai followed him with the camels, urging them on as fast as he could, to prevent them from sinking too deeply in the mire. However, that did not help much. A scream arose. The cord by which one of the camels was tied to another in front of him was drawn too tight, and cut his nose, owing to his having lost his feet. Up rushed the men to help him. Off came his load, and he was hauled up. Then on the string of camels proceeded again. The ground was so soft and soppy that when a camel lifted his foot, the hole closed up again. The rain came down in a deluge. The clouds covered us as with the darkness of midnight. Not a ray, not a glint of light broke through. Men and animals alike were dripping wet. Breathing was difficult and painful. What a ghastly land! It was amazing to me that the camels pulled through at all.

Even the mules began to get into difficulties; one of them stuck fast in the morass, and it cost us no end of trouble to get her out. Not only had men refused us their assistance, but the very elements, the earth itself, were conspiring to torture us to death. We should never reach those refreshing pastures, that blessed rest that we dreamed of at nights! How on earth would Chernoff's wretched camels ever get through? I fully made up my mind that not a single one would survive the two passes and the shifting mire, which every additional shower would of course make worse and worse.

At length we reached a pretty big stream. Where it came

Hewing a Path Down off the Ice.

from, and where it went to, we could not see; the snow was so thick, and the rain came down in such torrents. One consolation, however, we had: the gravelly bed was firm, and we were no longer in danger of being swallowed alive. We were all so thoroughly soaked, that splashing down the middle of the stream could not make us wetter than we were. A little bit lower down I observed some grass on the right bank, and there too, Shagdur picked up a big earthenware vessel. From its size the Lama inferred that it had belonged to strangers, and not to the nomads of the neighbourhood; *they* would not drag about with them such a big thing. It had evidently been left by the yak hunters in what was a permanent camp.

Of the two camels which had been left behind, only one succeeded in reaching camp; the other stopped just below that miry pass, and Hamra Kul proposed to stay with him all night. The poor beast was literally swallowed up in the mud, and all attempts to get him out failed. Hamra Kul sent to ask me what he was to do. I instructed two men to return to him with food and fuel, and to stay all night beside the camel, and in the morning, when the ground was frozen a little, they were to try their best to get him up with spades and felts. Besides that, I promised I would also send back all the other men to help them; for about half a mile lower down Li Loyeh had discovered good pasture, so that we should stay there all the next day. But all our preparations to save the poor beast, which was otherwise sound and well, were unavailing. The men found him in the morning dead, frozen fast in the treacherous soil.

During the course of the next day, Sirkin and Shagdur, who had been out hunting, reported that two or three miles further on the valley was studded with low hills, covered with beautiful grass, much better than any we had hitherto come across. Turdu Bai, in fact, spent most of the day down there; he could not tear himself away from the pleasure of seeing the camels eat. There was grass enough, he declared, to last for a month, and a good long rest was the only thing that could save the caravan. Upon hearing this, I immediately made up my mind that that was the place for our headquarters camp. There the tents should be erected, the loads stored, and the whole entrenched. Then, after determining the position of the place astronomically, we would put the finishing touches to our Mongolian equipment, and make a start for Lassa. And it was high time. Two or three of the Mussulmans, who had been out collecting fuel, had heard a shot. Probably we had neighbours, and it would be as well to keep a sharp look-out.

Originally I had intended taking with me to Lassa both the Buriat Cossacks as well as the Lama; but since our approach had now certainly been reported by the yak hunters we unexpectedly stumbled across, I dare not leave my main camp with only one Cossack to defend it. Even though the probability was slight, that the Tibetans would make an attack upon our base, still it was more prudent to be prepared for any eventuality that might happen; and it might be a long time before Chernoff came up with the rest of the caravan. I decided, therefore, to leave Cherdon behind; his repeating rifle would be a formidable addition to the defences of the camp. I was extremely sorry to have to tell him my decision, and put it off as long as possible. I knew it would be an intense disappointment to him, for amongst Lamaists the pilgrimage to Jo (Lassa) counts as high in point of sanctity as the pilgrimage to Mecca does amongst Mussulmans. But, by way of comforting the poor fellow, I told him there was little likelihood of our breaking through the jealous cordon which the Tibetans undoubtedly kept upon their city, and I promised him that he, as well as his comrades, should visit some holy temple or another before the journey came to an end. Now a Cossack does not, as a rule, show what he thinks or feels; he simply answers, "Thank you, sir." His one law is obedience. But I understood only too well what this change of plan meant for honest Cherdon.

This decision meant also a great difference to us three pilgrims, in that it diminished our strength by one-fourth. Still the enterprise was altogether so risky, that it would make very little difference whether there were three of us or four.

On the 24th of July we moved down to the place where the Cossacks had found the promising pasture. The distance was barely two miles; but on the way my mind was assailed by anxious thoughts. Would this be the last occasion on which I should travel with my caravan? Should I ever see them again? Would they be left alone in peace until I returned?

The glen descended steeply, the river tumbling from step to step in foaming cascades. We crossed it repeatedly. The grass on the hills through which it wound its way gradually improved. Not that it ever became thick and continuous, but it grew in patches, and was fairly sappy and luxuriant, especially on the slopes that were exposed to the southern sun and sheltered against the cold north winds. The place I chose for the important camp was the flattened top of a rounded hill, close to the left bank of the river, at an altitude of 16,822 feet. But although the grazing was all that the men promised, the camp was badly chosen from a strategical point of view, seeing that it was commanded on all sides by the hills which surrounded it. If a band of Tanguts took it into their heads to open hostilities, they could scarcely wish for a more favourable situation.

I appointed the 27th of July for the start. On the last evening I locked up the valuable boxes I was leaving behind me, except the chronometers, packed in cotton wool in their respective cases. These I left in charge of Sirkin, after instructing him to observe the utmost caution in winding them up. And he was cautious, much too cautious ; the very first evening after we left one of them stopped, because Sirkin was afraid to wind it up fully, for fear of breaking the springs. And the same thing happened to the other one the second day. However, no great harm was done, for I had subsequently an opportunity to repeat the observations which I took here at Camp no. XLIV. During my absence it was also Sirkin's business to take charge of the meteorological observatory, and this he carried through without a hitch. In the presence of all the men I formally nominated him chief of the headquarters camp, directing them to obey his orders as though they were issued by myself. To Turdu Bai, however, owing to his skill and experience in the management of camels, I reserved the right to propose a shift of camp whenever he should deem it advisable. He thought that they could remain where they were for ten days, and then make a short flit. It was further agreed between us that when they moved they should leave at this camp a document, telling us in which direction they had gone and how far, and at each successive camp a similar document.

I talked to each of the men separately and exhorted them to do their duty. Li Loyeh had his own private plans. He had asked permission to accompany me to Lassa, and when I gave him a decided refusal, he begged to be allowed to return to Charkhlik by the way we had come, over the mountains—a distance of 570 miles. Then came Mollah Shah and Hamra Kul, who said they wanted to go with him. Realizing better than they did the utter absurdity of the thing, I quietly answered them that they were perfectly at liberty to do as they pleased. But under no circumstances could I spare them horses, so that Li Loyeh, who was the only one who had his own horse, could alone ride. I promised to give them provisions, besides which Li Loyeh had his own gun of native manufacture. Then I took out the general map I had made of the journey, and pointed out to them each separate station where we had encamped all the way from Charkhlik, and wound up by sketching to them the probable issue of their mad attempt. Mollah Shah, who was an old man, would be the first to give in, and would be left behind, for he could not suppose that the other two would hamper themselves with a sick man. Then it would be Li Loyeh's turn, for he was not over and above strong. Hamra Kul, being a big powerful man, might, I said, if he were fighting for his life, succeed in struggling back to Charkhlik, but he would never do it. He would be torn to pieces by the wolves in the Arka-tagh. I wished them a successful journey, and prayed that Allah would keep His protecting hand over them.

Now, whether it was that this sketch made a deep impression upon them, or whether they came to take a more sensible view of the matter—anyway, in the evening they appeared at my tent, and penitently flinging themselves upon their knees, besought me, in the name of all that was holy, to let them remain with me, which I of course granted. I never ascertained what evil it was had entered into them, and I was too much taken up with my own enterprise to get to the bottom of it. They swore that it was simply a longing for home; but the same day Sirkin discovered in one of the glens behind the camp the fresh track of a man, who sometimes walked, sometimes rode, and during the last night or two the dogs had barked furiously. It was already whispered in camp that the Tibetans were spying upon us, and had us under constant observation. This, however, I did not believe, because kulans showed themselves now on the one side and now on the other of our route, and the track Sirkin noticed might equally well have been made by them. A score of ravens were very busy flitting about the camp—under the existing circumstances no very happy augury.

Finally, I had a talk with Sirkin, and unfolded to him the serious nature of the risk we were running. He listened silently, and gravely shook his head. "If we are not back in two and a half months' time," I said, "you are to break camp and return to Charkhlik, and from there go to Kashgar." I did not really think we should lose our lives; but I must of course prepare for the worst eventuality, and make the best arrangements I could for securing the safety of my maps and note-books. I gave him the key of my treasure-chest, so that he might have the means wherewith to equip a fresh caravan at Charkhlik. I also gave him the general map I had made of our route, although the sense of locality possessed by the native Mussulmans would be quite sufficient to enable them to find their way back. Although there was, of course, little likelihood that a single camel would survive the journey back, still some of the horses might possibly struggle through, and Sirkin knew which were the boxes he had to save at all costs. And no matter how long they might remain at Camp no. XLIV., they were to keep strict guard both day and night, and the animals were never to be let out to graze without two armed men and two or three of the dogs accompanying them. After that I went to bed, for the last time for several days under "civilized conditions." I dropped to sleep at once, and did not wake until Shagdur came and called me next morning, and said it was time to start.

X.

A Dash for Lassa.

The Forbidden Land of the Holy Books.

CHAPTER XVII.

THE START FOR LASSA.

During the two days we rested at Camp no. XLIV. the five mules and four horses which we intended to take with us had been looked after with especial care. They were reshod, and their saddles and rugs repaired. The whole of our baggage was squeezed into two Mongolian boxes. The only instruments I carried with me were three mariner's compasses, two watches, an aneroid, two thermometers, three pairs of coloured wire spectacles, and the Verascope camera, with eight dozen plates. In addition the following articles were absolutely indispensable :—The sheet of the map of Asia, containing Lassa, by the General Staff of the Russian Army, small note-books for my diary, and others for the itinerary, ink, paper, and pens, measuring compasses, razor and soap, scissors, a lantern, an axe, a dozen stearine candles, and boxes of matches, some medicines, ten yambas (£75 to £100) in silver. Our provisions consisted of flour, rice, talkan, and meat; but I only took ten tins of preserved foods, just for the first day or two, and each tin as it was emptied was filled with stones and dropped into a lake or stream for safety's sake. Our weapons consisted of a Russian repeating rifle, a Berdan rifle, and a Swedish army officer's revolver, with 50 cartridges for each. Besides this, we each carried upon our persons a number of small things which the Mongols never go without—for instance, round my neck a rosary, and a *gavo* (a case for holding a sacred talisman), with an idol inside, whilst at my girdle hung a case-knife, Chinese ivory chopsticks to eat with, a skin tobacco-pouch, a long pipe, and tinder and flint. Each man was provided with a double suit of clothing, for we were not likely to travel far without getting wet through. All our utensils such as cooking-pots, jugs, cups, etc., were of genuine Mongolian make. We selected the smallest and lightest of the yurts to sleep in, and last, but not least, the Lama made a comfortable cloak of thick white felt for use whilst doing sentry-go at night. Everything that would have been likely to excite the suspicion of the Tibetans was hidden away in one of the boxes underneath our stock of provisions. Most of them were of such a character that, in case of urgent danger, they could, without serious hurt, have been put under water. But things would have to get pretty bad before I should willingly consent to part from my instruments and note-books.

When Shagdur called me, I made haste to don my disguise, stuffed the instruments I should want on the journey away into their respective hiding-places, and felt that I was now a Mongol indeed. Even from the very first I was quite at home in my new coat, which was of a dark-red colour. It was soft and comfortable; and the only thing I missed about it were the many convenient pockets with which my ulster was provided. The compass and route-book I simply stuck inside my coat, trusting to the girdle to keep them in place. My head-covering consisted of a yellow cap, with turned-up flaps. For some time past I had been wearing the coarse, clumsy Mongol boots, so as to get them easy and comfortable; besides, I had found them very serviceable on wet ground, because of their thick soles and turned-up toes.

It was a bright, sunny morning, and the air full of flies and butterflies, so that I did not require my big yellow overcoat. The horse I had chosen to ride upon was my favourite white one. It was now perfectly well again, and I was in the act of adjusting the soft Mongolian saddle, when Sirkin came up behind me and addressed me in Mongolian; but he was taken rather aback, and quickly checked himself, when he saw that it was I. He had taken me for the Lama. The mistake rather flattered me: it showed me that my disguise was not amiss.

All the dogs were tied up except Malenki and Yollbars, who were to go with us. Our little caravan was loaded up, we mounted, and were off. Sirkin turned his head away to conceal his emotion; Hamra Kul wept like a child, and followed us a little way on foot, tramping unheedingly through the river in his distress. Camp XLIV. disappeared behind the hills. We rode at a smart pace down the glen. Should we ever see that peaceful spot again? I did not doubt the Almighty Hand which had hitherto guided my steps across the deserts and over the mountains. Shagdur simply revelled in the prospect of the

The Author in Mongolian Dress.

adventures which were now beginning. As for the Lama, he was as unruffled as a bowl of sour milk, and when, according to the understanding arrived at at Kum-köll, I asked him if he wished to stay behind, he refused to hear of it. He would not desert me, he said, but would go with me even though it cost him his life.

Shagdur rode a yellow horse, and the Lama the knowing little mule which we very nearly lost the year before, beside the lake where the two cairns of stones were erected. My two comrades led the pack animals, while Ördek, who rode the fourth horse, gave an eye to the loads. I was taking the last-named with us to watch the animals the first two nights, after which we should have to watch them ourselves. Cherdon and Turdu Baï also went with us for two or three hours, and then, after a last farewell, they too turned back.

The glen we travelled down was narrow, and hemmed in by steep hills. For the most part the current ran in a single bed, but in places was divided into several arms. The volume of the stream was immensely increased after the last two days of sunshine, which had caused the glaciers to melt faster. At the very beginning of the journey we crossed the river no less than nine times. At the sharp turns its banks shot down vertically, and several brooks, fed by natural springs, joined it from the left. The prevailing rock was red sandstone; but it was so disintegrated that the hard rock was a rarity—it was mostly gravel and big stones that we saw. Owing to this the entire landscape wore an aspect of redness. At one spot on the right bank two small heaps of stones appeared to indicate a ford, and, sure enough, close by we discovered traces of a hunters' camp—namely, three smoke-blackened stones arranged for the support of a cooking-pot. Another evidence of the presence of visitors was a dead yak, which had been shot not very long before, though it was now dried up, and either that very day, or the day before, there had been a bear prowling about it.

After fording the river two or three times more, we emerged upon an open expanse of country, with no mountains in sight except in the extreme distance. Here we left the river, which turned to the north-east, whilst our route lay to the south-east. The southern faces of the mountains behind us bore far less snow than their northern faces. Kulans, hares, and marmots, in addition to a single wolf, were the principal creatures we noticed on the open plain. Upon reaching an open basin beside a spring (*namaga*), where the grass was luxuriant, we pitched our first camp. One reason why we stopped there was that one of the mules was beginning to limp badly. I made the fire, whilst the men did the rougher work. The horses and mules were hoppled by means of a rope going from one fore leg to one hind leg, so as to prevent them from straying too far. After that we prepared our simple meal of roast meat, rice, bread, and tea. When the meal was served, we ate it with our hands and the Chinese chopsticks, and drank out of a little wooden Mongolian cup; spoons and forks were luxuries we did not defile our boxes with. Our Lama, however, had no appetite; in fact, he seemed to be in a decidedly bad way, and complained of headache. It would be very hard if he was going to fail us now after we had got him so far; but he was so very much out of sorts, that I was really afraid he would have to return with Ördek.

I spent the afternoon stretched out on the ground, and got a good baking from the sun; but at eight o'clock we all went to bed, for the simple reason that we had nothing else to do. While we three pilgrims crept into our tent, which we shared in brotherly fashion together, Ördek kept an eye upon the animals. There was a bright moon, and how glad I was we had it during the trying nights that awaited us. I decided to take Ördek with us yet another day, for our Lama was really far from well. He reeled in his saddle, and had to keep getting off and lying on the ground.

The surface was hard and very favourable, and we did 24 miles with the greatest ease. Although the hills and valleys we passed on the way were scantily furnished with grass, yaks and kulans were remarkably numerous. Occasionally we counted them by the hundred; but then there was any amount of moss and herbs, which our tame animals would not look at. Every now and again one of us would ride on in advance to the top of the next rising ground and take a peep over on the other side; but as yet we saw no signs of human beings. Not that we were now anxious to shun them; on the contrary, if we came across a nomad camp, or mounted men, we should first endeavour to get Ördek away unperceived, so that he might return to Camp no. XLIV., and then, like the honest pilgrims we were, we should ride straight towards them. We were now travelling east-south-east, having before us, on the eastern horizon, a gigantic snow-capped mountain-mass, with a beautiful blue lake

Our Start from the Headquarters Camp.

at its foot. Upon reaching the lake side, which we had meant to follow to the south-east, we were turned back by vertical sandstone cliffs, which rose sheer out of the water, and were of the same brick-red colour which was so characteristic of the Tibetan landscape thereabouts. After a wearisome detour over a series of low hills we once more struck the lake, and found ourselves confronted by fewer difficulties. Concentric rings of beaches and terraces round the shore showed, at a glance, that the lake was shrinking, and consequently must be salt. And, as a matter of fact, it was absolutely destitute of life, and the ground all round it perfectly bare—there was not even so much as a blade of grass.

We did not want to tire our animals too much, and it began to be time to think of stopping; but it was no use looking for fresh water anywhere near the salt lake. However, after advancing for some distance along a kulan track, we caught a glimpse of another lake, somewhat smaller, but, strange to say, containing fresh water, although its surroundings were just as flat and dreary as those of the salt lake. Here we made our second camp. Our Lama was now a good deal better, and we were all in very good spirits. For some time we sat round the fire and chatted, and discussed our plans for reaching the holy city. I reckoned out how long our march had been, and how much farther we had to go. The Lama described the strictness with which the Tibetans examined, in Nakkchu, all pilgrims who arrived from Mongolia; we therefore thought it best to avoid that route, and, road or no road, make our way as best we could to the eastern end of Tengri-nor, and thence go down upon Lassa by the pass of Lani-la. In this way we should strike the great pilgrim road between Nakkchu and Lassa, and so could mingle with the stream of pilgrims unobserved.

Then followed a comical scene: my head was to be shaved. I sat down on the ground beside the fire, and Shagdur played Vandal's havoc with my hair. After he had cropped me as close as the scissors would go, he soaped my head well all over, and then Ördek appeared on the scene with his razor. Within a few minutes my head was as bright and smooth and round as a billiard-ball. Shagdur and the Lama looked on, intensely interested. Then I laid hold of my moustaches, and in a trice they were off, although I confess I thought it was a pity to spoil in this ruthless way the appearance of a not bad-looking fellow. I congratulated myself that I was allowed to keep my eyebrows and eyelashes. When the process of spoliation was completed, I confess I looked perfectly hideous—worse than Cæsar's bust. But there was nobody to see me, and my appearance was quite in keeping with those bare, close-shaven uplands.

But I was not yet done with, for our Lama still had to have his turn. Like an experienced quack and old hand at the business, he began to rummage amongst the paper pokes and pouches, in which he kept his medicaments, and then with a light touch smeared my face all over with grease, soot, and brown colouring matter, until it shone like a cannon-ball in the sun. A little hand-glass, which I had with me, speedily convinced me that I looked the genuine thing. I was almost afraid of my own self, and had to study my visage a long time before I succeeded in convincing myself that the Mongolian baboon I was looking at really was the same person as my father's son. After the concoction had dried my complexion became a dirty grey.

CHAPTER XVIII.

A NIGHT ATTACK.

OUR camp stood on a tongue of land between the two lakes, and in a quite open situation, except for a few low hills on the south-west. Here we regarded ourselves as absolutely secure, for we had not observed the slightest traces of human visitors, and our dogs were perfectly quiet. About five o'clock the wind set in from the north, and drove clouds of sand and dust across the salt lake and over our camp. We of course took refuge in the yurt, and by eight o'clock, it being then almost dark, we crept in under our furs and felts. Ördek was about 200 yards away, guarding the horses and mules. He was to remain up all night, so as to give us an opportunity to get a last good sound sleep, and in the morning he was to return to Camp no. XLIV.

At midnight the tent-flap was lifted. Ördek put in his head and cried in a terrified whisper: "Bir adam kelldi!" "There's a man!" His words acted like an electric shock. We all three jumped up, seized our rifles and revolvers, and rushed out. The storm was still raging; the moon hung pale amid tattered, swift-flying clouds. Ördek led the way, telling us as he ran how he had seen a dark spectre stealing in amongst the horses. But he was so terrified that, instead of shouting an alarm, he had run off to the tent to tell us. The consequence was that we of course arrived too late. In the dim light of the veiled moon we could just discern two dark mounted shadows hurrying off, driving two loose horses in front of them. The next moment they disappeared behind the hills. Shagdur fired, but without effect. Then he, the Lama, and Ördek hastened in pursuit of the robbers, whilst I remained behind to guard the camp; perhaps it was even now surrounded by the accomplices of the depredators. My men returned in about an hour, after what had proved a bootless errand.

We at once held a council of war. The first thing was to count our animals; all the mules and the two worst horses were still there, quietly grazing. But our two best horses, my white one and Shagdur's yellow one, were missing. From the tracks it would appear that three mounted men had stolen upon the camp in the teeth of the wind. They had approached on foot, leading their horses, which they hid in a depression or dry watercourse that ran down into the lake. From there one of the men approached the camp alone, creeping on his hands and knees, until he came quite close to the two outermost horses. Then, suddenly jumping up, he drove them down towards the lake, where his two companions were waiting with their own horses. Then mounting, they galloped off over the hills. It was just at this moment that we saw them as we rushed out of the tent. I think I was never more annoyed in my life. To have our horses stolen from under the very nose of our own watchman, with two big savage dogs to help him! My first impulse was to abandon the expedition to Lassa altogether, and make the thieves pay dearly for their temerity. I felt inclined to track them down, even though it should take weeks, and then surprise them in the same way. I entirely forgot to scold simple Ördek; he had always proved a capable man hitherto. But his real place was in the desert, and similar uninhabited regions; he was in some respects right when he said that men are the worst enemies you have to contend with —far worse than tigers and sand-storms.

But after a while my indignation cooled down, and I was able to take a calmer view of the situation. We again followed the trail to the top of the hills, and there found it disappear amongst the hard gravel. Shagdur could with difficulty be restrained from pursuing the thieves; his weapon actually burned his hands. He was desperately loth to lose his horse, which he had cared for like a child. But he also quieted down when I told him that these men, whether they were professional thieves or simply yak-hunters who thought the opportunity too good a one to be lost, would certainly not stop until a late hour the following night. Besides, there was not the remotest prospect that we with our stale horses would be able to overtake them. They were our best horses they had taken, and their own animals were no doubt full of go. and

A Night Surprise.

habituated to the mountain-air. And then they knew the lay of the country, while we were entirely ignorant of it; so that they would be able to take advantage of the river-courses and gravel-beds, both to hide their own trail, and to lead us astray with blind ones. Finally, if two of us pursued them, and two stayed behind, we should still further weaken our little company, which was much too weak even as it was. That idea must, therefore, be abandoned; it was too risky. We might congratulate ourselves that the robbers had been content with two horses; and I consoled Shagdur by telling him that had I been in their place I should have stolen *all* the horses, so as to render it quite impossible for us to pursue.

This was a lesson to us. The difficulties of the enterprise were now upon us in real earnest, and we must make up our minds to be more vigilant. Even in the midst of these lonely, dreary mountains, a band of robbers had sprung up, as it were, out of the very ground, and carried off our horses without sc much as a dog barking. In all probability they had no connection with the yak-hunters whom we saw at Camp no. XXXVIII. it was much more likely that the footprints which Sirkin notice in the valley, and the shot which the Mussulmans heard abor the same time, had something to do with our midnight visitor And no doubt they had kept us steadily in sight since the Being afraid to tackle the big caravan, they had retired into som hidden glen, and there lain in wait for the opportunity which they no doubt foresaw would sooner or later come. They had watched us, the little pilgrim band, set out, had followed us stealthily at a distance, dogging us like wolves from behind the hills, and, finally, had availed themselves of the storm which came on to accomplish their nefarious purpose. But we were determined to profit from the experience. From this moment onwards we must live as if we were in an enemy's country, and be prepared, at any hour of the day or night, for an attack from the most unexpected quarter.

Sleep was out of the question for the remainder of that night; so we made a little fire outside the yurt, and crouched round it. Wrapping ourselves in our overcoats, and lighting our pipes, we sat and talked, the moon peeping out at intervals from between the lowering clouds. Towards daybreak we boiled the kettle for tea, and that, together with rice and bread, constituted our breakfast. Then we made an early start. I and Shagdur mounted the remaining two horses. As for Ördek he sat over the fire weeping, beside himself with terror at the thought of having to return the 40 miles back to Camp no. XLIV. alone, on foot, and unarmed. He begged and prayed that he might go with us, and promised that he would keep better watch in future. Then, finding me inflexible, he asked that he might have the revolver; but our midnight adventure had convinced me that it was not advisable to travel in that region without weapons.

I hurriedly scribbled a note to Sirkin on a leaf which I tore out of my diary, telling him what had happened, and enjoining him to keep a vigilant look-out. Robbers were prowling about the neighbourhood, and as they were apparently well informed as to our circumstances, he would have to maintain the strictest watch both day and night, and take particular good care that the caravan animals were not stolen away from him. And, in conclusion, I ordered him to let Cherdon, Li Loyeh, and one other man pursue the thieves, but not to waste more than a week over it. All other information he would be able to obtain from Ördek, who would show them where to pick up the trail. Ördek stuffed the letter into his girdle, and was given a box of matches, so that he might light a fire when he stopped for the night. When he parted from us he looked like a condemned criminal setting out on his last dread procession to the scaffold. But no sooner were we mounted than we saw him stealing along at a half-trot along the lake-side. He thought, I suppose, that it would rain robbers all day, and any moment a bullet might come whistling through the air and pierce him to the heart.

Later on, when our Lassa expedition was ended, he told me how he got on on his way back. All that day, the 29th of July, he did not stop a single moment; nor did he dare to follow our trail in the open, but stole along like a wild cat, through the ravines and watercourses, no matter how they winded and doubled. All day he kept longing intensely for night; but when night came, and the rain poured down in torrents, he was afraid of the darkness, and thought every moment he would be set upon by cut-throats. Two or three times he was nearly frightened out of his wits by kulans peacefully grazing. Then he would stop and crouch down, and roll himself into a ball like a hedgehog, and lie breathlessly still for a time. At last, however, in the pitch-dark night, he came to the throat of the valley where the camp was, and after that he literally ran. The river beside him rumbled in its deep bed, completely

Shagdur, the Author, and Shereb Lama in Pilgrim Attire.

drowning all other sounds. All the way he kept thinking he heard somebody pattering behind him. Every stone hid a lurking miscreant aiming at his heart. How in the darkness and the rain he managed to find his way down the steep slope he did not know. He just kept hurrying on, stumbling, falling, picking himself up again, and time after time forded the river, getting wet to the waist.

Even then his troubles were not ended, for upon approaching the camp, he was as near as possible shot by the sentry, who gave the alarm. But, luckily, Ördek called out to him, and the sentry recognised his voice. The other men came out and crowded round him in amazement, overwhelming him with questions. But for a long time Ördek was not able to answer them ; he was so utterly overcome with fatigue, and dropped breathless, like a wet rag. He had never touched the piece of bread he took with him, nor did his appetite come back until after he had slept through the whole of the following day.

Ördek's story and my letter naturally aroused the fears of the men in camp, and caused them to dread the worst, seeing that only the second night out we had thus been exposed to attack. The incident, however, produced one good result. The men were henceforward always on the alert, and had any robbers been so ill-advised as to think of paying them a visit during the night, they would have met with a very warm reception.

Early the next morning Cherdon got ready to start. He took with him Turdu Bai and Li Loyeh ; poor Ördek was not in a condition to go. In spite of the rain, our trail was distinctly visible the whole of the way, and they also managed to hit upon the robbers' trail. About 20 or 25 miles from our camp the latter had stopped early in the morning, and there been joined by several other men, accompanied by 15 yaks. After that they took to the water, and rode such a long way on gravelly ground and in the streams that Cherdon and his companions never succeeded in picking up the trail again.

CHAPTER XIX.

A WET NIGHT-WATCH.

BUT to return to our pilgrimage. After Ördek left us, we steered our course south-east and east-south-east, and travelled close upon 24 miles. The mules could easily have done more, but we had to think of the horses. On the shores of a sheet of water, close beside the spot where we encamped, we observed indications of sheep having grazed at a comparatively recent date. Thence we struck up a broad valley, where there was an abundance of pasture. A little distance away, in a notch in the hills, on the right, were about 200 yaks. We stopped, and through the telescope looked about for the herdsmen, for the animals appeared to be tame. But when we approached nearer, the yaks took to flight. Now, wild yaks are never found very near to human dwellings; accordingly we might count upon having another two days before we came into contact with the Tibetan nomads.

All the glens and watercourses seemed to converge towards the south-west, where, no doubt, there was a lake. Kulans and antelopes were very numerous. But throughout the march the landscape did not vary—an open expanse, bordered on the south by low mountains. We halted beside a little brook, and as there were now only three of us, I gave a hand with the unloading and putting up of the tent, and, in fact, did anything there was to do. Whilst Shagdur and the Lama looked after the animals, and hoppled them, I gathered dry yak droppings in the skirt of my voluminous Mongol coat—and found it a very interesting occupation. When I had done, the other two pilgrims congratulated me upon the big heap I had managed to get together in such a short time.

It was now no longer "Vasheh Prevoshoditelstvo," for I had strictly forbidden Shagdur and the Lama to show me any outward tokens of respect; on the contrary, they were to treat me as if I were their groom. Shagdur was to pose as the leader of the

An Encampment of the Three Pilgrims

party, and when we camped it was his duty to issue all commands. Speaking Russian was strictly tabooed; nothing but Mongolian issued from our lips. Shagdur played his part splendidly, and I think I may say I acted mine not amiss. At first my good Cossack was reluctant to issue orders to me; but eventually his scruples sat very lightly upon him. As for our Lama, he had no need to personate any character at all; he had simply to be what he actually was—a Lamaist Lama. Mine was the hardest task, seeing that I had to perform two rôles at one and the same time—first that of a Mongol, secondly that of a menial. After having so honourably done my duty as collector of fuel, I had my dinner, drank my tea, smoked my pipe, and lay down and slept like a log until eight o'clock. When I awoke I was alone; the other two men were driving in the animals for the night. But both Shagdur and the Lama were less cheerful than usual. Whilst I was asleep they had seen three Tibetans, who came over a pass in the east, and rode past our camp towards the north-west. Once they had stopped as if to confer together, after which they turned towards our camp; but eventually they disappeared behind a hill, and were not seen again. Their conduct was highly suspicious; they were no doubt waiting for the night. We were now convinced that we were dogged by spies, and that mounted scouts continually patrolled the line of our march. But whether the men whom Shagdur had just seen were acting on their own initiative or by the command of others, we, of course, did not know.

At half-past eight we picketed the animals to a rope stretched between two pegs. The plan on which we arranged our camp that night was the plan we observed throughout. As night-attacks would almost certainly be made against the wind especially seeing that we had dogs with us, we placed the tent so as to have its one opening on the side that was sheltered from the wind, and the animals were picketed some five or six feet in front of it. As soon as it grew dark, we let the fire die down, and brought in the boxes, cooking utensils, saddles, &c., which lay outside. On the other side of the horses and mules we chained the big black dog, Yollbars; while Malenki, a big black and white savage beast, was fastened on the other side of the tent, a little distance away.

We divided the night into three watches of three hours each —9 to 12, 12 to 3, 3 to 6, and as a rule I took the first, and the Lama the last. Consequently I was the first to go on night-duty;

and this night, at any rate, I experienced no difficulty whatever in keeping awake. For one thing I had already had a good sleep, and in the next place I was kept on the tenter-hooks in momentary expectation of an attack. The other two were fast asleep and snoring before nine; they were both tired after the excitement of the previous night. I began my vigil, backwards and forwards, backwards and forwards, sometimes close to the tent, sometimes further away. Never shall I forget the numberless heavy footsteps I took hour after hour between Malenki and Yollbars. The minutes crawled. I counted the turns I took—5, 10, 15, 20—and that only took ten or twelve minutes. Oh, those weary, weary nights! Then I sat down and played with Yollbars, who barked and jumped with joy when I patted him. Then I stopped and stroked the horses, and after them the mules. Then I went and cheered up Malenki a bit. Then I—but why enumerate the tiresome devices I successively adopted for killing time?

The morning had been warm, and at intervals copious showers fell, but the afternoon had been tolerably fair. At 9.30, however, a furious tempest came on. The sky turned as black as ink, the lightning flashed from behind the clouds, and the thunder rolled and rumbled amongst the mountains and over our lonely camp with demoniacal fierceness. The worst of all was the rain; it came down like a deluge. I have never seen it rain faster. It lashed the tent and rattled against the canvas as if it would rend it to pieces, while the tent inside was filled with a fine spray like that from an *eau-de-cologne* bottle, wetting everything. But the sleeping men paid no heed to either dampness or rain; they only pulled their coats up a bit higher, and went on driving their pigs to market for all they were worth. Outside the big splashing raindrops played a loud but merry and musical tune on the Mongolian saucepans and saucepan-lids, which were still standing beside the fire.

For some time I continued my slippery promenade, backwards and forwards, between the dogs, until, feeling at length as wet as a drowned cat, I took shelter inside the tent. The moon was now of little use, for the clouds were wedged together in a compact mass, and the rain came down as if it never meant to stop. However, it was not absolutely dark; the moon did shed a faint, diffused light, just sufficient to show the shadows of the caravan animals, a trifle darker than the background of the night behind them, so that I was able to keep an eye upon, at any rate, their numbers.

Then, lighting my pipe and setting up a candle-end behind the lid of a small box, I jotted down my reflections on the joys and beauties of the night! One sentence, and then a turn round the camp; then back again to the light; another sentence, and another round! The rain drip, dripped off my coat-sleeves, my cap was glued to my bald head as if the two had been cast together in one piece, while my artistic countenance, after these repeated drenchings, bore a close resemblance to a zebra's skin. The temperature did not fall below 4°.0 C., or 39°.2 Fahr., so we had no ground to complain of the cold. The rain continued to stream down without intermission; its monotonous patter-patter drowned all other sounds. But, hark! what was that? A plaintive cry in the distance! Were the Tibetans going to set up the same hyæna concert that the Tanguts did at Karasharuin-kubb (Khara-nor) in 1896? No, it was only Yollbars expressing his disgust at having to lie out in the persistent rain. Another alarm! What was *it?* Nothing more than a distant roll of thunder. And time after time was I thus deceived by the thunder and the rain, and time after time I rushed out, with my revolver cocked under my cape, and stood and listened intently through the falling rain. Then, when all was quiet again, I returned to my candle-end. It was perfectly wretched, especially when my pipe refused to burn; it too had caught the prevailing fashion, and, like everything else, was wet.

Although the rain did not abate, the pigs began to want less forcible driving. We shall have a glorious ride to-morrow! I thought to myself. The monotonous breathing of the mules began to make me feel drowsy, and my eyelids grew heavy; but I never forgot myself for more than five minutes together. Had I failed in my watch I should have been overwhelmed with shame, and should have despised myself.

Every now and again, when the rain tickled them, the animals whipped their flanks with their tails, and occasionally the dogs growled softly. Every time they did so I at once jumped up and took a turn round the camp. At 11.30 I went out, firmly resolved not to come back again until my time was up; and I stayed out until well over 12. Shagdur slept so soundly that I hadn't the heart to wake him, and had just persuaded myself to let him have an extra half-hour, when all of a sudden both the dogs began to bark furiously. The Lama awoke and hurried out with his rifle. I cocked my revolver. We put out the light. We stole round the mules in the direction where we suspected the danger to lie. There we distinctly heard the tramp of horses; the Lama even declared he heard the barking of a dog in another direction. He was just going to fire, but I stopped him. I was determined I would not be the first to begin hostilities; but if the Tibetans made an attack upon us—well, that would be quite another kettle of fish.

That there were horsemen within a few hundred yards of us could no longer admit of a moment's doubt. Leaving the Lama beside the tent, I awoke Shagdur, and we both proceeded down the wind, quietly, cautiously, listening every few paces. Then we distinctly heard a horse departing. After that everything was quiet, and the dogs gradually settled down.

Now it was Shagdur's turn. I heard him splashing through the slush as I crept into my damp sheep-skin. Nights like this are more exciting than instructive—more interesting to read about than to experience. "But you will soon get used to it," I thought to myself, and I very quickly dropped off, and slept well and soundly.

Our Lama, who had had the last watch, came and called us at five o'clock; he thought riding would be preferable to sitting still and indulging in matutinal *dolce far niente* amid such surroundings. I cannot say that we felt particularly brisk or lively after the novel experiences of the night. The air was raw and damp, and we were wet and chilly, and everything smelt sour and nasty. But then it all formed part of the piece; it was the little touches like these that impressed us with the reality of the thing. Nobody had ever heard speak of Lassa pilgrims who were exactly what you might call "Scented darlings!" For my own part, I began to think we were getting along swimmingly. In situations like ours, impressions are apt to be a good deal influenced by the sun. You have a burning desire to see where you are going to, and what your surroundings are like. The night, with its deceitful shadows, is obnoxious even to those who have not the slightest fear of the darkness.

When I started on this crazy expedition my Mussulmans evidently considered that I had somehow, somewhere dropped a goodly portion of the common sense with which Mother Nature had endowed me. And truly it *was* a crazy project, I will admit, to risk so much, my life included, merely for the pleasure of seeing Lassa, a city which, thanks to the descriptions of Indian Pundits and Buriats, their maps and photographs, is far better known, both in respect of its topography and its appearance, than most other towns in Central Asia. But, after two years of quiet, peaceful rambling through the uninhabited parts of the continent, and after my long stretch of strenuous labour, I will honestly confess that I felt an irresistible longing for an adventure which should have a genuine spice of danger in it. I was fascinated by the idea of getting myself involved in difficulties which it would tax all the powers of manhood in me to get out of again with a whole skin; in fact, I wanted to have a good tough tussle with fate. I wanted to pit my alertness, my courage, my resourcefulness, and my resolution against the strong hand of destiny. In a word, it was adventures I sought for, far more than I sought to get to Lassa. My friend the Lama had described the holy city to me so thoroughly that I was almost sick of it. I wanted to see the Tibetans—I wanted to talk to them—I wanted to get to the bottom of their rooted detestation of Europeans. A few years ago an uncritical young man astonished us with tales of his having been tortured in Tibet; but I was in no degree deterred by his sensational stories—for the simple reason that I did not believe them. It would be a gain for everybody concerned if people who find it difficult to stick to the plain truth would leave the writing of books alone.

As you might expect, none of us had a very good appetite that morning, especially as it consisted of nothing better than bread and tea. But after our pipes were lit, and we were well started in the saddle, the day passed in the usual manner. However, it was rather trying to my patience to plot the route from the back of a beast that moved like an antiquated family-coach. The day was as dull and gloomy as the night had been, without a glimpse of sunshine. The skirts of the heavy black clouds hung so low down that we kept expecting to see them burst—crash!—upon the earth. The downpour, however, turned out, when it did come, to be less formidable than we had expected—only a little occasional splatter of rain, with a determined hail-squall between, whilst we were crossing the mountains on the south.

During the course of the morning the Lama announced that he saw a black tent away in the south-east, and wanted to go to it to gather information; but I preferred to keep on. Upon entering the glen which led up into the mountains, the ascent increased rapidly, until it soon became a stiff climb. Quitting the brook which trickled down it, we rode zigzag up the hills of red, disintegrated sandstone. In two or three places we observed camping-grounds which had been recently used, and there was a cairn on the summit of the pass. Over on the other side we went down by a very steep declivity into a broad glen leading to the south-east. A little way down, in an expansion of the glen, we came across the dead body of a sheep, with its load on its back, consisting of salt packed in a two-ended sack. It had evidently been left behind by a Tibetan sheep-caravan, which had been up to the small lakes where our robber friends had paid their respects to us, to fetch salt, which, as I have already said, lay thickly around some of them. We had, indeed, observed traces of sheep in the locality. As we advanced the deserted camp-fires became more and more frequent, as well as the bones of the animals upon which the Tibetans had dined. Moreover, a herd of yaks had recently travelled up one of the side-glens we passed.

Upon reaching a point where our glen swung away to the south-west, we turned our backs upon it, and struck up into the next mountain-range. Here Shagdur soon hit upon a frequented track, and from the top of the pass to which it led us, we again commanded a wide prospect to the south, though it was not a very encouraging one—being merely an endless succession of mountains and mountain ranges as far as the eye could reach. Not a man, not a black tent, not a herd or a flock within sight. A little longer, then, we were to be still free from inquisitive glances; though all the time we had a presentiment that hidden spies were dogging our footsteps, and never lost sight of us. The sky was gloomy and heavy as lead, and the hours crawled wearisomely past. Day though it was, we were still on the stretch. We knew nothing whatever about the country we were traversing, we knew nothing whatever about its circumstances or its people. Yet we were convinced that, sooner or later, the unexpected would happen. Never for one moment durst we relax our vigilance; a critical moment might come when we least of all expected it. From the pass we again followed a path which was perfectly distinct, and evidently much used, until we reached a valley that abounded in marshes, pools, natural springs, brooks, and rivulets, with luxuriant grass. The yak-dung had been turned over to dry, so that whoever did it meant to come back again. And there were signs of nomad camps in every direction.

As the grass seemed to thin out further on, and there happened to be a suitable position from the strategic point of view

In the Pouring Rain and Mire.

for our solitary camp, we decided to stop where we were. The wet tent was reared on a neck of land, about 230 feet across, between two small lakes. We viewed the approaching night with a certain amount of uneasiness. We felt that something would happen, we wondered what. The usual routine over, we lay down and tried to sleep ; though, for my own part, I heard the rain streaming down in torrents all the time ; indeed I felt it drip—drip—dripping from the canvas down upon me.

At eight o'clock we tethered the animals in the usual way. The air was still, but it rained as it only rains in Gilan and Mazanderan (the two Caspian provinces of Persia) ; in fact, the only place where I have seen rain anything like it was at Asterabad. But this night proved much worse than the preceding : it was as though hundreds of gutters were emptying themselves without cessation over our little camp. But then it was the regular rainy season in that country, and we had no right to complain. If you kept watch, as I did that night, for four hours at a stretch, and got drenched to the skin till you hadn't a dry stitch on you, you would no longer need to ask what is meant by a good, thorough, honest, well-intentioned rain. Sometimes I sat in the tent-door for a little shelter. To hear the rain beating on the mules' pack-saddles was like the swish of clothes in a wash-tub ; it ran off them in a stream. When the animals shook themselves, it was like the spray of a waterfall. Every now and again they pricked their ears, and the dogs growled menacingly.

I let Malenki loose for a bit, that he might go and hunt up a bone or two at a camping-ground close by, for during the last two or three days neither he nor Yollbars had had anything to eat except bread. All at once one of them began to bark, and very soon the other joined in too. But it was a false alarm : one of the mules had struggled loose, and was taking a walk up the nearest hillside. I, of course, went to fetch her back ; but it was easier said than done. She was fresh and lively, and kept me dodging about the hillsides a long time before I succeeded in getting hold of her halter. Her escapade demoralized one of her companions, who followed suit. Again it was a nice business to catch her. For a good half-hour or more I could not complain that I belonged to the "unemployed."

When I was awakened, after only a couple of hours sleep, on the morning of the 31st of July, to help with the packing up and reloading, the rain was still coming down with the same lusty energy. There was, however, nothing for it : the order was inexorable: "Mount at daybreak." And so away we posted to the south-east across a difficult and heavily rolling country. There was not now a single dry rag throughout the whole of our little caravan; the rain could not make us any wetter. But, oh! we did long for just a little sunshine to come and dry us. Yet we never saw anything of it that day; the grey and lowering clouds never lifted, though they did distinguish themselves by an extraordinary generosity. When I got into my soft saddle, the water squelched out of it, and my boots were soon so full that every time I moved them, the water inside swished backwards and forwards. When I lifted my arm, it was like wringing out a wet clout. Wretchedness, thy name is Rain in Tibet! Oh, if only it had snowed instead!

The route we were following plainly led, we now saw, to Lassa. After crossing five passes, the trail joined another which came from the west, and was freshly trampled by a big herd of yaks; and as the heavy rain soon blotted out all animals' footsteps, we concluded that the herd in question must have passed quite recently—maybe that very morning. If we made haste, we might ibly overtake the caravan.

CHAPTER XX.

FIRST MEETING WITH THE NOMADS.

BEFORE we got very much further, we saw, away in the far distance, a number of black dots: they were yaks. A little while after that a flock of sheep loomed up out of the semi-darkness; then a tent, which had hitherto been masked, came into view on the edge of a brook. Whilst I and Shagdur continued our journey, the Lama rode across to the tent to see what he could make of its inmates. We assumed, of course, that they were Mongol pilgrims, and thought that we might perhaps travel in company with them. But they turned out to be Tanguts, making a pilgrimage from the temple of Kum-bum, in north-west China. They were travelling very slowly, resting one or two days at every camp, and considered that it would take them still a fortnight to reach Lassa. They manifested a far too lively interest in us, and pumped us about everything—who we were, how many we were, where we came from, where we were going to, and so on, and so on. They had 50 yaks with them, two horses, and three dogs; but these last quickly repented their desire for a nearer acquaintance with Yollbars and Malenki.

The flock of sheep consisted of no less than 700, and were only guarded by an old woman, who, however, was apparently quite accustomed to pilgrims, for she exhibited not the least fear of us. She might very well have done so, for after all the rain and mud and mire we looked little better than tramps. The worst knights of the road would have had no cause to blush for us, for the very last traces of refinement in our appearance had been punctiliously but thoroughly washed away. The old woman told us that in the next glen we should find a black tent, where we could obtain everything we wanted, above all, information about the road to Lassa.

And, sure enough, we found the tent in the spot she indicated, and encamped about three-quarters of a mile from it, choosing, for safety's sake, an open situation. The Lama at once went to the people in the tent, and returned well satisfied with his visit. The tent, which he found guarded by dogs, was inhabited by a young man and two women, who, however, refused to sell us either sheep, or milk, or fat, or tsamba, on the ground that it was a sacred day. If, however, we would wait patiently until the morrow, we might have everything we wanted; but, seeing that we were peaceful Mongols, they gave him there and then some dry argol, or yak-dung. The Lama brought a bagful of it with him; and it was a good thing he did, for our own supply was so wet that we should hardly have been able to make a fire without it. In reply to his question, as to whether they would sell us two or three horses, the people answered that that rested with the master of the encampment, and he was just then absent from home.

Scarcely had the Lama finished his story, when the man in question appeared on a hill-side not very far away. As soon as he saw us, he stopped and scrutinized us closely. The Lama, however, went and invited him to our tent, and he came without ceremony, showing no fear whatever, and squatted down on the wet ground just opposite the tent-opening. Sampo Singhi, for that was his name, was a man probably about forty years old; his face black rather than sunburnt, beardless, and wrinkled; his dirty hair as black as a raven's wing, and the rain trickled off it down upon the ragged sack-like cloak he wore; boots of coarse felt, which had originally been white; pipe and tobacco-pouch hung from his girdle; everything from top to toe unspeakably filthy—such was the appearance of the first Tibetan we came into contact with. He was bare-headed and bare-legged, except for his boots—in other words, he was minus inexpressibles. It must have been pretty cool, riding about in those rains clad in such primitive attire.

He kept blowing his nose incessantly with his fingers, and with an amazing display of energy; and we, for safety's sake, did the same, for we did not know but that these demonstrative acts of politeness were imperatively demanded by Tibetan etiquette when you met a stranger. The picture we made in that streaming rain was one which would have rejoiced the hearts of the gods. Pity there were none to see us!

Sampo Singhi pried, without the slightest shyness or compunction, into all our belongings; so that it was a good thing I stuffed away my instruments and diary before he came. He was

A Young Tibetan Shepherd.

particularly pleased with our tubs, which were narrow at the top and broadened out towards the bottom. He remarked, with the air of a connoisseur, that the Mongols always had tubs like those. Of me he manifested not the slightest suspicion; but then I was nearly as dirty as he was. The acquaintance

An Older Tibetan.

made, and confidence established, our Lama succeeded in squeezing out of Sampo Singhi the information that the site of our camp of the previous day, between the two small lakes, was called Merik; and a river which we had seen that day in the east was called Garchu-sänghi. The spot at which we were then encamped was called Gom-jima, and the nearest mountain-range in the south-east, Haramuk-lurumak. He told us also that for two days more we should hardly be likely to meet many nomads, but on the third day their tents would be numerous. If we travelled by short, slow stages it would take us twelve days to reach Lassa; but if we travelled at the rate we had done that day—we did very nearly 26¼ miles—we should reach the city in eight days. Yes, he said, the road we were following led right enough to the pass of Lani-la.

Shagdur and the Lama were both snuff-takers, and Sampo Singhi was induced to take a good strong pinch. But he ought not to have done it; it was naughty of him. He began to sneeze, and sneezed and sneezed as though he never meant to stop. Nor was he the least bit put out when we laughed at him. He asked, quite innocently, whether we were accustomed to put pepper in our snuff; but he was not to be tempted to indulge in a second pinch.

Suddenly bethinking him of the responsibilities of his position, Shagdur roared out at me: "Boy, don't sit there with your mouth open. Go and fetch in the horses." We did not know whether Sampo Singhi understood Mongolian or not; but, at all events, he manifested not the slightest astonishment when I jumped to my feet, ran up the hill-side, and began to drive the animals towards our tent. Fortunately he took his departure before I had been at it very long, otherwise he had sense enough to have asked himself, what does that fellow know about mules? For no sooner did I get them all together, than Sarik Kullak, or "yellow-ears," took it into his head to gallop back to the abundant pasture from which I had fetched him. I followed him, and brought him back; but when we got to the spot where I had left the other mules, behold! they were gone. The mules were masters of the situation. Finally, I managed to catch three of them, and took care to keep fast hold until I had them safe on the picketing line.

In the evening the sun, when setting, condescended to honour us with a parting glance from underneath the heavy masses of cloud, and about nine o'clock the moon peeped out for a few short minutes. But soon after ten the wind got up in the west, and I had to turn my attention to the tent. A little later on the rain began to stream down again, steadily, resolutely, persistently. It was as much as ever I could do to see the animals. That night, however, we were a good deal easier in our minds. Since our unexpected meeting with the yak-hunters, we had not come across any of the natives, although we felt that they were hovering about our path like evil spirits, and once had even caught us napping. Now, however, we had the peaceful nomads for our nearest neighbours; besides, Sampo Singhi assured us that there were no robbers in that part of the country. But for all that we did not relax our vigilance one whit; the only difference was that I now ventured to light the brazier inside the tent. It made our already abominably dirty dwelling still more dirty by adding soot to the mud.

On the 1st of August I was awakened with the words: "Three Tibetans are coming to see us!" I made haste to get up and hide away any little articles that lay about and might have betrayed the presence of a mysterious stranger. The approaching visitors were two men and a woman, and their errand, it was evident even at a distance, could only be a peaceful one, for they were leading a sheep behind them, and carried several things in their hands. Sampo Singhi was again the principal spokesman, as he arranged his various delicacies round our fire. "Beautiful things—beautiful things!" he exclaimed. After our scanty fare of the last few days, we should feed like princes! He had brought us a big piece of *mar* (fat), a bowl of *sho* (sour milk), a dish of *chorá* (powdered cheese), a can of *oma* (fresh milk), and some *bema* (clotted cream). What more could we wish for? And, truth to say, they were all first-rate except the cream, which was very little different from a packet of hairy, sooty pieces of skin, squeezed tight together. Powdered cheese is one of the main ingredients in tsamba, the others being flour, tea, and lumps of fat or butter—all mixed in the proper proportions, and stirred together in one dish. I must confess I never succeeded in cultivating a thorough liking for this delicacy, though the Mongols set such immense store by it. On the other hand, I cannot speak too highly of the sour milk. It surpassed all my previous conceptions in that line; and when it was all done, had some Fortunatus come to me and offered me a choice amongst all the delicacies of the earth, without hesitation I should have chosen just another bowl of sour milk. It was thick, and white, and tart. Tibetan *sho* is unsurpassed by anything of the kind in the world!

But the time came to pay for these fine things, and Shagdur drew forth a few pieces of Chinese silver. Sampo Singhi took them and weighed them, and pronounced them beautiful, but declared that he never accepted anything but silver struck at Lassa. As we had no such money, we tried him with blue

Chinese cloth, and that bait took. Sampo Singhi stroked it tenderly, passed it through his fingers, examined it closely, studied its effect at arm's-length—in a word, he was enraptured with it. His noble spouse's little eyes were alight with covetousness. We had brought with us two bundles of this cloth expressly for purposes of barter, and Sampo Singhi complacently assured us he would be satisfied with one of these. Then began the usual Asiatic higgling and bargaining, which resulted in Sampo Singhi finally contenting himself with a third of a bundle—9⅓ yards. But no matter how we tempted him, he would not part with any horses. When this important business was settled, each party congratulated themselves that they had got the better of the other!

At my suggestion our Lama then asked Sampo Singhi to kill the sheep, and cut it up; he might then, as a reward for the hospitality and friendliness he had shown us, keep the skin for himself. He was delighted with the suggestion. With carefully veiled indifference, I watched how he set about it. Flinging the animal on its left side, he tied together three of its feet, leaving the left fore-foot free; then he wound a thin soft leather strap several times round its nose, pulling it tight; next, placing the animal's head in such a position that its two horizontal cork-screw-like horns touched the ground, he put his feet on them. The sheep lay motionless as if in a vice. Then Sampo Singhi stuck the thumb and fore-finger of his right hand into his victim's nostrils, his object being to kill it by suffocation. I took a stealthy peep at my watch to see how many minutes it would take, though I afterwards forgot to note down the time; but I do remember that it took a good many minutes, and that I suffered unspeakably, as I witnessed the poor animal kicking and struggling in the convulsions of death. The whole time the old man kept repeating at a desperate rate: "On maneh padmeh hum." It put me in mind of the Mussulmans' method of killing sheep, for they also, whilst reddening the knife-blade with innocent blood, as if at one and the same time to quiet their own consciences and flatter their Creator, generally gabble a string of prayers in praise of the Almighty!

At last, however, the sheep ceased to struggle; its legs relaxed, and Sampo Singhi got up. It was hard to witness this cruelty without taking steps to stop it. However, I dare not betray my feelings; besides, it would have profited little to interfere with time-honoured customs. After that we breakfasted together on the milk foods which we had bought, and I let the dogs stuff themselves with meat, as a reward for their faithful services at night. As for Madame Sampo Singhi, she was so enraptured with her piece of cloth, that she quite lost her appetite, and could do nothing but nod good-naturedly first to one of us and then to another, time and time again. She was dressed in a similar manner to her lord and master, except that her coarse black hair was gathered into two long plaits hanging down her back, though for the most part it stuck out like rats'

A Tibetan Woman.

tails in every direction all over her head. How on earth she contrived to get so amazingly dirty as she was, I could not for the life of me understand; but oh, how I *did* envy her! I suppose my skin was of finer texture—at any rate, the rain persisted in washing it "clean." But upon that good lady's cheeks the filth was plastered so thick and firm that she might have forced potatoes in it with every prospect of success. I imagine the pores of a Tibetan's skin are atrophied—at all events, they never can discharge their proper functions rightly.

When we started again Sampo Singhi good-naturedly helped us to load up; and our tent, after all the rain it had absorbed, was twice its ordinary weight. The honest nomad wished us a successful journey and a pleasant visit to Lassa, and did it, our Lama said, in such courteous terms, as showed that he was no stranger to the elegancies of Lamaist manners. Evidently he had no desire to detain us; otherwise he would have given us some warning of what we should have to face before the day was over. He simply said, however, that we should have to cross a pass, and that the road to Lassa was everywhere quite easy to follow, and that was all. We promised to look him up when we returned, and did so, but failed to see him, as he had moved his household Penates to fresh pastures green.

When we started, about nine o'clock, the clouds lowered heavy as lead over the earth, boding nothing good, and it was only half light. On the other side of the hills and knobby mountains we struck the river Garchu-sänghi, which on a closer inspection of it looked anything but inviting. As we proceeded, its glen narrowed rapidly, and the dense masses of water rolled along with a hollow rumble between their containing cliffs. The path was in places very difficult, crossing over the shoulders of the crags by dangerous pathways. Here marmots and hares were particularly numerous, and our dogs put themselves to a vast amount of unnecessary trouble in their passion for disturbing them. Five minutes after we left Gom-jima, the inevitable rain begun again, and we were very soon wet through. It would soon be a novel experience to feel dry. The ground was simply one illimitable morass. Our animals splashed and squelched and plumped their way through the slush. Over a final pass and down a steep slope, and the country once more opened out; for as far as the rain would permit us to see there were no mountains in the south. But leaving the Garchu-sänghi on our left, we soon turned south-east, taking precious good care not to wander off the track into the deep, tenacious mud. After proceeding a good distance in this new direction, we found ourselves moving straight down upon the right bank of a river, so big and so broad that at first we took it for a lake, especially as the rain prevented us from seeing the opposite bank. But above the sharp splashing of the rain-drops on its surface we soon detected a hollow, rumbling roar, as of a vast flood in movement. The yellow muddy colour of the water also told us plainly that it was a river; and as we stood on the brink, and saw it rolling its overwhelming masses west-south-west, we realized that our fate was sealed. There was no other way except to ford it.

It was, in short, no other than the Sachu-sangpo, which had been previously crossed in this neighbourhood by M. Bonvalot, Prince Henri d'Orléans, and Mr. Rockhill; but in consequence of the enormous rainfall it had swollen amazingly, and was divided into at least a score of arms, each of them big enough to make a respectable river. Four of these were, indeed, so formidable that I thought it would be almost impossible to ford them. Without a moment's hesitation and without making the least examination of the ford, our Lama, who always led the way, rode straight into the water, and we of course followed obediently in his footsteps. However, everything went off all right—for a time. The river was not more than three feet deep, except in one or two places, though every moment I kept expecting to see the Lama, who rode the smallest mule, disappear amid the turbid flood. After scrambling about half-way over, we stopped to rest a minute or two on a mud-bank, where the current flowed more gently and was barely a foot deep. Up to this point I had been in a state of great anxiety, but now felt considerably relieved. My self-congratulation was, however, of a precarious character. We had half the river behind us, it is true, but the other half was still before us, and there we were, in the middle of that vast, roaring, racing, foaming flood, rolling down its immense volumes upon us as if it meant to sweep us away like straws. With these broad expanses of water moving swiftly past on both sides of us, it was not at all easy to keep one's head and ward off giddiness.

The Lama, digging his heels into his mule, once more plunged into the boiling current. Ten paces and the animal was immersed to his tail. Up went the rider's knees, to keep the water out of his boots. Almost at the same instant the mule which carried our two skin-covered boxes was in difficulties. The boxes, being watertight, lifted her off her feet, and the current, swinging her half-round, carried her with it. She was, of course, drawn by the suction into the swiftest part of the current, till nothing of her was visible except her head and the two boxes. I gave her up for lost. But in some extraordinary manner she contrived to get her footing again. By that time she was quite close to the left bank, up which she managed to scramble unaided, although she was a very long way down stream.

As soon as we saw what had happened to the mule, Shagdur

and I shouted frantically to the Lama to turn back; but he did not hear us. The river churned and foamed around him as if he were a paddle-wheel. He merely hoisted his knees higher up on his saddle, and patted his mule as she sank deeper and deeper into the water. I can only say that the contempt of danger which on this occasion he displayed was nothing short of heroic; for you must remember he was dressed, as indeed we all were, in a big, heavy sheepskin, saturated with rain, and was, besides, unable to swim. For my own part, I had fastened up my coat and loosened my girdle, so as to be ready to fling them off at a moment's notice. Although I by no means wanted a bath—that is to say, deliberately wished for one—I was fully prepared for a dip, for in that incessant rain we got stiff and spiritless, and the weather was much too cool to tempt one to take a bath, especially now, when everything in the nature of personal cleanliness was so diametrically at variance with our Mongolian principles.

But fortune favours the brave, and we very soon saw our Lama's mule beginning to rise out of the water, and the young man soon after dropped his feet into the stirrups. For us, with our bigger horses, the passage was not so dangerous.

The Sachu-sangpo, however, as if in revenge for our audacity, was resolved not to let me off without a wetting. "If you dare try," it said, "to penetrate to the holy of holies of Tibet, you shall at least have reason to remember your insolence in defying the hindrance which I put in your way." The last of the arms, one of the four biggest, although not more than 100 feet across, was deep and very swift. The Lama and Shagdur were already safely across, for I was lingering behind. Without noticing which way they had gone, I struck straight across towards the spot where I saw them standing. My horse sank in up to the flanks. Higher and higher rose the water. Ugh! here it was pouring into my boots! Now it was over my knees. Now it was at the top of my saddle. Very soon there was nothing left above water but the horse's head and neck. The Lama and Shagdur screamed themselves purple trying to make me understand which way the ford ran. But not a sound did I hear owing to the roaring of the river. Now it was up to my waist. I was just going to slip off my horse when his feet went from under him, and he began to swim. Instinctively I laid hold of his mane; as it turned out, it was the very best thing I could have done; for he soon touched bottom again, and, making a desperate effort, succeeded in scrambling up the steep bank, the water pouring like a tide off both horse and rider. I had had my bath, a thorough one and no mistake. But the strain made me shaky in the knees for a long time afterwards.

This wetting made, it is true, very little difference to us, for we were all thoroughly drenched to the skin already by the rain; yet somehow rain is preferable to being dipped bodily with your clothes on into a running river. All our belongings —tent, boxes, clothing, food—were in the same condition. After this adventure our little party, standing on the bank, cut a sorrier figure than ever. Still, it was a good thing to be safe on the other side of the river. Nobody could tell how long this ever-blessed rain would continue, and until it stopped the river would certainly not fall. It had taken us twenty-six minutes to cross from one side to the other; but then we had forded the stream slowly, and portions of the river-bed, between the arms, were not covered with water. As I counted them, my horse took 716 steps in those parts of the river only which were actually under water; in other words, the stream, if continuous in breadth, would have been close upon 550 yards wide. To calculate the volume of a river so split up as this was, and under such circumstances as those we crossed it in, was not to be thought of. I should, however, estimate it approximately at 8,000 or 9,000 cubic feet in the second. It is only in the rainy season, and then not very often, that the Sachu-sangpo attains such enormous dimensions. Anyway it is one of the largest rivers in the interior of Tibet. I am not, of course, speaking of those which find an outlet to the ocean, but only of those which have the whole of their course from source to mouth within the country itself. At a later period we were again destined to form a close acquaintance with this river, namely, in the lowest part of its course.

The valley through which it flowed stretched 85° west of south, but was soon lost to view in the blur of the rain. Grey, chill, dreary—such was the landscape that faced us when we turned our dripping backs upon the Sachu-sangpo. My boots were now painfully watertight—until it occurred to me that there was really no need for me to haul along with me the great weight they contained. This was not, indeed, the first time that I had carried water in my boots. One previous occasion was in the Desert of Takla-makan in 1895; but then it was to save a man's life. Now, however, nobody's life was at stake, and we certainly could not complain of want of water. I stopped and emptied my boots, and then hung them on the saddle behind me, and rode barefoot. The boxes were less tenacious reservoirs; the water was already dripping out of them, and went on dripping until we encamped. And this we soon did, for we had all had enough for that day. We found a grassy hill, where the rain had penetrated the ground without converting it into a morass, and there, beside a little brook, we halted. Before dark the brook had swollen out to three times the size of what it was when we arrived, and I drew a sigh of satisfaction as I thought of what the Sachu-sangpo would be like behind us. It would have been utterly impossible to cross it then. I was sure that Sampo Singhi had deliberately abstained from warning us, either lest we should stay too long on his pasture-grounds, or because he did not wish to accompany us and show us the best place for fording the stream. I must simply call the Camp no. L., for I do not know what was the name of the locality. And truly a cheerful camp it was! All our baggage was saturated, and several of our things destroyed. Our Lama was most concerned about his medicine-chest—that is to say, the cloth and paper bags in which he kept his medicaments and other remedies. For a little while we were puzzled how to get a fire. There was plenty of yak dung, but it was so wet it would not burn. But after stripping off the outer wet layers, and wrapping the inner cakes in dry paper, we at last succeeded. Then I took off my clothes and at the risk of scorching them dried them at the anything but odoriferous argol fire.

Pitiless and unemotional, night wrapped her wings about the earth, and the moon was unable to send even one transient gleam to light up the rain-drenched uplands of Tibet. When I began my four hours' wearisome watch, it was chill and gloomy and dark and windy, and it rained as if—as if the sluice-gates of heaven were pulled up and burnt! The tent canvas flapped like a sail in an unsteady wind. I fancied I heard stealthy footsteps approaching. Then it was horsemen charging down at full gallop. Twice during the night, and from different directions, I heard shouts. Perhaps they were the pilgrims from Kumbum; but, no, surely they would never be so foolish as to try to cross the Sachu-sangpo.

What with watching at night and the stretch we were kept upon all day, the suspense was beginning to play upon our nerves. There was now no longer any secret about our being on the way. We were already amongst the Tibetans, and each succeeding day brought us nearer to a crisis. We were, it is true, slowly but surely approaching our goal; but we were getting tired—very tired. In fact I almost longed that we might be stopped in some way or other. I would give worlds to sleep my sleep out. On the other hand, I thought that having surmounted two such difficulties as the attack of the robbers and the passage of the Sachu-sangpo, fortune would surely go on and favour us to the end, and permit us to reach Lassa.

That night also one or two of our animals broke loose during my spell of watching. Both my companions were sleeping heavily. Our Lama, strange to say, was now in good heart, and took a cheerful view of our prospects, and yet at first he had not been willing to come with us. Shagdur was calm, but grave. They were both splendid fellows, just the sort of men to have with you in an enterprise like that which I was embarked upon, if it was not to have a disastrous termination. When midnight came, I gave poor Shagdur not one minute's grace. Whilst he, after examining his rifle, crept out into the rain, I crept into my miserable bed. He was too giddy with sleep, I was too drowsy, for us to talk. We changed places without exchanging a word.

CHAPTER XXI.

YAK CARAVANS.

OUR Lama whiled away the tedium of his watch by converting a preserved fruit tin into a lamp, fashioning a wick out of a rope-end, and feeding his lamp with mutton fat. That was the only light we had on the morning of the 2nd of August. During the day a remarkable thing happened: it stopped raining! The sky was, it is true, threatening enough, but it cleared up towards evening. Our poor animals were, however, unable to do more than 15½ miles. Both the horses were completely done up, and two of the mules had sore backs.

We now followed the little brook beside which we had encamped until we came to a small pass. Then, after traversing a chaos of hills, we once more reached open country, and in the far distance, that is, to the south-east, soon perceived a mysterious black patch on the horizon. When we approached nearer to it, it turned out to be a herd of yaks, belonging to a caravan encamped on a hillside immediately overlooking the road. The herd numbered about 300, all pack animals.

The men of the caravan, 25 in number, having no tents, sat round their fires in the open air. Their baggage, which consisted of cube tea, sewed up in sacking, was stacked up in a dozen piles beside them. They were carrying it from Kumbum, in the west of the Chinese province of Kan-su, to Tashilumpo, on the Brahmaputra. They would therefore soon turn off to the right, that is, to the south of the highway to Lassa. They were only travelling by night, halting during the day to let their animals graze. That is unquestionably an excellent plan when you know the way, and are not making maps. A troop of fierce dogs, which came rushing to meet us, were received by Yollbars and Malenki in a fashion which inspired even their owners with respect. We were riding quietly past their stacks of tea, when several of the men came down to the roadside to look at us. Thereupon we stopped. They were all naked to the waist, their coats being flung back from their brown chests and shoulders, and held in place by the girdle. Their first question was "How many are you?" as though they wanted to know which side would be most likely to win in case of a scrimmage. Then they asked: "Have you anything to sell? Where do you come from? How long have you been on the road? Where are you making for?" And when we told them "Lassa," they thought it a perfectly natural thing that we should do so. All the same, I overheard an old man, as he

A Tibetan Caravan-man.

pointed to me and nudged his neighbour, utter the solitary word, "Peling!" *i.e.*, European!

They were a rough-looking crew, a good deal like robbers. With their dirty-brown complexion, and thick black hair, which was often gathered into two pigtails, they were not unlike North American Indians. One of them understood a little Mongolian and asked good-naturedly, "Ämur sän baneh?" or "How do you do?" Most of them, however, paid not the slightest attention to us, but remained beside their camp-fires, drinking tea and smoking, as though there was nothing at all uncommon in the sight of pilgrims. The men who interviewed us, however, invited us to stop and encamp beside them; but we were not ambitious for company, and after a few minutes' further conversation we resumed our march.

My horse now so far gave up that he was unable to keep pace with the mules, so that after going about a mile further, we judged it prudent to stop and pitch the tent beside a spring in the open, about a stone's throw south of the road. The latter was now a regular highway, and afforded evidence of a lively traffic.

It was a splendid afternoon; the sun warm—nay, quite hot—and we spread out everything we possessed to dry—clothes, sheep-skins, wraps, rugs, etc.—and a gentle south-west breeze helped the sun. However, not long after this we once more heard the thunder, and in a little it was followed by a fierce squall of hail, and this again was succeeded by a sharp burst of rain; so that we had to bundle our belongings hurriedly together and pitch them helter skelter into the tent. Most of the thunderclaps had a peculiar metallic sound, which died away slowly in the far distance, like the echo of a church bell. I have never heard anything like it before. It was only immediately over our camp that the storm raged; the country all around was bathed in bright sunshine. That evening we sat a long time over our fire, discussing our position, and decided at the first opportunity to exchange our exhausted mules and horses for fresher animals—even yaks would be better than nothing.

During the last few days nothing of a suspicious character had happened in our neighbourhood; but our Lama thought that the yak-hunters would almost certainly send intelligence to the chief of Nakkchu, and in that case he would at once despatch special messengers into every part of his province, with instructions to keep a sharp watch upon the roads that led to Lassa. Once we reached the more inhabited districts, where the people were accustomed to pilgrims, we should be less likely to attract attention. That night we kept careful watch, for the escort of the tea caravan, ten at least of whom carried firearms, had not inspired us with an over-great degree of confidence. Had they chosen to fall upon us in the darkness our position would have been desperate indeed. Although it was urgently desirable that we should push on as fast as possible, we nevertheless decided to rest the 3rd of August where we were. The locality was called by the Tanguts Amdo-mochu, and they said that for a yak-caravan it was a journey of five days thence to Nakkchu, and seven to the pass of Lani-la.

I was awakened at nine o'clock next morning by my companions, after a thorough good night's rest. They said the tea caravan was approaching, and would be worth looking at; and, in truth, it was an extremely original and picturesque sight. They marched in military order, and in divisions of 30 or 40 yaks each. The animals travelled slowly, with short pottering steps, but kept rank without occasioning much trouble

A Tame Yak, the Animal I Rode from Leh to Kara-korum in 1902.

to the two or three men who were in charge of each detachment. If a yak chanced to stray from the ranks one of the drivers would stretch out his arms towards it, and whistle shrilly, and the beast would at once return to its place. The men urged on their animals with short, shrill, staccato cries. Considering the strength of a yak, their loads were light. All the men travelled on foot, and none of them were in the least degree inquisitive. Although they went close past our tent not one stopped and peeped in; they were too intent upon their business.

Our Lama went and spoke to two or three of them. They said that by way of a change they had rested the past night, and were now marching by day; also that, having reached a region where the grass was more abundant and of a better quality they could let the yaks graze during the night, particularly as it was moonshine. They again invited us to get ready and accompany them to their next camp. This travelling company from Kum-bum were Tanguts, men of the same race as the Tibetans, and speaking the same language. The entire caravan—the yaks, the men, their clothes, their weapons, their dogs—all were perfectly black, and they were accompanied by black shadows, for the sun now came out. It was like a procession of demons! They were, as I have said, on their way to the holy temple of Tashi-lumpo, and the bazaars of Shigatse, where they would sell their tea.

With the whole day before us we meant to have a thorough good rest. As this was the first real opportunity we had had to get our belongings dry, we spread everything out in the sun on sheepskins and cloaks, and with the thermometer at 14°.6 C. or 58°.3 Fahr. it was appreciably warm. I even took off most of my own clothes, and put them also in the sun. Then we filled our boots with warm, dry sand, so as to make them reassume their proper shape. That day I had the indescribable pleasure of cooking our dinner. After cutting the pieces of meat into thin rashers I roasted them in butter from Sampo Singhi's "farm," and they made a very delicate dish, flavoured as they were with powdered cheese and salt. The sour milk was unfortunately all done, but we had some tea and raisins for dessert. The latter were discovered by our Lama when he was rummaging amongst his precious medicine bags. He had brought them with him all the way from Charkhlik, but had never produced any of them before. The rest of the day I spent basking in the sunshine with my pipe, and a saddle for my pillow. I have seldom felt so indolent as I did on the 3rd August, 1901. Shagdur and the Lama slept most of the time; though we took care to keep our animals within sight all day.

The Lama, with the mien of an artist, painted my head all over down to the roots of my hair, and even inside my ears. For future use he provided me with a little box of brown paint and a small brush, so that when necessary I could, with the help of my bright watch-case, touch up the colouring myself. For I admit it is annoying when you, like a conjuror with his one-two-three! change your skin, to find a pink patch showing, much as if a piece of a ball-beauty's dress were to get pasted on a chimney sweep's nose.

The only language we used was Mongolian; neither I nor Shagdur ever uttered a word of Russian. Before going farther we thought it best to be prepared with the answers we should give in case we should be cross-examined by the Tibetans. Our story was to be that we were all Buriats from Sakhir, and had travelled through the land of the Khalkha Mongols and Tsaidam. Our Lama would on no account allow himself to pass for a Mongol: he was a Buriat, and, lest he should be recognised again by his acquaintances in Lassa, he put on darkened wire spectacles like those I wore, but he intended to keep out of their way as much as possible. The man he was most afraid of was the chief lama of the temple in which he had pursued his studies. If he were recognised he expected the consequences would be serious. The Tibetans would allow us to return, but would detain him, under the pretext that he was a Lassa lama, and would then punish him as a traitor who had showed the spies of the Europeans the way into the forbidden territory. Whether we were resting or whether we were crossing the unknown mountains he gabbled incessantly his prayers to the eternal gods, and argued the point with his conscience again and again.

He took the greatest interest in Christianity, and repeatedly asked me to tell him about my faith. As far as he could see, there were many points of contact between Christianity and Lamaism, and I had quite as good a right as anybody else to make the pilgrimage to Lassa. His knowledge was confined to what he had gleaned from the holy books of Tibet and Mongolia, and seeing me engaged about so many things of which he had never hitherto had the slightest conception, such as investigating the nature of the earth's crust, studying the heavenly bodies, and reading strange books, he came to the conclusion that I was at least as good as a lama, and that the authorities at Lassa ought to thank me if I chose to pay them a visit. The Dalai Lama was omniscient: he knew who we were, and why we were travelling to Lassa; indeed, he knew what we talked about every day. He would see to it that no ill happened to me; but what his attitude would be towards our Lama himself was another and a very different question. If my God was Almighty, would I pray to Him that He would preserve the Lama's life and limbs, for it was solely for my sake that he had embarked upon this perilous adventure. I assured him that he might be perfectly easy. Whatever happened we should all stick together; I would never desert him.

Between sunset and the moment when the moon began her nightly journey through the star-lit vault of heaven there was one hour of intense darkness, so that we were quite relieved when at length she showed her face. I had the first watch—from 8 to 11. It was so peaceful and still, there was not a sound far or near. By way of a change the Lama and Shagdur slept outside the tent. The nearer we came to the scene of danger the calmer I became. It is far easier to be in the midst of peril than to wait for and anticipate its arrival.

Starting again at five o'clock on the morning of the 4th of August, we directed our course to the south-south-east, and traversed a fairly open country, be-ribboned with rocks. Upon reaching a point where the road bifurcated, we stopped in perplexity; but finally decided that the road to the left must lead to Lassa, and the road to the right to Tashi-lumpo. But, after riding about an hour along the former, we found that it swung away sharply to the east, and so concluded that it led to Nakkchu. Accordingly we turned back to the other road, and soon had proof that we were in the right way. For we met a caravan of a hundred yaks, all lightly loaded, and driven by half a dozen armed men on horseback, and they were coming from Lassa. The men wore big tall yellow hats, with wide brims, and had goats and dogs with them; but they seemed afraid of us, and hurried on past us as fast as they could.

Our mules had picked up tremendously after the good grass and the day's rest. But whether it was that they considered the yaks more sociable, or that they thought them comical creatures—anyhow, they turned suddenly about and joined the caravan. The yaks, however, were of a different way of thinking—probably they had never had any previous close acquaintance with mules—for off they started across the plain, followed by their owners and three of our mules, all at full gallop. The Tibetans whistled, we shouted, while our dogs and the dogs of the yak caravan improvised a bloody melée, so that the utmost confusion and uproar prevailed. At last, however, we managed to get hold of our rebellious animals, and order was once more restored. But some perverse spirit of evil seemed to have taken possession of one of our mules, a brute called Dungan, because she was bought from a Mohammedan Chinese. A little while afterwards, without any pretext whatever, she suddenly set off at a wild gallop, until everything she carried on her back, saddle included, littered the plain behind her. We caught her, and loaded her up again; but, as the same manœuvre was repeated twice again, we finally led the frisky jade in a rope. The rest had also done my horse so much good that he easily knocked off the 22½ miles we did that day. Our Lama slumbered and snoozed in his saddle, and kept making the most comical lurches, so that every moment I expected to see him measuring his length on the ground; but somehow or other he never lost his balance.

The weather was magnificent, and the two days' unbroken sunshine had thoroughly dried the ground, as well as made our loads very considerably lighter. The track now led up to a low, easy pass, marked by an obo, constructed as usual of slabs of

Our Lama in Conversation with the Natives.

sandstone, and bearing the inevitable inscription *On maneh padmeh hum!* The ground was, however, riddled all over with the runs and holes of a species of small rat, causing the horses to stumble, and making riding difficult. But their folly in undermining the highway cost some of them their lives, for our dogs hunted them incessantly. Malenki ate them up—bones, skin, and all; but Yollbars contented himself with giving them a nip in the back of the neck and a final toss in the air. The slopes on both sides of the pass were dotted with flocks of sheep and herds of yaks, with several black tents amongst them; but we saw none of the occupants.

Over on the other side of the pass we dipped down into an

open, saucer-shaped valley, fringed round with distant hills. Here from one of the tents, there emerged an old man, with whom our Lama conferred. But the nomad positively refused to either sell or let on hire his horses. Curmudgeon that he was, he even refused to let us buy milk. He had plenty, he said, but it was not for sale ; he wanted it all for himself. As we advanced the track grew broader and more distinctly marked ; but it was a remarkable fact that we never met any person travelling alone, either on horseback or on foot. It seemed to be the practice in that country to travel only in large companies. There was an abundance of grass, and in every direction large herds of yaks, horses and sheep, with shepherds and herdsmen in charge of them.

CHAPTER XXII.

PRISONERS.

THE tents now became much more numerous, being dotted about like black points all over the country. In one place there were as many as fourteen, all standing close together. Outside each tent there was as a rule a big pile of argol or yak dung, stacked up for winter use, though sometimes it was spread out, so as to dry the better. After a while we again passed the big tea caravan, encamped beside a small lake. We did not see anything of the men in charge of it. Probably they had gone to the nomads' tents to talk, and smoke, and drink tea. We thought it prudent, however, to continue for about an hour further, and then encamped beside a small hamlet of four tents. Our Lama paid a visit to one of them, and came back bringing with him a piece of fat and a *domba* (Mongolian bowl) of sour milk, which he had obtained in exchange for a Chinese porcelain cup.

Meanwhile we were visited by a young Tibetan, an extremely friendly and communicative fellow, who talked incessantly, although we did not understand a single word he said, until our Lama came and interpreted for us. Our uninvited guest said that he was a man of Amdo, and his dialect was very different from that spoken at Lassa. He told us the names of the nearest mountains, though I will not answer for the accuracy of his information. He said that the lake which we saw in the south-east was called Tso-nekk—that is, "Black Lake"—a name which was very likely correct, for it is a common enough designation throughout Central Asia under various forms, such as Kara-köll, Khara-nur, etc. The road we were following would soon divide, he told us, one branch going to Lassa, the other to Tashi-lumpo; and there was yet another road farther to the east, which joined the great highway to Lassa.

We were very anxious to get rid of the stranger, for we took him for a spy, who had been sent to learn all he could about us; but as the man refused to take the hint, Shagdur and I retired into the tent and, closing the flap, had our dinner, leaving the Lama to entertain the guest. At dusk, however, the fellow succeeded in tearing himself away. He had turned his horse loose to graze, and went to catch him ; but it was easier said than done. The horse went off southwards, and for as long as ever we could see them, even with the help of the telescope, the horse was trotting on ahead and his would-be rider pegging away industriously behind him. In reply to our enquiry whether there were robbers in that part of the country, our young friend replied, "Not for us Tibetans ; but for you, who come from so far off there is no safety ! "

On Monday, the 5th of August, we covered 22 miles, and our camp that night was no. LIII. We were still pursuing the same direction (south-south-east), and soon after starting reached the shore of the lake of Tso-nekk. Almost every brook and water-course we crossed that day ran down towards this lake. Then we crossed three more passes, and so reached an extensive plain, encircled by mountains, which, especially in the south and south-east, reached a high altitude. Here we halted in the vicinity of twelve black tents. This was the limit of our journey ; thus far we were to go, but no farther—that is to say, 162 miles from our headquarters camp, and one to five days from Lassa. It was now warmer. At one p.m. the thermometer registered over 20°.0 C., or 68°.0 Fahr.

During the course of the ride we were astonished that our passage nowhere excited any attention, and that nobody came and spoke to us, although we saw Tibetans sitting outside several of the tents beside their fires, with the little children playing with the lambs and puppies. Nor did any of the curious come to visit us when we pitched our tent beside the little brook ; not that we were anxious for visitors or burning to be cross-questioned. For my own part I should have preferred to go and greet our neighbours in their own tents, but thought it on the whole wiser to keep away from them.

After a thorough shaving, painting, and massaging with fat, I had my dinner and went and lay down. Just at dusk Shagdur came in and woke me up, saying there were three Tibetans approaching. The Lama and he went to meet them, while I stayed behind. It was now quite dark, and there was a fine drizzle, and as the sky was clouded, I was quite unable to make out our animals, nor could I see any of the men. My companions were absent a long time, and I was beginning to be uneasy about them, when Shagdur at length turned up. He was, as usual, calm, but the fact of his addressing me in Russian showed that he had serious intelligence to communicate. "Things look bad for us," he said. "I did not understand a word they said, but they kept repeating incessantly 'Shved Peling,' 'Chanto' (Mussulman), 'Buriat,' and 'Lassa,' one after the other. I left them talking. The Lama is almost weeping, and is crushed with humility, and bows at almost every second word."

Soon after this the Lama himself came hurrying in, tremendously excited, and quite downcast. For some time he was unable to speak; but after he had calmed down a little his words came by jerks, and in a trembling and broken voice. To judge from his headgear, one of the men was a *noyyin* (chief or officer). His bearing was quite pleasant and polite, but he had spoken in a decided, authoritative tone, which brooked no contradiction; and yet, added the Lama, his eyes were treacherous. The chief said that three days ago they learnt that a Shved Peling, that is a "Swedish European," was on the way to Lassa; also that some yak hunters, who had just reached Nakkchu, had reported that a number of Europeans, strongly armed and with a big caravan, were coming south over the mountains. Then the poor Lama had been overwhelmed with a multitude of questions. Did he know anything about these Europeans? Were any of them with him? How many did his company number? How many animals had they? Had they any weapons? Where did they come from? Where were they going to? Why had they chosen this back road which Mongols never travel by? "You had better answer me truly," said the chief. "How can you, who are a Lama, keep company with these unknown strangers?"

Our Lama replied that he had been commanded by the *amban* (governor) of Kara-shahr, to act as interpreter to the European caravan as far as Ladak. The caravan was up in the mountains, nine days' journey distant, and whilst the caravan animals rested, he and two companions had received permission to visit Lassa.

The chief then put several searching questions about the main caravan, to all of which our Lama gave truthful answers, for he took it for granted that the Tibetans already knew all about us through their spies. He told him how many baggage animals we had, and that the men in the main camp numbered three

"Europeans" and fourteen Mussulmans. The chief's decision was this: "You must stay where you are. To-morrow I will come to your tent, and we will discuss the matter again. I will bring with me a Mongolian interpreter, so that he can talk to the other two. As for provisions and horses or yaks, we will consider all that to-morrow."

It was already late, and after picketing the horses and mules as usual, we sat round a brazier and discussed the situation. The first thing was to prepare for the cross-examination next day, and Shagdur was very insistent that the Lama should act as interpreter.

What interested me most was to learn where they got the words "Shved Peling" from. My first thought was that some rumour of my project had filtered up from the English newspapers in India; only Shved was not an English word, whereas it was a Russian word, namely, the Russian equivalent of "Swedish." Then I thought of the big caravan of Mongol pilgrims which passed our camp at Temirlik in the autumn of 1900. Could they have somehow picked up the word? But at that time nobody, not even the Cossacks, had any idea as to my future plans, and I could only suppose that the Mongols, when talking to Shagdur and Cherdon in their own language, had asked whether I was a Russian or an Englishman, and had been told I was a Shved, or Swede, a word which could not be translated into Mongolian. These people, I concluded, had carried the news to Lassa, being well aware that the warning of the approach of such undesired guests would be well rewarded. And the yak-hunters, whom we saw at Camp no. XXXVIII., would confirm the intelligence that the European caravan was approaching.

There was, however, a third possibility, namely, that our Lama, during his conversation with the Tibetan chief, had been himself the first to use the word. In that case, our Lama was acting treacherously, and Shagdur actually asserted that he would not trust him for anything he could see. His demeanour the whole time struck him as being very strange, and the purport of his conversation seemed to be of a corroborative character. The whole affair was shrouded in mystery. The only points which were certain were, that somehow or other the word "Shved" had become known to the Tibetans without their understanding precisely what it meant. To me, however, the addition of the word "Peling," which signifies "European," and has through some channel or other been introduced into Tibetan as the equivalent to the Persian "Fereng," or "Ferenghi," made it perfectly plain what they intended. This was the first—and I am certain it will be the last—time in my life that I was not proud to be called a Swede. However much I tried, I was reluctant to believe that the Lama was behaving treacherously. I did not believe it then; I do not believe it now. The little cloud of suspicion under which he for a moment rested was soon dissipated, and I never let him suspect, even by a chance word, that the barest suspicion had ever been entertained against him. Perhaps it was for this reason that afterwards, throughout all the long journey right away to Astrakhan, he showed a devotion

A Group of Tibetans.

and fidelity which might be taken as a penance for a moment's weakness, or as if intended to atone for a passing cowardice, which, whilst it exposed me, seemed to secure him a means of retreat in case of need. One thing, however, spoke tremendously in his favour. It was his interest, as much as it was ours, to get through the ring of guards, scouts, and spies, who watched all the roads that led to Lassa from the north, without his own identity being recognised. If we were discovered and made prisoners, his position would be infinitely more serious than ours; for if I thought well to take off the mask, and proclaim myself a European, nobody would dare to injure me; whereas the Lama would have been held responsible for acting as guide to a European in disguise, and would perhaps have been tortured to death. For this reason I do not believe that he betrayed us to the Tibetans. Besides, it is extremely likely that, even before the 5th of August, our arrival was expected. At one of the nomads' tents a man enquired whether we had seen any Europeans on the road, and the reader will remember one of the men with the tea caravan pointed to me and called me "Peling!"

For my own part, I was glad that the uncertainty was coming to an end. Something was going to happen; but what? We were now thoroughly committed to the adventure, and we should soon hear what fate had in store for us. With so many neighbours all around us, we might perhaps have thought we were safe against an attack, but nobody could tell what even they might be planning against us, and—well, for the present it would be wise not to relax our vigilance. We therefore picketed our horses and mules as usual, and kept a good watch. All through the night the dogs kept barking in the nomad encampments, the fires of which we saw glimmering through the darkness all around us. Our Lama thought that the nomads were going about from tent to tent, carrying the news of our arrival, and discussing what was going to happen.

The next day, the 6th of August, our fate was, therefore, to be decided. Immediately after sunrise three Tibetans came to visit us, though they were not the same as the three inquisitors of the night before. After tethering their horses at a suitable distance from our tent, by linking their forelegs together with a leathern throng, they came and squatted down beside our fire, and began to fill their pipes with tobacco, which was light-coloured, dry, and fine-grained. Their real business seemed to be to examine the colour of my eyes, for no sooner did I take my place between them than they asked me to take off my blackened spectacles. Now, they were no doubt convinced that all Europeans are fair, and have blue eyes. Consequently they were quite astonished to discover that my eyes were as black as their own. They were evidently satisfied, for after a series of friendly nods, they went on talking, and talked quick and fast. Then they asked to see our firearms, a request that we complied with with the greatest alacrity. They could not fail to be impressed with them. Shagdur showed them his repeating rifle, and explained to them how it was used, and I did the same with my revolver; but when we showed them how to insert the cartridges, they shook their heads, and begged us to put the murderous things away.

Shortly after that they became convinced that they would be safer at a distance, though before going they thought well to inform us that it was a three months' journey from where we were tö Lassa. Their object plainly was to deter us from continuing our journey; possibly they hoped we might turn back of our own accord. But I instructed the Lama to tell them that we required no information on that point. We were as well informed about the country as they were. Then they got up, and moved slowly and watchfully—walking backwards all the time—to their horses; nor did they mount until they thought they were well out of range of our rifles.

After that we had peace for half an hour; then we perceived four other men approaching on foot. Three of them had long black hair, and were very dirty, and were armed with swords, and carried pipes; but the fourth was a tall lama, with close-cut grey hair, and he wore a red robe and a yellow cap. He appeared to be a thorough "gentleman." He never cast a single inquisitive glance at me, nor did he ask one indiscreet question. All he wanted to know was the strength of our main camp, which we at once told him.

The old man, who wore an air of great respectability and showed some knowledge of the world, replied, with disconcerting firmness, "You will stop here three or four, or at the most, five days. This morning we sent messengers to the chief of Nakkchu, to ask whether we are to let you go on or not. In answer we shall either have a letter with instructions how to act, or our chief, Kamba Bombo, will come here himself. In any case, until then you are our prisoners. If we were to let you go on, and it afterwards turned out that you are people who have no right to go to Lassa, we should forfeit our lives. The chief of Nakkchu is the next in authority above us, and we must be guided by what he orders."

I proposed to send a special courier to Lassa to ask permission to proceed, but the old lama refused. He said it might take a month to obtain an answer that way. Then I proposed that we ourselves should ride on to Nakkchu. This also was refused. Our interviewers no doubt considered that once out of their sight, we, instead of going to Nakkchu, should be sure to press on to Lassa. And he finally cut short all negotiations by declaring decisively that there was no need to discuss the matter further: they knew what they were about, and we were in their power. It was clear they were perfectly well aware that we belonged to the big caravan which was approaching from the north, and it was equally clear that they were fully informed about everything concerning us, and only wished to test the truth of our statements.

Before he went the old man bought a teacup from us, and told us that he would be happy to supply us with anything we wanted. During the course of the conversation our visitor let drop what rank it was he held amongst the Lamas. Whatever it was, it made a profound impression upon our modest Shereb Lama; for he at once got up, placed the palms of his hands together, and touched the old man's brow with his own. On both sides the usual formalities of politeness were observed, and neither party was sparing in their assurances of friendship and regard. At length these guests also took their leave.

We now hoped that we should be left in peace for the rest of the day; but within a minute or two something happened which filled us with a certain degree of uneasiness. There was a small group of tents about half a mile away, and from every direction we perceived little bands of horsemen approaching them, each man armed to the teeth with spear, lance, sword, and long black musket, with a forked rest to fire it from. Some of them wore tall white felt hats, with brims, others dark scarves round their heads, and all were enveloped in cloaks, brown, red, black or grey. They looked more like bandits or highway robbers than anything else; but they were evidently soldiers, mobilised to meet the threatened invasion of southern Tibet. Where had they come from with such amazing suddenness? They seemed to have sprung like mushrooms out of the ground. The vicinity of the nomads' tents grew quite black with horsemen. We counted one, two, three, up to 53 men. They took counsel with the liveliest gesture. They dismounted and put up a big white tent. They gathered round the fires in little groups. But all the time not one amongst them appeared to pay the slightest heed to us three poor pilgrims—rather an ominous circumstance that! We watched them with the greatest interest through the telescope. Our Lama was greatly downcast, and thought they were about to take our lives. Had they really contemplated anything of the sort, we were, we knew, comparatively powerless; but I thought if they really did mean to make a clean sweep of us, they could do it without

The Tibetans Charging Past Our Tent.

all that amount of ceremony, and would have a better chance of success if they attacked us at night.

The day was dull, and cold, and rainy, and every now and again the view was obscured by the mist and the blur of the rain. We were wondering and speculating as to the meaning of the Tibetans' measures, when, as if in answer to our enquiry, they executed a manœuvre which was not at all calculated to dispel our fears. After seven of them had set off at a smart pace eastwards, probably to Nakkchu, and two others had disappeared in the direction of Lassa, the rest galloped in a compact body across the plain, straight towards our tent. For one moment I really did think it was all up with us. We held our weapons ready, and sat or stood at the entrance to our tent. The Tibetans, flourishing their lances and spears above their heads, and uttering the wildest whoops, charged straight down upon us. The horses' hoofs beat ominously upon the bare ground, and the clods flew in every direction around them. Some of the men, who brandished swords, seemed to be issuing words of command. When they arrived within a few horses' lengths of the tent they pulled their horses round, some to the right, some to the left, and, thus split into two wings, returned to the point from which they started. This manœuvre they repeated two or three times, whilst a few scattered horsemen were all the while circling round our camp. Their object clearly was to inspire us with a proper degree of respect; and in this surmise we were shortly afterwards confirmed, when they dismounted and began to shoot with their long black muskets.

At two o'clock in the afternoon there was another change in the proceedings: the Tibetans, mounting again, and wrapping their cloaks about them, for it was raining in torrents, rode away towards the north-west—that is to say, in the direction from which we had come. At this I was seriously alarmed, and feared they meant to make an attack upon our headquarters camp whilst we were separated from it, and I felt strongly urged to turn back and go to my men's assistance.

As soon as the Tibetans had taken their departure and the coast was clear—at least in our immediate neighbourhood—two nomads put in an appearance from the nearest tents. They brought with them fat and sour milk, and explained that they were forbidden by their chief to receive anything in recompense. I wanted to give them a porcelain cup; but they said that without the chief's assent they durst not accept it, although later on they returned, and said they might have it, the chief had no objection.

In this way we were entertained all day long by our neighbours. The last and most pertinacious were, however, four men who arrived about three o'clock in the afternoon. One of them was exceedingly impudent, and examined closely everything he could lay his hands upon. Amongst other things he unearthed a mariner's compass, which interested him immensely. He asked what it was, and when I described it to him minutely he exclaimed, "Just so, just so; the Chinese have things like that." Once or twice he pointed to me and said, "That man is not a Buriat." He was painfully inquisitive, and asked how it was we had chosen that back way, instead of travelling by the ordinary pilgrim high roads. "Don't you know," he said, "that you may lose your heads for coming this way? Everybody who goes to Lassa this way has his head cut off." Our Lama thought to get out of the difficulty by explaining that we had travelled in company with a big caravan from Lop-nor, and that we intended continuing to Lassa. The man answered, "You must first obtain permission of the Governor of Nakk-chu." But on the whole these men too, spies though they were, were friendly and unconstrained, and promised to bring us various necessaries on the morrow. As we were unable to get rid of our troublesome visitors in any other way we went and lay down in our beds; but even that proved of no avail. The sky clouded and grew quite dark, and then the rain began to pour down in torrents. Upon that all four crept inside the tent, where we were already sufficiently cramped for room without them. And they stayed until dusk, for the rain came down in dead earnest, and was mingled with hail and snow. As our tent stood on a gentle slope, we soon had to go out and dig a trench all round it to lead off the water. After that we sat over our pipes and wooden bowl of sour milk, and chatted till ten o'clock, our damp, cold quarters feebly lighted by a miserable tallow candle. The rain pattered monotonously on the canvas; it was pitch dark outside, and the wretched weather made the dogs surly. Relying upon the old Lama's assurances that there was nothing to fear from robbers, we that night turned our animals adrift, and left them to look after themselves. I conjectured, however, that no one would want to deprive us of the means of leaving the country; on the contrary, their one concern was to get rid of us as speedily as possible. The Tibetans offered to send us four watchmen; but we declined—it meant spies. During the night we saw several camp-fires glimmering faintly through the blur of the rain, especially along the road to Lassa. We afterwards learnt that there were that night no less than 37 outposts keeping guard all round us.

We now slept all three at one and the same time, no longer troubling ourselves about either animals or rain. It was the reaction from the forced ride and the fatigue of the past week or so which made us sleep. At daybreak next morning I was awakened by the murmur of voices; it was the first relay of Tibetans come to visit us. And all that day, the 7th of August, they kept it up, one group coming after another, so that we seldom had even so much as half an hour to ourselves. No sooner did one band depart than a fresh one appeared, and the same man seldom came back a second time. It was like a continuous changing of guards. Our very inquisitive friend of the day before came again, bringing us a bowl of sour milk, a sack of first-rate, well-dried *argol*, and a pair of bellows—this last a very welcome gift. Another Tibetan stayed with us a good three hours, drinking tea, feasting on tsamba, and smoking—in fact, he made himself quite at home. His face was surrounded by a perfect forest of black hair, which stuck out in tufts in every direction, without the slightest pretence at arrangement. The "love locks" which hung over his eyes were shortened, though that did not at all add to the beauty of his countenance. His back hair was, however, gathered into a plait, the end of which was adorned with two or three *gavos*, or cases for holding idols, and with ribbons, on which coloured pearls or stones were stitched. When he rode on horseback, he wrapped his plait round his head or round his hat. We subsequently saw many others who wore their hair in the same fashion. This man, who seemed as if he never would go, showed plainly enough that he was a spy. Indeed he was so frank as to ask us not to run away during the night, otherwise he would lose his life. He told us it was five days more to Lassa; but we subsequently ascertained that there was a properly organized post along the road, with stations where horses could be changed; for when we sent a special messenger, he returned on the second day—that is to say, he took one day to travel to Lassa, and one day to return. The name of the valley in which we were encamped was Jallokk, and that of the mountain nearest to us in the west Bontsa.

When this tiresome person at length left us, we saw three horsemen come to meet him, and then they all four remained for a good half-hour in conversation. The three mounted men were evidently questioning the spy about the observations he had made, and about the questions we had put to him. After that all four turned round, and drove our mules and horses away to another pasture-ground. Early next morning there was not one of them to be seen; but towards noon they again put in an appearance not far away. Evidently they had been driven off to prevent us running away during the night.

Amongst others who came to visit us was a long-haired old man, bent with the weight of many years, whom the other Tibetans treated with a certain amount of reverence. Although he was very long-winded in his talk, and spoke half the time in a sort of whisper, nevertheless the other Tibetans listened to him with the greatest attention. Our Lama picked up the following words which fell from him. "These three men," he said, "are not what they should be. They must not of course go to Lassa. In two or three days Kamba Bombo will be here, and then we shall see. Meanwhile we must take care that they want for nothing, and we must give them everything they need Nobody may take anything in payment. If they should make an attempt to escape, the guards must at once come and tell me, no matter when it is. Amgon Lama has consulted the holy books, and has ascertained that these men are questionable characters, and must not be allowed to go to Lassa. The hunter Onji saw them long ago amongst the mountains in the region of Merikjandsem, and he says they are an enormously big company. Intelligence was at once sent to Lassa."

"Did Amgon Lama believe that that man was a Buriat?" asked one of them, as he pointed to me.

"He said he couldn't tell," answered the old man.

Every explanation he made was received by the others with the remark, "Lakso, lakso!"—a word which signifies obedience, subjection, and reverence all combined. Our poor Shereb Lama had it constantly on his lips when talking with the Tibetans; in fact, he almost trembled before them. His attitude was painfully submissive, and his voice whining. He now pictured our future in the darkest colours, and feared the very worst.

To-day, again, there were numbers of horsemen constantly coming and going all over the neighbourhood. The whole country was manifestly up in arms. One of our guests confessed quite openly that it was because of our big camp in the mountains. Another said they were only patrols and scouts sent out to watch and see that no enemies forced their way into the country. I was not half so anxious about ourselves as I was about the headquarters camp. Had we not been prisoners in the hands of the Tibetans, I should have at once gone back to strengthen their defence.

It poured with rain all night; and next morning, the 8th of August, I was awakened half suffocated by smoke. The tent was full of it, and the rain came in like a fine spray; it was, in fact, a regular raw, cold morning. Back with the tent-flap, then,

Tibetan Horsemen.

and let the fresh air come in! The rain might do its worst. That morning at any rate it was a comfort to be ready the moment we awoke, without having any further toilet to perform. The layer of fat that was last rubbed into my face was now covered with a thick coating of soot!

Our stream of visitors continued as on the previous day, and proved a great trial to our patience. The first to arrive were five men with a sheep. They asked us if we required anything further, and we ordered fat, butter, fresh and sour milk—all of which they brought in far greater quantities than we could use, even when we called in the dogs to help us. They then asked us whether our big camp was sufficiently near to the nomad tents for it to be supplied with such provisions as our men might need. This was at any rate reassuring, and I began once more to doubt whether the call to arms was aimed at our main camp. We were also told that Kamba Bombo of Nakkchu and Nanso Lama were on their way, and would arrive next day. Then the cross-examination began all over again; but I told them plump and plain that they might wait until Kamba Bombo came. Whatever he wanted to know I would tell him. It was no business of theirs who we were. If they didn't stop their string of silly inquisitive questions we would not let them come into the tent any more. This disconcerted them; they bowed, cried depre-

A Tibetan Soldier.

catingly, "Lakso!" and put out their tongues. Our Lama declared that they stood terribly in awe of me. I admit our situation struck me as being not unlike that of Charles XII. of Sweden in Turkey. We had penetrated into a foreign country, a ridiculously small troop opposed to overwhelming numbers. The people of the country would not allow us to go where we wanted to go, and yet they were anxious to get rid of us at all costs.

Our Lama, however, was gloomy and despondent. He had a lively recollection of Kamba Bombo of Nakkchu, and of the thorough way in which he had searched the caravan of Mongol pilgrims with which our Lama formerly travelled to Lassa. If

Kamba Bombo should happen to recognise him again, his fate was sealed; and even if he did not recognise him, our Lama's destiny was not a little uncertain. He told me about a Mongol Lama, who for some transgression or other forfeited his right to visit the holy city, and who by way of atonement for his offence was ordered to travel from Da-kuren (*i.e.*, Urga) all the way to Lassa in the attitude of prayer—that is to say, on his knees. Flinging himself prone, with his hands stretched out on the ground in front of him, he drew his knees up towards his hands; and then flinging himself forwards again, with his hands stretched out in the same way, again drew his knees up to them; and in that way travelled the whole of the long wearisome distance—a task which took him six years to accomplish. And when he arrived within his last day's march of the city-gate, the Dalai Lama refused to allow him to enter. A second time, and yet a third time the man performed this painful penitential journey on his knees, until they became as hard and horny as the callosities on the knees and breast of a camel. Still the Dalai Lama's heart did not soften. "And now," our Lama concluded, "seeing that I have sinned in guiding you here, what will happen to me? Even if I escape with my life, my career will be ruined, and I shall never see Lassa again."

During the course of the day, Ben Nursu, the spy of the day preceding, and the day before that, put up a tent two or three hundred yards to the south of ours, and there, as he honestly admitted to us, took up his quarters so as to be able to keep his eye upon us. About noon we saw some 15 horsemen gallop to the east. We assumed that they were gone to meet Kamba Bombo, who probably was not now very far away. In the afternoon we slept for a couple of hours, being for that period actually left in peace; in fact, we had nothing else to kill the time with, except sleeping and eating and getting our meals ready. Waiting in inaction like that was exceedingly trying to our patience, and we longed for the arrival of Kamba Bombo. The only thing that consoled us was that we escaped riding in the everlasting rain, when everything was so cold, and raw, and wet, and dreary.

CHAPTER XXIII.

CROSS-QUESTIONED BY KAMBA BOMBO.

FRESH, strange, inquisitive faces kept cropping up one after the other without cessation, though one person there was who stuck to us like a leech, and that was Ben Nursu. He used to have his meals with us—in fact, he almost lived with us. But we made some use of him by setting him to blow the fire with the bellows when it rained. Hardly one of our visitors came without bringing something eatable with him; in fact, their care for us was, like their attention, touching to a degree. According to what they told us, all this was done by command of the Dalai Lama. From this we inferred that the authorities in Lassa were kept informed every day of all that took place in our camp. The mounted men who kept coming and going in the direction of Lassa were couriers and special messengers. We were also told that the supplies which the nomads brought us would be subsequently paid for by the Government in Lassa. It was on this same plan that their soldiers were supported in the field. The latter are privileged to take whatever they want from the nomads, who are subsequently recompensed by the authorities in the capital. Thus our peaceful journey had created a terrible commotion in the country. Jallokk had become a sort of standing camp; it swarmed with scouts, spies, couriers, messengers, outposts—mounted men, in fact, of every description.

About two o'clock the sun flung aside its veil and peeped out for a little. Seven old men were at this time sitting round the fire outside, keeping us company. Whilst we were thus quietly talking, all of a sudden a band of mounted men appeared in the south-east. They were riding hard, and riding directly towards our tent.

"Ha!" cried the old men; "that's the *bombo* (governor) of Nakkchu."

We rose to receive the strangers, but when they drew nearer our visitors said it was not the governor himself, but his Mongolian interpreter, accompanied by four chiefs of the neighbourhood and their respective followings.

The interpreter was by nationality a Tibetan, and his Mongolian was a good deal more halting than mine; but he was a cheerful and amusing fellow, and not in the least degree inquisitive. He told us that as soon as the news of our arrival reached Nakkchu, Kamba Bombo had at once commanded him to ride on in advance, and he, the governor, would follow after as fast as he could. Thereupon the poor interpreter immediately mounted, and with his escort rode day and night through the rain until he came to Jallokk. And then, without even pulling up at the Tibetans' tents, he had ridden straight to us.

Once more our cross-examination was begun, and for the twentieth time we gave a detailed description of our headquarters camp, and of the strength of our force. Although the Tibetans had without doubt spied out our caravan, and knew all we could tell them about it, it was nevertheless difficult to induce the newcomers to believe our statements. They had got it into their heads that our main camp did not represent the whole of our strength, but that it was nothing more than an advance guard, which would be followed presently by a force of several thousands. This fear thrust into the background all inquiry as to my real nationality. The interpreter said it did not matter where we came from, or what tribe we belonged to. To Lassa we should not be allowed to go under any circumstances; we must turn back to our main camp in the mountains. No harm would, however, happen to us, for the Dalai Lama had issued orders to that effect.

After this Shagdur and I began to talk away at him in Mongolian, until the poor interpreter must, I am sure, have been ready to give his ears for a moment's peace. We told him that the Dalai Lama had never forbidden Buriats who dwelt in Russian territory to make the pilgrimage to Lassa. If Kamba Bombo presumed to prevent us from continuing our journey, it might cost him his head. There was no need to send to him, for we refused absolutely to negotiate with anybody except a high dignitary from Lassa. Every word we said was translated by the interpreter for the benefit of his companions, who began to look quite serious. As for Russia and India, they had no very clear conceptions about them, so that what we said about the power and greatness of those powers made no impression upon them whatever. Finally we agreed that they might send a messenger to Kamba Bombo, with the request that he would hasten, though only under the condition that another messenger went off to Lassa. The interpreter was a thorough gentleman except in one particular; he kept asking us for brandy, a commodity we did not possess. We told him it was a queer country we had stumbled into, where peaceful strangers could not travel without being set upon by robbers. He seemed to know about the theft of our horses already, and assured us that the animals should be replaced to our complete satisfaction, adding that if we wanted anything, we need only mention it and we should have it. We had told him that the chiefs of our standing camp were two "Europeans." He asked us what were their names. We told him Sirkin and Chernoff, and he wrote the names down. But when he asked us what our own names were we told him that that had nothing to do with him. We only told such things to men of distinguished rank.

After this emissary at length left us we sat up a long time as usual, discussing the events of the day and the prospects for the immediate future. As for our horses and mules, we no longer troubled ourselves about them. They were, so to speak, boarded out with the Tibetans, and we did not even know where they were.

On the 9th of August our shallow valley was again the scene of life and movement. A number of mounted men and patrols were engaged in driving the flocks and herds up into the mountains on the south-west, until the whole neighbourhood rang again with the shouts of the men and the hoof-beats of the horses, the bleating of the sheep, and the angry grunting of the yaks. At the same time small bodies of horsemen started off both towards Nakkchu and towards Lassa. We could not make out what all this meant; it looked as if the nomads were flitting to fresh pastures. But Shereb Lama, to whom everything just now presented itself in dark colours, thought they were clearing out so as to make room for the charge of the cavalry who were to ride us down.

At ten o'clock our friend the interpreter arrived again, attended by three other men. I asked him to send the latter away; there were several important matters to be considered, and I thought we could do it more comfortably without them. Against this he, however, protested most energetically; he considered it too risky to be left alone with such questionable characters as we were. Besides, he had come on a special errand, and as soon as he had delivered it he wanted to return. Kamba Bombo of Nakkchu had, it seemed, arrived with a large suite,

Tents of Tibetan Chiefs, White with Blue Borders. (Photographed on a Later Occasion.)

and wanted to see us. At the same time quite a village of tents was being run up about a mile to the south on the road to Lassa. One of the tents, a white one edged with blue, was of considerable dimensions ; the others which surrounded it were of smaller size. From several of them columns of smoke began to curl up. Crowds of horsemen were swarming all round the village, and our Lama was unable to put down the telescope and tear his eye away from the scene. Clearly his apprehensions were rising. The interpreter now invited us, in Kamba Bombo's name, to shift ourselves, our tent, and all our belongings, and establish them close to his own tent ; further, he invited us to go and dine with the powerful governor. The banquet was already in preparation. The place of honour was to be given to a sheep roasted whole, and there were cups for tea and bowls of tsamba ; and as soon as we arrived each of us should be honoured with a *haddik*, *i.e.*, a thin, light-coloured scarf which the Mongols and Tibetans are accustomed to confer upon distinguished guests as a token of respect.

Without a moment's hesitation I replied that if Kamba Bombo had the least spark of politeness about him it was surely his duty to come and visit us first. Besides, we had never heard speak of him, and did not know what right he had to assume authority over us. He need not for one moment suppose that we should obey his request to move our camp ; if he wanted to be near us, he was perfectly at liberty to come and pitch his own tent beside ours. We had no business with him, and had not sent for him. If he wanted to see us and talk to us, he was free to come to our tent whenever he chose. Our few days' stay in Jallokk had already taught us more than enough of the impertinence of the Tibetans. We were not likely to go and make ourselves neighbours of Kamba Bombo and his following unless we were actually forced to it. We were peaceful strangers from the north, and had a perfect right to make the pilgrimage to Lassa. We only wanted to know whether the road to Lassa was open to us or was not. If it was not, we should at once return to our main camp, and leave Kamba Bombo to answer for the consequences. All this, and a good deal more to the same effect, I flung at the head of the poor interpreter, until he wished himself, I am sure, miles away. His position of intermediary was certainly no bed of roses. He begged and prayed us to alter our decision and to go back with him ; but we were inflexible,

"The banquet is all ready," he said, "and they are waiting

for you. If you do not come, I shall be blamed—perhaps disgraced and dismissed."

He importuned me for over two hours; but as I refused to alter my decision, he at last rose and mounted his horse. Even in the saddle he paused and once more besought me to think the matter over, pledging himself that no harm should come to us. I simply told him it was a matter of perfect indifference to me what excuse he chose to make to Kamba Bombo, but to his banquet we should *not* go; and if the governor did not see fit to come and visit us, he should never see a glimpse of our faces. Thereupon the interpreter saluted, and took his leave and rode away.

This answer in reply to a friendly invitation may perhaps seem harsh and impolite, and you may think it was not seemly in three poor pilgrims to ruffle their feathers in this way against a powerful and distinguished governor. He was the ruler of Nakkchu—the province is also called Nag-tshu, and stretches beside the river of the same name, *i.e.*, the Upper Salwin—and it was his duty to examine all caravans, and scrutinise all travellers, pilgrims, and wayfarers who approached Lassa from Tsaidam by the great highway over the pass of Tang-la. If he did not exert his authority now, when real danger was approaching in the shape of a large and strong caravan, he would be sure to lose his appointment—perhaps even his life. Besides, it was pretty clear that he had been specially commanded from Lassa to quit his post for a few days, and go to Jallokk and ascertain precisely how matters stood there.

And in truth the harshness of our answer was in no sense dictated by a love for turmoil or disturbance. But ever since we had been stopped, the Tibetans had adopted a warlike attitude towards us. They had summoned troops, and with them made a direct display of strength against us. For my own part, I will confess that I could forgive them if they had been annoyed by our enterprise, for it really was meant to deceive them. Nobody could have blamed them if they had reasoned thus about it: "Here is a European who is trying to steal into Lassa in the disguise of a Buriat; and here is a Lama, who has actually studied in Lassa, come with the stranger as his guide. Come, let us make an example of them, and show the world that schemes of this kind are bound to turn our badly." As late as the 9th of August we were still in ignorance of our fate. The only thing we knew with absolute certainty was that under no circumstances should we be allowed to reach the capital. We naturally wondered, therefore, whether the preparations which we saw being made, and the restlessness which had taken possession of the Tibetans, really did not point to some sort of a decisive *coup*. Was this invitation at bottom only an attempt to entice us into a trap? When people go to a banquet it is customary to go unarmed. Perhaps the Tibetans were merely seeking a pretext for separating us from our weapons, of which we knew they entertained the profoundest respect. If it really was their intention not to let us escape alive from our imprisonment, we were firmly resolved we would at least make good use of the cartridges we had with us. Europeans had been known to disappear in Tibet; the last were Dutreuil de Rhins and Rijnhard, although it was not so close to Lassa as we were now. A European in disguise was naturally exposed to much greater danger, for if in the future any reckoning should be demanded with regard to him, the Tibetans would be able to reply, and quite justly, too, "We did not know he was a European; he called himself a Buriat." Thus, although several of our new-found friends had assured us that our lives were in no danger, and that no serious harm would befall us, nevertheless, in the light of these circumstances, I admit I was anything but convinced of our safety. Although I had not hesitated to expose myself to a very great danger amongst this people, who were so persistently hostile to Europeans, and although I had carried the enterprise to the utmost possible lengths, I was all the same desirous to bring the adventure to an honourable termination, and, if need be, before we would allow them to crush us, we were resolved we would up and, like the Vikings of old, "play like men."

Left thus to our own meditations, we sat for a couple of hours or so discussing the peril of our situation. During this time nobody came near us; we were as still as the grave. But the tents of the governor of Nakkchu were all alive. Men were constantly coming and going. They were determining our fate. What were they saying? What was to be the issue of their deliberations? We felt that a crisis was at hand. Perhaps Kamba Bombo was affronted by the rude answer I had sent him—perhaps he was even now preparing to give us a stern lesson. The wait seemed interminable; the suspense was fearful. I still remember it as if it were only yesterday.

At the end of two hours, or rather more, the ranks again

formed up round the white tent. The Tibetans appeared to be in desperate haste. They loosened their weapons. They mounted. Then a long black line of horsemen streamed out from amongst the tents and rode towards us at full gallop. It was not raining just at that moment, so there was nothing to prevent us from witnessing uninterrupted what was in truth a really magnificent spectacle. The Tibetans approached rapidly, keeping their horses steadily at the gallop. At first we only heard a confused hollow rumbling; but very soon we caught the swift thud, thud of the horses' hoofs beating the ground. It was as though a living avalanche were sweeping down upon us. A moment more and we should be annihilated. We held our weapons ready; but to see us standing there calmly waiting outside the tent, nobody would have suspected the terrible sense of uneasiness with which we were consumed.

On came the Tibetans in one long line stretching across the plain. In the middle rode the chief on a big handsome mule, though all the rest were on horseback. His staff of officials, military, civil, and priestly, who rode immediately behind him, were all dressed in their finest holiday attire. The wings consisted of soldiers armed to the teeth with gun, sword and lance, as though they were taking the field against a hostile tribe. We counted close upon 70 in all.

Then a small body detached themselves from the line, and quickening their pace, arrived two or three minutes in advance of the rest. They dismounted and saluted. One of them was my friend the interpreter, who simply announced that his Excellency Kamba Bombo was about to honour us with a visit. The great man himself arrived, and pulled up immediately in front of our tent. In a moment his attendants were out of the saddle, and had a carpet spread on the ground for their chief to step upon. He took his seat on a pile of cushions, which his servants held ready, and by his side sat Nanso Lama, a distinguished priest of Nakkchu.

I walked quietly forward and invited him into our tent. He at once entered, and after a little hesitation accepted the seat of honour I pointed to, a wet maize sack in the middle of our ill-smelling, almost mouldy, effects. His countenance expressed both cunning and sly humour; he blinked his eyes, and chuckled to himself. He was a man of about forty, little and pale, with a worn, tired look, though he was evidently delighted at having us safe in his toils. He knew it would be

"Not Another Step Towards Lassa."

a great feather in his cap when he reported his success to Lassa. His dress was tasteful and elegant, and he had evidently put it on specially for the occasion, for it was spotlessly clean. His servants removed his outer garb, consisting of a red Spanish cloak and a red *bashlik* or hood. He then stood forth arrayed in a suit of yellow silk, with wide arms, and a little blue Chinese skull-cap. His feet were encased in Mongolian boots of green velvet. In a word, he was magnificent. One of his men brought in pen, paper and inkhorn, and again the cross-examination began. Kamba Bombo was much less interested in us than in our headquarters camp and the strength of the caravan. He plied the pen himself, for he intended to send a detailed report to Lassa. Then he examined our belongings; but, strange to say, he never once expressed a wish to see the inside of our boxes; he was quite satisfied when we told him they contained our provisions. He seemed to have perfectly made up his mind with regard to myself, and even considered it superfluous to put any questions to me of a personal character. Shagdur, upon being questioned, adopted the tone of a field-marshal in giving his replies. He said he was a Russian subject and a Buriat, and as such had a perfect right to go to Lassa. The Russian authorities would regard it as an affront if we peaceful pilgrims were hindered from making the pilgrimage; nobody had any right to interfere with us.

But Kamba Bombo laughed, and said: "You need not think you can frighten me. I am going to do my duty. I have just had express orders from the Dalai Lama with regard to you, and I know better than you do what I have got to do. You will not go to Lassa. You will not go another day, not another step, towards Lassa. If you do you will lose your heads," and he drew his hand significantly across his throat. He added, that if he allowed us to go, he would lose his own life. "It doesn't matter the least who you are, or where you come from. Your actions are in the highest degree suspicious. You have slunk in by a back road, and must just go back to your headquarters."

We saw that we should have to obey; there was nothing else to be done. Shagdur then told him about our horses having been stolen. At first Kamba Bombo equivocated, and said he could not be answerable for what happened outside the boundaries of his own province. Shagdur replied, "Oh, so that country does not belong to you; perhaps then it belongs to Russia?" At this Kamba Bombo grew angry, and said that the whole country belonged to the Dalai Lama. Shagdur was afterwards immensely proud of the reply he made. The chief now rose, and taking Shagdur with him, went and sat down on the cushions outside. After a little while I was called out. Kamba Bombo was willing to procure two new horses, but I must pay for one of them. I simply laughed in his face, and, turning on my heel, walked back into the tent, saying, such presents would not do for us; it must be either two horses or none. Thereupon Kamba Bombo promised to give us next morning two others in place of the two we had lost.

On the whole he was very friendly and polite, not the least bit put out at having been disturbed, and compelled to ride over himself in this way. He was an excellent fellow to have to deal with: he knew his own mind and had a will of his own. Who I really was he never distinctly understood. I fancy, though, he must have believed that under the disguise of my threadbare Mongolian coat somebody out of the common was concealed, otherwise he would not have turned out with so much pomp and ceremony. The Tibetans are in constant communication with China, indeed they are nominally subject to that power, and China maintains a representative at Lassa, and a *yamen* or official residence in the vicinity of Potala, the temple palace of the Dalai Lama. There can be no doubt that the Lassa authorities had heard of the events which had recently occurred in China, and knew what stern vengeance had been exacted for the murder of Baron von Ketteler at Peking, and so considered it prudent not to injure a European..

Whilst this conversation was progressing, the other Tibetans crowded round us, and kept making comments and observations. They carried their swords in handsome silver-mounted scabbards, decorated with corals and turquoises; silver *gavcs* or cases for *burkhans*, that is, little images of Buddha; bracelets and rosaries; and in the long plaits of their hair, various parti-coloured ornaments—in a word, they were decked out in the handsomest finery they possessed. The more distinguished amongst them wore big white hats, with plumes in them; others had scarves wound round their heads, while the rank and file were bare-headed.

Shereb Lama was quite overpowered by all this grandeur. He lay prone on his knees with his gaze fixed immovably on the ground, and when the chief questioned him, which he did right sharply, was unable to meet Kamba Bombo's eye. His answers

Tibetan Cavalry.

were short and hurried, as though he had no longer any secrets to conceal. What he actually said we did not know, for they spoke Tibetan ; but afterwards he told us that Kamba Bombo sternly reproached him for having come with us, and said he ought to have known that no European would be tolerated in Lassa. His name was recorded in the black books of the temples, and he would never be permitted to set foot within the holy city again. If he attempted to enter it hidden amongst a pilgrim caravan, he must take the consequences. He had been faithless to his priestly dignity, and was a traitor.

Finally I proposed that I, with the help of our Lama and the interpreter, should write a letter to the Dalai Lama, who, if he really knew who we were, would, I asserted, be very pleased to receive us. But Kamba Bombo answered that it was quite unnecessary ; he himself received orders every day direct from Lassa with regard to us, and for a man in his position it would be unseemly to offer advice to the Dalai Lama ; it might lead to his dismissal, if not worse.

Thereupon he politely took his leave, swung himself up into his richly-decorated saddle, and rode away at a smart trot, followed by his large staff. By this it was twilight, and the troop soon disappeared from our gaze, and with them my hope of setting eyes upon the Mecca of Lamaism. The stars twinkled brightly over the white temples of Lassa ; not a breath of wind disturbed the peaceful serenity of the night, and only a dog barked occasionally in the far distance.

CHAPTER XXIV.

SENT BACK UNDER ESCORT.

THAT evening we sat up a long time talking. Our Lama was downcast and taciturn; but Shagdur and I were in excellent spirits. It is true we had failed in our attempt to enter Lassa; but we had the satisfaction of knowing that we had done our very utmost. When you meet with insuperable obstacles, it is then time to turn back, and you need have no compunction at doing so. Still, it was odd that the Tibetans released us without a single rough word.

Early on the 10th August we bade the nearest of our guards fetch our horses and mules to the tent; for we had decided to start back that morning as soon as we could get away. But as no messenger appeared from Kamba Bombo, I resolved to go to him alone, although Shagdur and the Lama both warned me against doing so. They thought we ought to continue to stick together as we had done hitherto. But, disregarding their advice, I rode at a gentle pace between the marshes towards Kamba Bombo's white-tented village. When I got nearly half way, I was surrounded by a band of armed horsemen, probably a score in number. Without uttering a single word they formed up in front of me and behind me, and when about half a mile from their tents they stopped, formed a ring round me, dismounted, and signed to me to follow their example.

After waiting barely a quarter of an hour, the same cavalcade as yesterday rode out from amongst the tents and approached us at the gallop, Kamba Bombo, in his yellow robes, riding in the middle of them. A carpet and cushions were spread on the ground, and he invited me to take a seat by his side. The interpreter was present, and we had a good talk.

This method of receiving me on neutral ground was a touch of etiquette which was as tactful as it was fully justified. The day before I had refused to accept Kamba Bombo's invitation, and he, no doubt, thought to himself: "I will show them they need not inconvenience themselves to come and visit me." He had likewise said: "You shall not take another step towards Lassa," and so he was come to prevent me. All my powers of persuasion were, however, not more successful now than they had been the day before. "I am not going to lose my head for you," he said. "So far as I myself am concerned, I don't care a pin whether you go to Lassa or not; but I have had my orders, and I am going to obey them." I then said to him, in a jesting tone: "You and I together could go there and back in a few days, and nobody be a bit the wiser." But he only laughed and shook his head, and cried: "Back, back with you! You must go back."

Then he blinked once, twice, three times, and uttered the single word "Sahib"; at the same time pointing south towards the Himalayas. It needed no interpreter to tell me what he meant. "You are an Englishman from India!" And say what I might, argue as I would, I could not get that conviction out of his head. Finding that he was not to be moved, I dropped the mask entirely, and admitted that I was a European, though not an Englishman; but that I came from a country in the north, a long way the other side of Russia; but he only laughed and kept repeating: "Sahib! Sahib!" Then I told him that I had with me two Buriat Cossacks and two Russian Cossacks, lent to me by the Russian Czar, and asked whether he believed that an Englishman would travel with Russian Cossacks, and whether he thought it likely that they would come from the north, when India lay to the south of Tibet. To this reasoning he replied in the same terms as before: "They are all Sahibs. If you have managed to get hold of a Mongolian Lama, you could easily secure a Buriat as well."

Two horses were now led forward, a dun one and a white one; these Kamba Bombo expressed himself as willing to present to me. "Let two of your men get on their backs and take them for a gallop," I said. They did so; but the horses, which were as lean as scarecrows, stumbled and looked anything but first-rate animals. I then turned to Kamba Bombo and asked him how he, a rich and distinguished man, dared to offer to me, who was at least as distinguished as himself, two such wretched jades. I refused to accept them; he might keep them for his own cavalry. Instead of being offended at this candid observation, he commanded two other horses to be led forward. They were plump and in good condition, and after they had been duly tried, I agreed to accept them.

After that we all rode back to our tent. Kamba Bombo sat for a good while, and ate raisins as a horse eats oats, and was entertained with tea, tsamba, and tobacco. We were surrounded by the whole of his staff, who made a fine show in their fantastic attire, their women's hats and long plumes intermingling peacefully with their warlike lances and swords. They made a gaudy picture in the sunshine; and all laughed, as in

Lamas Blowing Trumpets.

duty bound, at the witticisms of their chief. We then exchanged some of our Chinese yambas for Tibetan silver money. Kamba Bombo had a pair of scales with him, and weighed very carefully the silver we handed over to him. After that we showed him our weapons, and they evidently made a great impression upon him. I told him it was not a bit of use his raking together so many soldiers; with their wretched muzzle-loading muskets we were not a bit afraid of them. If it came to hostilities, they should bear in mind that we could shoot down three dozen of them whilst they were loading. But he asserted that they did not want hostilities; they only wanted to keep unauthorised strangers outside the frontiers of their country.

Then I asked him straight out why he durst not come to my tent without being attended by an escort of 70 men; was he really so horribly afraid of me? "Not at all," he answered; "but I know you are a distinguished sahib, and I have been instructed from Lassa to show you the same respect that we show to the highest dignitaries of our own country."

After waiting a long time, and waiting in vain, for a *deus ex*

A Lama Playing on a Drum and Metal Plates.

machinâ to open up for us the way to Lassa, I at length rose and gave orders to load up. This, with the help of the Tibetans, was accomplished in next to no time. Kamba Bombo then presented to me an escort of three officers and a score of men, who were to accompany us as far as the northern boundary of the province of Nakkchu. He assured me that as long as this escort was with us we need not trouble ourselves about anything; his men would look after our animals and provide us gratuitously with all the provisions we needed. And he wound up by making me a present of six sheep, a stock of milk-foods, and a number of bowls and dishes of fat. Then we said good-bye to this great chief, who had been at one and the same time so friendly and so inhospitable, and who had so inflexibly barred our way, and set off to return by the road we came. "Yes, my good Shagdur," I said—the fine fellow's courage and fidelity never wavered for a moment—"it is true we have not got into Lassa; but we have preserved our lives, for which we have every reason to be thankful."

After going some distance, I turned round in my saddle, and saw Kamba Bombo and his men poking and ferreting about the spot where our tent had stood. A few cigarette capsules and tag-ends of stearine candles would no doubt confirm them in the conviction that it was Europeans they had had to deal with. It was not until we had ridden for an hour or more that we fully understood how many men our escort consisted of, for first one turned back and left us, and then another, the last being our friend the interpreter, who importuned me incessantly for brandy.

Our escort really consisted of two officers, Solang Undy and Anna Tsering, with a junior officer and 14 soldiers, armed with sword, lance, and musket. Besides these there were also six other men, who were not soldiers, and whose duty it was to lead the pack-horses which carried the commissariat, and drive before them a flock of half a score sheep. We rode at a good round pace, and I was greatly amused to observe how the Tibetans executed the orders given to them. They rode in front of us, they rode behind us, they rode on both sides of us, and never let us a moment out of their sight. If they could have done so, I am convinced they would have ridden above our heads and under our feet, so as to prevent us from climbing up to heaven or suddenly diving off to the nether world.

The day was well advanced, for we did not get started until two o'clock. Again and again the Tibetans stopped and suggested that we should encamp; evidently they did not mean to hurry themselves. But they were now under my command, and so, leaving our baggage animals behind us, I, Shagdur and the Lama rode on until we reached the vicinity of the lake of Tso-nekk. The Tibetans had promised to be answerable for our belongings, and sure enough they brought them up without grumbling. It was dusk when we halted. Our escort had with them two black tents, which they pitched one on each side of ours and close to it. As soon as the camp was quiet, the animals were turned loose to graze under the charge of a couple of the Tibetans. Then I went and had supper with Solang Undy and Anna Tsering. The latter was a young man, with an exceptionally pleasant and sympathetic face. Both were, like nearly all the Tibetans, beardless; and Anna Tsering, with his long, black, dishevelled hair, looked very like a girl.

For some time that evening their tents hummed like a beehive: it was the Tibetans reciting their evening prayers, awak-

A Lama Reading.

ening in our Lama melancholy recollections of the evenings he had spent in Lassa, where from every temple there used to go up at that hour of the day one voluminous swell of prayer. He feared he should never hear it again.

All night long it poured with rain; but except for that our rest was not disturbed. When we arose in the morning, there were all our animals ready waiting for us; but everything was wet and heavy, and the ground greasy and slippery from the rain. Although it looked threatening all that day, the 11th August, it did not come down again. When the sun shone out, it was almost oppressively hot; at least it burned through my thin Chinese cap. Most of our escort wore nothing more than a coarse shirt, a sheep-skin, and big boots. They had a very convenient and practical way of dealing with the second of these. When it was warm, they slipped out their right arm and pushed down the sheep-skin, so as to leave the arm and upper part of the body exposed; but when it turned cold they pulled it up over their shoulder again.

Their horses were small and plump, and had very long hair; but, in spite of their short, tripping steps, they got over the ground rapidly. Yet they stumbled a good many times and flung off their loads, or bolted with them, dragging them along the ground. As, however, the men were watchful and alert, and, as will readily be understood, accustomed to caravan-travelling, things were soon put to rights again.

One of the chiefs had brought with him a long-haired yellow greyhound, with a blue ribbon and bells attached round its neck. Before we started I advised him to leave the animal behind; but he peremptorily insisted upon taking it. Before we got very far, however, Yollbars had a go at the brute, and mauled it fearfully. The greyhound, bleeding, limping, and howling, was then taken back in a string by one of the soldiers. The men of our escort stood terribly in awe of both our dogs. Even when they were mounted, they used to ride off directly Yollbars showed himself anywhere near, and when we pulled up at night they durst not dismount until we had tied up our dogs.

It was exceedingly annoying to have to retrace our own footsteps; but our Tibetans helped to shorten the road. I never grew tired of watching those wild men in their picturesque attire—their behaviour, their method of riding and managing their horses, of lighting their fires and cooking their food—everything they did, in fact, both in camp and on the march was interesting. All except the officers were the very image of highwaymen. Whilst on the march several of them rolled up the long plaits of their hair, and tucked them under their broad-brimmed hats. Two old men, lamas, wore their hair short, and as they rode, incessantly turned their *korlehs*, or prayer-wheels, mumbling *On maneh padmeh hum!* without for one moment tiring, their voices rising and falling in a monotonous, sleepy sing-song. By this we had to some extent won the confidence of our escort, and they watched us less jealously. They chattered a good deal and were noisy, and evidently enjoyed the little trip.

A Lama with a Prayer-wheel.

Shagdur was very often surrounded by a group of soldiers, jesting and joking with them right heartily. They laughed fit to split their sides at his attempts to speak their language.

Solang Undy wore over his shoulder a red cloth scarf with four big silver *gavos* sewn on the back of it, and carried at his belt his sabre, knife, steel and tinder-box, tobacco-pouch, pipe, and various other small articles, which rattled and jingled every time he moved. Amongst those I observed a small pair of nippers, with which he used carefully to pull out the hairs that dared to show themselves on his chin. His beardless face was seamed with wrinkles, making him look like an old woman. Carefully wrapping the plaits of his hair in a red handkerchief, he rolled the handkerchief round his head, and on the top of it balanced his felt hat with a big feather in it.

After riding 3½ hours, the Tibetans stopped and dismounted, asking whether we had any objection to a short rest for tea. My two fellow-travellers voted for pushing on, but I preferred to let the Tibetans do as they wished, so that I might have an opportunity to study their habits. They said they had not had time to get their breakfast: and certainly their assertion was fully borne out by the honour they did to the dishes.

With their swords they carved three clods out of the soft, grassy soil, and upon them placed the pots in which they boiled the water for their tea. They had with them a supply of dried argol, so that the fires were soon alight. Then they produced pieces of boiled mutton wrapped up in cloth, and prepared their tsamba of fat, butter, tea and small pieces of meat. As for us, we contented ourselves with sour milk. Whilst we were at breakfast our escort informed us that they were only ordered to accompany us as far as the river Garchu-sänghi, the boundary of the province of Nakkchu. After that they did not seem to care in the least where we went. We invited them to go with us all the way to our headquarters camp, but for that they had not the slightest inclination. They said they had only to obey orders; and it was easy to perceive that they fought very shy of our caravan, and of the force which they believed awaited us there. Thus in that particular part of the road which I may call the "robber-zone," we were to be left to look after ourselves. As it was now pitch dark at night, very different from the moonlight nights of our journey towards Lassa, we did not quite relish the prospect.

After all the rain we had had the ground was, if possible,

still softer than before. The horses stumbled, floundered and stuck fast at almost every step. We seldom saw any of the occupants of the nomads' tents; our guards seemed purposely to avoid them, for they always encamped at some little distance away. Such provisions as they wanted were fetched by one or the other of them as they rode past.

That afternoon, when we stopped for good, the men of our escort procured from somewhere two additional tents, and were also joined by six more men. It was a quiet, beautiful evening, with the stars twinkling through a light veil of cloud. The camp-fires burned clear and bright under the gentle persuasion of the bellows; and the smoke from our own fire curled up through an oblong rift in the top of the tent. Altogether our camp that afternoon presented both a picturesque and an animated scene, especially as the Tibetans were full of talk and laughter.

Had Kamba Bombo been with us that night he would have discovered excellent grist for his mill, for I produced my watch and mariner's compass. The Tibetans were completely mystified by the ticking of the watch, and never grew tired of listening to it. I told them it was a *gavo*, with a little live *burkhan*, *i.e.*, talisman, or image of Buddha, inside it. As soon as they were satisfied that my Verascope camera was not a revolver, nor any sort of mysterious infernal machine, they took no further notice of it. The camp that night was called Säri-kari.

In spite of the short marches they made, our Tibetans were early astir on the following morning. They were evidently enjoying the trip, and wanted to make it last as long as possible. In proportion as we approached the frontier of the province, our guards allowed us increasingly greater freedom. They often let us ride by ourselves a good bit behind their main force; though it was never very long before we perceived two or three mounted men following a long way in the rear. Next day we crossed the spacious valley where we first came in contact with the tea-caravan. Throughout the march I was put forcibly in mind of our merry sledge-parties at home in the winter months. Every horse had a jingling bell round its neck, and the monotonous tinkle, tinkle had a very drowsy effect upon me. But just before we reached our former camp, No. LI., the Tibetans swung off to the right and entered a little glen called Digo, where they stopped amongst the high luxuriant aromatic grasses. We had only been in the saddle 4½ hours, and I thought they were merely halting for tea again. But no, they had had enough for that day, for up went the tents. When I thought of our poor lean horses and mules I raised no objection. In fact it was quite a relief, as well as a novelty, to be exempt from the responsibilities incident to the leadership of a caravan, and after our late fatigues, and the strain and anxiety we had undergone, the long night's rests did us a world of good. So long as we were favoured with the escort, we could afford to take things quietly; after they left us we should be able to make as long marches as we liked.

The rest of the day was as beautiful as the spot we encamped

Tibetan Soldiers.

in. We set the end of the tent that looked towards the north open, so as to let in the light breezes which wafted down the winding glen; but the other end we kept shut, for the sun was decidedly hot. I lay and slumbered for some time, partly listening to the babble of a little brook which mingled with the talk and laughter of the Tibetans, partly playing with the beads of my rosary, and watching the rods of sunshine, which filtered in through the top of the tent, as they glinted on their polished surfaces. The thermometer went up to 19°.1 C. or 66°.4 Fahr. In fact, it was quite idyllic and summery, the last summer day we were destined to have.

The Tibetans were masters in the art of travelling comfortably and cheerfully. As soon as the order was given to halt, a troop of servants ran forward, and in a marvellously short space of time had the officers' tent up. Their saddles, bridles, saddlebags, and other accoutrements were flung carelessly on the ground round about, and their muskets placed across the forked supports, so as to keep them off the damp ground. As the weather was so fine everybody sat outside, and with the interest of adepts studied the preparation of their meals, an art that Asiatics love to practise above all others. They were unsurpassed in getting argol alight, and with the help of the bellows very clever in directing a tongue of flame against the side of their kettle, so that the water used to boil in next to no time. They prepared their tsamba in small wooden bowls very like our Mongolian bowls. Some of them used to knead the mass with their right hand, and add powdered cheese to the concoction. When they ate meat, they held it with the left hand and shaved off small pieces with a knife held in their right hand—much as an English farm labourer eats his bread and bacon. Anna Tsering used for this purpose an English penknife "made in Germany," which came, he said, from Ladak.

I was very anxious to secure specimens of several parts of their equipment and outfit, but they asked such exorbitant prices for them I could not deal. For a sword in a silver mounted scabbard, studded with turquoises and coral, they demanded 50 *liang* (about £8 6s. 8d.), although it was not really worth more than 11 *liang*. For a prayer-mill they demanded 100 *liang*. When I enquired about their muskets and lances, they told me they belonged to the Government, and they durst not sell them, at any price. We spent a good many hours in their tents; but they never once put foot inside ours. I suppose Kamba Bombo had forbidden them to do so, for I had said I wished to be left as far as possible undisturbed.

At nine o'clock that evening the thermometer registered 9°.1 C. or 48°.4 Fahr., and at seven o'clock next morning 7°.8 C., or 46°.0 Fahr. That day, the 13th August, there were only eight soldiers left, and they came in from the north, each leading a spare horse. They had probably been to reconnoitre, and conferred a long time with their chiefs before we got started. We now crossed the Sachu-sangpo again; it carried only one-fourth the volume it did before. This time we forded it without the slightest mishap, for the Tibetans knew exactly where the ford was; still, in the deepest places the water came up to the horses' girths. The men of our escort pulled off their boots before entering the river, and put them on again when they were safely across.

A short distance from the right bank we came to fresh springs and good grazing, which we somehow missed on the outward journey, and there we put up for the night. We had thus done three out of the nine stages, although these three had taken us four days. Next morning the Tibetans were to leave us; but we were now on such friendly terms with them that we did not at all like the idea of parting from them; we felt we should actually miss them. We tried to persuade them to go a little bit farther; but they had done their duty, and would do no more. I threatened that, after they were gone, I would stay a little time beside the Sachu-sangpo, and then turn back, and once more make for Lassa. "Just as you please," they answered. "We were ordered to conduct you to the frontier, and we have done so."

That afternoon Solang Undy, Anna Tsering, and an old man Dakkyeh paid their first visit to our tent, and feasted upon tea and raisins. As they were now on the other side of the frontier, they no doubt thought they might allow themselves certain liberties. Dakkyeh was the little old man who once, during the course of our detention, laid down the law so positively in our tent. He was perfectly prodigious; with his bronzy-brown, furrowed, dirty, beardless face and his long, bushy, uncovered hair, he looked more like a broken-down European actor than anything else. Whenever he saw me out came his tongue as far as ever it would stretch, and up went his thumbs into the air, a delicate attention which I replied to by imitating him, and I did it with such *aplomb* that Shagdur nearly killed himself with laughing.

I now succeeded in securing a few small trifles from the Tibetans, such as a dagger, two copper bracelets, a ring, a spoon, a pouch for gunpowder, and a flute, all for two or three yards of cloth. Cloth, Chinese porcelain cups, and knives were the most advantageous commodities for barter in that part of the world. That night we slept as long as ever we could, for after the Tibetans left us, we should have to do our own night-watching. I slept thirteen hours; and when I awoke, the Tibetans asked me whether we meant to stay there or not, and when I threatened to stay, they offered to go with us until we met some other nomads. Accordingly we rode on to the vicinity of Sampo Singhi's camp, to a spot called Gong-gakk, the chief of which bore the name of Jangdang.

With regard to the political and administrative relations of that part of Tibet, I was unable to obtain any very precise information; very probably they are not definitely fixed. I was told that the Sachu-sangpo formed the boundary line between the country of the Dalai Lama on the south and the Chinese Emperor on the north; but that the chief Jangdang was independent of both states. That the Sachu-sangpo did form an important dividing-line was evident from the fact that the Tibetans only escorted us as far as that river, and were indifferent where we went to after we were across it, as also from the fact that Kamba Bombo said he was not responsible for the robbers who stole our horses on the north side of it. When asked about the frontiers of Tibet, the Tibetans told us that in the west they coincided with the frontiers of Ladak, that east of it was eight days' journey to the boundary of China, and to the south three months (!) to the frontier of India, or Hindi as they called it. In the east of the country were two densely-populated districts, called Tsamur and Amdo; while the country to the west was called Namru.

As soon as we encamped the chiefs sent off a couple of men, as they said, to the nearest villages of Namru, and in the evening these men returned, bringing with them two or three big bowls of sweet and sour milk. The Tibetans also offered to give us all their surviving sheep; but we only accepted two, they would merely have been a hindrance to us during the forced and hurried marches we intended to make after our escort left us. Every afternoon or evening when we stopped the chiefs used to send out scouts into the neighbourhood. In all probability they were afraid our main caravan had advanced farther south, and they were anxious lest we should join forces with them, and make a concerted attack upon them, and after that cut our way through to Lassa.

Close by was a large yak-caravan, which was on its way home to Nakkchu after fetching in a load of salt.

The 15th August was the day of the separation. Our friends tried to induce us to stay yet another day, under the pretext that in the evening they expected two or three men from Namru, who would be certain to go with us if we wanted them, and watch our animals at night until we reached our own main camp. We preferred, however, to start. Solang Undy and

Anna Tsering advised us, if robbers ventured to approach our tent in the darkness simply to shoot them down. It was clear they were in no sense in collusion with the horse-thieves, for they had the profoundest possible respect for the efficacy of our fire-arms.

As we were saying good-bye Solang Undy offered to take four men and go with us to Sampo Singhi's tent; so off we all set together up the glen. On the way we met two mounted men, who turned about and likewise accompanied us. These men also were scouts, who had been out to see what our caravan was doing, and they now reported with the liveliest gesticulations the results of their observations. Although Sampo Singhi's tent still stood where it did, Sampo Singhi himself was not at home. Here our companions finally stopped. They invited us to stay the night over; but we could not accede to their invitation. We took a friendly leave of them and rode over the nearest pass to the north-west, and never saw anything more of them.

CHAPTER XXV.

BACK AT HEADQUARTERS CAMP.

ALTHOUGH our animals were in bad condition as well as exhausted, we, nevertheless, rode on at a steady pace, feeling somewhat lonely, and each wrapped in his own thoughts. The country was uninhabited except for two or three flocks of sheep and herds of yaks grazing on the adjacent hills. We stopped about an hour before sunset beside a fresh-water spring that bubbled up in a meadow, so as to give our horses an opportunity to graze before dark. The weather, which had so long been propitious, changed all at once. The sky darkened in the south-east, and unearthly-looking clouds of a flame-yellow colour, and as thick as a desert sand-storm, mounted up over the hill-tops. That meant queer weather, we thought. The wind approached nearer and nearer; it howled, it whistled. Down came the first pellets of hail, and it turned as dark as midnight.

Meanwhile we had picketed the horses and mules immediately in front of the tent-opening. The weather being what it was, it would be necessary to keep the most vigilant watch; besides which, owing to the storm, the night would be a couple of hours longer than usual. Perhaps, after having got us across the frontier, our late friends the Tibetans would no longer look upon us as guests, but would consider us hostile intruders, whom it would be meritorious to plunder. The weather could not very well have been worse. At eight o'clock the hail turned to rain, and it came down in torrents. The wind drove it against the tent with great fury, and it beat so violently upon the ground that the noise completely drowned the stamping of the horses and the drowsy footsteps of our sentinel. And it was intensely dark—impossible to see our hand before our face; where our animals stood picketed, less than three paces from the tent-door, it was simply one indistinguishable wall of blank darkness. The rain drove in as well as the wind, and all our matches were damp, so that we were unable to have even the comfort of a single candle. The tempest howled and whistled and whined. We sat crouched together in our sheep-skins, rocking backwards and forwards, and longing in vain for daylight. All our firearms were loaded and ready for use, and our dogs tied up close beside the horses. From that spot it was a five hours' ride to our former camp, No. XLVIII., and from it a seven hours' ride to No. XLVII., but when we reached No. XLIV. we should be home again.

At eleven o'clock the rain slackened, and I went out and had a peep at Shagdur, who sat crouched under his felt rug amongst the horses, and was drenched to the skin. Just as I joined him he cautioned me to be silent and listen. There was a sound like human footsteps down beside the spring. And sure enough, I heard them too ; but they were pattering steps. Then Shagdur suggested it might be a kulan, but I thought kulans would not venture so near to the Tibetans' flocks and herds. The footsteps came nearer, pattering, stealthy. Shagdur held his rifle ready. But it turned out to be only Malenki, who had been down to the brook to drink. This seemed to indicate that there was no immediate danger, so I turned in again and slept like a log till five o'clock. When the other two men called me it was quite fine.

At first we kept east of our former route, and I resumed my mapping. The surface was far easier than the old way, and there was a distinct tract along the west bank of the Garchu-sänghi. For some distance we followed the trail of a mounted man with two dogs. He must have gone that road quite recently, for their footprints had been made since it ceased to rain. Who was this mysterious horseman ? What was he after ? Where had he gone to ? Was he a member of a band of marauders who had appointed a rendezvous in the mountains ? It looked as if our footsteps were being dogged again. Perhaps the miscreants were only waiting an opportunity to fall upon us.

But as the trail appeared to lead into the heart of a range of formidable mountains, we soon abandoned it and steered a more westerly course ; that is to say, we travelled north-west. Soon after passing Camp no. XLVIII., with its little lakes, the contour began to rise, and kulans and antelopes made their appearance. We liked their company a great deal better than we did that of Tibetan horsemen armed to the teeth.

At length we stopped, after travelling 21½ miles. If we meant to get home in four days we ought to have done more than that, but our animals were dead beat, except the two new Tibetan horses, which we had to picket with special care to prevent them from breaking loose and running away back to their companions. The regions we were approaching were growing barer and barrener. The only people we could expect to meet here were yak-hunters and roving thieves. The hour or two after the tents were pitched were the pleasantest of the twenty-four. That was the only time when we obtained a little quietude, and could eat and smoke and talk in peace. As soon as it grew twilight we had to be on the alert, and as soon as ever it was dark we had to arrange the watches for the night.

That night everything was perfectly quiet. A long way off in the west the summer lightning played on the horizon, though there was no thunder. In fact, the night was so still that I was almost afraid of it. The faintest sound travelled a long distance; except for the low murmur of a rivulet, and the breathing of our own animals and my companions there was not a sound to be heard. The Lama kept talking in his sleep, and uttering Sirkin's name in a plaintive tone, as if he were calling upon him for help. As soon as day dawned we turned the animals loose to graze; this and a spell of a couple of hours in the evening was all the grazing we were able to give them, and they were generally hungry. It was for this reason that they were always straying off the path, thus making it difficult for us to keep them together.

On the 17th of August we were in the saddle nine hours, and covered nearly 25 miles. It was not very fast travelling; but then the country was in places extremely difficult—a continual up and down, with soft ground underfoot. This time we kept a good deal to the west of our former track, and ascended, by a gently sloping glen, the big range that we had crossed on our way out. On the other side of the pass we descended by another glen, which ran towards the west, and was most of the way shut in by perpendicular cliffs. In fact, it took us a good deal too far to the west; but once in it we were unable to get out again. Occasionally we saw yaks, evidently wild ones, although it was strange they should venture into such a rat-trap of a glen. That afternoon we put up our tent on a projecting crag, with deep ravines all round it, and felt pretty secure against attack. We had now little more than 40 miles left to our main camp, and with each day that passed our safety increased, although the Lama was of a contrary opinion, for the main camp was, he thought, very likely invested by the Tibetans.

The 18th of August was a hard and toilsome day. It cost us desperate efforts to get over the big range, though on the way out we had crossed it without any appreciable difficulty. The country was exceedingly broken and irregular, and we traversed no end of trenches, marshes, and miry pools, where the animals dropped in up to the fetlocks. All the watercourses were alike directed towards a little salt lake in the west-south-west. The entire region—hills and mountains alike—was of a brick-red colour, the predominant geological formation being

A Camp in the Tibetan Highlands.

red sandstone. Another pass, and we dipped down into a depression in which lay yet another lake. Here the surface was exceedingly trying. It was as if for centuries past all the mud and mire had been washed down from the adjacent heights, till it covered the plain to an immense depth. There was not a foot's breadth of hard rock anywhere. Fortunately for us it was fine weather; had it been raining, it would have been utterly impossible to advance. We were here a good bit west of the lake where our horses had been stolen. Between two and four in the afternoon, two of the mules showed signs of distress, and we pulled up to give them a little breathing-space. Meanwhile we ourselves dismounted, and drowsed and basked in the sun. The air was still, and the thermometer registered 19°.6 C., or 67°.3

Fahr. in the shade, a temperature sufficiently warm at those altitudes to make us somewhat afraid of sunstroke. An hour later and it was hailing, and we were again in the middle of winter. After the rest it was harder work than ever to get into the paces again. The continual marching and night-watching were terribly trying.

Just as we were slowly approaching the top of a hill, Malenki rushed off to a neighbouring hill and began to bark furiously. Fearing there were people there, I hastily rode after him, and nearly stumbled on top of a bear, which was busy at work scratching out a marmot. As soon as he caught sight of me he leapt up and went off at a trot, followed by the dogs. The latter soon overtook him, whereupon Bruin faced about and prepared to give Malenki a hug. At this the dog turned tail and raced back to us. Yollbars, however, danced round and round him for a long time.

As the animals were going slower and slower, we found it necessary to stop at the first grass we came to. The sky looked forbidding, for the clouds were of the same red or fiery yellow colour as the earth. Then followed another long wearisome night. This time we had not only to keep watch against the Tibetans, but also against bears. The message of the night is always sublime, except when you have to guard horses in Tibet. For the future I should always feel a certain amount of sympathy with the men who were out with the animals on night duty. Each of us kept watch in his own particular way. I used to write, sit in the tent door, and make the round of the camp at intervals. Shagdur used to wrap himself in his sheep-skin, and go and sit amongst the horses and smoke. The Lama used to pace backwards and forwards, mumbling prayers in a sing-song tone. We were now only about 20 miles from camp, but as our beasts had already done 300 miles, there was little likelihood that we should be home next night. Still, if all went well we should get near enough to be within reach of its protecting arm.

Next morning, after turning the animals adrift for a good browse, we went back and finished our sleep. When we started again we hoped to see on the other side of the first pass the broad open valley in which we had spent the first night of the journey, but instead of that the pass showed us nothing but a confused assemblage of hills. The surface below the pass was the very slough of despond. We were forced to get off and walk and hop as well as we could from one sandstone slab or mossy clump to another, or else we dropped in up to the knees. The poor beasts! their bellies actually grazed the ground; it was like marching through a river of mud. Every time we observed a spot that looked rather dry, we used every effort to reach it, so that we might get a moment to catch our breath and re-adjust the loads. This hideous pass was followed by two others equally as bad. Had I had the smallest suspicion of it, I should of course have stuck to our old route, which appeared to be a sort of foot-bridge leading across the quagmire.

At last, however, although we were all pretty nearly completely

A Camel Sinking in the Quagmire.

done up, we struck a little glen which led us out into the open valley we were so eagerly longing to reach. When we stopped, we found that, whilst ploughing through the mud, we had managed to lose the spade. The Lama went back to look for it, but returned without it, though he did not return altogether empty-handed, for he brought back with him an old Tibetan tent-pole, which came in wonderfully useful for making a fire. The country abounded in partridges, hares, and kulans, and, as was usual amongst those unhospitable mountains, the ravens appeared to be the principal inhabitants.

It was delightful to ride over firm ground again. For some little distance nine kulans kept us company. Upon reaching the top of an eminence, we rested a few moments to take a look round us. There was no smoke, no black dots, no signs whatever of our caravan or its animals. The region was as silent and deserted as when we saw it last, absolutely nothing to indicate there were human beings within many miles of the spot.

Although the sun was sinking rapidly, my companions seemed to think that we could reach home before dark. As a rule we used to drive the mules all together in a clump , but here, as the pasture was better, we kept them tied in two strings one behind the other. Shagdur led three of them, and the Lama the other three, while I urged them on in the rear. Shagdur was a long way ahead when my white riding-horse, though I was not at the moment on his back, suddenly fell and was unable to get up again. I thought his last hour was surely come; but the Lama smeared his nostrils with butter, and forced him to munch garlic. Big tears rolled down his cheeks; Shagdur said it was because he was unable to finish the journey. This decided the matter; we encamped for the night, and turned the animals loose to graze. The night passed peacefully. The dogs never growled once, but we observed no traces of our men's camp-fires.

On the 20th of August we started off again in the pouring rain, though it inconvenienced us but little, for the surface was almost everywhere hard and firm. Even the white horse managed to hobble along with us. Soon after passing the red hills near which we made our first camp on the way out, we heard two rifle shots, and a short time afterwards a third. Then we saw a yak lumbering up over the hills. We at once directed our steps towards it, and soon perceived two black dots advancing behind it; after a little the telescope showed us they were mounted men. Were they Tibetans? No, for they were riding straight towards us. We stopped and watched them, and after a while recognised Sirkin and Turdu Bai. We at once dismounted and waited until they came up. They almost wept with joy at the success of their day's sport; when they started out in the morning they little dreamt what "bag" they would make before night. It was very fortunate for us that we did thus stumble across them in the wilderness, for it would have been difficult for us to find them, now that the rain had completely obliterated their trail.

Some little time back Sirkin had flitted the camp into a side-valley on the south side of river; but it was so masked by the formation of the ground that it would have been difficult to find it without help. We all rode on together, and after a while perceived Kutchuk, Ördek, and Khodai Kullu running to meet us, with tears in their eyes, and crying "Khodai sakkladi! (God has preserved you!) Khodai shukkur! (God be thanked!) We have been like orphans while you have been away!" Their delight was quite touching.

An hour later and I was sitting once more in my comfortable yurt, with my trunks around me, and my nice warm bed all in order. After the month's privation and hardship we were delighted to return to "civilisation." Sirkin reported that one of the horses had died and that the others had not yet recovered,

Caravan Animals Grazing.

but the camels were very much stronger. He had, as I have already said, let the chronometers run down, having been afraid to wind them up for fear of breaking the springs. As a consequence of this, the first thing to be done was to return to Camp no. XLIV., from which we started when we set out for Lassa, because I had already determined its position astronomically. This meant, of course, the loss of a few days; but the horses and mules which had been with us would be all the better for a rest. During our absence it had rained nearly all the time. The men had occasionally made short excursions about the neighbourhood, and shot some kulans. Chernoff had succeeded so well in his task that when he arrived, on the 2nd August, he brought nine camels with him; he had only lost two camels and two of the horses. One of the former was my old veteran from the Keriya-daria, 1896.

All the men were well, and in the very best of spirits that evening. They confessed that after Ördek returned they had feared the very worst, and scarcely dared mention our names, but simply waited and waited. Yolldash nearly barked himself into fits with joy, and at once resumed his place by my bed-side. As soon as I had inspected the camp, I asked Cherdon to get me a bath ready. He filled the biggest tub he could find with warm water, and carried it into my yurt. If ever a thorough ablution was necessary, it certainly was in my case, for I had not washed for 25 days. The water had to be changed several times. It was quite a treat to put on clean European clothes from top to toe, and take a long last farewell of my Mongolian rags. After a good dinner, and after writing up the events of the day, I went to rest with a good conscience, and enjoyed *con amore* the peace and comfort which surrounded me.

I was satisfied to have made the attempt to get into Lassa; and neither then nor now do I regard the attempt as a mistake. There are hindrances which no power of man—individual man—is able to surmount. It was upon such that my venture had stranded. Compared with the month which we had just lived through, the few weeks that followed stood out as, comparatively speaking, a period of rest. Everything was pleasant and easy; even the rain pattering on the roof of the yurt was a pleasant thing to listen to, and the monotonous song of the night-watchman lulled me to sleep. I was glad I had not to go out and keep guard over horses. As I dropped off, I heard Shagdur and the Lama snoring righteously in their tent.

Next morning nobody had the heart to waken me, so that it was mid-day before we got started. As we advanced along the right bank of the river, I noticed that my men had built up stone pyramids on every outstanding eminence, and in the distance they looked like Tibetans. These were intended to guide us had we gone back to Camp no. XLIV. If any Tibetans saw these landmarks they would, I am afraid, accuse us of having planned a highway by which a large army would soon travel to invade their country. I also noticed an obo up a side valley; it was as usual built up of a number of sandstone slabs, with the usual formula, "On maneh padmeh hum," incised upon them. Upon reaching the camp we pitched our tents on the same sites they had occupied before.

The journey to Lassa seemed like a dream. Here I was sitting on precisely the same spot and amid precisely the same surroundings as a month before; the yurt was standing on precisely the same circular plot, the supports of the theodolite stood in precisely the same holes, and the river babbled as before. It was as if only one or two days had passed. All those long nights of watching and anxiety were forgotten; the venture was nothing more than an episode, a parenthesis, in the course of the journey.

After this there followed several days of rest. It rained and snowed incessantly, and I was not able to take all the astronomical observations I wished. I was, however, anxious to be off again southwards, impatient to reach inhabited districts where we could get some assistance, for it was perfectly evident that our animals would not be able to advance very much farther. Not far from the camp Turdu Bai and Cherdon showed me a place where, on the very day of our departure, they surprised a band of Tibetan hunters. Those heroes had however been so startled that they went off in a panic, leaving behind them 17 pack-saddles, a tent, and the whole of the meat which constituted the produce of their chase. Everything was still exactly as they left it, except the meat, which had, no doubt, proved acceptable to the wolves and ravens. You may imagine what wild rumours these panic-stricken fugitives would circulate as soon as they reached inhabited regions. They would, of course, greatly exaggerate, and assert that an entire army of Europeans was on its way to invade the country; as indeed we heard ourselves at Jallokk.

Although discipline had been maintained during my absence, after my return I sharpened it up a little more. Our animals were grazing in a valley a mile or two away. One night, when Chernoff rode out to them he found the watchmen asleep. He thereupon discharged his rifle, startling them not a little, and after that gave them a good drubbing. Next day the culprits came and complained to me; but instead of giving them any countenance, I hurled at their heads a new rule which I formulated on the spur of the moment—"Any man who shall hereafter be caught sleeping at his post shall be awakened by a bucket of cold water." Six Mussulmans were told off to keep watch every night, two and two turn about, and it was the business of the Cossack who happened to be on duty for the day to see that the men were duly relieved in succession. As a consequence of Chernoff's action Mollah Shah and Hamra Kul wanted to return to Charkhlik, but quieted down when I made them realise the folly of the idea. Quarrels and bickerings like these cannot very well be avoided in a large caravan, in which inclination and taste differ according to the views and customs of Christians, Mussulmans, and Mongolians.

I now appointed Cherdon my cook; Shagdur was to rest for a time, and also the Lama, who was gloomy and thoughtful. The old man, Mohammed Tokta, who had for some time been unwell, grew worse at the end of a week, and complained of pain in his heart. I recommended him to keep perfectly quiet. The whole camp was now in the best of spirits. The Cossacks made a *balalaika*, or stringed musical instrument, and with it, a Tibetan flute, a temple bell, makeshift drums, the musical-box, and some singing, they contrived on the last day of the holiday to organize, amid the pouring rain, a concert which earned tremendous applause, any lack of harmony being more than counterbalanced by the energy displayed.

XI.

Across Tibet to Ladak.

A Chain of Highland Lakes.

CHAPTER XXVI.

SOUTH AGAIN.

On the 25th of August we made a fresh start, and bent our steps south in quest of new experiences and new adventures. Our goal was now Ladak, but I was firmly resolved that I would not turn to the west until I was absolutely compelled. We knew that the Tibetans were on the alert, and the whole country in a state of siege; the troops were already mobilised, and we might safely reckon upon coming sooner or later face to face with them. But until we did, our course was south.

Strange to say, during the night that preceded our departure three of the horses turned queer, though none of the three had accompanied us to Lassa. One staggered and fell repeatedly; another actually died before we got out of camp; and the third, which I had ridden only four days before, just managed to struggle over the first pass, when down he went, and never got on his feet again. It was a depressing beginning, and proved conclusively that sooner or later we should be dependent upon the Tibetans. When I was called it was snowing fast, and when we started the rain was coming down in torrents. The day's march proved to be one of the very worst we had ever had. The entire country looked like one gigantic dumping-ground for the mud and slush of half the cities in the world. Horses, mules, camels, and men all sank deeply into it, and were unable to find firm foothold. The poor camels, linked one in front of the other, constantly stuck fast and broke their nose-ropes. And all the time it went on raining, raining, raining, as if it would wash the very hills themselves away. Over on the other side of the pass things mended a little. Thanks to the scanty sunshine, the southern slopes were generally better than the northern.

Next day both the weather and the country improved, but it was still a barren region, and ill-supplied with game. As the ground looked levellest towards the south-south-west, we bent our course in that direction. Some 20 to 25 miles west of our route was a small mountain group, capped with snow, and bearing rudimentary glaciers on its shoulders; and, very exceptionally, it was continued southwards by a chain overtopped by an occasional snowy peak.

Some time back Chernoff had reconnoitred that part of the country, and he now came to tell me that near a spring a little bit farther on he had observed distinct traces of camels. When we passed the spot on the 27th August, he pointed it out to me, and sure enough there had been a large herd of camels grazing there. Where they came from, and to whom they belonged, was a puzzle we never cleared up. Turdu Bai declared he had never been there with our camels. Perhaps they belonged to a Mongol caravan, which had strayed thus far out of its way. That same day we must also have crossed Captain Bower's route, but had no possible means of identifying precisely where. On our right was a long shallow lake, also lying north and south, while to the south another mountain-range ran at right angles across our route; but we only managed to reach its foot, and there pitched Camp no. LXVII. The autumn had already begun; the thermometer registered a minimum of $-5°.1$ C., or 22°.8 Fahr., while during the day it did not rise above 7°.9 C., or 46°.2 Fahr.

When the men were loading up on the 28th, one of them came to me and said that Kalpet, a native of Keriya, was missing. Upon enquiry, I learned that Kalpet the day before had complained of pain in his chest, and had lagged behind. The men believed he had followed slowly on in our trail, and had reached camp after dark without anybody observing him. But now he was nowhere to be found. I therefore sent the animals back to graze, and despatched Chernoff and Turdu Bai on horseback with a mule to bring the man in, no matter in what condition they found him. He might have been taken suddenly ill on the road; in any case, he must be in a bad way, seeing that he had not been able to follow us, and had had nothing to eat for 24 hours. Chernoff and Turdu Bai returned at the end of a couple of hours, bringing the poor fellow with them. We nursed him as well as we possibly could, and when we at length got under way, we let him ride on the mule.

Although the ground was firm, the day's march was extremely tiring, because of the great number of passes and ranges we had to cross. The morning was fine; but about eleven o'clock it clouded over, and after that snowed smartly at intervals.

Camp no. LXVIII. was 16,628 feet above the level of the sea. At nine p.m. the temperature was down to – 1°.9 C., or 28°.6 Fahr., and during the night it touched – 6°.2 C., or 20°.8 Fahr. In the morning the ground was slightly frozen and covered with thick rime-frost like snow, though it disappeared quickly when the sun rose. The mountain-ranges again ran from west to east. We crossed three by low, but difficult, passes; a fourth was pierced by a stream, and we accordingly followed its bed. The sites of old encampments were again very common, being indicated partly by the usual three stones for supporting the cooking-pot, partly by the bones of wild yaks

Sirkin's Kökkmek Goat.

and arkharis (wild sheep). Other signs went to show that that part of the country was visited by nomads as well as by hunters. Hares were plentiful, as were also yaks and wild sheep. One poor puss was chased by all seven dogs, and Yolldash caught her. Yollbars usually took these things quietly until the victim was caught, and then he displayed a superabundance of energy. Finding good pasture near one of these old encampments, we granted our tired animals an extra day's rest. The weather was perfect, the smoke went straight up, and our exhausted animals revelled in the good grass.

Shagdur and Turdu Bai, whilst reconnoitring towards the east, discovered a series of *ilehs*, or boundary-marks, built, some of them of stone, and others of sods. They extended a long way to the south, and stood so close together that Shagdur thought they were intended to mark the boundary of a province, more especially as there was no indication of a trail, which they might otherwise be supposed to indicate. Sirkin shot a *kökkmek* goat, which I photographed, and then Shagdur shot a second. This last, as well as a pretty little *yureh* (*Antilope Cuvieri*), were set up in the evening, with the help of sticks and other supports, in the natural position the animals assume when leaping; and in the morning they were frozen so hard that they stood by themselves. This was done that I might have an opportunity to photograph them. Seven or eight wolves prowled about the camp all night, howling in a most unearthly way.

A Frozen Deer and Goat.

We had, however, reached a much more hospitable country; the ground was firm, pasture commoner, the contours dipped towards the south, and we no longer had occasion to force difficult passes. The temperature, too, was higher, sometimes as high as 18°.2 C., or 64°.8 Fahr. All the streams of the district converged upon a little salt lake that lay south-west of our course. Beside it were some unusually big eagles, with their young ones scarce able to fly. The latter were set upon by our dogs, but defended themselves so successfully with beak and claws that the assailants were forced to retire baffled.

That night, in the still, clear, bright moonlight, a flock of wild-geese flew over the camp towards the south-east; they were

A Visit from the Shepherds of Jansung.

no doubt on their way to spend the winter in India. On the 1st of September we crossed the next mountain-range, which was built up entirely of soft material, and exhibited rounded forms throughout, by a pass 15,929 feet above sea-level. From its summit the view southwards was unusually broad and open, though on the horizon a slight deepening of colour suggested another range; but, except for that, the surface appeared level for fully two days. The country was very much greener than hitherto; nevertheless, there were no nomads; all the encampments we passed were old ones. After doing 12½ miles, we halted beside the first watercourse that contained water. Next morning the camp was astir at four o'clock. Further south the men pointed out some black dots, which they took for wild yaks, but which a glance through the telescope proved to be horses. Our Lama and the three Cossacks who were not on duty rode off to see what they were; though the Lama soon came back, leading his horse, for it had broken down. The strange horses were fat and in good condition, but shy. There appeared to be nobody in charge of them, nor was there any indication that anybody had gone off on the approach of the Cossacks. Apparently their owners considered the country quite safe, though we should not have dreamed of turning horses out without somebody to keep an eye upon them. However, the little excursion brought one advantage, in that it led to the discovery of still better pasture-grounds.

Early next morning our Lama, Shagdur, and Sirkin went out in quest of the Tibetans, who we suspected could not be very far away, for the hills about a mile farther on were dotted all over with probably a thousand sheep, besides a herd of yaks. Shortly after noon our Lama came back with a *domba*, or "bowl," of milk, and behind him appeared the two Cossacks, literally driving on before them three Tibetans, who were leading their horses, and one sheep. My men had stumbled upon a tent containing 13 inhabitants, most of whom alleged they were neighbours come on a visit. When my men appeared, the entire company took to their heels and fled in different directions; but as they went off on foot, they were easily caught and driven, as I have said, towards us. But they were too terrified to be very communicative, and the little information we were able to extract from them was not very valuable.

They said the district was called Jansung, and the *bombo*, or "governor," who lived near the big lake of Selling-tso, would cut their throats if they sold us any of the necessaries of life, and they distinctly refused to do so. But after Shagdur—he hated the Tibetans, since they had prevented us from going to Lassa—had given one of them a taste of his riding-whip, they proved more complaisant, and agreed to let us have a sheep and a bowl of milk. They had so recently arrived that they had not yet had time to prepare sour milk, and the fresh, untrodden appearance of the grass around their tent corroborated their statement.

"Where are you going to?" asked one of the men.

"To Ladak," answered our Lama.

"Then you are a good deal out of your way. You can't go more than a day's journey farther south. Your road will be stopped by the lake of Selling-tso, around which are much people." Their immediate chief was, they said, Banching Bogdo, who dwelt at Tashi-lumpo, but they did not know how many days journey it was to that temple. To the east, Kamba Bombo ruled over the province of Nakkchu, and to the south-east the Dalai Lama over the country around Lassa.

The three men approached our camp with evident trepidation. We invited them to take their place on a felt carpet just outside the yurt, and served them with tea and bread, which, after some hesitation, they accepted. For the sheep, which was at once slaughtered with the usual Mussulman ceremonies, we paid them in Lassa money, and gave them a porcelain cup for the milk. They could not sell us any horses, they said, because the horses were not theirs. They sat the whole time as if upon thorns, although our Lama did his best to reassure them by telling them no harm should happen to them. As soon as we had got all we wanted out of them we let them go, and they were up in their saddles in a moment. In the meantime I had got my camera ready, and our Lama diplomatically detained them with a final question, as well as by holding one of the horses by the bridle, and by that means I managed to snap the three half-wild riders. They were bare-headed, though armed with swords. The moment the Lama released the bridle, they pulled round and galloped off with dangling rein, looking behind them as if they were afraid they would hear a bullet whistling on their track. As soon as they thought themselves safe out of range, they slackened speed, and began to talk vivaciously. They no doubt wondered what strange people these were who had behaved so nicely towards them.

Our Lama Detaining the Three Tibetans.

On the 3rd of September we travelled 18 miles south-south-west, across an open, flat, level country, studded with numerous pools and small lakes, and clothed in many parts with first-rate grass. There was no hindrance in our path, and I assumed that Selling-tso lay between ourselves and the low hills which glimmered indistinctly on the southern horizon. We now kept all together, the sick camels not being allowed to lag behind. At intervals there were big flocks of sheep with their shepherds, but no dogs; these were all kept beside the tents. The Lama and Shagdur visited one of the tents, and brought back a domba of sour milk. As we advanced, the black tents of the nomads became more and more numerous, and in some places actually formed villages. As the Cossacks were leaving one of these villages, they were followed by a horse which had broken loose, and was particularly lively. Its owner and another man, besides an old woman, two young women, and a boy, came running after it to catch it; but when they tried to approach it with a rope it bolted, and came to us. At last we had to turn out and help the people to recover their property.

The young women wore their hair divided into an endless number of small plaits, which hung from the forehead down the back and sides of the head in the shape of a fan, the ends being fastened to a strip of red cloth decorated with various kinds of ornaments. From the middle of the strip of cloth another broad, embroidered, multi-coloured strip hung straight down the back. They were bare-headed like the men, and, like them, wore sheep-skin and boots. Where the natural roses should have adorned their cheeks, they had rubbed into their skin some brownish-red colouring matter, and thus given rise to two cakes of thick shining varnish. Two or three of their tame yaks, upon being attacked by our dogs, sought refuge in the middle of a pool, till the water came up to their jaws. Then, as they had only their heads exposed, and they were protected by a pair of very respectable horns, the dogs, after swimming round them a time or two, were forced to beat a retreat. This extempore aquatic pantomime excited the utmost hilarity amongst the men of my caravan.

Early that morning, six soldiers with white hats had suddenly appeared on our left flank. and thereafter accompanied us, but at a respectable distance. Another body ot seven now appeared on our right hand. Thereupon the first band rode in a long sweeping curve behind us, until they joined hands with the second band, and after that both bands together circled round our caravan, sometimes before us, sometimes behind us, sometimes to the right, sometimes to the left, sometimes riding slowly, at others galloping. I suspect they were executing some sort of manœuvres with the object of terrifying us. But when we simply continued to move steadily on, they approached within a couple of hundred paces of our rear, and entered into lively conversation with our Lama and Shagdur, who hung back to talk to them, after which they dismounted and entered one of the tents.

Meanwhile we arrived at the bank of a large river flowing from the east, which I soon recognised again as the Sachu-sangpo. The question was how were we to get across its broad stream. The Cossacks went in search of a ford. Whilst we were waiting for them, Ördek took off his clothes and waded through the river at a point where it was divided by a mud island. In the nearer arm the water came up to his neck, but in the farther arm it only reached to his arm-pits. When he returned, he tried another place; but had to take to swimming. Here then it was impossible for the camels to get over, especially as the bottom consisted of treacherous mud.

Meanwhile the Tibetans had come up, and riding to the top of the hill beside the river, saluted with loud cries the obo which crowned it, and then turned and watched with the greatest interest what we were about. Naturally they did not volunteer to give us any information, and we on our part did not ask them for any. After a short march beside the river, I commanded a halt, and bade the men pitch the tents. We at once unpacked the boat and put her together, and then, with Ördek for my boatman, I sounded the river to see how deep it was. As soon as we discovered a suitable ford, we intended to stretch a rope across the river and back again, and so ferry all the baggage over in the boat, while the camels waded across without their loads and pack-saddles. Meanwhile the Tibetans moved a short distance below our camp, and there sat watching us as mum as mice, thunderstruck at our having in some mysterious way conjured forth such a wonderful thing as a boat. At one time we thought of crossing in the darkness and silence of the night, so that next morning we should have disappeared; but we abandoned the idea because of the risk of the camels catching cold. In the evening, however, I made up my mind that we would not cross the river at all but would travel down its right bank till we came to the Selling-tso, which we would then skirt by the western shore, because Littledale had formerly travelled along its eastern shore.

The evening was still and bright, the silence broken only by the ripple of the stream, the tones of the balalaika, and the barking of the Tibetans' dogs. We saw the soldiers' bivouac fires on a hill to the north-west of our camp.

Next morning whilst we were busy measuring the volume of the river—it amounted to 2,402 cubic feet in the second—the chief of the district turned up with a band of soldiers, and for

Tibetan Women.

some time watched with speechless amazement what we were about. Then, singling out the Lama, he demanded to know distinctly what our intentions were, and assured us that if we would travel direct to Ladak, he would not only procure us guides for the first ten days of the journey, but would also sell us horses and sheep, and everything else we required ; but if it was our intention to go to Lassa we must wait till he sent a courier there to bring back an answer, and that would perhaps take a month. If, however, we pressed on straight for Lassa, he should forbid the nomads to sell us anything whatever, and at the same time he and his soldiers would do all in their power to prevent us.

If he did not do so, he and his men would lose their heads. "And serve you right, too," I observed. Whereupon he laughed, and remarked that it would no doubt be advantageous to us, though hardly altogether pleasant for them. Finally I told him we wanted neither him nor his guides; we knew perfectly well where we were, and which way we wanted to go.

"Yes," he answered undismayed, "you may indeed take our lives; but as long as we retain them, we shall do our best to hinder you from going further south."

The camels were driven in, and the caravan started, having orders to keep as near as possible to the right bank of the river. Then I and Ördek embarked in the little skiff to drift downstream. The trip was one of those delightful interludes in my Asiatic travels like the journey down the Tarim two years before. Immediately below our camp the river made a sharp bend, so that for a short distance we were actually drifting towards the east-north-east. The hill from which the Tibetans watched our proceedings consisted of conglomerate and red and green sandstone, and plunged steeply into the stream. The river was here narrow and the current exceptionally swift, and when it carried us close in under the precipice the Tibetans greeted us with wild shouts. I was afraid they were going to bombard us with stones, and was very glad when we got past that ugly place.

After that the river nowhere flowed through a rocky conformation, but became perfectly straight, being enclosed between terraces of clay 12 to 16 feet high. The adjacent country grew flatter and more desolate as we advanced. At the same time the river-bed widened out, and was beset with an increasing number of mud islands, which divided it into several channels. Ördek began to ply his oar, and down the Sachu-sangpo we danced at a lively pace. After a while, however, the muddy stream turned towards the south-west, and we had on our right a low range of hills, the hollows and declivities of which were dotted over with tents, and flocks of sheep, and herds of yaks. We could not see the caravan for the high bank, but Chernoff rode along the top of it, and so maintained communication between us. In the afternoon a keen south-west wind got up and made the river rough. This hindered us, while at the same time we were smothered in clouds of dust. The next time the caravan reached a suitable pasture they halted, and their example was followed by the Tibetans, who had faithfully dogged their footsteps all day.

Now that our sick camels had no passes to climb, they kept up pretty well. Mohammed Tokta was, however, in a very bad way; he appeared to suffer from an affection of the heart. Kalpet was pretty much in the same condition, still and quiet. He had no friends amongst the other men, and they said he was not ill at all, he was only malingering. One of them beat him because they had to do the work which he formerly had done. I confess I did not know what to believe; for, strange to say. the man had a voracious appetite. Fortunately I did not reproach him; I contented myself with asking Chernoff to keep an eye upon him, and I was glad I did so. I should have been

Two Shepherd Boys.

sorry if I had behaved unkindly to him, for the man really was ill, and he was friendless as well.

Next morning, the 5th September, the weather looked threatening, and although a fresh breeze set in about noon—you could feel distinctly that it blew off water and not off the steppe—the atmosphere remained clear. At one place the river was narrow and confined, and lintels of sandstone ran athwart its course and broke its current into cascades. We passed them, however, without difficulty. About the same spot a deep ravine came down out of the mountains in the north-west; but, although it only contained a little stagnant water, it was difficult and even dangerous for Chernoff to ride across; its bottom consisted of extremely soft mud. The banks in this part of the river's course were as much as 22 feet in height, and very often perfectly vertical, and gapped by a vast number of narrow ravines and gorges. The depth was here pretty constant at about three to four feet. It was plain the lake had once been a good deal bigger than it was then, and the stream in that part of its course was cutting its way through its own former sedimentary deposits.

Then the river took a sharp turn to the north-east, and after a long, tiresome curve flowed almost due south. Here its bed contained only two or three mud peninsulas, and the banks increased to over 26 feet in height, though subsequently they decreased in proportion as the river-bed broadened out from 350 yards to a quarter of a mile. Through this peculiar funnel-shaped channel the wind blew dead in our faces and the skiff pitched violently; so that, although Ördek laboured unweariedly at the oar, we made scarce any progress. In the distance, that is, to the south, the banks diminished in height, opening out a boundless vista, at once enchanting and sublime. We were now close to the Selling-tso; though how close it was impossible to tell, owing to the atmospheric reflection of the water. Although the range which stood on the east shore of the lake was distinctly outlined, nevertheless it appeared to be hovering in the air, on a stratum of the atmosphere which quivered and undulated in a most confusing way. It was just the same with the camels which were marching about a mile west of us: they seemed to be stalking along on long, thin stilts, and the entire caravan to be treading on air.

Finally the river opened out into a broad estuary, half a mile to a mile wide, and very soon both banks disappeared, and before us stretched the immense blue-green lake of Selling-tso. Here the banks were not more than four inches high, and the mud came up level with the top of them. The river was grey and muddy, and contrasted sharply against the beautifully clear, and undoubtedly salt, water of the lake. This last was, however, at first so shallow that we were forced to make a long detour before we could reach the north-west shore, where some of our men were waiting for us with horses. At the same time the wind blew so crisply from the south that the surface of the lake was ruffled all over with white-crested, curling wavelets. We found it advisable to take off our boots and haul the skiff up into a creek, and an hour later we were comfortably settled in our new camp.

The caravan also had had a good day, although the Tibetans had been annoying. Twice the Cossacks rode up to tents near the line of march for the purpose of buying provisions, but the scouts hurried there before them, and forbad the people to trade. On another occasion they met a caravan of 200 sheep laden with salt, and were negotiating with the owners when the Tibetan captain rode up and in a tone of authority absolutely forbad his countrymen to sell them anything. The Cossacks, who were more hot-headed than I am, instructed the Lama to tell the Tibetans that if they only pursued us for the purpose of preventing us from procuring supplies, they had better keep

Tent of a Tibetan Nomad in a Recess of the Mountain.

out of range, for they would be instantly shot down. After that they did not show themselves again for the rest of the day. Thus the caravan was able without further hindrance to approach three tents and encamp beside them. The occupants, twelve in number, were very open-hearted, and readily sold us a sheep, some milk, butter and fat. Evidently the curmudgeon of a chief, who thought he could starve us out of the country, had not been near them. Later on these people paid a visit to our encampment, and were regaled with tea and bread and tobacco, and we also gave them a number of small presents, including a couple of knives, a compass, and two pieces of cloth, with which they were perfectly enraptured. They called the locality Shannig-nagbo, or the "Black Cap."

Here we rested one day. I thought it wise to take advantage of the opportunity, and early in the morning bought several sheep; but I was only just in time, for at nine o'clock there arrived a troop of something like 50 horsemen, who proceeded to put up two tents, with blue domes, a mile or so away. About an hour after noon they sent a message to us, and our Lama went out and talked to them about half-way between the two camps. In reply to their message, I said that, if their most distinguished chief did not wait upon me personally, I should positively decline to have anything to say to them. After that the man did put in an appearance, followed by ten soldiers carrying swords. But we had the utmost difficulty in inducing him to enter our kitchen-tent, where tea, bread, and tobacco were set out on a stool. The Tibetans declined, however, to touch what we offered them. I suppose they thought it was not right to accept anything from people who were travelling through their country without permission.

Then began the usual fruitless discussion. The old chief, who was really a very nice, modest old gentleman, with a pleasing countenance and sincere style of speech, begged that we would stay where we were at least four days, whilst he sent a special messenger to Lassa to get instructions from the Devashung, or Holy Council. I told him we had not time to wait, and intended resuming our journey again next morning.

"Then we shall follow you," he said, "and stop you from going to Lassa. We shall soon be reinforced."

"If you do stop us," I replied, "you will have to shoot; but remember that we also have fire-arms."

Then the honest old fellow shook his head, and declared that they never thought of shooting, and he added that such hard words ought not to be exchanged between us. I offered him two or three presents, but he declined them, saying, "If you will only wait four days, I shall have great pleasure in accepting your gifts, and I will give you others in exchange for them; besides, I will procure you whatever supplies you want, as well as caravan animals to take you to Ladak."

In the afternoon Kalpet came to me snivelling and complained that one of the men had beaten him. I enquired into the matter, and warned the other men to be kind to him, and enjoined Chernoff, who was head-man of the caravan, to look specially after him. I was really very sorry for the man, for I never saw a creature more utterly forlorn. I shall never forget the look of hopeless depression that sat upon his features when he came to me, nor the way his eyes lighted up when I took his part, and gave him drugs from my medicine-chest. When I went to see him later on, he was eating the national rice-pudding with a good appetite, so that I concluded he was only suffering from a passing attack of mountain-sickness.

CHAPTER XXVII.

DEATH AND BURIAL OF KALPET.

When on the 7th September we started from Camp no. LXXV. and the steppes of the "Black Cap," one of our camels, a veteran from Kashgar, which had accompanied me on several of my desert journeys, was no longer able to rise, and had to be killed and abandoned. When the caravan was all loaded up, the Bombo came and made a last desperate attempt to induce us to stay where we were. But when I told him curtly that our road led to the south, he said no more and went away.

We followed the shore of Selling-tso west-south-west, the surface being hard and level. On our right was a steep ridge, and along its foot rode the Tibetans, now over 60 in number. A troop of two score antelopes fled at our approach; and just when the lake appeared to terminate, we rode into some excellent grass, thick, sappy and a foot high; we at once stopped to let the animals graze a little. Thereupon down galloped the Tibetans. Then they dismounted, unsaddled, and turned their horses adrift. Up went their tents, and in a very short space their fires indicated that they were getting their breakfast ready.

Then, leaving our outwitted pursuers behind us, we struck away from the lake and travelled south-west across four ancient beach-lines, each most distinctly marked by an immense ridge of gravel, the last and highest of them being more than 160 feet above the existing level of the lake. Selling-tso is thus rapidly drying up. After that we travelled along tolerably level ground for some time, until we reached a fresh ridge which dipped north-west towards another lake. Here we found ourselves on the edge of a very remarkable depression, elliptical in shape, with pools of fresh water in the middle, and a flock of sheep grazing round a solitary tent. Immediately to the south was a steep ridge, stretching from east to west, and some 500 or 600 feet high. As we were making for its western end, eight Tibetans suddenly made their appearance on a hill, and sat watching us. But when shortly afterwards they disappeared, it struck us that we must be on a peninsula ; evidently they felt sure of us for some little time to come at any rate. Thereupon I sent on Sirkin and Shagdur to reconnoitre, whilst we followed slowly after them. When they turned back and met us, they told us that the two lakes were in reality one, and that we were in fact on a peninsula which turned its broad, steep brow to the south. We therefore turned back to the north-north-east.

We encamped near a little tented village on the shore at a

Kalpet's Bed on the Back of a Camel.

place called Tang-leh, the people of which were very friendly, though they stubbornly refused to sell us anything. Thereupon I showed them four bladders of lard, which Cherdon had found in a crevice of the rock, though he left six others behind him, and asked them what was the price of them. "Three *tsos** each," they answered; but as the price was too high, we let them keep their lard, though the Lama observed, by way of a parting shot, that if we had been less pleasant people, we might quite easily have taken the whole ten bladders, and they been none the wiser.

The Tibetans encamped about a mile from us, with the

* The tso, about 7½*d.*, is the current silver coin of Lassa.

exception of 15 men, who came and put up their tents close beside ours. It rained fast almost all day long, and two or three times the westerly squalls were so violent that we were forced to stop and wait until they passed over. In spite of the rain, however, the Tibetans went through various manœuvres and warlike games on horseback, and then tested their marksmanship.

Kalpet was a good deal worse, and had to be tied on his horse to prevent him from falling off. Chernoff was his nurse, and rode by his side. Next morning the sick man besought us to leave him behind, a request which we did not of course comply with. Instead of that we transferred him to the back of a camel, making him as comfortable as we could with felts and cushions.

Had it not been blowing so smartly, I should have preferred to cross the lake in the skiff; but as it was, I was constrained to accompany the caravan along the northern shore, which stretched in a pretty straight line to the west. As soon as we began to load up, the Tibetans also set about striking camp, and when we were a mile or two on the road, the old Bombo, with 12 men, rode up to us, and made yet another attempt to induce us to travel straight to Ladak. But when I told him I should go which way I pleased, and was not to be frightened by him and all his soldiers, he appeared very much dejected, and announced that he should leave us to our fate, and go home to his own tents. I heartily wished him a successful journey; and the whole troop then disappeared, and we had the rare pleasure of being left in peace for the rest of the day. However, well on in the afternoon, two horsemen, evidently scouts, turned up in the distance, though they soon disappeared again amongst the hills. Here again the ancient beach-lines were distinctly marked; you could in places ride along them for hours together. The lake extended a very long way to the south, and then turned to the south-west and south-south-west. Here there were a great number of mud islands, and the water between them was fresh, indicating that a river entered the lake somewhere close by. This we very soon reached, and Shagdur quickly found an excellent ford, with a hard, gravelly bottom. The water was as clear as crystal; consequently the river must issue from another lake higher up the valley. Shagdur, whilst out reconnoitring, shot four wild-duck, and here they came floating down the river. We picked them up; but two others, which were only wounded, managed to struggle past us. Cherdon,

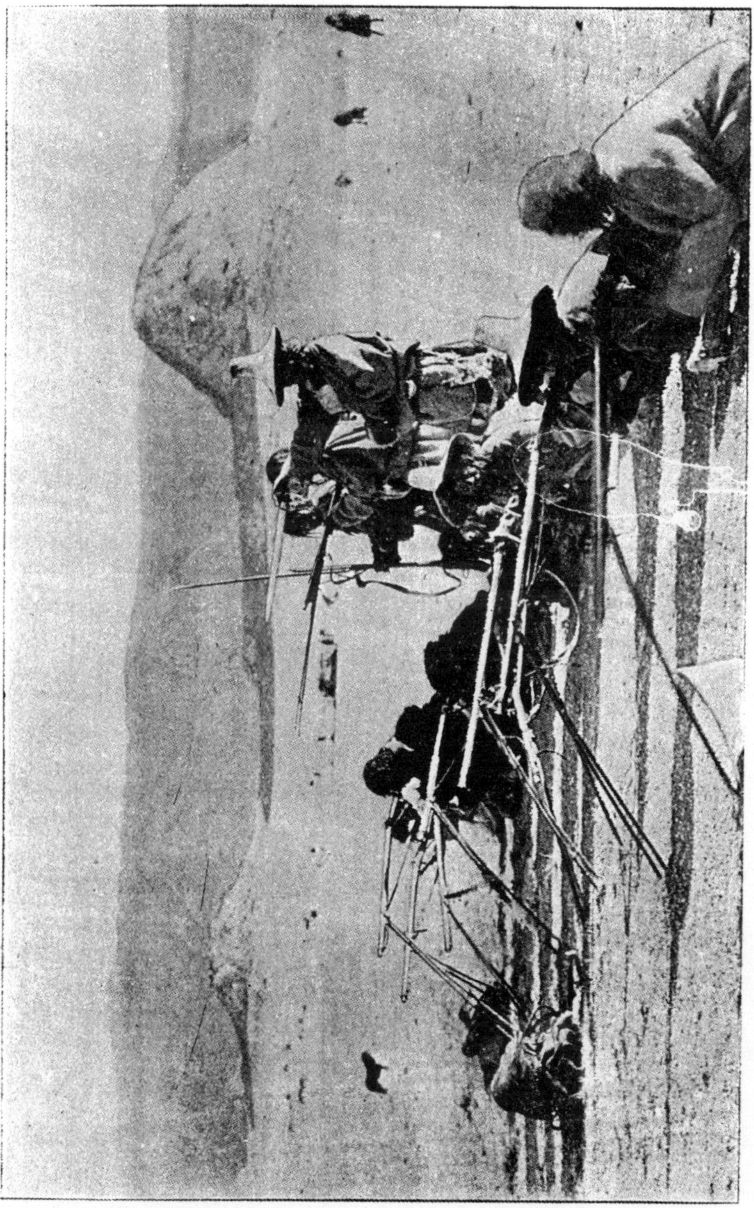

Charge of the Tibetans at Yaggyu-rapga.

[VOL. II.—*To face p.* 437.

daring and reckless, rode straight into the river after one of them, and cut its head off with his sabre. The other, however, disappeared among the flocks of gulls, which dotted the waters of the estuary in vast numbers. Their presence seemed to point to fish; and as the spot was in every way too inviting to be passed, we pitched our tents on the summit of the right bank.

No sooner was the camp arranged than two black lines appeared advancing rapidly from the north-west and the north-east; they were the troublesome and pertinacious Tibetans, 53 from the former direction and 13 from the latter, and they were leading after them a large number of pack-horses. They had clearly been to fetch fresh supplies of food, and to equip themselves for a longer campaign. Crossing the river by the same ford that we did, they galloped past our camp at full speed, some in front of the tents, others behind them and between them, as though they intended to annihilate us in one tremendous charge. As they rode they whooped and flourished their hands above their heads, but to us they paid not the slightest regard. They did not even bestow upon us so much as a single glance, as they raced through us like a whirlwind. And yet they were very picturesque in their variegated attire and white hats, their ornamental saddles, silver-mounted scabbards, and red flags fluttering from the forked rests of their muskets. Immediately beyond us they halted and held a long palaver, gathering in three groups round their leaders, who appeared to be instructing them how to use their weapons. Every now and again there came a peculiar whoop, like a word of command. Then finally they ran up their tents and lit their fires.

The Tibetans pitched their camp on a gentle rise completely commanding our tents, and the Cossacks noticed that at dusk they planted all their muskets in a line, with the muzzles pointing in our direction. We wondered if they meant to open a fusillade upon us during the night. As soon as it was dark, therefore, I took Shagdur and the Lama with me, and we went to the Bombo's tent, where I received a polite welcome, and was invited to partake of tea and tsamba. Within one minute the tent was packed full of Tibetans. I declined his refreshments because he had not accepted those I offered to him. "Reh! reh! reh!" (true! true! true!) he exclaimed. He then asked me what my name was. I replied that if he would tell me what the river was called he should know my name; but he scorned the transaction. Later on, however, we learnt that it was the Yaggyu-rapga. In answer to my question, whether it contained any fish, he answered, "Yes, plenty." I promised, therefore, to remain where we were over the next day, on condition that they, as a proof of their assertion, delivered at my tent at daybreak a moderate-sized fish. They promised to do their best, and borrowed a net from us, though they had, of course, no more idea how to use it than a baby.

At daybreak next morning there appeared at my tent door some of the Tibetans carrying the net, with a little mountain *asman* (fish) fast in its meshes. They were immensely proud of their capture, and declared it had nearly cost them their lives. Some of our own watchmen had, however, seen the Tibetans go down to the river at daybreak, where, waiting until they saw a gull in a favourable position, they threw stones at it just after it had swallowed a fish, and so forced it to disgorge. However we stayed the day there, as we had promised to do, but it was to fish.

Leaving Cherdon and all the Mussulmans, except two, to guard the camp, I and the other three Cossacks, with Kutchuk and Ördek, our experienced Lop fishermen, went to try our luck. Loading the skiff on a camel, we rode, followed by a crowd of Tibetans, up the right bank, till we came to a bend in the river, where there were two cataracts, one three or four feet high, the other just about one foot. At this spot the channel was narrow, being forced across and between sills of clay, mud, and gravel-and-shingle, and the water deep and of a blue-black colour. Here in a gentle eddy, just below the lower cataract, we put down our net; then launching the boat, we paddled round it in a sweeping curve, and beating the water with the paddles, frightened the fish into the meshes. In this way we caught two or three fish at each haul. After catching 28 I went away, leaving the others to continue the sport. Meanwhile the Cossacks angled from the banks, and they, too, were successful. Chernoff also shot a couple of wild duck, which we retrieved with the skiff. In a word, we had a most delightful day, a welcome break to the long, tiring marches of the caravan. Although it often hailed smartly, the squalls in no way inconvenienced us. The Tibetans sat all along the bank watching us, and, black as they were, looked like a string of crows on a barn roof. Taking Ördek with me in the skiff, we drifted at a rattling pace down to the Selling-tso. Here I got out and

Our Camp at Yaggyu-rapga. In the front line Vanka the Ram, and the Dogs Yollbars, Malchik and Hamra.

walked home, leaving Ördek to paddle and punt the skiff back to camp. We measured the river, however, and found its volume was 1,222 cubic feet in the second.

That evening the Bombo and 30 Tibetans came to visit me in my tent, bringing with them two sheep and three pails of beautiful milk, a reward, no doubt, for our having stayed the day over as they begged us. We let them listen to the musical-box, and see several of our "sights," and the Bombo now condescended to accept the presents I offered him. Meanwhile the Cossacks were looking on at the Tibetans shooting. The distance was not more than 45 yards, and the target was a little piece of wood fastened to a stake; but out of 30 marksmen not more than three hit the target. The Cossacks then offered to try; but the Tibetans refused to allow them, and for a very good reason. That day we had fish for dinner, to everybody's satisfaction. The Tibetans have no taste for delicacies. "Eat fish!" they cried. "You might just as well eat lizards and worms! They are all the same sort of thing."

When I awoke next morning, the Lop-men had already been out fishing; so that I was able to breakfast off fish instead of roast duck, as I had intended. The morning promised well, being bright and sunny; but very soon after we started the heavy banks of cloud, which hung on the horizon, advanced to meet us, and finally shook out their contents over us. It hailed, it rained, it turned raw and cold, and the ground became wet and slippery. Nor was that the only thing which depressed our spirits that day. The Tibetans were very tiring with their perpetual insistence that we should turn back. Besides that, our two invalids were rapidly getting into a serious condition. Kalpet, in particular, was very much worse.

The mountain-chain which ran south of the Yaggyu-rapga, was cleft by a natural and imposing rocky defile; and through it we penetrated to the south-east, the cliffs on each side of the defile being vertical and sharply outlined. Above them on the right circled a royal eagle, probably the same we had seen the day before preying upon the wild geese; but the pretty rock-pigeons hopped about on the ground without the least fear. Kulans and orongo antelopes were very common; and, like the fish, they appeared never to have been disturbed by man. The eastern extremity of the mountain-chain projected like a peninsula into the lake. At its southern foot we forded a large river called the Alla-sangpo, and then had once more on our left the light blue waters of the Selling-tso. Every now and again we caught glimpses of a labyrinth of mountains in the south-west; though for the greater part of the time it rained and hailed so incessantly that it was almost as dim as twilight, and I had to steer our course entirely by the compass. The country was like one boundless marsh. The Tibetans chose another route, and we finally thought it advisable to follow them. But when we did they stopped, thinking, no doubt, "Oh, they may just help themselves!" Once it cleared for a few minutes, sufficiently to let us obtain a view of the broad bosom of the lake, with a few scattered tents beside it, and big flocks of wild geese along the beach. We recognised again several features which we had passed on the opposite shore, especially the little range of hills on the peninsula that we traversed by mistake.

We were just on the point of turning towards a saddle in the south-south-east, when Kutchuk and Khodai Kullu came riding back to tell me, breathlessly, that Kalpet was a good deal worse. I hurried on and found him lying on a carpet on the ground, with the other men gathered round him. He was more dead than alive, and gasped for water; but as we had none near at hand, we offered him milk, and let him drink all he wanted. His face was a sickly yellow, his lips white, and his eyes glittered, though they wore, at the same time, a glazed expression. It was raining fast when we encamped beside a big pool of rain-water. One of the tents was converted into a hospital, and inside it we made Kalpet comfortable. He lay perfectly still, without appearing to suffer any pain. I gave him a small dose of morphia to help him to sleep. The old man, Mohammed Tokta, who was also placed in the hospital, was suffering from some ugly disease. His body was blown up and his face swollen; nor was he made any better through witnessing his unfortunate comrade's struggle with death.

That evening our friend the Bombo again came to visit us, and when we requested him to procure us some milk from the nearest nomad encampment, he replied that small-pox was raging there, and we might go and get it if we liked, but he, for his part, distinctly declined to do so. This time he brought with him three new individuals, amongst them a very funny old lama. The newcomers said that they came direct from the special emissaries whom the Dalai Lama was sending to prevent us from going to Lassa. And then began the usual prayers and entreaties that we would not advance farther, and so bring misfortune both upon them and upon ourselves. The emissaries from Lassa were not very far away; in fact, we might expect their arrival within two days. But I was immovable; I said it was shameful to treat peaceful visitors in that way, and invest us with hundreds of soldiers, armed to the teeth. We were not come to wage war upon them, and had honestly paid for everything we took. But I refused to give them any clue to my plans before the emissaries arrived. At this they were greatly chopfallen, and looked quite distressed.

Just at seven o'clock a squall came on, of so furious a character that the tents threatened to collapse under the weight

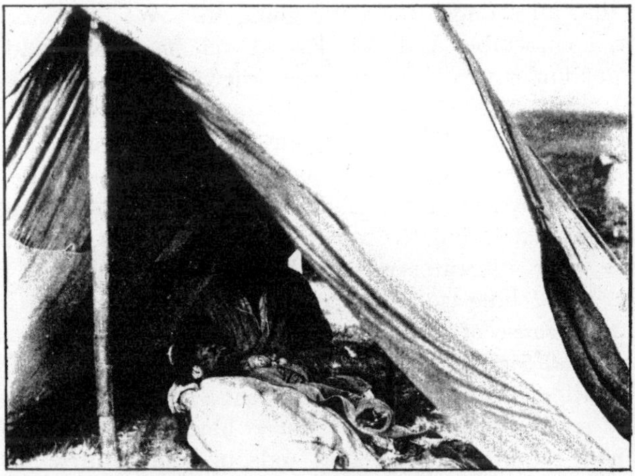

Our Hospital.

of the rain and the hail, and everything that was lying loose about the camp went whirling aloft. The Tibetans happened to be on their way back to their own tents, and so got another cold douche in addition to the one I had given them. When I made my last visit to the hospital that night, Kalpet was sleeping quietly; but Mohammed Tokta complained of his heart. The first thing I did when I rose on the 11th September was to visit the two invalids again. Mohammed Tokta was just the same, clear and sensible, sometimes even "joky"; but he told me he was gradually losing feeling in his fingers. Kalpet, however, was in a much worse condition. He had difficulty in breathing, his cheeks were hollow, though his eyes still retained their glitter. To me it seemed as if he could not last much longer; but he talked sensibly, and said it was a *kattik kessel* (hard sickness) he had got, and that he had been a good deal worse ever since he was beaten by one of his comrades some days ago. As a matter of fact, it had been nothing worth speaking about, although the mind of the dying man had seized upon it, and he could talk about nothing else. The unfortunate man who had the blow upon his conscience would have given a good deal to have undone it. Gradually Kalpet's consciousness left him; he no longer talked, but lay and stared straight before him, oblivious of everything that went on around him. I was thinking of staying another day; but it was such a disagreeable place that all the men voted for going on. We therefore made a soft, comfortable bed for Kalpet on his camel, and once more got under way. All the men knew we had death with us in the caravan, and consequently our spirits were depressed and gloomy. Travelling south-east, we perceived, from the first low saddle we crossed, a lovely lake, with ragged shores, embedded amongst low mountain ranges. Its water was as bright as crystal, and the aquatic plants and fish in it showed at once that its water was fresh, and consequently it could not be the Selling-tso. As, however, its western shore looked difficult, because of the steep rocks which lined it, I thought it best to send Sirkin and Shagdur on to reconnoitre. Whilst we were waiting, there came on a violent squall of hail, and we threw a felt rug over Kalpet to protect him. The three Tibetans who had recently arrived now rode up and assured me that there was no road along the west side of the lake; but if we insisted upon continuing there was a path along the northern shore, leading to the east. I suspected some trick, but did not very well see how I was to help myself, especially after the Cossacks came and confirmed what the Tibetans said.

We accordingly continued our way along the northern shore by what proved to be a decidedly zigzag route. There was, indeed, a trail behind the hills leading due east; but the Tibetans kept all the time behind us, and never showed us where it was. Hence we doubled the head of every creek and circled round every promontory and peninsula, without knowing in which direction the lake trended. In this way, although we took many unnecessary steps, I had the opportunity to obtain a detailed map of the capricious outline of the lake. We never saw more beautiful scenery in all Tibet: the creeks and fjords

Kalpet lying Dead on his Bier.

cut deeply into the land in every direction, penetrating the low, picturesque, and rugged mountains which shot abruptly down into the lake. At intervals there were small islands, knobbed like the backs of dolphins. Here there were no ancient beach lines; the freshness of the water suggested that this lake, Nakktsong-tso, as it was called, discharged into some other salt lake situated still farther to the south. Some of the creeks were semicircular in outline, and the lake lapped very pleasantly amongst the water-worn gravel which littered their shores.

After wandering about in this way for two or three hours,

The Funeral Procession.

we suddenly came upon the Tibetans, who had pitched their camp on the shore, and were making their usual halt for tea. They had gained upon us by taking the short cut behind the hills. We went on past them, and continued until the lake definitely swung away to the south-east. There the mountains also retreated from the lake, leaving a broad, level expanse of hard gravel. We terminated the day's march beside a group of tents at the east end of the lake, and there we again found the Tibetans, they having once more slipped past us, and their tents were already up.

Kalpet had spoken several times on the march, calling particularly for Rosi Mollah, his fellow-townsman from Keriya.

He had asked for water; he had asked to be turned over when he got tired of lying in one position. He had cried out loudly and distinctly that the camel was going too fast; but for some little time before we approached the end of the march he was silent. At last the men stopped his camel, and the Mollah listened. Then he rode on to fetch me. There was no longer any doubt; my poor servant had ceased to breathe. His features were calm, and his eyes had lost their glitter. In fact, he was already cold, although it was scarcely an hour since he last asked for water. The Mollah closed his eyes and we went on again. The Mussulmans had as usual sung to relieve the monotony of the march; but now they plodded on as silent as the grave, and nothing was heard save the footsteps of the animals as they tramped along the sand and gravel of the lake-side and the weary breathing of the camels. The caravan was converted into a funeral procession, the dead being borne on a living catafalque.

When we passed the Tibetans' tents, some of them came to meet us, and said we should have a long way to go to reach the next pasture. I told them we had a dead man with us, and must bury him in the ground. They received the intelligence quite calmly, and pointed out the best place for a grave.

As soon as the tents were erected, I consulted the Mollah and Turdu Bai with regard to the burial. They proposed that it should be put off till the next morning, and should then take place with the customary ceremonies. The body was left all night in the white tent, being watched by one of the men. The next morning, the 12th September, was gloriously bright and fine; only occasionally did a light, fleecy cloud drift across the sky, and a fresh breeze ruffled the surface of the lake. The grave was already dug, and Hamra Kul, Mollah Shah, and Ördek were swathing the body in a sheet after duly washing it. Their faces, with the exception of their eyes, were covered with white bandages to prevent them from inhaling the smell of the dead. Outside the tent sat Rosi Mollah, reading aloud from a prayer-book. The grave was only about three feet deep, with a kind of shelf on one side of it for the body. Then the funeral procession started, Kalpet being wrapped in a white felt, and borne on a camel's pack-saddle by Mollah Shah, Islam, Li Loyeh, Khodai Kallu, Ördek, Hamra Kul, and Kutchuk. Putting down the bier by the graveside, they lowered Kalpet cautiously into his final resting-place. Mollah Shah and the Mollah stepped

Kalpet's Grave.

down into the grave to put the finishing touches to the corpse as it lay on the shelf; then the Mollah addressed a few words to the departed, saying, "You have been an honest and faithful Mussulman. You have never done any of us any wrong. We miss you greatly. We bewail your loss. You have been a good and faithful servant to Tura (*i.e.* the author)."

After the two men stepped out of the grave, the pack-saddle was placed across it and covered with a felt carpet, the corners of which were kept in place by clods of earth. Then they piled the soil on the top of the carpet. The first rain, or the first wandering yak which chanced to come that way, would of course cause it to collapse. When the mound was completed, and a monument put up at its head, consisting of turves with stones on the top of them, the Mussulmans kneeled down round the grave, and, putting their hands before their faces, prayed silently, while the Mollah repeated certain forms of prayer for the dead. The spot where Kalpet was buried is marked on my map with a black cross. The mound is by this, no doubt, levelled down, and the flocks and herds of the nomads wander across it, while the wolves howl in the mountains in the dreary winter nights.

After the burial Rosi Mollah came to me and said, "Before we separate at the end of the journey, will you please give me a certificate, to the effect that Kalpet died a natural death, so that his brother in Keriya may not think that I or any of the others slew him." This I promised to do, and did do later on, as well as sent Kalpet's wages to his brother.

The Tibetans, who had been spectators of the burial, observed that we took a great deal of unnecessary trouble about it. "Why don't you fling the corpse out to the wolves and ravens?" they said, that being their own practice, as we witnessed on a subsequent occasion. The Mussulmans then burnt the tent in which Kalpet's dead body had lain, as well as his clothes and boots. In his case all the customary observances of the funeral were duly carried out; whereas when Aldat died he was buried simply as he was.

CHAPTER XXVIII.

THE EMISSARIES FROM LASSA.

THE day which followed this sad opening turned out bright and smiling, and the earth upon which men lead such a fugitive and uncertain existence again unfolded before us one of its most beautiful scenes. Once more we passed through a rocky defile or gateway, catching on our left yet another glimpse of the Selling-tso, and beheld from the crest of the low pass a wide expanse of open country, bounded in the extreme distance by mountains. Thence we directed our course due south, the Tibetans still hanging upon our rear. On the left of our route were some black tents, as well as two white and blue ones. Thither our self-constituted escort betook themselves, and as we in our turn approached them, a troop of horsemen galloped out and announced that two high dignitaries had arrived from Lassa, and begged us to stop, as they wished to have an interview with us. At first I refused, and said we had nothing to do with these emissaries, and would continue. But upon observing the large numbers of men who were riding about the tents, and reflecting that they came direct from Lassa, I thought it on the whole more prudent to stop, and at least hear what they wanted. Accordingly I begged the Tibetans to tell their chiefs that I would speak with them if they would come to me.

Shortly after this two elderly men in red robes approached on horseback, each horse being led by four attendants on foot. Stopping, but without dismounting, they greeted me politely. They looked quite friendly and good-natured; presumably the reports which they had heard of us during the last few days had been satisfactory. They said they had very important communications to make to me, and I positively must pitch my tents near theirs. To this, after raising a good many objections, I finally assented. Then they turned round and rode back to their own tents.

After waiting a long time for them to return, I sent our Lama to them to say that it was *they* who had requested us to stop, and if they really had anything important to say to me they had better make haste, or we should continue our journey. This stirred them up. Their camp was all commotion. The two emissaries hurried out, mounted, and rode towards us—the distance was only about 150 yards. For safety's sake they were surrounded by a strong escort, armed with swords, though they left their firearms behind them. Dismounting, they again greeted me politely, and stepped into our kitchen-tent, which on such occasions was generally cleared and brightened up with a variegated Khotan carpet. Upon this I and the two emissaries took our places, while the Cossacks, Tibetans, and Mohammedans formed tightly-packed rings all round outside. Our Lama, who acted as my interpreter, took his seat between us.

The elder of the two emissaries was called Hlajeh Tsering; the younger, Yunduk Tsering. They announced that they were members of the Devashung, or Holy Council, of Lassa, and had been sent by it to prevent me from going to that city. They knew I had already tried to get there another way with two companions, but had been stopped and conducted back across the frontier by Kamba Bombo's men; and their language was now precisely the same as Kamba Bombo had used. "You shall not advance another foot to the south," and for three long mortal hours this ultimatum was repeated in every possible variation. "We have millions of soldiers," said Yunduk Tsering, "and we shall prevent you." I asked them what they would do if we persisted in advancing in spite of them. They answered, "Either you or we will lose our heads. In our instructions it runs that we shall have our heads cut off if we let you go on. The whole country is full of soldiers." As far as our heads were concerned, I begged them to be under no apprehension; they could not touch us, partly because we had the assistance of higher powers, partly because we were armed with terrible weapons of destruction.

Both emissaries were greatly excited; they shouted and gesticulated, and got very hot; and when I, in spite of that, kept cool and quiet, and answered their threats with a dry laugh, they were ready to burst with indignation. "Kari-sari" (What does he say?), they asked incessantly. "He says he means to go south." "Mig yori" (if he has eyes), they shouted, "he shall see to-morrow how we will stop his caravan." "Mig yori! mig yori!" was incessantly on their lips, but I simply laughed and repeated after them, "Mig yori. To-morrow, when we march south, see to it that your muskets shoot straight, for by heaven you shall have a hot time of it!" Then they tried a new tack, and in pathetic tones earnestly besought me not to advance any farther. If we would only go back the same way we had come, they would procure us guides, and provisions, and everything else we wanted—in fact, all would then be well.

Now I had no intention of pushing matters to extremes; in fact, I had had enough of Tibet, and was now only anxious to reach Ladak, or rather, let me say, home—I mean my Swedish home by the waters of the Skrägård. But not to throw up the game too suddenly, I once more told them all their attempts were in vain—I was determined to go on. "Very well, then," they said—"very well, we will not shoot you and your men, but all the same we shall render it impossible for you to advance."

"How shall you manage that?"

"Ten or twenty of our soldiers will hold fast each of your men, and ten or twenty more will hold each camel, and we will hold them until they cannot stand."

"And what if we shoot you?"

"It will make no difference; we shall be killed all the same if we let you go on. We have received special orders from Lassa."

"Show me your orders, and I will stop."

"Willingly," they cried, and at once sent for the paper from their tents.

The document, which was a remarkable despatch, was read aloud by Yunduk Tsering, our Lama reading over his shoulder to check him. After the missive had been read aloud and translated once, we went through it again, slowly, paragraph by paragraph, whilst I wrote it down in Mongolian, with Latin lettering. The address on the outside of the folded document was this:

"In the year of the Iron Cow, the 6th month, the 21st day. This writing for the hands of the two governors of Nakktsong. It is from the Devashung, and is sent by post. It must be in their hands the 7th month, the 22nd day."

And then followed the document itself:—"In the year of the Iron Cow, the 6th month, the 19th day, there arrived from the governor of Nakkchu a writing (to the effect) that Lama Sanjeh, secretary of the Mongol Tsangeh Khutuktu, besides several pilgrims, were making a pilgrimage to Jo-mitsing in Hamdung, and that he, together with Tugden Darjeh, made certain communications to the governor of Nakkchu (that is, Kamba Bombo).

"The governor of Nakkchu has communicated the said intelligence to the Devashung. Tsangeh's secretary said, when he was setting out on his journey, he saw European men, and travelled in their company a piece. After they bought a quantity of clothing, they travelled on further. In the bazaar he saw two Russian men. 'Where travel you to?' he asked them. 'Are you lamas?' 'We are lamas,' they answered. The Khalkha Mongol, Shereb Lama, the healer, was in their company, and guided them. On the road he saw six Russian men travelling. A large number of camels and other men were also on the road.

"Let writings be sent with haste to Namru and Nakktsong, that it may be everywhere known that from Nakkchu inwards, for as far as my (*i.e.*, the Dalai Lama's) kingdom extends, Russian (European) men cannot have permission to travel south. Writings must be despatched to all the chiefs. Watch the frontiers of Nakktsong. It is necessary to watch the country closely bit by bit.* It is positively unnecessary that European men come into the Land of the Holy Books to spy around it. They have nothing whatever to do in the province which obeys you both. If they say it is necessary (know) that these two chiefs must not travel south. Compel them to turn and go back the way they came."

This missive cleared up certain points which had hitherto been obscure. Lama Sanjeh and Tugden Darjeh belonged to the caravan of Mongol pilgrims who passed through Charkhlik in May, 1900. Before that they had met with my two Buriat Cossacks and Shereb Lama in Korla and Kara-shahr, and the information which they had given, and which was embodied in the document, was in the main true. By "a large number of camels and other men" was meant our big caravan under Chernoff and Turdu Bai.

As soon as they reached Nakkchu, they told Kamba Bombo what they had seen, and the latter at once despatched a courier to the Devashung at Lassa. The messenger reached Lassa on the 19th of the 6th month, and on the 21st the fiery cross was speeding through the country north and west of the capital, especially through the provinces of Namru and Nakktsong, bidding the Tibetans maintain vigilant watch, and prevent any and every European from penetrating into the country. The

* This passage runs thus in Mongolian :—"Nakktsäng-tsonguin tsakhar hara, gadser gadser sän harreha kerekteh." The province is thus called Nakktsäng-tsong; but the name we always heard used was Nakktsong, just as the lake was always called Nakktsong-tso.

words "the province which obeys you both" proved that the document which had just been read to me was especially directed to the two emissaries who stopped us at Nakktsong-tso, and who were clearly the governors of Namru and Nakktsong respectively. From other information which we received it appeared that at the time when Kamba Bombo's report reached Lassa these two men happened to be in the capital, and their instructions were handed to them in person. Thus they were in possession of a number of details with regard to my dash for Lassa, and the way in which we had been stopped by Kamba Bombo. By "these two chiefs" were undoubtedly meant Sirkin and Chernoff, for when we were stopped by Kamba Bombo's men, we told them we had left two Europeans in our main camp, who would exact vengeance upon them if any harm happened to us. It was as we feared; the Mongol (Turgut) pilgrims had played us a dirty trick, though even without their tattling we should not have succeeded, for both Kamba Bombo and Hlajeh Tsering told us, they had received several independent reports from yak-hunters who had seen us.

In reply to this, all I could say was that I acknowledged the document, and that they were perfectly right to prevent us from going further, and I honestly told them that the policy of isolation which they were pursuing was the only means by which they could preserve their country from destruction. "All round Tibet," I said, "north, south, and west, Europeans have either conquered your neighbours or made them subject to themselves, and the same process has now begun in China. Your country is the only one in Asia which still preserves its independence intact." "Reh! reh!" they answered, "that is precisely how we wish it to remain! We are very sorry for you, that you cannot go to Lassa, but we must obey orders. So far as we are concerned, we should have been far better pleased if we had been ordered to accompany you to Lassa, and there show you all there is to be seen."

With the view of clearing up the situation, I asked them if they had any objection to send my Chinese pass to Lassa and wait with me for a reply. They said, "We cannot do it at any price, and for two reasons. In the first place, the Emperor of China exercises no authority whatever in our country, and in the second place the Devashung would suspect us of acting in your interests, and the least we could expect would be that we should be deposed from office."

Hlajeh Tsering Smoking his Pipe.

Shereb Lama's name was mentioned in the document, and here they had him before them in the flesh. They told him that if it had not been for my sake they would have seized him and handed him over to the authorities in Lassa, who would have inflicted upon him the punishment he so richly deserved for having guided a European towards Lassa. His name was now in very evil repute in the Holy City; it was written down in the "book of the suspect." It would be best for him if he never showed himself in the Holy City again; and with magisterial authority they laid down the law strongly to our poor Lama. But he, now that the die was cast, spoke out boldly and without reserve, abusing

Hlajeh Tsering and Yunduk Tsering.

the two emissaries unsparingly, and asking by what right they dared to use such language towards a lama who was not a Tibetan subject. He had received permission from the Chinese governor of Kara-shahr to accompany me, and also the consent of the prior of the monastery there; and when he returned he would tell them how he had been treated. As the quarrel looked like ending in blows, I produced the big musical-box, and, with the help of its soothing strains, reduced their discordant feelings to harmony.

Hlajeh Tsering was, however, the beau ideal of a gentleman, the perfect picture of a good-natured, indulgent, easy-going, favourite old uncle. Every member of our caravan, not excluding the Lama, was perfectly enchanted with him. I hope nobody will take exception to the phrase, if I say that he was far more like a wrinkled old woman than the distinguished governor of a province. Just look at the portrait of him which I drew (p. 457). His perfectly hairless face, the manner in which he wore his hair, his pig-tail, his head-attire, with its button of authority, his long ear-rings—all contributed to give him such a decidedly feminine appearance, that I asked him in all seriousness whether he really was not an old woman. This insinuation, which would have seriously offended any other man, seemed, on the contrary, rather to tickle Hlajeh Tsering, for he smiled mischievously, nodded, and twisted his parchment face into the most comical grimaces, put his hand before his eyes, and ended by laughing until the tears ran down his cheeks. "No!" he assured me, he was not an old woman, he was a man.

At seven o'clock that evening I, accompanied by Shagdur and the Lama, visited Hlajeh Tsering, in his tent, and stayed until midnight. This time we no longer discussed business, but laughed and talked and jested like a couple of students. Amongst other things we boasted of our weapons, and I proposed to try Shagdur's sabre against a Tibetan sword. After the trial the latter was gapped like a saw, though subsequently we found that the Tibetans did possess several swords made of excellent steel. Hlajeh Tsering also showed me two or three exceedingly useful revolvers which he possessed.

His white tent, with blue stripes and bordering, was neatly and tidily furnished. At the farther short end was a kind of low divan, made of cushions and bolsters, and in front of it stood a low table, upon which we were served with tea, sour milk, and tsamba. On the right-hand side of the divan, when you sat upon it, stood a small moveable shrine, with various *burkhans* (images of Buddha), gilded, and in part swathed in *haddiks* (scarves of honour), amongst them being the *burkhan* of the Dalai Lama. Two or three oil lamps were burning in front of it, and beside them were small trays of brass, containing various kinds of light refreshments, which were offered to the images, as is the custom in all the big temples. No sooner did any of us take a sip of tea than, hey presto! a servant ran forward and filled the cup up again, even though it would hold no more than ten or a dozen drops. Hlajeh Tsering had a special attendant to look after his pipes. His favourite was a long Chinese pipe, and when I gave him a tinful of my tobacco he was perfectly enchanted with it.

Yunduk Tsering, a man of about 45, was less endowed with intelligence. It was he who thought he could frighten me with big words, by dishing up his innumerable multitudes, and counting his soldiers by millions. I never had the least desire to become involved in hostilities with them, for I had only four Cossacks, and, as will readily be understood, I had neither the right nor the wish to use violence. If we had been so rash as to embark on any such mad and reprehensible undertaking, it would have been the easiest thing in the world for the Tibetans, with their immense superiority in numbers, to have entrapped us in some pass, and annihilated us. But the Czar had not lent me his

Hlajeh Tsering and Yunduk Tsering.

Cossacks for the purpose of creating disturbances in Tibet, but simply to serve as a guard for my own personal protection. Hence it was a point of honour with me to take them home, and return them to their quarters, as sound and uninjured as when they joined me. Yunduk Tsering, therefore, corpulent and bloated as he was, was not only slenderly equipped with brains, but I will even call him silly. In the course of our numerous discussions and disputes, he used repeatedly to draw his hand edge-wise across his throat, by way of illustrating what would happen to us if we persisted in pressing further to the south. He tried my patience to such a degree, that at last I called him point blank " a silly ass " !

Both emissaries were neatly and elegantly attired, and brought several different suits with them; some warm, some light, some intended for state occasions, and others suitable for everyday wear. The style was Chinese, that is to say, tunics and jackets or vests of silk or wool. The illustrations on pp. 459 and 461 show them dressed in gala attire.

CHAPTER XXIX.

THE NAKKTSONG–TSO.

ON the 14th September I left the camp, and began one of the most glorious lake-trips it has ever been my lot to make. Taking Kutchuk with me, and the skiff on a camel, I rode west to the shore of the adjacent lake of Nakktsong-tso. Strange to say, the Tibetans did not molest me; but then I had told them I was only going fishing. I left orders with the caravan to stay where they were that day, and on the following morning to proceed to the west side of the lake, and there wait for me at the spot where we had been turned back two or three days before.

Fifty-two degrees west of south there was a little rocky islet peeping above the blue waters of the lake. Towards it we directed our course, and it took us several hours to get there. The lake appeared to extend a long way in front of us. But I enjoyed the magnificent views, the lap-lapping of the bright, rippling water against the skiff, the beautiful weather, bright, cheerful, and warm (14°.2 C., or 57°.6 Fahr.); but even more enjoyable than these was the consciousness that I was safe from the amiable inquisitiveness and touching solicitude of the Tibetans as to the direction in which we intended to travel. The maximum depth along the line we took was 41½ feet.

The little crag was crescent-shaped and rose about 160 feet above the surface. At its western extremity stood a stone slab, indicating, I have no doubt, some winter track across the ice. A little strip of thick, luxuriant grass grew along its foot, and was now, at any rate, safe from interference, for the Tibetans possessed nothing in the shape of a boat by which to reach it; but the droppings of yaks and sheep showed that it was sometimes visited in the winter, when the lake froze, and so became connected with the shores. The limestone cliffs plunged steeply down on every side, the angle of inclination being 47° north and 43° west; this being the prevailing slope of the entire region.

The top was crowned with three cairns of stones, and afforded us a splendid and very useful view of the southern reaches of the lake. As we were not likely to visit them, I seized the opportunity to draw a sketch map of the lake in that direction.

Whilst we were tramping towards "Kalpet Sound,' Nakktsong-tso had appeared to extend a long way to the south; in fact, right up to the foot of the rocky ridge which blocked the view in that direction. But it now turned out that the islet was only about a mile distant from the southern shore; the illusion being due to the refraction of the air, which caused the extremely low steppe that stretched between the lake and the foot of the mountains to disappear. We perceived that it was covered with green pasture, and was sprinkled over with black dots—yaks, horses, and sheep; and besides eight black tents, there were also two stone buildings, probably local temples.

Beyond the island in the west three wild, irregularly formed crests appeared to rise from a larger island, or perhaps they—well, that was precisely what we were to find out presently. From the southernmost of the three spurs a low promontory jutted out a considerable distance into the lake. Having doubled this, we steered 80° west of south, and kept on in the same direction until nightfall. Immediately on our right we had the most southerly of the three mountain spurs. It was like a gigantic wall built up of immense, rugged blocks of stone, and in places rose sheer from the lake, which was shallow, or seldom more than six and a half feet deep. Further west the lake contracted, and we seemed to have entered a *cul de sac*. Narrower and narrower grew the lake. We passed the west end of the first spur. We passed the west end of the second spur—it culminated in a fantastic sort of pinnacle. By this we were only about half a mile from the southern shore; but what was this we had on our right hand? Was it an island, or not? These questions we kept asking ourselves at each stroke of the oars. Still on and on we rowed into the mysterious sound, until the scraggy promontory, which reflected itself in the still, bright surface of the lake, deepened its tints to purple and red where the setting sun fell upon it. In fact, the water was so transparent that the algæ and aquatic plants at the bottom were as easy to see as the plants in an aquarium.

We were following the shore-line, which now swung off to the north-west. As the strip of grass along its margin was untouched, we again hoped it was an island, so that we might spend another peaceful night free from the worrying attentions of the Tibetans. Opposite the western extremity of the second spur, that is on the other side of the water, towered an imposing mountain-knot, and at its southern foot, only a few hundred yards distant, we suddenly perceived a stone hut, with smoke rising from it. A solitary dog rushed out of it down to the lake-side and began to bark vociferously.

By this it was twilight. We paddled steadily along the tranquil sound, until the barking of the dog died away behind us. The cliffs, shooting up perpendicularly on both sides, flung back sharply the echoes of every stroke of the paddles. It was like rowing through an immense rock-built temple consecrated to Nature and Nature's God. Above head between the stupendous mountain walls a couple of royal eagles were sailing slowly round and round, poised on widespread, motionless wing.

All at once the sound appeared to come to an end; but no, it was only a low tongue of land stretching about seven-eighths of the way across the passage. Behind it the waterway still continued towards the north-west, though the jutting crags prevented us from seeing very far ahead. And then night dropped her veil over the scene, and lovely though it was, hid it from our eyes. It was time to stop and land. Now to turn in in an unknown country, and amongst strangers of whom we knew nothing, was not altogether pleasant, even though I had my revolver with me. As soon as we had drawn our boat safe on shore, we set to work to explore our immediate surroundings, and to our great satisfaction soon discovered that the tongue of land left a passage-way about 150—160 feet wide along the south foot of the mountains, so that we were effectually cut off from the natives, who, having no boat, would be unable to interfere with us. There was plenty of dry and excellent argol, and we soon had a comfortable fire burning, its light blue flames being as noiseless as St. Elmo's fire; for argol never crackles like wood. The night was bright and still, and we spent it quite peacefully crouched together in our sleeping-skins. Next morning, as soon as the sun tipped the summits of the cliffs on the west side of the sound, we were on foot again, and lit a fire, and put on the water to boil for tea. Thanks to Cherdon, we were well supplied with food in the shape of a whole roast goose, and two or three cakes of bread; and this was not the first time that I and Kutchuk had camped together. The little pools along the shore were sheeted with ice; but it soon grew warm, and at one p.m. the thermometer touched 14°.4 C., or 57°.9 Fahr.

Nor was it long before Kutchuk's blade was once more cleaving the water, and we were skimming along towards the north-west. I can scarcely imagine anything more sublime and, at the same time, enchanting, than the cliffs we were travelling between—it was like a Venetian lagoon flanked by ancient palaces of Cyclopean masonry. Time after time our view was curtailed by the jutting crags, and we repeatedly thought we had reached the point where we should have to turn back; but the defile wound on and on, and the natural canal continued to open up one perspective after another. The depth did not exceed 11½ feet, and the breadth was in general not more than a couple of hundred yards. All this time we were fortunately travelling north-west, the right direction to bring us to the rendezvous.

But upon doubling a projecting headland on the right we were greatly astonished to perceive some yaks and horses. As we shot past the headland, three men came rushing down to the shore, and shouted and threw stones at their animals to drive them inland. At the foot of the next headland on the right two black tents made their appearance, and beside them stood a man, a woman, and a boy, all of whom displayed the utmost amazement at seeing such strange visitors in their locality. Here, if anywhere, they should have lived in peace, for their dwelling was almost entirely surrounded by water. Seeing these nomads where we did, we assumed that they dwelt upon a peninsula, and that we should soon have to turn and row all the long way back again. In fact, we thought we could hear the Tibetans crowing over us as we rowed deeper and deeper into the bottle-shaped channel. One of them ran to the top of the nearest headland: was it that he might witness our discomfiture when we reached the end of the fjord?

But once again the sound widened out, and yet another deep vista unfolded itself towards the north-west. By this the skiff was leaking, and we had to bale. Whilst we were busy with this it came on to snow, though shortly afterwards the sun peeped out again. All of a sudden the depth increased to 38¼ feet, and after that the view opened out still wider, and again our hopes revived. Perhaps, after all, we should be able to struggle out into the lake without being forced to turn back. But all at once our spirits sank to zero: the sound suddenly came to an end, terminating in low flat land. We got out and dragged our boat as far as we could through the shallow water into a wedge-shaped bay, and there stuck helplessly fast. Kutchuk, taking off his nether garments, waded through the soft deep mud and climbed the nearest hill to look round. The first thing he observed was a river coming from the south, and entering a smaller lake, which appeared to be connected with the Nakktsong-tso. Thereupon we drew the skiff on shore, took it to pieces, and in a couple of journeys carried it and our baggage across the neck of land, 500 or 600 yards wide, which separated the bay from the river, an entertainment which cost us three full hours. However, even that was better than turning back. The river was divided into two arms, and immediately opposite its mouth the lake was choked with mudbanks, on which hundreds of gulls were busy. We now rowed towards the north-east, having on our left an especially imposing cliff. It was still a sound we were in, though broader than the one we threaded before; here the cliffs formed monumental gateways.

At length our eyes were gladdened by the sight so long wished for. Behind a pier-like sandy headland, on which a score of gulls stood, glittering white in the setting sun, we perceived the widespread dark blue waters of the Nakktsong-tso. Thus we had at last succeeded. Strictly speaking, it was a peninsula we had rowed round, and its only connection with the mainland was the narrow isthmus across which we carried our boat. The isthmus evidently consisted of alluvial mud, deposited by the river, and it had gone on accumulating until at last it completely choked up the sound. Except for this the locality where we saw the nomads would have been a perfect island. Thus Nakktsong-tso, which on several of the maps does not figure at all, while on others its position is greatly in error, proved to possess a very remarkable configuration. That is to say, it formed a watery ring or circle, like the lake of Yamdok-tso south of Lassa; and while it was tolerably wide in the north, in the south it was as narrow as a fjord.

On the other side of the pier-shaped sandy headland the depth increased suddenly from 10 feet to close upon 73. We rowed 60° east of north, and later on in the afternoon encountered a head wind and a "high sea." When the sun sank to the level of the horizon behind us, the water over those reaches which were only 10 feet deep changed from dark blue to a vivid green, through which we saw lacustrine growths below as distinctly as if we had been looking through a mirror. Our goal was a cape on the northern shore, whence we ought to be able to see the signal-fires of our camp. But the cape lay right in the teeth of the wind, and the shades of night were gathering fast about us; hence we were forced to put in to shore at the first spot we could reach. The night was again exceptionally clear, with a vivid moon, though the wind blew cold and keen; yet what cared we for that, once we were snugly tucked away like marmots in our warm furs? Fortunately, during these two nights that we camped out, it did not rain. We were tired, and the lullaby of the lake soon hushed us to sleep. I shall not readily forget those beautiful nights under the bright sparkling sky of Tibet, with its thin, pure mountain air, and the hushed music of its entrancing scenery.

That night the thermometer went down to a bare 2°.0 C. (or 35°.6 Fahr.). On the following morning we again started early with a strong east wind dead against us. It was cold and uncomfortable, and the lake ran so high that we had to keep close in to the shore. Then to cap all, five minutes after we started, we were overtaken by a terrific storm. The hail came down in such quantities that the inside of the boat was soon white all over; though immediately after it began the wind dropped and the waves subsided. The squall lasted for over two hours, and all the time seemed to hang directly over our heads. Behind us the sky was black and the mountains shrouded in white, while to the east the landscape was bathed in bright sunshine. We ourselves were enveloped in a sort of twilight, halfway between winter and summer. Gradually the hail changed into snow, which fell as soft as thistledown and clung to the canvas of the boat. For a couple of minutes the sun peeped out, then crept behind the clouds, and once more showed itself; all this time the snow continued to fall thick and fast, and the lake was greatly agitated. The water was of a most wonderful blue-green colour, a lambent and impressionable element, through which, in spite of its agitation, we were able to study with perfect distinctness every feature of the bottom of the lake.

Being compelled to rest awhile on a promontory, I walked to the top of the rising ground to have a look round, and there on the northern shore, sure enough, was the caravan straggling along, dogged by the black swarms of the Tibetans. Soon after resuming our journey, we came to an island on our right; it was of considerable size, and a score of horses were grazing on it. Here two capes nearly met, one jutting out from the island, the other from the mainland opposite, like the carbon sticks in an electric lamp. The strait between them was so shallow that the boat scraped the bottom. Here again there were large flocks of gulls fishing amongst the broken water, which frothed and foamed like a cataract in a river. This was the fjord that gave access to the island.

An hour later and we were opposite the camp. It stretched all along the shore; men and horses being sprinkled over every hill-side, while every now and again the columns of smoke which rose from the fires were snapped across and partly blown away by the wind. We had five tents, the Tibetans nineteen; but most of the latter were encamped round a fire in the open air. All my men were down on the shore to meet me, the Cossacks receiving me as usual with a military salute. I greeted them, as I always used to do in a morning, in the three languages—"Sdrazdvicheh!" to the Cossacks; "Salaam aleikum," to the Mussulmans; and "Amur sän baneh" to our Mongol Lama.

When they found I did not return, the Tibetan emissaries grew terribly uneasy, and redoubled their sentinels round our camp. The first evening Hlajeh Tsering went to the Cossacks, and asked them what had become of me. They answered, without blinking or turning a hair, that I had rowed over to the southern side of the lake, whence I proposed to make a dash for Lassa, and they were ordered to stay where they were till I returned. Upon this the emissary was immensely put out, and hastened to send out patrols in every direction, especially to the south. But during the course of the second day they must have found out that we were still on the lake, for they forbade the nomads who dwelt along its southern shore to render us any assistance. During the day's march they several times counted my men, and always found that two of us were missing.

Although they could not quite understand how things hung together, they suspected that one of my men had taken the horses round the lake, so that I and one or two of my attendants might ride to Lassa. In consequence of this they dealt more stringently with the caravan, and refused to supply them with provisions, and doubled the outposts at night. Nor did they relax these measures until they perceived the skiff labouring shorewards through the breakers. Their strength now amounted to close upon 200 men, not counting several patrols which had not yet returned; whereas we were only 18, that is to say, one against ten, or, if I counted the Cossacks only, one against fifty.

The Tibetans must have a very despicable opinion of us Europeans. Most travellers who have advanced as far as the "holy sphere" have arrived in such a pitiable and destitute condition, that it has only been with the assistance of the Tibetans themselves that they have been able to struggle out of the country. The Tibetans had never seen a strong caravan in good condition, one strong enough, I mean, to travel without asking their permission. I was, I admit, strongly tempted to play them a trick by crossing the lake secretly and making a dash for Lassa; it would have been quite easy to smuggle two or three horses away from the pasture in broad daylight. However, as I should really have gained little, probably only two or three days' march at the most, I abstained.

The Land of the Burkhans, the southern part of the Land of the Holy Books, is taboo to Europeans; it is the patrimony of the Dalai Lama, a sacred land, his own peculiar property. It is not that the lamas are more fanatical now than they were in the days when they welcomed the Jesuit missionaries; and certainly they are not less tolerant at the present day than in 1845, when Huc and Gabet spent several months in Lassa. Their policy of isolation during the last half century or so has not been dictated by religious, but by political motives. Their tactics, peaceful, but so far successful, have aimed at guarding their frontiers against Europeans, and conducting their unbidden guests politely, but firmly, out of the country. Still, Tibet will have to meet her destiny. So long as the Tibetans are inhabitants of the same planet as we are, they will have to reconcile themselves to our desire to know all about them, to study their religion and its sacred writings, their temples, their manners and customs, to explore their country and its approaches, to map their majestic mountains and sound their capricious lakes. So far, however, they have not fallen victims to specious representations about the growth of commerce—that is to say, the importation of tobacco, spirits, opium and fire-arms. They say, in effect, "Away with all your luxuries, with your steel, your gold and silver! All we want is to be left alone in peace in our own country."

When I said, "I will take the southern road to Ladak," they answered, "There is no southern road." When I spread the map out before them and pointed to the road, they objected, "Well, there is a road; but it is only for us. You may not travel through the Land of the Burkhans." And when I protested, "You are inhospitable," they hastened to answer: "Your land is for you; we have nothing to do there. But our country is for us; you must therefore leave it, and go home to your own."

It must have been a very expensive business to maintain a force of 200 men on a war footing, to say nothing of the loss caused by the men's absence from their own homes, and the care of their herds. But the expense did not trouble them, provided they were able to keep the intruder outside their borders. All this occasioned them an immense amount of trouble, and yet, in spite of it all, they were always friendly and polite. Their jealousy of strangers is only aimed against Europeans. Chinese, Ladakis, and the adjacent Asiatic races all have free entrance into Tibet. Hlajeh Tsering's cook was a Dungan or Mohammedan Chinese, who understood a little Chanto, or Turki, and had been in East Turkestan. The Mohammedans call everybody who does not profess Islam "Kapers," that is to say, "Heathens," equally whether they are Asiatics or Europeans; but the Tibetans exclude from their country none except Europeans, consequently their isolation is political, not religious. A Chinaman, a Japanese, a Buriat, an Indian Pundit like Nain Singh or Krishna, a merchant of Leh, none of these would experience any difficulty in entering Lassa. And when an Asiatic has been properly instructed, he has been able to bring home valuable reports of what he has seen. Hence, as I have already said, we know Lassa better than any other city in Central Asia, with the possible exception of Kashgar, Kulja, and Urumtchi. One who has been the guest of the lamas in Urga, Kum-bum, Himis, and other temples in Ladak, can testify that in each of these places he was received with the greatest hospitality, and never perceived any signs of intolerance whatsoever.

After a bright still evening it came on to hail about ten o'clock, and then turned to snow, and snowed all night, so that it was quite strange to hear the crunching of our night-watchman's footsteps as he trod his rounds. Next day, the 17th September, the snow quickly melted in the sun, though not on the northern faces of the hills. In the extreme south a stupendous pyramidal peak, which far overtopped all its neighbours, was a cone of glittering white, and being perfectly regular in formation, it bore a close resemblance to an extinct volcano.

I now ordered the caravan to proceed to the mouth of the Yaggyu-rapga. The camel on which Kalpet had died fell ill, and would soon die in its turn, because, as Turdu Bai said —and he understood all about camels—it had carried a dead man. The weather was so fine it tempted me on to the lake again; and I was only too glad to escape a whole day's march. This time Ördek was my boatman. Putting the skiff and baggage on horses he rode north across the narrow neck of land which parted the Nakktsong-tso from the Selling-tso. This isthmus was of a remarkable character. The water-parting lay immediately north of the Nakktsong-tso and only 30 or 40 feet above its level; but to reach the Selling-tso was a ride of a considerable distance, and in the course of it we descended 150 to 160 feet, so that the latter lake lay about 120 feet lower than its neighbour. I assume, of course, that the Natkksong-tso must have an outlet, although I failed to discover it. Possibly it has an underground connection with the Selling-tso. As we went down towards the latter, we again observed the same distinctly marked beach-lines that we had noticed when we approached its shores before.

The low-lying strip of sand next the lake was so muddy, that we were forced to wade a long way out before we could get our boat launched. The depth was trifling, seldom more than ten feet. The bottom consisted of greyish-blue clay, without a trace of vegetation, and the water was of a cheerful, spring-like green, and was arched over by a bright, sunny sky. Nevertheless, the only feature of the landscape that stood out sharply and distinctly was the broad peninsula which had forced us to turn back a few days before; we now saw that it was prolonged eastwards by a series of small pointed rocks, which seemed to hover just above the water. By directing the telescope to the left we were able to follow the caravan and its Tibetan escort. The latter had almost doubled in strength during the course of the day, owing to the arrival of several small reinforcements of mounted men. Above their heads hung a heavy, black hail-cloud, which, judging from the shafts of alternate light and dark that stretched down from it to the earth, kept persistently pouring out its contents over them the whole of the time. Not a drop, however, fell where we were.

We steered at first north-north-west, until we had rounded the promontory where the Alla-sangpo entered the lake; after that we went due west, making for the bifurcation of the mountain spurs which shut in the valley of the Yaggyu-rapga on the south. The sun was setting behind the mountains, causing

View Across the Chargut-tso, Looking West.

them to stand out like a black silhouette sharply outlined. It was quite dark when we reached the big camp, the fires of which gleamed like the gas-lights in a little town.

On the 18th September I gave orders to start early. Whilst we were loading up, some of the Tibetans came forward and asked us to stop over the day; Hlajeh Tsering and Yunduk Tsering were obliged to return, and it would be in our own interest if he bought our horses and arranged for the hire of yaks before they finally left us. I answered that it was a matter of indifference to us where they went; *we* were going on without delay. "In which direction?" they asked. I pointed west, up the valley of the Yaggyu-rapga. "It is impossible for you to advance that way," they asserted, "you must go to the north-west." Our answer was to make an instant start up-stream, keeping to its northern or left bank. The valley was grand, embraced as it was between the imposing mountain-spurs. From the summit of a hill, soon after starting, we obtained a delightful view of another large lake in the west, richly diversified by rocky islands, headlands and creeks; to all appearance it was almost as complicated as the Nakktsong-tso.

Ere we had advanced very far we were overtaken by the Tibetans, riding in troops of 15 to 20. Wherever we turned our eyes there were the black horsemen, with the red flags fluttering from the forks of their musket-rests.

Upon approaching nearer to the new lake, we perceived that the line of cliffs on our right stretched out some distance into the lake, and formed a peninsula with perpendicular faces. It would be impossible to get round it. The Tibetans, however, showed us a pass, and a very difficult one it was, in some places so steep and rough that had a camel slipped he would have been like a raw beefsteak by the time he got to the bottom. From the summit of the pass a new and glorious view burst upon our eyes towards the north-west, across another portion of the lake which was likewise beset with picturesque peninsulas and rocky islands. Down the slopes rolled the black troops of the Tibetans like a succession of avalanches, enveloped in clouds of dust. Spreading themselves along the regularly-formed strip of shore, they speedily ran up their tents, and the smoke was already curling from their camp-fires when we arrived.

Camp no. LXXXIV., on the eastern shore of the Chargut-tso (15,135 feet), was one of the best and most comfortable I have ever pitched my tent in. No matter which way we turned, the view was one to charm the eye and gladden the mind. To look west, deep into the fjords of the lake, was like looking into the vistas of a forest of stone. The islands and craggy headlands grew lighter and lighter in tint as they receded in the far distance, and the whole scene was bathed in sunshine. The Tibetans, with their picturesque attire and warlike equipments, were just the figures that this rugged landscape demanded.

The strip of beach was like the high street of a busy town —full of life and colour. Without counting ours, there were 25 tents, and yet the greater part of the native soldiery were gathered around fires in the open air. The shore was alive with men and horses. I only remember one occasion on which I dwelt in a larger camp, and that was in 1890, when I travelled in the train of Shah Nasr ed-Din to Mount Elburz. The numbers of our escort had gone on increasing until they approached 500 men. At dusk Almaz came in alone. Kalpet's camel was dead—Turdu Bai was right.

We could not quite make out what the Tibetans were after. Our faces were now definitely set towards Ladak ; why then had they called together such a large force ? Did they mean to make an attack upon us by night ? At any rate we appointed strong guards for that night, and held our weapons in readiness. About an hour after midnight I was awakened by an unpleasant dream. I was lying on my right arm, which was stretched out along the ground, and the hand grew numb and without feeling, and was icy cold. By chance I happened to touch it with my left hand, and being only partly awake, I fancied the Tibetans had flung a dead body into my tent. In a moment I jumped up and struck a light, and found the tent empty ; then, as soon as my thoughts cleared, I saw how the matter stood.

Here beside this beautiful lake we stayed two days, and the time passed all too quickly, what with visiting the Tibetans and entertaining them, and discussing the pros and cons of the route to Ladak. I said frankly that I proposed to go my own way, and should refuse to receive instructions from anybody. But the Tibetans declared we should have an escort all the way, and they undertook to procure us everything we wanted until we reached Ladak. Hlajeh Tsering, having heard that Kamba Bombo had given me two horses, made me a similar present ; besides which, he said that, as our caravan had been so fearfully decimated, 40 yaks were always, by special command of the

The Tibetan Emissaries' Guard at the Chargut-tso.

Dalai Lama, to be at our disposal. Strange that the Tibetans should be so friendly and courteous, for this was the second time I had attempted to approach the forbidden land. Under similar circumstances almost any other Asiatic race would have promptly made an example of us; but the Tibetans are far too good-natured and inoffensive to resort to violence; they never advanced beyond threats and the empty alarums of war.

At noon on the 19th September the Tibetans provided a magnificent spectacle for our entertainment. I had told Hlajeh Tsering that I wished to photograph him and his colleague, and after that the whole of his force of cavalry. They complied with my request with the greatest of pleasure, and at once called out 200 or 300 of their men. They drew them up in rank and file, but it was anything but an easy thing to get them to stand still. When I asked them to raise their swords and lances into the air they obeyed instantly; but the action awakened their warlike instincts, the horses grew restive, and the whole troop burst away as if charging home in an attack, uttering the fiercest war-cries as they galloped. It was in truth a wild sight to see them racing across the steppe, their accoutrements jingling, their weapons flashing in the sun. My photographic ambitions had perforce to rest until their warlike ardour subsided, and they were made to understand that when it came to photographing, there was no need for them to make such a display of energy or shout so desperately loud.

CHAPTER XXX.

STORM-STAYED IN THE CHARGUT-TSO.

THE 20th of September was the day fixed for starting on the long journey to Ladak; but the Tibetan emissaries begged us to wait until next morning, when they would accompany us some days on the road. The 20th was one of their great religious holidays, and they wished to stay quietly in their tents. To this request I acceded, and all the more readily because the enchanting waters of the Chargut-tso had for me an attraction I could not resist, and yet the treachery of the siren lurked behind its smiling face.

This time I selected Khodai Kullu to be my boatman, and we directed our course towards the outermost extremity of the craggy peninsula which bordered our bay on the south. Thence we pushed out towards the open part of the lake, but were driven back by a storm from the west. As soon as we saw the sky begin to darken we at once turned back, and, at the risk of tearing our boat to pieces against the sharp-edged stones, effected a landing on the steep, rocky shore of the peninsula. I was not going to be detained a prisoner there, so, bidding Khodai Kullu launch again, we set off to paddle back to camp diagonally across the bay, which by this was in a state of considerable commotion. The lake, indeed, ran so high that one moment we were down in the "trough of the sea," and the next were balancing on the crest of a lofty wave. The boat pitched and shivered and creaked alarmingly, and we travelled at a terrific pace, our progress being watched with the closest interest by a crowd of Tibetans gathered along the shore. We could see them when we rose to the tops of the breakers; they were watching us in silence, and with their hearts in their mouths. And, to tell the truth, we were not without anxiety ourselves. One moment we lunged forwards, and I thought we were going to be dashed to pieces against the shore; but the next moment we were being sucked back by the receding wave. The next time we were borne shorewards, Khodai Kullu, who held himself in readiness, leapt nimbly out, and at the same moment all four Cossacks plunged into the water, and literally carried me ashore between them. It was a smart piece of work. The Tibetans came hurrying up to convince themselves that I was alive and unharmed.

As soon as the storm subsided, we put out again, and succeeded in taking a series of soundings. Indeed, we stayed out until after dark, and had to finish our measurements by torchlight. As we drew in to shore, our bay presented quite an animated spectacle. Fires were blazing all round its shores, giving it the appearance of an illuminated harbour, and the smoke

Tibetan Soldiers Gambling beside the Chargut-tso.

from them was being wafted across the lake, where it hung like a greyish-blue veil above the now placid waters. Then the moon came out and flung a broad ribbon of quivering silver across the lake, and so added the magic touches of her glamour to the already entrancing landscape. As we pulled ashore we heard the gossip of the men and the Tibetan soldiers. They were drinking tea, smoking, and playing dice.

When I was called on the 21st of September, the thermometer stood just at freezing-point. The lake was as smooth as a mirror, and with its long chain of projecting rocky headlands looked like an immense fjord or river. It was such a bright, beautiful autumn morning, I just longed to be out on the water, especially as it would take me away from the noise and confusion of the 500 Tibetan soldiers.

Taking with me Kutchuk and provisions for three days, as well as warm felts and such instruments as I should require, I once more embarked on the Chargut-tso. The caravan started about an hour later, the Tibetans accompanying them in small detached parties, which kept riding all round them. But we soon lost sight of the long black strings of moving animals behind the intervening mountains. My men had instructions to encamp somewhere near the western end of the lake, and there wait until we joined them. The Tibetan emissaries were uneasy at this new lake-trip, and wondered what it meant. They did not like it at all.

We had barely been started a quarter of an hour when a fresh breeze sprang up in the west, and the face of the lake clouded over. Then it grew crumpled; then it began to rise; and finally it broke into waves. In short, we were in for another gale, and had to suspend our soundings and look after our own safety. It was too late to turn back; and even if we could have done so, there was nobody left at the old encampment to help us ashore. Nor was there a headland along the south shore behind which we could seek protection. All we could do was to row hard in the teeth of the storm, until we could obtain shelter behind the nearest craggy islet. However, I managed to obtain a couple more soundings. The maximum depth amounted to 138 feet. Every breaker we encountered drenched us to the skin. The water ran off my cap, and I had hard work to see through my spectacles. Note-books, felts, all our paraphernalia were as if they had been dipped in the lake. We toiled like galley-slaves, struggling against both wind and lake. At length, however, we got under an islet, where the waves were not so high. Close underneath it the depth was no less than 111½ feet. We were rather exhausted when we stepped on shore, but we made haste to pull our little boat well up out of the reach of the waves. Were she to be washed away, we should be in a most precarious position.

The little islet we landed upon was shaped like a saddle; that is to say, it consisted of two rounded knobs, with a depression or isthmus between them, not more than 350 yards across. I walked to the western side of the islet, and—I blessed my stars I was not just then at the mercy of the tempest. Having ascertained what sort of a place it was we were imprisoned on, we set about making ourselves comfortable. The boat set up on end afforded a certain amount of shelter against the wind, and a felt did duty as an awning, for all this while the sun was pouring down its golden rays out of a turquoise blue sky. By a fortunate impulse I had brought a book with me. Kutchuk dropped off asleep, and soon began to snore. Meanwhile the wind howled and whined in the crevices of the rocks. Having nothing better to do, about three in the afternoon we set to work and gathered sufficient yappkak and argol—there was plenty of both—and made a fire and had tea. At intervals Kutchuk got up and went to the western end of the islet, to see what the lake looked like;

Our Camp on the First Island in Chargut-tso.

but he always came back with the intelligence that the boat could not possibly live amid such a seething tumult. With the help of the telescope we were able to make out large flocks and herds, and several tents, along the northern shore of the lake.

Evening was approaching, and yet the wind showed no sign of abating, and the breakers continued to thunder against the west end of the islet. I had chosen this method of travel with the view of escaping the noisy confusion of the march, and enjoying the quiet beauties of Nature in solitude. Now, however, I was only anxious to get back to my people. Even the worst uproar of the camp would be better than being held a fast prisoner on a tiny island in the middle of a Tibetan lake. The sun set, bright, smiling with malicious glee. Deep shadows dropped down upon our little encampment, though the eastern shore of the lake was still bathed in brightness. Soon the shades of night began to creep up the mountain-sides. For a while their summits glowed scarlet; then the glow faded, and night, blue and cold, held Nature in her silent ban. What would we not have given for a glimpse of the ring of camp-fires which had lined the bay the night before! But our sole illuminant was the moon, half way towards the full.

Perhaps the wind would drop during the night. We went to sleep early, Kutchuk having orders to waken me about a couple of hours after midnight. It was often quite calm in the early morning, and if it were so next morning, we meant to seize the opportunity and row across to the southern shore. Kutchuk called me at 4 a.m. The stars were twinkling brightly, but the gale was blowing as hard as ever. We soon had a fire going, for there were nine degrees (Fahr.) of frost, and the hot tea went down famously. Then we sat on the shore, silent, musing, waiting for day to break. At length the open spaces of the sky behind the mountains began to lighten; and suddenly, as in a transformation scene, there was the sun streaming above the mountain-tops like a ball of burning fire.

But the storm, instead of subsiding, still continued to increase in violence. It was a regular "trade-wind," and blew strong and steady without relaxing a moment, while at intervals light frigates of clouds went sailing swiftly across the lake. When my book was finished I amused myself by making a map of the lake as far as I could survey it to the east and west. Whilst we lay and droned the day away on the eastern end of the islet, the western end was full of the roar of a mighty waterfall, the waves beat up so portentously high. Then I mapped the island, whilst Kutchuk gathered fuel. Then we had dinner. Then we anchored my shelter with big stones to prevent it from being blown away. Then I went to the south-west edge of the island, where the cliffs descended vertically into the lake, and sat and listened to the thunder of the waves. I closed my eyes, the better to enjoy my day dreams. Every beat of the enraged water against the iron-bound coast seemed to cry in mockery, "What do *you* want in this holy land?" Then I climbed to the top of the northern knoll to bid adieu to the sun when he set. Finally we built up a big fire, and practised the art of *dolce far niente*.

About 6.30 p.m. the violence of the wind seemed to abate,

and our hopes again rose. At 7 p.m., there was no doubt about it, the gale was nothing like so violent, although the clouds, which had massed thicker together, streamed away at the same giddy pace as before, the moon sailing on over them like a swift-keeled silver schooner. We began to study the weather with quickened interest. We went repeatedly to the western side of the island, but the lake still presented an unbroken expanse of plunging waves. Due west of us was another little rocky islet, the bearings of which I had already taken. We hoped we might at least manage to reach it before the moon set. Gradually the wind dropped, and we made haste to pack up.

Doubling the south-east corner of the island, we had on our

The South Shore of the Western End of the Second Islet.

right the steep face of the cliff, hanging like a spectre—it was faintly lighted by the moon—over the waters of the lake. At the same time we became exposed to the after-swell of the gale, though, fortunately, it was not at all dangerous. But it was so dark that we were unable to obtain a glimpse of our port, the next little craggy islet; it was merged in the mountainous background behind it. I knew, however, that it lay 87° west of south, and in that direction I steered, whilst Kutchuk rowed.

But calm and still though it was, it was anything but pleasant to row across an unknown lake in the dark. The water was as black as ink, the contours of the shore indistinguishable, the sky a deep blue-black, and the clouds drifted silently and gloomily as shadows over our heads. The only relief to the universal dimness was the band of silver moonshine dancing softly on the heaving water. The boat was heavily laden and deep down in the water, for we had packed into her as much fire-wood as she would hold. I was, however, very comfortable in the fore half. The sounding-line lay ready to hand, and my watch, compass, velocity instrument, and itinerary note-book were all placed so as to be within the radius of the lantern. Thus I was enabled to take my observations at leisure. The maximum depth was 123 feet; we got it quite close to the first islet, but the contour of the lake bottom gradually rose as we approached the second islet. We had already passed the biggest of the promontories on both the north and south sides of the lake; we could not now be very far from our goal. But the minutes passed, and yet we did not fetch it. Could we have gone past it in the darkness? Scarcely, for I had taken accurate note of its bearings. No; there it was, scarce a minute's distance in front of us. I thought we had been steering towards a peak at the western end of the lake. It is so confusing to row in the dark, even though one has the moon to help one.

We went to rest with the intention of continuing again at daybreak; but long before that Kutchuk came and told me it was blowing again as hard as ever. For want of anything else to do I explored the little island. In outline it formed a right-angled triangle, with its hypotenuse facing north-west, though it was not more than 1,100 feet long. The southern part of the island consisted of a thin stratum of red conglomerate, and its shores were littered with rocks of the same material. The highest point did not exceed 50 feet, and it was crowned by a couple of piles of stones. The temperature at noon was over 15°.0 C., or about 59°.0 Fahr., and in the sheltered spots the gnats were dancing.

At 12.30 p.m. it was perfectly quiet, but heavy black clouds, with long trailing fringes, charged with rain, were looming up in the west. Evidently a fresh storm was brewing. But by far the hardest part of the lake still lay before us. Which was it wiser to do; to go or to stay? Our provisions were nearly done. I have never made a lake excursion under more unfavourable circumstances. It seemed as if all the bad weather throughout the whole of Tibet were being forced to take the path across the Chargut-tso, or as if the gorge in which the lake lay were a sewer for carrying off all the dirty weather in that part of the world.

By two o'clock in the afternoon we had everything packed and on board; but then the storm burst again, and it was a lucky thing for us we had not left the island. It rained for a while, then another storm swept over the country to the south of the lake, leaving all the mountains white in its track. But at the end of about an hour the weather suddenly cleared, and the lake rapidly subsided, except for a gentle swell near the shores. At the same time the sun began to droop, and the Chargut-tso looked lovely. Surely it could not be dangerous to make a dash across it; we might surely hope to get behind one of the sheltering headlands on the south before a fresh storm burst. Kutchuk rowed his hardest, whilst I continued my soundings and steered. The maximum depth I obtained at this time was 157½ feet.

Yet no sooner did we leave the sheltering headland behind us, than once again the sky darkened in the west, and the thunder began to rumble amongst the mountains to the south, where it was either snowing or raining smartly. At the same time yet another storm was venting its rage on the more distant mountains that bounded the lake on the north. On the lake itself, however, it was still fine, and the sun set amid a wreath of fleecy clouds. Then there rose above the perpendicular cliffs of the south shore, towards which we were steering, a threatening steel-blue bank of cloud. Meanwhile the atmosphere grew ominously quiet. The clouds appeared to stand still and pour out their contents in one and the same place. But we were not to get off so easily. Underneath the clouds appeared the unmistakable harbingers of another approaching storm. That is to say, their lower edges turned a fiery yellow, as though some gigantic conflagration were raging behind them. I scanned the shores anxiously. There was not a sheltering cove within sight. It would have been wisest to turn and run before the storm, until we again fetched the islet we last left. Our little craft would outride any storm, provided only she rode with it. But our supplies were nearly exhausted, and what would happen if we were to be shut up on that island without food, possibly for two or three days? No, we must luff, and manage as best we could with what protection we could find under the cliffs on the southern shore.

After a few preliminary puffs, down swooped the tempest like a hawk upon a defenceless dove. In with the sounding-line—away with the compass—out with the oars! It will be a fight for our lives! Our boat creaks—she quivers! Bang! bang! she smites the on-driving waves as they rush upon her like berserks to the fray. Her hull is but canvas—will it hold? It bulges—it will burst—it must burst! Still, in a lake of that size, there was a limit to the height to which the waves would rise, and so far our little craft had safely ridden over the biggest of them. Never did I exert myself so desperately as I did then. By dint of a long, steady, regular pull, we gained one inch, or maybe two, at each stroke; for several days afterwards my hands were badly blistered. But the tempest was growing more furious—it was being forced through the mountain funnel in which our lake lay. "Pull away, Kutchuk! The shore is coming nearer, there is no danger! But—man alive—look out, here comes a big one!" A huge curler broke right along the stroke side. Our boat was half full of water. Backwards and forwards it washed with every pitch, with every roll. "Mind, Kutchuk! Here comes another!" If it goes on at this rate though we shall be drenched to the skin. We clench our oars till our knuckles whiten under the strain. We literally lift the boat upon our oar-blades. It can't go on much longer like this. We are sitting in water, the boat is actually half full, and the seas keep breaking over her bow. We shall go down—and soon. "Get your life-belt ready, Kutchuk! I've got mine ready!" "No, Tura, we *can* keep up till we reach that headland. Ya Allah!" Kutchuk was right—we did reach it—thank God! It was a perfect miracle we escaped disaster. I have never been so near it in any other of my boat-excursions in Central Asia, and that is saying not a little.

As soon as we came under the shelter of the headland the waves were less high, and we were able to take it more quietly. We just reached shore as it grew dark. It is, of course, no great feat to navigate a stormy lake in the dark if you have a good sound boat under you; but it is an altogether different thing when you have only a canvas skiff to trust your life to, and the gale is rending the clouds to tatters, and the wizardry of the moonshine is tipping each hissing and spitting wave with an unearthly light, and the dark, smooth hollows between suggest unfathomable depths—dark, cold and hungry!

No sooner did we land than the wind dropped. Then it began to rain, and it went on raining all night. We reared up the boat so as to make a sort of carriage-hood over our heads, and lighted a fire and dried our clothes. Then we

A Storm on the Chargut-tso.

went to sleep, and after our herculean exertions each of us slept like a top.

On the 24th of September, after breakfasting off the only crust we had left, we rowed away west again in fine weather. The lake soon narrowed and came to an end in a trumpet-shaped river-mouth. Entering this, we rowed on for about half a mile, and then emerged upon another large lake. The Tibetan emissaries had called it the Addan-tso, but the nomads whom we encountered on its shores gave it the name of the Nagma-tso. Observing some horsemen a long way off to the north, we hoped they were our own scouts looking for us; but they soon disappeared, and evidently without having seen us. However, we were steering diagonally across the lake towards the northern shore, which was at no great distance away.

As I have already described so many of our adventurous lake-excursions, I will now only add that on the way across the Addan-tso we were overtaken by a third storm, which literally drove us ashore, so that our boat filled and we had to jump out, carrying with us what we could snatch up first. But fortunately the rain held off; and when we spread out all our felts and rugs, and took off our own clothes, and after wringing them out held them up in the strong wind, everything was very quickly dried. After that we stayed quietly where we were for several hours. At length, however, I grew so hungry that I got up and started to walk towards the nearest nomad tent. But I had not gone very far when Kutchuk called me back, and pointed towards the little stream that connected the two lakes. Turning, I saw two horsemen, with three pack-horses. They had already perceived us, and were riding directly towards us. It was Cherdon and Ördek, who had been looking for us for two days all round the Addan-tso. All the men were extremely anxious about us. Chernoff and the Lama were looking for us round the Chargut-tso, and about an hour later they too joined us. Sirkin had ridden back the day before to see if we had by any chance turned up at the old camp from which we started. Not being able to find traces of us anywhere, they were beginning to fear the worst, and were debating what they should do if I did not return. One thing, however, they were resolved upon, and that was not to leave the locality without finding fragments of the boat or others of our belongings.

Cherdon had had several little adventures. Patrols of Tibetans were out in every direction, they also looking for us;

and in two places he had counted as many as eight tents standing together, guarding the roads to Lassa. On our way back to camp we were met by several bands of Tibetan horsemen, who, after greeting me politely by putting out their tongues, turned and escorted us in triumph to our own tents. The camp lay in a latitudinal valley, one which Littledale also probably traversed. The old man, Mohammed Tokta, was worse. One of the Tibetans had died; we saw the corpse flung out for the vultures and ravens to feed upon. Although there was little more than the skeleton left, it was a loathsome sight. One of our camels also was dead. Hlajeh Tsering invited me into his tent, where he received me as though I had been a victorious general, and entertained me to a "magnificent banquet," presided over by the images of his god, wreathed in a cloud of incense.

Except for two or three short river-trips, this was the last time I used the little skiff in Tibet. I still preserve a very lively recollection of the days I spent on the Selling-tso, Nakktsong-tso, Chargut-tso, and Addan-tso; they made such a delightful interlude in the long monotony of the caravan marches. Although my investigations can only be regarded as preliminary, still they were sufficient to afford a useful general idea of the hydrography of that beautiful lacustrine region. If the surface of these lakes were to be raised some 150 to 180 feet, their basins would be converted into genuine fjords, like those of the western coasts of Norway and Scotland. Probably the region was once glaciated, though at the present day apparently no traces survive of either glacial striations or scratches, of moraines or erratic blocks. The surface rocks are disintegrated, and all evidences of glaciation, supposing they once existed, have been swept away and destroyed. The Addan-tso was the highest, as well as the largest lake of the region. It received several streams from the adjacent mountains, especially from the immense snowy ranges on the south; and it discharged its superfluous drainage into the Chargut-tso. This lake again sent its overflow through the river of Yaggyu-rapga into the Selling-tso. There it stays and evaporates; thus Selling-tso is the only one of the lakes that is salt. What connection there was, if any, between the Nakktsong-tso and the Selling-tso I was not able clearly to ascertain. The former may possibly communicate by a subterranean emissary; possibly it may empty itself into another lake situated farther to the south, which we did not see.

On the 25th of September our friends, Hlajeh Tsering and Yunduk Tsering, who had been with us since the 12th, were to take their leave. Each of them sent me his *haddik*, or "scarf of honour," and wished me a "successful journey." Then they came to say good-bye in person, and assured me that all the stores I wanted, as well as guides and pack-animals, would be provided for me by order of the Dalai Lama. When our caravan was loaded up and all ready for the start, I paid a hurried farewell visit to the Tibetan chiefs, and gave them various presents, such as revolvers, knives, compasses, and pieces of cloth. I expressed my regret at not being allowed to go through

Tents of the Tibetan Emissaries.

to Lassa, and sent my compliments to the Dalai Lama; but I promised them I should carve out my route for myself, and should not necessarily follow that which my guides wanted me to take. I told them bluntly that I would not permit the two officers who were to command our escort to assume a tone of authority towards us; they must just content themselves with inquiring every morning which route I desired to adopt. If they made themselves disagreeable I threatened I would stuff them into two of our trunks, and take them all the way home with me.

Hlajeh Tsering answered that he and his brother officer intended to remain, with a few hundred mounted men, twenty days in the spot where we was then encamped. I saw at once that that was simply bluff, meant to deter us from turning back, and therefore replied that I intended stopping at the next fresh-water lake, and waiting until it froze. To this he replied in his turn that they could quite well stay a year where they were. Thereupon I proposed that, as we both seemed to have so much time to spare, we might as well keep one another company; and so, with a good laugh on both sides, we dropped the game of brag. Hlajeh Tsering was eating meat-balls in his own tent. Yunduk Tsering sat in his tent, with his secretaries and a whole pile of papers in front of him. He was not only drafting a detailed report to the Devashung in Lassa, but was also sending on instructions to the local chiefs all the way to Ladak.

CHAPTER XXXI.

YAMDU TSERING. A SIDE EXCURSION.

OUR road ran west through a latitudinal valley nearly 20 miles broad, with imposing mountain-ranges lying parallel to it on both the north and the south. The weather was raw, cold, and windy, and the pasture very indifferent. Nevertheless, we counted 32 black tents, or, say, 150 inhabitants, in the course of 16¾ miles. The valleys in the south of Tibet were unquestionably more densely inhabited than the northern districts; in fact, in the latter direction the inhabited country did not extend very far. Our escort was by this reduced to 22 men, under command of a chief named Yamdu Tsering, with whom I quickly became on a friendly footing. The place where we encamped the first night was called Shalung; it lay east of a lake bearing the name of Jaggtseh-tso, and receiving at its western extremity a river called Boggtsang-sangpo. As this last occurs on the map of both Nain Singh and Littledale, it may be assumed that the other names also are right. Nevertheless, I was able to identify only a very few of the names which Littledale gives.

On the 26th of September we travelled as far as the mouth of the Boggtsang-sangpo. The river was divided into several arms, and the pasture on its banks was so plentiful that we felt a day would not be lost if we stopped amongst it. Out of our original 39 camels we had only 22 left, and all of these were suffering from fatigue; while everyone of the horses that survived was in a pretty bad way. During the day's march of 17¾ miles we observed a very large number of flocks of sheep, but only 16 tents. The country also abounded in game—*e.g.*, kulans, antelopes, partridges, hares, and wild geese, so that our hunters kept us well supplied with meat. The new lake, Jaggtseh-tso, was a good deal smaller than those we had recently travelled beside, and its water intensely salt. The circular markings all round its shores indicated that it too was drying up. In one place the former beach-lines numbered no less than seven, and all were distinctly marked, one behind the other.

During the next few days we kept close to the Boggtsang-sangpo, and crossed it in one locality by the same ford by which Littledale did. Captain Bower's route, which we had touched at the Nakktsong-tso and the Chargut-tso, now ran a good deal farther to the north, and we never came in contact with it again. Nain Singh's route lay quite as far to the south. So that by following the course of the river I have just mentioned, I was able to avoid the routes of the three travellers who previously to myself had visited this part of Tibet. Our knowledge of the country would, of course, be increased if I struck out an entirely fresh route; though it was often impossible for me to tell whether I was keeping clear of Littledale's route or not. The map which that distinguished and capable traveller made was unfortunately drawn on too small a scale to enable me to recognise the topography of the regions he traversed. For this reason, and because my map was being constructed on such an incomparably larger scale, I regarded even those tracts in which I could not avoid travelling over the same ground as my predecessor as, for cartographical purposes, unexplored country. Littledale's map shows neither the Nakktsong-tso nor the Chargut-tso; and though Bower's map does show them both, it does not show the Selling-tso. Bower travelled between the Nakktsong-tso and the Chargut-tso, but he failed to elucidate the relation between the two. Of the Addan-tso he knew nothing whatever, nor does he show any outlet from the Chargut-tso; and he apparently considered that the Yaggyu-rapga entered the Chargut-tso, whereas it really flows out of it. I am not here criticising the cartographical material for this part of Asia; I am merely seeking to explain why it was essential for me to take several regions which are crossed by the well-known red route-lines as being still for my purpose a *terra incognita*. One of the chief objects in exploring an unknown country is, of course, to obtain materials for a map of it, and if a map is not reliable, it is virtually of little use. Both Bower's journey and Littledale's afford wonderful proofs of exploring skill and endurance; but with respect to mapping, Nain Singh's work is a long way the best, though even his map urgently needs revision.

Our first day beside the Boggtsang-sangpo was favoured with glorious weather—perfectly still, a serene and flawless sky—just

The River Boggtsang-sangpo, looking South-West.

the sort of weather we ought to have had on the Chargut-tso. And yet the night was cold, $-8°.0$ C., or $17°.6$ Fahr. Riding as we were towards the west, the left side of the face was so burnt by the sun that the skin peeled off, whereas the right side was icy cold, and it was the same with regard to the left foot and the right foot.

On the 29th September we did 18 miles, and encamped close beside the river, in which my Lop fishermen let down their nets. At dusk up came the Tibetans, and reared their tents immediately over against ours. The next day we travelled along the southern bank. The river was here very sinuous and deeply

Shagdur and Ördek Fishing in the Boggtsang-sangpo.

scarped. The mountains which bounded its valley on the south were called Nangra. For two or three hours Shagdur was missing; but when he overtook us, he flourished a bunch of five fish triumphantly in the air. As soon as the camp was settled down, therefore, I lent the Lop-men the skiff, and they drew the river at the sharper windings; but the men who angled were the more successful. The current ran quietly and slowly; in fact, when there was no wind it was perfectly smooth, so that it had the appearance of being a larger stream than it in reality was. The sunset was superb. Not in consequence of any reflection of the clouds, for the day had been bright and warm; but there was a matchless illumination in the east, with sharply accentuated lights and shades, and magnificent modelling in relief.

Our general order of march was now, under ordinary conditions, three days tramping and the fourth a rest-day. The 1st October was one of the last character, and most of the men spent it fishing. Shagdur was the most successful; he captured 18 fish, and then, by way of a change, went out and shot an antelope. Turdu Bai stood all day long holding his fishing-rod in his hand, and fished away with the serene patience of a born angler, and grinned most benignly when he came to show me his catch. Our Lama preferred to read his holy books (*nom*). The Boggstang-sangpo now carried a volume of 187 cubic feet in the second.

The night of the 1st October the thermometer went down to $-11°.0$ C., or $12°.2$ Fahr. Winter was fast approaching; we must make haste to get to Ladak. We encamped again next night, the fourth in succession, beside the Boggtsang-sangpo. Its breadth was only 19½ feet, but its depth was very considerable. Hardly were the tents up than the fishing-rods were hard at work. During these days we lived principally upon fish, I almost exclusively.

The 3rd October was our last day beside the river; we left it on our left hand. I should like to have taken a more southerly route; but the country was too mountainous for our camels. From Camp no. XCV. we obtained a glimpse of the mountain which Littledale called the "volcano of Tongo"; though I was told its name was Erenak-chimmo. Seen from a distance it did resemble a regularly formed volcanic cone. Whilst the caravan plodded along its own appointed track, escorted by the Tibetans, I, Chernoff, and the Lama rode to the mountain I have just mentioned. We reached its foot across a couple of conglomerate acclivities, and having ridden as far up its side as the horses were able to climb, got off and walked. But we soon had enough of mountaineering, and stopped and took a good rest. The bare rock only cropped out in a few places; it consisted of granite, crystalline schist, and porphyry, though other rocks were represented amongst the loose pieces scattered about over the mountain-side. But the mountain was not a volcano, and never has been a volcano; it was merely a link between the parallel ranges. From its summit the only recognisable features were the dominating snowy peaks and the valleys which we had ourselves traversed all the way from Jaggtseh-tso. All the

The Valley of the Boggtsang-sangpo.

rest was one indistinguishable chaos of mountain peaks, ridges, *massifs*, spurs, ranges. Immediately to the north were several crests which presented the most fantastic outlines—pinnacles, denticulations, crenelated walls. It was so pleasant and peaceful up there amongst the winds and the skies, quite away from the caravan and its petty intrigues, that I just longed to remain two or three days.

In the eastern gable-end of the third of the short crenelated crests which I have just mentioned, we discovered a round grotto, divided into an inner and an outer apartment by means of a low wall of stone slabs. The entrance was about 9¾ feet high. The thick canopy of soot which adhered to the roof seemed to indicate that the cave had been inhabited for a vast period of time, and the floor also was covered with sheep-dung. There we stayed a short time, enjoying the picture that was presented when we gazed through the opening of the grotto. The valley below was flooded with sunshine, while we were in the shade, and cool, and sheltered from the wind. The inevitable Tibetan formula was hewn upon some of the slabs. Perhaps the cave had been occupied by a hermit, who had dedicated his life to the service of the deities of the mountain. On the northern flank of Erenak-chimmo we likewise came across an exceptionally fine obo, the largest we had hitherto seen in Tibet.

On our way back to camp, whilst riding towards a very easy pass, we stumbled across Hamra Kul in a ravine. He lay motionless on his side as though he were dead. I went and looked at him; he complained greatly, and declared he could not walk. However, I knew exactly where the shoe pinched; for on the previous day he had been deposed from his position as leader of the horse-caravan, because he had been found negligent, and Mollah Shah had been appointed to succeed him. The Tibetans had pitched their tents on the other side of the pass (16,451 feet), and they now came and complained to me that my men had paid no heed to them, when they warned them there was no pasture for a long distance to come. This, of course, I could in no wise help. I found my men encamped at a spot called Churing, where Mollah Shah, who had been a member of Littledale's caravan, knew where he was; and as if in proof of the fact that it was the same locality, we picked up an ass's shoe, a thing which could not possibly have been dropped by any other caravan except Littledale's.

The 5th of October, when we advanced 15 miles towards the west, was one of the worst days I can remember. There had been over 24½ degrees (Fahr.) of frost during the night. The brook beside the camp was frozen, and I was awakened once or twice by the sheets of ice crashing together. It was killing work riding against the wind, which in the bitter cold cut like a knife. We were chilled to the bone, paralysed with cold, prostrated. The sun shone most of the day, it is true, but its effect was neutralised by the wind. Everybody, both in my caravan and amongst the Tibetans, walked, otherwise they would have been frozen. For my own part, I confess it was fatiguing in the extreme to have to walk at that altitude and against such a powerful obstacle. When all feeling had departed out of my hands, I used to stop for a while in some ravine, and turn my back to the wind and have a quiet smoke. It will surely be a horrid winter, I thought, seeing that the autumn was beginning with such intense cold. The worst of it was, that nearly every one of our horses and camels was beginning to lose flesh. One of the young Charkhlik camels, which gave up that day soon after we started, was nothing more than skin and bone. After leading him myself a little way, I left him in charge of one of the men, and rode on; but I had not gone very far, when I came upon two other camels, which were unable to keep up. And still further on I passed Kutchuk doing his best to urge along two exhausted horses. All the latter, as well as every one of the mules, were galled.

Our sick-list was at this time greater than ever it had been before. Hamra Kul, who was left on the road the day before, was brought in by two good-hearted Tibetans. Tokta Mohammed was neither better nor worse: he sat tied on his horse silent and patient, leaning forward upon a cushion. Almaz suffered from sore eyes, and complained that he was almost blind; but he quickly recovered when I gave him a little cocaine and a pair of darkened spectacles. With wind like that we needed to have exceptional eyes if we were not to suffer from them. I do not believe it would be so very horrible to freeze to death; you would just sink into a state of lethargy and pass away without any very special degree of pain. That evening Khodai Kullu was likewise reported unwell; he suffered from shivering fits and headache, for which I gave him a dose of quinine. At this rate we should soon have half the caravan on the sick-list. Summoning Yamdu Tsering, therefore, I told him, that the

A Mountain Group North of Camp no. XCII.

time was come for him to provide us with the yaks which the Dalai Lama had promised; and he at once undertook to supply them without loss of time.

The native sheep-folds, of which we saw several during that day's march up a tributary of the Boggtsang-sangpo, consisted of a semicircular wall of stones, with their higher parts facing the prevailing westerly winds. The interior was generally hidden under a thick layer of sheep-dung, against which the grey walls showed up in decided contrast. Upon being brought to a standstill in the district of Setcha (16,563 feet) by a pretty large river, Ahmed, Islam, Hamra Kul, Mollah, and Chernoff were all behindhand, with three camels and two horses, and it was long after dark when they came in. The first camel had been killed, the second left until next morning, and only the third succeeded in crawling into camp. One horse had died; the Kashgar horse was found dead next morning, 6th October; a third collapsed during the next day's march. The caravan was dwindling with alarming rapidity. During the night the thermometer dropped to −14°.9 C., or 5°.2 Fahr., and the river was frozen hard enough to bear. We only did a short march; for upon reaching pasture we stopped, although it offered only very indifferent grazing. At this rate, we could hardly hope to reach Ladak before Christmas.

At Camp no. XCVIII., where the yaks were to join us, we set to work to rearrange all our baggage to suit them; that is, we had to tie it up in smaller loads, for a yak cannot carry as much as a camel. As early as 9 p.m. the thermometer was down to −10°.6 C., or 12°.9 Fahr., and during the night it dropped as low as −17°.9 C., or −0°.2 Fahr. This was definitively the beginning of winter, and winter lasted seven months!

On the 7th October, under the pretext of seeking for better pasture, though my real object was to escape travelling over the same ground as Littledale, I took Chernoff, the Lama, Li Loyeh, and Kutchuk, with four mules, five horses, and a proportionate quantity of supplies, and struck out a more southerly route. During the night eighteen excellent yaks had put in an appearance; this released most of our animals, and especially the sick ones, which now travelled without loads. Shagdur was appointed chief of the caravan, with instructions to halt a few days at the first pasture he came to. All the invalids were mending, except Mohammed Tokta; but of his recovery there was not much hope, although he kept up his courage in a wonderful way.

Just as I was about to start, a band of Tibetans rushed forward, and seized hold of the reins and halters of our horses and pack-animals. We could not—we should not—go south; it was as much as their lives were worth. I bid the Lama tell them that if they did not instantly let go, we should use our revolvers. Thereupon they drew back; but nevertheless pursued us some distance on foot, insisting that the country to the south possessed neither pasture nor practicable path. But as we gave no answer, they finally turned back and left us.

On the other side of a low pass in the nearest range we struck the upper course of the river Churing, now frozen over. Chernoff speared five moderate sized fish with his sabre, but in his zeal fell in and got an icy bath. Turning, we saw a band of a dozen Tibetans, under command of Tsering Dashi, racing down the steep declivity of the pass. They soon overtook us, and kept close at our heels for the rest of the day. It seemed as if we were never to get away from their everlasting chatter and the unceasing jingle, jingle of their bells. The rest of the Tibetans remained behind with our caravan, under command of Yamdu Tsering. The inhabitants of two or three tents we rode past rushed out in consternation when they saw such strange people passing. Tsering Dashi pointed to a pass in the north-west, exclaiming, "the only one possible"; but we were not to be lured away, we continued our own course up the stream. We were at last forced to halt because a white horse gave up; but we turned the time to account by fishing. In the evening a fresh troop of Tibetans arrived, and the two bands conferred together in the most animated fashion. At daybreak next morning their force was still further increased, and amongst the newcomers was old Yamdu Tsering None of them had any tents with them, but all sat and froze in the open air. The poor old man looked perfectly miserable; he had been riding most of the night, and was cold, dispirited, and heavy-hearted, because of all the trouble we occasioned him. Once more he came and begged me to return to the caravan; but when he found he could not prevail upon me, he added, that he had ordered his soldiers to tear the loads off the animals' backs; if we would not go where they wished, they were no longer under any obligation to serve us. But his statement was plainly untrue; if it had been true, Shagdur would have been certain to send me a messenger.

As we still continued to press on south up the valley, Yamdu

A Mountain Group North of Camp no. XCII. (continuation of Illustration on p. 505.)

Tsering announced that he really would go back and drive away his yaks. "As you please," I answered, "but you had better beware of my Cossacks." Mounted men again swarmed about us on every side; a fresh mobilisation had taken place. What an unconscionable amount of trouble we were giving to poor old Yamdu Tsering!

On our way up the valley we saw several other nomad tents. Whenever their inhabitants became too curious, it only needed a wave of the hand from one of the soldiers, and they instantly disappeared. Extraordinary the understanding which existed amongst these half-wild people! It was as though there existed a sort of freemasonry amongst them. They rendered the most implicit and blind obedience to their deities, and to their superiors in authority, and seemed to be absolutely insensible to bribes. At any rate, we were unable to persuade even one of them to show us the road south. Imagine a country which does not contain a single traitor!

We pitched Camp no. C. beside the lake of Jandin-tso, in which the river Churing had its origin. Its surface was slightly frozen, but the wind afterwards broke up the ice. The lake itself was fed by fresh springs, and close beside them Chernoff shot a wild-duck. On the 9th October the lake was again frozen, and the day turned out bitterly cold, with a cutting head wind. At this time there was only six Tibetans left with us. They came and politely asked me what my plans were. I answered by pointing towards a glen which opened in the west-south-west. No sooner did we strike into it than three of our escort rode off to inform Yamdu Tsering. The pass at the head of the glen was of considerable height, and afforded a magnificent view of the majestic mountains around. Due west of us towered skywards the stupendous mountain-group of Shah-ganjum, sheeted throughout with perpetual snow. It consisted of three "humps," the middle one being the highest, and in the pure transparent atmosphere had a most imposing appearance. We halted beside a marmot warren in a district called Amrik-va. The wind howled fitfully and it was bitterly cold; in fact, every bone in our bodies ached with cold.

Next morning the wind was still playing its incisive accompaniment amongst the craggy buttresses and clumps of moss. The sky was as pure as the purest turquoise, and yet the "trade wind," the most trying of the many evils of that ill-reputed land, never for one moment proved faithless to the law of its existence.

Our route led across several easy passes, through dark wild mountain scenery. Kulans, antelopes, and wolves abounded everywhere. At last, however, the glen opened out and we descended towards the north-west. That night we stopped under the shelter, as we fondly hoped, of a detached mountain group; but the gusts came plunging down from the heights above like spinning waterfalls. From some of the ranges which were snow-clad the snow was swept off in trailing streamers of white powder, which glittered intensely bright in the sunshine.

But on the 11th October the condition of our horses forbade any further advance towards the south. We had penetrated to too high altitudes; it was time to return to our caravan. Accordingly we turned their heads towards the north-west, and rode across a wide open valley that lay immediately below the eastern foot of the magnificent *massif* I have just mentioned, the Shah-ganjum, with its four rudimentary glaciers. Littledale, who passed it on the north, calls it Shakkanjorm.

Half-way across we were met by Yamdu Tsering, who through his couriers had kept constantly in touch with us ever since we left the caravan. Strange though it may sound, both he and I were glad to meet one another, and our mutual greetings were of the most cordial description. He could now see for himself, I told him, that I had no evil intention in making this excursion to the south. He protested that he felt sorry I should have the toil of travelling over so many passes, and all for nothing; he was so terribly afraid I should be tired!

After meeting him, we continued north-west through a transverse glen, and found the caravan beside a little brook of spring-water, which, although small, was deep and clear and full of fish, so that I again had fish for dinner. All, animals as well as men, were well, except our old invalid, whose body was swollen up as with dropsy. I treated him as best I knew how; but he declared he did not want to be cured—he only wanted to see me once more and then he was ready to die.

We finally parted from Yamdu Tsering and Tsering Dashi at Camp no. CIII. on the 13th October. Their orders were to accompany us to the boundary, and it was here their task ended; for we were now arrived, it seemed, at the boundary between the provinces of Nakktsong and Bomba, this last a name which occurs also on Littledale's map. They asked me to give them a certificate to the effect that they had performed their duty faithfully, and to my satisfaction. This proved that they had been

Our Lama on the Left ; Yamdu Tsering and Tsering Dashi on the Right.

ordered to treat us courteously. After their departure we were to be taken over by a fresh chief, Yarvo Tsering by name.

When we started, I failed to see Yamdu Tsering and his colleague, so that I was unable to give them the revolvers and knives which I had selected as presents for them. I had already paid the yak-owners, and they were gone; but until the fresh relay turned up, we had to look after our baggage ourselves. We found them, however, in the pleasant valley of Ramlung, accompanied by the two old chiefs, who evidently did not intend to be deprived of their presents. From that valley we had an extensive prospect towards the east; at sunset the distant

Loading up the Yaks.

peaks disappeared in a ruddy illumination suggestive of a prairie fire. The sky was bright above head, but dark blue on the eastern horizon—the reflection of the higher regions where it was already night. In the foreground, the tents of the Tibetans, some black, others blue and white, stood up sharply against the hard, yellow grass, where the men were busy amongst their picketed horses. We only travelled ten miles that stage; indeed, under the prevailing circumstances it was seldom that we now did more than twelve miles a day.

On the 14th October we made a fresh start with 22 fresh yaks, hired at the rate of one *tsos* * a day for each animal, the

* We received in this part of the country eight tsos in exchange for one liang or tael (about 3*s.*) of Chinese silver, a transaction in which we were, of course, cheated.

whole under the charge of 30 attendants. The Tibetans tried as much as they possibly could to curtail the length of the day's journey; but I was one too many for them, for I always chose the new camping-ground myself. Water was becoming scarcer and scarcer, and sometimes it was impossible to find the springs without the help of the Tibetans. Shagdur, with the alertness and resourcefulness that never failed him, procured us both fresh milk and sour milk from a nomad, whose tent he discovered in a nook amongst the hills. The contour sank gradually towards the north; sometimes we were able to count as many as six parallel chains one behind the other. We were at this point travelling south of Littledale's route. At the spring of Sholung, on the evening of the 15th, we found a fresh relay of yaks waiting for us, and on the following day fresh bands of soldiers sprang up as if by magic out of the ground. The old yak-men began to haggle about the price; they insisted upon being paid in Lassa tsos, for they did not, they said, understand anything about Chinese silver. But when I answered them that it must be Chinese silver or nothing, they soon proved more tractable.

Cherdon's horse died, and only a very few of the others were able to carry their riders. Four men were, in fact, riding mules; the mules were standing the journey far better than the horses. Mohammed Tokta's feet were so swollen that we had to cut off his boots and wrap his feet in felts. We had not one drop of water all day long, and the pasture was extremely scanty, and the country more thinly inhabited. Nevertheless we were kept supplied with sheep, as many as we wanted. Not far from camp that evening we perceived 200 kulans grazing in one place in the valley.

On the 18th October we did an interesting stage of twelve miles towards the south-west. The Tibetans, with all the yaks and our baggage, struck into a ravine which pierced the range that formed the southern barrier of the latitudinal valley, saying that we too must follow them; there was only a little pass to cross. That was all very well for the yaks, but it was killing work for the camels. Hence, we declined to follow them, but continued along the mountain foot, although in doing so we had to cross an endless number of gulleys and ravines. From the spur where we turned south, we perceived that we had come quite close to the salt lake of Lakkor-tso. Littledale, whose route ran a good way north of this lake, observed that the greater number of the salt lakes of Tibet are undergoing the process of desiccation. Lakkor-tso was a conspicuous example of this; for its former beach-lines were easily discernible up to a considerable height above the surface of the lake. The successive levels formed flat shelving tracts edged by ridges, behind which there were very often lagoons. The present shores of the lake were white with salt, which, being dry and powdery, was whirled up by the wind, until it looked like clouds of steam or drifting flour. On our way to the river Sommeh-sangpo, which flowed westwards into the lake, we crossed several creeks, then dry, but inclosed between high banks, and not seldom filled with

Camp no. CIII., at an altitude of 15,946 feet.

cones and pyramids of salt, the remnants of former thick deposits, upon which the wind had long exercised its erosive power. We encamped by the river-side.

On the south we still had the same vast and rugged mountain-chain, forming apparently for several days to come an insuperable barrier to the advance of our camels. Here we were obliged to shoot the dog Hamra; he would not let us sleep o' nights. If there were no Tibetans to bark at, he used to bark at our own night-watchmen and our own caravan animals. Here, also, two horses died, and, strange to say, two she-camels gave birth prematurely. Turdu Bai attributed that to the extreme degree of cold ($-15°.4$ C., or $4°.3$ Fahr.), and to the fact of their having drunk cold water at an unseasonable moment. Here, again, we were met by a fresh convoy of yaks, with their drivers. As early as 9 p.m. the thermometer was down to − 10°.0 C., or 14°.0 Fahr., and the river froze so sharply that we heard the ice cracking during the night and the pieces grinding one against the other.

CHAPTER XXXII.

VIA DOLOROSA.

On the 30th of October the "trade-wind" began at 9.30 a.m. The reason I call it this is that it set in every day with appalling regularity. After midday it increased in violence, until it blew a perfect hurricane, and like a desert hurricane swept such vast volumes of sand and dust before it that at times the landscape was completely obscured. It was quite a picture—the chalky white clouds driving in over the Lakkor-tso from its western extremity and streaming off again at its eastern end, while the waters of the lake beat tumultuously against the beach underneath. So strong was the wind alongside the lake that the camels actually staggered, and mounted men reeled in the saddle. Our journey resulted, at any rate, in the discovery of two important climatic laws for that part of the world—(1) the rainy season coincided with the latter part of the summer and the early part of the autumn; and (2) the latter part of the autumn and winter were characterized by wind, the west wind predominating.

Every now and again away went a felt, a sack, or other loose object, and had to be recovered and lashed on again. My map was nearly wrested out of my hand, and torn to shreds and tatters. We lost another of our horses, one of the Lassa lot. At this time we were travelling down the Sommeh-sangpo, having an imposing mountain-range on both our right and our left. Eventually, however, the river turned northwards, and doubling the end of the range on that side, entered the Lakkor-tso, close beside a deposit of salt, with big white hills which gleamed like flour. An hour later and we were on the edge of the steep shore; this we skirted along a high terrace, until we reached another river, which came from the south-south-east, and likewise entered the lake. We spent the night on the left bank of the new stream. All the mountain slopes in the vicinity were scarred with horizontal lines, which, in certain lights, stood out like black rulings.

During the next day's march an extraordinary incident happened. The old man Mohammed Tokta was somehow left behind, without anybody noticing it, until Hamra Kul, who was lagging a long way in the rear with two or three tired horses, came across him in a hollow. He explained quite genially that, feeling tired, he had simply rolled off his horse, which had thereupon quietly continued as if nothing were the matter. Hamra Kul, of course, brought the old man on along with him, and when he got him into camp wrapped him up comfortably

Laying out Mohammed Tokta.

in felts and sheepskins. In the evening I went as usual to see how he was getting on, and make sure that he wanted nothing that we had it in our power to supply him with. Sometimes I used to give him a small dose of sulphonal, to make him sleep. This time, however, he was to sleep both long and heavily without any artificial aid. To all the questions that I put to him he returned perfectly rational answers; and when he said that he liked milk best, I ordered one of the men to give him all we had, and he drank a large bowlful. Then I asked him how he felt, and he smiled in quite a friendly way. But before the sun rose next morning he was stiff and cold. Nobody knew exactly when he passed away. Mollah Shah, who had the last watch, had gone off to collect fuel. Death visited the old camel-

Our Camp near the Western Shore of Lakkor-tso.

leader in his sleep; his eyes were closed, and he had not moved a muscle since the evening before.

This poor old man's death was a relief to all the survivors; for since his body had swelled up and assumed such a disagreeable black colour, we had ceased to entertain the slightest hope of his recovery. He had been ill for four months, and his own life had become a burden to him; so that his decease was really a release. Mohammed Tokta was a thoroughly honest man. Although he was the cause of a good deal of trouble to his comrades, I never heard any of them say a single unkind word to him. They were all fond of the poor old man, because he himself was always so friendly and cheerful, and made no fuss about his illness. During the last few evenings of his life, in spite of my express command to the contrary, he tried to sit up and salute when I went to visit him.

The other Mussulmans at once set about making preparations for the funeral; in fact, the grave was already dug before I was awakened with the intelligence that the old man was gone. After the corpse was washed, it was dressed in the clothes the old man wore, and then wrapped in a sheepskin and carried on a pack-saddle to the grave, where it was deposited with the same ceremonies as at the burial of Kalpet. This made the fourth death amongst my attendants since I began this series of journeys through Central Asia and Tibet. This incident did not, of course, tend to make our two remaining invalids, Almaz and Ahmed, feel any the better.

This mysterious illness, which carried off all three of the men I lost in Tibet, was not occasioned by any fault in our commissariat. We always had plenty to eat, and the food was nourishing. So long as we were in Tibet we never suffered for lack of fresh meat, especially after we entered inhabited regions, for we were always kept well supplied with sheep and lard by the inhabitants of the country; and I have surely said sufficient to show that we never neglected an opportunity when there were yaks, kulans, and antelopes to be had for the shooting. Add to this that latterly we had a very pleasant variety in fresh and sour milk, butter, and fish; while of the stores of rice, flour, and talkan, which we brought with us from Charkhlik, we still had an abundance left. We started, it will be remembered, with supplies for ten months, and we had not yet been on the march more than five and a half; in fact, we had quite sufficient of such things to last till we got to Ladak, although, as a matter of fact, they did not quite do so. But that was because, when the camels began to break down, we tried to rally them by giving them bread and rice. Indeed, before we received such splendid help from the successive convoys of yaks, we had occasionally been obliged actually to squander our provisions, so as to diminish the loads a little, or else throw some of our stores away.

The real cause of the disease was the rarefaction of the atmosphere, which at those altitudes is only half as dense as it is down at sea-level, and the consequence is the blood does not imbibe sufficient oxygen to maintain vitality. The fact is, we were living under altogether abnormal conditions—conditions for which our respiratory and circulatory systems were neither constructed nor adapted. Irregularities occurred in their functions, and those who were not sufficiently sound and strong ran, of course, a great risk. The heart laboured under great pressure, and if its muscles and tissues were not naturally strong, it was unable to force the blood to the extremities of the body. A distinguished Swedish physician has explained to me that that was the reason why the feet and legs of my men perished first; he thought that if it had been possible to keep the patient in a perfectly horizontal position, he might perhaps have been saved. But during a caravan journey it is, of course, extremely difficult to nurse sick folk in a perfectly satisfactory manner. You ought, of course, to halt and wait until they are restored to health. But in a country like Tibet such a course would often obviously put the entire caravan in jeopardy. The traveller has no alternative except to carry his invalids with him, and that naturally taxes their strength very severely.

The yak caravan got under weigh early in the morning, with one of the Cossacks as its escort. Next followed the ailing camels and horses, all without loads. And as soon as poor old Mohammed Tokta was buried, the rest of us left that melancholy spot, carrying with us my instrument cases on two or three of the camels that were still fit for work. We were only about 480 miles from Ladak, but at the slow pace we crawled along, the road seemed interminable. The last to leave were myself, Shagdur, and Sirkin, and we rode up the slope of the mountain which rose west of our late camp, our object being to measure the height of the ancient beach-lines above the existing level of the lake. The levelling mirror was fixed at five feet above the ground, and the distance between the points observed was reduced constantly, so that the line, which I eventually obtained

Camp no. CXIV. ; the Mountains on the South Side of the Valley.

formed a parabola. The ancient beach-lines, eight in number, on the slope of a hill on the opposite side of the valley, were incomparably the most sharply and distinctly marked. But both on this and on several other occasions I satisfied myself that the beach-lines were, as a rule, much more strongly developed on the western than on the eastern slopes, indeed on the latter they were frequently absent altogether; while on the northern and southern faces they were only moderately marked. What, then, was the cause of this uniformity? There could only be one, namely, the "trade-wind," which drove the waves with considerable violence against the eastern

Lamas blowing Trumpets.

shore, effectually obliterating the beach-line; whereas the western shore was sheltered from the breakers.

The result of my measurement went to show, that the highest of the ancient beach-lines was no less than 436½ feet above the existing level of the lake. And as the area of the lake would naturally diminish in proportion as its level dropped, we must have travelled several days across the bottoms of former lakes. The mountain we measured consisted of fine-grained crystalline schist of a dark colour, though higher up it was composed of compact quartzite.

After crossing yet another little pass, we approached yet another salt lake, exactly like Lakkor-tso—the same white shores and green waters—except that it was considerably smaller. The whole of its western half was exposed, and covered by very extensive deposits of salt as white as snow. We quitted its basin by a pass similar to that by which we approached it. Immediately below the pass we found Hamra Kul, with two dying horses. One of these, a dappled grey from Korla, I ordered him to kill at once; the other managed to struggle into camp. That journey through Tibet was an endless series of sufferings for both animals and men. Distress and pain dogged our every footstep. It was enough to make one weep tears of blood to witness so much misery, especially as we could do nothing to prevent it. Of the 45 horses and mules with which we started, we had now only 11 left.

The evenings were beginning to be cold. Kutchuk, who lived in my "kitchen," became very popular by keeping up a huge argol fire, and supplying the other men with a few embers to start their own fires with.

It was no doubt wise to make short journeys; still it was making a mockery of wisdom to restrict ourselves to such short marches as we did on the 22nd October. After about three miles the Tibetans halted, and urged us to follow their example, alleging it would be three days before we should reach grazing again; besides, that day or the next night they expected a fresh convoy of yaks to arrive, as well as some sheep. The cumulative force of these arguments being too strong, we stopped; but I gave the Tibetans to understand that when we came to reckon up, I should not count that as a complete day's work. To this they replied submissively, that I might arrange that as I pleased.

When we resumed our march we crossed the salt-pans, with their pyramids and "tables" of salt, three or four feet high, which glittered so intensely white that we were obliged to put on darkened spectacles because of the reflection. Intermingled with these was an occasional fresh-water pool, now coated with ice. Behind a mountain to the south-west, called Marmi-gotsong, lay the monastery of Marmi-gombo. Every now and again long-drawn trumpet blasts echoed from it and reverberated grandly amongst the mountains and across the lakes. A storm raged both that day and the day following. Even when it was dying away in the afternoon, the wind blew with a velocity of over 33½ miles an hour. Although we were still marching south-west, we were well to the south of Littledale's route. At Camp no. CXII., beside the river of Shaggueh-chu, we again heard trumpet-blasts to the south, blaring out like

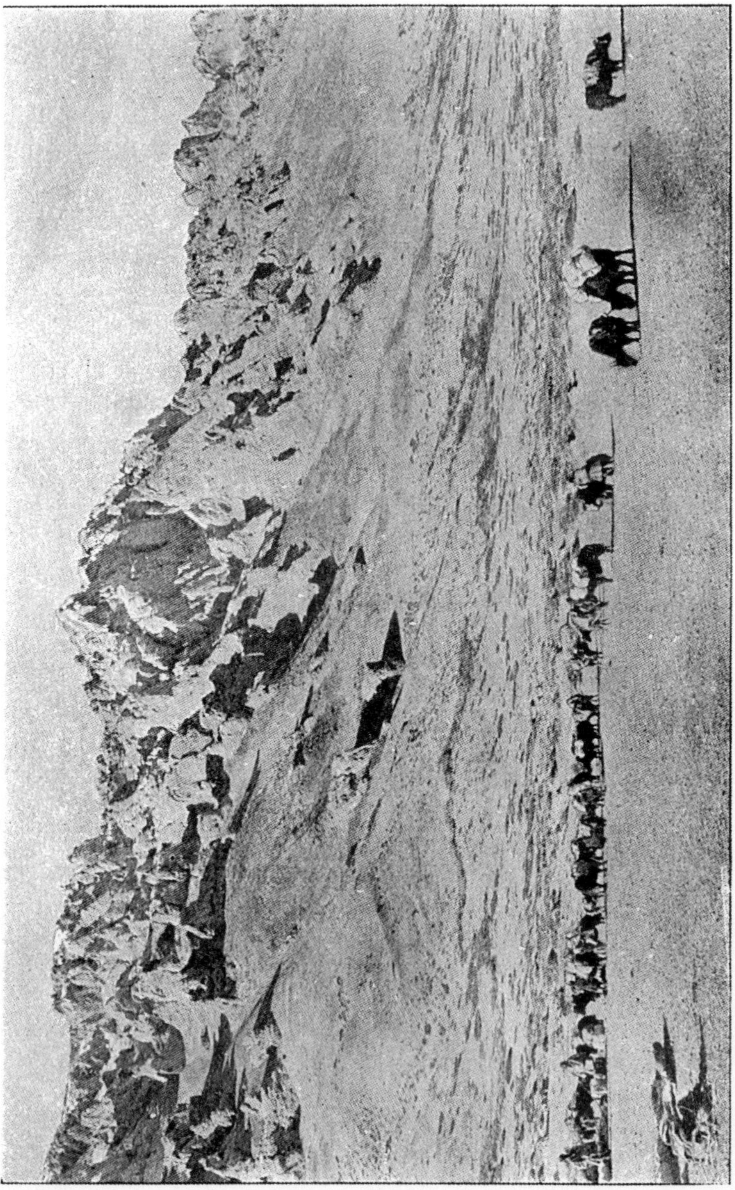

Camp no. CXIV. ; the Mountains on the South Side of the Valley.

fog-horn. I was strongly tempted to visit the temple; but the Tibetans positively refused to accompany us.

On the 24th October we were again marching between wild, craggy mountain-ranges, amid scenery that was both fantastic and sublime. We encamped beside a little pool called Omantso, immediately below a flat-topped pass (15,814 feet), in the province of Sagghet-sang, inhabited by the Senkor tribe, a name mentioned by Littledale. Three camels lagged behind that day, and only one of the three was able to reach camp. That night the thermometer fell to –18°.8 C., or –1°.8 Fahr. Next morning, even before we got started, we found it necessary to kill another of the horses. Six of the camels were not up to the mark, and were left to follow on with the yaks, and Almaz, who was still unwell, was allowed to ride the best of them. Just as we overtook them one of the six gave up; the two men, who were left with him, being unable to get him up again, finally cut his throat. Very soon a second lagged behind, with one of the men in charge of it, and yet a third followed suit. Still further on the dromedary was left at a patch of grass, to be picked up by the party in the rear. Thus Almaz only brought in one camel with him, the mother of the foal born at Charkhlik; the foal was the best of all, but then we fed it on bread. We had only 18 camels left out of 39; all the others lay dead beside the road we had travelled. All four Cossacks were now riding on mules. The only men who rode horses were myself, Turdu Bai, Mollah Shah, Li Loyeh, and Turdu Ahun, Hamra Kul's sixteen-year old son, who acted as servant to the Mussulmans. The rest of the men sometimes rode on camels, but generally walked.

Thus decimated, we pursued our way between the immense cliffs, which overhung our route like mediæval castles suddenly converted by wizardry into stone. All the ranges wheeled towards the north-west, just as the Himalayas and the Kwen-lun do in the same meridian. That evening we again encamped beside a little frozen lake underneath a pass called Bonjin-tso. Our yak leader was one Davo Tsering, a funny, good-natured little man, who could not understand what advantage it would be to him to cheat us.

Death still continued to play havoc in the caravan. We killed one camel in the morning, and three others lagged behind during the course of the day, Turdu Bai staying with them until ten o'clock at night. He was to see after them again in the morning, and if they were then unable to continue, he had orders to put them out of their misery. He and Sirkin, who rode back to fetch them, returned without them. One of the three was our only dromedary.

The weather still continued fine on the 27th October, and the "trade-wind" was still blowing, although not quite so violently. The route was quite level and good, and all our camels managed to do the day's march, though it was quite as much as some of the horses were able to accomplish. Some of the camels, however, were suffering from their feet, and wore stockings of kulan skin. The country soon began to open out again, and at intervals we saw nomads. Davo Tsering rode beside my bridle-rein, and, with admirable freedom from prejudice, gave me all the information I asked him for. He used to say, with all the dignity of a full-blown dominie, "Now write down that that mountain is called so-and-so." He afterwards asked the Lama on the quiet what I thought of him.

At this point our route and Littledale's separated, after having coincided for a short distance only. Beyond this the English traveller pursued a more southerly route than we did to Rudok, and then followed the southern shore of the Pang-gong-tso to Ladak. To the north-west we saw the lake of Doddap-tso; and in the locality of Na-ngamba an obo, consisting of a stone cist, 13 feet long, filled with *maneh* slabs and yaks' and sheep's horns, and bearing a little red flag on the top. Camp no. CXVI. was pitched on the western shore of the ice-clad freshwater lake of Oman-tso.

On the 28th October, we rode up and down, up and down the undulations of the surface until we reached the end of the latitudinal valley we had been traversing so long. From the pass at the end an entirely new world was opened out before us, and the old world we had known so long, and had had such bitter experiences in, closed behind us like a book. The predominant feature of the landscape before us was the circular lake of Perutseh-tso or Yim-tso. Our camp beside the Perutseh-tso was the best we had had since we left the Charkhlik-su, nearly six months before. The grass was high, thick, and tender; and there was an abundance of *balgun* bushes, so that we had no lack of good fuel; nor was there any deficiency of water. The camp soon assumed a cheerful aspect under the ring of big blazing fires the men built up, and it was not only cheerful, it was warm; and sadly we needed them, for the thermometer

Camp no. CXIV. ; the Mountains on the North Side of the Valley.

dropped to $-20^\circ.1$ C., or $-4^\circ.2$ Fahr. Only one camel failed to come up with the rest, and that was the mother of the foal; but when the men went back to the lake in the evening to fetch her, she was already stiff and cold. Thus there were only 14 camels left. Upon reaching camp, another of the horses died. Here Davo Tsering took his leave of us, declaring that he had no warrant to receive the present I offered him.

This made the ninth day we had travelled without giving ourselves a single day's rest. The grazing had never been good enough to tempt us; to make up for it we stayed at this camp four whole days, and all the animals picked up wonderfully. The men of the next relay of yaks sold us three small sacks of corn, brought from Ladak, for the sum of 4 *liang* (=13s.), which was, of course, too much; but although it was all gone in an hour, it did our poor beasts good. The new yak-leader told us that he was a Tajinur Mongol, and was born a few days' journey south of Kuku-nor, but his parents, whilst on their way to Lassa on a pilgrimage, sold him, when about five years of age, to a Tangut couple who were childless. How much they got for him he did not know; but our Lama said that the regulation price was 20 *liang* (=£3 6s. 8d.), and that transactions of this kind were not at all uncommon. Sometimes the Tanguts sold their children to the Mongols. Our man had, of course, been brought up as a genuine Tibetan, and did not know a single word of Mongolian.

The first day after our long rest we managed to do 16 miles, the going being level and good; in spite of that, however, one of the horses gave up soon after we started and had to be killed.

The weather was bitterly cold; to ride was like freezing us to death, the wind was so icy and so penetrating. Although the stream of the Ombo-sangpo was completely frozen over, the ice was not strong enough to bear us. The Tibetans tried it first; but when we saw how their horses and yaks slipped and slithered about, and even went through, we set to work and cut a channel through the ice for the camels. The night at Camp no. CXVIII. was gloriously bright and still; the thermometer registered $-15^\circ.4$ C., or $4^\circ.3$ Fahr. Stars of even the fifth magnitude were distinctly visible on the horizon; while stars of the first magnitude glittered with the brilliancy and sparkle of diamonds. Occasionally we heard the howling of the wolves, and it was both a cold and a hungry howl.

When we got up on the morning of the 3rd November,

we found that all our camels except two had taken themselves off back to the rich pasture of Perutseh-tso, and we lost a good deal of time in fetching them back. When we were at last ready for starting, we continued west, crossing first the plainly-marked and beautifully formed ancient beaches of the lake of Luma-ring-tso, and finally the extensive salt deposits which immediately surrounded the little lake itself, which was of course salt. We encamped on the shore of the next lake, Tsolla-ring-tso, separated from Luma-ring-tso by a narrow neck of land. In spite of the intense cold, the shores of these two lakes were for the most part fenny and treacherous, owing to the presence of fresh springs. Luma-ring-tso is quite erroneously marked on Nain Singh's map. He makes it some 33 miles long, instead of which it is only about 3½ miles; but then he never saw the lake himself, for his route lay a long way to the north of it. It was not likely that it had shrunk so much since 1873, the year in which the celebrated pundit made his memorable and important journey.

As the shores were so dangerous, we thought it wiser to tether the camels at night. Two of the horses, however, walked in, and when, after a world of trouble, we succeeded in getting them out again, they looked as if they had been modelled in mire. In spite of the long rest they had recently had, several of the horses were again in a queer way. The white horse, which I rode during the latter part of the journey towards Lassa, and which seemed to be dead beaten on 19th August, but had nevertheless recovered, gave up again next day, and I was just on the point of issuing orders to kill him, when the leader of the Tibetan caravan hurried up, and begged me to give him the horse, which I, of course, readily did.

That day we should, we knew, strike the border of Rudok. In fact, at the western end of the lake there were already seven tents standing, with a number of people about them. An impudent old man came forward and said, we could not advance any farther; there was good pasture in an adjacent glen, we might go there and share it with their horses and yaks. We were encamped close to the Tibetans, and our Lama at once went off to find out what was the matter. He returned in a state of great excitement. The chief of the Rudokis was, he declared, a perfect bully: he had demanded a pass from the Dalai Lama and swore that if he did not produce one, he would not allow us to march through his territory. This Bombo, or governor, of the province was reported to be on very good terms

Our Camp beside a Frozen Marsh, in the beginning of November.

with the Devashung or Supreme Council at Lassa, and was a sort of superintendent of the gold mines of Chokk-jalung,* where he resided during the summer, though in the winter he dwelt in the town of Rudok.

I sent for the man to come and see me. He arrived with a large suite, dressed in full uniform, and his manner was extremely arrogant. I invited him to take a seat on a felt carpet which I had had spread on the ground just outside my tent, though I myself remained inside, sitting near the brazier. For a little the man hesitated whether he should accept such an ambiguous compliment or not, but finally sat down, and

The North Shore of the Lake of Tsolla-ring-tso.

demanded to see our pass from the Dalai Lama. I answered, that we had never seen that magnate, and consequently could not very well bear any pass from him.

"I have not heard a word about you," he went on, "nor do I know who you are. I have had no report about you from Lassa, and I have no orders to furnish you with yaks. But I do know this, that Europeans are under no circumstances allowed to travel through Rudok."

* This was a place situated two or three days' journey south-west of the locality where we just then were. In the winter the mines are said to be almost deserted, though in summer 300 men are wont to gather there from all quarters, some of them coming all the way from Lassa. Chokk-jalung is considered to be the highest place in the world that is inhabited all the year round.

"If you are a high official, you ought to know it is your bounden duty to help us on our way to Ladak."

"I owe no obligation to suspicious personages, who carry no pass; but, if you like, I will write to Lassa, and you can wait here ten weeks until the answer comes back."

"Capital," I answered; "that will suit us splendidly; our animals are thoroughly exhausted and want rest. Write to Lassa by all means; we have plenty of time to spare."

"Very good. You understand that if I let you go through my province I shall lose my head?"

The man's manner was calm, dignified, and decided; but, as compared with our friends near Lassa, he was at the same time nothing short of impudent. The Cossacks were simply boiling with rage; they were longing to get home, or rather were dying to get away from that cold, windy, mountainous region. However, I calmed them down, for I realised that I had no right whatever to wage war upon Rudok. Besides, our opponents were too strong for us; even now they mustered more than 100 well-armed men. On the other hand, I did not want to be driven farther north, for I should there come into contact with one or other of the routes of Nain Singh, Capt. Bower, Capt. Deasy, or Capt. Wellby and Lieut. Malcolm. Still less did I wish to be forced to do as Capt. Deasy once did, burn the greater part of my baggage, tents, stores, and boat.

On the contrary, I rather welcomed the prospect of a 2½ months' delay. I was utterly worn out, and greatly in need of rest. So I took counsel with the Cossacks, and we soon arranged a plan for the winter. In two or three days' time we would go back to the rich pastures of the Perutseh-tso, and there construct a fortified camp. The locality was so interesting that I should never be at a loss for occupation, and the men would find plenty to do at first in building a high turf wall all round the encampment, and in digging a moat all round outside it. Then they might erect an outlook tower of the same materials. Then we would have a rest, we would hunt, make excursions, and nurse up our animals again, and when spring came would push out due south. I almost blessed the over-zealous Bombo for forcing me to enter into fresh plans with regard to Tibet, although in point of fact I had already had more than enough of that inaccessible country.

Next morning I announced to the chief our intention to return to the east, and he offered no objection. On the other

A Scene in Western Tibet.

hand, the Tajinur yak-caravan man declared that his orders were to convey us to the boundary of Rudok, not eastwards; but I saw a way by which that difficulty might be overcome. Meanwhile, however, the Bombo changed his mind, and informed us that he would procure us both yaks and provisions, if we would promise not to go near the town of Rudok. To this I readily agreed, for I had no intention of going to Rudok; that town lay on the route which Littledale had followed. After that we of course dropped the plan of the fortified camp, and prepared to resume our journey.

CHAPTER XXXIII.

TSO-NGOMBO OR THE BLUE LAKE.

HERE we put aside everything we could possibly do without and gave them to the Tibetans, and on the 6th November climbed over a pass (15,940 feet high), and found springs and grass on its north face. On the 7th the weather was splendid, and we were mercifully spared the annoyance of the incessant wind. But by way of a diversion the Tibetans began to squabble with our Lama, calling him a "dog of a heathen" for trailing about with "those Russian fellows." Our Lama grew so angry that he laid about him with his whip, and I bade him tell them that if they kicked up a row again, we would tie them fast on the camels' backs until they were "sea-sick"—and polite. We never saw a soul all day, nothing except a few old camp-fires. At night we encamped beside the spring of Tsebu. Silent—silent as the grave it was that night; I almost fancied I could hear the prickling of the intense cold as the frost fastened itself into the ground. Except for the long-drawn, melancholy howls of two or three wolves, the eerie stillness of the night was unbroken, for you could scarcely count the monotonous echo of our night-watchman's footsteps as he made his cold, weary rounds.

During the two following days we rode alongside a lake, which swarmed with wild geese and wild duck, then over a low pass into the deeply-eroded bed of the Ravur-sangpo, which had its origin in natural springs, and disappeared in the large valley that lay at our feet. The leader of the yak-caravan told us that the vicinity of Aru-tso, a lake situated four days' journey to the north, and mentioned by Captain Bower, was haunted by robbers from Amdo, Nakkchu, and Nakktsong. The year before a band of five had been seized at Ravur-sangpo, and put to death by command of the chief of Rudok. Except for those men the district was uninhabited. Our informant was a jocular old man: he used to ride beside me singing, and would often delight my men by imitating the gurgling of the camels.

On the 10th of November the thermometer registered $-26°.5$ C., or $-15°.7$ Fahr. We lay rolled up like mummies in our sheep-skins and furs, but even then we were unable to keep warm. We did twenty miles—quite a feat for us; we had not done anything like it for weeks. Our satellites wanted of course to stop and rest after we had gone six miles; but as we were just then met by a fresh relay of men and yaks we let the first lot go. We could not very well blame them for wanting to get home and inside their warm tents as soon as they could, the poor beggars were not blessed with inexpressibles! Leaving Cherdon and three of the Mussulmans, and all the Tibetans

Our Lama Quarrelling with the Leaders of the Yak-Caravan.

except four, to look after the yak-caravan, the rest of us rode on. We traversed a level valley. The day passed, it grew twilight; it was dark—not a drop of water all day! At length we met Shagdur, who had ridden on ahead to reconnoitre, returning with a little sack of ice. We continued as far as the frozen brook from which he obtained it. Li Loyeh, who had also been out in another direction, shot a wolf.

On the 12th the Tibetans put up their tents at the western end of a small lake which was covered with a thick coating of ice, alleging "there would be no water again for two days." We filled four sacks with good ice, and disregarding their energetic protests, calmly pursued our way. Whilst engaged at the lake we had observed two or three horses and men on a hillside a few miles to the north; but when we reached the spot they had disappeared. Our Tibetans asserted that they were robbers and had hidden themselves in some ravine, and they urged us to rout them out and shoot them. Shortly after that we perceived two more sitting round a fire, roasting a joint from an orongo antelope. They were simply peaceful, inoffensive hunters, nothing more. About an hour later we halted, and up came the yak-caravan, with its whistling, singing escort, and Shagdur carrying on a lively and playful conversation with them. The clever fellow had in a surprisingly short time picked up sufficient Tibetan to be able to talk fluently with the men of our succes-

View South-east from Camp no. CXXIX.

sive convoys. The yak-men were quite right. It *was* two days before we found water again, in a garrulous little stream. Had it not been for the information which the Tibetans gave us we should very often have been hard put to it for water. During the night of the 13th–14th November it froze sharp at the sides of the stream. It was become a rare thing for us to hear the sound of running water. What a contrast there was between this region and the country towards Lassa. There it poured with rain almost every day, and we ploughed our way through what was little better than a morass; here we actually had to hunt for water.

Next day we rode some distance up beside the Raga- and then turned away from it to the right. Soon after t

Tibetans wanted to stop as usual, although we had only done a very short march. They were to be relieved there, they said, by another convoy, and it would be as much as their lives were worth to go farther than they were ordered to go. I simply put the yaks in the hands of my Cossacks, with instructions to drive them on to our next encampment. The Tibetans meekly followed, and came and encamped beside us. There we rested two days, and bought sheep and milk from the nomads.

On the 17th November we travelled north-west up a valley, which eventually contracted into a narrow and picturesque gorge; this was littered with gravel, and terminated in a pass,

Vicinity of our Camp of 21st and 22nd November.

with a frozen pool. There the dun horse which Chernoff had brought from Keriya died. At nine a.m. the thermometer stood at $-18°.6$ C., or $-1°.5$ Fahr.; while at midnight it was $-24°.4$ C., or $-11°.9$ Fahr. Stinging cold, as well as inhospitable, amongst these dreary, desolate Tibetan mountains!

The last of the little camel foals was unable to reach Camp no. CXXX. (altitude, 16,602 feet). He fell, and we had to kill him. The little beast never throve after his mother died, even though we took the utmost care of him, feeding him upon bread and paste and milk, and keeping him well wrapped up at night, close beside the camp-fire. The hardiest and most enduring of our animals were the two sheep—Vanka, the ram, which had accompanied us for over two years, and a white one from Abdall. None of the men had the heart to touch them; they looked upon them as comrades, and would, I verily believe, have perished of hunger sooner than kill them.

At our next camp, Yam-garavo, there was an abundance of excellent, dry yappkak, which proved extremely welcome for fuel, especially as during the night the thermometer dropped to $-26^\circ.5$ C., or $-15^\circ.7$ Fahr. It was positive cruelty to the men who were out watching our animals; their sheep-skins were nothing like sufficient to keep out the cold. However, at this place at all events, they were able to indulge in the luxury of a

Terraces of Gravel-and-Shingle.

fire all night. All day we had to fight against a murderous wind, which penetrated to our very marrow, for the thermometer never rose above $-4^\circ.0$ C., or $24^\circ.8$ Fahr. We were absolutely forced to walk sometimes to keep from freezing, although it was terrible work for the heart and lungs, except when going down the declivities. At this camp another horse died. Poor beasts! their lives were simply a burden to them, and they themselves nothing but a source of trouble to us; but so long as there existed any hope we did not like to kill them, or even abandon them.

Still amidst a chaos of mountains! On our left, that is, to the south, we still had the imposing range which had accompanied us all the way from Nakktsong-tso, and hid from our sight the "Forbidden Land of the Holy Books." Yet although we were thus surrounded on all sides by gigantic mountains, snow-fields were a comparative rarity, and not a flake fell. We were simply panting for a good fall of snow; we were tired to death of the everlasting wind and the bright sky. We were still 240 miles from Leh. Everybody was longing to get there, especially myself, for I wanted, if it was at all possible, to despatch a telegram to my people in Stockholm before Christmas Eve.

During the night of the 20th–21st November the thermometer dropped to $-28°.2$ C., or $-18°.8$ Fahr. Next day we did $17\frac{1}{2}$ miles, but in the evening had to fetch ice some distance with the

Open Country at Tsangar-shar.

yaks, and then melt it over the fire before we could obtain water. That night we were kept awake by a dozen wolves which howled dismally all round our encampment, and were answered by our dogs.

On the 23rd November we lost another camel, so that we had only thirteen left, or exactly one-third of the number with which we started from Charkhlik. The last to succumb was one of the veterans from Kashgar, which had accompanied us across the Desert of Cherchen, and both times to Altimish-bulak. Our route now lay intermediate between the route of Captain Bower and the route of Nain Singh. Upon reaching Tsangar-shar the valley which we had been following opened out, and tents and flocks appeared in several directions. Here we picked up a fresh convoy of yaks, the leader of which was a fine old fellow. He undertook to guide us to Panggong-tso and along its northern shore; and I promised to give him a revolver if he did not lie more than he possibly could help. "I am too old to lie!" was his simple rejoinder.

For some days we travelled beside the river Tsangar-shar, which abounded in fish. Shagdur and Chernoff especially distinguished themselves as anglers, and time after time brought me a bunch of beautiful fish, frozen as hard as a stone. Although at first tolerably open, the valley soon contracted, and began to pick its way between picturesque crags and immense terraces of gravel-and-shingle. The river was sometimes open, but more frequently covered with a thick sheet of ice, which only needed sanding to convert it into a very serviceable bridge for our camels. In one place the stream widened out into a lake, which filled the valley from side to side, except for a narrow strip of firm ground on the north, only just wide enough to allow the camels to pass. Almost immediately below this lake the river emerged into daylight from underneath its icy coverlet, and there we pitched our tents. I am very fond of hearing the sweet, refreshing tinkle of running water.

That evening we had the privilege of witnessing a beautiful scene. The moon rode high and poured down a flood of vivid light, bringing out with great distinctness every detail of the spur of the mountains; owing to the dazzling sunshine and intense shadows we had been unable to distinguish them clearly during the day. Now, however, every triangular snowfield and every feature of the bold rock sculptoring stood out in the sharpest and vividest relief.

Here one of Kamba Bombo's horses went and blundered into the river, and we had great difficulty in getting him out again. I had him dried beside a big fire, and then swathed in felts, but he died within a couple of hours. Next morning Li Loyeh's horse was discovered to have died during the night. They found him lying between the tents, blown out and frozen hard. We had believed that if any horse survived the journey it would be Li Loyeh's, because of the care which its owner bestowed upon it, though he now confided to us the fact that he had never paid for it. Not far from our next camping-ground Turdu Bai's old black horse died; and during the day's march the last also of our Tibetan horses. Four all at one swoop! Thus of the

Double Terraces of Gravel-and-Shingle.

horses with which we started from Charkhlik, as well as of those we acquired on the road, we had left only one, namely, the big white animal that I was riding.

It is, indeed, a most serious undertaking to keep together a big caravan in Tibet. Travelling in that country is nothing like so easy a business as people think; nor is there any pleasure associated with it. You travel so many miles at the cost of so many lives, men, horses and camels; and it is not without reason that we mark travellers' routes red on our maps—their journeys have been made at the price of blood. Were I to put a red cross on my map at every spot where a life was

The Cossacks Angling on the March.

lost, it would be easy to trace the route of my caravans across the centre of Asia.

Those who, from the advantage of a comfortable easy-chair and a warm fire, sit in judgment upon a journey of this description, and weigh up its results, may readily acquire some conception, though only a very faint one, of what a journey through Tibet is like without going all the way to Tibet. They have only to travel in the depth of winter a few score miles away from their own doorstep, along a country where there are no roads or paths, with a temperature of twenty degrees below zero Fahr., and ride a horse that stumbles at every step, and when they stop at night, sleep in a cold, fireless tent, with the wolves howling all round them in the sheer, unconquerable wilderness. Yet even that would be infinitely short of what Tibet is like; but it would, perhaps, be sufficient to make such people a little more charitable in the opinions they pronounce. For my part, I would rather cross the Desert of Gobi a dozen times than travel through Tibet once again in winter. It is impossible to form any conception of what it is like: it is a veritable *via dolorosa!*

Compared with these formidable difficulties of the road, the country and the climate, the disputes and differences which are inevitable in a caravan composed of men of different races and different creeds, are positively mere trifles. To expect Mussulmans, Tibetans, Mongols, Buriats, and Christians to work harmoniously together under all the vicissitudes of such a journey would be to expect the impossible. One night it happened that Li Loyeh and Ördek, when keeping watch together, visited the Tibetans in their tent to smoke opium. Next morning the Tibetans came to our Lama and complained that after the two men had gone they missed a stick of opium worth ten liang (= about 31s.), and accused them of stealing it. The Lama hesitated to trouble me with such a small matter, but as they were very insistent, he at length did report it. I at once sent Chernoff and Shagdur to examine and overhaul the baggage of the two suspected men, and to search their clothes from top to toe; but no opium was found upon them, and we drove the Tibetans away, saying they lied. Li Loyeh and Ördek were, of course, hotly incensed with the Lama for having reported the matter, and determined to be revenged upon him, and this is the way they set about it. They went and persuaded Sirkin that the Lama had bribed them to make me believe that Kalpet's death was due to Sirkin's ill-treatment. Sirkin, as may readily be imagined, was perfectly astounded at this unwarranted and unjust accusation, and at once came and complained to me. Now, it was neither an easy nor an agreeable thing to disentangle a petty intrigue like this with calmness and sound judgment, especially when my teeth were chattering with cold in the early hours of the morning. Somebody was, of course, bound to be dissatisfied. When I look back upon all the difficulties which beset my path, I am amazed at my success in bringing even the shattered remnants of my caravan out of that land of woe to the comparatively sunny tracts from which the waters stream amain to the warmer climes of the Indian Ocean.

Still proceeding down beside the Tsangar-shar, we soon had

The Temple-Village of Noh.

actual proof that we were descending to lower altitudes, for on 27th November we encamped at only 14,368 feet above the sea. We still lived to a great extent upon fish. Chernoff and Shagdur vied with one another in their efforts at catching them: they harpooned the fish with their sabres and with Tibetan lances as they marched along. On one occasion Shagdur contrived to give himself a thorough ducking in the icy-cold water; venturing too far out upon the ice, his mule went through with him. Fortunately, I happened to be not far away, and built up a big, roaring fire, and made him warm himself and dry his

Our First Encampment beside the Tso-ngombo.

clothes. Otherwise, he was so reckless and hardened, he would have continued as if nothing had happened.

At length the craggy barrier which we had hitherto had on our left hand came to an end, and the river took a sharp turn to the south, just at the spot where the temple-village of Noh, called also Ojang, stood on the left bank. The buildings included a very picturesque little temple in red and white, adorned with bulbed cupolas, flags, gilded pinnacles, and other ornamental appendages. The houses were built four-square, with flat roofs, and were as a rule surrounded by white-washed walls, with red edgings at the top. They also were decorated with flag-poles and streamers. The floor was covered with felt carpets; the smoke escaped by a hole in the roof; and outside were big piles of wood stacked up for the winter. Our Tibetans told us before we reached the temple that nobody was permitted to touch this wood; it was the lamas' property. Bathed as it was in bright sunshine, Noh presented quite a pretty picture, with the bifurcation of the stupendous mountains for its background.

The gravel-and-shingle terraces approached quite close to the left bank, and it was not easy to guide the camels over them without immersing them in the deep, cold water. We were travelling west, but still along the foot of the cliffs, where the springs yielded water with a temperature of 15°.9 C., or 60°.6 Fahr. A low pass, marked by a cairn with flags stuck on the

View S. across the Second Lake of Tso-ngombo.

top of it, brought us out above the eastern end of the lake of Tso-ngombo. Beyond it on the south were several pyramidal peaks capped with snow, while westwards stretched the lake with its capricious outlines—creeks, bays, capes, islands, and steep, craggy shores. It was, however, only a few miles wide. We encamped close down beside the lake on a level shelf, where there was a little grass. A caravan of sheep from Ladak was already resting there, but at our approach they moved on. About half a mile from our camp was a little islet with plenty of good fuel. Our Tibetans spent the night there, for it afforded them shelter as well as an abundance of firing—as indeed it did us—and in the evening their immense fires flung a fiery-red glare across the glittering ice. All night the ice cracked and groaned from the tension it was labouring under, until it sounded like a fog-horn blown now from one quarter, now from another. A well-spring kept open several holes in the ice close to the island, and there we caught a number of fish.

Next day we gave ourselves a rest, and measured the depth of the lake between the shore and the island; the maximum was 20¾ feet. The leader of our yak-caravan announced that he was ordered to despatch a courier to Leh, so that when we reached the frontier of Tibet and Kashgar we might find everything we needed ready waiting for us. I seized the opportunity

The Middle Basin of Tso-ngombo.

to send a letter to the British Joint Commissioner for Ladak, with the request that he would forward succours of yaks, horses, and provisions. When the messenger disappeared in the darkness on his little, long-haired steed, I confess I did not envy him his ride, and particularly so when next day we saw the path he had ridden along.

On the 30th November, whilst the men who travelled on foot struck diagonally across the ice, the rest of us had an interesting march along the north shore of the lake. This last consisted of four distinct basins, connected by short rivers. The stream which connected the second basin—itself icebound, like the first—with the third basin, was as level and regular as an artificial canal, about forty feet broad and not deeper than ten feet. Its water, which flowed extremely slowly, was of an emerald-green colour and as bright as crystal. The bottom was covered with aquatic vegetation, and shoals of black-backed fish, with their noses pointing indolently and carelessly up-stream, hung in the deeper pools. The fourth basin, which was the biggest, extended a long way towards the west and north-west, and was entirely free from ice, a fact probably due to its great depth. It was shut in by high, rugged mountains, amongst which the camels' bells echoed melodiously, frightening the flocks of wild-duck which rocked on the curling waves. The

A View of the Western Tso-ngombo.

shore was strewn with fragments of rock and beset with steep, gravelly screes, making it very difficult for the camels to advance. We encamped the first night at a spot called Bal; and from Noh to Bal our route coincided with that of Nain Singh, though at the latter place we left it again. During the march we met a caravan of 200 sheep, laden with corn from Ladak. It was quite a pleasure to see how orderly they marched and how easy they were to manage; and no slope was too steep for them, although they bore quite heavy loads. The Tibetans carry on a considerable trade across the frontier of Kashmir, bartering 100 sheep, laden with salt, for 80 sheeploads of corn. At Bal the thermometer went down to $-20°.9$ C., or $-5°.6$ Fahr., during the night; and before morning a terrific storm swept over us from the north.

On the 1st December we were obliged to kill another of our camels, though it was hard to put an end to our veterans now we were so near to the end of the journey. We kept close to the lake shore, following faithfully all its windings, although that frequently took us over very difficult gravel terraces. This last division of the lake was long and narrow, and resembled a Norwegian fjord. As we advanced between the precipitous and broken cliffs which shut it in on both sides, one magnificent mountain scene after another unrolled itself before our eyes, over-

A Difficult Bit beside the Tso-ngombo.

topped at intervals by some dominating snowy peak. The waters literally swarmed with wild-duck, and became churned into white foam when the birds, startled by our advance, skimmed along and settled farther out in the lake. The surface was quite free from ice, except for a few thin, ragged patches in the sheltered creeks and corners. We counted five distinct beach-lines; the lowest, which was very deeply incised, formed a shelf along the side of the precipice. Finally, however, the mountains receded and left room for a beach of level but soft ground.

An hour later we reached the first of certain specially difficult places of which we had been forewarned—namely, a rocky headland, which plunged sheer down into the lake. That evening the men carried over all the baggage on their shoulders, and next morning the animals were piloted past the headland one by one without their loads, first the mules and horses, and then the camels. The yaks, however, preferred to climb over the dangerous acclivities.

Next morning just before sunrise a curious phenomenon appeared on the opposite, or south-east, shore. The lake "smoked"; that is to say, dense clouds of chalky white steam rose up off the water and spread themselves out over its surface. Whether these were caused by warm springs, or were simply due to the fact that the surface of the lake was warmer than the atmosphere, I do not know. The thermometer dropped to $-18°.3$ C., or $-0°.9$ Fahr., and the temperature of the water was two or three degrees above freezing-point. But shortly after the sun rose the mist dispersed.

The breadth of Tso-ngombo varied, of course, according to the configuration of the inclosing mountains. Although some of the men went on first to level the road by filling up holes and toppling loose blocks of rock into the lake, we nevertheless experienced a good deal of trouble in clearing the worst places. One of the most difficult was a steep scree littered with big fragments of rock, where the instrument cases kept catching against the stones, until we at last unloaded them and carried them ourselves.

Camp no. CXLI. was pitched beside the encampment of a sheep-caravan, consisting of two black tents, surrounded by the animals' loads and stacks of wood. Here I measured the height of the former beach-lines: the highest was 64 feet, the lowest 14¾ feet, above the existing level of the lake.

On the 3rd of December I sent Chernoff across the lake in the skiff to sound the depth along a line which I had previously marked out for him: the soundings gave 98½ feet. Meanwhile I and Cherdon rode along the shore until we came to a sound or strait, some 550 yards across, and frozen over. There we waited for the boat. We had been told that before the day was over we should come to a perpendicular cliff which it would be absolutely impossible for the camels to get over. Finding this little sound frozen, it occurred to me that we might take the whole caravan across to the south side of the lake, and so avoid the difficulty. Chernoff examined the ice to see if it would bear; but to make quite sure, we chopped holes in it—

it was $5\frac{1}{4}$ to 6 inches thick. (At the same time we sounded a maximum depth of $96\frac{1}{4}$ feet.) We continued our investigations a considerable distance along the south side of the lake without discovering any obstacle. Meanwhile the caravan had come to a standstill and was waiting. Still, not satisfied, I put Ördek ashore, bidding him light a fire if he should come to a place it would be impossible for the camels to get past. On our way back to the caravan, we perceived no less than three fires blazing along the shore we had just left. There was no help for it then; we must proceed as best we could by the northern shore. When Chernoff rowed across to fetch back Ördek, he again sounded

The Dangerous Path Along the Mountain Side; some of the Yaks on the Path, Others Above it.

the lake, and obtained a maximum depth of $97\frac{1}{2}$ feet. From this I inferred that it was traversed throughout its entire length by a trough or trench about 100 feet deep.

Turdu Bai now went to examine the difficult place which prevented our advance, and reported that he did not see how the camels could any way be got past it in safety. Now seeing that the region was so well stocked with plenty of strong dry timber and brushwood, I determined to make a ferry-boat, and, binding it together with our camels' pack-saddles and ropes, see if we could not in that way carry the entire caravan past the obstacle. I hoped we could make a ferry-boat big enough to bear at least one camel. At any rate, it *must* do, for I did not intend to go back to Bal, and from there travel in Nain Singh's footsteps to Niagsu. If only the ice had borne just round that tiresome promontory! But no, it was open water, said Turdu Bai.

However, that night we had some 36° of frost (Fahr.), and next morning large areas, which the night before had been open water, were coated over with ice. I at once sent off every man who could be spared to gather wood to make the ferry-boat, and when we reached the spot we found a big stack ready waiting for us. There was ice even round the dangerous impediment, though it was barely $1\frac{1}{8}$ inches thick. As soon as the tents were pitched, Sirkin and two or three other men climbed up to have a look at the promontory from the top. Their opinions were divided: Sirkin thought that the passage could be managed, if we cautiously steered the camels over one by one. Then I went and examined it myself; it was nothing short of suicide to attempt it. The smooth black slates sloped down into the lake at an angle of 43°. It is true there was a sort of path, consisting of flat slates laid along a kind of shelf, and held up on the outer side by poles and logs as much as six or seven feet long, but none of them looked to me strong enough to bear the weight of a camel. Sometimes, too, the path zigzagged up and down the break-neck declivities; most of our tired camels would assuredly have lost their heads, and turned giddy, and rolled down into the lake.

No; either we must build the ferry-boat and break the thin ice, or we must wait until the ice was thick enough to bear us. As the thermometer at one p.m. was already down to $-4°.5$ C., or 23°.9 Fahr., I hoped that the last eventuality would come to pass. At six p.m. the ice was no less than two inches thick. The Cossacks set to work to construct a make-shift sledge of pack-saddles, tent-poles, timber, and ropes, and covered it all over with felts. This was Shagdur's idea; if the ice should not prove strong enough for the camels to walk round, we could perhaps haul them past the cliff on the sledge.

The wind whistled through the bushes and crevices, roaring for all the world like a gale sweeping through one of our Swedish forests. The ice was growing stronger every hour. It now bore three men, whereas in the morning it would barely support one. We resolved to try our ferry-boat, by packing into it as many men as would together be equal to the weight of a camel. Then two other men started to drag it sledgewise round the pro-

Carrying the Baggage across the Ice on a Make-shift Sledge.

montory. As soon as the ice began to crack, out jumped the Lama, then I followed him, then Tokta Ahun, and so on, according as the ice grew thinner and thinner. As each deserter hopped off, he was greeted with salvoes of laughter from the heroes who remained. The ice was bright and glassy, and without a bleb; we could distinctly see the fish darting in and out amongst the aquatic plants at the bottom. Every now and then there was a rumbling along it as if somebody were firing cannon, and the sound died away slowly, slowly, a long way down the lake. We saw we should have to wait another day, to give the ice time to form.

During the next 36 hours we studied the thermometer with

Converting the Skiff into a Sledge.

the keenest interest. That night it recorded −19°.3 C., or −2°.4 Fahr.; at seven o'clock the next morning −11°.1 C., or 12°.1 Fahr.; at one p.m. −5°.1 C., or 22°.8 Fahr.; at nine p.m. −8°.9 C., or 16°.0 Fahr.; and during the night of the 5th-6th December, −20°.9 C., or −5°.6 Fahr. I got up an hour before daybreak to take an astronomical observation. As soon as that was concluded, the men carried all our baggage except my own tent and the cooking-tent round the promontory on the sledge. The ice was now three-quarters of an inch thicker. Meanwhile, the yaks climbed over the top of it; but then they are marvellously sure-footed creatures. They may slip, but they never lose their foothold. Still their owners were obliged to exercise the utmost vigilance to prevent them from horning one another over the precipice.

Chernoff once more sounded the depth of the lake, being drawn across it by Ördek and Khodai Kullu in one-half of the skiff, converted for the nonce into a hand sledge. The former dropped through and only just managed to save himself by clinging to the edge of the boat. The maximum depth was 70¾ feet; and the excursion showed that relatively warm springs must gush up near the southern shore.

Before we got round that troublesome promontory we lost yet another camel, thus leaving us with only ten. The ice was now 3¾ inches thick; and first thing in the morning we strewed 28 sackfuls of sand on the surface to prevent the camels from slipping, and then made haste to lead them round before the sun got up. The passage was accomplished without mishap. After that we fetched round the remainder of the baggage; and, having loaded up, once more pursued our way west. The track led round dangerous headlands, across small expanses of drift sand, and alongside regularly rounded bays. I myself walked all day long, for my horse was, like all the rest, in not very good trim. This part of the lake was quite open; evidently the formation of the ice advanced from the east towards the west.

Once more the Tso-ngombo narrowed, and at length it terminated, except that its fresh water was carried on further into the salt lake of Panggong-tso by the river Aji-tsonyak. On the northern bank of this stream, shortly after it quitted the former lake, we encamped for the night. I shall not readily forget the sublime beauty of that wild Tibetan lake, with its imposing dimensions and steep crags, peeping over one another's shoulders to mirror themselves in its silvery water, or the pure, glassy brightness of its ice.

CHAPTER XXXIV.

FROM THE PANGGONG-TSO TO LEH.

CAMP no. CXLIV., which was exactly one hundred days from our main camp in the mountains, was not altogether without importance. We had been told, that we were to be met there by a fresh relay of yaks from Ladak. But we saw nothing of them; and as the Tibetans wanted to go home, we had to keep an eye upon them to prevent them.

On the 7th December we encountered an ugly storm, which smothered us with sand. Chernoff went out in the skiff, and sounded the western end of the lake along four lines, the maximum depth he obtained being 104¼ feet. There was an abundance of vegetation in the lake. It discharged a volume of not more than 133½ cubic feet in the second. We had intended starting again on the 9th; but found that all the yaks had run away, and their trail was obliterated by a fresh storm, so that we did not find them again until towards the close of the day. Their leader, Loppsen, by name, agreed, however, to accompany us along the northern shore of the Panggong-tso, until we met the relief column from Ladak. It was high time we had succour; our supply of rice, flour and talkan had come to an end several days before, and we were living exclusively upon meat, having bought seven sheep at a neighbouring encampment. It was there Yolldash made some especial friends, so that we had to tie him up to prevent him from running away. The highest beach-line that we measured near the camp was 177 feet above the level of the river. It was evident, that the two lakes had formerly been connected, and, like all the other lakes in Tibet, were undergoing desiccation.

We started again on the 10th December; and whilst the caravan travelled along the north shore of the Panggong-tso, I and Ördek rowed down the river. The stream moved almost imperceptibly, keeping close to the foot of the mountains on the south. The temperature had dropped to $-25^{\circ}.7$ C., or $-14^{\circ}.3$

Fahr., yet the river was not frozen; whence I inferred there must have been some warm springs somewhere thereabouts. According to the high water marks, this branch of the river must have carried some 370 cubic feet of water in the summer, or three times as much as it measured at the date of our visit. Lower down the lake was completely covered with ice, except for one narrow strip of green-blue water. The river must have spread itself out over the top of the salt water.

After that we crossed over to the mountains on the north side of the valley. They consisted of green and black schists, and several springs trickled out at their foot. There we were

The Skiff on Lake Panggong-tso

able to command an uninterrupted view of the lake. The configuration of its shore-line was the same as that of the Tso-ngombo. There were the same spurs jutting out into the same capes, and enclosing between them the same small triangular or crescentic patches of level ground, with sparse scrub. The stones at the foot of the screes along the margin of the water were coated with a layer of white ice, full of bubbles. This was due to the impact of the waves upon the shore, for the spray froze immediately it touched the ice-cold rock. We found the caravan comfortably established on a flat peninsula called Siriap, where bushes were very plentiful.

Next day, the 11th of December, it was so still and fine that

Gulang Hiraman and his Ladakis.

I sent my two best boatmen, Chernoff and Ördek, to row south-west across the Panggong-tso and sound its depth. In case they should not be able to reach the next camp before dark, they took provisions with them to last for a day. The sky was covered with heavy black clouds, so that there was a sort of twilight all day; and the mountains all round were shrouded in fresh fallen snow. Our route was almost doubled in length by the peculiar "festooning" of the lake shore. Every spur or offshoot of the main range ended in a peninsula or headland, jutting out across the lake; and in some places the passages round the promontories were so difficult that we had to level them down with spades and pickaxes before the camels would face them. In one place the strip of shore only just afforded room for one sheep to pass, though fortunately the lake at that spot was not deep, so that the camels were able to get round it in the water. Although snail-shells had been numerous further east, where the fresh water issued from the Tso-ngombo, here they existed in far less quantity.

At our next camping-ground, where the drinking water was very little better than that of the lake, we were reduced to gathering the ice off the stones on the shore. At dusk we discovered that the camels had gone back, but we found them at the narrow passage I have just mentioned, for they had forgotten that just there they had gone through the water. They were trying to get back to the rich pasture beside the Tso-ngombo. After that we kept them tied up, and gave them a good feed of corn.

Next day, although the thermometer did not drop below $-7^{\circ}.5$ C., or $18^{\circ}.5$ Fahr., the entire neighbourhood was enveloped in a blinding snowstorm, so that we were unable to obtain even a glimpse of the southern shore. The lake ran exceedingly high, for the wind, being forced through the long narrow valley, swept across it unhindered with redoubled vehemence. We only did a short stage, but it was more difficult than any we had yet made beside this series of lakes. The difficulty was caused by a huge offset from the range, which shot down into the lake almost vertically. There was, it is true, a path over the top of it, a path which was usually followed by the yak caravans; but it was not practicable for camels. We pulled up for a while at the foot of the cliff, and whilst Sirkin examined the shore close down by the water's edge, Shagdur rode up to the top of the promontory. The former reported, that there was no possibility of getting round down below; but Shagdur said, that although the path over the top had a very ugly look, we might perhaps be able to manage it. Meanwhile the yaks clambered up with wonderful agility and sureness of foot. When they reached the top, fifteen of them were unloaded, and brought back to fetch my boxes, tents and other baggage; which they took right over to the next camp on the other side. Then they returned and fetched down their own loads.

Meanwhile the axes and iron bars were at work preparing a zig-zag pathway for the camels. Although the relative altitude was not much above 650 feet, it took us a good many hours to get the beasts over, for we had to take them one by one and proceed with the utmost caution. The pass, which was crowned by a cairn of stones with little flags stuck in it, afforded a magnificent view of the whole of the Panggong-tso, backed on the south by the world of snow-clad mountains which acted as the containing wall of the basin of the Indus. But we did not linger there a moment longer than needful, for the pass was swept by a keen and murderous wind from the west. It was only possible to stand by planting our feet wide apart. Whilst jotting down my notes, I turned my back to it, and made the utmost haste, lest my fingers should turn stiff, and then hurried down in the hope of getting shelter behind some projecting rock. But in this I was disappointed: the slope faced the west and was consequently fully exposed to the tempest. It was an awful descent! Sometimes I was forced to creep on my hands and knees, and at others cling tight to the rocks to prevent myself from being blown over the precipices. Turdu Bai had gone on first, leading two of the camels; but I met him returning, he was perfectly bewildered. After a long search, we discovered a place where it would be possible to make a path, although it would take a considerable time to do it. As, however, it was already twilight, Turdu Bai and some of the other men prepared to spend the night on the mountain-side with the camels. Next morning, however, we piloted them all down successfully.

Owing to the gale, our boatmen on the other side of the lake had been unable to rejoin us; but as we saw them from time to time through our glasses, and the flare of their camp-fire was readily visible at night, we were not uneasy about them.

At Serdseh, on the border-line between Tibet and Kashmir, a great and welcome surprise awaited us in the relief caravan, which had been sent to meet us by order of the Vezir Vezarat.

Camp no. CXLVIII. Beside the Panggong-tso.

the governor of the Maharajah of Kashmir in Ladak. It had gone first to Mann, a village on the south side of the lake immediately opposite Serdseh; but hearing nothing of us there, it had turned back and tried the north side. As if by magic, our position was completely altered. There stood twelve horses and thirty yaks, entirely at our disposal, and there were sheep, flour, rice, dried fruits, milk, sugar, even corn for our animals. What more could we want? My caravan was on its very last legs, and this opportune help just saved it. Our long spell of privation and hardship was at an end. It was like a breath from

The Camp of 16th December, 1901.

the warm plains of India, a greeting from hospitable friends, a reminder, as it were, of home!

The leaders of the caravan were two Ladakis—Anmarju, who spoke Persian fluently, so that I was able to talk to him, and Gulang Hiraman, a comical, good-natured old man, whose face beamed like the rising sun with benevolence. All the other men were also Ladakis, except one, who was a Hindu. Here I dismissed the last of the Tibetans, paying them well, and giving them all the old saucepans, cups, jugs and clothes that we no longer had any use for, as well as a revolver. It was not without a touch of melancholy that I saw them turn their backs upon us; in spite of all the toil and trouble we had caused them, they had rendered us most excellent service, and been both friendly and honest. Thus snapped the tie which had so long bound me to Tibet. That night, when the sun set and the shades of night crept up in the east, they seemed to swallow up the land of the Dalai Lama, with all its secrets and mysteries and unsolved riddles. But in my portfolios and note-books I possessed that which softened the bitterness of the parting, namely, information calculated to shed light upon parts of Tibet which had hitherto been completely unknown.

The leaders of the relief caravan surprised me by offering me each a silver rupee. Notwithstanding the comicality of the proceeding, I understood the friendly sentiment by which the givers were animated and dropped the coins into my pocket, intending of course to pay them back with interest. We encamped side by side, close to the spring which bubbled up on the very edge of the lake, its temperature being 16°.2 C., or 61°.2 Fahr., although the temperature of the air was - 6°.0 C., or 21°.2 Fahr. The water it yielded was quite warm, steamed in fact. I had a thousand questions to ask about Ladak, Kashmir and India, and it was late when we went to bed. We made a huge fire on a prominent headland as a signal to Chernoff to return; and next day he arrived safe and sound, after having measured two bathymetrical lines across the lake, and obtained a maximum depth of 155¾ feet. From this place I sent off a special courier to Leh, a journey they told us of eight days.

Before proceeding further, I must relate what happened to Yolldash, the dog which had so faithfully shared my tent and travels all the way from Osh. He spent the night as usual on the felts at my feet, and at sunrise got up, shook himself, and went out. He generally used to lie and sun himself outside the yurt until the caravan started; but that morning he ran up over the mountain on the east and—never came back. Khodai Kullu saw him tearing back along our trail as hard as he could put foot to ground. He had, as I have already mentioned, formed a close intimacy with some canine friends at a tented village amongst the lakes, and for the past two days we had kept him tied up to prevent him from running away. But he had after all given us the slip. He would have a long trot of a good thirty miles beside the Panggong-tso before he reached his inamorata. Poor Yolldash! I wonder whether he has forgotten me, and all the care and kindness I bestowed upon him during the two and a half years he was with me. I know that I, at any rate, missed

The Temple of Tanksi,

him terribly; and so did the men, though they upbraided him with ingratitude.

Whilst the caravan took another road further to the north, I, with Anmarju, Chernoff, and the Lama, proceeded beside the lake, following a giddy path over several difficult passes. When the rest of the caravan rejoined us, they had only nine camels with them. I felt sorry for the poor beast that dropped when almost within sight, as it were, of straw and corn. That night

Musicians and Dancers at Drugub; beside a Chorten.

it snowed in real earnest, and next day, the 16th December, the landscape wore a perfectly wintry aspect. From the pass above the camp we obtained a bird's-eye view of the lake; it was like a deep trench, cradled amid snowy cliffs. Although there were 18° of frost (Fahr.), and the camera was stinging cold to the touch, I nevertheless took some negatives. Turning our backs upon the grand lake of Panggong-tso, we rode across the sandy steppe which, with its sand-dunes, stretched away from its western extremity; then proceeded south-westwards up a gentle valley, until we came to a low pass or sill, marked by two stone coffers, with large *Maneh* slabs and streamers. On the other side we went down by a deeply-scarped glen, littered with gravel and stones, and encamped on the border of a little ice-bound lake about 200 feet below the level of the Panggong-tso. We were now within the basin of the Indus; the water which trickled down that glen would eventually, after countless vicissitudes, issue in the Indian Ocean. For two-and-a-half years we had been travelling through the self-contained drainage areas of Central Asia. It was quite cheering, therefore, to know that we had at length reached a region which drained into the ocean. The little sill which I have mentioned lay 2 mm. difference of atmospheric pressure above the Panggong-tso, and had a most interesting lesson to convey when compared with the ancient beach-lines which lay 177 feet above the Panggong-tso. There was a time when this lake discharged its waters into the Indus, though now, owing to climatic changes, it is cut off from it. Hence it has turned salt, and its fresh-water mollusks have died out.

On the 17th I said good-bye to the caravan and pushed on in advance to Leh, taking with me Anmarju, Chernoff and Cherdon, and three horses to carry the baggage, and men on foot to look after them. It was pitch dark when we rose in the morning, but the active little Ladak horses were ready waiting for us with their saddles on, and off we went at a sharp trot. I wanted to reach Leh in four days, so that I might get a telegram home before Christmas Eve; but to do that, we should have to ride twenty-four miles each of the four days. As we advanced down the valley, farms and cultivated fields began to make their appearance. At Tanksi, where we changed horses, I was struck by the temple and monastery of Jova, situated very picturesquely on a detached crag. Having photographed it from below, we proceeded on to Drugub (12,858 feet), where we spent our first night. There a troop of musicians, with drums and flutes, and wearing masks, came and played and danced in the courtyard in our honour. It was most strange to be sleeping again under a roof.

Next day the road led up and up back again towards the clouds, that is to say, to the difficult pass of Chang-la. At that season of the year it was, as a rule, blocked with snow, though in the winter of 1901-2 it happened to be open, the snow lying thinly and in patches. The ascent was difficult, nothing but blank walls of bare, grey rock. It took us several hours to reach the top (17,671 feet). The descent was even more precipitous, winding

Gulang Hiraman on his Pony.

as it did zig-zag down amongst a perfect chaos of scattered granite fragments. By the time we got down to the stone huts of Taggar it was pitch dark.

How strange it was to meet fresh faces, to see villages and arable fields fenced round with stone walls, temples crowning the jutting crags, and to hear the wind whispering through the poplars and willows! All these, as we advanced, became more and more numerous. My Cossacks began to look upon me with a certain degree of wonder; they were palpably impressed by the fact of my having found my way to these strange people, of whom they had never heard before, and not less so by the

View from the Temple of Tikkseh.

friendly reception which they gave me. Down, down we went to lower regions, the air growing denser and the temperature milder. As we advanced, those wonderful Buddhist tributes to the gods, the stone kists—compared with which the obos of the Mongols are mere child's play—increased both in number and in size. One of them, which crowned a low ridge, was five feet high, ten feet across, and no less than 850 feet long, and every inch of it on both sides was covered with stone slabs, bearing in endless reiteration the sentence, "On maneh padmeh hum." What a time it must take to raise such a monument to the deities! I suppose the lamas who, with a patience surpassing Job's, sit and perpetuate this eternal apothegm in stone, console themselves with the thought that when they are no more the very stones themselves will speak.

The temple and monastery of Jimreh occupy a marvellous situation on an outstanding crag, near a large and rich village situated below it. At length, after passing another chain of villages, we struck the Indus, winding like a serpent, with green, transparent, though broken, water at the bottom of a narrow trench, 150 to 160 feet deep. Here, at an angle above the river was a Maneh kist 10 feet high, 30 feet across, and no less than 1,365 feet, or more than a quarter of a mile, long. Deluded mortals! What a stupendous waste of labour! If these gigantic monuments of human folly were ranged end to end they would make a small Chinese wall.

Here, at this same spot, I was met by Mirza Mohammed, the *naib*, or secretary, of the Tesildar of Leh. He was a very amiable and genial man, and spoke Persian fluently, and many were the marks of kindness I was to receive from him in the immediate future. From this point we travelled at first along the right bank of the Indus, down its broad and spacious valley, until we came to the caravanserai of Tikkseh. High above the village, far from the noise of the world, lay the monastery of Tikkseh-gompa. The monks who numbered forty to fifty, kindly sent and invited me to become their guest; but I preferred to stay where I was—there was a fireplace (!) in one of the rooms of the inn. However, I paid them a visit on the following morning. Their terraces and balconies, which would have excited a painter's envy, commanded a view of the broad and spacious valley of the Indus that was overpowering in its grandeur.

Whilst on our way to Tikkseh we had been met by three messengers, one of them a woman. They carried their messages wrapped about the ends of little sticks—a sort of fiery cross. One of these people brought a telegram from the Resident of Kashmir, at that moment staying in Sialkot, running thus: "Warmest congratulations on safe arrival. Message sent to His Excellency Viceroy; trust arrangements made satisfactory."

From the moment I set foot on British territory the proofs of kindness and hospitality which were showered upon me increased from day to day. We reached Leh, the capital (4,000 inhabitants), tired and covered with dust on the 20th December. Here I was met by the Tesildar, Yettumal, a Hindu of an exceptionally distinguished presence, dressed, except for his tall white

The Town of Leh.

turban, in European garb. Speaking fluent English, he bade me welcome to the territory of the Maharajah, his master, and handed to me a polite telegram from the Vezir Vezarat. We

One of the Courtyards of the Temple of Tikkseh.

Lamas of Tikkseh. The Man on the Right is the Prior of the Temple.

rode first to the day bungalow, or hotel, where Englishmen visiting Leh generally put up. Although it was a neat, comfortable house, I preferred to accept Mirza Mohammed's, which was formerly the church of the missionary Weber, and possessed separate rooms, where my Cossacks could bestow themselves comfortably, besides a large courtyard and abundance of room for both men and animals when my caravan should arrive. A room was soon got ready for me, with a fireplace in it, besides a carpet, bed, table and chairs; and here Yettumal handed over to me my bulging mail-bags. It was eleven months since I had heard a word from Europe, so that the feelings of eagerness and anxiety with which I looked forward to news from home may well be imagined. I broke the newest letter open first, and having satisfied myself that all were alive and well at home, I was able to go quietly through the budget in chronological order. I read on and on; I read all night, and the sun was high in the heavens before I turned in next day. I was deeply grieved to learn of Nordenskiöld's death. Yettumal, in welcoming me, had used the words "King Edward." I did not know what he meant; it was a name I had never heard. I was ignorant that Queen Victoria had been dead nearly a whole year.

The first thing I did after reaching port in Leh was to send telegrams to King Oscar of Sweden, to Lord Curzon, and to my parents, and the reply of the first-named reached me on Christmas Eve. It was couched in friendly and encouraging language: "Many thanks for telegram, and for the interesting letters sent before. I heartily rejoice in happy arrival on British territory, and hope you will soon come home. I and mine are well. Hearty greetings.—KING OSCAR." I had already written to Lord Curzon from Charkhlik, *viâ* Kashgar, asking that I might, on arriving at Leh, lift a loan of 3,000 rupees. This sum I found waiting for me. I had also said something about the possibility of a short visit to India, and I now received a long and pleasant letter from the Viceroy, concluding with these words: "I have only one thing to suggest, and that is that you come down to Calcutta, where I shall be staying from January till the end of March, and give me the pleasure of seeing you as my guest at Government House, and hearing from your own lips all that you have seen and done." After I had answered this kind invitation with an acceptance, Lord Curzon telegraphed back: "Congratulate you upon your safe arrival after most arduous journey and great discoveries. Am delighted that we shall see you here.—VICEROY."

Thus I was to pay a short visit in India, and see again Lord Curzon, whom I had met a few years before. He was present

The Last of our Camels Arriving at Leh.

at the meeting of the Royal Geographical Society in December, 1897, when I gave the lecture on my former journey. But seeing that I had before me a ride of 240 miles to Srinagar, the capital of Kashmir, I thought I might very well allow myself ten days' rest before starting, and they passed all too quickly. I was overwhelmed by the many and great kindnesses shown me by the missionaries at Leh, Messrs. Ribbach and Hettasch, and their wives, Miss Bass, and the Mission Doctor, Dr. E. Shawe, who was unremitting in his attentions to the sick men of my caravan. I visited the missionaries every day, and have seldom known a station conducted in so exceptional a manner and with such promise of success. We spent Christmas Eve together in the cosy little room attached to the church. The apartment was one blaze of light, and the Christmas tree, hung all over with little wax candles, reminded me of many a happy day of my childhood. The little church was full to overflowing, and Mr. Ribbach preached in Ladaki, and the audience, dressed in their best, listened reverently and joined in the Psalms. Although I did not understand a word of what the preacher said, I have seldom been present at a more solemn and affecting service. My senses were hypnotised by the cheerful glitter of the lights, and my heart deeply stirred by the sweet and soothing tones of the organ. I had such an immense deal to be thankful for, now that my labours were at an end, and I was once more amongst Europeans.

The caravan arrived on Christmas Day. The last nine camels which had successfully climbed over the pass of Chang-la were now at liberty to rest. The noise in the streets made them rather shy, but they were soon at home in the peaceful courtyard, and I had the pleasure of seeing their eyes light up when they caught the scent of the luscious clover, which I had had brought in for them. The inhabitants of the little town, who had scarcely ever seen camels before, climbed to the top of the walls that surrounded the courtyard, and gazed with the utmost amazement at the strange, long-necked, hump-backed animals.

My plans for the immediate future were soon formed. Whilst I ran down into India, the caravan would stay at Leh and rest. I did not, however, require more than three of the Mussulmans, so that it just fitted, when the rest of them came and asked that they might return home *viâ* Kara-korum and Yarkand. I paid them their wages, with substantial additions, as well as a present of clothes, provisions, and horses to ride on; and hired a *karakesh*, or horse-owner, a native of Yarkand, who undertook for a certain sum to guide them to his native town. Then Sirkin, who was longing to get home to his wife and children, came and asked whether he might accompany them. This also suited me very well, because it gave me an opportunity to send letters to Consul-General Petrovsky at Kashgar. Accordingly, the following men here left me—Mollah Shah, Hamra Kul, Turdu Ahun, Rosi Mollah, Li Loyeh, Almaz, Islam, Ahmed, and Ördek, the last named being told off to act as servant to Sirkin. With their train of baggage horses, their guide, and his two servants, they made quite an imposing caravan, as, on the 29th December, 1901, they rode out of Leh. In spite of his longing to get home, Sirkin shed tears when I gave him my hand in farewell, and thanked him for the very great services he had rendered me.

I left Chernoff behind in charge of my caravan at Leh, Cherdon remaining with him as meteorologist, while Turdu Bai, Kutchuk and Khodai Kullu, the best of the Mussulmans, were retained to look after the camels, the mules, and my old riding-horse respectively. I gave them plenty of money to "keep house with," and Yettumal promised to see that they wanted for nothing. Dr. Shawe and the other missionaries also promised to look after them during my absence. Mr. Ribbach took the greatest interest in our Lama, who also stayed behind, and the two were very soon on a confidential footing. Shagdur I took with me to India having first obtained the Viceroy's consent to do so.

XII.

To India, Kashgar and Home.

CHAPTER XXXV.

A VISIT TO INDIA.

HERE I ought perhaps to conclude my narrative, seeing that I have reached parts which are well known, and have been described, and well described, by travellers of world-wide reputation. Still, for reasons which I need not specially emphasise, I cannot conclude without giving some account of what was one of the pleasantest episodes, if not indeed the very pleasantest episode, of the whole journey.

On the morning of the 1st January, 1902, four active little Ladaki horses stood impatiently pawing the ground outside my quarters. I and Shagdur rode two of them; the other two carried our luggage, and were driven by men on foot. Yettumal ordered his secretary, Mirza Mohammed, to accompany me. How uncertain is life! and yet how much more inscrutable is death! It was destined that I should not have an opportunity to thank the Tesildar, Yettumal, for the many kind services which he rendered me, for when I returned to Leh, he was dead and cremated, and his ashes scattered on the sacred waters of the Ganges.

To Srinagar, the capital and summer residence of the Maharajah of Kashmir, was a journey of over 240 miles. Horses were changed at every station or bungalow (*pangla*), sometimes oftener, so that we could travel as fast as ever we liked. But I was too tired to rush it, and seldom did more than one stage in the day; hence it took us 11 days to reach Srinagar. The first stage was to Niemo, where we found a very comfortable caravanserai, with an airy *bala-khaneh*, or upper storey, which reminded me of my travels in Persia. After that we descended among the cultivated fields and orchards of Saspul, the latter full of apple and apricot trees. Beyond that point the road ran along the right bank of the Indus, which was walled in by tremendous precipices, 1,500 feet high at least. The views which successively unfolded themselves were sublime. The masterly way in which the river had carved a path through the mountains appealed especially to my artistic instincts. The water was clear, and of a dark green colour; and as we rode for the most part some 150 feet above it, the river was spread out before us like a map. Sometimes it flowed in tranquil silence; it was then deep and broad. Sometimes its channel was contracted; then it boiled headlong down the cataracts, and hurried with a thundering roar amongst the stones which littered its bed. Sometimes it was frozen over, the ice being used as a bridge by the natives. The left side of the valley was continually in the shade, owing to the lofty precipices by which it was shut in. But at the entrance of the valley of Hippti there was a gap, through which the sun poured like a cascade, causing the light green water of the Indus to glisten like an emerald. The effects due to the brilliant sunshine followed one another with amazing rapidity. Up and down the path wound capriciously along the mountain-side, mostly at a giddy height; and sometimes it was so narrow that two people could not pass each other without great peril. Whenever we approached a sharp angle, our coolies ran forward and uttered a loud, shrill cry of warning, to keep the road clear.

Upon reaching Kalachi we turned up a little side-glen, leaving the valley of the Indus on our left hand. The path was often dangerous. Sometimes it clung to one side of the glen, sometimes to the other, crossing the river at the bottmo on little tottering wooden bridges. One of these looked so unsafe that we preferred to cross on the ice beside it. Just beyond the bridge of Sampa-nezrak a spring gushed out of the rock, and its water, freezing as it emerged, had covered the path with a little mound of ice. Here one of the baggage horses slipped and fell, and would have rolled down the precipice had I not caught hold of his tail just as he was hovering, and held him fast until the men ran to my assistance. A little further on we came to the Lamaist monastery of Lamayuruz, built in a peculiar and picturesque position on the summit of a razor-backed cliff of gravel-and-shingle, cleft by deep ravines. It is merely a question of time; but some day it will plunge into the depths below. At the bottom of the gorge there were an immense number of *chortens* ("stone pyramids"; see ill., p. 581), as is generally the case near the temples in this part of India.

On the 4th of January we crossed over the two passes of Fotu-la (13,450 feet) and Namika-la (13,010 feet), and when we reached the village and bungalow of Mulbekh it was pitch dark.

There we had an extraordinary reception, being met by a train of torch-bearers, whose torches shot up showers of sparks through the apricot trees, tingeing their branches a fiery red. At Kargil, where we were met by another nice, pleasant Tesildar, I was greatly astonished at being received by forty young girls dressed in holiday attire. Each of them carried a dish with something to eat upon it, it being the custom of the country for the guest to touch each dish, and, if so disposed, to slip a few annas under the food.

I had been told before leaving Leh that the pass of Zoji-la is nearly always closed in winter, and that I might there be

An Old Ladaki.

turned back; but this winter the snowfall happened to be a good deal less than usual, and upon inquiry by telegram we learnt that the pass was not at all dangerous. At Kargil we picked up a first-rate pass-climber and headman of coolies in Abdullah, a native of Ladak, who spoke Turki, or Yarkandi, as they called it there; and in the village of Draz we hired 50 coolies, with their spades and pickaxes, to go on first and mend the path where it was rendered slippery by the ice. There was a station at Matchui, quite close to the pass—a perfect God-send it must be for travellers who have the ill-luck to get snowed up, as happened a few years ago, and before the house was built, to the former Vezir

Vezarat of Ladak. He had made himself hated by his extortions, and the people on both sides of the pass were only too delighted at the opportunity to keep him shut up out of harm's way for two whole months, during which time he nearly perished of hunger, for he had a large retinue of coolies with him.

On the 9th of January we crossed over the Zoji-la, the worst pass I have ever seen, although its altitude did not exceed 11,500 feet, that is, more than 6,000 feet lower than the Tibetan passes we had lately had to deal with. Upon reaching Matchui, we left our horses and crossed the snow on foot, which crunched loudly

On the Way up the Zoji-la.

under our feet, for the thermometer was down to – 22°.0 C., or – 7°.6 Fahr. The Ladakis tied soft snow-shoes under our feet to prevent us from slipping, and we scrambled after them to the summit of the pass, which was so flat as to be scarcely perceptible. Shortly after that, however, we went down by a break-neck descent to the station-house of Baltal; the path zigzagged backwards and forwards down the face of an almost perfect precipice. We had to keep a very sharp look-out, and be careful not to lose our heads—a slip would have been fatal. The snow had melted where the sun touched it, making the ice-clad pathway exceedingly dangerous, even after the coolies hewed out steps with their ice-axes. Zoji-la is an important line of division, both orographically and climatically, between Tibet

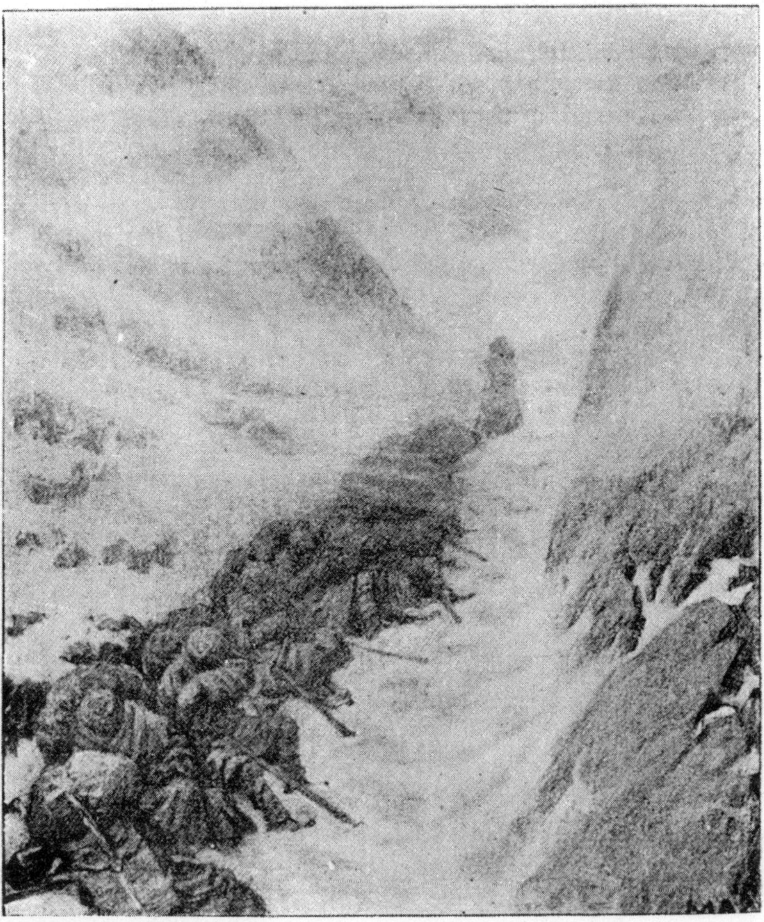

My Coolies Resting During a Snowstorm on the Pass of Zoji-la.

and Kashmir. When you stand on the summit of the pass you have the glen of Baltal at your feet, and to me it was an especial pleasure to hear again the mysterious murmur of the dark pine-woods—it put me so much in mind of my Northern home.

I shall not attempt to describe the beautiful country we rode through during the last two days—the dark green woods, the quaint towns, foaming rivers with their picturesque bridges,

A Dancing-Girl of Kargil.

in the background the glittering snowy mountains—the whole canopied by a turquoise-blue sky. The glowing descriptions which I have read of the lovely valleys of Kashmir really paled beside the reality.

At Srinagar I was received with genuine English hospitality by Captain E. Le Mesurier and his amiable wife, and in their society I spent two or three days I shall not soon forget. On the 14th of January we started again. Srinagar lies 5,250 feet above the level of the sea, and thence we were to descend, by a couple of secondary passes, to lower altitudes, until we finally reached the hot plains of India. The road ran first through the valley of the Jehlam, across the pass of Murree (Murri), and so on down to Rawal pindi. The road is a masterpiece of engineering, and in point of natural beauty far surpasses the Gruzinian (Georgian) military road across the Caucasus. To race down its thousand zigzags was a refinement of travel—indeed, I am almost tempted to call it a forbidden delight. The *tonga*, or travelling-cart, rested upon two moderate-sized wheels, and was provided with a roof and awnings at the side. It had two seats, with a back common to both. I and the driver sat on the front seat, and Shagdur on the back seat with the luggage. At the end of the strong, slightly turned-up pole there was a cross-bar, which was fastened by straps to the horses' saddle-pads, an arrangement which allows you to change horses in two or three minutes. It seldom took us more than half-an-hour from station to station. A few minutes before we reached the station, our driver used to blow a short, but tuneful, fanfare on his horn, and when we pulled up there stood a fresh pair of horses ready waiting for us. The pole was lifted from the panting, steaming pair we had just driven behind, the new ones were backed into their places, the straps were buckled, and away we went again at a gallop. As a rule the driver had far harder work to hold in his horses than to urge them on, so that I was not always quite sure whether they had bolted or not. So long as we were in the open country between Srinagar and Baramula there was no danger, but when we entered the gorge by which the road wound down the slopes of the Jehlam valley, there were plenty of places to make a man feel giddy, if that way inclined. The road went down steeply, and the horses literally tore along. On the right was a precipice, dropping sheer into the river, which churned and foamed at its foot, the only protection being a barrier two feet high. On ahead the road seemed all at once to come to an abrupt end ; but no, it swung sharply to the left. Yet on went our driver, without tightening rein. I thought the man was mad. We should go headlong over the precipice. Even though the horses managed to clear the corner, the cart must, it seemed, certainly pitch over and fling us out like a trio of loose apples. Just as I thought we were going to take a headlong spin through empty space, the horses slackened speed. But the corner was taken so finely that I was amazed we got round it alive. At this and similar corners the clear notes of the hunting-horn always rang out musically and distinctly as a warning to any other tonga that might be racing towards the same corner from any other direction.

Upon approaching Murree, the glory of the drive was increased tenfold, for we passed into the thick shade of a magnificent forest of Coniferæ. We now began to get down to lower levels; the air grew heavier, the breezes, which played amongst the hills at sunset, were softer and more balmy. But never for one moment did we slacken in our headlong race. It was already dark when our tonga began to rattle through the long straight streets of Rawalpindi. We drove direct to the railway station, for it was only an hour before our train started. After being so long accustomed to the silence of the desert and the stillness of the mountain wastes, it was to us a very strange thing to hear the shrill whistle of the railway engine.

At Lahore I stopped three days, incognito, of course, for I did not possess a single stitch of clothing that I could wear in good society. I rigged myself out afresh from top to toe, and, although somewhat weather-worn and sunburnt, was in a trice converted into a faultlessly-groomed gentleman. After that there was no longer any need of an incognito. The last evening I dined with Sir W. Macworth Young, the Lieutenant-Governor of the Punjab, and felt as if I had never been anything else but a society lion all my life.

What shall I say about Lahore—about Delhi, Agra, Lucknow, Benares? I will say nothing. All that I must leave to people who have time to study those marvellous and mystic cities; volumes might be written about each of them. I was merely a bird of passage, and only stopped one or two days at each. Although flying like a wild goose past the Taj Mahal, I could not, even in passing, withhold my admiration of the burial-mosque of Shah Jahan. It was unquestionably the loveliest work of art I have ever seen. The boasted glories of Constantinople, of Isfahan, Mashhad, Samarkand—all pale beside it. It is a summer dream in white marble, a piece of purest sky converted into stone. And Benares? Never shall I forget the boating-trips I made alongside its quays and stairways, those broad steps where every morning at sunrise thousands of pilgrims go to bathe in the hope of recovering health and strength. And then the Brahmins who worship the river, and recite over it their complicated prayers, and the aged people of the land who journey thither to die beside the sacred Ganges! In the midst of these bathing pilgrims and happy, playing children, I saw them washing a corpse in the river, ready for burning on the funeral pyre, to the strains of their own peculiar music. There is nothing to equal a row on the Ganges by moonlight. As I lay back dreaming in the stillness of the night, my imagination was excited by the holy city and by the thousand and one stories of its hoary, legendary past.

At Lucknow I was awakened one morning by Lieutenant Didrik Bildt, the only Swede I met in the course of my visit to India. And a thorough Swede he was, too ; I was proud to call him my countryman. In his charming company I spent one never-to-be-forgotten day in Lucknow, visiting with him all the sights and objects of interest.

Shagdur's growing amazement at all he saw and heard was to me a source of great enjoyment. It was, of course, only natural that a simple Buriat Cossack from Siberia should be impressed by all he saw and heard amongst these ancient cities of the Great Mogul, with their palm-trees, and pagodas, and bazaars crowded with noisy multitudes, showing in their dress every shade of colour under heaven. He asked me all sorts of questions about everything he saw, repeated to me his observations and speculations, and was unable to find words to express the fulness of his amazement. When we met a train of elephants in Lucknow, he could scarce believe his own eyes, and asked whether these colossal things really were living animals, and not some sort of machine, constructed in a different way from railway engines. To convince him that they really were alive, I asked the keeper to stop one of his animals, and then, stepping into an adjacent bazaar, bought a bunch of sugar-cane, and went and fed the elephant. The way the beast examined thoroughly every piece tendered to him, and cleverly rejected what was not good to eat, soon convinced Shagdur that the elephant was a real live animal.

Upon reaching Calcutta early on the morning of the 25th of January, I was met at the station by a Viceregal carriage, with four servants, wearing scarlet and gold liveries and lofty white turbans. Another vehicle took charge of Shagdur and the luggage. We drove direct to Government House, where I was conducted to a room on the second floor. I have never lived amid such grand surroundings as in the Viceregal Palace of India. The reception-rooms were adorned with costly works of art, the floors covered with soft Indian carpets, the walls hidden behind large oil portraits of the kings and queens of Great Britain, of Indian Maharajahs and Persian Shahs, all bathed in the brilliancy of the electric light. My bedroom, a vast apartment, had a private balcony, kept cool by an immense awning, from which I was able to drink in the fragrance of the palm-trees in the park. It also commanded a magnificent view of Calcutta, and beyond, right away to the jungles in the delta of the Hugli. The heat was distinctly perceptible in Bengal. End of January though it was, to a "Tibetan" like me it was even oppressive, so that I was beyond measure delighted to have a bath-room all to myself, and I made good use of it several times a day.

I arrived on a Sunday, and an adjutant at once came to tell me that his Excellency the Viceroy was expecting me at the Palace of Barrakpur, two hours by steamboat up the river. Accordingly, after breakfast I was taken there, in bright summer weather, with

Huts Below Baltal.

a crisp breeze, on the steam launch *Maude*, with the pleasantest company that could be wished—Colonel Fenn, body physician to His Excellency the Viceroy, and Mrs. Fenn; Colonel Robertson, British Resident in Mysore; and Mr. C. S. Bayley, Resident in Indore, Central India.

Barrakpur, which was furnished with that elegance and distinction of taste which are so characteristic of the English, stood in the midst of a tropical park. We were received by Lord and Lady Curzon and their two fascinating little daughters, in a large, cool, shady arbour. Lord Curzon welcomed me with the cordiality of an old friend, and presented me to the charming lady who shares his dignities. At lunch he proposed my health, and congratulated me upon the success of my journey. After I and my host had spent two or three hours discussing geographical questions, I was taken for a drive in the neighbourhood by

Lady Curzon, who handled the ribbons with as much skill as grace.

The ten days that I had the honour to be Lord and Lady Curzon's guest will always count amongst the brightest and happiest of my life. Not only did I receive every day fresh and embarrassing proofs of kindness and hospitality, but Lord Curzon, one of the most distinguished students of the geography of Asia, entered with the liveliest and most appreciative interest into the various incidents of my journey, the scope and significance of which he fully realised.

We in Europe have very little conception of what it means to be Governor-General of India, with almost absolute power over 300,000,000 subjects, or very nearly as many as are ruled by all the Sovereigns of Europe together. It is an august—an incomparable position, and compels admiration of a kingdom which is able to offer such a unique honour to one of its sons. Lord Curzon realises fully the responsibility which rests upon him, and takes an earnest view of his duties, sacrificing all his time and all his strength to the functions of his office. The whole of his time, except an hour or so for meals, was spent at his study-table. He had not a moment to spare for sport or social pleasures. Once when he accompanied us to the theatre he slipped away before the close of the first act, and hurried back to resume the cares of office. Lord Curzon's study was a large and tastefully furnished room, full of books and despatches, arranged on different tables and bookshelves. Here he did me the great honour of inspecting the scores of map-sheets which I had brought with me from Ladak, and I am not likely to forget the exceedingly kind, and even flattering, observations that he made upon them.

During my stay at Government House, two or three state dinners and state balls were given, with a splendour and magnificence which would not suffer by comparison with similar events at any of the great Courts of Europe. One day a German and an Austrian warship came steaming up the Hugli. This led to a breakfast to the officers at Government House, and was followed by several hospitable gatherings on board both ships and at the German Club. Mr. Voigt, Swedish-Norwegian Consul-General at Calcutta, gave a successful and enjoyable dinner in my honour.

During my nine years' wanderings in many parts of Asia my experiences have been many and of divers characters and complexions, but I do not ever remember such a great contrast between those I was now experiencing and the months that immediately preceded them. For two and a half years I had been cut off from the world, isolated amid the deserts and mountains of Central Asia, enduring exposure and fatigue, hardships and privations of every kind, and here I was, lapped in the luxury and refinement of a consummate civilization. For years I had led a solitary existence; now I made new acquaintances at every step. A little while before I was working and travelling in 50°-60° (Fahr.) of frost, and climbing mountain-ranges 16,000—17,000 feet above the level of the sea, the only denizens of which were the arkhari and the wild yak; now I was strolling under the palm trees on the shores of the Indian Ocean, amid the fabled splendours of the tropics. Only a little while ago, and I was living in the filthy smoky tents amongst the Tibetans; now I was enjoying all the refinements and delicate graces of English home life, intoxicated by the scent of roses, entrancing music, and the conversation of beautiful ladies. The Tibetans had treated me as a suspicious and dangerous individual; here in India I was literally overwhelmed with hospitality and kindness. When a new engagement beckoned me, I literally had to drag myself away from the kind friends with whom I happened at the moment to be staying. In fact, I was everywhere made perfectly and thoroughly at home. These successive departures and leave-takings imparted the only tinge of sadness to what was otherwise in every respect a most delightful and memorable trip.

During the last few days of my stay at Government House there were two distinguished visitors, namely, Sir Ernest Cassel and Professor Oscar Browning, of Cambridge, with whom I had several bright and happy talks.

The Indian press had welcomed me with such flattering marks of attention that I was inundated with invitations—to Darjiling, Ceylon, Mysore, Peshawar, from Major Younghusband, my old friend of Kashgar (1890), the Swedish missionaries, and many others. But I did not forget my caravan and my Cossacks, waiting patiently in Leh. Still there were some invitations which I could not resist, although by this means my stay in India was somewhat prolonged. Unfortunately, my faithful Cossack, Shagdur, contracted a fever, and was very weak the whole of our stay in Calcutta. He was very comfortably installed in a tent with a boarden floor, bathroom, and electric light, in the park, and was attended by Colonel Fenn and his assistant, Emir Baksh, who had accompanied Mr. Forsyth on his mission to Yakub Beg, of Kashgar, in 1873. I left Shagdur in their care, whilst I made a trip further south, arranging to meet him at Rawalpindi on my return.

After saying good-bye to Lord and Lady Curzon, I left Calcutta on the 5th of February, and travelled to Secundarabad, near Hyderabad (Haidarabad), to see my chivalrous friend of the Pamir Boundary Commission of 1895, Colonel McSwiney. He was stationed at the military camp of Bolarum in the Nizam's territory, where there was an English force of over 8,000 men. I spent three right happy days with Colonel McSwiney, who entertained me with military parades and picturesque displays of cavalry, amongst which tent-pegging by torchlight and in the glare of huge fires particularly interested me.

At Bombay I was the guest of the governor, Lord Northcote, and his charming wife. With them also I spent four days which I shall not readily forget. My apartment, which was again provided with a balcony, was at the very extremity of Malabar Point, and thus I had the ocean all round me, except on the north, where a narrow tongue of land led to the Parsees' "Tower of Silence." It was like living on board ship, a marvellous change for one who had been so many months in the interior of Asia. I never grew tired of listening to the cadence of the waves, as they beat against the foot of the cliff. Oh, how I longed to return home on their buoyant swell! It would have been infinitely preferable to climbing back up to the dreary, inhospitable mountains of western Tibet, and travelling all that long way across the two continents. I confess it cost me an effort to put the temptation from me; but I could not desert my caravan, and abandon wantonly the results of my journey. So, after a visit to the caves of Elephanta, with our Swedish-Norwegian Consul, Mr. Bickel, and a dinner at the house of the German Consul, Count Pfeil, and another with the French Consul, M. Vossion, I took leave of Lord and Lady Northcote, and returned to Delhi. I was exceedingly sorry to miss the learned Russian Consul, M. V. Klemm, who, eleven years before, had shown me such great kindness at Bokhara. He had just gone away on a short leave of absence, and although he was to be back in two or three days, I was unable to await his return. I was the more sorry because I owe him especial thanks for the generous offer he made me with regard to Shagdur. He proposed that if my young Cossack, who evidently could not stand the climate of India, was not strong enough to go back with me to Leh, he would send him on the first opportunity, and at the expense of the Consulate, to Colombo, and thence to Vladivostok, from which port he could easily reach his own home.

On my way to Rawalpindi I only stopped once or twice. At Jaipur I was met by the Maharajah's carriage, and had a splendid trip on one of his magnificently caparisoned elephants to the ruins of Amber. At Jaipur all the houses were rose-coloured, and all the inhabitants dressed in pinks and reds. It was like the blush of the morning in a garden of roses. There I was shown the greatest hospitality by Mr. Cobb, the British Resident.

The Maharajah of Kapurtala invited me by telegraph to visit him at his palace at Kartarpur, and there I spent two extremely pleasurable days in making excursions by carriage, by boat, and by elephant, accompanied in each case by His Highness himself. One of the days happened to be my birthday, and in honour of the occasion His Highness had a band of music, champagne, and other nice things at the dinner. My stay in Kartarpur was like actually living a piece of the Thousand and One Nights.

At Rawalpindi I picked up poor Shagdur, who, in consequence of his illness, did not derive half the pleasure from his visit in India that I had intended him to have. Colonel Fenn had sent him on from Calcutta in charge of a native assistant, and at Rawalpindi he had been again kindly taken in hand by Captain Waller and Major Medley, the well-known Asiatic traveller. The latter spent a good many hours talking Russian with Shagdur, so that Shagdur was perfectly delighted with him. Major Marshall, of the Army Medical Corps, who attended him, advised me to get him up into the mountains as soon as possible. But he was still so weak he could not sit up in the tonga, so that I could do nothing but wait patiently. As for myself, I was in clover. All the officers, from General Sir Bindon Blood, who had just returned from South Africa, downwards vied with one another in showing me attentions. Unfortunately I missed Dr. M. A. Stein, whose headquarters were at Rawalpindi. He had recently returned from his important and successful journey in East Turkestan. But happily I was able to make his acquaintance by correspondence, and before the year 1902 came to an end I had the pleasure of meeting him in London.

At length Shagdur was sufficiently well for us to make a start. We drove up to Srinagar by the same road and in the same way that we had driven down two months before. At the station-house of Ghari I met Sir Robert and Lady Harvey, and spent a most delightful afternoon in their company.

Thanks to the exceeding kindness of Captain and Mrs. Le Mesurier, Shagdur had another rest of five days at Srinagar, during which he picked up immensely in the fresh cool air of Kashmir. This gentleman and his wife were the first and the last English people I met during my long trip into India, so that the first impression which I received of the ruling race in that great dependency was both cordial and sympathetic, and it was with real and deep regret that I said good-bye to them—they were so unspeakably kind and nice, both to me and to my Cossack. The Captain, who was Joint Commissioner for Ladak, sent a telegram to Leh, ordering everything to be in readiness against our arrival, and especially that measures of precaution should be taken at Zoji-la. Mrs. Le Mesurier was in every respect an accomplished lady, and she had besides made a thorough study of the geography of Kashmir, and of the manners and customs of its inhabitants.

CHAPTER XXXVI.

HOME VIÂ THE MONASTERY OF HIMIS.

On the 6th of March we started again for Leh. I engaged two palankins called "dandies," each with eight bearers, and used mine as far as I possibly could; but Shagdur had such a decided objection to that method of travel that, weak as he was, he preferred to ride.

At Sonamarg I received telegrams from Capt. Le Mesurier, the Vezir Vezarat, as well as from Kargil and Leh, warning me on no account to attempt the pass of Zoji-la. The first-named very kindly invited me to return to Srinagar. But be the risk what it might, go on I must. The pass is more difficult from the Indian side, for you have to climb on foot *up* the ugly precipices. This time, too, we were unable to use the summer road, as we did when we came down, but were obliged to take the deep ravine into which the avalanches crash down every winter from the overhanging cliffs, and kill so many people. The utmost caution is at all times necessary. It is best to travel early in the morning, whilst the snow is still frozen; it is in the afternoon that the avalanches fall, after the snow gets softened by the sun. Nobody ever attempts to force the pass in snowy weather, for it is then that the peril is greatest.

On the 10th of March we were up at daybreak; it was still pitch dark, raw, and bitterly cold, and the stars still glittered brightly in the frigid steel-blue sky. The mountains and the snows were only just faintly perceptible. We were soon ready. First went 63 coolies and men to help smooth the road, walking in Indian file (see illustration, p. 600); after them followed several horses, carrying the men's provisions, and, last of all, we ourselves on horseback, escorted by the Naib-i-tesildar of Ganderbal and his suite. As it grew slowly lighter, the white snow-fields became more and more distinctly perceptible, and the spruces stood out blacker and blacker against them. Every now and again somebody would tumble head over heels in the snow, which gradually grew deeper. On we went, climbing up and up, step by step. The crust of the snow was still firm enough to bear men on foot; but it soon turned soft and let us through. When the horses no longer felt firm ground under their feet, but floundered about like porpoises, we all got off and walked. At Baltal we were met by Abdullah and twenty-three experienced and trusty mountaineers.

The next day we traversed the dangerous gorge. It was no longer recognisable, the masses of rock with which it was choked

A Young Woman of Ladak.

being buried under fallen avalanches to a depth, it was said, of 500 feet. In winter, therefore, the road runs over the top of this stupendous accumulation of snow, while in summer the gorge is absolutely impracticable. I and Shagdur were hauled and pushed to the top of the pass, down which swept a keen, cutting wind, like a waterfall, whirling up the snow in blinding clouds. But once happily past the most dangerous spots, all peril was over. Although the snow still lay deep, it was no longer drifted as it was in the pass. After every fresh fall the people trample a path, until eventually the track consists of a mere succession of deep holes. If you can manage it without losing your balance, it is best to walk on the little ridges between the holes, but as a rule people keep to the holes themselves.

In this way we struggled for four days across the pass and its approaches, until we were able to use yaks, and subsequently horses. For three days and three nights we were snowed up at Kargil, and the people endeavoured to amuse us with dancing girls and boisterous music. We reached Leh on the 25th March, and found all well. All the men whom I had dismissed had returned, except Sirkin and Ördek, saying that the pass was blocked with snow. Sirkin and Ördek had, however, succeeded

The Entrance Door of the Temple of the Doggtsang Raspa.

in forcing their way through, and they eventually reached Kashgar in safety.

It was my intention to rest at Leh for two or three days only, and then hasten northwards over the pass of Kara-korum; but the fates were against me. Shagdur had a violent and serious relapse, and Doctor Shawe diagnosed it as typhoid fever. There would be no possibility of his being able to travel under any circumstances for two or three months. He was fearfully weak and emaciated, and for two nights was delirious. Thus we were detained day after day. I fully realized that I should have to leave him, but I would not do it till the poor fellow was pronounced out of danger; and there were two days during which we had almost given up hope. But about the middle of April he got the turn, the crisis was passed, and he only needed a couple of months' rest and nursing in the mission hospital, where Doctor Shawe would have him under his own eye. I did all I possibly could for the invalid's comfort. I gave orders to Li Loyeh to stay with him, and be his servant, promising that if he did his duty well, he should have an extra reward when he reached Kashgar. They were to stay at Leh till the summer, and accompany a merchant's caravan to Yarkand, and thence

The Prior of Himis.

continue to Kashgar. I gave Shagdur two hundred rupees for his support, and if he should need more, Consul Klemm undertook to advance it.

It was hard to part from him. When I went into his room for the last time, on the 5th of April, it was full of warm and pleasant sunshine. Shagdur was of course sorry he was not able to accompany us to the end of the journey; but he saw that he must rest quiet until he was thoroughly well. I tried to look at things from the bright side, and comforted him with the promise that, as far as it depended upon me, I would take him with me on my next journey. This cheered him up; he said it would be the greatest happiness and honour that life could give him. At length I wrung his hand and tore myself away, committing him to God's care. Then the dam burst; he turned his head away to hide the tears. I hurried out, so as not to let him see the moisture that was glittering in my own eyes. And, of a truth, I did feel it intensely—the long uncertain separation. I was also really very sorry to leave the Ribbachs, the Hettaschs, and Doctor Shawe. They had shown me such exceptional kindness and rendered me such ungrudging help. The memory I carried away with me of their mission-

The Temple Court-yard at Himis.

station was that of an ideal establishment of its kind. Nor was it an easy thing to say farewell to our old and faithful veterans, the nine camels which survived, the only ones which had got through to Leh. During the three months they had already rested from their hardships they had grown fat and plump, and now ate their food with the utmost relish. But it was impossible to take them over the Kara-korum in winter. I sold them, therefore, for a mere song to a merchant from Yarkand, who was returning home in the following summer.

Great though the contrast was to go down from the Tibetan plateau, with its 16,000–17,000 feet of altitude and its rigorous winter, to the hot summer of India at the sea-level, the transition which now took place in the opposite direction was not less abrupt. It was really surprising, that I kept free from every trace of fever; but to counterbalance the immunity on that score, I was exceedingly tired, and was longing intensely to get back to my peaceful study in Stockholm. I decided, therefore, to travel as far as I possibly could in a palankin, that is to say, as far as the foot of the pass of Chang-la. Borne by four stout

A Lama Attired for a Religious Festival.

fellows I swung away out of Leh, and, dipping below the hills, we soon left behind us the picturesque little town, with the palace of its former kings crowning the crag that overhangs it. As the men sped down towards the Indus at a swift pace, they sang a characteristic antiphonic measure; that is to say, the leader sang a short strophe, whereupon the others joined in with a monotonous sleepy refrain. But the song stimulated them and helped them to march in time. On the 6th April we advanced down the left bank of the Indus; that is to say, I and my two attendants, the Lama and Kutchuk. The caravan,

The Idol of the Doggtsang Raspa.

with the hired horses, kept to the main road over the Chang-la, and then followed the right bank of the stream. At length we turned away from the Indus, and travelled south and south-west up the gravelly scree of the southern mountain-range, and then entered the valley of Himis, passing on the way a number of picturesque *chortens* (p. 581), as well as several rows of round or oblong stone kists. As we advanced, the valley grew narrower, and turned almost due west; the grey rocks

A Lama Wearing a Mask.

being dotted with solitary groups of poplars and the mountains wreathed with snow. Soon the famous temple of Himis came into sight. It resembled a cluster of houses arranged like an amphitheatre, or, rather, plastered like swallows' nests against the face of the precipice. After scrambling up winding paths, and threading various gangways and courtyards, protected by breastworks, we at length reached a little door in the wall, and met with a friendly reception from the prior. He was a little old man, with a thin grey beard and a big ugly nose, but his smile was the perfection of kindliness and good nature. His name was Ngavang Chö Tsang, and his title, Himi Chaggtsot.

I never in all my life saw such a labyrinth of rooms and cells, courtyards and passages, and steep narrow stone stairways, as there was in this temple complex. It would be difficult to give anything like an intelligible description of its plan. In fact, there was no intelligible plan; each little wing seemed to have been built just where there happened to be the most room to spare at the moment. We were taken through a gateway, up a steep acclivity paved with flat stones and shut in between high walls. We turned sharply round a corner, and were swallowed up in a dark passage which led to a series of small courtyards. We climbed up a staircase, and obtained a glimpse of the interior of a temple, the gilded idols being only just perceptible in the dim religious light. We stepped out upon a terrace, and were amazed at the glorious view which burst upon our sight; and when we glanced behind us we were once more amazed that the temple-town had not been long ago crushed flat by a fall of the cliff, which overhung it so threateningly at the back. Then we were led up another staircase, along other passages, through other pokey cupboard-like apartments, until we got perfectly bewildered. It was like wandering through a maze or an enchanted cave. I could find my way about in Government House, Calcutta, much more easily than here, although there I was some little time learning the "geography" of the place; though when I came to the big oil-portrait of Feth Ali Shah I knew I was on the right way to my own room. But here in Himis I would defy anybody to find the way except the monks and friars who belonged to it.

The first apartment into which I was taken had a ceiling supported by picturesque wooden columns, and contained the idol Dollma, with big glowering eyes. In front of the image, which was said to be three hundred years old, were ranged row upon row of little brass bowls containing water, rice, corn, flour, lard and butter. I made a hurried sketch of it from the other side of the apartment (see p. 619). This was said to be the most revered idol in the monastery. Two lamas lay prostrate before the image of the Doggtsang Raspa, which was gilded and draped with a cloak. On the right of it was Lama Yalsras, and on the left Sanjas Shaggja Toba. The temples themselves, of which there were seven, were called *dengkang* (in Mongolian *doggung*), and the rooms where the monks read their *noms* (sacred books) were called *tsokkang* (in Mongolian *sumeh*).

The Kitchen at Himis.

The monks keep a little lamp burning perpetually in a huge goblet-shaped brass bowl filled with yellow fat, which they call *lochott*. The walls were hung with religious paintings in the shape of standards, often several, one above another; while from the roof were suspended a number of draperies called *chuchepp*. Long triple-pointed pennons called *pann* wreathed the columns, and baldachins, shaped like gigantic parasols, were fixed above the images of the gods. Drums, bells, cymbals, and long wooden trumpets also formed part of the equipment of the temple. It was like walking through a museum, one that I would gladly have carried away with me. The book-shelves

In the Valley of Sheyok.

groaned under the volumes of noms, or Buddhist scriptures. All the other temples were furnished in a similar way with images of the gods and *chortens* of silver, set with rubies, turquoises and gold. Through a trap-door in the floor I was shown the *bakkang*; that is to say, the "armoury" of the temple, where the monks kept their vestments, masks, hats, spears, drums, trumpets, sackbuts, and a thousand other things, which they use at the great religious dances that take place every year in July. Two or three of the lamas good-naturedly put on their festal attire, and sat, or rather stood, as models to me whilst I sketched them. The kitchen, or *tabbtsang*, which they used on the occasion of their great summer festival, contained five gigantic cooking-pots, or "coppers," and several smaller ones, set in brick-work over a huge fireplace. The prior showed me everything himself, and did it with impressive dignity; and wound up by conducting me to a guest-room in a small and comfortable pavilion just below the monastery. When I visited him in the evening in his own apartment, the

A Flute-player at Sheyok.

narrow passages and corridors, seen in the yellow-red flare of the torches, were wonderfully like grottoes and caverns in a lime-stone mountain.

The old man told me that Himi-gompa, the name he gave to his monastery, was built three hundred years ago by Doggtsang Raspa, a lama who lives perpetually like the Dalai Lama. The present Doggtsang Raspa was, he said, nineteen years old, and for three years he had been living the life of a hermit, absolutely and entirely alone, in a very small gompa or cave in the mountain-side in the district called Gotsang. He had still three years to spend there. Thus for six whole years he would never see the face of a human being and never take a step outside of his prison. A serving lama, who lived close by, would keep him supplied with food, pushing it in to him every day through a small aperture, while a spring of water in his cell furnished him with water. But the two men were not allowed to look at one another, nor were they ever allowed to speak. Should it be necessary to make any communication of importance to the Doggtsang Raspa, it would be written on a strip of paper and left in the aperture.

The enforced recluse spent his time in meditation and in studying the holy scriptures of his faith. I asked what would

The Pass of Kitchik-kumdan near Kara-korum.

happen to him if he fell ill, and was told, by way of answer, that he was so holy he never did fall ill; and if he had done so, he possessed a remedy that was effectual against all the sicknesses in the world. Every Doggtsang Raspa before him had gone through the same process of purification. At the end of the six years he would come down to Himis, and when he died, his spirit would pass into a new Doggtsang Raspa.

There were about three hundred lamas attached to the monastery, and most of them spent the winter at other *gompas* or monasteries, and at Leh. They were, however, all supported by the monastery of Himis, which is rich and possesses a large extent of cultivated ground. A few years ago a Russian traveller astonished the world by the pretended "discovery at Himis of a manuscript describing the life of Jesus." But as he has already been sufficiently exposed, I need not say anything further about him. The following afternoon, when I left the temple, the prior made me a present of various stores, and a sheep, for which he would not allow me to pay him. He himself accompanied us on horseback as far as the bridge across the Indus; and at Taggar we picked up the caravan.

The return journey through Asia and Europe would supply sufficient material for another long chapter of travel; but I must here break off my narrative, though there are just a few things which I ought to mention. Having ascended the valley of Sheyok, or Sheok, with yaks, we came to the pass of Karakorum (18,564 feet); thence we crossed the passes of Sughett-davan and Sanju with horses, rested a couple of days at Kargalik and Yarkand, and at length reached Kashgar on the 14th May, 1902. Spring was dight in all her beauties when I again sat with my old friend Consul-General Petrovsky in his well-remembered garden, and talked over my experiences in Central Asia, and thanked him for the incalculable services he had rendered me on so many occasions during the past years. Mr. Macartney and Father Hendricks were also both intensely interested in my story. At the same time I made the acquaintance of two newly-arrived Swedish missionaries, Messrs. Andersson and Bäcklund, who had thrown themselves zealously into the work of the mission, and had every reason to be satisfied with the fruits of their laborious and self-denying efforts.

But I had no time to linger. A clasp of the hand, and I must hasten westwards over the mountains. Kutchuk and Khodai Kullu returned to their huts in the Lop country, carrying with them a handsome recompense for their faithful service. At Osh I parted from honest old Turdu Bai, warmly recommending him to Colonel Saitseff, in whose hospitable house I was once more received with open arms. It was hard to part from Malenki and Malchik. I went into the yard to say good-bye to them before driving down to the railway station in Andijan, and their wondering, questioning eyes followed me as if they understood that we should never see one another again. At Chernyayeva I took heartfelt farewell of that fine fellow Chernoff, who was to travel *viâ* Tashkend to Vernoye. Cherdon and the Lama accompanied me across the Caspian Sea. The good-natured Shereb Lama was taken terribly aback when he saw the paddle-wheels of the big steamboat begin to carry us out towards the open sea. These two accompanied me as far as Petrovsk, whence they were to continue to Astrakhan. In that city the Lama intended to settle down in a Kalmuck monastery, Consul Petrovsky having joined with me in recommending him to the governor. Shereb Lama durst not show himself again in Karashahr, and Kamba Bombo had forbidden him once and for all ever to enter Lassa again. Cherdon was to take the Siberian railway to his home in Transbaikalia.

I found it very hard to part from them all. We had been together such a long time. The tears they shed bore witness

A Portion of the Glacier of Kitchik-kumdan.

also to the feelings with which they parted from me. I have heard from some of them since, and was especially glad to know that Shagdur had got at least as far as Osh, within the boundaries of the Russian Empire. General Sakharoff, of St. Petersburg, has several times very kindly given me information about my faithful Cossacks, and quite recently I received a letter from Colonel Saitseff, which I was unable to read without emotion. It contained a description of Shagdur's account of his impressions of the journey, especially of the dash for Lassa and the trip to India. I was very pleased to learn that he retained an affectionate recollection of me.

King Oscar honoured all four Cossacks with a gold medal

each, which he had specially struck for the purpose, and which they received the Czar's permission to wear. Their own Sovereign, the Czar, bestowed upon them the distinction of the Order of St. Anna, together with a present of 250 roubles (£26) each. The King of Sweden also sent gold medals to Turdu Bai and Khalmet Aksakal, and a silver medal to Faisullah. At an audience which His Majesty the Czar Nicholas II. graciously accorded me at Peterhof, he expressed the great satisfaction it had been to him to hear how pleased I was with his Cossacks, and that their conduct from the first day to the last had been so irreproachable. I sent an official report about them to General Kuropatkin, the Imperial Minister of War.

I will not attempt to describe the feelings which swept over me when, on the 27th June, 1902, the *Von Döbeln* steered in amongst the islands of the Swedish skärgård. How often and often I had wondered whether I should ever again see those dear old grey rocks, associated as they were with so many happy memories of my childhood! It was three years and three days, and far more than 1,001 nights, since I said good-bye to my father and mother and other members of the family. There they were, waiting for me on the same quay from which they had waved to me their farewells. Summer was come again in all its beauty, and the lilacs were once more in bloom as they were when I started. The long years which had passed in the interval seemed like a dream; it was as if I had only been away for a few short days. Everything was exactly as it used to be.

The very next day I was received in audience by King Oscar, who has always supported my plans with such munificent generosity, and I may even say with fatherly kindness. To him I related the story of my travels, adding yet another stone to the building which I hope is still far from being finished.

THE END.

INDEX.